The World's Christians

Who they are, Where they are, and How they got there

Douglas Jacobsen

WILEY-BLACKWELL

A John Wiley & Sons, Ltd., Publication

This edition first published 2011
© 2011 Douglas Jacobsen

Blackwell Publishing was acquired by John Wiley & Sons in February 2007. Blackwell's publishing program has been merged with Wiley's global Scientific, Technical, and Medical business to form Wiley-Blackwell.

Registered Office
John Wiley & Sons Ltd, The Atrium, Southern Gate, Chichester, West Sussex, PO19 8SQ, United Kingdom

Editorial Offices
350 Main Street, Malden, MA 02148-5020, USA
9600 Garsington Road, Oxford, OX4 2DQ, UK
The Atrium, Southern Gate, Chichester, West Sussex, PO19 8SQ, UK

For details of our global editorial offices, for customer services, and for information about how to apply for permission to reuse the copyright material in this book please see our website at www.wiley.com/wiley-blackwell.

The right of Douglas Jacobsen to be identified as the author of this work has been asserted in accordance with the UK Copyright, Designs and Patents Act 1988.

Wiley also publishes its books in a variety of electronic formats. Some content that appears in print may not be available in electronic books.

Designations used by companies to distinguish their products are often claimed as trademarks. All brand names and product names used in this book are trade names, service marks, trademarks or registered trademarks of their respective owners. The publisher is not associated with any product or vendor mentioned in this book. This publication is designed to provide accurate and authoritative information in regard to the subject matter covered. It is sold on the understanding that the publisher is not engaged in rendering professional services. If professional advice or other expert assistance is required, the services of a competent professional should be sought.

Library of Congress Cataloging-in-Publication Data

Jacobsen, Douglas G. (Douglas Gordon), 1951–
 The world's Christians : who they are, where they are, and how they got there / Douglas Jacobsen.
  p. cm.
 Includes bibliographical references and index.
 ISBN 978-1-4051-8889-0 (hardback : alk. paper) – ISBN 978-1-4051-8887-6 (pbk. : alk. paper)
1. Christianity. I. Title.
 BR121.3.J33 2011
 270.09–dc22
                                                                          2010049301

A catalogue record for this book is available from the British Library.

Set in 10/13pt Minion by SPi Publisher Services, Pondicherry, India
Printed in Singapore by Ho Printing Singapore Pte Ltd

1 2011

Praise for *The World's Christians*

The historian Douglas Jacobsen has written a remarkably thoughtful, insightful, lively, and near-comprehensive account of the sprawling, vivid, internally plural, and wildly complex phenomenon of world Christianity. In an era when almost every religion has "gone global," Christianity remains the world's largest and most culturally and geographically diverse religion. Rivaled only by Islam for influence in geopolitical affairs, it shapes the sensibilities of Pentecostals who own small businesses in Latin America, Catholics and Anglicans who fight the scourge of HIV-AIDS in Africa, evangelical missionaries in the Middle East, and underground worshippers in China. For students of politics, culture, development, and conflict – for anyone interested in the evolution and prospects of the hundreds of Christian-influenced or -inflected societies around the world – *The World's Christians* is indispensable.

R. Scott Appleby, Professor of History, University of Notre Dame

Contents

List of Illustrations   vii
Preface   xiii

Introduction   1

Part I: Who They Are   **7**

Introduction

1   The Orthodox Tradition   13

2   The Catholic Tradition   26

3   The Protestant Tradition   38

4   The Pentecostal/Charismatic Tradition   50

Part II: Where They Are   **63**

Introduction

5   The Middle East and North Africa: Barely Surviving   67

6   Eastern Europe: Nationalism and New Mission   88

7   Central and South Asia: Confidence and Complexity   110

8   Western Europe: Thin, but Alive   132

9   Sub-Saharan Africa: Hope and Despair   155

10   East Asia: Piety and Politics   180

11   Latin America: After Monopoly   203

12   North America: Faith in a Free Market   225

13   Oceania: Experiments in Identity   248

Part III: How They Got There   267

Introduction

14   The Ancient Tradition: Beginnings to 500   269

15   The Great Division and the Age of the East: 500 to 1000   293

16   The Rise of the West and Decline of the East: 1000 to 1500   319

17   Christianity in a Global Era: 1500 to the Present   346

Index   375

List of Illustrations

Figures

Figure I.1	The four major contemporary Christian traditions	8
Figure I.2	Development of major historical Christian traditions	9
Figure 1.1	Where Orthodox Christians live	14
Figure 1.2	Holy Trinity Orthodox Cathedral (Sibiu, Romania), interior of main dome	15
Figure 1.3	Holy Trinity Orthodox Cathedral (Sibiu, Romania), nave and iconostasis	16
Figure 1.4	Key events in Orthodox history	24
Figure 2.1	Where Catholics live	27
Figure 2.2	Key events in Catholic history	36
Figure 3.1	Where Protestants live	39
Figure 3.2	Key events in Protestant history	48
Figure 4.1	Where Pentecostal/Charismatic Christians live	51
Figure 4.2	Growth of Pentecostal/Charismatic movement	60
Figure II.1	Nine cultural-geographic regions of the world	64
Figure II.2	Where the world's Christians live	65
Figure 5.1	Map of Middle East and North Africa	69
Figure 5.2	The Ottoman Empire at its peak, c. 1800	70
Figure 5.3	Where Christians live in Egypt	78
Figure 5.4	The Armenian genocide	81
Figure 5.5	Palestinian Muslims and Christians demonstrate at Al-Yarmuk refugee camp in Damascus, October 9, 2009	84
Figure 6.1	Map of Eastern Europe	89
Figure 6.2	Map of post-World War I Communist Europe	91
Figure 6.3	Three religious subregions of Eastern Europe	94
Figure 6.4	The Lord's Ark Catholic Church (Nowa Huta, Poland)	101

Figure 6.5   Population estimates of Orthodox Christians
              in the Russian Federation   104
Figure 7.1   Map of Central and South Asia   111
Figure 7.2   Where Christians live in India   117
Figure 7.3   Christians take part in a prayer meeting to protest against
              the killings of Christians in the Indian state of Orissa,
              in New Delhi, 27 December, 2007   120
Figure 7.4   An Indian shouts slogans in front of a mock crucifixion during
              a protest rally in New Delhi to demand government job
              reservations for "dalit" or oppressed Christians   127
Figure 8.1   Map of Western Europe   133
Figure 8.2   Chiara Lubich, Founder of Focolare   135
Figure 8.3   Padre Pio celebrating the Mass   136
Figure 8.4   Western Europe showing Catholic, Protestant, and religiously
              mixed regions   138
Figure 8.5   Francesco Franco and wife taking communion at
              Sunday Mass (1952)   141
Figure 8.6   Two of the most important Western European theologians
              of the twentieth century, Karl Rahner and Karl Barth   147
Figure 8.7   Anglican Communion: numbers by region   150
Figure 8.8   Members of the Church of England attending worship
              on a typical Sunday   151
Figure 9.1   Sub-Saharan Africa   156
Figure 9.2   Map of Africa showing European colonial claims, c. 1920   158
Figure 9.3   Christianity in sub-Saharan Africa (% of population)   163
Figure 9.4   Christianity in sub-Saharan Africa (number of adherents)   163
Figure 9.5   Christianity as a percentage of total national population   164
Figure 9.6   Distribution of Christian population in Nigeria   170
Figure 9.7   Nigerian Anglican Archbishop Peter Akinola   171
Figure 9.8   Carrying the tabot to be rechristened during the festival of Timkat 177
Figure 10.1   Map of East Asia   181
Figure 10.2   Archbishop Jaime Cardinal Sin at a rally in Manila, 2000   188
Figure 10.3   The EDSA I protests, Manila, Philippines, 1986   189
Figure 10.4   Map of Indonesia showing distribution of Christians   193
Figure 10.5   Reformed church (next to mosque) in Malang, East Java, Indonesia 194
Figure 10.6   Christians attend Sunday service at Shouwang Church
              in Beijing's Haidian district, October 3, 2010   199
Figure 11.1   Map of Latin America   204
Figure 11.2   The religious profile of Latin America in 1900 and 2005   205
Figure 11.3   Padre Marcelo Rossi participates in an outdoor mass,
              November 2, 2000, in São Paulo, Brazil   217
Figure 11.4   Catholic fighters of the Cristero Rebellion (1926–29)   218
Figure 11.5   *Evangélico* (non-Catholic) Christianity in Mexico   219
Figure 11.6   The island nations of the Caribbean   221

Figure 12.1   Map of North America   226
Figure 12.2   Percentage of the Canadian population (by province) reporting
               no religious affiliation   228
Figure 12.3   Religion in the USA using "American" categories of description   230
Figure 12.4   Religion in the USA using four world Christian traditions
               as categories of description   230
Figure 12.5   Church attendance rates by state   231
Figure 12.6   Bishop T. D. Jakes of the Potter's House Church   238
Figure 12.7   Where Catholics live   240
Figure 12.8   Where Mormons live   244
Figure 13.1   Map of Oceania   249
Figure 13.2   Map of Melanesia, Micronesia, and Polynesia   254
Figure 13.3   T. W. Ratana   257
Figure 13.4   Frank Bainimarama (leader of 2006 coup)   259
Figure 13.5   The religious profile of Australia   261
Figure 13.6   Entrance to Saint Shenouda Coptic monastery
               (New South Wales, Australia)   263
Figure 13.7a   Hillsong Church, Australia   264
Figure 13.7b   Pastor Bobbie Houston from Hillsong Church, Australia   264
Figure 14.1   Timeline for the Ancient Tradition   271
Figure 14.2   Roman Empire at peak, c. 120   280
Figure 14.3   Timeline of Christianity and the Roman Empire   281
Figure 14.4   Head of the giant statue of the Emperor Constantine
               in the courtyard of the Palazzo dei Conservatori, Rome, Italy   283
Figure 14.5   Estimated growth of Christianity as a percentage
               of the Roman population   284
Figure 14.6   Sasanian Empire, c. 250   287
Figure 14.7   Timeline of Christianity in Persia   289
Figure 15.1   The Great Division   294
Figure 15.2   Christian "East" and "West" and the general geographic locations
               of the four major traditions, 500–1000   295
Figure 15.3   Byzantine and Arab Empires, c. 800   304
Figure 15.4   Timeline of Orthodox Church in the Byzantine Empire, 500–1000   306
Figure 15.5   Timeline for Church of the East, 500–1000   308
Figure 15.6   Charlemagne's domain   314
Figure 16.1   Ten General Councils of the Catholic Church, 1123–1512   320
Figure 16.2   Fourteenth-century Italian Renaissance poet Dante Alighieri
               holding his book *Divine Comedy* against a backdrop of Hell,
               Purgatory, and Paradise in a 1465 painting by Domenico Michelino   324
Figure 16.3   The path of the Black Death   326
Figure 16.4   St George's Carved Stone Church (Lalibela, Ethiopia)   330
Figure 16.5   Changing Christian–Muslim boundary line in Spain, 800–1492 333
Figure 16.6   Map of the Crusader states, c. 1150 and c. 1200   334
Figure 16.7   Latin Empire in former Byzantine territory, 1204–61   337

Figure 16.8   The Mongol Emperor Hulegu with his Christian wife, Sorkaktani-beki   341
Figure 16.9   Timeline of Christian decline in Persia   343
Figure 17.1   Dirk Willems rescuing his pursuer   352
Figure 17.2   William J. Seymour with other leaders of the Azusa
Street revival   353
Figure 17.3   Portuguese and Spanish empires, sixteenth century   360
Figure 17.4   African slaves brought to the Americas, 1650–1860   365
Figure 17.5   Hong Xiuquan, leader of the *Taiping Tianguo*   368
Figure 17.6   Global map of the Cold War, c. 1980   371

Tables

Table 2.1   Global organization of Catholic Church   33
Table 2.2   Global distribution of Catholic parishes and priests   34
Table 3.1   The main "families" of Protestantism and their global presence   44
Table II.1   Christians as percentage of the population in the nine world regions   65
Table II.2   Relative size of the four Christian traditions in the nine world regions   66
Table 5.1   Christian profile of the Middle East and North Africa   73
Table 6.1   The main Orthodox churches of Eastern Europe   90
Table 6.2   Estimated size of Christian traditions in the Balkans today   96
Table 6.3   Christian populations in Catholic Central Europe   99
Table 6.4   Estimated size of Christian traditions in Russian region today   103
Table 7.1   Religious profiles of nations in North Central Asia   114
Table 7.2   Distribution of major religions in South Asia   115
Table 7.3   Estimated size of the five major Christian subgroups in India   122
Table 8.1   The four main Christian traditions in Catholic Europe   139
Table 8.2   Levels of religiosity in Catholic Europe   139
Table 8.3   The four main Christian traditions in Protestant and religiously
mixed Europe   146
Table 8.4   Levels of religiosity in Protestant and religiously mixed Western Europe   147
Table 8.5   Ten largest denominations in the United Kingdom   152
Table 9.1   Social and economic data for 10 largest African nations   160
Table 9.2   Growth of four Christian traditions in sub-Saharan Africa   165
Table 9.3   Religious affiliation in the 10 largest nations in sub-Saharan
Africa today   166
Table 9.4   Denominational profile of Nigerian Christian population   169
Table 9.5   Denominational profile of South African Christian population   176
Table 10.1   Distribution of three major world religions in East Asia   185
Table 11.1   Christian profiles of the 10 largest nations of Latin America   207
Table 11.2   The 10 largest non-Catholic churches in Mexico   220
Table 11.3   Religious profiles of five largest independent Caribbean nations   222
Table 12.1   The mainline Protestant denominations in the USA   232
Table 12.2   Historically black churches with more than one million members   237

Table 13.1   Religious profile of Melanesia   255
Table 13.2   Religious profile of Micronesia   255
Table 13.3   Religious profile of Polynesia   256
Table 16.1   Major Muslim empires, indicating general
             attitude toward Christianity   339
Table 17.1   Modern European empires   359
Table 17.2   Distribution of Christian population by continent,
             1800 and 1900   367
Table 17.3   Distribution of global Christian population by continent,
             1900 and 2000   373

Plates

Plate 1   Matthew the Poor/Yūsuf Iskandar
Plate 2   Coptic Pope Shenouda III
Plate 3   Ancient Armenian church near Lake Van, Turkey
Plate 4   Aerial view of St Sava Serbian Orthodox Church (Belgrade, Serbia)
Plate 5   Hill of Crosses, Siauliai, Lithuania
Plate 6   The Queen of Heaven, the Black Madonna of Czestochowa
Plate 7   Christ the Savior Church, Moscow, destroyed in 1931
Plate 8   Christ the Savior Church, Moscow, rebuilt in 2000
Plate 9   Orthodox Cathedral of the Ascension, Almaty, Kazakhstan
Plate 10   Cathedral of the Epiphany (CSI), Dornakal, India
Plate 11   Young Muslim demonstrators shout slogans as they march
           in central Paris
Plate 12   Pope Benedict XVI (R) meets France's President Nicolas Sarkozy
           at the Vatican, December 20, 2007
Plate 13   Victims of the Rwandan genocide lying outside a Catholic Church
Plate 14   Members of the Cherubim and Seraphim Church (AIC), West Africa
Plate 15   Yoido Full Gospel Church, Seoul, Korea, July 27, 2008
Plate 16   Zhongguancun Christian Church, Haidian District, Beijing
           (TSPM/CCC)
Plate 17   Golden Lamp Church, Linfen, Shanxi province, China;
           now closed by the authorities
Plate 18   Our Lady of Guadalupe
Plate 19   Universal Church of the Kingdom of God, Brazil
Plate 20   "This Home is Catholic" (*Este Hogar es Catolico*) door sign
Plate 21   Rick Warren's Saddleback Church, Lake Forest, May 20, 2008
Plate 22   Martin Luther King, Jr. preaching at Mason Temple, Memphis, Tennessee
Plate 23   Paul Gauguin: *Two Tahitian Women*, 1899
Plate 24   Paul Gauguin: *Haere Pape*, 1892
Plate 25   Detail of a painting of Tiwi art, Northern Territory, Australia
Plate 26   Icon of Symeon the Stylite

Plate 27   Ancient cross marking the purported burial site of St Thomas in Mylapore (near Chennai), India
Plate 28   Icon of the "Nine Saints" painted on a church wall in Ethiopia
Plate 29   Icon of the Triumph of Orthodoxy, Cretan School
Plate 30   Icon depicting Saints Cyril and Methodius, Varna
Plate 31   Thirteenth-century reliquary of the arm of St George
Plate 32   Andrei Rublev icon of John the Baptist
Plate 33   A page from Jefferson's pasted-together Bible
Plate 34   Baroque church, Steingaden, Germany
Plate 35   The Christian King Nzinga Nkuwu (João I) of Congo

Preface

Roughly one third of the world's population is Christian – more than two billion people in all – and the diversity within this community of faith is stunning. Christians are members of thousands of different churches, speak hundreds of different languages, and are present within almost every country and culture on earth. Christianity has been a world religion for centuries, but the global dispersion of Christianity has increased dramatically in recent years. This book surveys that expansive terrain, mapping the complex contours of Christianity, documenting its dimensions, and painting a portrait of the largest contemporary religious movement on earth.

I first decided to write this book more than 20 years ago while I was attending a meeting of "Third World" theologians held at Princeton University. What was then still being called the "Third World" has since become the first world of the global Christian movement. More Christians now live in Africa, Asia, and Latin America than in Europe and North America, and that southern shift in the movement represents more than mere geography. The Christian movement is changing and moving forward in ways that are very different from the past, and it is constantly becoming more diverse, but the many different kinds of Christians around the world continue to be linked together by their shared desire to follow the way of life that Jesus of Nazareth articulated and embodied when he lived in Palestine two thousand years ago.

Much of my research during the last two decades has been spent trying to understand these new global developments, and in many ways it has felt like trying to catch a train as it is pulling away from the station. Realities on the ground are changing all the time, and literally thousands of academic works have been produced that try to document and analyze those changes. Scholars often say that their own work is possible only because they have been able to stand on the shoulders of others. In this case, it feels much more like being carried along by a great crowd.

I learned long ago, in graduate school at the University of Chicago and in my initial foray into teaching at the University of Illinois, that understanding a subject with enough depth to explain it clearly to others is a challenge. When the subject is as complex as world

Christianity, this challenge is immense. The amount of information is overwhelming, and yet making things too simple runs the risk of misrepresenting reality. Finding the right balance between information overload and oversimplification can be difficult, but to whatever degree that balance has been achieved here, I have my students at Messiah College to thank. In my classes on the history of Christianity and on contemporary Christianity in Africa, Asia, and Latin America, they have helped me distinguish between what is important and what is merely intriguing and between what is significant and what tends to confuse with too much nuance and detail.

This work has also been tremendously enriched by interactions I have had with Christians around the world. Visits to more than 50 nations have allowed me to experience first-hand some of the amazing diversity that exists among the world's many different kinds of Christians, from attending a crowded Catholic mass in China, to participating in raucous worship with Pentecostals in Zimbabwe, to being moved to tears by the music of an Orthodox choir in Romania, to joining in devotion with pilgrims at the shrine of La Negrita in Costa Rica, to singing hymns with a Presbyterian congregation in Northern Ireland, to hearing the Orthodox Patriarch of Antioch describe the difficulties of being a Christian in the Middle East while I was in Syria. It would be impossible to name all the people and organizations that made such experiences possible, but it is an understatement to say that I am truly grateful.

The goal of this book is to describe the world's Christians as fairly and accurately as possible, without skewing that picture one way or the other. In a sense, then, this book is a kind of scientific field guide that identifies all the different "species" of Christianity around the world. As is true for any good field guide, geography and numbers matter. This volume, accordingly, tries to categorize and count all the various types of Christians found in the different regions of the world. Grouping and enumerating individual Christians is not an easy task. Even though most Christians know and are willing to say, for example, if they are Orthodox, Catholic, Protestant, or Pentecostal/Charismatic, estimating the country-by-country numbers can be surprisingly difficult. The *World Christian Encyclopedia* (2nd edn, 2001), edited by David B. Barrett, George T. Kurian, and Todd Johnson, along with the online World Christian Database, which constantly updates the information provided in the encyclopedia, is both the logical place to begin and a rich mine of information. However, the numbers given in the *World Christian Encyclopedia* and the World Christian Database do not always agree with other sources of information about the world Christian population, including church membership and attendance records, national census figures, regional and national surveys (when available), and statistics provided by international governmental and nongovernmental organizations.

The numbers included in this book are my own best estimates based on a careful comparison of all the sometimes conflicting information that is available. Other scholars might reach slightly different sums since there are a variety of valid ways to assess the data, but the figures provided here have been compiled with great care. The most significant difference in this regard has to do with the number of Pentecostal/Charismatic Christians. It is not uncommon to read claims that Pentecostal/Charismatic Christians now account for 25 percent or more of the world's Christians. But the only way to arrive at that number is to double count millions of people who are also counted as Protestants or Catholics. The percentages used in this book do not allow for that kind of double counting. To make everything add up to 100 percent, some adjustments have accordingly been made both to the Pentecostal/Charismatic numbers and also to Protestant and Catholic numbers.

In the end, however, numbers provide only the skeleton of the story that needs to be told. Religion is personal. It involves deep-seated emotions, lifelong habits of devotion, and distinct ideas about who God is, how the world is put together, and what it means to be human. To understand Christianity as a living religion requires awareness of that personal dimension, and this book attempts to put the flesh-and-blood substance of everyday faith onto the bones of the world Christian movement as it is defined by the demographic data. Doing so requires empathy, the willingness to suspend one's own beliefs and values and to enter into the world of the other as much as possible. No one can do this perfectly – the other always remains other, and no one can fully understand what it means to walk in the shoes of someone else – but given the religious conflicts and controversies that exist around the world, it is imperative that we try. My hope is that this book will serve as a fair introduction – both empirically grounded and empathetic – to the world's many different kinds of Christians and the hopes, fears, and challenges they face in their lives.

Introduction

The Christian movement began with just a handful of people, maybe a few hundred, who had known Jesus while he was alive and who looked to him even after his death as their religious teacher and guide. Jesus was born in a remote part of Palestine at the eastern edge of the Roman Empire, and during his lifetime his following never extended beyond that region. Most of his closest associates were of modest means, and many – perhaps most – were illiterate. All in all, there was little to suggest that someday this movement would span the globe, yet it has. Today Christianity, the religion of Jesus, is the largest and most widely disseminated religion in the world.

All Christians seek in some way or another to follow the teachings of Jesus of Nazareth. The term "Christian" comes from the honorary title "Christ," which was given to Jesus by the early church and means the "anointed one." Christians see Jesus as being the Chosen One who came to proclaim "good news" (the "gospel") to humankind, to announce God's love for the world and God's desire to redeem the world from sin, sorrow, and all that is wrong. But Christians also believe that Jesus was more than a mere messenger. In some sense, he was the message himself. He was, in his person, the redeeming presence of God on earth, the Messiah foretold in ancient Jewish scriptures. And it is that belief that has been the main driving force behind the growth of Christianity through the centuries and around the world: that, in Jesus, God came to earth to help and to heal the woes of humankind.

The historical Jesus was an unlikely leader. He lived his first 30 years in relative obscurity as the son of Mary and her husband Joseph, a carpenter in the small town of Nazareth. Then, for just a few years before he was killed, he took on the role of a wandering Jewish prophet and teacher, first in the rural region of Galilee and later in Jerusalem.

His message was simple but profound. Jesus affirmed much of the Judaism of his day, including the Golden Rule ("do unto others what you would have them do unto you"), but Jesus frequently added his own twist to those teachings. Some of these additions – the

The World's Christians: Who they are, Where they are, and How they got there, First Edition. Douglas Jacobsen.
© 2011 Douglas Jacobsen. Published 2011 by Blackwell Publishing Ltd.

folksy way he referred to God as "abba" (best translated as "daddy"), his willingness to bend the law to human frailty, his claim that he was able to forgive sins – were troubling to traditional Jews. His message was also troubling to Rome. Jesus spoke of a coming "kingdom of God" and described his own actions as the dawning of that kingdom. He instructed his followers to give appropriate respect to Caesar, the Roman Emperor, but he also told them to give their entire lives to God, a qualification that clearly limited any loyalty owed to Caesar. And, while he did not seek political power for himself, he refused to cower when he was arrested and questioned by Rome's political appointees in the region. All of that seemed potentially subversive to an empire that demanded absolute obedience, and Rome responded vigorously, as Rome always did. Using the gruesome spectacle of execution on a cross, the Empire eliminated Jesus and sent a public message to his followers that the show was over.

Most local residents thought that was the end of the matter. Another pesky prophet had come and gone, and life would now return to normal. But killing Jesus did not stop the movement. His closest followers soon became convinced that Jesus had survived his crucifixion or, as they put it, he had conquered the grave and triumphed over death. They reported that they had seen him alive, in a glorious resurrected body, and that he had commanded them to continue the work he had started. They were to preach the gospel throughout the world, to every person, in every tongue, in every nation.

The fourth-century historian Eusebius of Caesarea says that the disciples of Jesus cast lots to determine where each of them should go. Eusebius says that Thomas was assigned to Parthia (now Iraq and Iran), Andrew to Scythia (the lands north of the Black Sea), and John to the province of Asia Minor (now Turkey). Peter, as the leader of the group, was given freedom to travel wherever he wanted. Eusebius did not always get his facts straight, and this particular story may well be fictitious, but his basic point is accurate. Within a century of Jesus's death the Christian gospel had been carried as far west as Spain and as far east as India.

Jesus never produced any writings of his own, but his spoken words, remembered and written down after his death in short books called "Gospels," quickly became the key texts of the movement, and even today portions of them are read every week in most Christian churches. While Christians believe that the entire text of the Bible is in some sense inspired, the words of Jesus are seen as special. Some versions of the Bible even print the sayings of Jesus in red ink, rather than black, so they stand out from the rest of the text. And some Christians call themselves "red-letter" Christians to underscore the emphasis they put on the teachings of Jesus within the context of the Bible as a whole.

Part of the appeal of Jesus's words and actions is that they require reflection in order to be understood. The words of Jesus necessitate self-examination and transformation and require "hearers of the Word" to become better people in order to make sense of what he said. When Jesus says things like "blessed are the poor, for theirs is the kingdom of heaven," for example, people have to ask themselves what it means to be poor or to be blessed or to be part of the kingdom of heaven, and there isn't one right answer because each person brings something different from his or her own life to those questions. It is this power to draw people in, to make them rethink and refashion their own lives, that has led many people, Christian and non-Christian alike, to value Jesus as a great religious teacher. Christians across the ages and around the world have also called Jesus savior and lord because they believe the power of the still living Jesus (now in heaven) has spiritually changed them in ways they could never change themselves.

The dynamic quality of Jesus's life and message – its probing open-endedness – has been a boon to the global spread of Christianity. Jesus taught by using parables, paradoxical sayings, and symbolic actions, and the history of Christianity is largely the story of how people and groups in many different cultures have come to their own varied conclusions about what those words and actions mean for them. The flexibility of this interpretive process has allowed people all around the world to read the Bible as if it was written specifically for them, and to be confident that the meaning they have found in the text is as valid and worthy as the interpretations of other Christians. In particular, Christians in cultures that have only recently encountered Christianity can see themselves as having equal access to Jesus and an equal right to interpret the words of Jesus in ways that make sense in their own unique circumstances.

This process of cross-culturally enlarging the meaning of the Christian message began early in the history of the movement. The first major transformation – moving from Hebrew to Greco-Roman culture – is visible in the pages of the New Testament itself, where the Apostle Paul and other writers try to explain the message of Jesus to Gentiles (people who are not Jews) in a language (Greek) that Jesus did not speak. And as the followers of Jesus moved further afield, engaging Persian, Indian, Arabic, Berber, Gothic, and Coptic cultures, the work of translation and cultural adaptation became ever more complex. The categories of thought and perception that exist in one culture never line up precisely with the concepts and ideas in another, and practices that are symbolically meaningful in one culture may have no symbolic power in another. So the act of translating the Christian message from one setting to another often involved rethinking that message in radically new ways, with each new context stretching the meaning and message of Christianity in different directions. The incredible diversity of Christianity that exists around the world today is the result of this process.

But despite the freedom that has been part of this history, and despite the amazing internal pluralism of the Christian religion, there are a few central items – a handful of things – on which all or almost all Christians agree. Thus, for example, Christians corporately affirm that Jesus was somehow both human and divine, and most believe that God is a "Trinity" consisting of three "persons" (traditionally called the Father, Son, and Holy Spirit) eternally bound into oneness by their mutual and indestructible love. Explaining the details of these two doctrines – how Jesus can be two yet one and how God can be three yet one – has always been a challenge for Christians, but most still affirm these concepts. Christians also believe that "salvation," however it is construed – and Christians construe it in many different ways – is ultimately a gift from God. Human effort towards salvation may or may not be necessary, but salvation is impossible apart from God's grace.

All or most Christian churches also share certain practices. One of them is weekly worship. Whether taking place on Sunday (for most Christians) or on Saturday (for some Christians), gathering for weekly worship is a nearly universal Christian practice. Not every Christian attends worship every week, but the opportunity is always available. Most Christians also believe that baptism – accomplished by either submerging a person under water or pouring water over their head – is the standard ritual of initiation that publicly marks a person as a follower of Jesus. Baptism symbolizes both the washing away of sin and identification with Christ's death and resurrection (going into the water and then rising out of it is like being buried and then raised from the dead). Some churches baptize babies while others baptize only adults, but baptism in one form or another is almost always required for full membership. Finally, all or most Christian churches celebrate the Eucharist (which is also known as Communion or the Lord's Supper) on a regular basis. This mini-meal, which takes place within the context of worship, consists of a small piece of bread and a sip of wine or grape juice, but it is rich with symbolism. It commemorates the last meal that Jesus ate with his disciples. It represents Christ's body that was broken and his blood that was shed on the cross – in fact, many Christians believe the bread and wine literally become the body and blood of Christ during the Eucharistic celebration. It reminds those who participate that they are part of a community of mutual care and affection. And it anticipates the banqueting in heaven that Christians hope someday to enjoy with God.

But while Christians throughout history and around the globe share some beliefs and practices and some hopes about the future, the diversity within the movement is simply stunning. The goal of this book is to explain that diversity: to describe the *who*, *where*, and *how* of Christianity around the world. Part I describes *who* the world's Christians are, focusing on the four major contemporary traditions: Orthodox, Catholic, Protestant, and Charismatic/Pentecostal. The experiences of believers from each of the four traditions will be described: what they believe, how they worship, how they sense the presence of God in their lives, and how they institutionally organize their communities of faith.

Part II – the largest part of the book – is organized geographically and describes *where* Christians are living in the world today. Nine distinct regions are identified, based on a combination of factors including geography, the similarity of Christian experience in each region, cultural practices, and the size of the total population in each given area. To some degree, the world's Christian geography follows the world's continental divides, but not entirely. Thus North America (minus Mexico) constitutes one region, Central and South America (including Mexico) form another, Australia along with New Zealand and the Pacific islands represents a third, and sub-Saharan Africa exists as a fourth separate and distinct zone of Christian experience. But the European continent is divided into two subregions (East and West) because the Christian population of the continent is so large and because the history of Christianity in these two regions has been so different. And Asia, the home of more than half the world's people, is divided into three subregions: East Asia, Central and South Asia, and the Middle East, with the last of these broadened into a larger region that includes the north coast of Africa. As these regions are examined, it becomes clear just how diverse and how dispersed the Christian movement has become. There is no longer any identifiable spiritual or geographic center of world Christianity. Instead, the Christian world is now "flat" in the sense of being roughly evenly spread around the globe. In this newly flat world of global Christianity, every region has the own power to influence other regions while simultaneously being influenced from elsewhere.

Part III describes *how* Christianity developed its current global shape. It includes four chapters, each covering 500 years of history. This is not a complete history of Christianity, but is instead an overview focusing on how Christians, both theologically and geographically, got to where they are today. This history also underscores the ever-changing dynamics and character of the movement. Some of the most important Christian communities of the past – for example, the Church of the East that once contained thousands of churches in a far-reaching zone extending from what is now Iraq all the way to China – are now teetering on the brink of extinction. Other Christian traditions have only recently come into existence – most notably, the Pentecostal/Charismatic movement – but they have expanded very quickly and already circle the globe. While Christianity has been a world religion for a very long time, its global shape has changed dramatically over the course of two thousand years, and it is still changing today.

Suggestions for Further Reading

Barrett, David B., George T. Kurian, and Todd M. Johnson (2001). *World Christian Encyclopedia*, 2nd edn. New York: Oxford University Press.

Campbell, Ted A. (1996). *Christian Confessions: A Historical Introduction*. Louisville, KY: Westminster John Knox.

Chidester, David (2000). *Christianity: A Global History*. San Francisco: HarperSanFrancisco.

Davies, Noel and Martin Conway (2008). *World Christianity in the 20th Century*. London: SCM Press.

Dougherty, Dyron B. (2010). *The Changing World of Christianity: The Global History of a Borderless Religion*. New York: Peter Lang.

Dupré, Louis and Don E. Salaiers (eds) (1989). *Christian Spirituality: Post-Reformation and Modern*. New York: Crossroad.

Hasting, Adrian (ed.) (1999). *A World History of Christianity*. Grand Rapids, MI: Eerdmans.

Irvin, Dale T. and Scott W. Sundquist (2001). *History of the World Christian Movement: Earliest Christianity to 1453*. Maryknoll, NY: Orbis.

Jenkins, Philip (2007). *The Next Christendom, The Coming of Global Christianity*. New York: Oxford University Press.

Jenkins, Philip (2008). *The Lost History of Christianity: The Thousand-Year Golden Age of the Church in the Middle East, Africa, and Asia—and How It Died*. San Francisco: HarperOne.

Kim, Sebastian and Kirsteen Kim (2008). *Christianity as a World Religion*. New York: Continuum.

MacCulloch, Diarmaid (2009). *Christianity: The First Three Thousand Years*. New York: Viking.

McGinn, Bernard, John Meyendorff, and Jean Leclercq (eds) (1985). *Christian Spirituality: Origins to the Twelfth Century*. New York: Crossroad.

Patte, Daniel (ed.) (2010). *The Cambridge Dictionary of Christianity*. Cambridge, UK: Cambridge University Press.

Raitt, Jill (1988). *Christian Spirituality: High Middle Ages and Reformation*. New York: Crossroad.

Part I   Who They Are

Introduction

To be a Christian is to be a follower of Christ, but not all Christians follow Christ in the same way. That fact is underscored by a quick survey of the social structure of contemporary Christianity. Christians are institutionally divided into more than 35,000 separate churchly organizations, ranging in size from the enormous Roman Catholic Church which has more than a billion members to the grandly named Universal Church of Christ which has 400 members worldwide, most of them in the USA and the West Indies. Every week, Christians gather at more than five million local churches and parishes to worship God. And that's just the formal structure. Informally, there are millions of additional Christian groups which meet in homes, schools, and places of work for Bible study, prayer, and mutual support. Each of these groups and each individual follower of Christ is in some sense unique, yet almost all of the world's two billion Christians are affiliated with one or another of four major Christian traditions that dominate the movement today: Eastern Orthodoxy, Roman Catholicism, Protestantism, and the Pentecostal/Charismatic movement.

The word "tradition" comes from the Latin world *traditio*, which means "to hand down," and religious traditions represent specific packages of beliefs, practices, and spiritual attitudes and emotions that have been handed down within different religious communities from generation to generation for years, if not centuries. This definition of tradition might make it sound as if religious traditions never change, but that is not the case. All traditions change, though most change slowly. In essence, a religious tradition is like a long, multigenerational conversation in which each new generation adds its own new insights and concerns, sometimes affirming and sometimes critiquing and revising what was done in the past. Over the course of two millennia, Christianity has produced a number of different major traditions, each with its own distinct sets of beliefs, practices, and spiritual affections. Some historical Christian traditions have become extinct, but the four traditions described in Part I are still quite vigorous and strong.

The World's Christians: Who they are, Where they are, and How they got there, First Edition. Douglas Jacobsen.
© 2011 Douglas Jacobsen. Published 2011 by Blackwell Publishing Ltd.

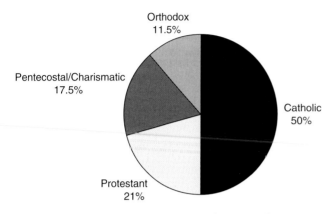

Figure I.1   The four major contemporary Christian traditions (% of total global Christian population)

Within the overarching category of being Christian, most individuals see themselves as belonging to one and only one of these four traditions. A person is either a Catholic or a Protestant or an Orthodox or a Pentecostal/Charismatic Christian. But while this general rule of thumb rings true for most Christians, there is sometimes fuzziness at some of the boundaries. Thus, for example, some people think of themselves as Orthodox Catholics (because they are members of Catholic Churches that use an Orthodox liturgy for worship) and others consider themselves to be both Catholic and Protestant, most notably "Anglo-Catholic" members of the Church of England. This kind of blurring of identity is especially common at the borders where the Pentecostal/Charismatic tradition touches the Protestant and Catholic traditions, with literally millions of Christians considering themselves both Catholic and Charismatic or both Protestant and Pentecostal. Even with these exceptions, however, most of the world's Christians can be classified quite easily into just one of the four major traditions.

The Catholic tradition has the largest number of adherents, including roughly half of all the Christians in the world. The Protestant tradition comes next in terms of size, followed closely by the Pentecostal/Charismatic movement. Eastern Orthodoxy is the smallest of the four major traditions. (See Figure I.1.) A full accounting of the world's Christians would also need to acknowledge a handful of other traditions that cannot be shoehorned into the big four. Some of these were once large and important Christian traditions such as the Church of the East (sometimes called the Nestorian Church) and the Miaphysite Churches (also known as the Oriental Orthodox Churches); see Figure I.2. Others are much smaller or of much more recent origin, such as the Church of Jesus Christ of Latter Day Saints (also known as the Mormon Church). These smaller alternative traditions will be discussed where appropriate in the regional and historical sections of this book, but they are not given separate treatment here.

Every Christian tradition has a beginning point, though the particular "birth date" of a tradition is not always easy to identify. The Pentecostal/Charismatic movement is the youngest of the four major traditions, and its beginning is the easiest to date, usually being associated with the Azusa Street Revival, which took place in Los Angeles, California from 1906 to 1908 under the leadership of the African American preacher William J. Seymour. October 31, 1517 is sometimes cited as the start-up date for the Protestant movement – the day when Martin Luther first posted his famous "95 Theses" protesting the practices of the Roman Catholic Church on the door of the church in Wittenburg, Germany where he served as both priest and university professor. The origins of the Catholic and Orthodox traditions are harder to date, both because these traditions are ancient and because each emerged slowly as the result of a long process of development

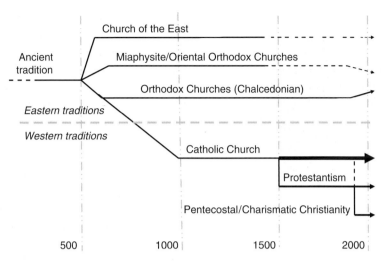

Figure I.2   Development of major historical Christian traditions

and consolidation. Many of the ingredients that make up these two traditions existed from the earliest years of the Christian movement, but those ingredients had to be mixed and baked for quite some time before they took on the specific characteristics that still define these traditions as they exist today. Viewed in terms of their contemporary identities, the Orthodox tradition can be said to have acquired its distinctively Orthodox shape around the ninth century, while the Catholic tradition developed its decisively Catholic identity sometime around the twelfth century.

The Orthodox Tradition

Today there are about 240 million Orthodox Christians in the world, accounting for roughly 12 percent of the world's total Christian population. They are part of a family of about 40 independent and geographically defined churches that all see themselves as part of a single Orthodox tradition. The Orthodox tradition is defined by its shared consensus rather than by a hierarchically imposed uniformity. Historically, the highest office within the Orthodox tradition is the Patriarch of Constantinople (also known as the "Ecumenical Patriarch"), but this title denotes honor and respect, not power or control. Most contemporary Orthodox Churches are organized along national lines, a fact that is reflected in names such as the Greek Orthodox Church or the Romanian Orthodox Church or the Russian Orthodox Church (which is the largest of the Orthodox Churches, having about 115 million members). For Orthodoxy, the liturgy (the service of worship in the church building) is at the center of lived faith, and Orthodox worship is a full body experience that involves hearing the words of the prayers, seeing the images (icons) of the saints that are painted on the walls and ceiling, and smelling the incense that wafts through the room from the censors swung back and forth by the priests.

The Catholic Tradition

The Catholic tradition is housed almost entirely within the single massive institution that is known as the Roman Catholic Church. This church is overseen by the Bishop of Rome, who is also called the "Pope" (meaning "papa" or "father"). The current Pope is Benedict XVI, who assumed office in 2005 after the death of his long-serving and popular predecessor, John Paul II. Because of its size and its hierarchical organizational structure, the Catholic Church can appear to be a monolith when viewed from the outside. But the term "catholic" means literally "from the whole," and the Catholic Church has always been a big tent where many different expressions of Christian faith and practice have been able to exist side by side within the wholeness of the church as a corporate body. The Catholic Church is the most ethnically and culturally diverse organization in the world, with more than 130 nations having at least 100,000 Catholics living within their borders. The five nations with the largest Catholic populations are Brazil (145 million), Mexico (90 million), the United States (70 million), the Philippines (65 million), and Italy (55 million).

Protestantism

The Protestant tradition is housed in a bewildering mix of thousands of different separate, independent denominations. Catholic and Orthodox Christians often consider the Protestant tradition to be unruly. In fact it is – but that is also the point. Protestants view faith largely as an individual matter, and Protestants are encouraged to read the Bible and determine what it means for themselves. As diverse and confusing as Protestantism can sometimes seem, the overall pattern is actually tidier than one might suppose. While Protestantism has tended to fragment with time, like-minded Protestants have also been busy gathering themselves together into a relatively limited number of major Protestant subtraditions. The largest of these are the Anglican, Baptist, Lutheran, Methodist, and Reformed subtraditions, and these five groups together account for roughly 85 percent of the almost 400 million Protestants in the world today.

The Pentecostal/Charismatic Movement

The newest of the four major contemporary Christian traditions is still in the early stages of formation. It has one core tenet: God is still active in the world through the Holy Spirit, so that miracles and spiritual gifts are an expected component of the Christian life. But while the movement's distinctive emphasis is relatively easy to describe, the boundaries of the movement are somewhat fuzzy, and they are fuzzy precisely because Pentecostal/Charismatic faith is defined by an emphasis rather than by a distinctively different set of beliefs. The question is how much emphasis a particular group has to place on the active work of the Holy Spirit in order to qualify as Pentecostal/Charismatic. Answers to that question differ considerably and, as a result, claims about the size of the worldwide Pentecostal/Charismatic movement vary widely. On the low side, some say that the movement now accounts for roughly 10 percent of the world's Christians. On the high side, some say 25 to 30 percent of the world's Christians are now Pentecostal/Charismatic in orientation. The 17.5 percent figure used in this book represents a middling estimate based on a careful region-by-region analysis of the numbers.

In the next four chapters these traditions are examined in more detail, with each chapter following the same basic format. First, the *spirituality* (the core convictions and lived experience) of believers in each tradition is described. Each chapter then explores how the Christian concept of *salvation* is understood. A third section focuses on the *structure* of the tradition, the movement's institutional and sociological organization. Finally, there is a brief outline of the *story* (or history) of the tradition. Taken together, these chapters provide a broad-brush description of contemporary Christianity. They answer the question "Who are the world's Christians?" by explaining how different Christians conceptualize God and salvation, how they have organized their churches, how they have institutionally housed and preserved their particular form of Christian faith, and how they have passed that faith down from generation to generation.

Chapter 1

The Orthodox Tradition

Orthodoxy has the longest history of the four major Christian traditions that exist today, and it preserves the ancient ideas and practices of Christianity more fully than any other tradition. In many ways, the past is still alive in Orthodoxy, so much so that some outsiders view Orthodoxy as locked in the past. But for its adherents, Orthodox Christianity is very much a living faith, connecting them to the present and future as much as to the past.

Geographically, the original heartland of Orthodoxy was the Middle East and the southern Balkans (the area that is now Albania, Bulgaria, Greece, and Macedonia). By 1500, however, under increasing pressure from Islam, the geographic center of Orthodoxy had moved north into Russia and Eastern Europe, where Orthodoxy remains the majority religion today. Three-quarters of all the Orthodox Christians in the world now live in Europe. In the twentieth century, Orthodoxy suffered greatly as most of Eastern Europe fell under Communist rule, but it endured and is currently enjoying a revival throughout the post-Communist world.

While Orthodoxy is the most geographically limited of the four major Christian traditions (see Figure 1.1), it too has become a global faith, with the Orthodox diaspora – the many communities of Orthodox Christians that now live outside of the Middle East and Eastern Europe – thinly circling the world. After Europe, Africa has the next largest number of Orthodox Christians, though most of the African Orthodox population (more than 90 percent) lives in just two countries: Egypt and Ethiopia. The Orthodox presence in Asia and Latin America (especially Brazil and Argentina) is generally small and spotty, but it exists. While the Orthodox population in North America and Australia is also relatively small, it is generally more robust. In North America, in particular, a significant experiment in Orthodox history is taking place. The Orthodox community in that region is highly complex – people from many different Orthodox Churches have moved to the area – and Orthodox leaders are currently trying to figure out how to unify all those Orthodox believers into a single "pan-Orthodox" movement. That process is prompting considerable theological

The World's Christians: Who they are, Where they are, and How they got there, First Edition. Douglas Jacobsen.
© 2011 Douglas Jacobsen. Published 2011 by Blackwell Publishing Ltd.

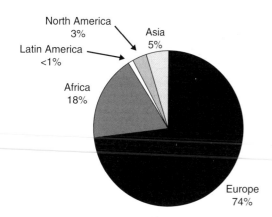

North America
3%

Asia
5%

Latin America
<1%

Africa
18%

Europe
74%

Figure 1.1   Where Orthodox Christians live (% of global Orthodox population living in each continent)

reflection and creativity in some circles (those favoring the Americanization of the tradition) and significant anguish in others (those wanting to hold on to the often deeply intertwined religious and ethnic identities of the past).

Spirituality

The spirituality of Orthodoxy focuses on worship, and to enter an Orthodox church is to enter a different place and time. Orthodox Christians view the liturgy (worship services held in the church building) as a way of participating briefly in the eternal worship of God that is always taking place in heaven. Most Orthodox churches have domed ceilings, and at the top of the dome there is an opening called the *oculus*. This is a symbolic eye into heaven and it is often encircled with windows. A huge icon (holy painting) of Christ as *Pantokrator* (the ruler of all) is painted in the oculus (see Figure 1.2), and Christ with the angels and apostles around him looks down on the gathered congregation where traditionally everyone stands, rather than sits, as a way of showing respect to God and to all the citizens of heaven.

Within an Orthodox church, one is surrounded by icons: icons on the ceiling, on the walls, on the screen or partition at the front of the church which is called an *iconostasis*, and on stands scattered throughout the building (see Figure 1.3). Icons portray not only Christ, but also Mary, the angels, and the great saints of the past. Other icons depict the stories of the Bible or important events in the history of Christianity. This panorama of images is intended to make those inside the building feel as if they are enveloped within a great community of faith, extending back in time thousands of years and looking forward together toward the future when God will welcome all the faithful into heaven. On the Orthodox way toward God no one walks alone. Rather, the journey toward God takes place in the constant company and with the ongoing assistance of others. That company includes both the living and the dead. In Orthodoxy, the boundary between the living and the dead is thin, and the Orthodox believe that the saints – holy men and women who have died – can still hear their cries for help and assist them in times of need.

In the same way that the line between life and death is thinned in Orthodoxy, the line between the sacred and the secular is also visually blurred in Orthodox iconography. The sacred and the secular interpenetrate, overlapping in time and space. Thus angels are everywhere in the icons because the Orthodox think they are everywhere in reality. The Orthodox believe that at the time of baptism every Christian is assigned a guardian angel for protection from evil and for guidance in the way of holiness and truth, but fallen angels (demons) are also ubiquitously present, seeking to turn people away from God and the path of faith. Because this spiritual world is hidden from view, humans tend to forget it. The liturgy and the icons remind people that they live within an invisible spiritual world of angels and demons just as literally as they live in the visible realm of the material world. In fact, the brilliance of the colors used in the painting of icons – and most of them were originally

Figure 1.2   Holy Trinity Orthodox Cathedral (Sibiu, Romania), interior of main dome.
Photo by author.

quite brilliant even though many old icons have grown dark with age – are luminous reminders that the spiritual world is as real, or more real, than the earth itself.

All of this communicates that nothing is ever done in secret. Life is lived in community. God is watching; Jesus is watching; Mary is watching; the angels are watching. And the saints are watching too. In fact, Orthodox icons – which are often displayed in homes as well as in churches – are understood to be not merely spiritual representations, but are also observers of humankind. The eyes of an icon are always painted last, and when they are in place the icon becomes, in a sense, alive – a living portal connecting the earthly community with the spiritual community of God and the saints.

The most revered figure in the Orthodox tradition, apart from Jesus and the Trinity, is Mary, who is called *Theotokos* ("God-bearer" or "Mother of God") because she bore God incarnate in her womb when pregnant with Jesus. Mary is venerated not only because she is the woman through whom God entered the world, but also because she models how every Christian should live. When the Archangel Gabriel told Mary that God had selected her to be *Theotokos*, she replied simply: "Let it be done to me, as I am your servant." God comes to people gently offering life in its fullness and, like Mary, each person must respond. In addition to modeling obedience, Mary also models holy suffering, since she endured watching her son being crucified. Finally, she is considered the most compassionate of all the saints, and icons of Mary communicate her desire to comfort all those who seek help in times of pain and distress.

Figure 1.3   Holy Trinity Orthodox Cathedral (Sibiu, Romania), nave and iconostasis. Photo by author.

Orthodox theology needs to be understood in the context of this emphasis on the visual and the communal. Within Orthodoxy, theology is a form of spirituality – a way of seeing the world and living in it – more than it is a philosophical explanation of belief. This is very different from the way theology is understood in most non-Orthodox Christian circles. Within the Protestant and Catholic traditions, in particular, theology usually consists of the logical explanation and philosophical defense of Christian doctrine. But Orthodox theology focuses on experience much more than it focuses on ideas or beliefs, and its primary "logic" is not philosophical, but relational, focusing on one's relationship with God and others. The purpose of Orthodox theology is not the achievement of intellectual understanding; the goal of Orthodox theology is to live in the holiness of God's presence, in the fire and warmth of the "Divine and Uncreated Light" of God.

The Orthodox tradition tends to favor an "apophatic" style of theology. Apophatic theology describes "who God is *not*" – the many ways in which God can be misunderstood – rather than attempting what theology can never accomplish: to capture God's character in human words. From the Orthodox perspective, the highest and best "theology" is a wordless theology of mystical communion with God that bypasses entirely the mediation of thoughts or ideas. A person cannot enter this encounter by thinking their way to it, but only through contemplation, clearing the mind of all thoughts and distractions in a way that results in receptivity to the divine and not in mere emptiness. The fourteenth-century Orthodox theologian Gregory Palamas explains: "Contemplation … is not simply abstraction and negation; it is a union and a divinization which occurs mystically and ineffably by the grace of God, after the stripping away of everything from here below which imprints itself on the mind, or rather after the cessation of all intellectual activity."[1] The Orthodox do not deny that there is a place for words and thought – a time to try to explain the spiritual realities of life insofar as they can be translated into human discourse – but that kind of theology of words is clearly secondary to theology as it is expressed and embodied in the experiencing of God.

Contemplative theology takes time and spiritual leisure; it is a natural fit for the monastic life. But many Orthodox laypeople also try to follow a way of life that involves continual prayer and longing for the presence of God. The most widely used contemplative practice in the modern Orthodox world is the "Jesus Prayer," a short prayer that says merely "Lord Jesus Christ, Son of God, have mercy on me." These words are often repeated in solitude, almost inaudibly, inhaling as one says the first three words and exhaling with the last four. Laypeople pray the Jesus prayer in the midst of daily routines, repeating it as they work or travel or eat their meals. The goal is to use this practice to slowly turn a prayer of the lips into a genuine prayer of the heart, cultivating a holiness of life and tranquility of spirit that is open to God's presence.

Orthodox spirituality has a focus on the higher world – the invisible world of God, the angels, and the saints – but Orthodox spirituality holds the earthly world in high regard as well. The Orthodox tradition teaches that human beings have both a material nature and a spiritual or divine nature, and both are good because both come from God. This is God's world, and it was created to be both appreciated and enjoyed. Ordinary life is honored in the Orthodox tradition. Time together with family and friends is considered a blessing, and the church itself is an extended family. Living together in the fellowship of the church requires times to fast, but also times to feast – times for repentance and sorrow, but also times for celebration, including the enjoyment of good food and wine. Rather than conflicting with the other-worldly emphases of Orthodox spirituality, this earthy spirituality grounds it in the here and now. Orthodox spirituality is deeply life-affirming and simultaneously nurtures an awareness that all of life is lived in God's holy presence.

Salvation

Compared to the Christian world as a whole, Orthodoxy holds a view of salvation that is broad and expansive. In non-Orthodox circles, salvation is often ascribed to the individual and to that person's reconciliation with God. For Orthodox Christianity, salvation is something that happens to the whole world. The goal of salvation is not merely reconciliation, it is also the *theosis* (divinization or deification) of individuals, of humanity as a whole, and ultimately of all creation. In keeping with this broad and active sense of *theosis*, Orthodox Christians would never claim that they are already "saved." Salvation in the past tense makes no sense; salvation is a process that draws one into a future of deeper communion with God and others. Orthodox Christians might say they are, by God's grace, on the path toward salvation, but in this life no one attains the fullness of salvation.

The word *theosis* – deification – is jarring to many people who are not themselves Orthodox Christians. The image of deification is meant to be jarring; it is meant to be stunning in its claim. The claim is that the unfathomable God of the universe, maker of all that is and ever will be, has chosen to enter into a special relationship of unity with humankind. In Christ, God became human so that humanity could become divine. The goal of salvation is unifying fellowship with the Trinitarian God who is the great lover of the world and everyone in it. The eighth-century Orthodox theologian Manṣūr ibn Sarjūn (also known as John of Damascus) explained it this way: "Those who, through their own choice and the indwelling and cooperation of God, have become assimilated to God as much as possible … are truly called gods, not by nature, but by adoption, as iron heated in the fire is called fire, not by nature, but by its condition and participation in fire."[2]

The image here is one of God as fire and of the deified person as a piece of iron that has become bright red through contact with the fire of God. In this process, the iron remains iron just as the human being remains a human being, but what one sees is not iron, but the fiery glow of God's presence. This image also reflects the fact that Orthodox theology has a genuinely positive view of human nature – significantly more positive than either Catholicism or Protestantism. Rather than seeing people as totally lost and overcome by sin, Orthodoxy sees humanity as weakened by sin in much the same way that sickness weakens people. Rather than being a total transformation, salvation is more like recovering from a disease and regaining one's natural strength. In fact, the consecrated bread and wine of Orthodox worship are sometimes described as "the medicine of immortality," the means through which God strengthens people for the spiritual journey that will take them back to God.

God's presence in anyone's life is an expression of God's love not just for that individual, but for everyone in the world and indeed for the entire universe. To be truly aglow with God's presence is to be filled with God's love for everyone and everything, and a focus on one's own individual salvation becomes unthinkable. In the Orthodox tradition, salvation or deification is a process of ever deepening communion with all of creation. Salvation reverses the human propensity to see the world in terms of self versus others. The Orthodox tradition insistently proclaims that no one can ever be saved alone, but only in the company of others.

The breadth of Orthodoxy's vision of salvation raises the question of universal salvation: Will everyone without exception eventually be "saved"? The technical term for this kind of universal salvation in the Orthodox tradition is *apokatastasis*. Some church leaders and synods have condemned *apokatastasis*, arguing that evil humans who reject God's grace will, like the demons, be damned forever. But others, including some of the most respected theologians in the history of the Orthodox tradition, like Gregory of Nyssa (4th c.) and Maximus the Confessor (7th c.), argue that everyone, even the demons, will eventually be restored to fellowship and unity with God in Christ.

Such debates have little to do with the personal journeys toward salvation of most Orthodox Christians. Their journeys begin with baptism, when a baby is welcomed into fellowship with God and others in the church. In the act of baptism an infant receives a new kind of life beyond the merely physical, beginning a new spiritual relationship with the parents, with the godparents who were part of the ceremony, with everyone who is already in the church, with the child's newly assigned guardian angel, and with God in Christ. As children grow up they slowly own their baptism for themselves, but they are not beginning from scratch. Even adult converts start in the middle, because others have helped them get going. No one comes to God alone.

Assisted by others in entering the path of salvation – a pathway that is itself a free gift from God – Orthodox Christians believe their own effort is necessary for progress to continue. There are two parts to that effort: first, sorrowing for the willful sin one discovers in one's own life (which can take many different forms) and, second, persisting in the practice of prayer (learning to push all of one's earthly thoughts and cares of life aside and simply *be* in the presence of God). But even here, Orthodoxy does not take an individualistic turn. It is in worship with others that one learns how to pray, and it is by feeding together on the bread and wine of the Eucharist – which is given even to children – that one receives the spiritual sustenance for continuing the journey toward salvation in the company of others.

Structure

Sometimes references are made to the "Eastern Orthodox Church" in the singular. While it is true that all Orthodox Christians see themselves as spiritual members of one church, there is no institutional entity called "the Eastern Orthodox Church." The Orthodox tradition is not housed in one church, but in a diverse family of related churches. At present, that family includes about 40 separate churches. Fourteen of these churches are designated *autocephalous*, meaning that other Orthodox Christian churches consider them to be fully self-governing and independent. These would include, for example, the Orthodox Church of Russia and the Orthodox Church of Antioch. A significant number of other Orthodox churches describe themselves as *autonomous*, which typically means that they exercise full control over their own affairs, but that their independence has not yet been recognized by the other Orthodox churches.

The familial sense of relatedness that exists among the Orthodox churches is different than the way Christians in the other traditions understand their connections with each other. The Orthodox view is, in particular, much more organic and less institutional than the way most Catholics and Protestants think. In fact, the Orthodox tradition has developed its own cluster of words to describe the distinctive sense of community that exists within the Orthodox world, including words like synodality, conciliarity, and *sobornost* (fellowship). All of these terms communicate essentially the same thing: Orthodoxy exists as a family of churches defined by their mutuality of respect, concern, and compassion for each other and for the work that God is doing in the world through each of the separate Orthodox churches.

Agreement on a few basic essentials is expected. For example, all Orthodox churches acknowledge the authority of the seven great councils of the early church and follow the same basic format for worship. But total uniformity is rejected. It is assumed that each autocephalous Orthodox church has the right to its own locally adapted national style of faith. It is also assumed that new churches will constantly be forming as the gospel moves into new cultures, and when these younger Orthodox churches mature they will eventually be granted the status of being independent or autocephalous. Like parents and children in ordinary families, tensions sometimes arise when a younger church seeks its independence and its older "mother church" may not yet be ready to grant autonomy. The situation can become even more complex and tense when several different Orthodox traditions are represented in one nation (as is the case, for example, in the United States) and lines of jurisdiction overlap. But the Orthodox tradition has a long history of negotiating these matters and almost always the issues are eventually resolved amicably.

Most Orthodox churches in the world today are organized along national lines, a relatively recent development fueled by two Orthodox convictions. One assumption is that each linguistically and culturally defined human community should have its own church so it can worship God in its own words and ways. A second assumption is that states and nations are to be respected because they exist by God's will and grace – they are ordained by God – and, because of that, Orthodox Christians have rarely engaged in overt political protest. Even during times of government persecution Orthodox Christians have typically acted respectfully toward their rulers, though they have sometimes strongly resisted government policies designed to change or control the Orthodox churches. In certain cases, the linkage between nationalism and Orthodox faith has become so strong they have practically merged. Theologically, the Orthodox tradition makes a distinction between a proper sense of cooperation with the state (called *symphonia*) and an improper veneration of or subservience to the state (called *phyletism*), but sometimes that distinction is difficult to define with precision.

One other large-scale issue related to the structure of Orthodoxy has to do with theology. In the sixth century, what was then the pre-Orthodox tradition experienced a division over the issue of how best to define the relationship of the human and divine in Christ. One party, the group of churches that would later become known as Eastern Orthodoxy, favored the wording of the Council of Chalcedon (which was held in the year 451). The other group, which rejected the Council of Chalcedon, became known as the Miaphysite tradition. (This history is discussed in some detail in Chapter 15.) Today the Miaphysite Orthodox tradition (sometimes called "Oriental Orthodoxy") is represented by the Coptic Orthodox Church, the Ethiopian Orthodox Church, the Syrian Orthodox Church, and the Armenian Apostolic Church. For years, these two groups (the Chalcedonian and the Miaphysite churches) considered each other heretics, but since the 1960s they have been in dialogue about possible reunification. Roughly 5 percent of the Orthodox Christians in the world are Miaphysite in theological orientation; the other 95 percent are Chalcedonian.

While these macrostructures of the Orthodox tradition are significant, it is important to remember that the real center of Orthodox organization is found on the local level, not the national or international. The local *see* or diocese is the most important institutional structure of Orthodox life. This is the heart of the church, where the faithful worship under the guidance and oversight of a local bishop. Every bishop is the spiritual equal of every other bishop. Thus titles like archbishop and metropolitan, which are given to bishops of important cities, are to some degree designations of honor and respect rather than power and authority. While archbishops and metropolitans do have special responsibilities within the Orthodox churches, they are not superbishops or minipopes and they never hand down decisions about matters of faith as if from on high. The goal is always to establish consensus among all the bishops. Bishops in the Orthodox tradition are unmarried, and most were previously monks. The transition from monastery to parish is usually not difficult. Small monasteries are scattered throughout the Orthodox world – there is almost always one somewhere nearby – and they are not isolated. Many laypeople visit the monasteries on a regular basis, and many monks serve as spiritual directors for local laypeople and clergy.

In contrast to the bishops, most Orthodox priests are married. Priests frequently need to give spiritual advice to the married members of their parishes, and it is assumed that unmarried men would be ill-equipped for the task. The extended family is tremendously important in the Orthodox tradition, serving as the most intimate social container of the Orthodox faith. It is in the family that children first learn of God, and it is in the family that Orthodox Christians learn the joys and difficulties of living in relationship or synodality. Many Orthodox church buildings reflect this familial ethos. While those outside the tradition tend to think of Orthodox churches as large and impressive cathedral-like buildings, the vast majority of Orthodox churches are small and intimate places. In village settings, a church may accommodate only 15 or 20 people, and almost every worshipper in the room will be related to everyone else, sharing the communion of Orthodox faith and spirituality as a natural part of life.

Story

The history of Orthodoxy is long and complicated, but it can be divided into four 500-year subperiods for ease of understanding. The first of these periods (up to 500) represents the prehistory of the movement, a time when the roots of the Orthodox Church were developing. The years from 500 to 1000 are the "formative age," when Orthodoxy first coalesced into its own separate and distinct tradition. This period can also be called the Early Byzantine Era because most of the key events took place in connection with the Byzantine Empire. The Late Byzantine Era (1000–1500) was a time of political decline for the empire, but it was also a time of theological advancement for the Orthodox Churches. Finally, the fourth era, starting around 1500 and continuing up to the present, is the "national church" period when the current state–church structure of Orthodoxy came into existence.

Prehistory: beginnings to 500

The deep roots of the Orthodox tradition extend back to the earliest Greek-speaking Christian communities within the ancient Roman Empire. The Roman Empire was bilingual, with Greek spoken by most people in the eastern half of the empire and Latin spoken in the west. Words and languages package reality, shaping the way people see the world. Greek-speaking Christians were more prone to think philosophically and abstractly about matters of faith, while Latin-speaking Christianity (which would eventually become the Catholic tradition) was generally more concrete and legalistic. To some degree this distinction remains in place even today.

But while the deep roots of the Orthodox tradition can be traced to the earliest years of the Christian movement in the Roman Empire, it makes little sense to speak about a distinctly Orthodox tradition during these years. The Christian movement as a whole was just getting started and many different and sometimes contradictory impulses were being expressed. It was only after the year 325, when the first ecumenical (general or universal) council of Christian leaders was held in the city of Nicaea (in the northwest corner of modern Turkey), that the earliest framework for the Orthodox tradition began to coalesce. Three more ecumenical councils would be held before the year 500, culminating in the Council of Chalcedon (451), and these four councils represent the common base for both the Catholic and Orthodox traditions.

The formative (or early Byzantine) age: 500 to 1000

The Byzantine Empire is the name given to the Eastern half of the old Roman Empire (roughly equivalent to modern Greece and Turkey) after the Roman Empire lost political control of Western Europe. The name change is also often associated with the transition of the Eastern Roman Empire, around the year 600, from a bilingual society (Latin and Greek) to a solely Greek-speaking nation. The Byzantine Empire lasted until 1453, so the formative age represents only the first half of Byzantine history. It was during these centuries that the Catholic and Orthodox Churches – the Latin-speaking and the Greek-speaking Christian churches of the old Roman Empire – began to drift apart from each other, slowly taking on their own separate and distinctive identities.

The reasons for this drift are complex and include political and cultural developments as well as emerging theological differences, but by the year 1000 it was clear that Orthodoxy and Catholicism had become independent of each other and were no longer simply different branches of the same large tradition. As if to mark this fact, the so-called "Great Schism" that took place in the year 1054 (an event that involved the Pope condemning the Patriarch of Constantinople and the Patriarch of Constantinople denouncing the Pope in return) is often seen as the formal point of separation between the two churches. But Orthodoxy's distinctive identity had really been forged several centuries earlier, during the 700s and the 800s when a tremendous conflict arose about whether icons should be allowed in the churches or whether they should be banned as idolatrous. The *iconophiles* (lovers of icons) won that contest, and icons have played a central role in Orthodox life ever since. While the Second Council of Nicaea, held in 787, settled this issue theologically, the final victory of the iconophile movement (often referred to as the Triumph of Orthodoxy) did not take place until 843, when the Byzantine Empress Theodora finally threw the full weight of the government behind the Council's decision.

The Orthodox tradition faced another challenge during this period that deepened and solidified its identity: the rise of Islam. Heretofore, Orthodox Christianity had defined itself by explaining how it superseded earlier forms of religion, presenting itself as an improvement on and correction of both Roman paganism and Judaism. But Islam was a new religion that saw itself as the successor of Judaism and Christianity. The initial reaction of Orthodoxy was to treat Islam as if it was a Christian heresy, hoping it would soon disappear. Rather than disappearing, however, Islam became stronger and soon took over much of the territory where Orthodoxy had previously flourished. This Muslim conquest of the Middle East changed the church's organizational structure. Before the conquest, the four Patriarchs of the great cities of Constantinople, Antioch, Alexandria, and Jerusalem had shared the leadership of the tradition. After the conquest, the Patriarch of Constantinople began to exercise greater authority because he was now the only Patriarch not living under Muslim rule.

The late Byzantine period

The late Byzantine period began on an upswing. The world of Orthodoxy was expanding northward as a result of the conversion of Russia, and the Orthodox Byzantine Empire seemed poised to reconquer much of the territory that had been lost to Islam. Under Basil II, who ruled from 976 to 1025, the Byzantine Empire made impressive gains in the East, in what is now Syria and northern Iraq, but then the tide changed and the Byzantine army suffered a huge defeat at the hands of the Seljuk Turks in the famous Battle of Manzikert (1071) in what is now eastern Turkey. That defeat marked the beginning of a long, slow decline in both the Byzantine Empire and its Orthodox church.

The weakening Byzantine Empire eventually felt compelled to ask the Catholic West for military assistance. That assistance came in the form of the Crusades which, at first, seemed to help. However, the armies of the Fourth Crusade (1204), rather than fighting against the Islamic forces in the region, attacked the Byzantine Empire itself, ransacking the city of Constantinople, raping Orthodox women, and stripping the churches of their treasures. Later a Latin-dominated puppet government was set up in the region with the intention of forcing the Orthodox Church to accept the supreme religious authority of the Pope. The Orthodox leadership never fully complied, and the Orthodox Church developed a deep and abiding suspicion of the Catholic Church that still impacts Catholic–Orthodox relations today.

Greek rule and Orthodox faith were restored in the region in the mid-1200s, but there was constant threat of attack from the Islamic Ottoman Turks. By the early 1400s, their situation was once again desperate and once again Byzantium turned to the West for help. And in repetition of the past, the Catholic West once again said that submission to the Pope was the cost of assistance. With no other option at hand, the Patriarch of Constantinople duly submitted to union with Rome at the Council of Florence in 1439. But despite that submission, no real aid was forthcoming, and Constantinople fell to the Turks in 1453, effectively ending the Byzantine Empire. Most Orthodox believers subsequently denounced the Council of Florence and repudiated any union with the Roman Catholic Church. The authority and prestige of the Patriarch of Constantinople also sustained serious damage because of complicity (even if it was essentially forced) in negotiating the union with Rome. Orthodoxy was clearly at a low ebb.

If there was any bright spot in the Orthodox history of this period, it was largely in the area of theology and spirituality, where the writings of Symeon the New Theologian (942–1022) and Gregory Palamas (1296–1359) helped shape a new "interior" expression of Orthodox faith and piety. Turning away from the abstract, philosophical, and scholastic theology of his contemporaries, Symeon stressed the inner experience of God, how humans search for and find the presence of God in life through the power of the Holy Spirit. Palamas similarly stressed the importance of the interior life, focusing especially on contemplation (including use of the Jesus Prayer) as a means of stilling the mind so that the light of God could be seen and experienced as fire within one's soul.

The national church period: 1500 to the present

After the fall of the Byzantine Empire, the Orthodox tradition became increasingly fragmented, and individual Orthodox churches began to identify with the individual nations within which they existed. The Orthodox Church of Russia paved the way. In the early 1500s, Russia (and its Russian Orthodox Church) tried to position itself as the new successor to the old Orthodox Byzantine Empire, even going so far as to call Moscow the "third Rome." But tensions and disputes within the Russian Orthodox Church weakened that claim. In the year 1700, the Russian Empire did away with the Orthodox Patriarchate altogether and made the Orthodox Church simply a branch of the national government under the control of a lay (nonordained) administrator. The Russian *Orthodox* Church became the *Russian* Orthodox Church, belonging to the Russian people and not to any other ethnic community. The interests of the broader transnational Orthodox community became secondary at best.

Similar national frameworks for Orthodoxy began to appear outside Russia in the 1800s as the Muslim Ottoman Empire, which had controlled most of Eastern Europe during the seventeenth and eighteenth centuries, began to weaken. As the boundaries of the Ottoman Empire slowly slipped back toward Turkey like a receding glacier, the various peoples of Eastern Europe one by one reasserted their older national identities and simultaneously wedded their Orthodox religious faith to those new identities. The result was the creation of a new European map of Orthodoxy that merged nationhood and religious affiliation. This is when, for example, the modern Greek state and the Greek Orthodox Church were created, and the same dynamic was at work in Romania, Bulgaria, and elsewhere. The typical pattern was for political independence to come first, followed by a local declaration of ecclesiastical autonomy. Then a new Patriarchate was established whenever the other Orthodox churches recognized that ecclesiastical independence. Thus, for example, Greek political independence was restored in 1832 and this was followed by a declaration of Greek Orthodox Church autonomy in 1833 and full autocephalous status in 1850. In Romania the process was slightly different, with ecclesiastical independence coming first (1865), national independence next (1877), and finally Romanian Orthodox autocephaly in 1925.

In the twentieth century, the Orthodox nations of Russia and Eastern Europe faced yet one more bitter trial: life under Communist rule. In 1917, Communists took control of Russia; after World War II, they extended that control to most of the rest of the region.

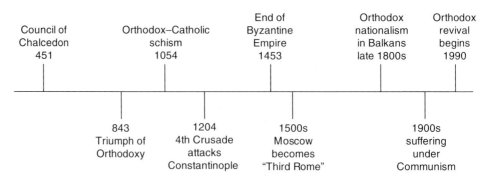

Figure 1.4   Key events in Orthodox history

Communists were atheists and were ideologically opposed to religion. Individuals were discouraged from belief in God, many churches were closed, and the religious education of children was often disallowed. This last restriction was especially harmful for Orthodoxy since the nurture of faith during childhood undergirds the Orthodox process of becoming Christian. Many churches declined in membership and attendance, sometimes drastically so, but Orthodoxy managed to survive. Since the fall of Communism in 1990, a revival of Orthodox faith has been underway, perhaps most prominently in Russia, but also in Romania, and to some degree in Bulgaria, Albania, and Serbia.

But the issue of nationalism remains, and nationalism in the modern Orthodox experience has sometimes verged on national worship. Orthodoxy's future will be determined largely by how it handles this issue. George Tsetsis, an Orthodox theologian associated with the Ecumenical Patriarchate, says:

> If Orthodoxy is to give a convincing concerted and united Orthodox witness in today's pluralistic world, then the rediscovery of an Orthodox conscience … that goes beyond ethnic and national cleavages is, I believe, an urgent matter. Orthodoxy will be credible only when all local autocephalous and autonomous Orthodox churches are able to speak and act *as one single body and not as separate ethnic or national entities.*[3]

That is both a harsh judgment and a high ideal, but it comes from deep within the Orthodox community itself and it reflects a genuine dilemma. The problem of nationalism in a now thoroughly globalized earth is forcing all the religious traditions, including Orthodoxy, to reassess their self-understandings and public roles in the world.

Notes

1 Gregory Palamas, *The Triads*, ed. John Meyendorff, trans. Nicholas Gendle (Mahwah, NJ: Paulist Press, 1983), pp. 34–5.

2 John of Damascus, *Three Treatises on the Divine Images*, trans. Andrew Louth (Crestwood, NJ: St Vladimir's Seminary Press, 2003), p. 106.

3 George Tsetsis, "Ethnicity, Nationalism and Religion," in Emmanuel Clapsis (ed.), *The Orthodox Churches in a Pluralistic World: An Ecumenical Conversation* (Geneva: WCC Publications, 2004), pp. 148–58; quote from p. 156.

Suggestions for Further Reading

Angold, Michael (ed.) (2006). *The Cambridge History of Christianity: Eastern Christianity*. Cambridge, UK: Cambridge University Press.

Binns, John (2002). *An Introduction to the Christian Orthodox Churches*. Cambridge, UK: Cambridge University Press.

Chryssavgis, John (2004). *Light Through Darkness: The Orthodox Tradition*. Maryknoll, NY: Orbis.

Clapsis, Emmanuel (ed.) (2004). *The Orthodox Churches in a Pluralistic World: An Ecumenical Conversation*. Geneva: WCC Publications.

McGuckin, John Anthony (2008). *The Orthodox Church: An Introduction to its History, Doctrine, and Spiritual Culture*. Oxford: Blackwell.

Parry, Ken (ed.) (2004). *The Blackwell Companion to Eastern Christianity*. Oxford: Blackwell.

Ware, Timothy (1997). *The Orthodox Church*. London: Penguin.

Chapter 2

The Catholic Tradition

The Catholic tradition is the largest of the four contemporary major Christian traditions, and its "catholicity" – its willingness to embrace difference and learn from others – has also made the Catholic tradition incredibly varied. Rather than forcing members to choose between one style of faith or another, Catholicism has typically opted to be a tradition of "both/and." Whatever is seen as having spiritual merit and value can be incorporated into Catholicism, even when the opposite emphases are also present within the tradition. Thus both celibacy and marriage are affirmed, and scientific inquiry is encouraged alongside the continuing acceptance of a range of superstitious local customs. Catholicism's both/and stance has also allowed it to adopt and adapt various ideas and practices from other Christian traditions. Some forms of Catholicism can thus look and feel quite Orthodox (veneration of icons and the respect given to Mary), while others can look and feel quite Pentecostal (speaking in tongues and belief in miracles), or even Protestant (Bible study by individuals and small groups). This same commitment to catholicity has also allowed Catholicism to welcome and appreciate spiritual insights and practices of many non-Christian religions and cultures.

The Catholic Church has high aspirations, but it has not always lived up to those ideals. This is, of course, true of all religious institutions and, indeed, of all secular institutions as well. No one lives up to all their ideals. So why even mention it? Because few other institutions have claimed so much. Up until the mid-twentieth century, it was common for the Catholic Church to describe itself as the one true church on earth, as the unblemished bride of Christ, and as the only pathway to heaven. These claims were made, however, by the same church that was the Church of the Crusades, the Church of the Inquisition, and more recently a church with a serious worldwide pedophile problem. It would be entirely wrong to judge the whole tradition on the basis of these lapses – and they are lapses, not the norm – but it would be equally mistaken to act as if they never happened. While some Catholic

The World's Christians: Who they are, Where they are, and How they got there, First Edition. Douglas Jacobsen.
© 2011 Douglas Jacobsen. Published 2011 by Blackwell Publishing Ltd.

Church leaders have found it difficult to acknowledge the imperfections of the Catholic Church and its tradition, most lay Catholics have not. Catholic laypeople have always known their church is imperfect, but they have loved it anyway. In fact, the willingness to admit one's own imperfections and to live together in community with other obviously imperfect people is one of the great strengths of the Catholic tradition at the grassroots.

Catholicism has been a global faith longer than any other Christian tradition. Up until 1500 almost all Catholics lived in Europe, but after that the movement expanded rapidly, first to Latin America and the west coast of Africa and later to Asia and North America. Today Latin America is the demographic center of the Catholic world, with almost two-fifths of the world's Catholics living in the region.

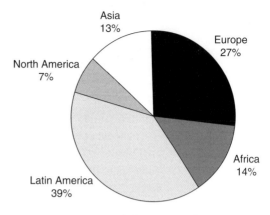

Figure 2.1   Where Catholics live (% of global Catholic population living in each continent)

Europe has the second largest Catholic population, while Africa and Asia are essentially tied for third place. North America, home to roughly 50 million Catholics, is the least Catholic continent in terms of overall numbers. (See Figure 2.1.)

Spirituality

Enormous diversity exists within Catholicism, including many different schools and sub-schools of spirituality. Thousands of books have been written about these different styles of Catholic faith and practice. The focus here will be limited to three dimensions that together provide some sense of the scope and range of Catholic spirituality: sacramental imagination, communal consciousness, and intellectual rigor.

Sacramental imagination

The Catholic tradition sees the world as infused with the presence of God. God is everywhere, and God is constantly calling the world and all the world's people to a higher and more holy way of life. This is the Catholic sacramental imagination. It sees the world as a place where both people and the material stuff of creation can become a means of divine self-revelation and a medium through which grace (God's free and unmerited assistance) is communicated to humankind. Thus the twelfth-century nun Hildegard of Bingen exuberantly described God as saying: "I gleam in the waters, and I burn in the sun, moon, and stars. With every breeze … I awaken everything to life."[1] Later, the nineteenth-century Catholic poet Gerard Manley Hopkins exulted that the world is "charged with the grandeur of God" ready at any moment to "flame out, like shining from shook foil."[2]

A sacramental experience of the world is one that communicates grace. It is an invitation from God to become "more" than one already is and to enter into a new depth of love and fellowship with God and all of God's creation. God's sacramental engagement with humankind is never a matter of imposition. God does not force grace on anyone;

it is an offer that must be actively received. Thus the Catholic tradition sees human cooperation – religious effort – as a necessary part of spirituality. But while grace is never forced on anyone, it does come with strings. God's grace is not given merely to enliven people or help them with their ills; God's grace is given for the purpose of drawing people closer to God and toward personal holiness. As the *Catechism of the Catholic Church* explains in its very first paragraph, "God draws close" to humankind in order to call individuals "to seek him, to know him, and to love him."[3]

The logic behind this sacramental vision of spirituality comes from the ancient North African Bishop Augustine of Hippo (354–430), who wrote at the beginning of his book the *Confessions* that "you [God] made us for yourself and our hearts are restless until they rest in you." According to the Catholic tradition, humanity was created to live in fellowship with God, and that fellowship is experienced in the present in the practice of prayer, which the Catholic *Catechism* defines as "a vital and personal relationship with the living and true God." The *Catechism* further explains that humanity's thirst for God is actually a response to God's own thirst for fellowship with humankind: "Whether we realize it or not, prayer is the encounter of God's thirst with ours. God thirsts that we may thirst for him."[4]

The *sacraments* of the Catholic Church are visible signs of God's grace. The seven sacraments – baptism, confirmation, penance, the Eucharist, the anointing of the sick, marriage, and holy orders (ordination to the priesthood) – communicate God's grace more directly and consistently than anything else in the world. These ritual acts largely follow the life cycle of faith. Baptism signals the beginning of faith and confirmation its coming to adult maturity. Penance and the Eucharist are repetitive acts that sustain the life of faith and help people to grow spiritually. And the anointing of the sick prepares one for what used to be called a "good death" – the ability to face the end of life trusting God and without fear. The sacraments of marriage and holy orders are somewhat different, representing alternative life directions: either to marry and live "in the world" or to become a celibate (unmarried and sexually inactive) priest wholly dedicated to God and the service of others. (While not taking "holy orders" per se, many lay monks and nuns also follow a celibate lifestyle of complete dedication to God and others that is similar to priestly service.)

The Catholic tradition also includes a variety of *sacramentals*, other actions that convey forms of grace in addition to the sacraments proper. Making the sign of the cross, being sprinkled with holy water, and receiving ashes on one's forehead at the beginning of Lent are all sacramentals. Catholics believe that the sacraments and sacramentals represent the most predictable and consistent means of receiving God's grace, but Catholics also believe that God's mercy can overflow these containers, making it possible for God's grace to suddenly appear in one's life in unexpected ways at times when people are in special need or specially open to God's presence in the world.

Communal consciousness

The Catholic tradition affirms the communal and interconnected character of human life. In particular, it stresses that the actions and attitudes of individuals affect those around them. Catherine of Sienna (1347–80) put it this way: "There is no sin that does not touch others, whether secretly by refusing them what is due, or openly by giving birth to the vices."[5] Virtues work in much the same way. While a virtue is first of all an individual characteristic – a disposition that allows someone to act in a morally good manner – the living of a virtuous life has the potential to impact others positively both by modeling good behavior and by eliciting gratitude from those who are positively affected by those good actions. Growing out of this vision of human interconnectedness, Catholics recognize the need for community within the church. In agreement with the Orthodox tradition, most Catholics assume that no one can be a Christian alone. Being a Christian is being part of the people of God who together are making their way forward in faith. It is in the community of the church that vices are slowly unlearned and that virtues are encouraged and nurtured.

The Catholic tradition takes this communal perspective one step further and applies it to society as well as to individuals. The assumption is that the accumulated moral choices of individuals in a society will slowly create a certain kind of moral ethos within that society that will, in turn, shape the morality of individuals. People who grow up in a materialistic culture are more likely to become materialists themselves, and people who grow up in a sexually liberal society are more likely to become sexually promiscuous. By contrast, cultures that emphasize spiritual, as opposed to material, values and that stress sexual self-control, as opposed to libertarianism, are more likely to produce citizens who are nonmaterialistic and sexually chaste. Consequently, public rules of behavior – especially the legal codes of nations that touch on explicitly moral matters – are seen as serious and relevant concerns for the church. Historically, the Catholic Church has often opposed government actions that decriminalize or encourage behavior deemed immoral by the Catholic Church. In recent years, some Catholics have taken public stands against abortion and gay/lesbian rights and others have been involved in antiwar protests and rallies for peace and justice. Whatever their particular causes, many of these participants are motivated by a spirituality that is deeply rooted in Catholicism's belief in the moral interconnectedness of the human community.

Intellectual rigor

Perhaps more than any other Christian tradition, Catholicism has affirmed the importance of bringing faith and reason together. The Benedictine monk Anselm of Canterbury (1033–1109) coined the phrase "faith seeking understanding," and those words have been a Catholic touchstone ever since. A hundred years later Thomas Aquinas (1125–1274), undoubtedly the most influential theologian in all of Catholic history, wrote that the goal of Christian intellect is to use reason and intelligent reflection to turn mere belief into genuine knowledge. The foundational affirmation of the Catholic intellectual tradition is that Catholic faith properly understood and human learning at its best will never truly conflict.

Faith has not always been properly understood and human learning has not always been at its best, so apparent conflicts arise all the time. History is full of examples, including the church's unfortunate condemnation of Galileo in the year 1616 for his sun-centered, rather than earth-centered, view of the universe. But 1616 is a long time ago, and the notion that faith and reason, or science and religion, exist in a state of perpetual warfare is a fundamental misrepresentation of the Catholic tradition. Most Catholic intellectuals believe that, over time, further reflection and better information will lead to coherence between faith and learning. How could it be otherwise when the God of creation, including the creation of the human mind, is also the God of Jesus Christ?

Seasoned by this relatively high assessment of human intellect, the Catholic tradition has developed a style of theology that differs significantly from the Orthodox tradition. The Orthodox tradition, as explained in the previous chapter, has been apophatic in its theological orientation, often choosing to remain silent rather than to speak and misrepresent God or Christian truth through the use of too many words or analogies. The Catholic tradition has taken almost the opposite approach. Though acknowledging that care must be exercised when using earthly images or ideas to describe God, the Catholic tradition says that use of those images and ideas is a necessary part of any robust articulation of the Christian faith. Rather than remaining silent, Catholic theology is more likely to pile images and ideas on top of images and ideas in its attempt to explore the depth of God's being and relationship to the world.

The Catholic tradition insists, however, that these earthly images and ideas be understood "analogically" when applied to God. An analogy describes one thing as similar to something else, but always in a limited way. Thus, for example, Catholics say that God created the world in something like the way an artist creates a work of art, but of course there are also differences. God does not have literal hands like an artist making a sculpture, and Catholics believe that God made the world *ex nihilo* ("out of nothing"), which is something no artist can do. Every other analogy has similar limitations, but these limits are not necessarily defects; they allow room for intellectual advance. For example, the Catholic Church has been able to accept the theory of evolution precisely because the analogy of God as creator is limited. It communicates that the world has an origin and purpose outside itself, but it does not necessarily imply that Catholics have any special knowledge about the details of how the world scientifically came to be. By affirming the importance of analogical thinking, the Catholic tradition acknowledges that there are many different ways to legitimately express a Christian understanding of God and the world. Rather than assuming that there is one and only one way of properly explaining the Christian faith, the Catholic tradition assumes that humanity's understanding of God has the capacity to grow and expand as knowledge advances and as new analogies are used to explore spiritual truths.

Salvation

Salvation in the Catholic tradition is set within a grand narrative of God's eternal love for the world. God made the world out of nothing, out of an overflowing abundance of divine love. And God created people as beings who were capable of experiencing that love and reflecting it back to God. Catholics believe that this original relationship of love between God and humanity was later disrupted by humanity's sin, but despite that disruption God's love for humankind continues and God is constantly trying to woo people back into the loving relationship for which they were created. This is why Christ said that the greatest of all the commandments is to love God with all one's heart, mind, soul, and strength. The love of God is "commanded" not because it is some kind of duty that humanity owes to God, but because people can only truly and fully be themselves when they exist in a mutually loving relationship with God.

For individuals, the day-to-day experience of salvation has a somewhat different focus: the forgiveness of and elimination of sin. Sin is an attitude or action that transgresses God's law or that directs humans away from life-affirming goals and purposes for which they were created. Sin often takes the form of wrongful attachments to crass desires and the seeking of material comforts which make people less than they were meant to be and which undermine the bonds of human care, affection, and solidarity. The Catholic tradition makes a distinction between *original sin* and subsequent sins. Original sin, which humanity inherited from the first human beings (Adam and Eve) who committed the first sin, consists of a lack of trust in and love for God. The various specific sins which people commit, ranging in gravity from *mortal sins* such as murder and adultery to *venial sins* such as white lies or occasional drunkenness, all flow from this underlying flaw in human nature.

As in Orthodoxy, salvation within the Catholic tradition is understood to be a process rather than an event. That process begins with the sacrament of baptism which undoes the damage of original sin and makes it possible once again to trust and love God. Overcoming various specific sins takes place through the sacrament of penance and reconciliation, which provides both a remedy for the sins people commit and a mechanism for moral advancement in the Christian life. Individuals first acknowledge the wrong they have done, then express sorrow (contrition) for their sins, and finally seek to "make satisfaction" that will right the wrong that has resulted from their actions. The church, through a priest, assures penitent individuals that their sins have been forgiven through the sacrifice of Christ's death.

The lifelong pattern of penance and reconciliation is called *conversion* or sometimes "conversion of the heart." This kind of conversion requires the death of the prideful self and the strict disciplining of one's desires and actions. It also necessarily involves pain and sadness for sin. Devout Catholics try to foster the process of conversion in their own lives through various acts of devotion and self-sacrifice, which can include saying the rosary (a sequence of prayers and meditations related to Christ and the Virgin Mary, often undertaken with the help of prayer beads), meditating on the *stations of the cross* (14 events associated with Christ's condemnation and crucifixion that are depicted in sculptures or paintings on the side walls of most Catholic churches), fasting, and even physical self-punishment. Some Catholics consecrate themselves entirely to God by taking religious vows and becoming monks or nuns. Other Catholics seek conversion of their hearts through prayer, meditation, service, and good works that laypeople can undertake without adopting all the rigors and restrictions of monastic life.

The most important ritual of conversion within the Catholic Church is, without doubt, participation in the Eucharist. The word "Eucharist" means thanksgiving, and the eucharistic celebration is an act of both participation in and thanksgiving for Christ's sacrifice which makes salvation possible. Catholics believe that the bread and wine of the Eucharist literally become the body and blood of Christ as a result of the prayer that is said by the priest during Mass (the Catholic service of worship where the Eucharist is celebrated). Holding his hands over the bread and wine, the priest says: "Bless and approve our offering; make it acceptable to you, an offering in spirit and in truth. Let it become for us the body and blood of Jesus Christ, your only Son, our Lord." As the unleavened wafer (called a *host*) is ingested, Catholics believe that Christ literally feeds their souls through the holiness of Christ's own body. Just as Christ's physical suffering on the cross somehow resulted in God's forgiveness of human sin, the physical presence of Christ in the host communicates grace to the recipient. Some devout Catholics participate in Mass every day. Mother Teresa, the saintly humanitarian from Calcutta, often said that the Eucharist was her spiritual food and that she could not get through a single day without it.

Holiness is the final goal of conversion, sufficient holiness that one can stand in God's presence and not be ashamed. Since most Catholics do not achieve such holiness while still living on earth, the idea slowly developed within Catholicism that there must be some place or some spiritual mechanism that would allow individuals to acquire the level of holiness needed to enter heaven after death. That place or spiritual mechanism is called *purgatory*. There is little, if any, reference to purgatory in the Bible, but Catholics view this doctrine as a necessary extension of other Christian and biblical teachings about salvation and holiness.

The Catholic Church has also wrestled with the question of whether salvation is available in any form outside the institution of the Roman Catholic Church. Historically, the most common answer has been "no," but starting in the sixteenth century, some Catholic theologians began to articulate a broader vision of salvation that allowed the possibility that some people who are outside the Catholic Church, even some who have never heard of Christ, might potentially end up in heaven because their lives demonstrate a "desire for baptism." Karl Rahner, one of the most important Catholic theologians of the twentieth century, called such people "anonymous Christians." The Catholic Catechism itself acknowledges this potentially wider scope of salvation by saying that while "God has bound salvation to the sacrament of baptism … he himself is not bound by his sacraments."[6]

The wideness of God's mercy is also a common theme in Catholic folk culture, where it is often expressed through the image of Mary as mediatrix of God's grace and forgiveness. A popular folk story tells of Jesus wandering around heaven to see how things are going and discovering that a number of people had made themselves at home who had no right to be there. He confronts Saint Peter, demanding an explanation, but Peter says: "Don't blame me. I slam the gate in their faces." Jesus is clearly not satisfied with this reply and presses for more information. Peter tells him, "You don't want to know," but Jesus states firmly, "Yes, I do." So Peter explains: "Fine. I keep them out, but then they go around to the back door and don't you know your mother lets them all in!"[7] Jesus is humorously portrayed in the story as a kind of strict policeman trying to keep sinners out of heaven rather than as the loving savior of the world, but God's deep love for humanity shines in Mary's maternal dispensing of God's love to everyone.

Structure

The Roman Catholic Church is the largest and most highly organized religious institution in the world. With a global membership of more than one billion, the work of the church is overseen by about 4,500 bishops, 400,000 priests, and almost a million religious men and women (monks and nuns). The Catholic Church owns and operates 125,000 schools worldwide, including approximately 200 full-fledged universities; it runs more than 100,000 charitable institutions (hospitals, orphanages, homes for the elderly and the needy). It is the only religious organization that governs its own country, Vatican City, the smallest nation in the world with a total territory of 108.7 acres. Europe was once the dominant center of

Table 2.1 Global organization of Catholic Church

World region	Total number of Catholics in region	% of world's Catholic population	Number of dioceses in region*	Number of parishes in region*
Africa	140,000,000	14	480	11,750
Asia and Oceania	132,700,000	13	675	25,750
Europe	277,000,000	27	725	127,000
Latin America	395,000,000	39	700	31,000
North America	75,000,000	7	265	24,000
Total	1,019,700,000	100	2,845	219,500

* Dioceses and parishes are constantly being created and disbanded. The numbers here are rough counts taken from http://www.catholic-hierarchy.org/ for the year 2009.

global Catholicism, but only about one quarter of the world's Catholics live there now. The most Catholic region of the world today is Latin America but there are also large Catholic populations in Africa, Asia, and North America. (See Table 2.1.)

The Catholic Church is geographically divided into nearly 3,000 separate and distinct ecclesiastical districts. Most of these are called dioceses, though some have other names such as eparchies, vicariates, and prefectures. A bishop or archbishop oversees every diocese, and the bishop of the oldest or most important diocese in a nation will often be called the primate of that country. In the last half century, local councils of bishops (some national and some regional) have become important entities within the global organization of the Catholic Church. The Council of Latin American Bishops (known as CELAM), for example, was instrumental in developing many of the basic ideas that later found systematic expression in Catholic liberation theology, and more recently the Federation of Asian Bishops' Conferences (FABC) helped prompt new discussions both of poverty and of the relationship between Catholicism and other religions.

Historically, the person of the Pope has been the most important guarantor of Catholic unity, and that remains true today. The main role of the Pope, as defined by the *Catechism*, is to serve as "the perpetual and visible source of the unity both of the bishops and of the whole company of the faithful."[8] The papacy is also the most important mechanism for preserving and promoting Catholic truth and this role of the papacy is related to the idea of papal infallibility. The doctrine of papal infallibility does not means that everything a pope says is binding on all Catholics. What it means is that whenever a pope solemnly declares some particular aspect of Catholic faith or ethics to be a dogmatic teaching of the Church – something that does not occur frequently and only when the pope is speaking "*ex cathedra*" – he is miraculously preserved from error by the Holy Spirit. The doctrine of papal infallibility was formally articulated at the First Vatican Council in 1870. Since that time, it has been invoked only once, in 1950, to declare the assumption of Mary (her miraculous ascension to heaven before she died), a fundamental article of faith for all Catholics.

Catholic bishops are morally and theologically subject to the authority of the Pope, who appoints them to office, but they have wide-ranging freedom to conduct business and

Table 2.2   Global distribution of Catholic parishes and priests

World region	Total number of Catholics in region	Number of priests	Number of Catholics per priest
Africa	140,000,000	29,000	4,828
Asia and Oceania	132,700,000	54,000	2,457
Europe	277,000,000	195,000	1,420
Latin America	395,000,000	61,000	6,475
North America	75,000,000	53,000	1,415
Total	1,019,700,000	392,000	2,602

Source: Based on numbers from http://www.catholic-hierarchy.org/ for the year 2009.

oversee the teaching and practice of the Catholic faith in their own dioceses. The Catholic Church is not organized like a business in which the Pope acts as a CEO who can fire and hire whomever he wants. Bishops are appointed for life and it is difficult to remove them from office. Authority is mixed with independence, and hierarchy is mixed with egalitarianism. The Pope has a special and powerful leadership role, but all the bishops of the Catholic Church – including the Pope, who is Bishop of Rome – are spiritual leaders who consult with each other about how best to maintain the church's faithfulness to Christ as expressed in the Catholic tradition.

Each diocese is divided into many parishes, and they are the heart of religious life for most Catholics. It is in this face-to-face world of the parish that Catholicism becomes a living faith performed in community with everyone else who is a member of that parish. Normally there is only one church building per parish, with one or more priests assigned to each parish to care for the spiritual needs of the local Catholic population. Currently there are insufficient numbers of priests to adequately staff every parish. In Latin America, there is only one priest for every 6,475 Catholic laypeople, and in Africa the ratio is one priest for every 4,828 parishioners (see Table 2.2). But the real numbers are actually worse than this since many priests are assigned to full-time jobs other than parish ministry. In some parts of the world, most notably in North America, a revival of the office of *deacon* (an ordained position that is open to married men) and the increasing use of lay ministers (many of whom are women) has become a means of helping to meet the need for pastoral care within the Catholic Church. Some Catholics have gone further, suggesting that the priesthood itself should be open to women and married men, but to date this option has been vigorously rejected by the Catholic Church hierarchy.

Story

Ancient roots

The Catholic tradition, like the Orthodox tradition, has a history reaching back 2,000 years. The deep roots of the Catholic tradition can be traced to the ancient tradition of the first centuries of the Christian movement. Along with Orthodoxy, Catholicism affirms the great creeds and councils of the ancient church, and the two traditions also share the same Bible. Yet a distinctly western, Latin-speaking variety of Christianity (as opposed to Greek-speaking) was beginning to emerge even during this earliest period of Christian history (up to the year 500). That Latin perspective is especially evident in the writings of Augustine of Hippo, and it is this Latin-speaking form of Christianity that forms the deep foundation on which Catholic tradition has been built.

Early medieval period

The years 500 to 1000 represent the time when the Catholic and Orthodox traditions began to formally and self-consciously distinguish themselves from each other. Beginning in the early fifth century, the western half of the old Roman Empire (contemporary Western Europe) fell into political decline. As political structures faltered and then collapsed, many Catholic bishops found it necessary to take on some local responsibilities of government, and the Pope, the Bishop of Rome, became one of the few individuals capable of exercising some kind of leadership over the region as a whole. The prestige and power of the papacy increased significantly in 781 when the Papal States (which, at the time, included most of the middle third of Italy) became a separate Catholic country governed by the Pope as its monarch. Today's Vatican City is the last remnant of this ancient Catholic nation.

The early medieval period was also when most of Europe converted to Catholic Christianity. The process began in 496 with the conversion of King Clovis of France and was mostly complete by the year 1000. During this missionary era, the beliefs and practices of Christianity were slowly translated into the many different languages and culture of the region, with each new translation adding new ideas and emphases to the accumulating Catholic tradition. One of the most notable of these developments was a new emphasis on the idea of sacrifice and the death of Christ. This found visual representation in the crucifix, which became an important object of Catholic devotion for the first time during this period.

Later medieval period

Catholicism developed its mature form as a religious tradition between the years 1000 and 1500. During these centuries, the Catholic Church slowly defined many of the doctrinal commitments that still characterize Catholicism around the world today, including the seven sacraments, transubstantiation (the belief that the bread and wine of the eucharistic meal become the actual body and blood of Christ), and purgatory. This is the era when celibacy was first mandated for parish priests, when the great Gothic cathedrals of Europe were built, and when the Crusades were fought with the hope of militarily reclaiming the Holy Land as Catholic territory. This is also when Mary assumed her special role of prominence within the Catholic tradition, a development that was encouraged by the Crusaders' interaction with the Christians of the East who had always held Mary in high regard.

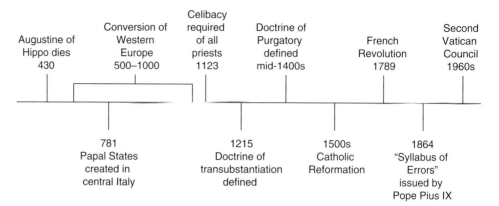

Figure 2.2 Key events in Catholic history

1500 to the present

The most recent period has been a time of challenge and response. The first challenge arrived in the form of the Protestant Reformation. The theological response of the Catholic Church – the "Catholic Reformation" – most clearly articulated at the Council of Trent (1545–63) was to clarify the essentials of Catholic belief and practice and in opposition to Protestant errors. The Council addressed a range of problems within the church, with the long-term result being a much more centralized and more efficiently run institution. The Catholic Church also expanded geographically during this time. The Catholic monarchs of Spain and Portugal led the way with the conquest of Latin America and the colonization of the west coast of Africa, but various missionary orders, especially the newly created Society of Jesus (the Jesuits), also introduced Catholicism to India and East Asia in the sixteenth and seventeenth centuries.

A second period of challenge began in the eighteenth century with the dawning of the Enlightenment, the rise of modern science, and the beginnings of democratic politics. The church felt threatened by these developments and especially by the anti-Catholic attitudes of the French Revolution (1789). The Catholic Church regrouped during the rule of Pope Pius IX, who held office from 1846 to 1878, the longest papal reign in history. His famous *Syllabus of Errors* (1864) denounced almost everything modern about the modern world, including democracy, freedom of the press, and secular (i.e., not controlled by the church) public education. Papal power increased dramatically during the nineteenth and twentieth centuries. One sign of this increasing power is that in the early 1800s, the Pope directly appointed fewer than 5 percent of the church's bishops. Today, every Catholic bishop is directly appointed by the Pope.

The authoritarian and antimodern posture that characterized the Catholic Church in the nineteenth-century church continued well into the twentieth when the new threat of atheistic Communism kept the church on guard. Beneath the surface, however, new and more progressive ideas about Catholic faith and life were being generated. Those new views were pushed to center stage when Pope John XXIII convened a Second Vatican Council (1962–5) to reassess the place of Catholicism in the modern world. He believed the church needed an *aggiornamento* (a major updating and reorientation) and that was the challenge he put before the bishops and other Catholic leaders who gathered in Rome. The proceedings of Vatican II were sometimes contentious, but in the end the 16 documents produced by the Council were well received, rearticulating the Catholic faith in contemporary language, encouraging a more proactive sense of Catholic identity, and internationalizing the organization of the church as a whole. Disagreements continue about how best to interpret the Council's main message, but there is no question that Vatican II opened new possibilities for the Catholic Church that are still being explored today.

Notes

1 Matthew Fox (ed.), *Hildegard of Bingen's Book of Divine Works with Letters and Songs* (Santa Fe, NM: Bear and Company, 1987), pp. 8–10.

2 Gerard Manley Hopkins, *Poems of Gerard Manley Hopkins*, 3rd edn (New York: Oxford University Press, 1948), p. 70.

3 *Catechism of the Catholic Church* (New York: Doubleday, 1995), p. 9.

4 Ibid., pp. 673–4.

5 Catherine of Sienna, *The Dialogue*, trans. Suzanne Noffke (New York: Paulist Press, 1980), p. 35.

6 *Catechism of the Catholic Church*, p. 352.

7 Adapted from Andrew Greeley, *The Catholic Imagination* (Berkeley: University of California Press, 2001), pp. 89–90.

8 *Catechism*, p. 254.

Suggestions for Further Reading

Allen, John L. Jr. (2009). *The Future Church: How Ten Trends Are Revolutionizing the Catholic Church*. New York: Doubleday.

Boekenkotter, Thomas (1990). *A Concise History of the Catholic Church*, revised and expanded. New York: Doubleday.

Buckley, James J., Frederick Christian Bauerschmidt, and Trent Pomplun (eds) (2007). *The Blackwell Companion to Catholicism*. Oxford: Blackwell.

Catechism of the Catholic Church (1995). New York: Doubleday.

Greeley, Andrew (2000). *The Catholic Imagination*. Berkeley: University of California Press.

Lamb, Matthew L. and Matthew Levering (eds) (2008). *Vatican II: Renewal within Tradition*. Oxford: Oxford University Press.

Linden, Ian (2009). *Global Catholicism: Diversity and Change since Vatican II*. New York: Columbia University Press.

McBrien, Richard P. (1981). *Catholicism*. Minneapolis: Winston Press.

O'Collins, Gerald and Mario Farrugia (2003). *Catholicism: The Story of Catholic Christianity*. Oxford: Oxford University Press.

O'Grady, John F. (2001). *Catholic Beliefs and Traditions: Ancient and Ever New*. Mahwah, NJ: Paulist Press.

O'Malley, John W. (2008). *What Happened at Vatican II*. Cambridge, MA: Harvard University Press.

Reese, Thomas J. (1996). *Inside the Vatican: The Politics and Organization of the Catholic Church*. Cambridge, MA: Harvard University Press.

Chapter 3

The Protestant Tradition

Protestantism is the most diverse of the four Christian traditions. Even a quick examination of global Protestantism reveals an astonishing degree of difference. Gathering in settings as varied as small house churches in China, huge megachurches in the United States, ancient stone cathedrals in Europe, and rented storefronts in urban Latin America, Protestants espouse a wide variety of views regarding theology, ethics, styles of worship, and spirituality. And yet, underneath all this quite obvious diversity, Protestants share one common focus: a commitment to recover and proclaim the gospel of Jesus as it is articulated in the Bible that by grace through faith forgiveness is possible and new life is available. Everyone has direct access to God through Jesus Christ.

Grounded on this shared vision of personal Christianity rather than on creed or institution, Protestantism is a very different kind of tradition than either Orthodoxy or Catholicism. Protestants have written creeds and have produced many different kinds of churchly institutions, but the center of gravity of this tradition lies elsewhere, in its commitment to the Bible as the basis for faith and in the personal, rather than communal or institutional, character of the individual's relationship to God.

Another common Protestant assumption is that Christianity belongs at home, in the marketplace, and the classroom as much as it does in the church. Protestants are world-affirming. They assume that God's message to humanity as it is found in the Bible has implications for all of life, far beyond the explicitly religious dimensions of life alone. This means there is a constant need for Protestants to read the Bible alongside their "reading" of the cultures in which they live, allowing scripture to critique and affirm those cultures and simultaneously using the insights of the world to extract new wisdom out of scripture. It is this back and forth movement – from the Bible to the world and then back again – that has allowed Protestantism to become such a complex global movement with its thousands of different denominations.

The World's Christians: Who they are, Where they are, and How they got there, First Edition. Douglas Jacobsen.
© 2011 Douglas Jacobsen. Published 2011 by Blackwell Publishing Ltd.

For the most part, Protestants do not call themselves Protestant in the same way that Catholics call themselves Catholic and Orthodox Christians call themselves Orthodox. If asked to describe themselves religiously, most Protestants identify themselves either by the name of their particular Protestant subtradition (i.e., Anglican, Baptist, Lutheran) or they call themselves simply "Christian." This is so much the case that in certain parts of the world – in both the United States and China, for example – saying you are a "Christian" is often intended to imply that one is Protestant rather than Catholic. Instead of being a "family name" that people use to identify themselves religiously, the term "Protestant" is more of a general label that applies to the movement as a whole. Saying one is a Protestant is a bit like saying one is a baseball fan rather than a football fan, but everyone knows the real core of being a fan is loyalty to a particular team (or in this case, a denomination or local congregation) and not to a sport in general.

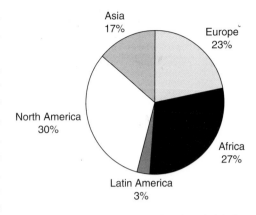

Figure 3.1   Where Protestants live (% of global Protestant population per continent)

That said, the term "Protestant" is an apt description of the movement as a whole. In its root meaning the word "Protestant" has two dissimilar but overlapping definitions. On the one hand, it can mean "to protest," and the name Protestants was applied to the original Protestant reformers partly because they protested certain Catholic attitudes and actions that they thought contradicted the core message of the gospel. But the word Protestant can also mean "to profess" or "to confess" what one believes to be true, and this more positive definition gets closer to the real meaning of the movement. A common synonym for Protestant in many parts of the world is "evangelical," meaning "of the gospel" or "good news." Thus Protestantism in Germany, the birthplace of the movement, goes by the name *Evangelische* and in Latin America Protestants are known as *evangelicos*. (The term "evangelical" can sometimes be confusing in this regard because in some countries, such as the United States and Britain, calling oneself an "evangelical Christian" is not synonymous with simply being a Protestant.)

Many people, including many sociologists, use the term "Protestant" as a catch-all label for all Christians who are neither Catholic nor Orthodox. In this usage, groups like the Jehovah's Witnesses and the Church of Jesus Christ of Latter Day Saints (Mormons) as well as almost all Pentecostal/Charismatic Christians would be labeled Protestant. This book does not follow that pattern. Since the Pentecostal/Charismatic movement has created its own new church structures, and since many of its adherents are as closely affiliated with Catholicism as with Protestantism, it is treated as a separate and distinct Christian tradition (as explained in the following chapter). Similarly groups like the Jehovah's Witnesses and the Church of Jesus Christ of Latter Day Saints that also see themselves as new and unique Christian traditions are also categorized as separate communities of faith, rather than indiscriminately lumping them into the Protestant camp.

The Protestant tradition began in Europe, and most of Northern Europe remains solidly Protestant today, but the demographic center of the movement has now shifted to North America and Africa. Protestantism is also gaining ground in Asia, but it still remains a very small movement in Latin America (see Figure 3.1).

Spirituality

Protestant spirituality focuses largely on the Bible. Protestants frequently refer to the Bible as the Word of God (with a capital "W"), and they expect God to speak to them through that Word. This was the experience of Martin Luther, who read the biblical words "the just shall live by faith" as a message from God that freed him from the fears of condemnation and hell that had haunted him all his life. In the twentieth century, that same focus on the words of the Bible energized the ministry of Billy Graham, the conservative American Protestant who became the century's best known and most widely traveled evangelist and who never tired of repeating the phrase "the Bible says." It is also echoed in the words used by pastors in the United Church of Christ (one of the most progressive denominations in the United States) when they introduce the reading of the Bible in Sunday worship: "God is still speaking."

For Protestants, the Bible contains the pure message of the gospel by which all of life, including faith itself, is to be judged, and reading the Bible is a spiritual discipline undertaken for the purpose of keeping one's vision of the gospel fresh and vibrant. From the beginning of the movement, the translation of the Bible into the local language of the people has been a priority. Protestants want to read the Bible for themselves. This is perceived as both a privilege and a responsibility. Protestants historically have called this the "right of private interpretation," the right to read the Bible and decipher its meaning for oneself. This Protestant affirmation was and still is a revolutionary concept. It is what drove Martin Luther, usually considered to be the founder of the Protestant movement, to stand in front of the Pope and the Holy Roman Emperor and declare his opposition to Catholic teaching by figuratively holding forth the Bible and saying, "Here I stand." This Protestant principle also helped to set the stage for modern conceptions of religious freedom as a basic human right.

But Protestants do not believe that all interpretations of the Bible are equally worthy and true. There are better and worse ways of reading and finding meaning in the Bible, and the different Protestant churches have seen it as their job to find the best one. In fact, the main reason they exist as different churches is that they have come to different conclusions about which interpretations are better and worse. In many churches these communal conclusions are ensconced in documents called confessions of faith, and these confessional statements delineate certain beliefs that are assumed to be beyond question. But even in the most confessionally minded Protestant churches there is plenty of room for creative reflection about faith and life based on a fresh reading of the biblical text.

Undertaking this work of reflection is the job of theologians, but in the Protestant tradition, virtually everyone is a theologian in some sense. Thus it is not only preachers and professors in seminaries (schools for training ministers) who "do theology." Many ordinary Protestants, not academically trained, see themselves as theologians too, and every day thousands of Protestant carpenters and office workers, nurses and accountants, day laborers and lawyers come home from work, take out their Bibles, and begin to study, hoping to glean something new that will deepen their faith and provide them with some new insight about the meaning of the gospel for today. Protestants also routinely gather in small groups for Bible study and prayer where they can learn from each other and test out their interpretations of the Bible on other people whose opinions they respect.

There is a great deal of interpretive freedom within the Protestant tradition, but almost all Protestant churches affirm five distinctively Protestant beliefs. First, Protestants affirm that salvation comes from God alone and that human effort cannot change an individual's standing with God. Second, Protestants affirm that faith or trust in God and God's grace is the core of religious life. Third, Protestants see the church as a fellowship of believers rather than as a hierarchical institution. Fourth, Protestants believe in the "priesthood" of all believers: even though churches may ordain ministers, everyone in the church is spiritually equal with everyone else. Finally, Protestants believe that every human institution, including the church as it exists on earth, is flawed and fallible. Perfection will only be reached in heaven.

These last two characteristics have been especially important in the history of Protestant spirituality, and they coalesce in the idea of vocation. To have a vocation, viewed from a Protestant perspective, is to be called by God to participate in the work of healing the flaws of this world and of caring for those who have been hurt by the world's current imperfections. This work can take many different forms. Some vocations are explicitly religious or church-related, but others may be quite "secular" in character, meaning they do not look religious on the surface. Thus it is possible, indeed it is highly likely, that many Protestant politicians, artists, teachers, police officers, home builders, salespeople, stay-at-home parents, and people in business see their work as a kind of religious vocation, dedicated to God and to serving others just as much as the activities undertaken by any missionary or pastor. This is very different from the Catholic tradition where, until recent years, the notion of vocation or serving God has almost always been associated with the priesthood or with the consecrated life of religious brothers and sisters. Protestants, however, believe that God calls people in many different ways to many different kinds of work, and that anything done in faith for the purpose of building the kingdom of God on earth can be considered a spiritually meaningful and significant Christian vocation.

From the beginning of the movement, Protestant spirituality has also included the singing of hymns. Sometimes hymn singing has been seen as a form of instruction for the uneducated – a way of communicating Protestant doctrine memorably and understandably. In some churches hymns still play that role, with worship leaders reminding congregations to "think about the words you are singing." But hymns in the Protestant tradition have also frequently been a means of putting one's faith into words, a way of testifying to the grace of God in one's life. This style of song is exemplified by the well known hymn *Amazing Grace,* written by John Newton (1725–1807), a former slave trader who later became an Anglican priest. The emotions of Newton's own dramatic conversion saturate the lyrics, and the lyrics are emotionally moving to singers: "Amazing grace, how sweet the sound that saved a wretch like me! I once was lost but now am found, was blind but now I see." Protestants often develop strong attachments to their favorite songs, and they can bristle when change is suggested. Thus it is not uncommon for a congregation to split over the adoption of a new hymnal, and many Protestant congregations around the world are currently embroiled in "worship wars" over the use of traditional hymns versus newer praise songs.

Salvation

The Protestant vision of salvation is simultaneously intimate and austere. It is intimate because salvation focuses on the personal relationship between the believer and God. Jesus is frequently portrayed as the friend of sinners, ready and willing to embrace all who turn to him, and salvation is pictured as a kind of homecoming or return to a God of love. Protestantism emphasizes the immediacy of God's grace. One by one, individual by individual, God redeems humanity, freeing people from the burden of their sins and befriending each one in turn. The only requirement is faith; the gift of salvation is free, with no cost beyond placing one's full trust and confidence in God.

But the intimacy of salvation is sometimes frightening in its starkness. Each individual has to meet God in stunning isolation. Everyone has to face God alone. The saints of the past cannot intervene, and Mary cannot mediate the encounter. Anxiety can be further heightened by Protestantism's bleak assessment of the unredeemed condition of humankind. People are declared to be "lost," they are "worms in the dust," they are "totally depraved." In the famous words of Jonathan Edwards (1703–58), the American Puritan and revivalist preacher, humans need to recognize that they are "sinners in the hands of an angry God" before they can appreciate the breadth of God's grace. Meeting God on those terms can be terrifying.

Many Protestants today have adopted a much more gracious and forgiving image of God, but the basic framework for salvation remains the same. The main issue is sin and how to deal with it. Protestants define sin in many different ways – as an expression of the innate egoism of human beings, as a transgression of God's moral law, as a failure to act when action is required – but however sin is defined, most Protestants use legal language to describe the result. People are "guilty" before God who is their judge, and that guilt must be removed before a new and positive relationship with God can begin. What makes acquittal possible is that Christ died for each individual's sin and rose again to plead that person's case before God. As a result, instead of seeing that person's sin and guilt, God now sees Christ's righteousness instead. It is Christ's righteousness, accessed through faith, that opens the pathway for individuals to be reconciled with God.

In terms of its basic components, the Protestant view of salvation shares much with Catholicism. But Protestantism sets itself apart by heightening the sense of damage wrought by sin and by insisting that forgiveness is the result of grace alone obtained through faith alone to the glory of God alone. Catholicism is uncomfortable with all those "alones." For the Catholic tradition, salvation always includes *both* divine grace *and* human effort. But for the original Protestant Reformers and for many Protestants today, faith is a matter of either/or: *either* God is the giver of salvation *or* people have to earn it for themselves, and Protestants think the second option is impossible.

Because they were convinced that people could never earn their own salvation, the original Protestant reformers were overjoyed when they discovered (according to their reading of the Bible) that salvation was entirely and only a gift from God. But this does not mean Protestants feel no need to perform "good works." In reality, most Protestant churches place a high value on living morally and serving others – they are in the business of encouraging "good works" – but they are quick to point out that such behavior has nothing to do with earning one's salvation. It is, instead, an expression of gratitude to God for salvation that has already been received as a gift.

While Protestants believe that salvation is obtained only and solely through faith in God's grace, they are also aware of how fragile the experience of faith can be. Almost all Protestants experience periods of doubt as well as times of confidence in God's mercy. Luther himself was sometimes beset with violent mood swings, ranging from ecstatic hope to abysmal depression. In light of this fact, different groups of Protestants have often tried to identify various sources of assurance that can undergird faith during times of trial. One common response has been for Protestants to engage in the regular confession of their sins. Catholics obviously do this too, but for many Protestants the confession of sin is included as a regular component of public worship, whereas confession in the Catholic tradition has usually been done in a private setting and confession is made to a priest. Another important Protestant way of dealing with uncertainty in matters of faith has been to emphasize the significance of correct doctrine in contrast to religious feelings. The reasoning is that faith is based on truth – that is, faith has to be placed in God rightly understood (the one true God) or else faith is nothing more than wishful thinking, and wishful thinking no matter how fervent it might be can save no one. The conclusion for some Protestants has been that having a true and proper understanding of God is what really matters, and as long as one's beliefs are correct (defined by some selected standard of measure) then one's faith is solid and one's salvation is assured even if the emotion of religious assurance is lacking. Various Protestant churches emphasize other markers of faith, including the ability to pinpoint a specific date and time when one was "saved" or "born again."

One of the main arguments that has historically divided Protestants relates to the way that God distributes faith to different individuals. One view, closely associated with the Reformed or Calvinist tradition, is *predestination*, which portrays God as having previously chosen some humans for eternal salvation, selectively providing them with saving faith, while simultaneously withholding faith from others. According to this view, salvation is entirely a matter of God's will and humanity has nothing to contribute to the process. While this was the majority perspective during the first century or two of the Protestant movement, many Protestants eventually came to see predestination as being out of synch with their vision of God as a God of love. They preferred to think that God offers salvation to everyone, and each person then has the option of either accepting or rejecting that offer. This alternative view was articulated most clearly by the Dutch theologian Jacob Arminius (1560–1609), and his understanding of salvation has been called *Arminianism* ever since. The great majority of Protestants in the world today affirm this Arminian or "free will" perspective.

More recently the central debate about salvation within Protestantism has focused not so much on the means of salvation as on what the notion of salvation entails. In particular, many contemporary Protestants question the older notion that equates salvation with being saved from eternal punishment in hell and gaining eternal life in heaven. Recent polls indicate that fewer than half of the Protestants in the world believe there is some place called hell, and perhaps only two-thirds or three-quarters of them believe in heaven. Instead of focusing on the afterlife, increasing numbers of Protestants speak of salvation as something

Table 3.1   The main "families" of Protestantism and their global presence

Family name	Largest global organization (year founded)	Countries represented	Number of member denominations	Number of global adherents
Anglican	Anglican Communion (1931)	160	44	80,000,000
Baptist	Baptist World Alliance (1905)	200	210	50,000,000
Lutheran	Lutheran World Federation (1947)	78	140	65,000,000
Methodist	World Methodist Council (1881)	107	130	40,000,000
Reformed/ Presbyterian	World Alliance of Reformed Churches (1970)	107	214	75,000,000

that takes place on earth in the here and now. For some, salvation is understood in political terms, as freedom from oppression and as freedom for work and dignity. For others, salvation has to do with personal wholeness, discovering what one truly values and then living authentically in the light of those values. And for some salvation is finding community, a group of people who care for each other and who share each other's sorrows and joys. The older idea of salvation as eternal life in heaven with God is still part of the mix – and it is still likely the most common view – but it is no longer the only definition of salvation.

Structure

Unlike Catholicism, Protestantism has no overarching institutional structure that holds the tradition together. It is embodied instead in a wide variety of church organizations that are all functionally independent of each other. The sheer number and diversity of Protestant church groups can be overwhelming, making it easy to get lost in the trees and to lose sight of the Protestant forest. From a distance, however, clusters of relatively similar churches come into view. Five distinct families of Protestant churches – Anglican, Baptist, Lutheran, Methodist, and Reformed/Presbyterian – currently account for more than 80 percent of all the Protestants in the world. In the last century or so, all five of these groups have created formal associations designed to facilitate fellowship and cooperation among the churches around the world that are part of their particular family (see Table 3.1).

A quite different means of making sense of the Protestant world is to divide it in half, with the ethnic, tradition-minded Protestantism that has flourished in Europe representing one side of this divide and the more free-wheeling, start-from-scratch Protestantism that has flourished in the United States representing the other.

Almost all the earliest forms of Protestantism followed the European model which resulted in the creation of a host of Protestant state churches in Scandinavia, Germany, Great Britain, the Netherlands, and Switzerland. Leaders of these Protestant state churches believed with Luther that while Christian faith was highly personal, it was also necessarily public and even political. Thus they continued to assume that in any given state one church should prevail as the official religion for everyone, and state churches of this kind also obviously had the responsibility for serving the spiritual needs of all the people in the nation. Those needs included instruction in right doctrine, opportunities for worship, and the administration of the sacraments, but they also included more practical concerns such as care for the sick, the poor, and the orphaned. In those nations that adopted the state church model, the church thus became not only a religious organization, but also the equivalent of a state office of compassion. For this reason, many countries in Europe continue to finance the work of the official state churches today. These churches have generally become much less religiously dogmatic than they were in the past and most now see themselves as ministering to the spiritual needs of everyone in society regardless of what specific religion those people might be.

In the United States a very different kind of Protestantism emerged. Early on, before the American Revolution (1776), there was an attempt to set up something like a state church in some of the 13 colonies. For example, the Anglican Church was the de facto state church in most of the southern colonies and the Puritan Congregational Church played a similar role in New England. But the model never took deep root in the new American setting. Too many different kinds of Protestants had settled in the region to make the monopolistic church state model possible. Eventually, separation of church and state became the norm and Protestantism became a wholly nongovernmental affair.

This disestablishment of religion (the separation of church and state) created a new spiritual marketplace where different Protestant groups were compelled to compete with each other for members. The name for this new Protestant arrangement is "denominationalism," with denominations seeing themselves as churches (plural) sharing one geographic domain in contrast to the European model of one church per nation or region. Denominational competition produced constant innovation, as new and old churches alike developed different theologies to articulate Christian beliefs and programs to attract adherents. As a result, Protestantism in the United States developed an increasingly start-from-scratch perspective, which allowed anyone to begin a new church or denomination based on his or her own peculiar views as long as they could generate a following. During the last century, this American style of denominational Protestantism has spread around the globe, becoming the dominant form of Protestantism everywhere except Europe.

Story

Protestantism has been in existence for only five hundred years, but those five centuries have been tumultuous. For ease of understanding, Protestant history can be divided into four periods: origins (1500–1650), new options (1650–1800), engagement with modernity (1800–1950), and the contemporary period (1950 to the present).

Protestant origins

The Protestant movement burst on the scene in the early 1500s in response to perceived moral failings and doctrinal errors in the Roman Catholic Church. The new approach was received warmly in many parts of northern Europe, and Protestantism soon spread from

Germany to Scandinavia, England, Switzerland, France, and Poland. In Germany, Martin Luther (1483–1546) was the main actor, and the Lutheran tradition codifies his thinking. A generation later, John Calvin (1509–64) helped articulate the Reformed tradition with the publication of his theological masterpiece, the *Institutes of the Christian Religion*. A more radical expression of Protestantism, known as Anabaptism, also emerged during these years in Germany and the Low Countries. Anabaptists emphasized adult rebaptism ("anabaptism" literally means to baptize again), separation of church and state, and pacifism; the largest group was the Mennonites founded by Menno Simons (1496–1561). Meanwhile in England, the Church of England slowly evolved from being an independent Catholic Church – King Henry VIII (ruled 1509–47) wanted the church in his realm to be Catholic, but governed by the crown rather than the pope – to being a middle-of-the-road Anglican Protestant church under Queen Elizabeth (ruled 1558–1603) that tried to blend the best aspects of Catholicism with the best insights of Protestantism.

In the face of various Protestant challenges the Catholic Church, which was accustomed to having monopoly status in most of Europe, responded vigorously. Catholic rulers across the continent took up arms to defend the true Catholic faith. Soon almost all of Europe was embroiled in a widespread religious civil war that continued for a century and a half. At times, Protestant armies squared off against Catholic armies, but sometimes Lutheran and Reformed Christians took up arms against each other, and Puritans (Reformed Protestants in England) sometimes clashed with more moderate Anglicans. The pacifistic Anabaptists were persecuted by almost everyone. By 1650 the region was exhausted, and the violence slowly abated. The political solution as defined by the "Peace of Westphalia" (1648) took the form of a new patchwork map of Europe that allowed political rulers in local states to determine the official religion for that domain. This is when Lutheranism was confirmed as the state church in Scandinavia, the Church of England (Anglicanism) became the public faith of England and Wales, and Reformed (or Presbyterian) Protestantism became the officially sanctioned religion in Scotland and in various parts of what is now Germany, Switzerland, and Hungary.

New options

The years 1650 to 1800 were a time of both consolidation and creativity for the Protestant movement. By 1650, the Protestant state churches of Northern Europe had mostly settled into a form of faith called *confessionalism*, a regionally based, theologically defined form of Protestantism that stresses proper worship and the teaching of right doctrine. Not much emphasis was placed on religious experience, on the need to rethink religious beliefs in the light of emerging knowledge, or on the responsibility of Christians to communicate the gospel to those who lived outside the borders of their own nations. While this form of Protestantism was acceptable to many, it was stifling to some.

Pietism developed as one of the alternatives to confessional Protestantism. The Pietist movement began in Germany, under the leadership of the Lutheran minister Philip Jakob Spener, and then it quickly spread elsewhere. Pietism stresses the personal and experiential aspects of Protestantism, including self-conscious conversion, dedication in prayer, careful study of the Bible, and moral self-discipline. Typically, the Pietist movement gave rise not to new independent churches, but to networks of devout believers who operated within the European state churches. The most prominent exception to this rule was the Methodist movement, which eventually broke away from the Church of England and became a new denomination. Historically, the most consequential aspect of Pietism was its emphasis on individual conversion, which led Pietists to launch the first missions for carrying the Protestant message to people outside of Europe.

A second, smaller group of Protestants known as rationalists also disliked the confessional model. Living in the Enlightenment era when intellectual elites were becoming convinced that reason was the only principle for guiding life, Protestant rationalists sought to reform Protestantism by applying reason to both historical Protestant beliefs and to the Bible itself. These rational Christians argued that too often in the past Protestants and other Christians had been closed-minded and narrow in their thinking. They agreed that the Bible was an important source of insight, but they also thought much could be learned from other sources of knowledge, including the natural world and simple logic. When reviewing the teachings of the Protestant churches of their day, Protestant thinkers such as John Locke and Thomas Jefferson found those doctrines both mistaken and inadequate. In response, they formulated their own new and generally quite moralistic (as opposed to doctrinal) understandings of the life and teachings of Jesus. Their legacy lives on in a broad variety of contemporary Protestant thinkers who emphasize reason and science as much as or more than the Bible in theological reflection on Christian faith.

Engaging modernity

The nineteenth and the early twentieth centuries (1800–1950) were a time of testing and transformation for Protestantism. Impetus for change came from many sources: new ideas from the realm of science (Darwinian evolution), new thoughts about society and economics (Marxism), new views of human psychology (Freudianism), and new interactions with other cultures. Social developments within Western society, ranging from the end of slavery to the industrial revolution to the Western colonization of the world to the development of new forms of communication to the rise of modern medicine, continually forced the Protestant churches to rethink their mission and role in the world. In an earlier era, Protestantism had been a major engine of change in the world; in this era, developments in the larger world became engines for change within Protestantism itself.

These were the years when the fragmentation of the Protestant movement reached an all-time high. As different Protestant groups responded differently to the challenges of the times, more and more new Protestant churches were created, each of them embodying alternative responses to social and intellectual developments of the period. As churches multiplied, the landscape of Protestantism became increasingly complex and the "marketing" of faith became a bigger and bigger concern. The many different Protestant churches could no longer assume a fixed clientele for their services, so increasingly they began to compete for "customers." In addition, the intellectual challenges of the times forced many Protestants to redefine their beliefs. Protestantism is a tradition that emphasizes the intellect, and the scholarly and scientific advances of the modern age were spiritually demanding. Eventually, this produced a kind of Protestant schism, with "modernists" (Christians

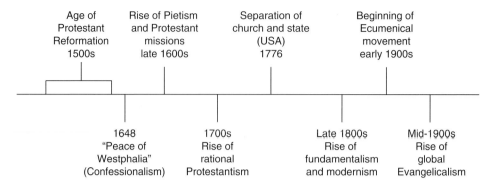

Figure 3.2 Key events in Protestant history

who generally welcomed the new knowledge that was coming out of the universities) at one end of the spectrum and "fundamentalists" (Christians who distrusted or rejected the new ideas of the time) at the other end.

The contemporary period

Since 1950 the worldwide dynamics of Protestantism have changed once again. Protestantism has become globalized, and most of its growth is now occurring in the southern hemisphere. Protestant theology has been reshaped by the contributions of women, people of color, and other previously disenfranchised groups who now express their own new and distinct ideas about what Christianity is and should be. At present, the two largest and most easily identifiable factions within Protestantism are comprised of those associated with the Ecumenical movement and those associated with the Evangelical movement.

The word "ecumenical" comes from a Greek word meaning "house" or "household," and the main focus of Ecumenical Protestantism, especially during the middle years of the twentieth century when it was at its peak of influence, has been uniting all Christians in one household of faith. Ecumenical Protestantism began within the global missionary movement when the proliferation of Protestant churches came to be seen as an impediment to effective communication of the gospel. Differences that divided the churches in Europe and America appeared meaningless or irrelevant in many other global settings and caused confusion among people who were hearing the gospel for the first time. These concerns eventually led to the creation of the World Council of Churches in 1948, a largely Protestant organization dedicated to championing "the visible unity of all Christians."

Since its founding, the World Council of Churches and the Ecumenical movement have been highly successful in helping many Protestant churches develop a deeper sense of commitment to and cooperation with each other. The movement has also expanded its vision of what ecumenism entails. Especially during the last 40 years, the notion of unity has been extended beyond Christianity to apply to the world as a whole. This means that concerns such as peace, justice, and human rights – issues that focus on treating everybody in the world fairly and equally – have become increasingly visible. In the mid-twentieth century, Ecumenical Protestants supported a number of liberationist movements around the world, including the Civil Rights movement in the United States and the antiapartheid movement in South Africa. More recently, Ecumenical activism has focused on issues related to gender and sexual orientation, including openness to those seeking ordination as Protestant ministers. Perhaps ironically, these justice issues have revealed deep tensions within the Ecumenical movement itself and those tensions have complicated the work of fostering unity among the churches.

Evangelicalism represents an alternative style of contemporary Protestantism. The roots of the Evangelical movement can be traced back to Pietism with its emphases on the need for personal conversion, the importance of studying the Bible, prayer, discipleship (following the moral and spiritual guidelines of Christianity in everyday life), and the task of mission (spreading the "good news" of Christianity around the world). The United States is the center of global Evangelicalism, but it is a worldwide phenomenon. For many years, Evangelicals were largely nonpolitical in their public behavior, focusing all their efforts on religious conversion. In recent decades, however, Evangelicalism has taken a political turn, giving special attention to "traditional values," which includes opposing the relaxation of laws related to abortion, sexuality, the family, and various other moral concerns.

While they are in many ways paradigmatic Protestants, Evangelical Christians have begun to complicate the idea of just who is and who is not a Protestant. Up until the 1960s, the Protestant identity of the movement was relatively clear – Evangelicals were conservative, revivalistic, or conversion-oriented Protestants – but since then leaders of the movement have tried intentionally to expand the definition of the term to include members of the emerging Pentecostal/Charismatic tradition as well. While it is true that Protestant Evangelicals and Pentecostal/Charismatic Christians have much in common, most scholars and theologians would also say that the two movements are not identical. Those differences will be explained in the following chapter which focuses on the global Pentecostal/Charismatic movement, the fourth of the major Christian traditions in the contemporary world.

Suggestions for Further Reading

Bebbington, David W. (1992). *Evangelicalism in Modern Britain: A History from the 1730s to the 1980s*. Grand Rapids, MI: Baker.

Cracknell, Kenneth and Susan J. White (2005). *An Introduction to World Methodism*. Cambridge, UK: Cambridge University Press.

Dillenberger, John and Claude Welch (1954). *Protestant Christianity: Interpreted Through Its Development*. New York: Scribner's.

Durnbaugh, Donald F. (1985). *The Believers' Church: The History and Character of Radical Protestantism*. Scottdale, PA: Herald Press.

Forell, George W. (1960). *The Protestant Faith*. Philadelphia: Fortress Press.

Gritsch, Eric W. (1994). *Fortress Introduction to Lutheranism*. Minneapolis: Fortress Press.

Kaye, Bruce (2008). *An Introduction to World Anglicanism*. Cambridge, UK: Cambridge University Press.

Leith, John H. (1981). *Introduction to the Reformed Tradition*. Atlanta, GA: John Knox Press.

Leonard, Bill (2003). *Baptist Ways: A History*. Valley Forge, PA: Judson.

McGrath, Alister E. (2007). *Christianity's Dangerous Idea: The Protestant Revolution – A History from the Sixteenth Century to the Twenty-First*. New York: HarperOne.

McGrath, Alister E. and Darren C. Marks (eds) (2004). *The Blackwell Companion to Protestantism*. Oxford: Blackwell.

Chapter 4

The Pentecostal/Charismatic Tradition

The Pentecostal/Charismatic or Spirit-filled movement is the youngest of the four major contemporary Christian traditions. The word "Pentecostal" comes from the story in the biblical book of Acts about the crowds who had gathered in Jerusalem, after Jesus's death, for the Jewish feast of Pentecost. The Holy Spirit is described as descending on the gathered followers of Jesus, filling them with spiritual power and giving them the ability to speak in unknown languages. The term "charismatic" comes from the Greek word *charism* meaning gift. Used in a Christian context the word refers to the various gifts of the Holy Spirit described in the New Testament, including the power to work miracles, to preach and prophesy, to speak in unknown languages and to interpret what is said, and to care for those in need. Pentecostal/Charismatic Christians see themselves as both filled with God's Spirit (as on the day of Pentecost) and endowed with all the different gifts of the Holy Spirit. They are Christians who expect to see God's miraculous power displayed on earth as part of normal, everyday experience.

The Pentecostal/Charismatic movement began about a century ago, but its growth has been phenomenal. Today almost a fifth of the world's Christian population identifies with this tradition. Those inside the movement say this growth has been brought about by the Holy Spirit, but a variety of social factors also help to explain the explosion of Spirit-filled Christianity around the world and especially among the world's poor. More than any other Christian tradition, Pentecostal/Charismatic Christianity allows people who have been beaten down by the world to feel loved and empowered by God – and the emphasis on feeling is important. Pentecostal/Charismatic Christians don't just believe in God; they claim to feel God's presence physically in their bodies. What also makes Pentecostal/Charismatic Christianity popular is its lack of expense. It needs no cathedrals or icons, and it needs no highly trained clergy. All that is required is a willingness to lift up hands and voices in praise of God, and this can occur anywhere, including the shabbiest of settings. Partly because it

The World's Christians: Who they are, Where they are, and How they got there, First Edition. Douglas Jacobsen.
© 2011 Douglas Jacobsen. Published 2011 by Blackwell Publishing Ltd.

offers so much for so little, Pentecostal/Charismatic Christianity has become the fastest-growing religion in the history of the world.

Because so many Pentecostal/Charismatic Christians are poor, some sociologists have labeled the movement a religion of the oppressed and they describe those involved as having turned to religion as a means of easing their social and economic distress. But not all Pentecostal/Charismatic Christians are poor, and even most who are poor would reject that interpretation of themselves and their faith. They would readily admit that faith helps them endure the harshness of life, but more importantly they would say it energizes them and provides them with a sense of power and purpose. The power of the Holy Spirit gives them the ability to bind demons, to heal the sick, to live at peace with their neighbors, and when necessary to stand up for their own rights. And God's call to action, received through dreams, visions, and prophetic utterances as well as through the words of the Bible, gives them a strong sense of divine purpose. Rather than seeing themselves as the passive poor who need God's help merely to survive, Pentecostal/Charismatic Christians see themselves as agents of God who are charged with transforming the world through the power of the Holy Spirit.

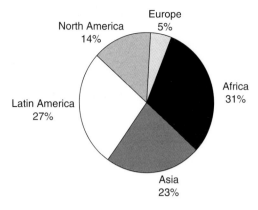

Figure 4.1   Where Pentecostal/Charismatic Christians live (% of global Pentecostal/Charismatic population living in each continent)

It is common to identify the beginning of the modern Pentecostal/Charismatic tradition with the Asuza Street Revival that took place in Los Angeles, California, starting in 1906, but the epicenter of the movement today is found in Africa. Almost one out of every three Pentecostal/Charismatic Christians in the world is an African. The second largest Pentecostal/Charismatic community is found in Latin America, with Asia close behind. The United States, where the Azusa Street Revival took place, now accounts for only a relatively small portion of the worldwide Pentecostal/Charismatic movement. The least Pentecostal area of the world is Europe. (See Figure 4.1.)

Spirituality

Pentecostal/Charismatic spirituality centers on experience: feeling God's presence within one's own body. The testimonies of millions of Pentecostal/Charismatic Christians say the same thing. When the Spirit of God entered their lives they were overwhelmed by a strange and wonderful power they had never experienced before. The early Pentecostal leader William Durham said:

> I was overcome by the mighty fulness of power and went down under it. For three hours [the Spirit of God] wrought wonderfully in me. My body was worked in sections, a section at a time. And even the skin on my face was jerked and shaken, and finally I felt my lower jaw begin to quiver in a strange way. This continued for some little time, when finally my throat began to enlarge and I felt my vocal organs being, as it were, drawn into a different shape. O how strange

and wonderful it was! and how blessed it was to be thus in the hands of God. And last of all I felt my tongue begin to move and my lips to produce strange sounds which did not originate in my mind.[1]

Another early Pentecostal leader, David Wesley Myland, said much more succinctly that the Pentecostal/Charismatic experience was like swallowing "God liquidized."[2]

Because Pentecostal spirituality is experiential and physical, human feelings are at its core. This is so much the case that some Pentecostal/Charismatic theologians say that an emphasis on "orthopathy" (right feelings) and not just on orthodoxy (right belief) or orthopraxy (right behavior) is what distinguishes the Pentecostal/Charismatic movement from the other major Christian traditions. While Pentecostal/Charismatic Christians emphasize the emotions, they are not simply emotivists. They are also *believers* who recognize the importance of doctrine while simultaneously arguing that words and rationality have limits and that the world is a much stranger and more wonderful place than words or rationality can ever fully comprehend.

Some scholars think of the Pentecostal/Charismatic movement as a new kind of Protestantism. They are reluctant to conceptualize this expression of Christianity as a separate and distinct tradition because like Protestantism it stresses the individual's relationship with God and the importance of the Bible. Although the two traditions indeed share some common concerns, it is unhelpful to conflate them. The relationship between Protestantism and the Pentecostal/Charismatic tradition is similar to the relationship between Catholicism and Orthodoxy: there is significant overlap, but at the level of their core spiritualities they differ. Thus Protestantism's focus on understanding – on describing faith in words, concepts, and clearly formulated doctrines – is very different from the Pentecostal/Charismatic tradition's focus on experiencing God beyond or outside the realm of words. Pentecostal/Charismatic faith is about being enveloped in the love of God; it is about being healed emotionally and physically by God's presence; it is about being "slain in the Spirit" (knocked unconscious by God's power); and it is about "letting go and letting God" – shutting off one's thinking and relaxing into the flow of God's Spirit within and around one's body. Self-control is a Protestant virtue, but it is precisely the willingness to sometimes lose control, even of one's own body, that allows Pentecostal/Charismatic Christians to experience God in the way they do.

William Durham's description of losing control under the power of the Spirit concludes with his lips producing "strange sounds which did not originate in my mind." This is speaking in tongues (or just "tongues"), and tongues have been part of the Pentecostal/Charismatic movement from the beginning. Originally, speaking in tongues was understood as the physical sign that one had received the *baptism in the Holy Spirit*, an experience defined as including the individual's complete "filling" by the Holy Spirit and the reception of new spiritual powers and gifts. The experience of speaking in tongues was such a definitive marker in the early years of the Pentecostal/Charismatic movement that it was frequently called the "tongues movement."

Today, speaking in tongues is optional in many Pentecostal/Charismatic circles. In this more contemporary perspective, the singular focus on the gift of tongues has given way to a wider sense of all the gifts of the Holy Spirit. These gifts include both the miraculous (such as claims to be able to heal the sick, predict the future, or raise the dead) and the relatively ordinary (such as the ability to teach or to lead or to encourage others). A similar moderation of opinion has taken place with regard to the baptism in the Holy Spirit itself. While many old-style Pentecostal/Charismatic groups still consider this baptism to be a unique and necessary experience – it is the thing that makes one a Pentecostal/Charismatic Christian – many members of the contemporary movement now assume that a person can arrive at the Spirit-filled life via a number of different pathways, not all of which involve a specific and dateable experience that is identified as the baptism in the Spirit.

Pentecostal/Charismatic Christians live with the miraculous, and they assume that God's wonder-working power will be displayed in the world on a regular basis. Signs and wonders, the various miraculous ways that God speaks directly to individuals and that God acts in the world, are part of ordinary life. Individuals in all the Christian traditions and in virtually all the world's religions believe that miracles sometimes take place, but Pentecostal/Charismatic Christians assume that miracles occur all the time. They are part of normal Christian existence. The belief is that God is constantly watching over humankind and that God is ready and willing to intervene even in the smallest details of life. So Pentecostal/Charismatic believers pray and expect God to respond whether the request is for a good parking spot when they are running late, for healing when a child is diagnosed with terminal cancer, for the redirection of a hurricane that is heading toward one's city, or for reconciliation when a personal relationship has been ruptured. Nothing is too small or too big to bring to God in prayer.

Pentecostal/Charismatic Christians know that God does not answer all prayers in the way they want those prayers to be answered. Pentecostal/Charismatic believers lose their jobs, their marriages fall apart, tornados hit their homes, the banks in which they put their money fail, they get sick, and they die. But often God does intervene, and when that happens, Pentecostal/Charismatic Christians tell each other about it. They testify about what God has done for them, and once one person begins to testify others almost always begin to tell their stories too. People love stories – it is part of being human – and people remember and retell the stories they have heard, especially if those stories are sources of encouragement and hope. So in the midst of life's sorrows, Pentecostal/Charismatic Christians pull out their miracle stories and remind each other that God loves them regardless of circumstances and that somehow, even in the worst of times, God can miraculously turn sadness and evil into good. When bad things happen, the Pentecostal/Charismatic reaction is not to doubt God's power, but to cling to God's love instead, waiting to see how God will eventually bring blessing out of adversity.

Pentecostal/Charismatic Christians assume that they are involved in a massive invisible spiritual war and that some of the pain they experience is the result of that warfare. Angels and demons clash around them, and Christians are called to join in the fray against the forces of evil. This is not meant as a metaphor. Many Pentecostal/Charismatic Christians believe the world literally is infested with devils and evil spirits intent on spreading fear and encouraging immorality, and many feel that they are living in the last days of human history when the battle with evil is becoming more intense. In the power of the Spirit and in Jesus's name, Pentecostal/Charismatic Christians are committed to binding the forces of evil and setting people free from the spiritual captivity to which they may have fallen prey. For "modern" people this will sound like pure fantasy; "modern" people believe the world consists solely of what can be seen and measured and that anything else is nonsense. But the great majority of the world's people, including many people in the purportedly modern West, still believe in demons, evil spirits, and the haunting presence of the dead. In such a world, the message of Pentecostal/Charismatic power can become literally a godsend, a promise of desperately needed protection that allows them to live free of spiritual fear, perhaps for the first time in their lives.

The great majority of the world's Pentecostal/Charismatic Christians are women, and the attraction can be found partly in the fact that the Pentecostal/Charismatic movement generally affirms that the Holy Spirit can empower women in the same way the Spirit empowers men. There is a gender equality built into the theology of the tradition. That assumption of spiritual equality has not always led to equality in church practices, but even in the most patriarchal churches Pentecostal/Charismatic women are confident that God can use them to do great things. Over the past century, women have played prominent roles in many Pentecostal/Charismatic churches, with perhaps the most famous being Aimee Semple McPherson, whose popularity in early twentieth-century America rivaled that of the hottest stars of Hollywood.

The broader appeal of Pentecostal/Charismatic Christianity for many women, however, may reside less in its distribution of power and leadership in the church than in its domestic significance. Simply put, it has helped to bring about improved home lives. Many Pentecostal/Charismatic churches teach that the man is to be the head of the home, but in order to be in charge spiritually a husband must be good and faithful. For women who live in patriarchal societies where male domination is a way of life, having this kind of moral responsibility placed on their husbands can be a huge step forward. Wives will gladly obey their husbands if it means they will stop spending their earnings on alcohol, stop their extramarital affairs, and become faithful spouses and responsible fathers. What is more, the language of Pentecostal/Charismatic Christianity provides husbands and wives with a way to negotiate marital difficulties without blaming each other. When tensions flare up, Pentecostal/Charismatic couples often ascribe the fault to Satan rather than to each other. Husbands and wives can then join forces to fight Satan and save their marriages at the same time.

Pentecostal/Charismatic Christianity emphasizes the miraculous and the supernatural, but perhaps the key characteristic that distinguishes it from other Christian alternatives is something quite simple and ordinary: joy. Joy is what Pentecostal/Charismatic believers say they feel in the presence of God, and they express that joy in the exuberance of their worship. Many Christian liturgies or services of worship can be dry, dull, and somber. Many Christians think of Sunday worship as an obligatory duty they must grudgingly perform. But this is not the case with most Spirit-filled Christians. In Pentecostal/Charismatic worship, people dance and sing, they clap their hands, they shout, they march around the room, they hug each other, they "get happy in the Lord," and they rejoice. Pentecostal/Charismatic believers know how to cry – in fact, tears are often considered a spiritual gift – but the predominant emotion is joy. Awash in joy, Pentecostal/Charismatic Christians don't go to church reluctantly out of a sense of duty; they go to church happily and willingly because it is fun to express their joy together. That sense of holy fun goes a long way toward explaining not only how the Pentecostal/Charismatic movement is different from other Christian traditions, but also why it is growing so rapidly.

Salvation

In the Pentecostal/Charismatic tradition, salvation has a focus on the future. There is no question that salvation entails the forgiveness of past sins and the righting of past wrongs, but the attention of Pentecostal/Charismatic Christians is on what is yet to come, on the blessings that God has ready for everyone who believes. In this regard, the Pentecostal/Charismatic movement has more in common with the Orthodox tradition that stresses salvation as deification than it does with the Catholic and Protestant traditions that tend to describe salvation largely in terms of sin and forgiveness. This future-oriented and growth-in-godliness perspective is reflected in the language of *fullness* that some Pentecostal/Charismatic Christians use to describe the experience of salvation. Salvation is not just about forgiveness, nor is it only about holiness understood as the absence of sin. Instead salvation in the Pentecostal/Charismatic tradition is about moving ever deeper and higher into the fullness of God and into the fullness of life that God intends for all people.

Yet salvation in the Pentecostal/Charismatic tradition is not solely about the future, it is also about the here and now. There is a widespread saying within the Pentecostal/Charismatic movement that God has provided "healing in the atonement," that Christ's crucifixion and resurrection did not merely address the spiritual needs of humankind, but humanity's physical needs as well. Pentecostal/Charismatic Christians are biblical literalists and when the Bible says healing is part of salvation they believe it.

In the early years of the Pentecostal/Charismatic movement, some leaders even instructed their followers that use of medical doctors or natural healing remedies was strictly forbidden because healing should come only from God. Using nonreligious means to deal with disease was construed as a lack of faith, or perhaps as evidence that one was not really a Christian at all. Over the years, this stridency concerning faith healing has slowly dwindled, and many contemporary Pentecostal/Charismatic Christians now believe that God often brings healing through a combination of modern medicine and faith.

This same kind of overlap between the earthly and the other-worldly, between the physical and the spiritual, is also at the root of the *prosperity gospel* which in recent decades has become increasingly prominent within global Pentecostal/Charismatic circles. Every week, literally thousands of Spirit-filled preachers tell their followers that God wants them to be rich. The standard message is something like this: if you want a nice house or a new car or stylish clothes, you have the right to claim those things in Jesus's name, and God will give them to you. The key is stepping forth in faith, and the typical recommendation is that a "seed" offering should be donated to the preacher's own church. Making this seed offering – which is often a substantial portion of a poor person's total assets – shows God the sincerity of one's faith, and the theory is that God will then grant the individual, in return, a bounteous harvest of wealth. Obviously, there is tremendous potential for charlatanism in this kind of preaching, and the prosperity gospel has accordingly received heavy criticism both from those outside the Pentecostal/Charismatic movement and from those within.

But from a Pentecostal/Charismatic perspective God really does want everyone on earth to enjoy the good things of life. A certain kind of self-denial is part of the Pentecostal/Charismatic message, and most Pentecostal/Charismatic churches underscore the need for members to avoid cheap and inappropriate pleasures, especially sexual pleasures. But it is not pleasure itself that is wrong. It is only harmful and sinful pleasures that are to be avoided, and those are to be avoided in part because they interfere with the ability to enjoy the much deeper pleasures that God has in store for those who remain morally pure. According to the Pentecostal/Charismatic view of the world, God wants people to flourish in all possible ways, including financially. Pentecostal/Charismatic Christians would agree with others that greed is a sin, that selfishness is a sin, and that pride in one's wealth can be a sin, but being wealthy itself can be a blessing from God.

Having said that, it is important to remember the social context in which most of the world's Pentecostal/Charismatic Christians live. More than three-quarters of all Pentecostal/Charismatic believers live in Africa, Asia, and Latin America, and by almost any measure, most of these individuals are desperately poor. "Prosperity" for them does not mean two BMWs in the garage and a mink coat in the closet. It means having enough food for today and possibly for tomorrow. It means having a roof that does not leak. It means obtaining a minimal level of education. It means having a job – any kind of job. When the prosperity gospel is transplanted to a wealthy culture it can appear to be nothing more than religiously sanctioned greed, but that is not the case globally. Most Pentecostal/Charismatic Christians understand how easily prosperity preaching can go awry, but they also genuinely believe that God wants people to prosper. To squelch the preaching of prosperity would thus be to deny part of the fullness of salvation, and no Pentecostal/Charismatic Christian would want to do that.

If there is an Achilles heel within the Pentecostal/Charismatic movement and its view of salvation, it is that all the grand promises of Christianity seem to hang by the very slender thread of human faith and will. Having faith – enough faith to believe in miracles – is a constant struggle, and lapses in belief or trust are sometimes seen as evidence that one is no longer Spirit-filled or that one may even have "lost" one's salvation. Taken to the extreme, these kinds of concerns can result in an almost neurotic fixation on the current vitality of one's own faith: is my faith sufficiently fervent to guarantee salvation and God's continuing blessing? For some, the pressure can become simply too much to bear, and many people have left the movement for that reason. Thus, alongside the ever increasing numbers of Pentecostal/Charismatic Christians in the world, there is also a growing contingent of post-Pentecostal/Charismatic Christians who have exited the movement in search of a less pressurized form of faith.

Structure

As a tradition Pentecostal/Charismatic Christianity is much more a grassroots movement than the three traditions already discussed. It has no central governing authority, and is bound together instead by a loosely shared vision of the Holy Spirit's work in the world. In the Gospel of John, the Holy Spirit is likened to the wind that blows wherever it wants without warning or predictability, and members of the Pentecostal/Charismatic tradition view their own movement in the same way. Yes, they plan and plant new churches in good organizational fashion, but they are also always on the lookout for new Spirit-led developments they could not have predicted.

From the very beginning, the Pentecostal/Charismatic movement has been entrepreneurial. People who think they have been called by God to start a new work simply go out and do it. No permission or consultation is needed. The assumption is that, just as many different flowers can grow in a field, so the many different Pentecostal/Charismatic organizations can flourish alongside each other; and if those groups are responding properly to the guidance of the Holy Spirit, the result will be compatibility and not conflict. That is the theory; it is not always the reality. Entrepreneurial movements tend to produce leaders who have very strong senses of their own authority and prerogatives. Egos of leaders can become immense, and that description clearly applies to some of the men and women who have led the Pentecostal/Charismatic movement. The temptation to either denounce or engulf other Pentecostal/Charismatic fellowships can be almost irresistible, and conflict has been a prominent part of the movement's history.

While all Pentecostal/Charismatic Christians share a common vision of the active work of God in the world, this shared vision has not produced uniformity in terms of either ideas or social organization. These diverse expressions of Pentecostal/Charismatic faith generally fall into four large categories or subtraditions: classical Pentecostalism, the Charismatic movement, neo-Charismatic churches and organizations, and Independent churches.

Classical Pentecostals represent the oldest layer of the Pentecostal/Charismatic movement. Begun in the early twentieth century, classical Pentecostalism is a form of Pentecostal denominationalism. Newly Spirit-filled leaders created new churches (for example, the Assemblies of God or the Church of God in Christ) where their Spirit-filled followers could worship God together with all the exuberance they could muster – exuberance that would have caused them to be expelled from many of the churches then in existence. Most classical Pentecostals believe that for the experience of baptism in the Spirit to be validated the recipient has to speak in tongues. They also tend to emphasize the importance of correct doctrine more than other Pentecostal/Charismatic groups. Structurally, classical Pentecostal denominations are well-organized institutions with easily recognizable lines of authority at both the congregational level and denomination-wide. As a group, classical Pentecostals number about 75 million worldwide.

Charismatic Christianity began in the 1960s. Charismatic Christians believe many of the same things as classical Pentecostals and behave in many of the same ways, but they feel no need to separate from the non-Pentecostal denominations to which they belong. Thus Charismatic Christians who are Baptists typically identify themselves as both Baptist and Charismatic, and the same would apply to all other denominations – Catholic, Lutheran, Methodist, and so forth. Because Charismatic Christians do not group themselves in separate organizations, they can be difficult to count, and the best anyone can do is roughly estimate how many members of the world's many different non-Pentecostal churches are Charismatic in religious orientation and identity.

The difficulty of counting Charismatic Christians can be illustrated by looking at the Catholic Charismatic Movement. One commonly cited source estimates that there are 120 million participants in the global Catholic Charismatic Renewal (CCR). This number includes about 14 million Charismatic Catholics who attend weekly charismatic prayer groups, 6 million more who show up once a month, and another 10 million who participate annually. An additional 15 million are tangentially involved, bringing the total to about

45 million adults. The larger number of 120 million is then generated by adding in all the children of the adults who are currently involved in the movement and by including everyone who has ever been involved in any way, even if they have subsequently left the movement.[3] All of these calculations can be questioned, and the real number of people who are active participants is much smaller. Similar questions arise when trying to count Charismatic Christians in all the other churches. Even with these qualifications, however, most scholars would estimate that the number of Charismatic Christians in the world probably equals or exceeds the number of classical Pentecostals.

Neo-Charismatic Christians are Spirit-filled Christians who, like classic Pentecostals and Charismatic Christians, believe that the Spirit of God is actively involved in the world doing miracles and changing lives. But they are less dogmatic about what counts as evidence of Pentecostal/Charismatic faith and they are generally more willing to embrace those who are seeking the Spirit as well as those who have already received the Spirit. With regard to speaking in tongues – a key issue for both classical Pentecostals and Charismatic Christians – most neo-Charismatic believers see this as only one among many spiritual gifts, and believe there is nothing especially significant about the experience. They assume that some people will speak in tongues, but many will not. What makes neo-Charismatic Christians relatively easy to identify is that since the 1980s when the movement first arose they have been busy creating a host of new denominations and organizations to house the movement. Different neo-Charismatic denominations or associations of churches can vary greatly in the emphases they place on the visible use of spiritual gifts. A person might attend one neo-Charismatic church and hardly ever see anything that seems decisively or dramatically "charismatic," but might attend another church and be blown away by the spiritual intensity of the experience – speaking in tongues, healing the sick, miraculous visions from God, and other spiritual manifestations that could include roaring like a lion or laughing uncontrollably in the Spirit. The global neo-Charismatic movement probably includes close to 100 million people.

Finally, there are a growing number of Pentecostal/Charismatic Christians around the world called *Independents*. These Christians are functionally Pentecostal/Charismatic in their spirituality and practice, but most would not use the words Pentecostal or Charismatic to describe themselves because those terms are Western. Most Independent Christians, as that term is being used here, live outside the West, and they see themselves and their churches as both autonomous (free from outside control, especially missionary control) and autochthonous (growing out of the local culture) in matters of faith. The most prominent representatives of this Pentecostal/Charismatic subgroup are the many African Independent or African Initiated Churches (AICs) that have appeared during the last hundred years, but there are also many Independent house churches in China and Independent Spirit-filled churches in Brazil. While the worship practices of many of these Independent groups resemble those of other Pentecostal/Charismatic churches, they usually also incorporate a variety of local customs and rituals that add a distinctive flavor to the mix. While virtually all of these Independent churches began as local Spirit-filled Christian movements, some have now developed into transnational organizations with congregations located in various cities and nations, including those of Europe and North America. At present, there are more than 100 million Independent Pentecostal/Charismatic Christians scattered throughout the world.

In terms of formal organizational structures, some Pentecostal/Charismatic Christians are content to live within the confines of their local congregations alone with no desire to affiliate with other congregations in some kind of denominational arrangement. The many unaffiliated Pentecostal/Charismatic congregations that one can find around the world vary greatly in size, ranging from very small churches, where only a small handful of believers gather weekly in someone's home, to the enormous Yoido Full Gospel Church in Seoul, Korea, which has a membership of more than half a million people. Some of these local congregations are run as spiritual democracies where everyone has a voice, but others are quite hierarchical in organization and the founder (often designated an "apostle") sometimes has almost total control over the group.

But while some Pentecostal/Charismatic believers are strict congregationalists, the majority of the world's Pentecostal/Charismatic Christians belong to organizations or associations that transcend the limits of a single congregation. What to call these organizations is an issue. Many Pentecostal/Charismatic Christians dislike the term "denomination" because it sounds too bureaucratic. They would prefer something more lively and interpersonal. Thus the Assemblies of God – the largest Pentecostal "denomination" in the world with approximately 55 million members – insists that it is a "cooperative fellowship" and not a denomination. This is semantics. Any sociologist would describe the Assemblies of God as every bit as organized and bureaucratic as any denomination, but for those inside the movement words matter, and words can make a difference in the way people feel about the organizations in which they are involved.

Beyond the denominational or "fellowship" level, the Pentecostal/Charismatic movement has generally had a hard time creating larger structures of association. The Pentecostal World Fellowship (PWF), founded in 1947, looks as though it should parallel other global Christian organizations like the Lutheran World Federation or the World Methodist Council. In reality, however, the PWF has a much smaller function. For most of its history, the only job of the PWF has been coordinating the triennial Pentecostal World Conference – a loosely organized conference and time of worship where Pentecostal/Charismatic Christians from around the world could meet and greet each other. Recently, the PWF has tried to broker a series of more formal agreements of cooperation among its 46 member churches regarding missionary activity, humanitarian efforts, government lobbying (especially concerning issues of religious freedom), and the mutual recognition of educational degrees from Pentecostal/Charismatic universities, seminaries, and Bible schools, but the going has been slow. Many Pentecostal/Charismatic groups value their independence too much to be bound by "paper agreements" with others.

Story

No particular aspect of the Pentecostal/Charismatic tradition is dramatically new. Virtually everything that is part of the movement has been evident previously within the history of Christianity; the filling of the Spirit, speaking in tongues, miracles, healings, prophecies, and other wonders are all part of the larger Christian story. What makes the Pentecostal/Charismatic movement distinctive is the way it has revived these practices and brought them together in a movement that focuses specifically on the power and activity of the Holy Spirit in the world today.

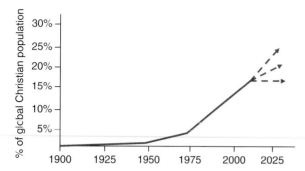

Figure 4.2   Growth of Pentecostal/Charismatic movement (as % of worldwide Christianity)

The coalescence of this new movement of the Spirit is often associated with a "revival" that took place at the Azusa Street Mission in Los Angeles, California during the years 1906 to 1908. The Azusa Street Revival was led by the African American preacher William J. Seymour. Seymour had been born a Catholic, raised a Baptist, and become an independent holiness preacher (focusing on how to obtain an experientially "deeper" Christian life) in his adult years. He received the baptism in the Holy Spirit after he moved to Los Angeles in 1906. He was an unassuming leader and would sometimes sit in front of the meetings at the mission simply praying in silence, never uttering a word. But miraculous things took place, and news of the events soon spread around the globe. People came from everywhere to see what was happening, and they left changed. Many were changed by a personal encounter with the Spirit of God, but they were also changed by the new friendships they established with other believers from all over the world. It was that network of friendships that turned the previously scattered phenomenon of modern Spirit-centered Christianity into a self-conscious movement.

But even though Pentecostalism became newly organized as a result of the Azusa Revival, Pentecostalism was not birthed there. It was birthed simultaneously in many different places at roughly the same time. One of the birthplaces of the Pentecostal/Charismatic movement was the Mukti Mission in Pune, India led by Pandita Ramabai, an internationally known Hindu feminist who had become a Christian. In 1906 and 1907 a spiritual revival, accompanied by miraculous events and speaking in tongues, spread through the mission giving rise to the first Indian Pentecostal center. In South Africa, Isaiah Shembe was busy forming his new independent *amaNazaretha* church about the same time, a church that was anticolonial and decidedly charismatic at the same time. In Chile, Willis Hoover created a new Pentecostal movement within the Methodist Church of that country, a movement that soon resulted in the formation of a new Pentecostal church. In Europe and China similar developments took place. All of which is to say that the Pentecostal/Charismatic movement has been multicentered and global from the very beginning.

The complete history of the Pentecostal/Charismatic tradition is still being pieced together, and it is difficult work because so much of the growth of the movement has taken place outside the recordkeeping cultures of upper-class Western society. Generally, the Pentecostal/Charismatic gospel has been handed on orally, person to person, by individuals who were often poorly educated or even illiterate. In much of the world for much of the twentieth century the Pentecostal/Charismatic movement was like a forest fire burning underground in the root systems of the trees, and it only burst into visibility relatively recently. Many non-Pentecostal Christian leaders were unaware of its existence before the 1960s, but since then it has exploded all around the world. The overall rate of growth has been staggering, especially in Africa, Latin America, and Asia.

The size and scope of the Pentecostal/Charismatic movement is uncontested, and no one doubts that the world is currently witnessing one of the most dramatic developments in all of Christian history. But where it all may be heading is hard to discern. Around 1990, some scholars were predicting that the Pentecostal/Charismatic movement would soon take over all of Latin America, replacing the dominant faith of Catholicism. But that did not happen, and the trend lines of Pentecostal/Charismatic growth now seem to be leveling out in some parts of the world. It seems unlikely that the Pentecostal/Charismatic movement has reached its peak and growth will undoubtedly continue for some time, but the key question seems to be shifting from simple growth to maturation, and it is an open question what maturation will mean for a movement that has so far lived on the vitality of its spiritual newness.

Notes

1   William H. Durham, "Personal Testimony of Pastor Durham," *Pentecostal Testimony*, 1(3), 7 (undated but almost certainly 1909).

2   D. Wesley Myland, *The Latter Rain Covenant and Pentecostal Power with Testimony of Healings and Baptism* (Chicago: Evangel Publishing House, 1910), pp. 25–6.

3   David B. Barrett and Todd M. Johnson, *World Christian Trends, AD 30 – AD 2200: Interpreting the Annual Christian Megacensus* (Pasadena, CA: William Carey Library, 2001), p. 275.

Suggestions for Further Reading

Alexander, Paul (2009). *Signs and Wonders: Why Pentecostalism is the World's Fastest Growing Faith*. San Francisco: Jossey-Bass.

Anderson, Alan (2004). *An Introduction to Pentecostalism*. Cambridge, UK: Cambridge University Press.

Burgess, Stanley M. and Eduard M. Van Der Mass (eds) (2002). *International Dictionary of Pentecostal and Charismatic Movements*, revised and expanded. Grand Rapids, MI: Zondervan.

Cox, Harvey (1995). *Fire from Heaven: The Rise of Pentecostal Spirituality and the Reshaping of Religion in the Twenty-First Century*. New York: Addison-Wesley.

Hollenweger, Walter J. (1997). *Pentecostalism: Origins and Developments Worldwide*. Peabody, MA: Hendrickson.

Jacobsen, Douglas (2003). *Thinking in the Spirit: Theologies of the Early Pentecostal Movement*. Bloomington: Indiana University Press.

Karkkainen, Veli-Matti (2009). *The Spirit of the World: Emerging Pentecostal Theologies in Global Contexts*. Grand Rapids, MI: Eerdmans.

Miller, Donald E. and Tetsunao Yamamori (2007). *Global Pentecostalism: The New Face of Christian Social Engagement*. Berkeley: University of California Press.

The Pew Forum on Religion and Public Life (2006). *Spirit and Power: A 10-Country Survey of Pentecostals*. Washington, DC: The Pew Forum.

Wacker, Grant (2003). *Heaven Below: Early Pentecostals and American Culture*. Cambridge, MA: Harvard University Press.

Westerlund, David (2009). *Global Pentecostalism: Encounters with Other Religious Traditions*. London: I. B. Taurus.

Part II   Where They Are

Introduction

Global Christianity is much too complex to digest in one bite. In order to make sense of things, the Christian world has to be divided up into reasonably sized parts. The next nine chapters do just that. They look at nine quite different and distinct regions of the world and examine the history and contemporary status of Christianity in each. A number of factors were taken into account in drawing this nine-region map of the world, including natural geographic divides; population size; differences of language, history, and culture; and the varieties of Christianity that exist in each region. Roughly in the order in which Christianity first appeared in each, these nine regions are: (1) the Middle East and North Africa; (2) Eastern Europe (including all of Russia); (3) Central and South Asia; (4) Western Europe; (5) sub-Saharan Africa; (6) East Asia; (7) Latin America; (8) North America; and (9) Oceania (see Figure II.1).

Two hundred years ago, 85 percent of the world's Christian population lived in Europe, and a hundred years ago 70 percent still lived there. Today, only slightly more than a quarter of the world's Christian population lives in Europe and 60 percent lives in Africa, Asia, and Latin America. The change has been tremendous. Some scholars speak of this as a great move to the south. Christianity is less and less a religion of the northern hemisphere and increasingly one of the global south. But that image doesn't quite capture the whole picture of what is going on. "Northern" Christianity, even though its global numbers have decreased, is far from dead, so the better image is to see the global Christian world as newly "flat." Christianity no longer has a worldwide center. Geographically Christianity circles the globe and theologically no one form of Christianity represents the norm. Christians anywhere can shape and influence Christianity everywhere. Figure II.2 shows how the global Christian population is distributed across the nine regions described above.

The experience of Christians in each of the nine regions varies significantly based both on the raw number of Christians who live there and on the size of the Christian community in

The World's Christians: Who they are, Where they are, and How they got there, First Edition. Douglas Jacobsen.
© 2011 Douglas Jacobsen. Published 2011 by Blackwell Publishing Ltd.

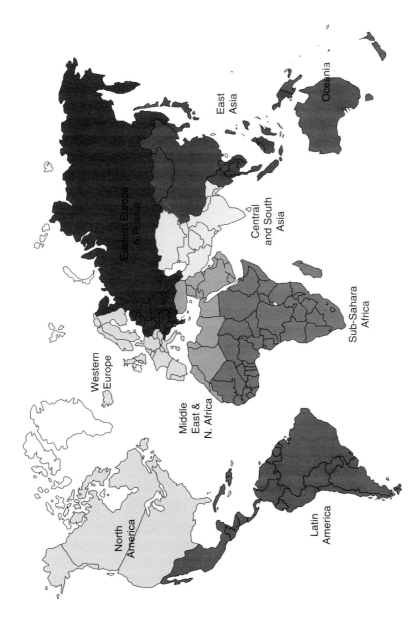

Figure II.1 Nine cultural-geographic regions of the world

comparison to the population as a whole. Christians now account for a majority of the population in six out of the nine world regions, the three exceptions being Central Asia, East Asia, and the Middle East and North Africa. Latin America is the most thoroughly Christian region by far with Christians accounting for more than 90 percent of the population. Table II.1 provides the numbers for all nine regions.

The experiences of Christians around the world also differ considerably based on how the four major Christian traditions are distributed globally. There are Orthodox, Catholic, Protestant, and Pentecostal/Charismatic Christians in each of the nine regions, but the regional distribution of these traditions is quite uneven. Table II.2 provides region by region numbers for all of the traditions. Orthodoxy is especially strong in Eastern Europe and in the Middle East and North Africa where Orthodox Christians outnumber those from other traditions by a factor of almost three to one. Catholicism is the dominant form of Christianity in Latin America (accounting for almost 80 percent of the total Christian population) and in Western Europe where there are twice as many Catholics as there are Orthodox, Protestant, and Pentecostal/Charismatic Christians combined. The situation in the remaining five regions (Central Asia, East Asia, sub-Saharan Africa, North America, and Oceania) is more mixed.

The chapters that follow describe each of these nine regions, one at a time, following the same basic format. After a brief introduction, the first half of each chapter focuses on the overall social, political, historical, and religious characteristics of the region; the second half of each chapter looks more closely at current events in several selected nations. But while

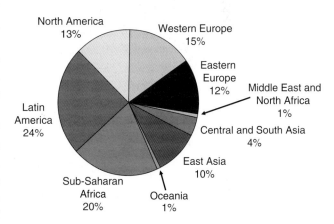

Figure II.2 Where the world's Christians live (% of the global Christian population by region)

Table II.1 Christians as percentage of the population in the nine world regions

Region	Total regional population	Christian population	Christians as % of total population
Middle East & North Africa	350,000,000	18,250,000	5.0
Eastern Europe	335,000,000	255,000,000	76.0
Central Asia	1,625,000,000	76,000,000	5.0
Western Europe	395,000,000	310,000,000	78.0
Sub-Saharan Africa	750,000,000	405,000,000	54.0
East Asia	2,100,000,000	205,100,000	10.0
Latin America	560,000,000	507,000,000	91.0
North America	330,000,000	260,000,000	79.0
Oceania	34,000,000	24,000,000	71.0
TOTAL	6,479,000,000	2,060,350,000	32.0

Table II.2   Relative size of the four Christian traditions in the nine world regions (number of adherents and percentage of all Christians in region)

Region	Orthodox	Catholic	Protestant	Pentecostal-Charismatic	All Christians in Region
Middle East	14,500,000	2,500,000	1,000,000	250,000	18,250,000
and North Africa	75%	20%	4%	1%	100%
Eastern Europe	175,000,000	64,000,000	9,000,000	7,000,000	255,000,000
	69%	25%	3%	3%	100%
Central and South	6,000,000	20,000,000	20,000,000	30,000,000	76,000,000
Asia	8%	26%	26%	40%	100%
Western Europe	2,000,000	210,000,000	88,000,000	10,000,000	310,000,000
	1%	68%	28%	3%	100%
Africa	35,000,000	140,000,000	115,000,000	115,000,000	405,000,000
	9%	35%	28%	28%	100%
East Asia	100,000	100,000,000	50,000,000	55,000,000	205,100,000
	<1%	50%	24%	26%	100%
Latin America	500,000	395,000,000	11,500,000	100,000,000	507,000,000
	<1%	78%	2%	20%	100%
North America	6,000,000	75,000,000	129,000,000	50,000,000	260,000,000
	2%	29%	50%	19%	100%
Oceania	700,000	9,200,000	10,300,000	3,800,000	24,000,000
	3%	38%	43%	16%	100%
TOTAL	239,800,000	1,015,700,000	433,800,000	371,050,000	2,060,350,000
	11.5%	49.5%	21%	18%	100%

this is the general pattern, individual chapters sometimes vary because the complexities of Christianity around the world do not always fit into the same conceptual boxes or categories.

Chapter 5

The Middle East and North Africa

Barely Surviving

Two thousand years ago the north coast of Africa was the breadbasket of the Roman Empire. Wheat grown in Africa was exported all over the Mediterranean world. That is no longer the case. The climate of the region has changed and what was once fertile, well-watered farmland is now largely desert. A similar change has taken place with regard to Christianity. During the first six hundred years of the Christian movement, the Middle East and North Africa were the heartland of the movement. Today, the region is in danger of becoming a Christian desert – a place where Christianity is present in only a few scattered oases and is absent almost everywhere else.

Christianity was born in the Middle East. This is where Jesus lived. He grew up in what is now Israel and the Palestinian Territories and for a short while he lived with his family in Egypt. This is also the land where the Christian church had its beginnings. At first, Jerusalem was the headquarters of the movement, but the new faith quickly spread beyond the region of Palestine. There were followers of Jesus in what is now Syria and Lebanon within a year or two of Jesus's death. During the next decades, partly as the result of the work of the ever-energetic apostle Paul, Christianity was introduced to the Arab tribes living in what is now Jordan and it was also preached in cities and towns all across the old Roman province of Asia Minor (present-day Turkey). Even earlier than this, Christianity had entered North Africa (Egypt and Libya), carried home by residents of the region who were in Jerusalem shortly after the death of Jesus and who were converted after hearing Peter preach the new gospel of Christ on the day of Pentecost.

For the next six centuries, the Middle East and North Africa remained fertile Christian ground and produced some of the most significant leaders of the movement. Augustine of Hippo, whose influence remains enormous even today, was a bishop in what is now Algeria. Tertullian, Cyprian, and the famous martyrs Perpetua and Felicitas all lived in Tunisia. Origen, who is considered by many to be the first Christian theologian, lived in Alexandria

The World's Christians: Who they are, Where they are, and How they got there, First Edition. Douglas Jacobsen.
© 2011 Douglas Jacobsen. Published 2011 by Blackwell Publishing Ltd.

in Egypt in the third century, and a hundred years later that same city was home to both Arius and Athanasius, famous antagonists in an ancient debate over whether Christ was truly God or not. Jerome, the author of the Vulgate (the first Latin translation of the Bible), lived in the Palestinian desert where, according to legend, he was protected by a pet lion. And the famous brothers Basil of Caesarea and Gregory of Nyssa (whose ideas were crucial for defining the Christian doctrine of the Trinity in the fourth century), along with their spiritually gifted sister Macrina, were born and reared in Cappadocia, which is now part of Turkey.

It was in this region, too, that one of the most important institutional innovations in all of Christian history took root: monasticism. Anthony of Egypt is often called the first monk. He left the urban comforts of Alexandria some time around the year 295 to move to the desert and become the first Christian hermit. He lived alone seeking to devote every waking minute of his life – and he tried to stay awake as much as possible – to the glory of God and to the self-discipline of his own desires. And he seems to have been successful. His reputation for holiness and spiritual power soon spread throughout the entire Roman Empire. In fact, he can be considered the first great Christian celebrity, as people from far and near came to see him, to seek his advice, and in some cases to stay with him in the desert as fellow followers of the harsh but rewarding way of life he modeled. So many came and stayed that it was said the desert blossomed with monks like flowers after rain. A similar development took place in Syria that perhaps even predated the rise of monasticism in Egypt. This Middle Eastern Syro-Egyptian monastic ideal would eventually spread through the entire Christian world, reshaping the Christian movement forever.

Then, in the mid-600s, the newly formed armies of Islam swept out of Arabia, conquering the eastern and southern coasts of the Mediterranean Sea. At first, the lives of Christians did not change all that much. Like Jews, Christians were considered *ahl al-kitab* ("the people of the book") and as such they were treated with tolerance by Muslim believers and were not forced to convert. Many Muslims considered Christians and Jews to be cousins in faith. They shared a monotheistic belief in one God and they all traced their deep roots back to Abraham.

But tolerance of another faith is not the same thing as religious freedom, and over time restrictions on non-Muslims tightened and social pressures to convert increased. In cases of marriages between Christians and Muslims, it was mandated that all children be raised Muslim. Conversion from Islam to Christianity was made illegal and this led, at times, to outright persecution of Christians. Christians were barred from constructing or repairing church buildings, many of which eventually became unusable. Finally, Christians were subject to a special tax that applied only to non-Muslim citizens. Obviously not all conversions to Islam were the result of social pressure, and some Christians became Muslim because they thought Islam was a spiritually superior faith. Whatever the route, Christianity began to decline in the region and that decline has been persistent. By the year 1000, the Christian percentage of the population, which had formerly included almost everyone, had likely been cut almost in half. By the time of the Crusades (the twelfth and thirteenth centuries) only about a quarter of the population was still Christian. Decline slowed after that and Christians still accounted for roughly 15 percent of the population in 1900. But the twentieth century was difficult and now only 5 percent of the region is Christian.

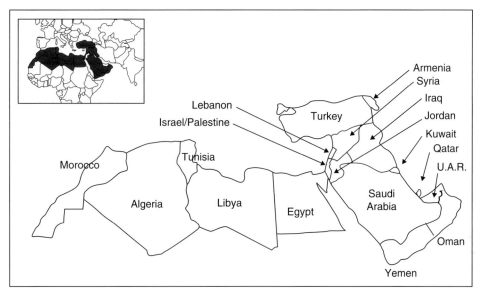

Figure 5.1 Map of Middle East and North Africa. Map by author.

Note: 17 countries: Total population 350,000,000 (5% of global population); Christian population 18,350,000 (5% of regional population, 1% of global Christian population): Orthodox 14,500,000, Catholics 2,500,000, Protestants 1,000,000, Pentecostal/Charismatic 250,000, other 100,000.

Today the region as a whole accounts for about 5 percent of the global population, but less than 1 percent of the world's Christians live here – roughly 18 million followers of Jesus scattered among more than 330 million followers of Muhammad. Rather than being the geographic center of the Christian movement, this is now the heartland of Islam. Christianity is surviving, but just barely, and the future looks bleak. Many wonder if there will be any Christians left a hundred years from now. The Christians of the Middle East and North Africa are, however, a tough and tenacious people. The desert spirituality of the monks of the past – a spirituality honed by survival in harsh conditions – continues to nourish and encourage the churches in the region.

The Region as a Whole

Religion is the main glue that holds together the 20 countries that make up this region of the world. This is the historical center of the *Dar al-Islam* – that portion of the globe where people have submitted to the rule of God as expressed in the message of the Prophet Muhammad. With the exception of Turkey, which was added in the eleventh century, this region has been under Muslim rule since the mid-600s. Western forces captured and held some of the coastal areas of the eastern Mediterranean for a while during the Crusades (the twelfth and thirteenth centuries), but these temporary Christian kingdoms were quickly reconquered by Islam. Today followers of Islam form the overwhelming majority of the population in every country, with only two exceptions: Israel and Armenia. Lebanon, which

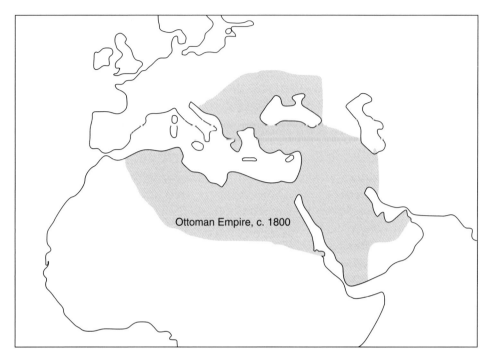

Figure 5.2   The Ottoman Empire at its peak, c. 1800. Map by author.

was created in the early twentieth century to be a homeland for Maronite Christians, and where Christians used to predominate, is now more than 60 percent Muslim. Taking the region as a whole, 95 percent of the population is Muslim and together they constitute 25 percent of all the Muslims in the world.

It is not just religion that holds this region together, however: the early Muslim rulers of this region were also held together by a shared cultural, ethnic, and linguistic identity. The term we use to describe that shared identity today is "Arab," although the people of the past rarely used that word to define themselves. They simply were who they were and felt no need to describe themselves using a specific label. Because of this shared cultural and linguistic heritage, the region under discussion here (with the exception of Turkey and Armenia) is thus also often referred to as the "Arab world." While there is a connection between the Arabic language and Islam – the *Quran* is written in Arabic, and strict Muslims feel that it should not be translated into any other language – it is important to remember that being an Arab and being a Muslim is not the same thing. In fact, many Christians who live in the area, especially those in Israel, Jordan, the Palestinian territories, and Syria, quite proudly call themselves Arab today. Christians were also at the forefront of the mid-twentieth century pan-Arab movement which sought to build a regional sense of identity on the foundation of a nonreligious, transnational understanding of Arab history, culture, and political goals.

A third overlay that describes this region of the world is that almost all of these countries were at some point in the past part of the Ottoman Empire (see Figure 5.2). The Ottoman Empire was based in present-day Turkey and had its capital in Istanbul. It rose to prominence in the 1400s and for the next two centuries it was the most powerful political regime in the world. After 1700, the empire slowly weakened, and it was finally dismantled in the early 1920s after having suffered defeat as part of the Central Powers in World War I. One significant aspect of the Ottoman Empire is that it was culturally and ethnically Turkish rather than Arab, and that fact shaped public policy. As "foreigners" in this largely Arab region, the Ottoman sultans refrained from imposing their culture on everyone else. Instead they allowed citizens to follow their own local cultures and customs as long as they were generally loyal and obedient to the state. This policy of tolerance was especially important for religious minorities.

The Ottomans revived the "*millet*" or "*dhimmi*" system of government for minority populations within their territory, an ancient Middle Eastern social arrangement designed simultaneously to protect certain rights of minority groups and to reinforce their inferior status within the population as a whole. Leaders of a *millet* community were responsible both for governing their people according to the group's own religiously defined laws and for making sure the group as a whole remained subservient to the larger kingdom or empire within which it was embedded. They were also responsible for collecting taxes and other governmental fees within their own community. Within the semiautonomous Christian *millet*, church leaders were expected to build and run their own schools; to oversee their own courts related to marriage, family, and inheritance; and to serve as representatives to the central government. At first, there was only one Christian *millet* in the Ottoman Empire, but over time a number of separate *millets* were organized, acknowledging the fact that the different Christian groups in the region did not see themselves as belonging to the same religious community. The *millet* system gave Christians a certain degree of freedom and it allowed them to live at peace with their Muslim neighbors, but it also separated them into visible communities of second-class citizenship. In that sense, it was both a blessing and a curse. What the Ottomans demonstrated, however, was that an empire could be effectively run by a central government without requiring religious conformity from all the residents of the empire. Many Christians in the region still see this Ottoman policy of unity-in-diversity as a possible model for the future.

The current map of the Middle East and North Africa is the result of both Ottoman decline and European meddling, primarily by Britain and France. The Ottoman Empire was a large and somewhat unwieldy political regime and some of the edges of the Empire – most notably the Arabian peninsula and Algeria – began to break away as early as the 1700s. During the next century, the Ottomans lost all of their remaining North African holdings. When the Empire dissolved entirely after World War I, the last remnant of the old Ottoman domain became the newly independent nation of Turkey, under the leadership of the so-called "young Turks" who were both secular and democratic in orientation. Britain and France divided the remaining Ottoman lands among themselves, creating a British "mandate" that included Iraq, Kuwait, Palestine, and Jordan, and a French "mandate" that included present-day Syria and Lebanon.

In the following three decades (1920s, 1930s, and 1940s) the countries that now make up the Middle East slowly evolved out of these mandated areas. Syria and Lebanon became independent in the mid-1940s, with Lebanon being specifically designed by the French to be a majority Christian state. Jordan was separated from Palestine in 1923 and became fully independent in 1946. The United Nations sanctioned the creation of Israel as a Jewish homeland in 1947, and Israel was established in 1948 – an event that immediately led to war and ongoing tensions. Finally, through a complicated series of events involving a long history of tension between Russia and the Ottoman Empire, the nation of Armenia became, first, part of the old Soviet Union (in the 1920s) and then independent in 1991 as the USSR fell apart.

The Christian Churches

The Christians of the Middle East and North Africa are distributed unevenly across the 20 nations that currently exist in the region. More than half live in Egypt. Armenia claims another 15 percent of the total Christian population, with smaller numbers found in Lebanon (8%) and Syria (6%). The oil-exporting countries that are members of OPEC (Algeria, Bahrain, Iraq, Kuwait, Libya, Qatar, Saudi Arabia, and the United Arab Emirates) taken together account for another 12 percent of the whole, but, with the exception of Iraq, almost all of the Christians in these oil-rich nations are foreign workers, not local citizens.

In terms of specific church traditions, the distribution of Christians is similarly uneven. The Coptic Orthodox Church in Egypt accounts for over half of all the Christians in the region. Coptic Orthodoxy is officially "Miaphysite" in its theology – believing that the human and divine were merged in the person of Christ – as opposed to being "Chalcedonian" – a theological position which affirms that Christ possessed two distinct and unmerged natures, one human and the other divine. This dispute dates back to the 400s (see Chapter 15), but it has divided Orthodox Christianity ever since. Churches that affirm Miaphysite views (sometimes called "Oriental Orthodox Churches") form only a small percentage of the global Orthodox communion, but they are a majority in the Middle East. The Armenian Apostolic Church is also Miaphysite, as is the Syrian Orthodox Church. In total, more than 70 percent of the Christians in the region identify with the Miaphysite tradition. Chalcedonian Orthodoxy (also known as "Eastern Orthodoxy"), which is the majority expression of Orthodox Christianity worldwide, makes up only 6 percent of the Christian population in North Africa and the Middle East. (See Table 5.1.)

The next largest Christian group in the region is the Catholic Church. Here, again, things are not as simple as they first seem. Less than half of the area's Catholics attend churches that use the "standard" Western (Latin) order of worship when celebrating Mass. The majority are "Eastern rite" Catholics. While Eastern rite Catholics acknowledge the spiritual authority of the Pope and are thus clearly Catholic, they use an Eastern (meaning Orthodox) liturgical format in their services of worship. Sometimes Eastern rite Catholic churches are called "Uniate" churches (meaning they are united with Rome), but that label is considered derogatory by most Eastern rite Catholics today.

The largest Eastern rite Catholic Church is the Maronite Church, which is located almost entirely in Lebanon, and claims about one million members. The ancient roots of this church can be traced to the hermit priest Maron who died in the early 400s. He began a monastic movement in the area of Mount Lebanon that slowly evolved into an independent church. The Church's first Patriarch, who took office in the year 687, was John Maron. The

Table 5.1 Christian profile of the Middle East and North Africa

Church	Membership	% of all Christians in region
Coptic Orthodox	10,000,000	55
Armenian Apostolic	2,750,000	16
Roman Catholic (total)	2,500,000	14
Latin rite Catholics	*1,000,000 (5.5)*	
Maronite Catholics	*1,000,000 (5.5)*	
Other Eastern rite Catholics	*500,000 (3.0)*	
"Greek" Orthodox	1,500,000	8
Protestant (total)	1,000,000	5
Syrian Orthodox	250,000	1
Pentecostal/Charismatic	250,000	1
Church of the East	100,000	–
Total	18,350,000	

relationship between the Maronite Church and the Roman Catholic Church was forged during the time of the Crusades and that connection has remained close ever since. In the Middle East, Western crusaders were often called "Franks" because so many of the soldiers came from France and, based on that fact, the Maronite Church has maintained especially close ties with the French Catholic Church. Given that long-standing relationship, it was not at all surprising that France wanted to protect its Maronite allies when it took control of the Lebanese-Syrian region following World War I. The current boundaries of Lebanon and Syria were drawn by the French specifically to establish Lebanon as a Catholic nation governed by a clear Christian majority. Since independence, Lebanon's constitution has guaranteed that the president will always be a Maronite, but changing demographics are calling that policy into question. Maronite Christians now make up significantly less than half the population (some estimates are as low as 25%) and their future in the country they used to "own" is now uncertain.

Most of the other Eastern rite Catholic Churches in this part of the world were formed as the result of eighteenth-century Catholic missionary activity which sought to woo Orthodox Christians away from their own churches and into communion with Rome. These churches, whose membership was drawn mostly from Armenian, Syrian Orthodox, and Greek Orthodox Churches, are all relatively small. Together they represent only 2 percent of the Christians in the region, but their existence is still resented by some Orthodox Christians who see them as the result of immoral "sheep stealing" on the part of the Roman Catholic Church.

One church that used to be quite large, but is now only a shadow of its former self, is the Church of the East, which is also known as the "Nestorian" Church. Originally centered in the Persian Empire (present-day Iraq and Iran), the Church of the East eventually spread throughout central Asia and even planted itself in China and parts of Southeast Asia. During the fourth, fifth, and sixth centuries, Nestorian churches and monasteries were built all across the region that now comprises Uzbekistan, Turkmenistan, Tajikistan, Kygyzstan, and Kazakhstan, with Church of the East missionaries establishing outposts as far east as the Chinese capital of Chang'an by the mid-600s. Most of this area eventually came under Islamic rule, however, and the Church of the East began to decline. The fourteenth-century Mongolian conqueror Timur Leng (known as Tamburlaine in the West) was especially hard on the church. Timur and his regime obliterated Christianity in most of Central Asia and in much of the Middle East as well. Today a mere handful of Nestorians remain, living mostly in Baghdad and in the northern borderlands where Iraq, Iran, and Turkey meet. The recent fighting that has taken place in Iraq has also had a profoundly negative impact on this community, and the overall numbers of Nestorians in the region may now be as low as 100,000.

Finally, about one million of the Christians in the Middle East and North Africa are Protestant. This group ranges from house-church Pentecostals to high-church Anglicans and also includes Baptists, Presbyterians, Methodists, Lutherans, Brethren, nondenominationalists, and almost every other kind of Protestant. Many of these groups began as missionary ventures, but they are all now locally led. Many also, however, continue to have close ties with Christians in the West. This can be a blessing, in terms of financial assistance and educational resources, but it can also be a curse in times of tension when connections with Europe and America may be viewed as consorting with the enemy.

The Christians of the Middle East and North Africa are very much aware of their minority status and through the years they have adopted a range of different survival techniques. Early in the twentieth century, many Christians supported the creation of secular governments in the area, following the secular nation-state model of Europe, hoping they would provide a public structure of life that would minimize their risk of persecution and maximize the potential for peaceful and prosperous coexistence with their Muslim neighbors. During the middle years of the twentieth century, some Christians – such as the Palestinian Greek Orthodox leader Ya'quob Farraj – thought the pan-Arab movement had the potential to open space for Arab Christians to live and flourish side by side with Arab Muslims. By the end of the twentieth century, however, both options (secularism and pan-Arabism) had largely dissolved, swept aside by a rising tide of pan-Islamism, a philosophy of regional unity that rejects secularism and assumes a shared allegiance to Islamic faith. This pan-Islamism has also become increasingly fundamentalist in orientation, leading contemporary Christians in the Middle East and North Africa to feel more isolated and threatened than they have for centuries.

Faith and Ethnicity

Historically, the Christian communities of the Middle East and North Africa have survived by wedding faith to ethnicity. The Armenians are an example. The Armenian Apostolic Church proudly claims its beginning in the conversion of the Armenian King Trdat who, in the year 301 CE, became the first political head of state to become a follower of Jesus. When monarchs convert they generally try to lead their people into their newly adopted faith, and that happened in Armenia with King Trdat. Armenian nationality and Armenian faith have now been merged for more than 1,700 years. A similar ethnic-religious dynamic has been at work in many of the other historical churches of the region. To be a member of the Coptic Orthodox Church is a matter of both faith and ethnicity. To call oneself a Maronite is to make a statement that is religious and political at the same time. To be identified with the Nestorian Church of the East is to name oneself in a way that is both spiritual and cultural.

Christianity in this part of the world is a religion into which one is born much more than it is a religion one adopts by choice. It is a religion of kinship, blood, and communal practices as much as (if not more than) it is a matter of doctrine. It is also a religion in which the community as a whole is the bearer of the faith, and not everyone is expected to evidence the same level of spiritual devotion. Religiously "nonpracticing" members of the community are thus still seen, and they typically see themselves, as full members of the community. No one is expelled for lack of fervor. In fact, the only way to leave the church/community is through conversion to another faith.

This linkage between peoplehood and faith has deep roots in the Orthodox tradition in which most of the churches in the region are located. Orthodox doctrine asserts that "no one is saved alone." The life of faith – the life of living, by God's grace, into holiness and redemption – is not something attained by oneself. Faith is a group experience that takes group effort, and that will finally result in the salvation of the whole. The Orthodox say that individuals are never complete in and of themselves, and that each person lives in complementary relationship with others. Fully cognizant of the reality of human interdependence, Orthodox Christianity has always respected the role of culture and country in human life, even to the point of assuming that each nation (defined in terms of culture and peoplehood, not necessarily in terms of modern nation-states) should have its own church that reflects the traditions and ways of life of that particular human community.

But the fusion of church and nation that is currently evident in the Middle East and North Africa also reflects, to some degree, Islamic influence. Within Islam there is no easy differentiation between religion and the state. Religion is about public life as much as it is about personal practice, and law and faith blend together. So it is no surprise then that when the forces of Islam took over previously Christian lands, they assumed that Christianity also involved a mixture of religious and political concerns. The *millet* system discussed above was the result. While Orthodox Christians may already have been predisposed to a communal understanding of faith, the *millet* system as administered by Muslim officials strengthened and reinforced this tendency toward communalism, adding a specifically political dimension to the ethnic communalism of Orthodox Christianity.

Over the years, the line between faith, culture, and politics has, for many of the Christians of the region, blurred into oblivion and, in general, that blurring has aided their survival. Having multiple overlapping sources of social cohesion – political, cultural, familial, economic, *and* religious – has protected the Christian minorities of the region from being either fully absorbed into or totally crushed by the larger Islamic population that surrounds them. But this blending of faith, culture, and politics comes with a cost, especially in terms of the Christian values of peaceableness and compassion. In the Middle East, being political can often involve guns as well as votes, and regional militias are often part of the political process.

One of the clearest examples of this merger of force and faith is found in the Maronite militias of Lebanon. While these Christian military units have undoubtedly helped the Maronite community survive, they have a reputation for ruthlessness that exceeds that of almost every other military organization in the area. It is hard, even for some Maronites, to square that brutality with the moral message of the gospel. Self-protection has led numerous religious communities in the Middle East and North Africa to arm themselves for the purpose of protection, but that is a dangerous path that does not necessarily guarantee survival. In fact, the problems being experienced by Maronites in Lebanon today are to some degree the result of having lost the respect of the general Lebanese population because of their overreliance on military force and their partisan political maneuvering.

Weariness and Decline

The Christians of the Middle East and North Africa are still surviving, but the number of Christians in the region as a percentage of the population is declining, and the pace seems to be accelerating. In the past century alone there has been a two-thirds drop from 15 percent of the total regional population in 1900 to 5 percent today. Roughly half of that decline can be attributed to the massacre of Armenian Christians that took place in Turkey during the early years of the twentieth century and to the mass exodus of Christians (about 500,000 – mostly European Catholics) from North Africa that took place during Algeria's war for independence from France in the 1950s and 1960s. But even after discounting the impact of those two relatively isolated but devastating events, the Christian population as a percentage of the region's total population is still no more than half the size it was a hundred years ago.

Anecdotal evidence suggests that the flow of Christians out of the region has increased in the last decade or two. No one knows with certainty how many Christians now remain. Generally, it is the wealthier and better educated Christians who have emigrated, since they have the means and opportunity to do so, and this brain drain has not made it easier for those who stay behind. Reacting to this loss of sorely needed gifts and talents, the Maronite bishops of Lebanon warned their followers in a public appeal that they would "not find what [they] are looking for in another land." They said there was no "cure" in leaving, but rather the only real cure was to be found in "coming back … to one's reason, conscience, homeland, and to each other."[1] Leaders of other churches share this sentiment. They are all asking their followers to stay put and not to flee the region in search of better places to live. But people are not necessarily listening.

At present, the worst situation may be in Iraq. The Christian population suffered alongside everyone else during the American effort to "liberate" Iraq that began in March 2003, but since the cessation of the American combat effort in May 2010, violence against Christians has increased. Christian leaders have been kidnapped and killed, and in the fall of 2010, gunmen from an extremist group called the "Islamic State of Iraq" attacked the Catholic Cathedral in Baghdad, killing 50 people and warning that more Christian blood would soon be shed. Shortly thereafter, 11 Christian sites in Baghdad were targeted for attack in a coordinated effort to "cleanse" Christians from the city.

Even before this particular round of violence, Sahar Gabriel, an Iraqi Christian and journalist, had predicted: "In 10 years there won't be a single Christian in Iraq, I think. Maybe less than 10 years."[2] Christians are leaving in droves; anyone who has a ticket out of the country is going. There were more than a million Christians in Iraq during the time when Saddam Hussein (1979–2003) ran the country. Now there are fewer than 400,000. This decline is troubling to many Iraqis, not just Christians. Christians and Muslims have lived together in Iraq for hundreds of years, and most mainstream Muslim leaders have expressed their commitment to defend the rights and lives of their Christian fellow citizens. But the government is divided, resources are still relatively thin, and the Iraqi police and defense forces are not particularly efficient. Promises of defense without the infrastructure to back them up may be genuine promises, but they are hollow. Because of that, many Iraqi Christians who do not have enough money to exit the country entirely are heading north to the Kurdistan region. This is the historical center of Christianity in Persia, and Kurdish leaders have said they will protect any Christians who move into their territory. It appears almost certain, however, that the south and central regions of Iraq will become "Christian-free" zones in the years ahead – a microcosm of what many Christians fear may happen to the Middle East as a whole.

Spirituality and Survival in Egypt

Weariness and decline have called forth two significantly different spiritual responses from Christians in the region. On the one hand, some have called for personal spiritual renewal, stressing the need to revive ancient monastic ideals so that ordinary laymen and women can use them as resources in their personal struggles of faith and survival. A rather different model stresses the need for Christians to adopt a "nationalist" political strategy that will unify the whole Christian community and provide group mechanisms for defending their rights. These two alternatives are apparent in many of the countries in the region, but they have been especially visible in the Coptic community in Egypt which represents more than half of all the Christians in the region and claims about 12 percent of the Egyptian population.

Within the Coptic Church two prominent leaders have been vocal proponents of these opposing views for more than 30 years. The well-known monk Matthew the Poor (1919–2006) represents the personal spirituality option, while Pope Shenouda III, the official head of the Coptic Orthodox Church, represents the nationalist stance.

Matthew the Poor (see Plate 1) was born Yūsuf Iskandar, but in his early adult years he decided to become a monk and adopted the name Matthew. He sold his lucrative pharmacy business, gave his money to the poor, and set off to the desert in imitation of St Anthony of old. For a while he lived at the St Macarios monastery in the Natrun valley, but in 1958 he left the monastery in order to found a new nonmonastic religious order for laypeople called *Mukarrasin*. Members of this order are to live as much like monks as possible, given the restraints of their jobs and their family responsibilities. Rather than mandating precise behaviors, the stress is on virtues like humility, prayer, and submission to God's will. Special emphasis is placed on avoiding anger and "turning the other cheek" when confronted with

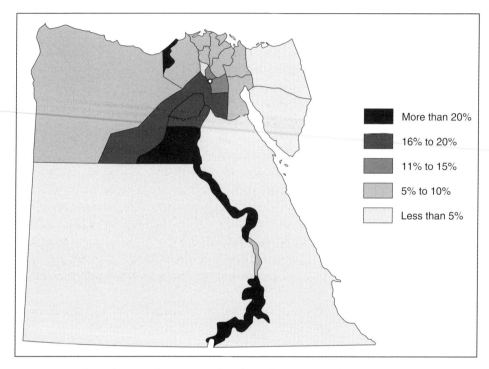

Figure 5.3   Where Christians live in Egypt (% of population that is Christian by geographic subregion). Map by author.

incidents of prejudice or persecution. For Matthew the Poor, such incidents are occasions for training toward martyrdom – the willingness to give up one's life without self-defense as public witness of one's faith in and reliance on God. In his various books and other publications, Matthew the Poor champions this way of life as the only genuine path to spiritual renewal and the only road that leads to eternal life with God.[3]

Matthew's view of the world is one in which God has complete control. God decides what will and will not happen and it is neither the right nor the prerogative, nor is it within the power, of any human being to change what God has ordained. The life of true faithfulness should accordingly be "a life of total submission and humility"[4] before God and others. If followed rigorously, this would be a recipe for religious sainthood, but it also allows believers to maintain their dignity by morally rising above those who harm or oppress them. For Matthew the Poor, this is the only reasonable way to live as a Christian in present-day Egypt. Any other option ultimately leads into error, either moral error in the form of anger and hatred directed against members of the majority Muslim culture, or spiritual error in the form of pride which ultimately sets one in opposition to God.

Pope Shenouda III (see Plate 2), who was formerly a monk like Matthew, has a very different understanding of what is possible, preferable, and practical for the Coptic community. But rather than adopting the monastic and other-worldly stance of Matthew the Poor – which Shenouda thinks is beyond the capabilities of most ordinary believers – the Coptic pope has opted for a much more this-worldly and realistic response to the pressure-filled life that defines Coptic Christianity in Egypt. (Note that the head of the Coptic Orthodox Church is called a "pope," the same term used to describe the spiritual head of the Roman Catholic Church. Translated literally, the word "pope" means simply "father." In the last Coptic papal election, Matthew the Poor was one of the other finalists who were considered in addition to Shenouda.)

Shenouda calls his own position Coptic Nationalism and says its goal is to provide Coptic Christians in Egypt with an alternative social universe in which they can live their lives with dignity, self-esteem, and a sense of achievement. This is far from Matthew the Poor's call for self-effacing, spiritual humility, an agenda that Shenouda considers both dangerous and futile. Shenouda believes that most Egyptians, whether Christian or Muslim, see Christian humility as nothing but weakness. This is corroborated by Boutros Ghālī, a well-known Coptic spokesperson, who recently told a researcher: "Let's face it, the Copts just don't have balls!"[5] Aware of how prevalent this kind of attitude is, Pope Shenouda feels Christians have to defend themselves or they will receive no respect at all. He believes that while, as an individual, a Coptic Christian may choose to forgo self-defense in matters that are purely personal, every Copt has a responsibility to defend the collective rights of the entire community whenever they are at stake.

In order for Shenouda's vision of Coptic nationalism to succeed, his first challenge was to confront the entrenched interests of the existing church hierarchy – the system of bishops and priests that ran the church. Before his tenure as pope, the Coptic Orthodox Church had only 13 bishops in all of Egypt. Most of these bishops were old men who ran their dioceses as personal fiefdoms. Given the size of their dioceses, these bishops could not possibly know all their parishioners, and many did not want to. After all, they were churchly princes and not social workers or community activists. But the latter is exactly what Shenouda thought they should be – priestly Christian social workers, intent on improving both the physical and the spiritual lives of all Copts. So he began a program of dividing up old dioceses and creating new ones all over Egypt. Today there are 64 dioceses in the church and almost all of the bishops are young men (there are no ordained women in the Coptic Church) who, having been appointed by the pope, share his ideals.

Shenouda's vision of Coptic nationalism is predicated on the notion that the church should be an all-encompassing reality for Coptic Christians – a spiritual nation within the nation where one's identity can be fully invested. Cradle-to-grave programs of churchly socialization include mass baptisms of babies intended to remind the community of its own fertility; Christian training for young people and university students designed to help them understand how and why they are different from their Muslim and secular acquaintances; an emphasis on collective prayer and fasting that builds community spirit; and very strict rules against divorce. The pope hopes to strengthen the family as the foundation of Coptic Christian identity and to make the Coptic Orthodox Church a place where every Copt can find meaning, make friends, strive to develop a good reputation, and seek status. "My only ambition," he says, "is to integrate every Copt – every single one of them – into the church."[6]

In many ways, Pope Shenouda's program seems to be working. The churches are crowded and people are enthused. They are proud to be Copts. But no one knows how deeply his vision of Coptic nationalism has really sunk in nor how successful Coptic nationalism will be in the long run as a defense against the wearying assault of fundamentalist Islam in Egypt. There is also some reason to fear a more concerted Muslim backlash if Shenouda-style Coptic nationalism becomes too strident. Shenouda himself seems to recognize this danger. The fiery rhetoric of his early career has given way to a more conciliatory public stance. The views of Pope Shenouda are also challenged by the gentle virtues of Matthew the Poor, and the Coptic community seems to recognize that they need somehow to keep both approaches alive. For the time being, Coptic nationalism seems ascendant, but no one knows when real persecution might suddenly arise and Matthew the Poor's spirituality of martyrdom may become the only remaining option.

Turkey and Armenia

The persecution that some Egyptians fear may be in their future is embodied historically in the experience of the Armenian church and the Armenian people. Throughout most of history, Armenia has existed more as an idea than as a geographic, political entity. The traditional homeland of the Armenian people is located in the mountainous region north of Syria, Iraq, and Iran in what is now eastern Turkey and the Republics of Armenia and Azerbaijan, but this territory has been ruled by many different nations and empires. The triangular region defined by the three points of Lake Sevan, Lake Van, and Lake Urmia constitutes the core of the ancient Armenian homeland (see Plate 3), but later many Armenians migrated to what is now south-central Turkey. Today, most of this region is devoid of any Armenian presence, with the exception of the Republic of Armenia itself.

This absence of Armenians is due to the genocide against the Armenian people that took place in the late nineteenth and early twentieth centuries. At the beginning of the nineteenth century all of this region, as well as most of the Balkans, was still under Ottoman rule. But slowly the peripheral parts of the declining empire were breaking away and declaring their own independence. These developments encouraged Armenians to contemplate their own potential independence, and they reached out tentatively to Russia hoping to find a larger nation willing to champion that cause. The Russians generally rebuffed them, and Turkish leaders were totally unwilling to contemplate the independence of the Armenian region. Places like Serbia, Macedonia, and Bulgaria might be allowed to go their own way, but the Armenian homeland was in the middle of Turkish land. So the "Armenian problem" became an internal Turkish affair, and the "solution" was genocide (see Figure 5.4).

Violence against the Armenians began as early as the 1890s, but the organized killing of the Armenian people began in 1915, during World War I. The Ottoman Empire had, by that point, essentially ceased to exist, and the nation of Turkey had been taken over by the Committee of Union and Progress (a group of new leaders known commonly as the "Young Turks") who sought to create a new secular Turkish Republic in place of the old Islamic empire. Driven by a heightened sense of ethnic nationalism instead of religious faith, the Young Turks fostered the idea that there was no place for Armenians in the new Turkey. They were ethnic and religious "foreigners" and they had to be eliminated so that Turkey would be free to be fully Turkish without the pollution of any Armenian presence. And so, the genocide began. The primary method was forced deportation. In town after town across

Figure 5.4 The Armenian genocide
Courtesy of the Armenian Genocide Museum-Institute

eastern Turkey, the Armenian population was rounded up and forced to leave. To minimize the risk of resistance, able-bodied men were often executed on the spot and then the remaining women, children, and older men were marched into the desert. Ostensibly the destination was Syria, but only about 20 percent of the Armenians made it that far. Many more died or were killed in the camps that were hastily erected on the border. Between one and two million Armenians were ultimately put to death in what the Armenians call "the Great Calamity."

To this day, the Turkish government refuses to acknowledge that the genocide took place. According to them, any significant violence against the Armenians during the early twentieth century was a justifiable response to troublemakers and revolutionaries intent on destroying the Turkish nation. Most scholars and unbiased observers, however, view the Armenian genocide as one of the clearest examples of ethnic cleansing in human history.

In the understanding of the Armenian Christians and the Turkish Muslims among whom they lived, religion and ethnicity are seen as intimately connected. The Ottoman Empire stressed that connection and, because of that, the Ottomans would have been very hesitant to perpetrate the kind of genocide against the Armenians that the secular Young Turks later orchestrated. Islamic law requires Muslims to respect the religious rights and identities of Christian minority groups living in their midst. Once the restraint of religion was removed, however, the Young Turks could demonize the Armenians on the basis of race alone and move ahead with their plans to eliminate them. If the genocide can thus be understood as a "secular" event from the Turkish side, it remained a profoundly religious event from the Armenian side, for the Armenians never adopted the idea that their religion and their ethnicity could be separated.

The results of the genocide continue to be reflected in the population profile of modern Turkey. In 1900, there were approximately three million Christians in Turkey (20 percent of the total population) and virtually all of them were Orthodox. Today less than 1 percent of the population is Christian. More than half of that decline can be directly attributed to the Armenian genocide. Other significant declines in the Christian population took place when Greek Orthodox Christians were deported during the Greco-Turkish War of 1922 and when Orthodox Christians fled Istanbul during a series of anti-Greek riots in 1955 that destroyed three-quarters of the Orthodox churches in the city. Today, only 250,000 Christians remain in the country. About 60 percent of those Christians are Orthodox. The rest are mostly Protestant, a group that accounted for only 2 percent of the Christian population in 1900.

As for the Armenians and their church, they are currently flourishing in the independent Republic of Armenia, but the past century has been rough. An independent Republic of Armenia existed briefly after the end of World War I (1919), but it was taken over by the USSR in 1920. During the early years of Communist rule, churches and religious schools were forcibly closed and religion was ridiculed. As was the case elsewhere in the USSR, pressure on the churches was relaxed during World War II as Stalin sought to promote Russian patriotism and support for the war effort by any means necessary. Given that relaxation of Communist control, a number of Armenians who had emigrated abroad returned to the country following the war, but the government instituted a new round of persecution in 1948–9, and many of the returnees were arrested and deported to work camps in Siberia. In the 1960s, a new movement for Armenian autonomy began to form in the region and finally a new Republic of Armenia – the only predominantly Christian nation in the Middle East – was proclaimed in 1991 after the collapse of the USSR.

The Armenian Orthodox and Apostolic Church (its official name) is currently divided into five semiautonomous jurisdictions (in technical Orthodox terminology, two of these are "catholicosates" and three are "patriarchates") with a worldwide following of about nine million. About 2.5 million Armenians live in the Republic of Armenia (along with nearly a million citizens who are not ethnically Armenian) and another 500,000 Armenians are spread throughout the Middle East. The remaining six million are members of the Armenian diaspora, many of whom are only marginally involved in the life of the church. Within Armenia itself, the Orthodox Church has the status of formally being designated the state religion, but religious freedom is also affirmed. In practice this means that non-Orthodox religions face some difficulties in carrying out their work, but generally most non-Orthodox groups are not actively harassed.

The Armenian Orthodox Church has a unique organizational structure. It is hierarchical, but it operates locally on a democratic basis with each congregation having the right to select its own priests rather than having them assigned by an overseeing bishop. The church can have this kind of hybrid system because the real core of the Armenian Orthodox Church lies elsewhere – in its ethnicity and not in its institutional structures. This is a church where God, faith, nation, and homeland all merge, and where the survival of the people and the church are seen as one and the same thing. The way that most Armenians view their own nation is similar to the way that many Jews view Israel – as a historic homeland which guarantees that both their faith and their people will survive. It should perhaps come as no surprise, then, that Christian Armenia is the one nation in the Middle East that has close diplomatic relations with the state of Israel.

Israel and the Palestinian Territories

No discussion of Christianity in the Middle East and the Mediterranean South Coast can ignore Israel and the Palestinian Territories. While representing only a fraction of the region's landmass – about 2 percent of the total – this small piece of ground holds enormous significance. This is not ordinary turf; it is "the Holy Land," venerated by Christians, Jews, and Muslims alike. As has been the case so often in human history when land is seen as holy, this is also a place where violence always lies just beneath the surface ready to break out at the slightest provocation. Alongside all the holy symbolism, however, the ordinary still matters. Ordinary Jews and ordinary Palestinians (both Muslim and Christian) have a host of ordinary concerns that shape their daily lives – issues of justice and survival, worries about making a living and raising a family, and questions about whether to leave or to stay in a land where conflict is so much part of daily life. In order to make sense of what is happening in Israel and the Palestinian Territories, it is necessary to keep these two dimensions always in view: the religious/symbolic and the ordinary/concrete superimposed on one another.

Christians represent only a small percentage of the population within the borders of Israel and the Palestinian Territories. This has been the case for many years, but their numbers are declining. In 1900, Christians accounted for about 10 percent of the local population; today they represent only 3 percent. Despite being a small community, the Christians in this region have frequently been at each other's throats, turning small disputes into major confrontations. This is illustrated in the way the Church of the Holy Sepulcher in Jerusalem – one of the holiest Christian sites in Jerusalem, built on the traditional location of Christ's crucifixion – is administered. Different rooms and sections of the building are claimed by four different Orthodox Churches: Greek, Syrian, Coptic, and Ethiopian. In the early 1800s, competition for building space and use became so intense that it was finally decided that a local Muslim family should be appointed the keeper of the keys to lock and unlock the building for services and other events, because none of the Christian groups trusted the others not to change the locks and claim the whole building for themselves. This arrangement continues even today.

In recent years, however, local Christians in Israel and the Palestinian Territories have drawn closer to each other and have developed much better working relationships. This is partly the result of deepening ecumenical convictions. Many Christians in the Holy Land, like Christians all around the world, have concluded that bitter denominational disputes reflect poorly on a religion that claims love as one of its central values. However, Palestinian Christians are drawn together not only by idealism, but also by their shared opposition to what they see as the unjust and oppressive policies of the Israeli government.

Figure 5.5   Palestinian Muslims and Christians demonstrate at Al-Yarmuk refugee camp in Damascus, October 9, 2009
© Louai Beshara/AFP/Getty Images

The state of Israel, like every other nation in the region, is a relatively modern creation. It was formed in 1947 when the United Nations partitioned the old British Mandate in Palestine into two new countries: a Jewish state of Israel and a predominantly Muslim state of Palestine. The history that led up to this momentous event was complex, but Zionism was central.

Zionism is the belief that the strip of land on the eastern edge of the Mediterranean Sea that we now call Israel and the Palestinian Territories belongs rightly, by history and divine fiat, to the Jewish people. Modern Zionism, like many other forms of modern nationalism, sprang into existence during the nineteenth century. For Zionists, the idea of "returning" to Palestine was a mix of longing for the past and hope for the future. It meant moving "home" and it also represented a way of leaving behind the pressures and fears, as well as the intermittent persecution, that was part of living in Christian Europe. In the late 1800s and the early 1900s, European Jews began to move to Palestine by the thousands. They bought property and developed an impressive network of cultural, economic, and religious associations intended to foster both mutual support and Jewish identity. The horrors of the Holocaust during World War II gave a new sense of urgency to the movement. Hitler's attempt at the complete genocide of the Jewish people had been nearly successful, and most Jews and many Christians in Europe and America came to believe that the creation of a secure homeland for the Jewish people was a moral imperative. It was in that context that the United Nations passed the 1947 resolution that partitioned Palestine and created the state of Israel.

While this action assuaged the conscience of the West, it infuriated many people in the Middle East. By what right, they asked, did the United Nations take this land from the Arab people and give it to the Jews? In the years leading up to partition, Zionists and other European leaders had frequently described the land as essentially devoid of people: a land without a people for a people without a land. But, of course, the land was not empty. The "return" of the Jewish people to the land of Israel (the notion of "return" itself is a charged word) accordingly required the displacement of at least some of the local Palestinian population. Much of this displacement was accomplished by the legitimate purchase of property from Palestinian families, but eventually violence was also used to empty the land of some of its Palestinian citizens. When the United Nations voted for partition, Palestinians felt betrayed by the rest of the world. Left to their own resources and feeling they had to fight back, the Palestinians attacked. Israel won that war and in the process enlarged the territory under their control. Since that time, Israel has won every other confrontation and its zone of control has been extended, leading to ever more frustration within the Palestinian community. There is no way to describe the history or current state of affairs in Israel and the Palestinian Territories in a neutral manner. The issues on both sides are so deeply laden with religious symbolism and legitimate moral outrage that it is impossible for any view to be "objective."

The very existence of the state of Israel has itself been a matter of concern and speculation for Christians around the world. One particular viewpoint, called *dispensationalism*, has been especially influential. According to this perspective, the new state of Israel is a fulfillment of prophecy and a sign that history as we know it is about to end. The rebirth of Israel is like an alarm clock going off, indicating the imminence of "the rapture," when God will transport all genuine Christians out of the world. After that rapture has taken place, the armies of the world will gather in the Middle East and the battle of Armageddon will commence. At the climax of that conflict, Christ himself will descend to earth, end the violence, judge the nations, and establish his thousand year millennial reign on earth. Millions of Christians around the world, and especially in the United States, believe this account of the future is simply true. It is considered to be history written in advance, literally how the world will end. For dispensational Christians, the messy realities of life on the ground in Israel and the Palestinian Territories can be largely ignored. All that matters is that Israel once again exists and because of that Christians can rejoice in the nearness of Christ's return.

Virtually all the local Christians who live in Israel and the Palestinian Territories would reject this dispensational vision of the future as harmful and mistaken. For them, the focus is not on God's grand symbolic plan for the ages, but on the ordinary matters they confront every day, matters of justice, suffering, and survival. Even more, they would reject the notion that the land of Palestine rightfully belongs to Israel either because God promised it to the Jews long ago or because it represents the miraculous fulfillment of prophecy.

If there is a central affirmation in Palestinian Christian theology it is that God has no favorites. While God may have had a special covenant with the people of Israel in the distant past, that covenant was never meant to be restrictive. It was a means to the end of the redemption of the world as a whole. Any special privileges that Jews may have had in the past have thus been superseded, and today God deals equally with all people. The key question for Palestinian Christians is where justice lies, and in answering that question, most would say unequivocally that justice lies with the Palestinian cause. This stance places the great majority of Palestinian Christians in political agreement with their Muslim neighbors.

On this issue there is little, if any, difference between the two communities. Naim Ateek, an Anglican priest and former canon of St George's Cathedral in Jerusalem, explains:

> Most Palestinians do not deny the evils of anti-Semitism or the vileness of the Holocaust; but they do feel that the solution of the "Jewish problem" – a Western phenomenon that had little or nothing to do with their home, Palestine – was achieved at their expense, by their loss of Palestine. Palestinians would argue, furthermore, that if people in different lands based their claims to territory on divine promises or conquests, our world would be a shambles [7]

For many years there was an easy alliance between Christians and Muslims in the Palestinian movement, an alliance made possible because that struggle was defined in secular terms as a partnership of Palestinian national identity. This was the position of the Palestinian Liberation Organization (PLO) and of the Fatah political party. Because of that secular orientation, Christians were able to hold a number of relatively visible leadership positions in the movement. But the rise of Hamas, an alternative explicitly Islamic Palestinian political party, has unsettled the equation and is changing the options. If Hamas continues to grow in strength and influence, it will be very difficult for Christians to continue to hold any public leadership roles within the Palestinian movement, even in Fatah, and the future of the Palestinian Christian community as a whole may become significantly more tenuous. Like almost every other Christian community in the Middle East and North Africa, the Christians of Palestine are beleaguered.

Hope?

Tensions between Muslims and Christians play a huge role in the lives of most Christians in North Africa and the Middle East, but there are exceptions to this rule. In some communities, Christians and Muslims still live side by side in peace and sometimes their religious practices even overlap. In rural Syria, for example, both Christians and Muslims visit the gravesite of the Sufi Muslim saint Nebi Uri seeking healing and advice, and members of both groups are welcomed with equal warmth by the sheikh who oversees the shrine. Similarly, at the nearby Orthodox Christian Convent of Seidnaya, Muslim and Christian neighbors come together in prayer, seeking help (mostly to conceive children) from the famous icon of Notre Dame.

What allows these interfaith friendships to exist? Sister Tecla, who runs the convent, says simply, "We are all children of God … The All Holy One brings us together."[8] That may be true. It is also true that people in general tend to lay aside their squabbles, religious or other, in the face of shared pain or suffering, and undoubtedly that is also part of what is happening in these cases. Regardless of what makes it possible, these examples show that Christians and Muslims can live peaceably together in the Middle East and North Africa. So, there is hope. But the rareness of such occurrences reminds us that the normal state of affairs is quite different. Antagonism and not peace generally rules and, for the Christian minorities of the region, that almost endless antagonism is becoming more wearying every day.

Notes

1 Monthly Statement of the Assembly of the Maronite Bishops, December 5, 2007. Online at http://www.irf.ac.at/dfs/query/query.php?radio_doc=1442&userlang=e&doclang=e (accessed November 4, 2010).

2 Sahar S. Gabriel, "Leaving Iraq: An Iraqi Christian," *New York Times,* March 19, 2009. Online at http://atwar.blogs.nytimes.com/2009/03/19/leaving-iraq-an-iraqi-christian/ (accessed November 12, 2010).

3 For background information on Matthew the Poor see S. S. Hasan, *Christians versus Muslims in Modern Egypt: The Century-long Struggle for Coptic Equality* (New York, Oxford University Press, 2003), pp. 89–94.

4 Matthew the Poor, *Orthodox Prayer Life: The Interior Way* (Crestwood, NY: St Vladimir's Seminary Press, 2003), p. 257.

5 S. S. Hasan, *Christians versus Muslims in Modern Egypt*, p. 112.

6 Ibid., p. 130.

7 Naim Stifan Ateek, *Justice, and Only Justice: A Palestinian Theology of Liberation* (Maryknoll, NY: Orbis, 1989), p. 104.

8 William Dalrymple, *From the Holy Mountain: A Journey Among the Christians of the Middle East* (New York: Henry Holt, 1997), p. 190.

Suggestions for Further Reading

Abu-Nimer, Mohammed, Amal I. Khoury, and Emily Welty (2007). *Unity in Diversity: Interfaith Dialogue in the Middle East.* Washington, DC: United States Institute of Peace.

Ateek, Naim Stifan (2009). *A Palestinian Christian Cry for Reconciliation.* Maryknoll, NY: Orbis.

Badr, Habib, Suad Abou el Rouss Slim, and Joseph Abou Nohra (eds) (2005). *Christianity: A History in the Middle East.* Beirut: Middle East Council of Churches.

Bailey, Betty Jane and J. Martin Bailey (eds) (2003). *Who Are the Christians of the Middle East?* Grand Rapids, MI: Eerdmans.

Betts, Robert Brenton (2009). *The Southern Portals of Byzantium: A Concise Political, Historical and Demographic Survey of the Greek Orthodox Patriarchates of Antioch and Jerusalem.* London: Musical Times.

Craig, Kenneth (1991). *The Arab Christian: A History in the Middle East.* Louisville, KY: Westminster/John Knox Press.

Dalrymple, William (1997). *From the Holy Mountain: A Journey Among the Christians of the Middle East.* New York: Henry Holt and Company.

Hasan, S. S. (2003). *Christians versus Muslims in Modern Egypt: The Century-Long Struggle for Coptic Equality.* New York: Oxford University Press.

Meinardus, Otto F. A. (1999). *Two Thousand Years of Coptic Christianity.* New York: The American University in Cairo Press.

Merkley, Paul Charles (2001). *Christian Attitudes Towards the State of Israel.* Montreal: McGill-Queen's University Press.

Patrick, Theodore Hall (1996). *A History of the Coptic Orthodox Church.* Greensboro, NC: Fisher Park Press.

Raheb, Mitri (1995). *I Am a Palestinian Christian.* Minneapolis: Fortress.

Sennott, Charles M. (2001). *The Body and the Blood: The Middle East's Vanishing Christians and the Possibility for Peace.* New York: Public Affairs.

Wagner, Donald (2001). *Dying in the Land of Promise: Palestinian Christianity from Pentecost to 2000.* London: Melisende.

Chapter 6

Eastern Europe

Nationalism and New Mission

Since 1990, the main story of Christianity in the 21 nations that make up Eastern Europe (Figure 6.1) has been one of revival. After decades of Communist domination that was decidedly biased against religion, the post-Communist era has been a time of religious recovery and advancement. Churches have been rebuilt, membership has increased, attendance at worship is up, and Christians are feeling more optimistic about the future than they have for generations. For years the most important concern of the churches was survival. Now they see themselves as having a new mission in the world: modeling what a modern, but still Christian, Europe could look like.

The Christian world as it is envisioned in Eastern Europe is one in which ethnicity and nationality remain significant. More than anywhere else in Europe, the sense of being a distinctive people living in a particular place plays a central role in Christian self-consciousness in this region of the world. This means that being a Christian in Eastern Europe often includes a strong sense of patriotism. While concerns about these two matters – faith and nation – can often blend comfortably and constructively together, there have been times when the mixture of Christianity with ethnic or national politics has become toxic, rekindling ancient antagonisms and encouraging violence. This toxicity was evident in the lands of the former Yugoslavia, where acts of genocide and "ethnic cleansing" took place in the 1990s.

In global Christian perspective, Eastern Europe is the center of Orthodox Christianity. Of the approximately 240 million Orthodox Christians in the world, 175 million (73 percent) live in Eastern Europe. Half of these Orthodox Christians are Russian, but millions more live in Belarus, Bulgaria, Greece, Romania, Serbia, and elsewhere. Orthodox Christianity is embodied in many distinct churches in Eastern Europe, including eight autocephalous

The World's Christians: Who they are, Where they are, and How they got there, First Edition. Douglas Jacobsen.
© 2011 Douglas Jacobsen. Published 2011 by Blackwell Publishing Ltd.

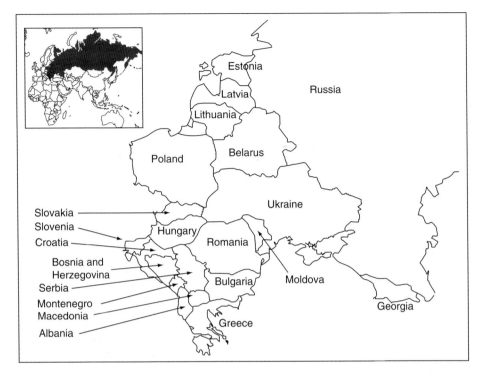

Figure 6.1   Map of Eastern Europe. Map by author.

Note: 21 countries: Total population 335,000,000 (5% of global population); Christian population 255,000,000 (76% of regional population, 12% of global Christian population): Orthodox 175,000,000, Catholics 64,000,000, Protestants 9,000,000, Pentecostal/Charismatic 7,000,000.

(totally independent) churches and at least 10 other churches that claim some degree of autonomy even though they are not fully autocephalous (see Table 6.1).

The Orthodox are not, of course, the only Christians who live in Eastern Europe. Roman Catholics (64 million of them) can also be found in this region, as can Protestants (9 million) and Pentecostal/Charismatic Christians (7 million). Relations among these different kinds of Christians have sometimes been strained, and antagonism between the Orthodox and Roman Catholic Churches, in particular, has often been bitter. Orthodox Christians in Eastern Europe tend to view the Pope as an aggressive "sheep-stealer," trying to woo Orthodox Christians into the Catholic fold by whatever means necessary. In the past – during the age of the Crusades and at intermittent times since then – this has included violence. Many Orthodox would say that today the main Catholic strategy is seduction, the use of idealistic rhetoric about cooperation and Christian unity to slowly pull people away from their Orthodox convictions and historical commitments. Apart from these tensions, what is shared by all of the Christians in the region (except for those in Greece) is the experience of living under Communist rule and now living in a post-Communist era. That shared experience obviously did not unite the churches, but it has provided them with a common challenge: reconstructing their identities and redefining their missions in a new era of freedom.

Table 6.1   The main Orthodox churches of Eastern Europe

Church	Status	Members in Eastern Europe (1995)
Albanian Orthodox	autocephalous since 1937	500,000
Church of Belarus	not autocephalous	5,250,000
Bulgarian Orthodox	autocephalous since 1961	6,500,000
Estonian Orthodox	not autocephalous	200,000
Church of Georgia	autocephalous since 5th century/1991*	3,000,000
Greek Orthodox	autocephalous since 1850	10,000,000
Hungarian Orthodox	not autocephalous	50,000
Latvian Orthodox	not autocephalous	500,000
Macedonian Orthodox	not autocephalous	1,200,000
Moldovan Orthodox	not autocephalous	3,000,000
Orthodox Church of Montenegro	not autocephalous	300,000
Polish Orthodox	autocephalous since 1948	1,000,000
Romanian Orthodox	autocephalous since 1865	19,000,000
Russian Orthodox	autocephalous since 1589	90,000,000
Serbian Orthodox	autocephalous since 1346/1920*	5,500,000
Ukrainian Orthodox	not autocephalous	29,000,000**
Total		175,000,000

* These churches had autocephalous status in the past, lost that status, and have recently regained it.

** There are currently three groups in Ukraine trying to become "the" Ukrainian Orthodox Church. This number includes all three.

Defining Eastern Europe

The division between Eastern Europe and Western Europe extends back in history to a time before the idea of Europe as a distinct geographic region had even been invented. The setting was the Roman Empire, and the division was linguistic. People in the Western half of the Empire spoke Latin and those in the East spoke Greek. In the late third century, this linguistic division was codified into a bureaucratic structure of government, and the idea of a Roman Mediterranean East and West emerged. After the fall of the Roman Empire (i.e., the barbarian conquest of the West in the late fifth century), this East–West division slowly evolved into the religious and cultural divide that still separates the Latin-based Christianity of Catholic Western Europe from the Greek-based Christianity of Orthodox Eastern Europe. The borderline between these two distinct cultural spheres has never been entirely clear, and it has fluctuated to some degree; however, the overall distinction remains palpable and real even today.

In terms of more recent history, one of the experiences that unites much of Eastern Europe (in contrast to the West) is a history of Islamic rule. Russia was subjugated by the Islamic Mongol Empire in the mid-thirteenth century, and the rulers of Russia continued to pay tribute to the Mongol's successor state, the Golden Horde, until the late fifteenth

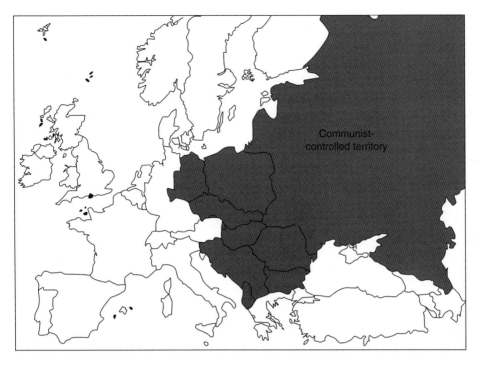

Figure 6.2   Map of post-World War II Communist Europe. Map by author.

century. In the fifteenth and sixteenth centuries, all of the Balkans, along with a wide swath of land north of the Danube River, were conquered (or made subject states) by the Ottoman Empire. At its greatest extent, the Ottoman Empire exercised control over almost all of what is now Greece, Albania, Macedonia, Bulgaria, Serbia, Montenegro, Bosnia-Herzegovina, Croatia, Hungary, Moldova, and parts of the Ukraine. The northern fringes of this territory (including Hungary, northern Romania, Moldova, and the Ukraine) were under Muslim rule for about 150 years, with most of the rest ruled by the Ottomans until the end of the nineteenth century.

Eastern Europe, in contrast to the West, also shared the experience of Communist rule. The Communist period lasted in Russia from 1917 to 1990, and in the rest of the region from 1947 to 1990. The one exception was Greece, which was never governed by Communists. The divide between Eastern and Western Europe was especially sharp during these years, with the continent being cut in half by the so-called "Iron Curtain" that divided Communist territory from the capitalist West. Life behind the Iron Curtain was harsh, and emigration was practically impossible.

Since the end of the Communist era, Eastern Europe has undergone considerable change, including the creation of nine new countries that did not exist in 1990. Bosnia-Herzegovina, Croatia, Serbia, Montenegro, and parts of Macedonia were formerly merged together in the Communist country of Yugoslavia, and a sixth region is still seeking independence: the Kosovo province of Serbia. Similarly, the Czech Republic and Slovakia were created from the former Czechoslovakia, while the nations of Belarus, Estonia, Georgia, Latvia, Lithuania, and Ukraine were created when the old Union of Soviet Socialist Republics (USSR) dissolved in 1991. Many of these new nations are defined by the ethnicity of their majority populations, but some of these ethnic groups have never before had a country to call their own. As a result there is a unique old–new character to these nations as they struggle to reclaim their old identities and to define new ones in a post-Communist Eastern Europe.

The Crucible of Communism

It would be difficult to overstate the effect of Communism upon twentieth-century Eastern European Christianity. Communism has been called a Christian heresy because, like Christianity, it posits a heaven-like future where everyone will live in peace and society will be perfect. But in contrast to traditional Christian teaching that says that God will be the power behind this utopia, Communism says that people must create this utopia for themselves. In the Communist view, God does not exist, and belief in God is evil because it undermines humanity's willingness to take control of its own future. Religions that protect the status quo must accordingly be actively rejected in order to overturn the unjust economic structures of society and to usher in the new world of Communist egalitarianism. Given their differences, Christianity and Communism were bound to clash, and that clash came first in Russia.

Communists took charge of Russia in the Bolshevik Revolution of 1917, and they quickly undertook the destruction of religion, which in Russia meant the Orthodox Church. Efforts to squash the church involved the dissemination of antireligious propaganda, the confiscation of church property, and the mistreatment of church leaders who were incarcerated, deported, intimidated via show trials, and often executed. As many as 600 bishops, 40,000 priests, and 120,000 monks and nuns were killed or died in prison during the first decade of Communist rule.[1] By the late 1930s, it seemed as if the job was almost done. Religion was near an end. At the turn of the century there had been more than 40,000 church buildings in the Russian Empire; by 1940 a mere handful were still operating as places of worship. But plans for the complete eradication of the Russian Orthodox Church were interrupted by World War II, when Soviet President Joseph Stalin decided that the religious nationalism fostered so effectively by the Orthodox Church could be harnessed temporarily for use in the war against Germany.

After the war, the influence of Communism expanded to almost all of Eastern Europe, and the battle against religion was renewed. In the Soviet Union, the antireligious rhetoric of the prewar years was revived, and antireligious policies were put in place throughout the newly organized Communist bloc nations of Eastern Europe. In 1967, Albania declared itself fully atheistic and banned religion entirely. Priests, pastors, and imams were arrested, and church buildings and mosques were confiscated or destroyed. In an attempt to eradicate every trace of religion, Albania even required everyone with a Christian name to discard it and adopt a new secular name in its place. The policies in Albania were extreme, but antireligious sentiment was part of public life in every Communist country.

Starting in the mid-1960s, however, the Communist governments of Russia and Eastern Europe began slowly to moderate their religious policies in ways that made life somewhat less burdensome for Christians. This does not mean that life became easy. Many restrictions on religion continued, Christians were sometimes still arrested and imprisoned, and churches were still sometimes seized and destroyed. But overall there was a lessening of pressure and a slight shift toward more religious freedom.

The reasons for this shift in policy are complex, but two factors were especially significant. First, the persecution of the churches could let up because it had largely accomplished its goal. Almost all the churches had been maneuvered into submission, and they no longer represented a serious threat to any Communist government. Second, a new generation of Communist leaders concluded that the persecution of religion was giving the Communist movement an unnecessarily bad public image. Religion, they believed, would eventually disappear on its own just as Karl Marx had predicted. If that was the case, why rush the process at the cost of making Communists appear to be trampling on basic human rights? A better strategy would be to give the churches a little freedom and then let the churches convince the world of Communism's goodness. So some churches were allowed to reopen, and some church leaders were given freedom to travel and speak, and those same leaders were encouraged to join the World Council of Churches and various international peace organizations where they could extol the virtues of Communism. For many Christian leaders this was like a bargain with the devil, but the possibility of gaining greater freedom for their churches convinced some of them that cooperation was the best if not the only option.

And then, unexpectedly, things really did begin to change for the better. In country after country, the Communist cause lost traction and religious faith began to revive. If an atheistic movement can lose its soul, then that is what seems to have happened with Eastern European Communism. The dreary reality of life under Communist rule simply did not live up to the utopian rhetoric of the leaders, and people turned away. In some cases, the churches helped push the Communists out of power through prayer protests. In other cases, the dynamics were more purely political. But what was the same everywhere was a resurgence of faith, and as Communism vacated the premises religion began to recover from years of oppression.

It would be an overstatement to say that Christianity is flourishing across Eastern Europe. The landscape is uneven, and church participation remains relatively low compared to many other regions of the world. Only 10 to 15 percent of the population attends church services weekly. But compared to levels of religious practice and belief during the years of Communist rule, the trend lines are heading upward, and most scholars predict that Eastern Europe's post-Communist religious revival will continue to strengthen in the years ahead.

Three Religious Subregions

To make sense of the Christian experience in Eastern Europe, it is helpful to divide the region into three different subregions, each with its own religious profile. The three subregions are: (1) the Balkans, (2) the predominantly Catholic nations of Central Europe, and (3) the Russian Orthodox sphere of influence (see Figure 6.3).

The Balkan subregion includes the countries of Albania, Bosnia, Bulgaria, Greece, Macedonia, Montenegro, Romania, and Serbia. Taken together, these nations account for roughly 18 percent of Eastern Europe's population, and about 85 percent of them are

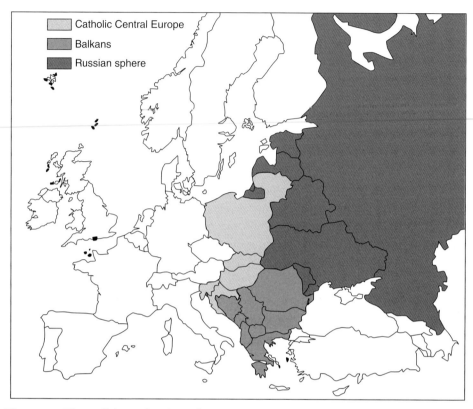

Figure 6.3   Three religious subregions of Eastern Europe. Map by author.

Orthodox. While Orthodoxy has a strong ethnic dimension almost everywhere it exists in the world, in this region there is a heightened sense of the connection between ethnicity and faith. This connection enabled the Orthodox Churches of the Balkans to maintain their identity during centuries of rule by Muslim Ottomans and later by Communist dictators, but it has also contributed to recent ethnic tensions, including violent outbreaks that have disrupted life in the former Yugoslavia.

The nations of Catholic Central Europe include Lithuania, Poland, the Slovak Republic, Hungary, Slovenia, and Croatia. A little less than 20 percent of Eastern Europe's population lives in this subregion, but it contains more than 90 percent of Eastern Europe's Roman Catholics. Poland is the largest and the most intensely Catholic of these nations. Taken together, these nations form the front line in the encounter between Western Catholicism and Eastern Orthodoxy, and the Roman Catholicism of this subregion often seems braced for religious opposition.

The Russian bloc of nations consists of Belarus, Estonia, Georgia, Latvia, Moldova, Ukraine, and the Russian Federation. Nearly three-quarters of all the Orthodox Christians of Eastern Europe live in these seven nations. The churches in this subregion have a distinctive identity as well, following a Russian style of Orthodox worship in contrast to the "Greek" style that predominates in the Balkans. Russian Orthodox Christians are proud of their history and tend to see themselves as the most loyal among all defenders of Orthodoxy. Even during the years of Communist rule, they perceived themselves as having a superior spiritual status within the Orthodox world.

Ethnicity and Faith in the Balkans

Orthodoxy in the Balkans is closely bound up with ethnicity and national identity. This linkage of religion and nationality is a common component of the Orthodox tradition that became more pronounced in the Balkans during the years of Ottoman rule. Under Ottoman rule, the Orthodox Christians of the Empire were all grouped into one subcommunity (*millet*) that was headed up by the Patriarch of Constantinople. As leader of the Christian *millet*, the Patriarch used his spiritual and political powers to help the Christians of the region maintain their own distinctive non-Muslim identity. One strategy was to insist on use of the Greek language in all church activities. This included not only the liturgy, but also confession, which sometimes had to be done through an interpreter. While this may have seemed wise in the eyes of the Patriarch, and while it may have drawn a sharp line between the Christian and Muslim populations, it also caused many non-Greek Christians to resent the Patriarch and desire their own national religious liberation from his control. As the power of the Ottoman Empire began to wane in the nineteenth century, the nations of the Balkans began to clamor for both political *and* religious independence. The first to achieve this goal was Greece, which asserted its political independence from the Ottoman Empire in 1832 and its religious independence from the Patriarchate of Constantinople in 1833. The other nations of the region followed suit, with Bosnia, Serbia, and Romania claiming independence in the late 1800s, and then Albania and Bulgaria in the early 1900s.

The Orthodox teaching of *symphonia* describes the ideal relationship that should exist between the church and state: they are to work together for the spiritual and material benefit of all the people. God has ordained one church for each people and God also ordains the governments of those people. In the Orthodox perspective, these two God-appointed entities – the church and the state – have a responsibility to respect each other and work with each other, even when the church dislikes the policies of the state and even when the state dislikes the priorities of the church. But while the Orthodox tradition recognizes a legitimate place for national churches and for religious nationalism, it also acknowledges that church–state relations can sometimes become too close. Excessive entwinement can lead to the sin of *phyletism*, subjecting faith entirely to the passions of national ethnic identity.

In the post-Communist decades, many of the Orthodox churches of the Balkans have been living in a fuzzy moral borderland between *symphonia* and *phyletism*. This is especially the case in the former Yugoslavia (the present-day nations of Bosnia-Herzegovina, Croatia, Macedonia, Montenegro, and Serbia) where ethnoreligious warfare killed thousands of people and destroyed hundreds of religious buildings and other national/ethnic landmarks during the 1990s. During the long rule of Josip Broz Tito (1953–80), Communist ideology and an insistence on cooperation across ethnic and national lines had held the different people of Yugoslavia together, but the country began to slide into chaos almost as soon as he was gone.

Table 6.2   Estimated size of Christian traditions in the Balkans today (as % of total population)

Country	Population	Orthodox	Catholic	Protestant	Pentecostal/ Charismatic
Albania	3,000,000	18	16	1	3
Bosnia-Herzegovina	4,000,000	16	16	1	1
Bulgaria	7,750,000	84	1	1	–
Greece	11,000,000	91	–	–	–
Macedonia	2,000,000	62	–	–	–
Montenegro	500,000	74	4	–	–
Romania	21,750,000	80	9	3	2
Serbia	10,000,000	79	5	1	–
Regional total	60,000,000	74	7	2	1

The Balkan history of the 1990s is complex and many facts are contested, but it seems clear that the revival of religion in the region has at times contributed to the escalation of violence. This is especially true in Serbia. In 1980, only about a quarter of the Serb population still identified as Orthodox, but since then the numbers have shot up. This growth has been partly a result of the end of Communist rule, but it is also part of the revival of Serbian national identity and territorial claims. Rediscovering ancient religious sites was part of the creation of a new Serbian state, and building or rebuilding churches was one way of marking territory. Perhaps the most impressive activity in this regard was the construction of the massive church of St Sava in Belgrade (Plate 4). Completed in 1989, this *hram* (an Orthodox memorial church) is believed to mark the spot where the remains of St Sava, the founder of the Serbian Orthodox Church, were burned in 1595 (long after Sava's death in 1235) by the Albanian-born Ottoman Emperor Sinan Pasha.

Commemoration of this event suited the new history Serbians were developing for themselves, a history that emphasized their persecution by Muslim and Catholic neighbors and that could be used to justify their efforts to cleanse the land of non-Serbians. (There is no question that Catholic and Muslim persecution is part of this history, but that history can be remembered and dealt with in many different ways.) While the church itself cannot be blamed for all the atrocities that took place during the fighting of the 1990s, the leaders of the Serbian Orthodox Church did little to stop the "ethnic cleansing" that took place, and in fact they sometimes encouraged the violence. An infamous example was a speech given by Pantelić Lukijan, Bishop of Buda, in April of 1991 that advised Serbian Orthodox Christians to "disregard the Gospel of Christ and turn to the Old Testament, which reads: An eye for an eye, a tooth for a tooth!"[2] Once justice had been achieved, he said, then Serbs could return to the rule of the gospel which encouraged forgiveness and mercy. That kind of rhetoric paved the way for the bloodbath that followed. The Serbian Orthodox Patriarch Pavle (1990–2009) also originally gave his support to the war effort, though he later changed his views and spoke out against the violence. While opinions are mixed, many Serbian Orthodox Christians still feel no shame about what took place. To their way of thinking, the life of the nation – and by extension the life of the Orthodox faith – was at risk, so the leaders who orchestrated Serbian attacks on Bosnian Muslims and Croatian Catholics were simply doing what had to be done.

While the Serbian case is unique, close connections between faith and nationalism – relationships that can lead to oppression of non-Orthodox believers – are evident throughout the Balkans. For example, in Romania there is a strained relationship between the Romanian Orthodox Church and the Greek Catholic Church (a Catholic "uniate" church formed in 1687 from the formerly Orthodox churches in the Transylvanian region of northern Romania). When the Communists took control of Romania in the mid-1940s, they banned the Greek Catholic Church because the government was offended by the anti-Communist stance of the Pope, and they reallocated its 1.5 million members along with its church buildings and other properties to the Romanian Orthodox Church. When Communist rule ended in 1989, the new government voted almost immediately to relegalize the Greek Catholic Church and ordered its property to be restored. But the Romanian Orthodox Church dragged its feet until 1999, when Pope John Paul II visited the country and met with the Orthodox Patriarch Teoctist (1986–2007). Since then, things have moved forward more smoothly, but many Orthodox Romanians still disdain the Greek Catholic Church for its submission to Rome and for originally "stealing" members from the Orthodox Church. And many Greek Catholics continue to have less than warm feelings toward the Romanian Orthodox Church for cooperating with the Communist government so willingly in seizing their church's assets and holding on to them as long as they could.

The history of Greece is very different from that of Romania, but a similar tension with Catholic Christianity is evident. In 1975 Greece adopted a new constitution that declared "every known religion is free and the forms of worship thereof shall be practiced without any hindrance by the state." Yet the government, with the active support of the Orthodox Church, continued to prohibit Catholic worship, using the argument that the only "known religions" in Greece are Orthodox Christianity, Judaism, and Islam. It took new legislation in 1999 to expand the category of "known religions" to include the Catholic Church. In the following year (2000), the government took another significant step toward genuine religious freedom when it decreed that government-issued identity cards would no longer include religious affiliation. The Greek Orthodox Church immediately protested, collecting more than three million signatures in an attempt to reverse the ruling. The Church argued that Orthodoxy is inseparable from Greek identity, so citizens should not be prevented from naming their religion on their identity cards. In a country that is more than 90 percent Orthodox, any requirement that citizens be publicly identified by religion can be construed as a threat to non-Orthodox believers. From the Orthodox perspective, however, it seems appropriate for non-Orthodox individuals to feel out of place in Greece. In their eyes, Greece is and ought to be Orthodox turf.

In recent years, many of the churches in the Balkans have taken a step back from the extreme nationalism that flared up immediately after the end of Communist rule. Some church leaders have even gone so far as to warn that the overnationalization of the churches represents a threat to faith itself, because it divides Christians from Christians and it subjugates the gospel to political control. The outcome of this debate is hugely important in terms of Christianity globally. While the churches of the West often seem to assume that simple church–state separation is the obvious solution, that answer does not fit realities on the ground in many regions of the world where the conjoining of faith, ethnicity, and nationalism is all but inevitable. Thus Christianity worldwide will be influenced by the models that Christians in the Balkans develop to address this issue.

Catholic Central Europe

The nations of Central Europe (Croatia, Hungary, Lithuania, Poland, the Slovak Republic, and Slovenia) also face tensions related to nationalism and faith, but here the dominant religion is Catholicism, not Orthodoxy, and that creates a different dynamic because of the international character of Roman Catholicism. Each of the six nations of Catholic Central Europe has its own distinct religious profile (see Table 6.3), but they are bound together by their joint history on the front lines of Catholic engagement with Orthodoxy. In the year 1054, mutual condemnations were issued by the Pope as head of the Catholic Church and the Patriarch of Constantinople as head of the Orthodox world, declaring each other's church to be heretical. In the aftermath of this Great Schism (as it later came to be called), these two old and venerated churches spent centuries viewing each other as spiritual enemies. These mutual condemnations were lifted by Pope Paul VI and Patriarch Athenagoras I in 1965, but tensions remain. The Orthodox continue to be vigilant against any perceived Catholic encroachment on Orthodox lands, and the Catholic Church continues to see itself as having a right to encourage conversions anywhere and everywhere in Eastern Europe.

The history and attitudes of the region are captured, perhaps in slightly exaggerated form, in the experience of Lithuania. Lithuania was founded in the thirteenth century by Catholic warrior monks, the Livonian Brothers of the Sword and the Teutonic knights, who waged a crusade against Orthodoxy and European paganism in the Baltic region at the same time as their peers were fighting a holy war against Islam (and to some degree against the Orthodox Church) in the eastern Mediterranean. Catholicism was imposed on the region by force, but so successfully that Catholicism became intertwined with Lithuanian identity. A hill of crosses, located near the town of Siauliai in northern Lithuania, serves as a physical reminder that this is Catholic Christian turf. During the period of Communist rule, the Soviets tried to destroy the site several times, removing the crosses and even plowing down the hill, but each time the hill of crosses was restored (see Plate 5).

This kind of crusader legacy does not, however, define the whole of Catholic Central Europe. In Hungary, for example, more than a quarter of the population has been Protestant since the sixteenth century, and over the years a spirit of accommodation has developed. This spirit of accommodation was challenged during the Communist years. At first, Catholics were singled out for harsher treatment than Protestants because Pope Pius XII had explicitly condemned Communism and because the Catholic primate (the highest Catholic official in the country) Cardinal Jozsef Mindszenty put up more of a fight than his Protestant peers. But after an initial period of rough persecution, the Hungarian government switched gears and adopted a policy of control based on rewards rather than punishments. The Communist government began subsidizing the salaries of pastors and priests, and in return the Catholic and Protestant Churches developed a new theology of "humility" that stressed the spiritual dimensions of faith and not criticizing the state.

Table 6.3   Christian populations in Catholic Central Europe (as % of total population)

Country	Population	Orthodox	Catholic	Protestant	Pentecostal/ Charismatic
Croatia	4,500,000	5	83	1	3
Hungary	10,000,000	–	62	21	5
Lithuania	3,250,000	5	85	1	1
Poland	37,750,000	2	90	–	2
Slovak Republic	5,500,000	1	70	7	5
Slovenia	2,000,000	2	82	1	1
Regional total	63,000,000	2	82	4	3

Since the fall of Communism in 1989, the relationship between the churches and the state has remained close, and relations between Catholics and Protestants have been cordial. Both Catholics and Protestants have benefited from new church–state agreements. While the Hungarian constitution guarantees religious freedom, this does not mean that all religious groups are treated equally. In fact, a two-tiered system of religious preference exists within the country. "Respected" religious groups – those that have been in the country for a long time like Catholics, Reformed Protestants, and Lutherans – are financially subsidized, while funding is being withheld from newer religious groups (such as Pentecostals) until they can prove their staying power and social usefulness to the state. In 2001, the Hungarian government funded roughly two-thirds of the annual budgets for the Catholic, Lutheran, and Reformed Protestant churches.

Poland

Poland has been Catholic since the tenth century and its relationship to Rome has always been close. Miesko I, the first Polish monarch to convert to Catholicism (in 966), asked the pope to put his country under the direct protection of the church in order to fend off the Germans who were trying to annex the territory. Almost 700 years later, another Polish king (Jan Kazimierz) facing a different enemy (Sweden) once again turned to the Catholic faith for protection and support. This time, however, the appeal was made directly to heaven through the icon of the Black Madonna (Plate 6) that was housed in the fortified monastery of Jasna Gora in the town of Czestochowa. The Swedes were subsequently defeated and, in 1656, King Kazimierz dedicated the whole nation to the Queen of Heaven.

Despite Kazimierz's action, Poland did not fare well in the centuries that followed. In fact, Poland did not even exist during most of the nineteenth century, when its various regions were parceled out to the Russian, German, and Austrian Empires. A strong sense of Polish nationalism persisted, however, and after World War I the country was reconstituted. As before, Catholicism was central to Polish identity. In 1926, a concordat with the Vatican gave the church control of the educational system and a significant role in defining the moral norms of society. The state also agreed to provide some financial support for the clergy, though this was modest (about 15 percent of a typical priest's salary) and the church had to make up the difference through donations from parishioners.

Most ordinary Poles thought of Catholic faith and Polish identity as one and the same, and the strength of that connection sometimes bubbled over into dislike for anything and anyone who was different – especially Poland's Jewish community, which prior to World War II accounted for about 10 percent of the nation's total population and 25 percent of the urban population. Polish national extremists often used anti-Semitic rhetoric as a means of ratcheting up Polish patriotic fervor. The Catholic Polish Primate Archbishop August Hlond warned in a pastoral letter of 1936 that hatred of others was a serious sin, but his comments did not stem the rising tide of Polish anti-Semitism that, during World War II, allowed the Nazis to kill Jews with so little interference. Nine out of every ten Polish Jews were eventually executed in the Nazi death camps of Auschwitz-Birkenau, Belzec, Chelmo, Majdanek, Sobibor, and Treblinka.

Following World War II, Poland was assigned to the USSR's sphere of influence. As was the case elsewhere in Eastern Europe, the Communist government in Poland sought to control and minimize religion's influence, but the degree to which this could be accomplished in Poland was limited. The bonds between Catholicism and Polish culture were simply too strong to break. A few priests agreed to cooperate with the state but most did not, and the church in general adopted a quiet but determined program of resistance to Communist ideology and atheistic values. One telling event took place in Nowa Huta, a new industrial city being built as a model of God-free socialism. The Catholic workers who were constructing the city wanted a church, and they took it upon themselves to build one for themselves using their own funds. They were assisted in their efforts by then Archbishop Karol Wojtyla of Krakov, who later become Pope John Paul II, and today the Lord's Ark Church of Nowa Huta stands as a monument to Polish Catholic persistence and pride in the face of Communist opposition (see Figure 6.4).

In 1989, when the Solidarity Movement, with the strong cooperation of the Catholic Church, finally brought Communist rule to an end in Poland, public support for the Catholic Church was at an all-time high. One poll conducted in late 1989 found that 90 percent of the Polish people had a favorable view of the Catholic Church. Almost immediately, however, that favorable impression began to fade. By 1998, 60 percent had come to believe that the Catholic Church had too much power in Polish society, and 25 percent said they had "no confidence" in the church at all. The Catholic Church that had served as a source of strength and support for all Poles during the Communist regime was perceived to have become interested only in its own narrowly defined moral agenda. At the top of that agenda is the criminalization of abortion. The church wants abortion to be declared illegal with no exceptions allowed, even in cases where rape was involved or where the life of the mother is at risk. By and large, Poles – even those who are Catholic – do not agree. A 2004 opinion poll found that 60 percent of Polish Catholics are prochoice despite the Catholic Church's strongly prolife stance.

Given this division of opinion, the Catholic Church in Poland is trying to discern where its emphases should lie. Pope John Paul II always hoped Poland would be a model of modern Christianity for the rest of Europe. Standing firm in its Catholic faith despite persecution and economic hardship, Poland had the potential to provide a religious alternative to what the Pope saw as the shallow secularism of the West. His one great fear was that Polish

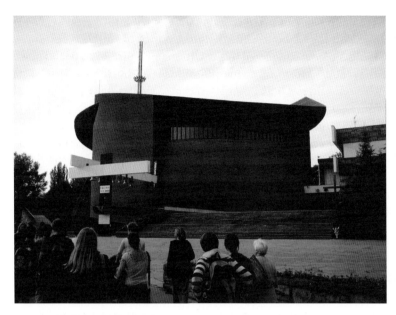

Figure 6.4   The Lord's Ark Catholic Church (Nowa Huta, Poland)
Source: http://commons.wikimedia.org/wiki/Image:Nowa-huta2.jpg

Catholics would be seduced away from the fervor of their faith by money and materialism. The Pope warned: "Don't let yourselves be caught up by the civilization of desire and consumption."[3] To some degree, Poles have ignored that warning. In the last two decades they have worked intensely to improve the economic standing of their country and their own wealth. In 1990, Poland ranked 100th among the nations of the world in GDP (gross domestic product, a common measure of national wealth). By 2000, it had climbed to about 75th place and today it is among the top 50 wealthiest nations in the world. But while seeking prosperity, the Polish people have also remained devout. In fact, by almost any measure, Poland remains one of the most religious countries in all of Europe. It is still possible that Poland may someday fulfill Pope John Paul's dream of re-Christianizing the rest of Europe.

Orthodoxy in the Russian Sphere of Influence

The Russian region of Eastern Europe – the countries of Belarus, Estonia, Georgia, Latvia, Moldova, Ukraine, and the Russian Federation – contains the largest concentration of Orthodox Christians in the world, and it has ancient roots in Christian history. Georgia was one of the first nations in the world to adopt Christianity as its state religion (in the early fourth century), and Christianity has been the dominant religion of Russia since the year 1000. Starting in the mid-1400s, the Russian Orthodox Church began to describe itself as the primary defender of Orthodoxy worldwide. According to the Russian view, Constantinople – historically the most important Patriarchate in the

Orthodox tradition – lost its premier status when it fell into "heresy" via a brief agreement to unite with the Catholic Church at the Council of Florence–Ferrara (1438–39). It was then subsequently conquered by the Ottoman Empire in 1453, and most Russians viewed that event as a form of divine punishment. Centuries earlier Constantinople had dubbed itself "the Second Rome" – the new capital of the newly Christianized Roman Empire – and after Constantinople's fall, Moscow began to call itself the "Third Rome" that would guide and protect Orthodox Christianity until the end of the world. This self-image of Russia as the defender of Orthodoxy in its entirety remains a prominent element in Russian Orthodox identity today, and relations with the Patriarchate of Constantinople continue to be strained because of that view.

Despite the grandiosity of its claims, the Russian Orthodox Church has had a rough history. In the seventeenth century, a huge dispute and eventual schism erupted in the Russian Church over changes in the liturgy introduced by Patriarch Nikon of Moscow (1652–58). Then, at the end of the seventeenth century, Tsar Peter I (also known as Emperor Peter the Great) reorganized the church in an effort to make it more modern and up to date. This reorganization included the elimination of the office of Patriarch and the creation of a new Synod structure for governing the church, which essentially transformed the church into a religious department of the state overseen by a government bureaucrat, called the *Oberprokuror*, who was a layperson. The Russian Orthodox Church was appalled by this new arrangement, which paid no attention to church law or to centuries of tradition, but they had no effective way to resist the Tsar and eventually they had to submit.

Things did not change until the early twentieth century, when pressure from the army and various opposition parties forced the Russian Tsar Nicholas to resign from office in 1917. In the political vacuum that was created, the leaders of the Orthodox Church saw an opportunity to restore the Patriarchate. Gathering together in a national council (*sobor*), they elected Tikhon as the Patriarch of the Russian Orthodox Church. But the same political vacuum that allowed the church to undertake this action also allowed the Communist Bolsheviks to come to power, and the results were disastrous for the church.

For the next seven decades, from 1917 to 1991, the Russian church suffered under the rule of Communism as party leaders actively persecuted believers, closed or destroyed most church buildings, and subverted the moral and spiritual leadership of the few clergy who were left. The intensity of oppression fluctuated, but it never stopped. By the late 1980s, only about a quarter of the Russian people said they still believed in God, and most young people had never been inside a church. But Communism was also becoming less compelling as the century progressed. What had begun as an optimistic political movement designed to change the whole world had devolved into bureaucratic drudgery, and in the late 1980s the Communist government finally stopped working. On Christmas Day 1991, President Mikhail Gorbachev resigned from office, dissolved the Soviet Union, and ended 74 years of Communist rule in Russia.

The dissolution of the Soviet Union prompted the creation of several new nations in Eastern Europe, and this fact has complicated the history of Orthodoxy in the region. Members of the old Russian Orthodox Church now live not only in Russia, but also in Belarus, Estonia, Georgia, Latvia, Moldova, and Ukraine. Each of these nations has its own distinctive religious profile (see Table 6.4), and each is also developing its own new

Table 6.4   Estimated size of Christian traditions in Russian region today (as % of total population)

Country	Population	Orthodox	Catholic	Protestant	Pentecostal/ Charismatic
Belarus	9,750,000	56	13	1	1
Estonia	1,250,000	17	–	17	2
Georgia	5,000,000	60	2	–	–
Latvia	2,250,000	30	17	17	4
Moldova	4,250,000	50	–	2	1
Russian Fed.	143,000,000	63	1	2	2
Ukraine	46,500,000	60	9	3	4
Regional total	212,000,000	61	4	2	2

sense of Orthodoxy's public role in society. The extremes are represented by the Russian Federation and Ukraine. Within the Russian Federation, the Russian Orthodox Church has reasserted its near monopoly status as the spiritual carrier of Russian identity, while Ukraine has adopted a much more pluralistic vision of church and society.

The Russian Federation

The Russian Federation is the largest Orthodox country in the world. Since the fall of Communism, the Russian Orthodox Church has been flourishing. By almost any measure, its situation is dramatically improved from what it was two or three decades ago. In 1989, there were only about 2,500 Orthodox Church buildings open for worship. Thousands had been destroyed by the Communist government, including the famous Christ the Savior Church in Moscow (see Plates 7 and 8). Since 1989, more than 17,000 churches have been newly built, rebuilt, or restored – including Christ the Savior – and more than 800 monasteries have reopened. In 1990, only 27 percent of the Russian population identified itself as Christian. By 1991, that number had risen to 45 percent and by 1998 it was close to 60 percent. Today about two-thirds of the population self-identifies as Christian (including both Orthodox Christians and others). In the 1980s, less than one quarter of the population attended services occasionally, but now that figure has almost doubled and more than 40 percent of the population attends church services at least once a year.

These are meaningful and impressive changes, but the impact of years of Communist rule has still not fully been undone. Orthodox Christianity is a religion of tradition and nurture and this framework of faith was seriously disrupted during the Soviet era. For decades, Russian parents stopped having their babies baptized, and most children received no religious instruction as they were growing up – not from the church, not in school, and not at home. In essence, individuals were raised in a religious void. As a result of this history, the Russian Church now has both new fervor and new needs when compared with the past. It has more fervor because adult converts are often more excited about their religion than

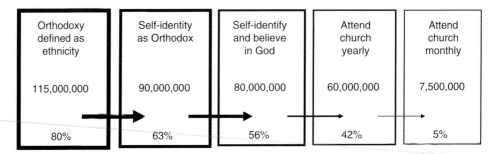

Figure 6.5   Population estimates of Orthodox Christians in the Russian Federation

those who have been slowly nurtured into it from birth. It has more needs because recent converts often have very little understanding of their own faith. The teaching institutions that are needed to rectify this situation are slowly being created, but it will take many years for the Orthodox Church to rebuild its educational infrastructure.

There are many different ways to count membership in the Russian Orthodox Church and different approaches yield very different results. One common way to count Orthodox Christians is to include everyone who is ethnically Russian. In Russia, this makes sense because this is the way Muslims are counted: everyone who is ethnically Turkish and lives in south-central Russia is considered Islamic whether they are practicing Muslims or not. The Patriarchate of Moscow uses this ethnically inclusive method for counting members and as a result it estimates the size of the church at roughly 115 million people (about 80 percent of the total population of the Russian Federation). If, however, the label of Russian Orthodox is restricted only to those who self-consciously identify themselves as Orthodox, the number drops to about 90 million people. (This is the figure adopted in this book.) But other distinctions can also be made. If we were to include only those Russians who claim to be Orthodox *and* who also believe in God, then the total would drop to about 80 million. And if some minimal requirement of church attendance (once every year or two) was added the number would fall to 60 million. Finally, if regular attendance at worship (once a month or more) was taken to be the marker of genuine Orthodox faith, the count would produce only about 7,500,000 people – a mere 5 percent of the total Russian population. (See Figure 6.5.) The membership lists of most churches include people who don't believe in God and who rarely if ever attend worship, but those numbers are somewhat higher in Russia than most other countries.

This mixed picture of Russian Orthodoxy – clearly recovering, but still somewhat thin and fragile – has led the leadership of both the church and the state to conclude that, for the time being, Orthodoxy needs some protection and assistance. This was not the original assessment of the first post-Communist government. Initially, the Duma (Russian Parliament) passed a Freedom of Conscience Act (1990) that declared that all the churches and religious organizations of the country should be treated equally, with the Russian Orthodox Church receiving no special favors. But after heavy lobbying by the Orthodox Church, that law was changed. An amendment passed in 1997 banned all missionary activity by "new" religious groups, with "new" being defined as any organization not registered with the government as of 1982. Since the country was still Communist in 1982 and only a small handful of churches were officially registered at the time, the new law essentially gave the Russian Orthodox Church a near-monopoly on religion in the country.

Taking advantage of that status, and doing all it can to link Orthodoxy with Russian national identity, the church has championed the reintroduction of religious education in the public school system. Classes on the "Basics of Orthodox Culture" are now required in many public schools, even in predominantly Muslim regions of the country. The focus of these courses is on history and culture as opposed to theology, but that still gives the Orthodox Church a huge advantage in its competition with religious rivals. What is taking place in the schools is also taking place in Russian society as a whole. While the organic unity that used to exist between the church and the state is permanently a thing of the past, a strong sense of cooperation between church and state is being reconstructed. Presidents Putin (2000–08) and Medvedev (beginning in 2008) have both expressed strong support for the church, going so far as to describe Russian Orthodoxy as the "fountainhead of our statehood, our great culture, our national soul, and the traditions of our people."[4]

Within the church itself, the picture is somewhat more complex. Russian Orthodoxy has a history of supporting public morality, charity, and peace, but it has also been known to foster elements of anti-Semitism and aggressive nationalism. Some of these tendencies have re-emerged in the post-Communist years, and some groups within the Russian Orthodox Church – most notably the right-wing organization known as the Russian Orthodox Movement – have made very strong statements about the need to reassert Russian greatness and to end "Jewish Fascism" once and forever. Because Russian Orthodoxy is relatively decentralized, it has not been easy to control this radical wing of the church. The late Patriarch of Moscow, Aleksy II, carefully choreographed public events to push these elements to the margins of the church, but Aleksy himself had a strong sense of Russia's mission in the world – a mission that included being a global counterweight to what he saw as the immoral freedom and godless materialism of Western Europe and North America.

Aleksy, who served as Patriarch from June 1990 until his death in September 2008, was a remarkable church leader who had enormous influence in politics and the military as well as in the church, and much of the revival of Orthodoxy in Russia – the building of new churches, the reopening of monasteries, and the good reputation of the Church – can be credited directly to him. He has been succeeded by Kirill I, who was enthroned in the Patriarchal office on February 1, 2009. Kirill will likely continue the same policies as his predecessor. While known internationally for his work with the World Council of Churches, Kirill is a theological conservative who shares Aleksy's distrust of the West and of the Catholic Church, but he also shares Aleksy's fears of the havoc that could be wrought by the radical right in his own Church. He has said that the main goal of his Patriarchy will be to further develop the *symphonia* between church and state that Aleksy did so much to reconstruct, and if he is successful the revival of religion in Russia will likely continue to expand in the years ahead.

Ukraine

With 47 million people, Ukraine is the second largest nation in Eastern Europe. The Ukraine was one of the most religious regions within the old USSR, and it remains significantly more religious than the Russian Federation today. But Ukraine is taking a very different path into the future than Russia. Rather than seeking to rebuild the alliance of church, state, and culture, Ukraine has decided to embrace religious freedom. The result is a flourishing of religious diversity unlike anything taking place in other predominantly Orthodox nations in the region.

For Ukrainians, religious diversity begins within Orthodoxy itself. According to the standard Orthodox view of the world, there should be only one Orthodox Church in each nation, but Ukraine currently has three different Orthodox Churches competing with each other. A majority of the Orthodox congregations (about 6,000) are affiliated with the Russian Orthodox Church through the Moscow Patriarchate (UOC-MP). During the Communist days, the churches in this group were simply part of the Russian Orthodox Church, but since the creation of the new Ukrainian state, the UOC-MP has been given more autonomy. For some Ukrainians, semi-independent status is not sufficient, however, and they want complete separation. This is the position of the Ukrainian Autocephalous Orthodox Church (UAOC), which was founded in the 1920s. Almost wiped out by Stalin in the 1930s, a small remnant of this church survived and reconstituted itself in 1990 after the fall of Communism. The UAOC now controls about 2,000 congregations in the country. Troubled by the divide between the UAOC and the UOC-MP, a third group of Orthodox believers tried to solve the problem in 1992 by creating yet a third Ukrainian Orthodox Church, overseen by a patriarch seated in Kiev (UOC-KP), which was intended to be a merger of the other two groups. However, only some Ukrainians heeded their call for unification, so the 1,000-plus congregations of the UOC-KP are now a third competing Orthodox Church.

While this confusion among the Orthodox is troubling to many Orthodox Ukrainians, it has been a boon to other religious groups. Roughly 60 percent of the population is Orthodox. If all of those people were united in one church, they could easily be tempted to follow the path of quasi-monopoly adopted by the church in Russia. Instead, their division has opened space for other churches to grow and develop.

One of the churches that has most benefitted is the Ukrainian Greek Catholic Church (UGCC), which has about 4.5 million members. The UGCC is a uniate Catholic Church, which means that it acknowledges the supremacy of the Pope and Roman Catholic doctrine in general, but continues to follow an Orthodox style of liturgy in worship. The origins of the UGCC can be found in the Union of Brest-Litovsk that was concluded in 1595. Seeking to bolster the Catholic forces of the Counter-Reformation, the Polish King Sigismund III Vasa, who also controlled the western Ukraine, basically forced his Orthodox subjects to convert to Catholicism. Allowed to keep their own ways of worship, many Ukrainian Orthodox believers went along with Sigismund's policy. In the 1800s, this identity was reinforced when the region was annexed by the Catholic Austro-Hungarian Empire, and once again the Ukrainians were allowed to keep their old traditions intact. During the years of Russian rule in the nineteenth and twentieth centuries the church was severely persecuted, but rather than undermining their faith this persecution etched Greek Catholicism deeper in their hearts. It also made the Greek Catholic Church a center of Ukrainian (versus Russian) patriotic sentiment, a disposition that has also helped it flourish in the newly independent Ukraine. Because Ukrainian Greek Catholics see themselves as members of a *national* Ukrainian church, and not just as a Catholic minority faith in a predominantly

Orthodox land, there is strong movement within the church favoring the relocation of the UGCC headquarters from the western Ukrainian city of Lviv to the capital of Kiev. Such a move is vigorously opposed by the Ukrainian Orthodox Churches, who see the UGCC as a kind of traitor church – a Trojan horse within Ukraine that is serving the Vatican's efforts to Catholicize all of Eastern Europe.

The religious freedom that came with the end of Communist rule benefitted all of the non-Orthodox Christian communities in the Ukraine, but none more than the Protestants. Among the Protestants, the Baptists have the longest history in the country, having first arrived in the mid-1700s. In Ukraine, the category of "Baptist," which encompasses about 2 percent of the population, includes both ordinary Baptists and various Anabaptist groups, such as the Mennonites. There has been a good deal of cross-fertilization between these groups, and Baptists in Ukraine are accordingly somewhat different than Baptists in the rest of the world. In particular, Ukrainian Baptists are distinguished by their commitment to pacifism (the refusal to kill or to fight in any wars) and to living apart from "the world" and all its sinful temptations. While religious freedom has made their lives easier, many old-style Ukrainian Baptists worry about its effect. They believe that suffering tests the loyalty of believers and that lack of suffering can lead to laxness. Communism was thus a mechanism for deepening faith, while the libertine culture of the West that is currently flooding into the country poses new dangers for those seeking to maintain their spiritual purity in a world full of sinful temptations.

But some Baptists have decided that the new post-Communist situation is more an opportunity than a threat, and they are busy refashioning their faith to make it more attractive to their Ukrainian neighbors. This new wing of the Baptist community has developed numerous connections with Christians in the United States, and many American-style innovations are evident. The stodgy clothes of their old-style Baptist peers have been discarded along with many of the gender-related rules that used to define decorum in worship. The new message is that "God is love," a message delivered via a host of innovative educational, musical, and social programs. But the moral and doctrinal core has not changed, and this branch of Ukrainian Protestantism is experiencing significant growth, in part because of its commitment to those standards. Numerous commentators have noted that the post-Communist era led to a collapse in the moral and spiritual standards of society; the cynicism necessary for survival under Communist rule combined with the new materialism of the post-Communist era to produce an anything-goes society. The rules and dogma of the Baptist churches, combined with the welcoming fellowship they provide, form an attractive alternative for many Ukrainians, a way of living morally, but still prospering.

A similar dynamic is energizing the Pentecostal/Charismatic community. The number of Pentecostal/Charismatic Christians in Ukraine is still relatively small – perhaps 5 percent of the total Christian population – but the movement is becoming more visible every day. In the capital city of Kiev one of the main promoters of the movement is Sunday Adelaja, a Nigerian-born Pentecostal preacher who founded a church called the Embassy of the Blessed Kingdom of God for all Nations (often shortened to the Embassy of God). The church drew its initial membership from the margins of society – almost all the original members were ex-drug addicts – but it has grown tremendously, and it is now one of the largest Pentecostal/Charismatic churches, not only in Ukraine but in all of Europe. It meets in a rented sports arena that is the only facility in the city large enough to handle the crowds.

Adelaja's vision for the church is expansive. He says the goal is to take "responsibility to improve the world and reform the Earth through the principles of the Kingdom [of God]."[5] The logo of the church is a globe with light shining out of the Ukraine to all other parts of the world, and the church lives up to that symbol by sending missionaries to a variety of other nations including Germany, the United States, and India. The message that is preached both in the church and by its missionaries is a holistic understanding of Christian faith that mixes healing and prosperity with care for the poor and needy. In bringing these concerns together, Adelaja's Embassy of God Church is reflecting developments in the Pentecostal/Charismatic movement globally. Around the world, many of the Pentecostal/Charismatic churches that are growing the fastest are those that combine piety and public service in ways that most traditional Pentecostal/Charismatic leaders find problematic. For these more traditional leaders, mixing spirituality, prosperity, and social service is a recipe for trouble, and recent developments at the Embassy Church have reinforced those concerns. In early 2009, Adelaja was indicted for fraud related to an investment company (King's Capital) that is associated with his church. These charges have not been proved, but they have cast a shadow over the church and its ministry.

Regardless of how Adelaja himself may fare, the sense of energy and excitement that has been part of the rhetoric at his Embassy Church illustrates a much larger pattern that is observable in the region as a whole. After years of suffering under Communist rule, Christians in Ukraine and throughout all Eastern Europe are becoming re-energized, ready to take a place at the forefront of the global Christian movement. Whatever their particular identity – Russian Orthodox, Polish Catholics, or Ukrainian Charismatics – they all feel called to a special role in Christian history. They see themselves as having a vital message that needs to be shared with the rest of the world, and no one expects them to be shy about promoting their different versions of Christianity in the years ahead.

Notes

1   Nickolas Lupinin, "The Russian Orthodox Church," in Lucian N. Leustean (ed.), *Eastern Christianity and the Cold War, 1945–91* (London: Routledge, 2010), pp. 19–39; see p. 34.

2   Quoted in Vjekoslav Perica, *Balkan Idols: Religion and Nationalism in Yugoslav States* (Oxford: Oxford University Press, 2002), p. 293, n. 164.

3   Quoted in Timothy A. Byrnes, "The Polish Church: Catholic Hierarchy and Polish Politics," in *The Catholic Church and the Nation-State: Comparative Perspectives*, ed. Paul Christopher Manuel, Lawrence C. Reardon, and Clyde Wilcox (Washington, DC: Georgetown University Press, 2006), pp. 103–16, quote p.109.

4   Quoted in "Prime Minister Putin says that the State shall Support the Social and Educational Mission of the MP," *Voices from Russia*, June 28, 2008. http://02varvara.wordpress.com/2008/06/28/prime-minister-putin-says-that-the-state-shall-support-the-social-and-educational-mission-of-the-mp/ (accessed July 23, 2008).

5   Quoted in Catherine Wanner, *Communities of the Converted: Ukrainians and Global Evangelism* (Ithaca, NY: Cornell University Press, 2007), p. 214.

Suggestions for Further Reading

Byrnes, Timothy A. and Peter J. Katzenstein (eds) (2006). *Religion in an Expanding Europe*. Cambridge, UK: Cambridge University Press.

Clark, Victoria (2000). *Why Angels Fall: A Journey Through Orthodox Europe from Byzantium to Kosovo*. New York: St Martin's.

Davis, Nathaniel (1995). *A Long Walk to Church: A Contemporary History of Russian Orthodoxy*. Boulder, CO: Westview Press.

Garrard, John and Carol Garrard (2008). *Russian Orthodoxy Resurgent: Faith and Power in the New Russia*. Princeton, NJ: Princeton University Press.

Hann, Chris and Hermann Goltz (eds) (2010). *Eastern Christians in Anthropological Perspective*. Berkeley: University of California Press.

Johnson, Juliet, Marietta Stepaniants, and Benjamin Forest (eds) (2005). *Religion and Identity in Modern Russia: The Revival of Orthodoxy and Islam*. Aldershot, UK: Ashgate.

Kloczowski, Jerzy (2000). *A History of Polish Christianity*. Cambridge, UK: Cambridge University Press.

Leustean, Lucian N. (2010). *Eastern Christianity and the Cold War, 1945–91*. London: Routledge.

Parry, Ken, David Melling, Dimitri Brady, Sidney H. Griffith, and John F. Healey (eds) (1999). *The Blackwell Dictionary of Eastern Christianity*. Oxford: Blackwell.

Perica, Vjekoslav (2002). *Balkan Idols: Religion and Nationalism in Yugoslav States*. Oxford: Oxford University Press.

Pospielovsky, Dimitry (1998). *The Orthodox Church in the History of Russia*. Crestwood, NJ: St Vladimir's Seminary Press.

Stan, Lavinia and Lucian Turcescu (2007). *Religion and Politics in Post-Communist Romania*. Oxford: Oxford University Press.

Wanner, Catherine (2007). *Communities of the Converted: Ukrainians and Global Evangelism*. Ithaca, NY: Cornell University Press.

Chapter 7

Central and South Asia
Confidence and Complexity

Christianity has always been a minority religion in Central and South Asia, but despite their small numbers, Christians in this part of the world have rarely lacked confidence. Religious self-assurance has been especially evident in India, home to 85 percent of the Christians in the region. Writing in 1937, V. S. Azariah, the Anglican Bishop of Dornakal, India, described Christians as "the conscience of the country … raising their voice against all corruption, selfishness, and oppression and lending their weight to all measures that help the moral and social regeneration of the people. Their presence is indispensable in the legislatures; India cannot do without them."[1] At the time Azariah was writing, Christians accounted for only 2 or 3 percent of the Indian population, a tiny fraction of the whole. A poker player might call his statement a bold bluff with a weak hand. Azariah thought it was simply the truth and had to be said. The thought of keeping silent for fear of repercussion probably never crossed his mind. He was an Indian and a Christian and he had the right to boldly express his opinion.

Azariah-style confidence can be a strength, but it does not guarantee survival. Tracking northward from India to Central Asia, we find a land where Christianity was once a flourishing and confident religion, but where few Christians remain today. This is true of Shi'ite Iran and in the Sunni Muslim states of Afghanistan, Tajikistan, Turkmenistan, and Uzbekistan. These countries were all part of the old "Silk Road," the major medieval corridor of travel between China and the Middle East. Energetic Christians – monks and merchants looking for lost souls and lucrative trade goods – were constantly traversing this land and in their wake Christian settlements sprang up all along the route. Ruins of Christian churches, monasteries, and cemeteries can still be found scattered throughout the region, and historical records indicate that Christians were respected as leaders in trade, civil service, and medicine. But over time the situation changed, and Christians came under harsh persecution. By the year 1500, few Christians were left.

The World's Christians: Who they are, Where they are, and How they got there, First Edition. Douglas Jacobsen.
© 2011 Douglas Jacobsen. Published 2011 by Blackwell Publishing Ltd.

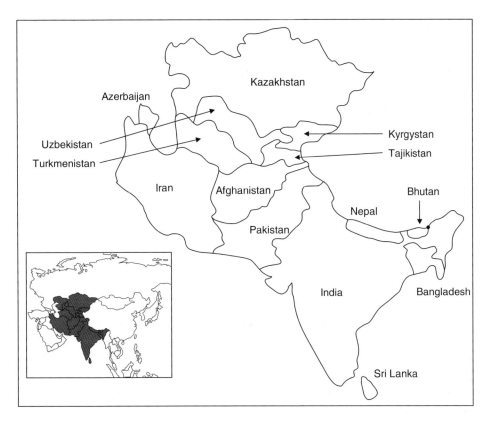

Figure 7.1   Map of Central and South Asia
Note: 14 countries: Total population: 1,625,000,000 (25% of global population); Christian population: 76,000,000 (5% of regional population, 4% of global Christian population): Orthodox 6,000,000, Catholics 20,000,000, Protestants 20,000,000, Pentecostal/Charismatic 30,000,000.

While it is always possible that a similar eradication of Christianity could take place in South Asia, that trajectory seems unlikely. Christian roots go deep in India, and Christianity has been present for almost two thousand years. Even Jawaharlal Nehru, the first Prime Minister of India, described Indian Christianity as being as old as Christianity itself. In fact, many Indians believe that Jesus visited India himself. There is no solid proof that such a visit ever took place, but it is possible, and in some ways the historical veracity of the story is less significant than the mindset it illustrates: Christ and Christianity are seen as Indian. Christians here are fond of saying that Jesus was Asian and that all of his earliest followers were Asian as well, so Indian Christians feel no need to apologize for their religion as if it was some kind of foreign import. They are Indian and they are Christian, and those two identities fit smoothly together.

The Christianity that has flourished in this part of the world has always been complex. Religion along the old Silk Road was a pluralistic affair, as it usually is in areas alive with trade and commerce. Different kinds of Buddhists, Muslims, Hindus, Jews, and members of various shamanistic religions lived and traveled along the Silk Road, and so did a variety of different kinds of Christians. So members of the Church of the East (Nestorian), the Syrian Orthodox Church, the Armenian Apostolic Church, Byzantine Orthodoxy, and later Roman Catholicism had to learn how to get along with both each other and with the various non-Christian religions they encountered on a daily basis. This is where Christian multiculturalism began, and Christians in Central and South Asia have known for centuries that Christians can be confident, creative, and at home in society even when their numbers are small.

The Region as a Whole

As a cultural and geographic area, Central and South Asia is somewhat less integrated, and perhaps less familiar, than the other regions discussed in this book. Few outsiders can, for example, name the six Central Asian republics that gained independence as a result of the collapse of the Soviet Union in 1991 (Azerbaijan, Kazakhstan, Kyrgystan, Tajikistan, Turkmenistan, and Uzbekistan). For many people, this vast terrain is a blank space on the map. It is the land in between the more historically enduring Chinese Empire to the east and the Roman, Persian, and Islamic Empires to the west. Here, in the middle, empires seem to arise and collapse almost overnight with names that are difficult to keep straight: Sasanids and Samanids, Khurusan and Khwarrazmshahs, Khtai and Chaghatai, Mongols and Moghals.

Central Asia, and to some degree South Asia as well, is an ethnic and cultural checkerboard where many different groups and subgroups live side by side. Over the years, these groups have built up complex sets of interrelationships, and personal identities reflect this complexity. Living in the same locality creates one kind of relationship, but bonds of language, tribe, ethnicity, and religion form additional layers of identity that can sometimes come into conflict with each other. In some situations religion or language may take precedence, but in different circumstances tribal or ethnic identity may become the key element. This fluid and flexible structure of identity has allowed huge empires suddenly to blossom into existence and then collapse almost overnight. Coalitions of identity and mutual interest can be formed and unformed very rapidly in this part of the world.

This multilayered sense of identity remains an important fact of life today, though the boundary lines that delineate the contemporary nations of Central and South Asia can sometimes mask the underlying social complexity. Yes, Uzbeks live in Uzbekistan, but so do Russians, Tajiks, Kazakhs, Tartars, and Karapalaks. Kyrgyz make up about half the population of Kyrgystan and the remainder is a mix of Russians, Uzbeks, Ukrainians, Tartars, and Kazakhs. India is even more complex. There are at least 18 language groups in the nation that include five million speakers or more, and the most common of these languages, Hindi, contains at least 50 distinct subdialects. Even in Iran, a place that appears relatively uniform on the surface, the official language of Farsi is spoken by only half the population. Village loyalties, tribal associations, caste and class membership, occupational ties, and religious affiliations overlay linguistic diversity. It is difficult to say anything "in general" about the region, since there are exceptions to every statement and contrary examples to be found almost everywhere. Broadly speaking, however, the region contains two major subdivisions: (1) predominantly Muslim Central Asia and (2) the Indian subcontinent, which is much more religiously and culturally diverse.

Muslims and Christians in Central Asia

Central Asia is predominantly Muslim, but two very different forms of Islam are present in the region. In Iran and Azerbaijan, Shi'a is the dominant tradition; in the other countries of the region, Sunni Islam predominates. The original divide between Shi'ites and Sunnis (somewhat akin to the Protestant–Catholic divide in Western Europe) took place very early in the history of the Islamic movement and the main issue had to do with the leadership. Shi'ites believed that the *caliph* (the global head of the Islamic community) should be a blood relative of the Prophet Muhammad, while Sunnis believed matters of piety and skill should take precedence over family relations. In the years since the original split, other differences have become prominent. Shi'ites have developed a tradition that emphasizes the possibility of martyrdom in the present while hoping for a messiah figure called the *mahdi* to appear in the future, while Sunnis place greater emphasis on law and philosophy. The relationship between these two groups has been antagonistic for centuries, and this has intermittently led to violence.

Since the 1500s, Iran has been the global center of Shi'ite Islam. During the twentieth century, the ruling shahs of Iran tried to modernize the country and its faith by encouraging Western-style education, economic development, and attitudes about gender. These changes produced resentment at the grassroots level where traditional Shi'ite values held sway, and that resentment allowed the exiled religious leader Ayatollah Ruhollah Khomeni to return to the country in 1979 and orchestrate an Islamic revolution that halted the secular drift of the country and restored the rule of Muslim law. Iran was declared an Islamic Republic and it remains so today. More than 95 percent of the population is Muslim, and 90 percent of those Muslims are Shi'ite. In Azerbaijan, the picture is relatively the same: 85 percent of the population is Muslim with roughly three-quarters Shi'ite. Very few Christians live in this Shi'ite-dominated area, except for a small community of Russian Orthodox in Azerbaijan (totaling just over 100,000 members) and a slightly larger group of Armenian Christians in an area that straddles the Azerbaijan–Iranian border.

In contrast to West Central Asia, North Central Asia (the so-called "land of the 'stans'") is primarily populated by Sunni Muslims. With the exception of Afghanistan, none of these countries existed a hundred years ago. The rest – Kazakhstan, Kyrgystan, Tajikistan, Turkmenistan, and Uzbekistan – were all part of the old Russian Empire. The contemporary boundaries of these nations, which do not correspond to any earlier divisions of the land in the area, were originally drawn in the 1920s during the transition from Russian imperial rule to the Communist-run Union of Soviet Socialist Republics (USSR). The Communist goal in creating these new republics was governmental administrative efficiency; the USSR was too big to be entirely ruled from Moscow. When the USSR dissolved in 1991, these pragmatically designed "republics" suddenly became new, independent nations. They have been trying to formulate reasonable national identities for themselves ever since, with mixed results.

Most of the population in this north central region of Asia is Sunni Muslim, and it has been for the last seven to eight centuries. Compared to their fellow Sunnis in the Middle East, those in Central Asia have traditionally been more moderate in their religious beliefs and practices. The Hanafi tradition of Islamic law, which stresses reason and common sense

Table 7.1 Religious profiles of nations in North Central Asia (% of total population)

Country	% Christian	% Muslim	% Nonreligious
Afghanistan	0	95	0
Azerbaijan	3	85	10
Iran	1	96	0
Kazakhstan	15	50	30
Kyrgyzstan	8	64	25
Tajikistan	1	83	15
Turkmenistan	1	88	10
Uzbekistan	1	77	20

more than some other Sunni subtraditions, defines the general religious framework. At the grassroots, Sufism, a spiritual tradition within Islam that places significant emphasis on the personal, interpersonal, and mystical elements of faith, also has significant influence. This region has a history of mutual Muslim–Christian toleration. This spirit of accommodation is rooted both in Muslim moral teaching, which encourages respect for Christians and Jews, and in the experience of living under Russian rule. Within the Russian Empire of the seventeenth to nineteenth centuries, Muslims in Central Asia were typically granted religious tolerance and allowed to practice their faith as long as they were loyal to the tsar. There were exceptions, times when forced conversions took place, but generally Russia was much more tolerant of Islam than were the Christian nations of Western Europe.

Under Communist rule (1917–91), attitudes toward religion changed. Both Christianity and Islam were suppressed. Religious practice declined and the number of persons claiming no religious affiliation increased dramatically. Since the fall of the USSR in 1991, mosques and churches have been rebuilt, but neither the Muslim nor Christian communities have fully bounced back. A sizeable portion of the population – 10 to 30 percent – remains nonreligious (see Table 7.1). Practicing Muslims now constitute half the population in Kazakhstan (the low) up to a high of 88 percent in Turkmenistan. The only countries with substantial numbers of Christians are Kazakhstan, where about 15 percent of the population is Christian (see Plate 9), and Kyrgystan, where 8 percent is Christian. The majority of these Christians are either Russian Orthodox or Ukrainian Orthodox, though some Polish Catholics live here (having immigrated to the region in the early 1800s) as do some German Lutherans (who were deported to the region by the Russians during World War II). In recent years, Western Protestant organizations have begun sending missionaries and other Christian workers to the area, but the numbers are small and their impact thus far has been minimal.

A unique situation exists in Afghanistan, which has always been a place apart. Its rugged terrain has allowed its tribal people to remain relatively independent, even when the land has been nominally under someone else's rule. Historically beleaguered, this is the one Central Asian country where Sunni Islamic fundamentalism has found a foothold. The Taliban, radical Sunnis who were allies of Osama bin Laden and his al-Qaeda organization, seized control of the country in 1996. Fiercely strict in their application of Islamic law, they

Table 7.2   Distribution of major religions in South Asia (as % of total country population)

Country	% Christian	% Muslim	% Hindu	% Buddhist
Bangladesh	1	86	12	1
Bhutan	0	1	18	80
India	6*	12	75	1
Nepal	2	4	72	9
Pakistan	3	96	1	0
Sri Lanka	9	9	11	65

* The official Indian census of 2001 claims that Christians constitute only 2.34% of the country's population, but this is clearly an underreporting.

ruled by intimidation and terror until they were driven out of power by the United States in late 2001. Even with a huge American military presence, post-Taliban Afghanistan remains a fragmented place where the central government exercises only partial rule over the country outside of the capital of Kabul. Religiously, more than 95 percent of the population is Muslim and less than 1 percent is Christian.

South Asia: The Indian Subcontinent

South Asia, the Indian subcontinent, includes the current nations of India, Pakistan, Bangladesh, Nepal, Bhutan, and Sri Lanka. Almost a billion and a half people live here – nearly a quarter of the world's population. It is religiously diverse, and each of the world's four largest religions – Christianity, Islam, Buddhism, and Hinduism – is well represented (see Table 7.2). More than 70 million Christians live in south Asia, about 40 percent are Pentecostal/Charismatic, roughly 30 percent are Protestant, 25 percent are Roman Catholic, and about 5 percent are Orthodox.

During the first half of the twentieth century this entire area was under either direct or indirect British rule. British control ended shortly after the conclusion of World War II, precipitated by the *swaraj* (self-rule) movement led by Mohandas (Mahatma) Gandhi. The transition to full independence went relatively smoothly for the nations of Nepal, Bhutan, and Sri Lanka, since they had always been semi-independent. A more complicated transition confronted the core regions of the British Raj, consisting of the three current nations of India, Pakistan, and Bangladesh.

Gandhi had hoped to establish a unified nation encompassing the entirety of the old Raj, but both the British and many local Muslims feared that in a unified state Muslims would experience prejudice in a land where Hindus formed the overwhelming majority of the population. As a result, the decision was made to partition the Raj into two nations: a predominantly Hindu country of India and a predominantly Muslim country of Pakistan. Pakistan, according to this plan of partition, was an oddly divided nation with a western territory (present-day Pakistan) and an eastern territory (present-day Bangladesh) separated by about a thousand miles. While the logic of this partition made sense on paper, the reality produced great suffering. Suddenly some Muslims found themselves living in areas that had been designated Hindu and some Hindus found themselves in areas designated Muslim. Feeling isolated and in potential danger, many of these "misplaced" people decided to migrate across the border to join their coreligionists. It soon turned ugly. Violence flared, people were killed, families lost track of each other, and long-lasting bitterness is the result. Twenty-five years later in 1972, Pakistan experienced its own partition, when Bangladesh (then called East Pakistan) became an independent nation after a civil war with its western counterpart.

At present, there are close to four million Christians in Pakistan, approximately 3 percent of the population. Most (about 75 percent) are ethnically Punjabi and many are former low-caste Hindus who converted in droves during the early twentieth century. Persecution of Christians is not uncommon in Pakistan, where they experience a double dose of prejudice for being both non-Muslim and poor. Sometimes Christians are described as "dirty," and Christian men, because they are not circumcised, have at times been unfairly accused of spreading HIV/AIDS and other diseases. In addition to the nation's Punjabi Christians, a significant Christian community can also be found in the mountainous tribal area along the Pakistan–Afghanistan border. More than half the Christians in Pakistan are Protestants. The profile of Christianity in Bangladesh is similar to that of Pakistan, but Christians make up an even smaller portion of the population, only about 1 percent.

The island nation of Sri Lanka (formerly Ceylon) presents a rather different cultural and religious profile. The island is divided along ethnic lines with the majority Sinhalese in the south and the minority Tamils in the north. Sinhalese outnumber Tamils about ten to one, but a Tamil resistance army called the Tigers waged an on-and-off war for independence for almost four decades, until finally conceding defeat in May 2009. The Sinhalese are predominantly Buddhist and the Tamil are Hindu, but Christianity has adherents in both groups. At present, 33 percent of the Tamils are Christian and 5 percent of the Sinhalese, which makes these two groups of Christians roughly the same size (700,000 to 800,000 each). Approximately 80 percent of Sri Lankan Christians are Roman Catholic. This commonality of faith has the potential to transcend the island's ethnic divide, and there is some hope that it might also help foster peace in the years ahead.

Christianity has only the smallest of toeholds in the Himalayan nations of Bhutan and Nepal. Bhutan is overwhelmingly Buddhist (about 75 percent) with Hindus accounting for almost all of the remaining population. Christians are nearly nonexistent. Nepal is the mirror image of Bhutan, being mostly Hindu (about 75 percent), with Buddhists as the second largest religious group in the country. Here, too, the Christian community is very small, only about 2 percent of the population.

Christianity and the Indian Nation

When India gained independence in 1947, it faced three enormous challenges. First, the nation had to become politically unified, something that had never been done before. Second, a form of governance had to be devised that would take into account the amazing diversity of the country. Third, a shared understanding of national and cultural Indian

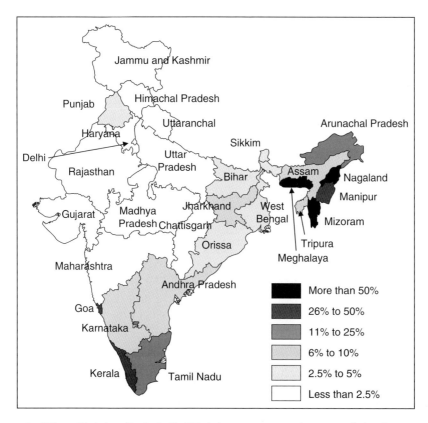

Figure 7.2   Where Christians live in India (Christian percentages of state populations). Map by author.

identity had to be developed. The process of dealing with these challenges has, at times, been ragged and even violent, yet India has managed to survive as the world's largest and most diverse democracy. Each of the three challenges has had implications for Indian religion in general and for Indian Christianity in particular.

The first challenge confronting India was and still is national unification. At the time of independence, Great Britain exercised direct control over only about two-thirds of the country. The rest of the country was divided up into more than 500 princely states that cooperated with British rule while maintaining political autonomy. These states ranged in size from the huge princedom of Hyderabad (roughly the size of Great Britain) to dozens of tiny principalities that were only a few square miles in size. The first order of business for the new Indian Prime Minister Jawaharlal Nehru was to figure out how to incorporate all of these semi-independent principalities into the new Indian nation. Most of the princes signed on to unification with little resistance, but some held back, hoping either to gain greater privileges for themselves or to become independent nations in their own right. The state of Kashmir, in the far north, was especially reluctant to join the new nation and was later claimed by both India and Pakistan, making it a flashpoint for continuing tension between the two countries.

While most of the princely states were eventually absorbed into the Indian union, the issue of governmental integration has never been fully resolved. Various groups and regions have, from time to time, agitated for more autonomy, special status, or full independence from India. In 1966, for instance, a new Punjabi state was created in recognition of the shared language and religion of the Sikhs there. A similar situation exists in the northeastern part of the country where ethnicity and faith – in this case, Christianity – have become catalysts for other separatist movements. Three states in this region have Christian majorities – Mizoram, Meghalaya, and Nagaland – and religion has been linked with movements for self-rule in all of them.

The history of Nagaland reflects the general situation in the northeastern region of India. Nagaland was made a state in 1961 in response to the armed uprising of the Naga people against Indian rule. The hope was that statehood would quell that violence, but a grinding civil war has ensued. The Nagas do not want to be a state within the Indian nation; they want full independence to become their own Christian nation – and they are overwhelmingly Christian (approximately 90 percent). Most Naga Christians are Baptists, but their Baptist faith is unique. While they revere Billy Graham and have close ties with a tiny, American fundamentalist Baptist college in Florida, many hang crucifixes on their walls and more than half of them are explicitly socialist or communist in their political views. This distinctively Naga-style socialist Baptist faith has united and sustained the Naga people in their resistance to Indian rule for more than 50 years. While most Indian Christians are proud to be Indian, the Christians in Nagaland insist they are not Indians and do not want to be part of any Indian nation.

The second major challenge facing independent India was to create a new system of law and government that could both facilitate democracy and encourage social stability within one of the world's most culturally and religiously diverse nations. At the time of partition, it was common for those outside the region to assume that India would define itself as a Hindu state in much the same way that Pakistan would be a Muslim state. But while Pakistan opted to become the Islamic Republic of Pakistan, India chose a different route, becoming simply the Republic of India with no religious adjective to describe its identity.

The Indian constitution acknowledges that India is a deeply religious nation, and seeks simultaneously to protect religious freedom and to minimize interreligious conflict. There are five clauses in the constitution that relate to religion. Four of these are unproblematic. They ban discrimination on the basis of religion, give religious groups the freedom to manage their own affairs, make it illegal for any person to be compelled to pay taxes in support of any particular religion, and forbid the teaching of religion in publicly funded schools. But the fifth clause, Article 25, has been the source of endless dispute. It stipulates that:

> subject to public order, morality and health and the other provisions of [the constitution], all persons are equally entitled to freedom of conscience and the right freely to profess, practice, and propagate religion. Nothing in this article shall affect the operation of any existing law or prevent the State from making any law regulating or restricting any economic, financial, political, or other secular activity which may be associated with religious practice.

What at first seems clear in this statement is murky by the end, and that murkiness has created problems.

The key issue is conversion. From the very beginning, starting with the constitutional convention itself, Indian Hindus have been concerned that Christians (and sometimes

Muslims) try to convert Hindus away from their faith. For Hindus, this is simply wrong. One's *dharma* (one's religious rule of life) is given at birth and cannot validly be contested. Being religious means submitting to the *dharma* one has received. Choosing to go against one's *dharma* is inherently irreligious and puts one's soul at risk. Understood in this way, conversion is the opposite of true religion. Many Hindus accordingly define genuine religious freedom as the right not to be tempted to convert, and they are deeply offended when people try to convert others through the use of what they see as false promises of spiritual or material gain that appeal to the baser instincts of humankind.

Christians have an entirely different point of view. Many Christians feel it is their duty to share their faith with others and to invite people to convert. Christian evangelism often includes promises of eternal life in heaven and it often seeks to embody the message it preaches in acts of care and kindness to others (e.g., help for those who are sick, aid for those in need, and education for those who lack schooling). These are not seen by Christians as inappropriate inducements to conversion, but merely as part of their faith. What is at stake, from the Christian perspective, is the right of individuals to choose whichever religion best fits their own needs and understanding of reality. For Christians, choice in religious matters is not immoral, but necessary – most would say that faith has to be freely chosen to be true faith at all. Seen in that light, it is immoral to try to box anyone into the faith they were given at birth.

This brings us back to Article 25 of the Indian constitution which was a grudging compromise, splitting the difference between Hindu and Christian views. One of the key Hindu leaders at the convention, Purushottamdas Tandon, stated bluntly that: "We have agreed to the right of conversion … [even though] we Congressmen do not think it at all right … that people should strenuously go about trying to convert peoples of other faiths into their own, but we want to carry our Christian friends with us."[2] The first clause guarantees the right to propagate the faith, which most Christians understand to include the right to engage in conversion-seeking activity. The second clause allows the government to limit certain conversion-related practices, which Hindus view as deeply troubling.

How well has this compromise worked? From the perspective of most Christians not that well, especially in recent years. Starting in the mid-1960s, a number of Indian states passed "freedom of religion" acts that criminalize any use of force, inducements, or fraudulent means of encouraging conversion. Most Christians do not object in principle to banning certain ways of encouraging conversion since they do not want to fill their churches with so-called "rice Christians" who convert only because of the material benefits gained. But they do object to "freedom of religion" bills in which the definitions of force, fraud, and inducement are so vague – some would say intentionally vague – that Christians can be hauled into court on ridiculous charges. In some places, promising a future life in heaven for those who convert can warrant criminal prosecution with penalties of up to three years in prison in addition to substantial fines.

While Christians are bothered by these new laws, they are more troubled by the recent social and cultural developments that have made them possible. This raises the third great challenge facing India since independence: how to foster a national sense of identity that unites the nation in a way that transcends the pluralities of life on the ground.

Historically, two rather different ideals have vied for prominence. One is rooted in a view of Indian identity that celebrates the cultural, religious, and ethnic diversity of the nation.

Figure 7.3   Christians take part in a prayer meeting to protest against the killings of Christians in the Indian state of Orissa, in New Delhi, 27 December, 2007
© Manpreet Romana/AFP/Getty Images

This pluralistic and publically secular approach has been politically championed by the Congress Party, which was originally led by Mahatma Gandhi and Jawaharlal Nehru. It is a vision of the nation that affirms that every group is special and has something to contribute to the vibrancy of Indian life. A second view of Indian national identity focuses very specifically on India as a Hindu nation and it makes *hindutva* (Hinduness) the core concern. Its most ardent articulator, Madhavrao Sadashivrao Golwalkar (1906–73), argued that every citizen of India ought to be given the choice of either adopting Hindu culture and Hindu religion or leaving the country. Those who choose to remain without conforming to the ideals of *hindutva* should be bound by legal sanctions and hedged in by social prejudice. Golwalkar tried to make the argument that *hindutva* is a cultural and not necessarily religious conception, but that distinction is hard to maintain in practice.

For the first four decades after independence, the Gandhian and Nehruvian view was dominant, as India tried to become a model of pluralistic democracy. In more recent years, however, the two competing ideals have sparred as equals, with the *hindutva* party often on top. The Hindu Right, known collectively as the Sangh Parivar (a term analogous to the Religious Right in American politics), is led by the Rashtriya Swayamsevak Sangh (RSS), which is a cultural association, and by the Bharatiya Janata Party (BJP), which is a political organization. The BJP was created in 1980 and ruled the country from 1998 to 2004 under the leadership of Prime Minister A. B. Vajpayee.

During these six years of BJP rule, followers of the Sangh Parivar openly encouraged violence against Muslims and Christians all across India, but especially in the so-called "cow belt," or Hindu stronghold, that runs across the middle of the country. Churches and mosques were destroyed and mob violence was organized against Muslim and Christian believers. Many Muslims and Christians were killed. While the government tried to distance itself from this violence, it was clear that many BJP politicians were pleased that Christians and Muslims felt threatened and that Hindus felt empowered. In the years since 2004, sporadic violence has continued. BJP and other Sangh Parivar activists have shifted their focus away from the national scene to the states, where they have helped enact many of the new "religious freedom" laws (discussed above) which have been used not merely to prevent conversions, but also to intimidate non-Hindus. It is no surprise that most Christians are strong supporters of the Gandhi–Nehru secular vision of the nation. They feel that they have every right to promote their religious and political views. They are, after all, not foreigners as the advocates of *hindutva* contend, but native Indians who should have the same rights as all other Indian citizens.

The Varieties of Indian Christianity

Christianity in India is, like the country as a whole, incredibly complex. Indians, in general, glory in religious pluralism, and Indian Christians passionately embrace their own internal pluralism. V. Chakkarai, a mid-twentieth-century Christian lawyer from Madras (now Chennai), put it this way:

> It is not possible to drill Indian nature with its varied types and temperament into one pattern. Different groups, marked by strong emotional and mental features, must be left to produce their own forms of worship; and no obstacles should be placed in the way … That one form of worship and only one should prevail from the north to the south amidst a diversity of peoples, is a dream; nay it is a night-mare. The true catholicity of Indian Christianity will make room for the widest and wildest diversities … A cold dull level of uniformity will never be welcome in India."[3]

Indian Christianity is indeed widely and wildly diverse, but five historical layers can be identified. The oldest layer is the St Thomas tradition of South India, followed by additional layers of Catholic, Protestant, Pentecostal/Charismatic, and "churchless" Christian influences. Today each of these historical layers has adherents numbering in the millions (see Table 7.3).

Thomas/Syrian churches

The various churches that have emerged out of the old Syrian (Church of the East) tradition date their founding to the first-century arrival in India of Thomas, the disciple of Jesus. Thomas is said to have landed at Cranganore on the west coast (about 150 miles north of India's southernmost tip). He preached throughout much of southern India and finally died and was buried at Mylapore near present-day Chennai. Scholars used to scoff at this claim, but it may well be true since an active sea route connected India with the Middle East during the first century. By the fifth century, India's Thomas Christians had established fraternal relations with the Syrian-speaking Church in Persia, so they are also designated as Syrian Orthodox. The first converts in the Thomas Christian tradition community were high-caste Hindus, and over time the Christian community essentially became its own new

Table 7.3   Estimated size of the five major Christian subgroups in India

Tradition	Estimated number of adherents
Thomas/Syrian	3,500,000
Catholic	16,500,000
Protestant	19,500,000
Pentecostal/Charismatic	15,500,000*
Churchless Christians	10,000,000
Total	65,000,000

* This number reflects only those who are members of explicitly Pentecostal/Charismatic churches. An additional 10,000,000 Pentecostal/Charismatic Christians are members of the Catholic and Protestant churches.

and relatively elevated caste in the local social structure. In the contemporary state of Kerala in southern India, approximately one-third of the people are Christians, and they are still distinguished by their relatively high social status.

Three and a half million Christians trace their spiritual roots to this ancient historical source, but Thomas Christians no longer exist as one community. Over the centuries, they have scattered into seven or eight different denominations, some remaining Orthodox in their identity and modes of worship and others associating with the Roman Catholic Church (for example, the Syro-Malabar Catholic Church, which has 500,000 members) or the Protestant tradition (for example, the Mar Thoma Syrian Church of Malabar, with just over a million members). Despite different allegiances, they are bound by a common ancient heritage, and allegations that Indian Christianity is an imported Western religion make little sense when directed at Thomas Christians.

Catholic Christianity

The second oldest layer of Christianity in India is Catholicism, a tradition that now claims almost 17 million followers. Catholicism was first introduced to India in 1498 when Vasco da Gama arrived off the west coast of India seeking "Christians and spices." Da Gama's search for spices is easy to understand. He was a merchant seeking wealth. His hope to find Christians was fueled by the widespread Portuguese and Spanish belief that there was a Christian monarch in the East, called "Prester John," who was a potential ally against the Muslims of North Africa and the Middle East. Da Gama was accordingly delighted to discover Christians in India, but his joy soon soured when it became clear that the Christians he had discovered were quite different from the Roman Catholics of Western Europe. Instead of being viewed as allies, Indian Christians came to be seen as heretics needing correction. After the Portuguese had established a military presence at Goa, they launched an Inquisition aimed mostly against local Indian Christians, designed to coerce them into the one true Catholic faith. This was Catholicism with an iron fist, and over the next two centuries more than four thousand Indians were brought to trial with nearly a hundred death sentences handed down.

While the Inquisition reigned in Goa, a rather different Catholic message was being preached further south along the fishery coast of Kerala and then later on the west coast of Tamil Nadu. Led by Jesuits like the Spanish Francis Xavier (1506–52) and Italian Roberto de Nobili (1577–1656), this alternative Catholic initiative displayed great respect for Indian sensibilities and spirituality. De Nobili not only learned the local languages, he also adopted Hindu dress and moral norms. He lived a simple life, became a vegetarian, and sought to persuade Hindu Brahmins to accept Christian faith on the basis of persuasion alone. De Nobili assumed that Hinduism and Christianity were not antithetical and he sought to blend the two. Some contemporaries thought he went too far in that direction and some of his views were later condemned, but the ideal of making Indian Catholicism fully Indian has never been repudiated by the Catholic Church.

Both of these tendencies – the dogmatic and the culturally sympathetic – remain operative in Indian Catholicism today. Some Catholic theologians like Raimundo Panikkar come close to embracing Hinduism as an equal, alternative path to God. On the other hand, the "Dominus Iesus" declaration issued by the Congregation for the Doctrine of the Faith in 2000 and written by Joseph Cardinal Ratzinger (who is now Pope Benedict XVI) argued that salvation is fully available only in the one true Catholic Church and that all other religious traditions, including other Christian traditions, are "gravely deficient." In terms of simple familiarity, however, what Indian Catholicism is best known for is something very different than either of these theological options: the compassionate ministry of Mother Teresa (1910–97) and her Missionaries of Charity. Mother Teresa, an Albanian who emigrated to India, dedicated her life to serving the poorest of the poor in Kolkata (Calcutta), caring for those she found dying on the streets so they could, in the end, die with peace and dignity. The recent publication of her letters, which revealed her own inner struggle of faith, has only deepened the respect and admiration many feel for her. More than anyone else, she has been the global face of Catholicism in India.

Protestantism

The third layer of Indian Christianity is Protestant. Protestantism was introduced as early as 1700, but it did not really take off until about 1800, after the English missionary William Carey and his Baptist colleagues had arrived in northeastern India. Carey's first goal was to convert Indians to Christianity, but his second goal, not far behind in his list of priorities, was to teach Indians to read the Bible for themselves, as he believed that the Bible itself would change India more than preaching. He translated the Bible into Bengali (one of the languages of northeastern India) and led the way in establishing missionary schools where Indians could learn how to read these newly translated scriptures.

Along with the desire to convert individuals, many Protestant missionaries also felt called to Christianize the culture of India. Schools were one means of doing this, as were hospitals and clinics, but direct social criticism was also involved. These Protestant Christians denounced the caste system, the practice of *sati* (the ritual immolation of widows on the cremation pyres of their husbands), child marriage, and temple prostitution. Much of Protestantism's social activism focused on the needs of those at the bottom of the social hierarchy, and this contributed to the massive conversions of Dalits and other social outcasts all across India during the late nineteenth and early twentieth centuries. The testimonies of these converts indicate that religious concerns – matters of salvation and spiritual empowerment – were predominant, but the social message of Christianity was inextricably intertwined with these more personal dimensions of faith. Protestant Christian activism in India was almost always paternalistic and often aggressively Western in tone. For the most part, Protestants now acknowledge that fact and are working diligently to become less Western and more genuinely Indian in character and composure.

Because it has no central authority, Protestantism tends to fragment. New denominations are launched every year. Almost all of these new groups start small, and most remain small for as long as they exist. Most of the Protestant denominations in India fall into this category, with less than 5,000 members each. But while many Protestant churches are the products of division, some denominations are born out of a desire to unite. Two of the biggest churches in India were formed in this way. The Church of South India (CSI) came into existence in 1947 through a merger of Anglicans, Methodists, Presbyterians, Congregationalists, and Reformed Christians and now claims 3,500,000 members. The Church of North India, which was created in 1970 and brought together even more denominations than the CSI, now has 1,500,000 members. Other large Protestant churches include the Baptists with 6,000,000 adherents (representing 30 percent of all Protestants in the country), United Evangelical Lutheran Church with 1,500,000 members, and the Presbyterian Church in India with approximately 800,000 members.

While Indian Protestants tend to have a local focus, many are also quite well informed about broader Christian trends in the world. European and American theologians are widely read, and global perspectives inform their faith. A number of Indian Protestants have also become world Christian leaders. M. M. Thomas, for example, served as moderator of the Central Committee of the World Council of Churches (WCC) from 1968 to 1975 and in that capacity he helped steer the WCC toward a more embracing understanding of the relationship between church and society. His vision of the Christian's role in the world was one of working with all people of good will, regardless of their faith, helping to build a new world characterized by peace, compassion, and mutual respect. For Thomas, evangelism was a relatively low priority. Other Indian Protestants would, of course, stress precisely what Thomas wanted to push aside: the centrality of conversion. Vinay Samuel embodies this alternative approach. He is an ordained CSI minister who has been active for many years in a variety of global evangelical organizations, combining what he sees as Christianity's responsibility to promote social justice and conversion equally.

Pentecostal/Charismatic Christianity

The fourth and most recent layer of Christianity in India is Pentecostal or Charismatic in nature, emphasizing the visible and miraculous power of the Holy Spirit. Globally this movement includes about 17.5 percent of all Christians, but in India the percentage is closer to 40 percent. The Indian Pentecostal/Charismatic movement began in 1905 at the Mukti Mission (or ashram) near Pune, which is just south of Mumbai. This center was run by Pandita Ramabai Sawaswati, a brilliant Sanskrit scholar who had become known worldwide for her book *The High-Caste Hindu Woman* (1887). She converted from Hinduism to Christianity after reading the Gospel of Luke. That particular Gospel emphasizes justice for the poor, and Ramabai's Mukti Mission, founded in 1898, was dedicated to the rescue and protection of "child widows" and orphans. It was also a place of Bible study and prayer, but in 1905 strange things began to happen. Some members of the community were "slain in the Spirit." Others spoke in tongues or reported that their skin felt as if it was inflamed with the presence of God. Many announced that they had been newly and wonderfully filled with the Holy Spirit of God. Ramabai interpreted these events as the beginning of a new and distinctively Indian way of being Christian, a way of being spiritually free and alive in a manner that differed considerably from the stiff and staid norms of traditional Western Protestantism.

The subsequent history of the Pentecostal/Charismatic movement in India has in many ways confirmed Ramabai's description of the movement. While Pentecostal missionaries from the West have been part of the story, the main plot has been indigenously Indian. The group Manna International provides a representative glimpse of Indian Pentecostalism. This church is jointly led by the husband and wife team of Ernest and Rachael Komanapalli. After spending some time in the USA for educational purposes, they returned to India in 1971 to pastor a 30-member Pentecostal congregation in Amalapuram in the state of Andhra Pradesh. The church in Amalapuram today seats 4,000 people, and the Manna International network in India consists of a thousand churches with more than 125,000 members. Despite the size of the headquarters church, this denomination as a whole is made up of mostly small congregations (averaging slightly over a hundred members each) that focus most of their energy on the spiritual and physical needs of people from the poorer sectors of society. The church preaches a "full gospel" message of salvation, healing, and the empowerment of the Holy Spirit, but it is also attuned to other human concerns. Manna International runs an orphanage, a home for widows, and a center for deaf people. It has also started a small Bible College in Hyderabad and broadcasts weekly radio and television programs throughout India.

A very different picture of the Indian Pentecostal/Charismatic movement is provided by the wide-ranging ministry of D. G. S. Dhinakaran (1935–2008), who was a highly respected leader in the mainstream Protestant Church of South India. The core of Dhinakaran's ministry is the "Jesus Calls" organization, which operates a very well-designed website offering 24-hour prayer support anywhere in the world. Dhinakaran claimed that his prayers could heal the sick, make the lame walk, and stop damaging downpours of rain. At mass meetings held in Chennai, he would routinely call out the names of people in the crowd and offer personal prophecy – commentary on their spiritual, physical, and emotional condition. In the mid-1980s he established television programs that can now be viewed throughout India as well as in the rest of Asia, the Middle East, and the USA. Dhinakaran was well known in international televangelist circles, and when people like the Armenian-American revivalist Benny Hinn visited India, Dhinakaran was often the local host. In some ways, Dhinakaran was a typical health-and-wealth TV preacher, but there was more to his ministry than that. His numerous accomplishments include the founding of an engineering college, Karunya University, which is fully accredited and now has more than 5,000 students (about 60 percent male and 40 percent female) in residence. Clearly committed to the social advancement of men and women across India, he was one of the best known Christian leaders in the country. After Dhinakaran's death, the Chief Minister (Governor) of the State of Tamil Nadu was one of the first to pay homage.

The Pentecostal/Charismatic movement in India is large and diverse. The small churches of Manna International are a far cry from the slick website of the Jesus Calls ministry, but both movements are authentically Indian. Both movements are also transnational, and that should not be surprising. There are few places left in the world where being indigenous means being entirely local, and that is especially the case with Pentecostalism. Played out in a wide variety of ways, the theological and social emphases of Pentecostal churches in India are empowering and confidence-building, especially to Dalits. To some degree, Pentecostalism in India is serving the same social function as the liberation theology of twentieth-century Latin America.

Churchless Christianity

A fifth layer of Indian Christianity points in a very different direction. Rather than being transnational or national or even local in scope, it is intensely personal and private. As many as 10 million people in India are churchless Christians, virtually invisible in terms of the public practice of their faith. Rather than joining with others in church gatherings to engage in the corporate worship of God, these followers of Jesus express their devotion to God entirely in private, seeing no need to parade their religious allegiances in the public domain.

Several factors contribute to the popularity of churchless Christianity in India. First, there is a long tradition within Hinduism of private worship and devotion to God or the gods. Identified with the Sanskrit term *bhakti* (meaning love or devotion), this tradition has been widely adapted by Christians. Its goal is the experiential union of the worshiper with God, and the distractions of public gatherings can make that union more difficult to achieve. But it is not just "Christians" who worship Jesus in this *bhakti* fashion; significant numbers of "Hindus" also worship Jesus as an avatar of the divine. The terms Christian and Hindu are placed in quotation marks here because in practice these two forms of devotion to Jesus can look basically identical, making any easy distinction between Hindu and Christian impossible. Other Indians conceptualize their devotion to Jesus in primarily moral and ethical terms. Being a Christian means following a "Jesus way of life." This involves trying to make one's whole life conform to the gospel, but it does not require communal gatherings for the worship of God. Finally, some Christians in India are churchless because to declare their faith in public would have extremely negative consequences. In many families, for example, it would be very difficult for a wife to say publicly that she was a Christian if her husband was not. In some cases, the same would hold true for children. Others refuse to be visibly identified with the church because it might open them to persecution or because they might lose government benefits if they are officially reclassified as Christian instead of Hindu. Whatever the reason for their churchlessness, there are many Indians who consider themselves followers of Jesus but feel no need to demonstrate that commitment through the act of joining a church.

Christianity and the Dalits

Within traditional Hindu society, Dalits (who were formerly called "untouchables") represent the lowest rank on the social hierarchy. The historical origins of the Dalits are not entirely clear, but most scholars believe they were the original inhabitants of the land who were pushed into a subservient role when the Indo-Aryan tribes of central Asia invaded the region around 1500 BCE. As Hinduism coalesced over the centuries, the social philosophy of Hinduism has provided a religious rationale for the oppression of Dalits. According to this traditional Hindu vision of life, the human community is organized into a social and spiritual pyramid with Brahmans and other high caste people at the top, lower caste respectable workers in the middle, and Dalits and other noncaste people such as the *adivasi* (tribal groups) at the bottom. Dalits make up about 20 percent of the Indian population.

While many terms have been used to describe Dalits (e.g., untouchables, *harijan*, the Scheduled Castes), Dalit is the self-chosen designation of the group. The word Dalit means to be broken and crushed, and Dalits have chosen that term because it communicates both a social identity and a moral claim. They are the oppressed, they are oppressed because others are their oppressors, and many are now demanding that their oppression cease. Historically Christianity played a significant role in fostering this new liberationist Dalit self-consciousness. The Christian message, as it was preached by late nineteenth- and early twentieth-century missionaries, included the claim that everyone was equally loved by God. Responding to that egalitarian message, thousands of Dalits converted to Christianity as a way of simultaneously rejecting the socially oppressive worldview of Hinduism and affirming their own worth as human beings. Once the notion of equality was let loose within the Dalit community, however, it took on a life of its own which was far larger than the Christian community. But while the main leaders of the movement for Dalit rights have not been Christians, many have acknowledged that Christianity was an important catalyst in the emergence of Dalit self-consciousness.

As a result of Dalit pressure, the Indian Constitution made social discrimination against Dalits illegal, and other laws have largely banned discrimination within Hinduism itself. The Indian government has, in addition, taken steps to help Dalits overcome the social restrictions that have historically been placed on them by developing a variety of educational and affirmative action programs. Ironically, however, Indian governmental policy now drives a wedge between the Dalit community as a whole and Christian Dalits as a subgroup within that community. While Dalits as a group are eligible for special benefits, Christian Dalits are banned from those programs. To receive Dalit benefits one has to be legally classified as a Dalit, but Dalits who convert to Christianity are reclassified as Christians and lose their official Dalit status. In effect, this policy acts like a huge tax on conversion. To convert is to give up one's Dalit rights, and that can be costly. This policy informally strengthens the hand of Hindus in Indian society, and the militant Hindu Sangh

Figure 7.4   An Indian shouts slogans in front of a mock crucifixion during a protest rally in New Delhi to demand government job reservations for "dalit" or oppressed Christians.
© Sunil Malhotra/Reuters

Parivar movement has used the policy to encourage Christian Dalits to reconvert to Hinduism and thereby regain their Dalit rights. In August of 2009, the state assembly of Andhra Pradesh passed a resolution asking the Indian federal government to change the law and allow Dalit Christians to keep their Scheduled Class rights. So far, no federal action has been taken.

How this plays out will have serious implications for the Indian Christian community as a whole. The current estimate is that well over half – some say 60 to 70 percent – of the Indian Christian community is Dalit. If there is any significant erosion of Christian faith among Dalits it will dramatically impact Christianity in general. Christian groups have been outspoken in their criticism of the current policy, saying it represents blatant religious discrimination, but the churches themselves have not necessarily been models of equality when it comes to Dalits. While social discrimination against Dalits is denounced in most churches, de facto segregation is still observable in many congregations. In some cases, this is encouraged by the architectural floor plan of older church buildings which often included separate spaces for high caste, low caste, and Dalit believers.

A more important development is that Dalit Christians themselves are becoming more articulate about how they envision the core beliefs and practices of Christianity. During the 1980s and 1990s, a new form of theology emerged within the Dalit community which centered on the claim that Jesus was himself a Dalit. According to this view, Jesus did not merely care for the poor and oppressed, he was one of the crushed and broken members of society himself. Some Dalit theologians argue that to truly follow Jesus implies fully cooperating with the Dalit political cause. While this Dalit version of liberation theology represents an important advance in Dalit thinking about Christianity, it is not uncontested. In fact, many Dalit Christians seem to favor a more Charismatic or even magical understanding of faith – one that places special emphasis on the power of the Bible as a physical object. Whether the issue is social justice or healing, it is the book itself – placed on the forehead of a sick person or held in the air – that is a source of power and strength. What is common to both of these versions of Dalit Christianity – the liberationist and the Charismatic – is that faith is understood as a source of power and empowerment, and this newly confident Dalit spirituality is challenging the churches as well as the whole society to live up to the ideals of equality both profess.

Jesus, Christianity, and Indian Culture

Many Indians have said they deeply honor Jesus, but they have serious questions about the ways in which Christians have tried to control the world's understanding of Jesus. They see a breach between the simple, moral message of Jesus and the complex theological frameworks promoted by the churches, and they see a divergence between what they would say is the core message of Jesus – showing love and respect to all, being nonjudgmental, turning the other cheek – and the churches' propensity to be aloof, judgmental, and defensive. Gandhi exemplifies this attitude as much as anyone. He had deep respect for Jesus as a moral teacher and religious guide, but he loathed organized Christianity, claiming that the churches had distorted the message of Christ almost to the point of preaching its opposite. Gandhi said that Jesus "belongs not solely to Christianity, but to the entire world,"[4] and he felt a responsibility both to free Jesus from the clutches of Christians and to call Christians back to the real Jesus of history.

Any attempt to understand Christianity in India has to take into account this widespread respect for Jesus, combined with deep antipathy toward institutionalized Christianity. In India the influence of Jesus is much wider than Christianity itself. The early nineteenth-century Indian scholar and religious leader Ram Mohan Roy (1774–1833) was a trailblazer in this regard. In 1820 he published a book entitled *The Precepts of Jesus: The Guide to Peace and Happiness*, which made the case that being a true disciple of Jesus meant following his way of life. While attracted to Jesus, Roy never joined any church and he continued to identify himself as a Hindu, sensing no tension at all between his respect for Jesus and his Hindu cultural and religious commitments.

Some members of the Christian community have echoed those sentiments. P. Chenchiah, a member of the "rethinking Christianity" group that was active in the 1930s and 1940s, put it this way: "No man can serve two masters. But every man can love two parents, father and mother." For Chenchiah, Christianity was father and Indian Hindu culture was mother, and he loved both. He hoped for a day when all the wisdom of the Hindu tradition could be fully integrated with the best insights of Christianity to produce a full and deep faith focusing on God as the "all in all to all of us."[5]

Most Indian Christians would consider Chenchiah's view to be extreme. They might see some points of overlap and compatibility between Christianity and Indian/Hindu culture, but they would also see areas of conflict. Generally speaking, Catholics have been more embracing of Indian/Hindu culture and spirituality, while Protestant and Pentecostal/ Charismatic Christians have been more cautious. Catholicism in general has a more positive disposition to culture and its relationship to faith, respecting culture as the scaffolding on which faith rests. Catholics also value material culture and thus they are at ease in a place like India where the material stuff of religion – statues, paintings of saints, flowers, bells, incense, umbrellas, ribbons, and holy buildings erected on holy sites – is so important. Protestants and many Pentecostal/Charismatic Christians, on the other hand, see faith and culture as being, at least in part, in competition with each other. They are suspicious of culture and worry that various cultural values, ideas, or practices will draw believers away from devotion to God. And Protestants, in particular, get nervous whenever faith is mixed with material culture. For them, it is the "word" – the Bible – that counts, and anything too material smells potentially like idolatry.

It is not surprising that Catholic festivals and celebrations in India look and feel rather more Indian than their Protestant and Pentecostal/Charismatic counterparts. Catholics in the village of Avur in Tamil Nadu, for instance, celebrate Easter each year by pulling a statue of the risen Christ around town in a massive chariot that looks exactly like the chariots that Hindus use to escort their gods around town on other festival days of the year. Christ is dressed in a *dhoti* and he wears a gold embroidered shawl around his shoulders, which is what any upper-class Hindu man might wear to a temple or special religious occasion. And the chariot is decorated with brilliant banners and hundreds of flowers which is, once again, an adaptation from Hindu custom. The differences – the visual indicators that set this particular chariot and its god apart from parallel Hindu celebrations – are subtle: a different choice of primary colors, a different pattern of weaving in the cloth, a different path around town to a different destination.[6] Most Catholics have no problem with any of this, and the parade itself is not much different from similar Catholic festivals at Easter-time in Europe or Latin America. If there is a difference here, it is that this Christ of India parades through the streets on Easter Sunday as the resurrected lord of the universe – which is, once again, precisely the attitude with which Hindus would carry their gods through town – rather than traveling the streets as the bloodied and beaten Christ of Good Friday.

Most Protestants in India would be appalled at this gaudy Catholic festival. They would see it as little more than Hinduism with a thin Christian veneer. But Protestants, too, affirm their Indianness in ways they consider proper and appropriate. One such way is through architecture. The Church of South India's Cathedral of the Epiphany, built in the 1930s in Dornakal (see Plate 10), for example, was designed to intentionally incorporate Muslim and Hindu features and to mimic the grand historic buildings of the region. Bishop Azariah, who helped plan the structure, said he hoped the building would give a "touch of magnificence"[7] to the lives of the mostly low caste converts who formed the membership of the church. Azariah wanted his parishioners to be proud of being both Christian and Indian.

Bishop Azariah and his church bring us back to the main theme of this chapter. Christians in this part of the world, and especially in India, are able to express their faith with confidence. Their attitude stands in stark contrast to the weariness of Christians in the Middle East and North Africa, where Christianity accounts for roughly the same percentage of the regional population. Far from feeling weary, Christians in India are upbeat, even exuberant. Though they express their faith differently depending on region, churchly tradition, and social status, the Christians of South Asia see themselves as playing a vibrant and valued role in the multicultural and multireligious dynamics of the world in which they live.

Notes

1 V. S. Azariah, *India and the Christian Movement* (New York: National Council of the Protestant Episcopal Church, 1938), p. 91.

2 Quoted in Sebastian C. H. Kim, *In Search of Identity: Debates on Religious Conversion in India* (New Delhi: Oxford University Press, 2003), p. 47.

3 V. Chakkarai, "The Church" in G. V. Job et al. (eds), *Rethinking Christianity in India* (Madras: A. N. Sudarisanam, 1938), p. 116.

4 Quoted in Robert Ellsberg (ed.), *Gandhi on Christianity* (Maryknoll, NY: Orbis Books, 1991), p. 28.

5 P. Chenchiah, "Religion in Contemporary India" in *Rethinking Christianity in India*, p. 214.

6 This ritual is described in Joanne Punzo Waghorne, "Chariots of the God/s: Riding the Line" in Selva J. Raj and Corinne G. Dempsey (eds), *Popular Christianity in India: Riting between the Lines* (Albany: State University of New York Press, 2002), pp. 11–37.

7 Quoted in Paul M. Collins, *Christian Inculturation in India* (Burlington, VT: Ashgate, 2007), p. 125.

Suggestions for Further Reading

Collins, Paul M. (2007). *Christian Inculturation in India.* Burlington, VT: Ashgate.

Dempsey, Corinne G. (2001). *Kerala Christian Sainthood: Collisions of Culture and Worldview in South India.* New York: Oxford University Press.

Fernando, Leonardo and G. Gispert-Sauch (2004). *Christianity in India: Two Thousand Years of Faith.* Delhi: Penguin Books India.

Frykenberg, Robert Eric (2008). *Christianity in India: From Beginnings to the Present.* Oxford: Oxford University Press.

Guha, Ramachandra (2007). *India After Gandhi: The History of the World's Largest Democracy*. New York: HarperCollins.

Kim, Kirsten (2004). "India," in John Parratt (ed.), *An Introduction to Third World Theologies*. Cambridge, UK: Cambridge University Press, pp. 44–73.

Kim, Sebastian C. H. (2003). *In Search of Identity: Debates on Religious Conversion in India*. New Delhi: Oxford University Press.

Kim, Sebastian C. H. (ed.) (2008). *Christian Theology in Asia*. Cambridge, UK: Cambridge University Press.

Raj, Selva J. and Corinne G. Dempsey (eds) (2002). *Popular Christianity in India: Riting Between the Lines*. Albany: State University of New York Press.

Webster, John C. B. (1992). *The Dalit Christians: A History*. Delhi: ISPCK.

Webster, John C. B. (2002). *Religion and Dalit Liberation: An Examination of Perspectives*. New Delhi: Manohar.

Chapter 8

Western Europe

Thin, but Alive

In recent years, sociologists and news reporters have frequently suggested that Christianity is in the process of dying in Western Europe. A quick tour around the continent might confirm that judgment. In a land where Christianity used to be visible almost everywhere, it can now require a determined search to find a church building – and when it is uncovered it may no longer be a place of religious worship, having been converted into a restaurant or retail shop or personal dwelling. Today, only about a quarter of the population in Western Europe is religiously active, another half has some kind of minimal connection with organized Christianity, and about a quarter are self-consciously nonreligious. Given those demographics, Western Europe no longer needs all those former churches.

Some people worry that Christianity may be fading from the mental landscape as well. Only half to three-quarters of Western Europeans now report that they believe in God (depending on how the question is asked) and significantly fewer than half believe in either heaven or hell. Familiarity with the stories of the Bible and basic Christian doctrine also seems to be evaporating. Many Western Europeans no longer know enough about Christianity to reject it intelligently. Rather than being opposed to faith, they have simply lost interest.

Western European Christianity is also declining in terms of global significance. In 1900, approximately 14 percent of the world's population lived in Western Europe, and they made up 40 percent of the world's Christians. The figures today are very much lower. At present, Western Europe accounts for only 6 percent of the world's population and for only 15 percent of the world's Christians. A significant portion of this shift in numbers can be explained on the basis of global birthrates: Western Europeans have been having fewer babies than people in the rest of the world. This is so much the case that some social commentators fret that Western Europe is committing cultural suicide by failing to reproduce. Since Christian membership has declined even faster than the population as a whole, it comes as no surprise that some people describe Western European Christianity as a dying faith within a dying continent.

The World's Christians: Who they are, Where they are, and How they got there, First Edition. Douglas Jacobsen.
© 2011 Douglas Jacobsen. Published 2011 by Blackwell Publishing Ltd.

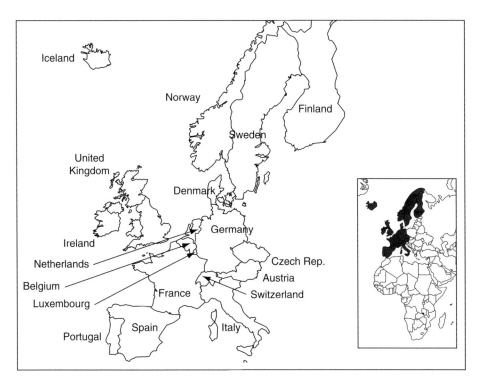

Figure 8.1   Map of Western Europe. Map by author.

Note: 18 countries: Total population 395,000,000 (6% of global population); Christian population 310,000,000 (78% of regional population, 15% of global Christian population): Orthodox 2,000,000, Catholics 210,000,000, Protestants 88,000,000, Pentecostal/Charismatic 10,000,000.

However, a closer look at the data reveals a more complex reality. While there is no question that Christianity has experienced a recession of sorts, there is still plenty of Christianity to be found. In fact, more than three-quarters of the population of Western Europe identifies itself as Christian and a sizeable number of those Christians attend church regularly. While it is true that only 3 or 4 percent of the population of Sweden attends church each week that is not representative of the region as a whole. More than 50 percent of the Christians in Ireland are weekly churchgoers, giving it one of the highest attendance rates anywhere in the world. And despite Sweden's very low rates of weekly attendance, 95 percent of Swedes show up at church at least once a year, if for no other reason than a baptism, wedding, or funeral.

The reports about declining belief in God are similarly uneven. The general trend over the last half century has been downward, but belief (and disbelief) in God varies considerably from country to country. Only about half of the population of France believes in God, and if asked specifically about a personal God (as distinct from some vague spiritual force behind the universe) that number falls to about one third. But in Ireland more than 90 percent of the population believes in God, and the figures for Italy and Spain are almost as high. What may be more significant is that the numbers seem to have stabilized in recent years. If future opinion surveys prove that to be true, it will signal that the decline of

Christianity in Europe may be coming to an end. Whatever the case, it is too early to write the obituary of Christianity in Western Europe. Christianity is quite obviously much thinner than it used to be, but it is definitely alive.

Signs of Vitality

The Christianity that exists in Western Europe is not merely the last remnant of the Christianity that existed in the past. A careful examination reveals that a variety of new growth is also taking place – little shoots of religious life that may or may not flourish in the future. Many of these newer Christian movements hold relatively traditional views of God and God's supernatural power, and they value traditional Christian activities such as taking the Eucharist, reading the Bible, engaging in personal prayer, and assisting those in need. But some new movements are much more progressive in character.

In the United Kingdom, the Alpha Course developed by clergy from Holy Trinity, Brompton, an Anglican church in southwest London, is a 10-week program designed to introduce participants to the central ideas and practices of Christianity. It is explicitly aimed at people who feel trapped within the mundane routines of secular life and who are looking for something more meaningful. The lessons assume that participants have received little if any prior instruction about Christian faith – which is the state of most Britons – so the Alpha Course is quite didactic in tone. The course is not intended to be a discussion group where people share their varied opinions, but rather is a class where people are taught what they should believe. While focusing on "mere Christianity" (the basic ideas and practices of Christianity that are common to all Christian traditions), the course also has a distinctly Charismatic flavor, devoting a number of sessions to topics like the filling of the Holy Spirit, speaking in tongues, and divine healing. It is estimated that about two million people in the United Kingdom have participated in the Alpha Course, making it one of the most successful Christian initiatives in the history of the country. The course has also been exported beyond the United Kingdom, with as many as 15 million participating worldwide.

A very different kind of grassroots Protestant vitality is found in various feminist initiatives that have been launched in Western Europe during the last two decades. Examples include the *Kvennakirrkjan* organization in Iceland, the *Oecumenische Vrouwensynoden* gatherings in Netherlands, and the *Sofia-mássor* liturgy developed for use in the Swedish Lutheran Church. Each of these movements provides an alternative expression of Christian faith that appeals to those who have found traditional forms of Christian faith to be inadequate for contemporary life and harmful to women. The leaders of these feminist initiatives insist that being fully Christian requires contemporary followers to transcend or transgress the traditional norms of church-defined Christianity, a very different approach from that of the Alpha Course.

Within the Catholic world, other signs of vitality are evident, many of which accentuate the role of laypeople. This new emphasis grew out of the Second Vatican Council (1962 65). Prior to Vatican II, Roman Catholics had tended to think of the Catholic Church as composed primarily of bishops, priests, and the religious (monastic brothers and sisters); everyone else was simply part of "the people." But the Council underscored the fact that "the people" themselves had an active role to play as the living embodiment of the church. This emphasis strengthened existing Catholic associations devoted to lay activism and inspired the creation of additional lay organizations.

In Italy, the rhetoric of Vatican II strengthened "Focolare," a movement founded in 1943 by Chiara Lubich (1920–2008) in Trento, Italy. Focolare (which means "hearth" or "fireplace") encourages small group study of the Gospels and traditional Catholic practices such as devotion to Mary, but its main emphasis is on fostering unity among all people. The "spirituality of unity," Lubich says, is something that can be embraced "not only by Catholics and Christians of other churches, but also by the followers of other religions and by people without any religious faith." The goal is to create "spaces of fraternity" where the "unity of the human family" can be rebuilt. While many *focolarini* (as the members of the movement are called) are traditional Catholics, membership is also open to Protestants and Orthodox Christians as well as to followers of other religions. The group has a formal membership of about 140,000 and a global following of more than two million, many of them in Western Europe.

Figure 8.2 Chiara Lubich, Founder of Focolare
© New City, London

The Community of Sant'Egidio is another lay ecclesial movement that has made headlines in recent years. Centered in Rome, Sant'Egidio was founded by Andrea Riccardi in 1968 while he was still a teenager. Based on his reading of the Gospels and meditation on the life of St Francis, Riccardi started a new organization for high school students that focused specifically on the needs of the poor. A key activity of the organization is "peoples' schools" held on Sunday afternoons and dedicated to the education of poor children living in urban slums. As the group has matured, it has become more broadly interested in issues of peacemaking and justice. Combining positive social action with personal fellowship and community, Sant'Egidio now has about 50,000 members worldwide, including both Catholics and non-Catholics who are attracted to Jesus but repelled by many of the trappings of official church Christianity.

Another old outlet for Catholic piety that is now in the process of renewal is the practice of pilgrimage. To go on pilgrimage is to travel to a shrine or other religious site for the purpose of seeking special help from God. One of the most frequently visited destinations in Western Europe – more than eight million people a year – is the small town of San Giovanni Rotondo in southern Italy. This is the site of the friary (monastery) where Padre Pio (1887–1968) served as a spiritual director and priest for many years and where he is now buried. Famous for possessing the stigmata – constantly bleeding wounds on his hands, side, and feet that mimic the wounds Christ received on the cross – Padre Pio was also reputed to be able to heal the sick, predict the future, and levitate while in prayer. Treated as a saint by many during his lifetime, Padre Pio was officially canonized by Pope John Paul II in June 2002. Drawn by his reputation for holiness, compassion, and spiritual power, Catholics come to the shrine at San Giovanni Rotondo seeking healing, guidance, and hope.

These varied religious activities and organizations – from the Alpha Course and *Kvennakirrkjan* to Focolare and pilgrimage – are illustrative of the fact that Christianity is

far from dead in Western Europe. Church as usual may be on the decline, but church as usual does not equate with Christianity in its entirety. The traditional churches of Western Europe represent one way of being Christian, and for many centuries that model served the region well. But time and again Christianity has had to develop new ways of organization, worship, and spirituality in order to meet the changing needs of people around the world – and this describes what is taking place in Western Europe. Times of transition are also, of course, times when faith can be lost. If the old containers of a religion disintegrate before new ones can be formed, the result can be the extinction of that religion in that particular location. Some scholars think that Christianity is on the brink of extinction in Western Europe, and they may be right, but signs of vitality indicate that a turn-around is possible.

Figure 8.3   Padre Pio celebrating the Mass
© The Art Archive/Alamy

Intellectualism, Secularism, and Christianity in Western Europe

If there is one characteristic of Christianity in Western Europe that marks it as distinct, it is its intellectualism. For centuries, Christians in Western Europe have insisted that their faith is not only in line with what Jesus taught, but that it is also demonstrably true. This attitude is captured in the phrase "faith seeking understanding," which was coined by the medieval bishop and theologian Anselm of Canterbury (1033–1109). In Western European Christianity, beliefs have been subjected to corroboration, clarification, and correction in the light of knowledge gained through rational reflection, scientific inquiry, and the pragmatic testing of values and ideas in the realm of ordinary life. According to Pope John Paul II in his encyclical *Fides et ratio* (1998): "Faith and reason are like two wings on which the human spirit rises to the contemplation of truth."[1] Western European Christianity has always stressed the need for educated, intellectual faith; anti-intellectual or purely emotional faith has never been the ideal.

This Western European Christian emphasis on reason and the intellect helps explain why secularism has had such an impact in the region. The term "secular" originally meant simply "this world" (in contrast to the eternal world of heaven), and it was the Christian tradition itself that first prompted Western Europeans to study this world on its own terms. Christian intellectuals envisioned the world as a freestanding creation of God – a world that was beautiful and mysterious, but one that was also governed according to a divine order that was awaiting discovery through rigorous empirical research. Most historians of science now agree that this Western European Christian vision of the fundamental orderliness of the world helped to pave the way for the development of modern science.

Ironically, the focus on science, reason, and the observable world that was nurtured by Christianity is in part responsible for the rise of secularism (understood as nonreligiousness) in the West. The French scientist and mathematician Pierre-Simon Laplace (1749–1827) is reported to have said, "God is a hypothesis I do not need." Even though many contemporary Christian theologians can readily incorporate modern scientific schol-arship into their religious thinking, it is evident that large numbers of Western Europeans have, like Laplace, simply lost interest in religious questions. The culture has moved from one in which belief in God provided the general background to all of life to one in which belief in God is an option for people who are "into that kind of thing" or who have time to reflect on the deeper meaning of life. But many people can live much of the time without any thought of God, the transcendent, or the spiritual dimensions of existence. It is not that Western Europeans are actively rejecting Christianity, since many Western Europeans still express support for Christianity in general. What is lacking is a sense of how Christianity connects with ordinary life. Many Christian leaders are asking whether Christianity can be reformulated in ways that will make sense to modern "secular" Western Europeans, and at present that question seems to have no clear answer.

A Christian Map of Western Europe

Christianity in Western Europe comes in two basic varieties – Catholic and Protestant – and, of these two, Catholicism is the larger by far. Catholics account for more than half the population of Western Europe and for two-thirds of all the Christians in the region. Protestants are a distant second, claiming about 28 percent of the Christian population. (The Pentecostal/Charismatic and Orthodox communities are both relatively small.) The general Catholic–Protestant division of Western Europe is visible in the geography of the region: most Catholics live in the southern part of Western Europe and most Protestants live in the north. There are exceptions, however: one of the most Catholic countries in Western Europe – Ireland – is located in the north. The countries of Germany, Netherlands, and Switzerland, which are all religiously mixed, fall roughly in between. (See Figure 8.4.)

Catholic Western Europe

Catholic Europe mainly comprises the countries of Austria, Belgium, the Czech Republic, France, Ireland, Italy, Luxembourg, Portugal, and Spain. More than 80 percent of Western Europe's Catholic population is found in these nine countries, and for the most part Catholics in these nations only rarely encounter any non-Catholic Christians. Orthodox, Protestant, and Pentecostal/Charismatic Christians represent a miniscule part of the popu-lation (only 3 to 4 percent combined), and even in the Czech Republic, which is the least Catholic country of the nine, Catholics still outnumber other Christians by more than ten to one (see Table 8.1). The Vatican is also located in this region, so even though Europe is no longer the demographic center of global Catholicism, it remains the administrative center of the Catholic Church.

While Catholicism is clearly the dominant faith across these countries, its strength varies significantly from country to country. One way of measuring this strength is to examine survey data asking how often people attend church, whether or not they believe in God, how often they pray or meditate, and if they identify themselves as being religious. A high number

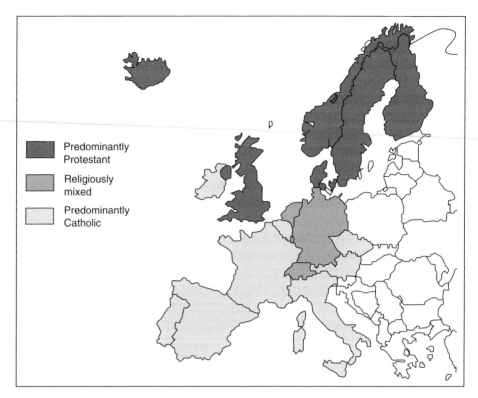

Figure 8.4   Western Europe showing Catholic, Protestant, and religiously mixed regions. Map by author.

of positive responses to these questions would indicate a generally higher level of religiosity in that country, while fewer positive responses would translate into a lower overall level of religiosity. Following this formula, Ireland, Italy, and Portugal stand out as more religiously devout than the rest of Catholic Western Europe, while the Czech Republic – where religious activity is still somewhat depressed following decades of Communist rule – and France are clearly less religious than the rest of the region. Austria, Belgium, Luxembourg, and Spain, despite having very different religious profiles, can all be categorized as being moderate in their religious fervency and practice. (See Table 8.2.)

Belief in God and practices like church attendance and prayer can be documented with numbers, but other less easily measured factors also shape Western European perspectives on faith and secularization. None is more significant than the way Catholics – at least the leadership of the Roman Catholic Church – view the European past. In the Catholic perspective, Western Europe and the Catholic faith are inseparably linked, as they have been since the year 800. That is when Charlemagne had Pope Leo III crown him as the Holy Roman Emperor, exercising political control over most of what is now Belgium, France, Italy, the Netherlands, Switzerland, and western Germany. Charlemagne's ascent signaled much more than the mere consolidation of a medieval Christian kingdom; it marked the beginning of a new regional identity. Before Charlemagne, what we now call Western Europe was still viewed largely as the hinterland of the old Roman Empire – an empire that had

Table 8.1 The four main Christian traditions in Catholic Europe (% of total population)

Country	Population	Catholic	Protestant	Pentecostal/Charismatic	Orthodox
Austria	8,000,000	74%	3%	3%	2%
Belgium	10,500,000	79%	1%	1%	–
Czech Republic	10,000,000	34%	3%	–	–
France	60,500,000	77%	2%	2%	1%
Ireland	4,000,000	80%	4%	4%	–
Italy	58,000,000	87%	1%	3%	–
Luxembourg	500,000	87%	1%	1%	–
Portugal	10,500,000	94%	1%	2%	–
Spain	43,000,000	94%	–	1%	–
Total	205,000,000	83%	1%	2%	–

Table 8.2 Levels of religiosity in Catholic Europe

Country	% Attend church monthly *	% Believe in God *	% Pray weekly *	% Religious person *	Overall religiosity
Austria	42	87	44	79	Moderate
Belgium	27	71	34	67	Moderate
Czech Republic	36	39	17	43	Low
France	12	61	20	47	Very low
Ireland	77	96	69	74	High
Italy	53	93	64	86	High
Luxembourg	80	73	32	63	Moderate
Portugal	51	96	62	88	High
Spain	35	83	37	64	Moderate

* Data from 1999 World Values Survey.

once circled the entire Mediterranean Sea. But by 800, the north coast of Africa had come under Muslim rule, and the remains of the Roman Empire in the East had shrunk to the much smaller Orthodox Christian Byzantine Empire. For the first time, people in the West were coming to see themselves as a distinct region of the world, set apart not just by geography but also by religion. In contrast to the Islamic lands of the south and to the Orthodox lands of the east, Western Europe was the land of Catholic faith.

Throughout the medieval period and up to the late 1700s, church and state in Catholic Western Europe were wedded together in a system known as Christendom. In this system, there was a functional division of labor, with the church responsible for spiritual and eternal concerns and with the state in charge of public order and basic human needs. But there was ample overlap. The Catholic tradition stresses the social character of human ethics and assumes that the overall moral climate of a society has a huge impact on personal behavior. In Christendom, governments were expected to provide clear moral boundaries for society as a whole. The Catholic Church defined those moral boundaries, and the state was supposed to codify them in law and enforce them.

Christendom's assumption of church–state cooperation was never seriously questioned until the eighteenth century, when the leaders of the French Revolution proposed a radically different model for European society. The main goal of the Revolution was to sever the relationship of church and state and to erect a new form of government based solely on the will of the people. No longer would the Catholic Church be allowed to dictate morals and belief; every person would make those decisions for himself or herself. The Revolution ultimately failed, and life in France and the rest of Catholic Europe more or less returned to the old order during the nineteenth century. Yet the church had been permanently affected, often adopting a defensive posture against perceived enemies that included democracy, church–state separation, public education, and even freedom of the press.

During the early years of the twentieth century this defensiveness slowly diminished. After the Second Vatican Council, the Catholic Church began to embrace the notions of modern democracy and religious freedom, while simultaneously developing a range of ecclesiastical, social, and cultural programs intended to shape the moral contours of Western Europe into accord with Catholic teaching. The general liberalization of European norms and mores that began in the 1960s exposed inadequacies in this approach. In the last 25 years, the pendulum has accordingly swung back, and the Catholic Church is trying to adopt a public posture balanced somewhere between the reactionary stance of the nineteenth century and the progressive changes that were favored in the years immediately after Vatican II.

Church and politics in Spain

Historically, Spain has been one of the most fervently Catholic countries in Western Europe, and it is the home of some of the most famous saints in Catholic history, such as the sixteenth-century founder of the Jesuits, Ignatius Loyola, and Teresa of Avila, the renowned mystic and poet. More recently, Spain was the birthplace of Opus Dei, an organization begun in 1928 to encourage Catholic laypeople – especially those in the professions such as banking, law, and higher education – to aspire to the same level of holiness as that sought by devout monks and nuns. It was also in Spain that the Cursillos de Cristiandad movement (meaning "little course in Christianity") was launched in 1944 to deepen faith and foster spiritual leadership among the laity through attendance at intensive three-day retreats. Spanish Catholicism has also had a darker side. In 1492, King Ferdinand and Queen Isabella demanded that all Jews either convert to Catholic Christianity or leave the country, a ruling that was not formally rescinded until 1990.

The prevalence of Catholicism in Spain, as strong as it is, has not always translated into respect for the hierarchy of the Roman Catholic Church. It has often centered instead on local saints, local apparitions of Mary, and local traditions of communal and family piety. Bishops and priests who have tried to bring local practice into closer accord with the official teachings of the Roman Catholic Church have often been resisted, resented, and even removed from office. In fact, there is a long tradition of outright anticlericalism in Spain, especially in the realm of politics, that has had terrible costs for the church. During the Spanish Civil War (1936–39), anticlerical Republicans specifically targeted

Figure 8.5   Francesco Franco and wife taking communion at Sunday Mass (1952)
© Dimitri Kessel/Time & Life Pictures/Getty Images

more than 6,000 priests, monks, and nuns for assassination in an attempt to break the political power of the Catholic Church.

The Spanish Civil War was brought to an end by General Francisco Franco, who then ruled as a semidictatorial president from 1939 to 1975. During Franco's rule, the Roman Catholic Church was restored to a position of prominence in Spanish society under the rubric of "National Catholicism." National Catholicism meant, among other things, that Catholicism was the only legally recognized religion in the country (although other faiths could be practiced in private), that the government paid the salaries of bishops and priests and basically underwrote the church's entire budget, and that the teaching of Catholic doctrine was required in all Spanish schools. National Catholicism also meant that Franco himself claimed the right to approve or veto virtually every clerical appointment in the country. This kind of conservative church–state alliance was consistent with the policies of the Catholic Church then current in most of Western Europe. There was great fear in the Vatican that the forces of democracy, socialism, and modern culture were antithetical to devout Catholic faith, and the church believed that strong state support for Catholic moral and religious values would be a bulwark against the advancing forces of sin and secularity.

This reactionary understanding of the relationship between Roman Catholic faith and modern society was eventually jettisoned by the Second Vatican Council, and the impact in Spain was immediate. Bishops and other church leaders were instructed to distance themselves from Franco and his autocratic ways, and new clerical appointments in Spain were almost always given to more progressive (pro-Vatican II) bishops and priests. Responding to these changes, Franco removed some of the restrictions against other religions in 1967, but he simultaneously reaffirmed the special privileges of the Catholic Church. It was not until several years after Franco's death that the Spanish Constitution of 1978 formally decreed the separation of church and state and promised full religious freedom for all citizens. Separation of church and state did not, however, mean separation of Catholicism from Spanish culture, and the church remained a strong presence in the country. In particular, Catholic doctrine continued to be taught in the schools and the Catholic Church continued to receive substantial funding from the government. Even today, roughly one-third of the church's budget is paid by the government, and this is further subsidized with a voluntary tax that the state collects on behalf of the church.

While other religious groups are now legally allowed to operate in the country, none of them has been granted a similar financial arrangement with the government. Until very recently, complaints about government foot-dragging were common, especially in matters related to the construction of non-Catholic religious buildings and permits for public events. Such dilatoriness may partly explain why non-Catholic Christianity remains a minimal presence in Spain, but it also seems that Spaniards (in contrast, for example, to Catholics in Latin America) are not particularly attracted to either Protestant or Pentecostal/Charismatic forms of Christianity. There are currently only about 300,000 non-Catholic Christians in the country, scattered into slightly more than 1,000 local congregations. Roughly 40 percent of these congregations are Pentecostal/Charismatic, with the next largest groups being, in order of size, Baptist, Brethren, interdenominational, and Presbyterian.

Since the 1980s, the dynamics have been changing both in the Catholic Church and in Spanish politics. The liberalization of social norms in the late 1960s and 1970s – especially those related to sexuality – and declining church attendance numbers convinced the Catholic leadership that the stance of Vatican II might have been overly optimistic. The election of Pope John Paul II in 1978 further shifted the landscape. While very much a supporter of human rights and religious freedom in Eastern Europe, John Paul II took a more conservative stance in the West. The Pope was particularly disappointed with the way the church in Spain had so easily given up political power in a country that was almost 90 percent Catholic. He began to appoint new, more conservative bishops who he hoped would be more convincing as religious leaders and more willing to reassert church authority in matters of public faith and morals.

With the generally conservative and prochurch People's Party (PP) in charge of the Spanish government from 1996 to 2004, this policy seemed to be working quite well. But the Spanish Socialist Workers Party (PSOE) unexpectedly won the elections in 2004, and the equation was upset. Led by José Luis Rodriguez Zapatero, the PSOE had campaigned on a liberal platform of economic reform, of withdrawal of Spanish troops from the war in Iraq, and of relaxation of laws related to divorce, abortion, and gay marriage. And they followed through on all their promises once in office. In 2007, the new government also changed the rules related to religion and values in the public school system. While continuing to allow religious education on a voluntary basis, the state mandated a new course in civics, called

Educación para la Ciudadanía, which focused on the importance of mutual tolerance in a pluralistic society.

The church was appalled and worried, and some leaders said the PSOE was launching a frontal attack on the Roman Catholic Church. The Archbishop of Madrid called the new government "a hotbed of sin." Pope John Paul himself said in 2004 that the Zapatero government was "promoting disdain toward religion" and that he would not allow the church to be silenced by threats or intimidation. During the lead-up to the 2008 elections, the Spanish Catholic Church organized a huge "Christian Family Day" protest in Madrid at which bishop after bishop fulminated against the PSOE and called on all faithful Catholics to vote the PSOE out of office and the PP into office.

But they may have overplayed their hand. The PSOE won the election, with 43 percent of the vote compared to only 38 percent of the vote for the PP. Prior to the election, the PSOE had defended itself by criticizing the Catholic Church for becoming blatantly partisan in its politicking, and by questioning how it could be accused of being anti-Catholic when the government was still underwriting about 30 percent of the Catholic Church's annual budget. The party also suggested that the bishops were simply out of touch with popular Catholic opinion. Public polls showed, for example, that roughly 70 percent of the Spanish population supported the PSOE initiative to legalize gay marriage. A wide variety of grassroots Catholic organizations, including some associations of priests, criticized the bishops for focusing on a handful of divisive issues while ignoring other issues of equal concern to working families. Survey data also suggest that these developments have had a negative impact on Spanish religiosity in general. In particular, the latest figures from the World Values Survey indicate that the percentage of the Spanish population attending church monthly dropped from 35 percent in 1999 to 22 percent in 2008. The numbers for almost all the other nations of Western Europe held relatively even during this same time span.

The outcome of the 2008 election has raised a series of tough questions for the leadership of the Spanish Catholic Church. What are its priorities? What is the best way forward? Has it created a rift between the leadership and the Spanish Catholic population as a whole? The history of the twentieth century shows that the Roman Catholic Church is still struggling to come up with an approach to politics and public life that can work in modern Western Europe. The fact that a strategy of direct confrontation failed so miserably in a country that is as solidly Catholic as Spain underscores the issue facing the entire region: how are Catholic faith and practice best nurtured in a pluralistic world in which being Catholic is becoming ever more a matter of choice rather than a permanent identity assumed at birth?

Christianity, Islam, and the limits of secularism in France

The increasing visibility of Islam in Western Europe is beginning to reshape questions of religion and public life. This is a concern in many countries. Germany worries about how to mainstream the more than three million Muslims (4 percent of the population) who live within its borders, the United Kingdom is concerned about calls by some of its Muslim residents (4 percent of the population) to introduce aspects of Shari'a law into the British legal system, and tensions between Muslims and non-Muslims in Netherlands (Muslims account for 5 percent of the population) have been at boiling point ever since the murder of film producer Theo van Gogh after he made a controversial 2004 documentary called *Submission* about the treatment of women in Islam. But the real case study for the future of Islam in Europe is found in France, where Muslims now make up about roughly 8 percent of the population – and the way Islam is treated in highly secularized France has significant implications for Christianity as well.

In terms of adherents, Islam is the second largest religion in France, ahead of both Protestantism and Judaism. Compared to the country's Roman Catholic population (47 million), the number of Muslims is small, but compared to practicing Catholics – when no more than one in ten French Catholics is attending Mass in a given week – the number of Muslims looks considerably more significant. Given that the French Muslim population has more than tripled since 1970, France as a whole is unsettled about demographic projections for 2025 or 2050. This uneasiness has been exploited by the National Front politician Jean-Marie Le Pen, who argues that immigration has to stop to keep the true French "Nation" (which he identifies as the historical, white, "indigenous" Christian citizenry of the country) from becoming extinct.

Le Pen's fear of "foreigners" is extreme, but many French citizens worry that the growing Muslim population may change France as they know it – and religion is at the core of this concern. The concern is not just that Muslims follow a different religion from that of the majority, it is that most Muslims consider faith and public life to go hand in hand. This understanding is at odds with the long-standing French policy of *laïcité,* the idea that religion and public affairs should not overlap.

The roots of *laïcité* go back to the "Declaration of the Rights of Man and of the Citizen" – a statement of political first principles formulated in 1789 at the beginning of the French Revolution – written partly to protect French citizens from the coercive social and political power of the Roman Catholic Church. The Declaration links individual religious freedom with public harmony, saying that "no one shall be disquieted on account of his opinions, including his religious views, provided their manifestation does not disturb the public order established by law." In force for a short time during the French Revolution, *laïcité* was set aside by Napoleon Bonaparte in 1801 when he signed a Concordat (a religious treaty) with the Vatican, restoring the Roman Catholic Church to a place of special honor in France. During the nineteenth century the religious activities of the Catholic Church were largely funded by the state, and non-Catholics – Protestants, freethinkers, and Jews – were treated as second-class citizens. The policy of *laïcité* was restored in 1905 under new legislation that ended the special status of Catholicism, mandated separation of church and state, and established religious freedom on the condition that public order is not disturbed.

The new visibility of Islam in France is calling into question the idea of *laïcité* – at least as it has been traditionally understood. The flashpoint has been the *hijab* (headscarf) and whether Muslim schoolgirls are allowed to wear it in the public schools (see Plate 11). Does the wearing of a *hijab* somehow "disturb the public order" of the classroom? There is no question that wearing the *hijab* is a public statement of religious affiliation, much like wearing a yarmulke or a crucifix, but historically wearing a yarmulke or a crucifix has never raised concerns. For many French citizens, however, the *hijab* is somehow more ominous, a symbol of radical Islam (in contrast to "ordinary" Islam) that is staunchly opposed to both modern French secularism and historical French Christianity. Some question if wearing the *hijab* is the free choice of the schoolgirls themselves or whether they are being forced to wear it by their parents or their religious communities. If that is the case, then the French state sees itself as having the responsibility to ban the practice because *laïcité* was formulated precisely to protect individuals against that kind of coercive religious power. Still others wonder if France is as genuinely secular as it claims to be and whether the fuss about Muslim headscarves might be an expression of latent Christian prejudice. The "headscarf controversy" began in the 1980s and became more heated in the 1990s. Eventually the French President and Parliament banned the display of any "ostentatious" religious symbols in the public schools. But if the French leadership thought a new law would end the issue, they were mistaken. Instead, the dispute has broadened into a wider public conversation about religion's place in French society.

The President of France, Nicolas Sarkozy (elected in 2007), has called for a fundamental re-examination of the place of religion in France (see Plate 12). Sarkozy, who heads the center-right Union for a Popular Movement (UPM) political party and describes himself as a "cultural Catholic," has suggested that France may need to adopt a more active or open secularism that is genuinely committed to religious freedom. Sarkozy's attitudes were shaped to some degree by his experience as Minister of the Interior, the agency that oversees the government's relationship with religious communities. At the time of his appointment, the Muslim community had no organized body for dealing with the French government, and Sarkozy helped them form a national Council of the Muslim Faith. He also suggested that the French government might provide partial funding for the construction and operation of French mosques. His reasoning was both idealistic and practical. On the one hand, he wanted "the Republic to be a Republic of real, not virtual rights. What good does it do to tell our Muslim compatriots that they have the same rights as anyone, if they have to pray in basements and garages?"[2] Since the French government, despite its commitment to *laïcité*, still pays for maintenance on all Catholic churches built before 1905, Sarkozy's proposal seems reasonable. Additionally, Sarkozy worried that lack of public funding was forcing the Muslim community to look elsewhere for support, typically outside of France and sometimes from extremist sources.

Many French leaders in the recent past have expressed concern about the potential problems caused by religion, but Sarkozy focuses on religion's positive contributions. He observes that religion often provides people with hope and moves them to care for the poor, and he praises the contemplative life of monks and nuns, saying that reflection on faith and life undertaken in solitude can be a helpful counterpoint to the frantic pace of modern existence. He also makes a case for the public funding of religion, arguing that "there is a contradiction between the desire to acknowledge the religions as a positive factor in society and completely denying them any form of public financing."[3] In other parts of the world, positively valuing religion is typically unrelated to public funding, but in Western Europe, favor and funding have almost always gone together. Addressing the issue of secularism and Christianity, Sarkozy says "we should uphold both sides – accept the Christian roots of France ... while defending secularism."[4] While each of these issues could be examined in detail, the real significance lies in the big picture of what is happening in France. That is, the mere fact that France is once again debating the place of religion in the public square is itself a powerful signal of how much the religious dynamics of the continent are changing.

Table 8.3 The four main Christian traditions in Protestant and religiously mixed Europe (% of total population)

Country	Population	Catholic	Protestant	Pentecostal/ Charismatic	Orthodox
Denmark	5,500,000	1%	85%	2%	–
Finland	5,200,000	–	85%	6%	1%
Germany	83,000,000	33%	35%	2%	1%
Iceland	300,000	1%	90%	3%	–
Netherlands	16,250,000	34%	22%	4%	–
Norway	4,500,000	1%	85%	8%	–
Sweden	9,000,000	1%	85%	5%	1%
Switzerland	7,250,000	44%	38%	4%	1%
United Kingdom	59,000,000	9%	52%	5%	1%
Total	190,000,000	22%	46%	4%	1%

Protestant and Religiously Mixed Western Europe

The nine Western European nations of Denmark, Finland, Germany, Iceland, Netherlands, Norway, Sweden, Switzerland, and the United Kingdom are considerably less Catholic than the nations discussed above, and they are also somewhat less Christian overall (see Table 8.3), with only 75 percent being Christian compared with close to 90 percent in the predominantly Catholic nations. In Scandinavia and Iceland, Protestants – almost all of them Lutheran – make up the great majority of the population and Catholics account for less than 1 percent. The United Kingdom is also overwhelmingly Protestant, though its dominance is slightly less and the Catholic and Pentecostal/Charismatic populations are slightly larger than in Scandinavia. In the religiously mixed countries of Germany, the Netherlands, and Switzerland, the numbers of Catholics and Protestants are roughly even, though church–state relations tend for historical reasons to be organized in a generally more Protestant than Catholic fashion.

Most of the Protestant churches in Western Europe began as state churches – that is, they were first organized from the top down as the result of decisions by national rulers to declare their countries Protestant rather than Catholic. In this regard, Protestantism in Western Europe is different from Protestantism in much of the rest of the world. In many regions of the world, Protestantism has grown from the ground up, producing a wild flowering of different churches. In Western Europe, by contrast, Protestantism has been a much more orderly affair and much more closely coordinated with the state. This has especially been the case in Scandinavia, but it holds generally true for the rest of Protestant Western Europe as well.

Viewing themselves as churches of and for the people of their lands as a whole, Protestant Christianity in these countries has tended to blend smoothly into the various national cultures of the region. Often this has had positive results. The fact that these Protestant nations have some of the best health and social support networks found anywhere in the world is a reflection of the way that Christian values, in this case generosity and care for others, have been infused into the legal systems and public policies of these nations. But this same close association of faith and culture also produced some terrible results, with none more horrific

Table 8.4 Levels of religiosity in Protestant and religiously mixed Western Europe

Country	% Attend church monthly *	% Believe in God *	% Pray weekly *	% Religious person *	Overall religiosity
Denmark	12	69	20	77	Moderate
Finland	14	82	40	67	Moderate
Germany	23	53	29	46	Low
Iceland	12	84	42	74	Moderate
Netherlands	25	60	33	69	Moderate
Norway	12	69	–	47	Low
Sweden	9	53	–	39	Very low
Switzerland	24	83	–	57	Moderate
United Kingdom	19	72	29	42	Low

* Data from 1999 World Values Survey.

than the way in which Christians in Germany welcomed and supported Hitler and his Nazi regime. Only a small handful of Protestant pastors took a stand against the Nazification of the churches. Known as the "Confessing Church," this Protestant opposition group emphasized the costliness of following Christ in a culture that had become evil. Its most famous member was Dietrich Bonhoeffer (1906–45) who was arrested following a failed attempt to assassinate Hitler and was executed in 1945, just a month before the end of World War II.

Because Protestantism in these countries has a history of being closely merged with the national culture, it is not surprising that these churches have tended to internalize the secularism of the surrounding culture more quickly and more deeply than has been the case in the Catholic nations. Church attendance in Protestant Western Europe is generally abysmal, belief in God is low (especially if the inquiry is about belief in a personal God), prayer is largely neglected, and only about half think of themselves as being religious persons (see Table 8.4). Conventional Christian morality seems to be on the wane as well. In most of the region – and especially in the more Protestant countries – few couples marry before having children. The latest records from Norway show that more than 80 percent of first children are born to single mothers. In the United Kingdom, half of all children are born out of wedlock.

Turning to the religiously mixed nations of Germany, the Netherlands, and Switzerland, it is noteworthy that these countries produced some of the finest biblical and theological scholarship of the twentieth century, including

Figure 8.6 Two of the most important Western European theologians of the twentieth century
8.6a(TOP) Karl Rahner
© Topfoto/Ullstein Bild
8.6b(BOTTOM) Karl Barth
Courtesy of the Karl Barth Archiv, Basel, Germany

the work of Protestants like Karl Barth (1886–1968), Rudolph Bultmann (1884–1976), Abraham Kuyper (1837–1920), Jürgen Moltmann (born 1926), and Paul Tillich (1886–1965). Catholic theology flourished in these countries as well, including the work of Karl Rahner (1904–84), Hans Küng (born 1928), Edward Schillebeeckx (1914–2009), and Hans Urs von Balthasar (1905–88). It may be that working in a religiously mixed culture requires theologians and biblical scholars to be more careful in their labors and less apt to accept the taken-for-granted assumptions of their own tradition. Perhaps not surprisingly, the churches of these countries have been at the forefront of the global ecumenical movement since the early years of the twentieth century, and the headquarters of the World Council of Churches is located in Geneva, Switzerland.

The Scandinavian state churches

The church–state Protestant structure that exists in Scandinavia was once the Protestant norm, but today it is globally unique. Denmark serves as an example. King Christian III (ruled 1534–59) made Lutheranism the official religion of the nation in 1537, and he placed himself in charge. Technically that still holds true – the Danish monarch remains the official leader of the state church – but now virtually all oversight of the church is delegated to the government office of Ministry of Ecclesiastical Affairs. The very fact that a state church still exists in Denmark is amazing, however, since Denmark is one of the least church-attending and least God-believing countries in all of Europe. It is also constitutionally committed to religious freedom. Nonetheless, most Danes seem perfectly content to maintain Lutheranism as the state religion.

Membership in the Church of Denmark is voluntary – as it has been since 1849 – but roughly 85 percent of the population still belongs. Only about 10 percent shows up for services on a monthly basis, but more than half of the population attends at least once a year. Formerly, the state treasury funded the salaries of clergy and the operating budget of the church, but today the Church of Denmark is largely self-funding. Members contribute a portion of their earnings to the church through a local tax, ranging from 1 to 1.5 percent of annual income. The state collects this tax on behalf of the church and then adds a modest amount from the general tax to make ends meet. This means that every Dane, whether or not a member, contributes something to the maintenance of the church. In other countries this might lead to widespread protests, but in Denmark no one complains about the arrangement. Three-quarters of the people express high levels of trust in the church, making Denmark one of the most church-friendly nations in all of Western Europe.

A similar situation prevails in the rest of Scandinavia. Like Denmark, Norway and Iceland also maintain formal state churches, and both provide some funding for their churches; the Norwegian and Icelandic churches enjoy other privileges as well. In Norway, for example, at least half the members of the national Cabinet must belong to the state church, and in Iceland the state requires all new housing developments to include a free gift of land for the future construction of a church. Finland has a slightly different arrangement with two official state churches: a Lutheran state church for the Finnish majority and an Orthodox state church for ethnic Russians living in the eastern region of the country. In the past Sweden had an official Lutheran state church as well, but the church was disestablished in the year 2000. However, even though it is no longer formally bound to the state, everyone knows that Lutheranism is still functionally the national church of Sweden.

For non-Europeans, the term "state church" has connotations of government control, state bureaucracy, and lack of freedom, but that is not descriptive of the Scandinavian state churches, and it is certainly not true in Denmark. In fact, the Danish Church is set up to maximize local control of all church functions. There is no central governing authority, and every bishop is fully autonomous in his or her diocese (the first female bishop was ordained in 1995). The only significant government-imposed limitation is that state clergy, as paid employees of the state, are not to make any official statements either supporting or opposing government policy or legislation. This kind of "gag order" on the clergy is in keeping with the traditions of the church itself. More than 150 years ago, the Danish church leader N. S. F. Grundtvig developed a people-centered theology for the church that emphasized the differences between faith and politics, and he concluded that the church's role is to concentrate on matters of faith and not on government policies. Grundtvig's position was widely embraced, and since then the main focus of the church has been on nonpolitical religious activities such as worship, youth education, and life-cycle ceremonies like weddings and funerals.

The origins of the state church tradition in Scandinavia are both principled and pragmatic, and they can be traced back to Martin Luther himself. When Luther first broke with the Roman Catholic Church in the early years of the sixteenth century, he had no intention of casting aside the centuries-old Catholic vision of the church as the provider of spiritual aid for all the people of the local region or nation. Luther wanted to correct what he saw as the theological errors of Roman Catholicism, but he had no desire to undo the regional character or undercut the civic responsibility of the local church. In Luther's view, the church was called to serve as a conduit of divine grace for all the people; it was not supposed to be a special club for those who were unusually devout.

The Lutheran principle of public service continues to define the tradition. In the secular context of contemporary Scandinavia, this means that the state churches now operate rather like state-owned utilities.[5] They are there for anyone who needs them, but they do not impose themselves on anyone. People go to church for special events – holidays like Christmas and Easter and special family events like weddings, funerals, and baptisms – but they feel no pressure to attend on a regular basis. Like other public utilities such as water companies or electricity suppliers, the state churches of Scandinavia do not typically elicit warm feelings of appreciation, but most people seem reassured by the fact that they are there.

For most people this seems to be sufficient, but not for all. Some Scandinavians desire a more fervent faith, and typically this has found expression in a form of Christianity called Pietism. Pietism is a term used to describe a style of Protestantism that focuses on conversion, the affective experience of God in one's life, the devotional reading of the Bible, and the gathering together of small groups for prayer and mutual encouragement. Many Pietists stress the power of the Holy Spirit, and a majority of Pietistically oriented Protestants in Scandinavia could just as easily be described as Pentecostal/Charismatic. Most Pietistic Christians in Scandinavia remain members of the state churches, but they augment their practice of faith with a variety of other spiritual activities. Some Pietistic groups have also constructed their own small chapels (*bedehus*) where they gather with like-minded believers for study and prayer. The influence of Pietism varies significantly from country to country, with the strongest representation being in Norway, especially in the "Bible belt" located along the southeast coast.

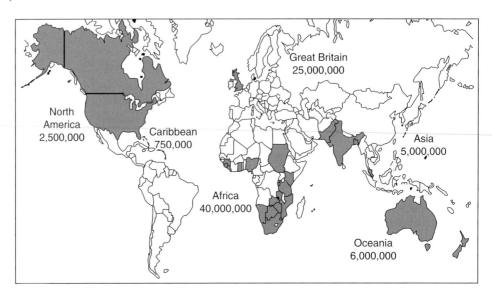

Figure 8.7   Anglican Communion: numbers by region (shaded nations have significant Anglican populations). Map by author.

Christianity in the United Kingdom

The headline story of Christianity in the United Kingdom in the twentieth century was one of decline. At the beginning of the century, the UK was perhaps the single most influential Christian nation in the world. It was the last of the great Western European colonial empires, and up until the end of World War II that empire – a mix of independent commonwealth nations, traditional colonies, and occupied territories – still circled the globe. For the most part, the British were colonial pragmatists. Their primary interests were in ease of governance and economic gain, rather than in promoting their own Protestant religion. Though religion was not overly emphasized, British-style Anglican Protestantism took deep root in much of the British imperial realm and has had a lasting influence. A map of the Anglican Communion today – all those churches that self-consciously identify with the Anglican (Church of England) tradition – reveals how deeply Anglicanism has taken root (see Figure 8.7). Almost 20 percent of all the Protestants in the world are now part of the Anglican Communion, and the numbers in Africa are particularly staggering: 40,000,000.

But while Anglican Christianity has spread like wildfire in some parts of the globe, precisely the opposite has been happening "at home." Rather than growing, the number of active members in the Church of England has been falling rather dramatically. Most reports still list the number of adherents within the British Isles as around 25,000,000, but that figure probably includes many people who would not describe themselves as church members. It is estimated that between 25 and 30 percent of Anglicans in the UK attended church on a regular basis in the year 1900. That that has dropped to about 4 percent today, with most of the decline taking place since the 1960s (see Figure 8.8). If regular attendance is viewed as the marker of active faith, active Anglicans in Africa probably outnumber active Anglicans in the UK today by about twenty to one.

The Church of England in the United Kingdom has always been internally diverse, a church where English men and women worshiped together despite their spiritual and theological differences. In recent years, however, it has been difficult to steer the church in a direction that will keep everyone together. Four discernible factions are evident: Anglo-Catholics, Evangelicals, Progressives, and the tolerant "Broad Church" that tries to glue the other three together.

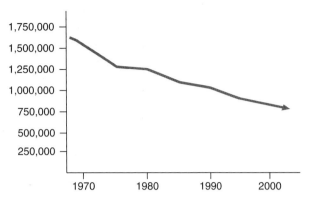

Figure 8.8   Members of the Church of England attending worship on a typical Sunday

Anglo-Catholics would like the Church of England as a whole to become more Catholic, and they have tried to create spaces in the church where Catholic-leaning Anglicans can feel at home. Their hope is that someday the Church of England will be able to reunite with the Roman Catholic Church without losing its distinctive Anglican character. In November 2009, Pope Benedict XVI announced new rules that made it easier for individual Anglican priests and bishops to be welcomed into the Catholic Church. Anglo-Catholics were simultaneously pleased and perplexed by this new policy. They appreciate the welcome that has been extended, but their goal is not simply to become Catholic, but to reunite the two churches. The pope's new policy may actually be a hindrance in that regard. A key issue for many Anglo-Catholics is the ordination of women as bishops. Currently the Church of England ordains women priests, but not as bishops. If that policy is changed – and it looks as though it will be – that action would largely close off any possibility of reunion with Rome. In that event, a good number of Anglo-Catholics may well leave the church, seeing conversion to Roman Catholicism as the only option left.

Evangelicals within the Church of England are probably the largest of the Anglican subgroups, representing perhaps 40 percent of the active members. Evangelical Anglicans are deeply concerned about what they see as the liberal drift of the church, especially regarding sexual ethics and gay and lesbian concerns. Tensions are high at the time of writing because many Evangelicals in the worldwide Anglican Communion boycotted the 2008 Lambeth Conference (a meeting of the global leadership of the Anglican Communion held once each decade) and instead attended a separate Evangelical Anglican meeting called the Global Anglican Future Conference (GAFCON) in Jerusalem. Many Anglican bishops in Africa feel that the Church of England has become apostate (supporting ideas and moral practices that contradict the gospel message), so much that they sometimes encourage Evangelical Anglicans worldwide, including those in the UK, to leave the church.

The third subgroup within the Church of England is the most recently formed and is progressive and socially liberal. Progressive Anglicans worry that the Church of England has been locked into an anachronistic past, something that has to be overcome if the church is to have any relevance in the future. In recent years, its focus has been on issues of gender and sexuality, favoring the ordination of gay and lesbian pastors (as both priests and bishops). What progressives fear most is often precisely what Evangelicals favor – close adherence to

Table 8.5   Ten largest denominations in the United Kingdom

Name of denomination	Membership
Church of England	25,000,000
Catholic Church	5,500,000
Church of Scotland	500,000
Church of Ireland	365,000
Methodist Church of Great Britain	330,000
Presbyterian Church in Ireland	300,000
Greek Orthodox Church	250,000
Church of Jesus Christ of Latter Day Saints	185,000
Baptist Union of Great Britain	140,000
Jehovah's Witnesses	125,000

doctrinal norms and sexual ethics of a past era that somehow are expected to strengthen the "traditional family." Anglican progressives are also deeply committed to the ordination of women as bishops, and that puts them more deeply at odds with both Anglo-Catholics and some Evangelicals.

Growing tensions among Anglo-Catholics, Evangelicals, and Progressives are making the task of the fourth group, Broad Church Anglican moderates, ever more difficult. Their calling is to hold the church as a whole together, but strategies are becoming harder to formulate. The Archbishop of Canterbury is the religious head of the Church of England and, almost by definition, the leader of the Broad Church movement since church unity is one of the most important responsibilities of the office. The present Archbishop, Rowan Williams, is a trained theologian of keen intelligence, and it will take all of his considerable intellectual and spiritual gifts to hold the Church of England and the global Anglican Communion together in the years ahead.

The Church of England represents just over 60 percent of the total Christian population of the UK. The rest of its Christians are scattered among a variety of other churches, but by far the largest is the Catholic Church, with about five and a half million members. (See Table 8.5.)

At various times and places during the last five hundred years, members of the Catholic Church have been subjected to persecution in the United Kingdom. The so-called "troubles" of Northern Ireland – a period of extreme tension lasting from 1968 to 1998 – is the most recent, involving both Catholic–Protestant violence and Irish armed resistance to British political rule. Apart from Northern Ireland, however, Catholic–Anglican relations were generally cordial in the twentieth century, much more so than in the preceding centuries. Currently, the Catholic Church seems to be maintaining its membership and involving most of its members in parish life relatively well, despite having a somewhat quirky administrative structure. Rather than being overseen by one ecclesiastical hierarchy, Catholicism in the United Kingdom is organized into three separate and distinct ecclesiastical jurisdictions: the Catholic Church of England and Wales (4,250,000 members), the Catholic Church in Scotland (750,000 members), and the Catholic Church in Ireland (500,000 members).

There are no other church groups in the UK that compare in size to the Catholic and Anglican churches, but most of them, regardless of size, have been affected by the same general disenchantment with organized religion that has decimated the Church of England. The only obvious exceptions are found among the many immigrant churches that now exist in most of the UK's cities. Many of these immigrant churches are vibrant and growing, and often they stand out like shining lights in the otherwise bleak British religious environment.

The Kingsway International Christian Centre in London is one of these new immigrant churches. Very few Londoners attend church, yet Kingsway packs in 10,000 worshipers every Sunday for a three-hour worship service. The church was founded in 1992 by the Nigerian-born Matthew Ashimolowo who preaches a pulsating Pentecostal/Charismatic message of personal salvation and the power of God. Originally a single congregation, Kingsway is quickly becoming a transnational denomination with branch churches popping up in the counties surrounding London as well as in the West African nations of Ghana and Nigeria. It is also slowly reaching out beyond the African and Caribbean immigrant community that forms the bulk of its membership to include white Britons as well.

The overall picture of Christianity in the UK confirms the image of Western Europe as a region where Christianity is slowly dying, but churches like the Kingsway Centre provide evidence to the contrary – that, in some places, Christianity is still very much alive. Viewing the situation in that way, it is easy to envision churches like Kingsway as small religious seedlings growing out of the cracks in a landscape that is otherwise paved over with secularism. But that image by itself does not do justice to the data. While Western Europe is clearly less publicly Christian than it once was, there is still plenty of Christianity around. That Christianity can be found in the Catholic Church, in the old Protestant state churches, in the newer immigrant churches like Kingsway, and in a host of other Christian initiatives that have begun or been revived in recent years. Given the massive degree of change that has taken place in the last half century, it is possible that Christianity is moving toward extinction in Western Europe. But it is just as possible that the decline of Christianity is actually part of a transitional trough that may turn upward in the future. Whatever the case, Christianity in Western Europe most certainly is not yet dead, and it continues to play a significant role in the Christian movement globally.

Notes

1 See http://www.vatican.va/holyfather/johnpaulii/encyc-licals/documents/hfjp-iienc15101998fides-et-ratioen.html.

2 Quoted in "Nicolas Sarkozy: La loi de 1905 est un monument," La-Croix.com (April 2008), http://www.la-croix.com/article/index.jsp?docId=2299411&rubId=4076# (accessed August 30, 2008).

3 Quoted in Carlo Cardia, "Even the République Needs Religion," Chiesa On Line (May 11, 2006), http://chiesa.

espresso.repubblica.it/articolo/55661?&eng=y (accessed August 30, 2008).

4 Quoted in "Sarkozy Sparks Debate in France Over Religion in Public Life," European Jewish Press (January 18, 2008), http://www.ejpress.org/article/23286 (accessed August 30, 2008).

5 This image comes from Grace Davie, *Europe – the Exceptional Case: Parameters of Faith in the Modern World* (London: Darton, Longman, and Todd, 2002), p. 138.

Suggestions for Further Reading

Atkin, Nicholas and Frank Tallett (2003). *Priests, Prelates, and People: A History of European Catholicism since 1750*. Oxford, Oxford University Press.

Buruma, Ian (2006). *Murder in Amsterdam: Liberal Europe, Islam, and the Limits of Toleration*. New York: Penguin.

Davie, Grace (2000). *Religion in Modern Europe: A Memory Mutates*. Oxford: Oxford University Press.

Davie, Grace (2002). *Europe – the Exceptional Case: Parameters of Faith in the Modern World*. London: Darton, Longman, and Todd.

Jenkins, Philip (2007). *God's Continent: Christianity, Islam, and Europe's Religious Crisis*. Oxford, Oxford University Press.

Madeley, John T. S. and Zsolt Enyedi (eds) (2003). *Church and State in Contemporary Europe: The Chimera of Neutrality*. London: Frank Cass.

Michalski, Krzysztorf (ed.) (2006). *Religion in the New Europe*. Budapest: Central European University Press.

Rémond, René (1999). *Religion and Society in Modern Europe*. Oxford: Blackwell.

Rosman, Doreen (2003). *The Evolution of the English Churches, 1500–2000*. Cambridge, UK: Cambridge University Press.

Ryman, Björn, Aila Lauha, Gunnar Heiene, and Peter Lodberg (2005). *Nordic Folk Churches: A Contemporary Church History*. Grand Rapids, MI: Eerdmans.

Taylor, Charles (2007). *A Secular Age*. Cambridge, MA: Harvard University Press.

Ward, Kevin (2006). *A History of Global Anglicanism*. Cambridge, UK: Cambridge University Press.

Chapter 9

Sub-Saharan Africa

Hope and Despair

Africa is the continent where human life began. It is the homeland of us all, and the forces of life run deep. Most African cultures assume the interconnectedness of life across time, and even those who have died are considered to have an active presence among the living members of the community. The birth of a child is seen as a blessing and the whole village is involved in the nurture and development of the young. Outsiders who visit Africa quickly observe that family and community are central to life in Africa and that hope is the glue of society. Although these core values hold true across the region, it is also true that Africa is a vast and diverse place. In particular, the countries of North Africa that rim the south coast of the Mediterranean Sea were exposed to influences so different from the rest of the continent that they are discussed elsewhere (see Chapter 5). This chapter focuses on the 43 countries that make up sub-Saharan Africa. These 40 countries have many overlapping concerns, but they also have many different stories to tell.

Kofi Annan, the Ghanaian former Secretary-General of the United Nations, once noted that it is important when speaking of Africa "not to mistake hope for achievement." And, indeed, realities on the ground in contemporary Africa can be cause for despair. The present condition of Africa is at least partly the result of a long and brutal history of interaction with the West (and also the Muslim Middle East), a history that involved the slave trade, followed by colonization, followed by various forms of loans and "assistance" that have rendered the continent economically weak, deeply in debt, and struggling with social and political problems that seem almost insurmountable. Africa is also facing a health crisis due to HIV/AIDS and malaria, along with a host of other diseases, which cost billions of dollars a year and cause horrific loss of life. And yet, despite all these troubles, most Africans still manage to be people of hope.

In most parts of the world, hope and despair are understood to be contradictory responses to life – one cannot possess both at the same time – but Africans manage to combine the two.

The World's Christians: Who they are, Where they are, and How they got there, First Edition. Douglas Jacobsen.

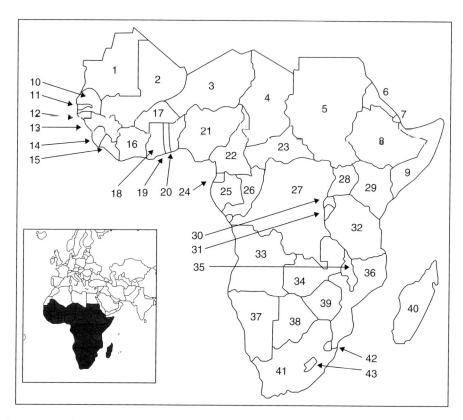

Figure 9.1   Sub-Saharan Africa. Map by author.

1	Mauritania	16	Côte D'Ivoire	31	Burundi
2	Mali	17	Burkina Faso	32	Tanzania
3	Niger	18	Ghana	33	Angola
4	Chad	19	Togo	34	Zambia
5	Sudan	20	Benin	35	Malawi
6	Eritrea	21	Nigeria	36	Mozambique
7	Djibouti	22	Cameroon	37	Namibia
8	Ethiopia	23	Central African Rep	38	Botswana
9	Somalia	24	Equatorial Guinea	39	Zimbabwe
10	Senegal	25	Gabon	40	Madagascar
11	The Gambia	26	Republic of Congo	41	South Africa
12	Guinea-Bissau	27	Dem. Rep. of Congo	42	Swaziland
13	Guinea	28	Uganda	43	Lesotho
14	Sierra Leone	29	Kenya		
15	Liberia	30	Rwanda		

Total population: 750,000,000 (12% of global population); Christian population: 405,000,000 (54% of regional population, 20% of global Christian population): Orthodox 35,000,000, Catholics 140,000,000, Protestants 115,000,000, Pentecostal/Charismatic 115,000,000.

This mixing of hope and despair is predicated on the belief that life is often paradoxical, that the experiences of life transcend logic. This understanding of life as paradox is reflected in the proverbs that have been passed down from generation to generation in many different African cultures. A well-known West African proverb asserts that "suffering and happiness are twins." In Ghana, people say "it is difficult to tell whether a swimmer is drowning or not." A proverb from Angola promises that "neither pain nor pleasure endures." And a Burundian saying reminds those who are suffering that "even a night with no rooster will eventually end."

The mixing of hope and despair that is part of African culture in general is also part of African Christianity. In fact, the dichotomies within Christianity may be even starker than those in society at large. On the one hand, Christianity has expanded in sub-Saharan Africa at a rate without parallel in world history, from fewer than 10 million Christians in 1900 to more than 400 million Christians today. Those numbers are staggering. Clearly there is something in the Christian message and way of life that is powerfully attractive in the African context, something that provides hope in an all too often bleak world.

Beneath the numbers, however, despair lurks in the shadows, and it occasionally bursts into full view. One of the worst eruptions of despair took place in the small central African country of Rwanda in 1994 (see Plate 13). Two ethnic groups predominate in Rwanda: the majority Hutus and the minority Tutsis. For most of the first half of the twentieth century, the Tutsis ruled the nation but from the 1960s to the mid-1990s, Hutus were in charge. Fearing that Tutsis were organizing to regain power through military means, and driven by intense ethnic hatred, the Hutu leadership of Rwanda handed out machetes and encouraged Hutus across the country to kill their Tutsi neighbors. The genocide began early in April 1994 and lasted until the end of May. When it was over, more than 85 percent of the Tutsi population was dead – 800,000 people in all.

What is particularly shocking from a Christian point of view is that at the time of these killings Rwanda was one of the most Christian nations in all of Africa, considered by many to be the jewel of the African Christian world. The Rwandan King Mutara IV had formally dedicated the country to "Christ the King" in 1946 and by the mid-1990s roughly 90 percent of the Rwandan population was Christian. Yet one of the worst genocides in modern history took place there. Some Hutu Christians did try to protect some Tutsis during the massacre, but virtually all the killers were Christians, and there were some instances in which Christian clergy from various churches and members of the Catholic religious orders aided Hutus in their hunt for Tutsis to kill. In the aftermath of the genocide, the Christian churches of Rwanda have struggled to understand their own complicity in the moral failure of the nation, and deep questions remain about the character of Rwandan Christianity. Christians across Africa must now ask themselves the nagging question: "If this could happen in Rwanda, what evil might suddenly erupt elsewhere in Christian Africa?"

Colonization and Independence

It is impossible to understand contemporary African Christianity without some understanding of the crucible of European colonization and decolonization. The European colonization of Africa began in the nineteenth century only a few years after the international

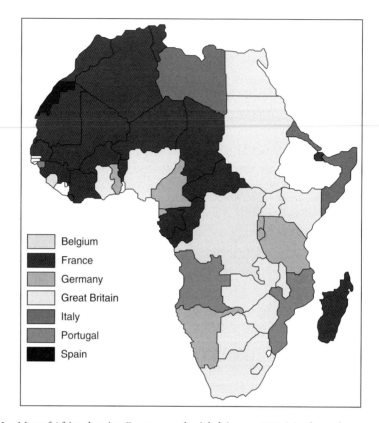

Figure 9.2   Map of Africa showing European colonial claims, c. 1920. Map by author.

trade in African slaves was brought to an end. Deprived of the free use of black labor outside of Africa, Europeans decided to put Africans to work for Europe's benefit within the borders of Africa itself. In some ways, participating in the colonization of Africa became a European fad. Once a few European countries claimed African land for themselves, the others felt compelled to do the same. In fact, the competition for colonies became so intense that it came to be called the "scramble for Africa" as country after country raced south to claim their little bit of the "dark continent" before it was too late.

The colonizing nations recognized that their competition for land could easily turn into armed conflict, and in order to reduce the risk of war, they convened a conference in Berlin in 1885 to parcel out the lands of Africa among the different interested European powers: Belgium, Britain, France, Germany, the Netherlands, Italy, Portugal, and Spain. By 1915, nearly every inch of Africa had been claimed by some European power. Ethiopia and Liberia were the sole exceptions to this land grab, but even here foreign influence was strong – Italy in Ethiopia and the United States in Liberia. Most national borders in contemporary Africa continue to follow colonial boundaries that were drawn up in the boardrooms and royal halls of Europe at the end of the nineteenth century, even though these borders often fail to follow logical geographic boundaries or traditional cultural and tribal zones.

The rush out of Africa began around 1960, with the European scramble out of Africa taking place even more quickly than the scramble in. Initially some European nations tried to slow the process, suggesting that Africans needed decades or even centuries to develop the skills of self-rule, but Africans would tolerate no such dithering and demanded immediate independence. In the end, the fear of revolution combined with increasing costs drove the Europeans to pack their bags and leave. In 1960 alone, 16 new nations came into existence. Within a decade and a half, almost all of Africa was independent. Zimbabwe and Namibia were among the few nations to obtain freedom later than 1975, winning independence in 1980 and 1990, respectively.

The rhetoric of African independence was grand. The continent's new leaders, many of whom had been educated at Christian mission schools, spoke about their nations in glowing terms, proclaiming them models for all humanity. They promoted the notion that Africa was a continent of natural socialism – a place where community was at the heart of life, where Jesus's Golden Rule (treating others as you would want to be treated yourself) was part of local tradition, and where people genuinely cared for each other. In Senegal, Léopold Senghor called this new African way of life *negritude*. In Tanzania, Julius Nyerere called it *ujamaa,* a Swahili word meaning "familyhood" or "cooperativity." Many of Africa's new leaders were also given honorific titles or claimed them for themselves. Ghana's President Kwame Nkrumah, for example, was called "Osagyefo," a word that means "redeemer." Nkrumah himself was a Catholic Christian, but some Ghanaian Christians were offended by the application of this particular term to an earthly ruler when it should be reserved for Jesus alone. Most Ghanaians, however, considered the term inoffensive, akin to calling someone the "father of the nation."

Regardless of the glorious rhetoric and the grand titles, the realities of life in Africa soon began to worsen rather than improve. Once installed in office, many of the formerly idealistic leaders of African independence became enamored with power and luxury, lining their pockets and those of their friends with enormous wealth while ignoring the needs of the poor. Economic ruin was often the result and frequently that ruin led to nondemocratic forms of government as government leaders tried to protect their wealth by ruling unopposed. In country after country, political dissent was crushed and one-party rule was instituted. But even if the leadership had been better, the transition to independence in Africa would have been difficult. Defined as they were by colonial boundaries that ignored the African social landscape, many of the new African nations were a mishmash of groups who shared little in common. National identity has always been difficult to construct in Africa because of this fact.

The geopolitics of the Cold War in the second half of the twentieth century created other challenges for democracy in postcolonial Africa. During this era the United States and the Soviet Union (USSR) were constantly seeking allies in their global competition. As the independent states of Africa came into existence, the new rulers were offered gifts, loans, and military assistance in exchange for their allegiance. The only condition was ideological agreement with either Western capitalism or Soviet Communism, and concerns like justice or nation building were often treated as inconsequential. Since the end of the Cold War in the late 1980s, the situation has changed. On the positive side, many African countries have experienced some improvement in the political realm. Without foreign support, leaders have had to become more accountable to their own people, and multiparty politics and democratic rule have become much stronger. But

Table 9.1   Social and economic data for 10 largest African nations

Nation	Total population	Median age (years)	Life expectancy (years)	GDP per capita (US$)	Literacy (%)
Nigeria	135,000,000	18.7	47	938	69
Ethiopia	77,000,000	18.1	53	221	36
DR Congo	58,000,000	16.3	47	150	67
South Africa	48,000,000	24.5	49	6,239	82
Tanzania	38,500,000	17.8	53	358	69
Sudan	36,500,000	18.9	59	1,262	61
Kenya	35,000,000	18.6	54	799	74
Uganda	29,000,000	15.0	52	368	67
Ghana	22,000,000	20.4	60	649	58
Mozambique	20,000,000	17.4	42	389	39
World average		28.0	66	8,125	79

the end of the Cold War also signaled a global decline of interest in Africa, and the continent's economy has suffered because of that neglect.

By almost all measures, life in Africa today is bleak (see Table 9.1). Per capita GDP for most African countries is about 10 percent of the global average – about 1 percent of the per capita GDP in the United States and Great Britain. Literacy, which provides a rough measure of education and overall well-being, and other socioeconomic measures are also low. AIDS and other infectious diseases have reduced life expectancy in most of sub-Saharan Africa to under 50 years (the global average is 66 years) and the median age for the continent is under 20 years (the global average is 28 years). The African experience is, of course, not uniform. Some nations, such as Botswana, Equatorial Guinea, Gabon, and South Africa, are doing quite well economically and politically, but other nations, like Burundi, Malawi, Sierra Leone, and Zimbabwe, are on the brink of collapse.

The international community has struggled with how to respond to African needs. The United Nations, a number of national governments, some corporations, and many humanitarian organizations have offered assistance, but the problems seem to grow despite these contributions. In addition to the significant aid provided by the United States and Europe, China and Saudi Arabia are also becoming more involved in Africa. China, in particular, has come to Africa looking for oil and other natural resources and it tends to ignore issues of human rights and social justice. This has made Chinese trade and economic assistance especially attractive to rogue governments such as those of Sudan under the rule of Omar Hasan Ahmad al-Bashir (begun in 1993) and Zimbabwe during the later years of Robert Mugabe's long tenure as president (begun in 1987).

One of the saddest ironies of African life is that the continent's economic woes are exacerbated by one of Africa's great strengths, the family. Most Africans believe that a large family is a blessing. But the blessing of having many children is turning into a curse for the continent as the total population increases. In 1950, there were 200 million people living in Africa. Today there are 750 million, and the population is projected to be 1.6 billion or more by 2050. Food production has declined in Africa during the last two decades and many African nations can no longer feed themselves, so the burgeoning population is making mere survival a little more difficult every day.

Christianity and Colonialism

Christianity and colonialism were closely connected in Africa. While Christianity had been present before the colonial era (most notably in Congo and Ethiopia), it was colonization that allowed Christianity to penetrate the interior of the continent. Europe's colonialist ambitions were predicated on an assumption that its own "advanced" culture should be imposed on all of Africa, and Christianity was clearly part of that culture. Yet the marriage between Christianity and colonialism was not always amicable or smooth. European colonial powers were far more interested in economic endeavors than religious conversion, and they sometimes even created roadblocks to limit the work of Christian missionaries.

The majority of the Catholic missionaries in Africa were from France, but the government of France was resolutely secular and made no attempts to facilitate the work of their missioners. The French authorities liked the fact that Catholic missionaries were willing to provide education on the cheap, but they were leery of everything else. On the Protestant side, England was the largest colonial power, and it too was relatively cool toward Christian missions despite being a self-professed Christian nation. British colonial policy was pragmatic, aiming to operate in the most efficient and least locally offensive manner. In many regions of British Africa, this meant placing restrictions on missionary activity in predominantly Muslim areas where conversions would have led to social unrest. While there were places in colonial Africa where church–state cooperation was the norm, especially in the areas controlled by Belgium and Portugal where the relationship between the church and the colonial state was quite cozy, these were the exception rather than the norm. In the end, however, the distance that often existed between Christianity and colonial rule was a boon for the spread of Christianity in Africa. That gap helped the African people to look past the ugliness of colonial rule and salvage something positive out of European Christianity. That refined nugget of positive Christian ideas and ideals became the core around which various new African visions of Christianity would eventually emerge.

Some credit for the Africanization of Christianity should be given to the missionaries who demonstrated genuine compassion and concern for the people of the continent and who put great effort into communicating the gospel in African terms. But the key people in this process were the many local African believers who became either catechists or self-appointed prophets to their own people. Catechists (most of whose names were never recorded) were unordained local believers who worked with Christian missionaries, translating and adapting the missionary message to make it more understandable and applicable to the local context. Riding their bicycles and carrying their Bibles from village to village, catechists took the gospel to venues where missionaries could never go. More than that, catechists functioned as folk theologians, reformulating the Christian message and way of life so it could grow more easily in the rich spiritual soil of African culture.

In addition to the catechists who worked in tandem with the missionaries, a host of Spirit-inspired African Christian prophets also appeared on the scene – individuals who felt no need to rely on Western missionaries for guidance or instruction. In fact, these local prophets often accused the missionaries of misrepresenting the gospel. Their criticisms emerged from their own reading of the various vernacular translations of the Bible that were published in most locations soon after the initial missionary encounter. Marriage was a significant source of conflict. Many African cultures are polygamous, and polygamy was frequently condemned by missionaries who said the Bible defined marriage as a relationship between one man and one woman, but literate Africans soon discovered that the Bible said no such thing. Polygamy may not be recommended, but the Bible – even the New Testament – never clearly condemns it. Many Africans eventually concluded that the missionaries were more concerned with their own cultural norms than they were with the literal meaning of the biblical text. In fact, reading the Bible literally was often a liberating experience for many African Christians.

Another frequent point of friction concerned the miraculous power of the Holy Spirit. When Africans read the Bible, they saw miracles everywhere – especially miracles of healing – and they also saw that God frequently spoke to people through dreams and visions. Receiving those revelations or working miracles required no special training, but only faith in God. Yet the missionaries seemed to downplay miracles, and often they insisted that Africans had to be carefully educated prior to preaching the gospel to others. Dreams, visions, and miraculous power were, however, common fare in African culture, and many African Christians felt the Bible gave them warrant to claim those gifts and use them for the work of God on earth.

When missionaries resisted these new local African interpretations of the Bible some of the catechists and prophets broke away from the missionary churches to begin their own new African Independent Churches (which are also often called African Initiated Churches or AICs). The first AICs arose in the 1870s, but the movement peaked in the mid-twentieth century. Sometimes the creation of a new AIC was precipitated by theological differences, but often Africans simply wanted to be in charge of their own churches. These organizations have taken slightly different forms in different regions of Africa. In West Africa, for example, the largely non-political Aladura movement (meaning "praying people" in Yoruba) has been especially strong, represented by groups like the Eternal Sacred Order of the Cherubim and Seraphim (see Plate 14) begun by Moses Orimolade in 1925. Elsewhere, politics and faith have mingled more easily. The movement toward independent churches has slowed significantly since the 1970s, largely because the leadership of most formerly missionary-run churches has now been transferred to local African pastors and bishops. The pressure for independence from white religious rule is no longer an issue.

Today about 80 million Africans – about one tenth of the total population and 20 percent of the Christian population – are members of an AIC, most of which have a strongly Pentecostal/Charismatic flavor. This should come as no surprise. In most AICs significant emphasis is put on the work of the Holy Spirit and the supernatural world looms large. The role of prophets is also emphasized, and many AICs are organized hierarchically with people assigned different roles in the churches based on their differing endowments of spiritual power and authority.

Church independence movements have generally been more common in Protestant circles than in Catholic. Catholic bishops and priests typically exercise more control over their parishioners than their Protestant counterparts, and the Catholic Church as a whole stresses the importance of obedience to the ordained clerical hierarchy. Schism is considered a sin. Nonetheless, a few Catholic African Independent Church movements have arisen, and the Legio Maria movement in Kenya, begun by Blasio Simeo Malkio Ondetto in 1962, is the best known. Its membership peaked in the mid-1980s, but it remains a viable movement today. One of the unique innovations of this church is the addition of a new office of church leadership known as "checkers" or "sniffers." The check-ers stand at the entrance to the church compound and each person desiring entrance kneels in front of them in order to be sniffed. The assumption is that the check-ers have the gift of literally smelling good and bad intentions, and their role is to keep those with bad intentions from joining in church worship. One characteristic of many African churches is an emphasis on the whole person and all the senses. The sniffers of the Legio Maria movement are an interesting example of how that can be expressed in practice.

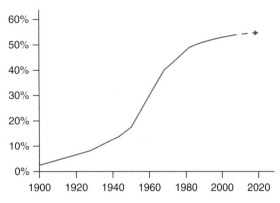

Figure 9.3   Christianity in sub-Saharan Africa (% of population)

The Growth of Christianity

The headline story of Christianity in Africa can be summed up in one word: growth. Never before has Christianity expanded so quickly in any region of the world. The trajectory is staggering. In 1900, there were roughly seven million Christians in Africa, making up about 5 percent of the total population. Today there are more than 400 million Christians in the region, and together they account for 53 percent of the total population. The great spurt in growth in terms of Christians as a percentage of the total African population took place in the middle decades of the twentieth century, from 1950 to 1970, during the era of independence. In 1950, only about 15 percent of the population was Christian, but that number had almost tripled to 43 percent by 1970. The growth of Christianity as a percentage of the population has crept up 10 more percentage points over the last 40 years (see Figure 9.3). More than half the countries in Sub-Saharan Africa now have Christian majorities (see Figure 9.5).

But while Christianity as a percentage of the African population may be leveling off, the actual number of Christians in Africa continues to skyrocket (see Figure 9.4). The reason behind this phenomenon is the gen-eral population explosion taking place on the conti-nent. Africa today has nine times as many inhabitants as it had in 1900. The next fastest growing region of

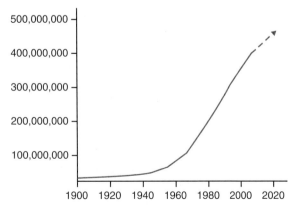

Figure 9.4   Christianity in sub-Saharan Africa (number of adherents)

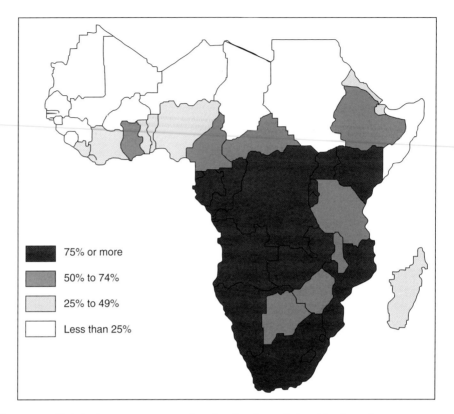

75% or more

50% to 74%

25% to 49%

Less than 25%

Figure 9.5　Christianity as a percentage of total national population. Map by author.

the world is South America, where the population has increased eightfold during the same time frame. By contrast, the North American population is two and a half times as large now as it was in 1900, and the population of Europe has hardly grown at all. Thus the massive growth of Christianity in Africa during the last several decades has been partly the result of continuing evangelism (i.e., people who are not Christians converting to Christianity), but it is also the result of Christian mothers having lots and lots of Christian children.

In addition to looking at Christian numbers in the aggregate, it is interesting to look at the comparative growth of the four major Christian traditions. Of the seven million Christians living in Africa in 1900, roughly half were members of the Ethiopian Orthodox Church, a quarter were Catholic, and another quarter were Protestant. All of these groups have grown significantly since then, as has the newer Pentecostal/Charismatic tradition, which was only just beginning around the year 1900, but Orthodoxy has seen the least growth, being only 12 times larger now than it was at the beginning of the twentieth century. In almost any other region of the world this kind of growth would be considered astonishing, but in Africa it is unremarkable. (See Table 9.2.)

When scholars today say that Christianity is moving south, it is this phenomenal Christian growth in Africa (and in Latin America) that they have in mind. In 1900, African Christians accounted for less than 2 percent of all the Christians in the world. Today, 20 percent of the world's Christians are African. In terms of specific denominational traditions, Africa now

Table 9.2   Growth of four Christian traditions in sub-Saharan Africa (total number of adherents)

	1900	*1950*	*1970*	*2005*
Orthodox	3,000,000	8,000,000	17,000,000	35,000,000
Catholic	1,500,000	14,000,000	51,000,000	140,000,000
Protestant	1,500,000	8,000,000	38,000,000	115,000,000
Pentecostal/Charismatic	–	1,000,000	18,000,000	115,000,000*
Total	6,000,000	31,000,000	134,000,000	405,000,000

* This includes all classical Pentecostal denominations and neocharismatic churches, most AICs, and
Charismatic Christians in the Catholic and Protestant churches.

claims more than 50 percent of all the world's Anglicans, 25 percent of all Reformed Protestants, 20 percent of the world's Lutherans, about 15 percent of the global Methodist population, and 14 percent of all Catholics. These changing statistics are translating into power shifts in a number of different global associations, most obviously in the Anglican Communion, where the African churches are no longer willing to let the Church of England and the Archbishop of Canterbury lead the way. More and more, the African bishops are calling the shots, and they are intent on making sure that their own conservative theological concerns are heard loud and clear in what they see as the liberal West.

Africa's Changing Religious Profile

The growth of Christianity in Africa has not only changed the face of global Christianity, it has also dramatically reshaped the African religious profile. When the twentieth century began, approximately 80 percent of all Africans could be classified as followers of African traditional religion. The remaining 20 percent were either Muslim (13 percent) or Christian (7 percent). Over the course of the century, the relative strength of the three groups changed dramatically. Today more than 50 percent of the population is Christian, 25 percent or more is Muslim, and only about 20 percent would still identify their primary allegiance as traditional African religion. Statistics for individual countries, of course, vary significantly (see Table 9.3).

The shift from African traditional religion to Christianity and to a lesser degree from Islam represents a huge alteration of the religious profile of Africa, but the raw numbers may overstate the amount of change that has taken place. Unlike Christianity and Islam, African traditional religion does not have clear parameters for determining membership. Rather than being something one joins or affirms as a matter of doctrine, African traditional religion was and is part of local culture. It is expressed in a variety of practices related to community cohesion, the agricultural calendar, lifecycle transitions, ancestors, fertility, healing, and help with personal difficulties. To be sure, many Africans who have converted to Christianity and Islam understand the act of conversion to be a radical break with the past. Because of this, many converts destroy the material objects (fetishes) that are used in traditional ceremonies – objects which have sometimes been handed down generation to

Table 9.3   Religious affiliation in the 10 largest nations in sub-Saharan Africa today

Nation	Population	% Christian	% Islamic	% Afr. Trad. Religion
Nigeria	135,000,000	46	44	10
Ethiopia	77,000,000	56	30	12
Congo (DRC)	58,000,000	93	1	3
South Africa	48,000,000	78	9	3
Tanzania	38,500,000	52	32	16
Sudan	36,500,000	18	70	12
Kenya	35,000,000	80	7	12
Uganda	9,000,000	86	5	4
Ghana	22,000,000	54	20	24
Mozambique	20,000,000	38	11	50

generation for decades or centuries – as part of their conversion. But other Christians and Muslims have continued to participate in the rituals and practices of African traditional religion to some degree and in certain circumstances. It would thus not be uncommon for an African Christian to consult a local traditional healer or participate in a coming-of-age ceremony. If queried about their religious identity, these same individuals would not hesitate to answer that they are Christians.

In fact, one reason that Christianity has grown so quickly is that it is attuned to the religious questions and concerns that permeate traditional African spirituality. This spiritual sensibility assumes that the world has two separate dimensions – the visible and the invisible – and that danger and ambiguity lurk in both spheres. The visible world is the world of life in the present. It is the world of sensory experience, practical rationality, and ordinary life. The invisible world is, by contrast, the abode of spirits and ancestors – beings that can either help or harm – and, more ominously, it is the world that witches manipulate to do evil in the world. Most Africans believe that everyone lives in these two worlds simultaneously and that the two worlds often interact.

Christianity, especially as Africans have adapted it to their own cultures, addresses both of these worlds. In the visible world, Christianity offers practical wisdom about how to interact with others and it provides assistance in the restoration of broken relationships. It offers education that involves training for life in general and, especially for women and for unmarried males, it can provide an expanded sense of personhood and social status. As for the invisible world, Christianity offers protection from evil spirits, disgruntled ancestors, and witches. It provides access to the miraculous power of the Holy Spirit and it promises eternal life in heaven with God. Christianity makes the world feel safe: Both the visible and the invisible worlds are under God's control, and human beings can flourish in the protection and blessing of God's grace. Given the choice between the ambiguity and fear that is part of traditional African religion and the assurances of Christianity, huge numbers of Africans have converted to Christianity. There is something in the Christian message and way of life that connects very deeply and very satisfyingly with the religious longings of the people of Africa.

Responding to supernatural spiritual power has been a special challenge for the Roman Catholic Church. While the Catholic Church clearly believes in miracles, the Catholic tradition has always been a bit uneasy with individuals who claim specific spiritual gifts. One of the best known cases in this regard is Emmanuel Milingo (born 1930). Milingo was named Archbishop of Lusaka, Zambia, in 1969. In 1973, he announced that he had received a special gift of healing from God and had the power to deliver people from demon possession. He then began to hold special meetings for healing and exorcism in Zambia and elsewhere. This would not have been seen as a problem in Protestant or Pentecostal/ Charismatic circles, but Milingo was a Catholic and a bishop. His special style of ministry raised significant concerns. Finally, the Pope felt compelled to remove Milingo from Africa, bringing him to Rome in 1983 as a Special Delegate of the Pontifical Council that works with migrant and itinerant people. It was hoped that this transfer would allow the Vatican to keep a closer eye on Milingo and his unique form of Catholic ministry. But Milingo was not easy to corral. After his removal from Africa, he has continued to practice his healing ministry around the world and he also took up the cause of priestly marriage, demonstrating his seriousness by getting married himself. His marriage has since been dissolved, but Milingo formed a new organization in 2006 called "Married Priests Now" to further the cause, and ordained four married men as bishops. The Vatican excommunicated Milingo for this act and finally defrocked him (took away his priestly status) in December 2009.

Marriage itself is another issue that is shaping the profile of Christianity in Africa and, once again, Catholics and non-Catholics face different challenges. For the Roman Catholic Church, marriage is a sacrament. There is one right way to perform that sacrament, and those who have not been married in a properly Catholic way – either because the marriage is polygamous or because it was performed in a traditional manner outside the Church – are often prohibited from participating in the other sacraments. This means that in some African countries, a majority of Catholic laypeople are not allowed to participate in communion during the celebration of the Mass. The only "legal" way to rectify this situation is to somehow sacramentally regularize the wedding vows of married Catholics, but there is no clear procedure by which to do that, and the shortage of Catholic priests nearly everywhere in Africa makes that an impossible task anyway. The Protestants and Pentecostal/ Charismatic churches (including the AICs) have not necessarily done much better. Some churches have simply turned a blind eye to the problem, while others have tried to come up with creative compromises. Thus, for example, some churches will allow wives who are involved in a polygamous marriage to attend church and participate in the sacraments, arguing that each of them has only one husband, but at the same time they will ban men from communing because they are married to more than one wife. Since the great majority of church members in Africa are women this policy works fairly well in practice, but it is clearly a stop-gap measure.

The African Christian community as a whole is roughly split between men and women, but the active membership of the churches tends to be overwhelmingly female in composition, partly because of policies related to marriage and partly because women generally express more interest in religion than men. African men tend to stay on the margins, either absenting themselves entirely from church or staying outside socializing while the women and children attend worship inside. Given that gender dynamic and the continent's very young median age, the "average" active African Christian can be described as an 18-year-old illiterate mother who is caring for two or three small children and who is also responsible for making sure the entire family has food to eat and clothes to wear.

All churches – Orthodox, Catholic, Protestant, and Pentecostal/Charismatic – are struggling to minister to the needs of the young women who constitute the core of the church, and they are doing so with different degrees of success. One hindrance in this regard is the fact that most African churches remain profoundly patriarchal in their structures and organization. Women are often barred from holding formal leadership roles and they are rarely asked for input when making church decisions. Despite those restrictions, women have, given their numbers, frequently been able to amass considerable informal power in the churches and some women have served as prophetesses, even starting their own independent churches. One of the most famous is Alice Lenshina (1920–1978) who founded the Lumpa Church in Zambia in 1953 – a Christian movement that was later crushed by the Zambian government. But informal power is not enough for some women, and the Ghanaian theologian Mercy Amba Oduyoye (born 1934), along with the Circle of Concerned African Women Theologians she helped found, has been at the forefront of advocating women's rights in the African churches. Oduyoye's critique of sexist practices is scathing. "I believe that the experience of women in the church in Africa contradicts the Christian claim to promote the worth [and] equal value of every person." Rather than promoting women's rights, she says "Christianity reinforces the depersonalization of women."[1] While others are more optimistic about recent progress that has been made with regard to the place of women in the church, everyone agrees that the future of Christianity in Africa hinges on how well it addresses the needs and desires of its female members.

Across the African churches, there is a common appreciation for how much the core concerns of faith dovetail with basic human needs. In Africa, giving someone a cup of water can save a life, and sharing one's food is an act of faith because so many people have no idea where their own food will come from tomorrow. While Christians in Africa are by no means indifferent to matters of belief, practical concerns are central. This practical orientation of African Christianity is expressed in the "African Creed," which was developed by the Masai of Kenya:

> We believe in the one High God, who out of love created the beautiful world and everything good in it. He created man and wanted man to be happy in the world. God loves the world and every nation and tribe on the earth. We have known this High God in darkness, and now we know him in the light. God promised in the book of his word, the Bible, that he would save the world and all the nations and tribes.
>
> We believe that God made good his promise by sending his son, Jesus Christ, a man in the flesh, a Jew by tribe, born poor in a little village, who left his home and was always on safari doing good, curing people by the power of God, teaching about God and man, showing the meaning of religion is love. He was rejected by his people, tortured and nailed hands and feet to a cross, and died. He lay buried in the grave, but the hyenas did not touch him, and on the third day, he rose from the grave. He ascended to the skies. He is the Lord.

We believe that all our sins are forgiven through him. All who have faith in him must be sorry for their sins, be baptized in the Holy Spirit of God, live the rules of love and share the bread together in love, to announce the good news to others until Jesus comes again. We are waiting for him. He is alive. He lives. This we believe. Amen.[2]

Christianity and Islam in Nigeria

Nigeria is the largest country in Africa in terms of population. It also has more Christians than any other African nation. The Nigerian Christian leadership is confident and energetic, and Nigerian Christian influence is evident throughout Africa as well as other parts of the world. For example, the largest church in the Ukraine is pastored by a Nigerian Pentecostal, and the Nigerian Anglican Church (which accounts for about a quarter of all the Anglicans in the world) now has several missionary congregations in the USA. A quick look at the denominational profile of Nigerian Christianity reveals considerable diversity, but in recent years there has been a decided shift toward Pentecostal/Charismatic forms of faith. Currently half the Christian population can be characterized as Pentecostal/ Charismatic. (See Table 9.4.)

The Pentecostal/Charismatic character of Nigerian Christianity has increased in step with the growing prominence of urban megachurches. Most of these churches, led by Spirit-filled Charismatic preachers, offer a wide variety of religious services to those who attend. Matchmaking is one important attraction for many younger people who have moved to the cities from the countryside and who find themselves, in the absence of traditional village matchmaking rituals, at a loss about how to proceed. It is not uncommon for Charismatic preachers to provide very direct advice about who God wants to be married to whom.

Table 9.4 Denominational profile of Nigerian Christian population

Group	Number of adherents	% of all Christians in country
AIC*	18,000,000	28
Anglican	17,500,000	28
Catholic	16,500,000	26
Pentecostal*	3,000,000	5
Baptist	2,500,000	4
Lutheran	2,000,000	3
Methodist	1,750,000	3
Ref/Presb	750,000	1
Other	1,000,000	2
Total*	63,000,000	

* There are about 10,000,000 members of the Protestant and Catholic Churches that can be considered Charismatic. If those are added to the members of the Pentecostal churches and the AICs, there would be roughly 31,000,000 Pentecostal/Charismatic Christians in Nigeria, half the Christian population.

In many of these churches there has also been an emphasis on the accumulation of wealth. Benson Idahosa (1938–98), who founded the Church of God Mission – a ministry which currently claims about a million members – was one of the first to move in this direction. Linking up with a variety of international Charismatic leaders like the Americans Jim and Tammy Bakker and their PTL (Praise the Lord) television show, Idahosa began preaching that God wanted to financially bless all who would donate money to God's work through his own church. While there are many ways to critique this wealth-focused style of Christianity as being both crassly materialistic and false in its promises, the reality is that membership in these churches tends to promote virtues like self-discipline and frugality that actually do allow people to gain employment or start their own business. "Wealth" in the context of Nigeria generally means something akin to minimal economic security rather than diamonds and flashy cars. Nigeria's Pentecostal/Charismatic leaders readily admit that God uses a variety of means to gift people with wealth, and education is one of them. To that end, Nigerian Christians have opened about 20 new private universities, almost half of them associated with Pentecostal/Charismatic churches.

The Christian population of Nigeria is large, growing, and active – and so is the Muslim population. Christians currently claim to represent just under half the population, while Muslims claim three-quarters. Since that adds up to well over 100 percent, at least one of these figures has to be incorrect. The likely reality is that the Muslim and Christian portions of the population are roughly equal in size, and the overestimate of the Muslim community is a political assertion – a way of claiming that Muslims should continue to have slightly more control over the central government than Christians, which is the historical pattern of rule in the country.

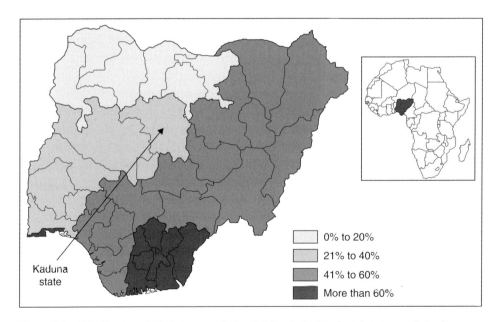

Figure 9.6   Distribution of Christian population in Nigeria (as % of total state population).
Map by author.

The Christian population of Nigeria is concentrated mainly in the southeastern part of the country and Muslims dominate the northwest, though neither religion has a monopoly in either area. Differences between the two religious groups are exacerbated to some degree by tribal differences. For the most part the Hausa are Muslim, while Christianity is more strongly represented among the Igbo (Ibo) and Yoruba. Finally, regional differences complicate the picture. During British colonial rule, the land that is now Nigeria was divided into three separate administrative units (North, South, and West) that were largely autonomous. The nation was united at independence in 1960, but regional autonomy has remained an issue. In the late 1960s this led to a bloody three-year civil war. Since then, the country has been relatively stable, but regional tensions are never far beneath the surface of public life. The strains are particularly acute in the Middle Belt that runs from east to west across the central region of the country, and Kaduna – the most central state in the nation (see Figure 9.6) – has been a hot spot of Christian–Muslim violence.

Figure 9.7   Nigerian Anglican Archbishop Peter Akinola
© RONEN ZVULUN/Reuters/Corbis

After independence, Nigeria was a secular state in terms of basic legal structure, but that situation changed in the late 1990s when several northern Nigerian states replaced their local secular legal codes with Muslim Shari'a law. Many Muslims welcomed this development, but Christians were deeply troubled and some began to migrate out of the region. Others chose to stay and fight. Each side blamed the other for being the first to use violence, and thus each side felt righteous about its own use of force. Anglican Bishop Peter Akinola (see Figure 9.7) has warned repeatedly that no Muslim should think their side has a monopoly on violence: Christians will defend themselves! Most Muslim leaders express the same feelings, so the cycle of violence continues. The central government has always had a hard time maintaining order, and the "safest" towns are often dependent on vigilante groups who are hired to keep the streets calm. In other words, self-defense (or preemptive violence) often appears to be the only way to protect oneself and one's community.

There is evidence, however, that at least some Muslims and Christians may be tiring of the mutual hatred and fear. In Kaduna, for example, an interreligious friendship has emerged between two high-profile former enemies: the Christian pastor James Movel Wuye, and the Muslim Imam Muhammad Nurayn Ashafa. Wuye used to be a violent Christian activist, urging his followers to attack their Muslim neighbors by turning the words of Jesus more or less upside down. Jesus said when someone hits you on one cheek, turn the other, but Wuye argued: "We've been beaten on both cheeks, so there's no other cheek to turn." Then, at a Christian conference, someone pulled him aside and scolded him roundly saying "you can't preach Jesus with hate in your heart." The words hit home, and Wuye's life was turned around. About the same time Ashafa, a member of one of Nigeria's Muslim militias, had a similar life-changing experience. After a local Sufi hermit was stabbed to death by Christians, Ashafa decided he was going to kill Pastor Wuye in retaliation. But then he heard a sermon by the local imam about Muhammad's denunciation of revenge, and he knew he had to change his ways. The two men eventually met at Ashafa's initiative, and they now travel around the country telling their stories and trying to help end Christian–Muslim violence in the country.[3]

The political situation in Nigeria may also be taking a turn for the better in terms of Muslim–Christian relations. The President of Nigeria from 1999 to 2007 was General Olusegun Obasanjo. Obasanjo is a Baptist who comes from the southwestern region of the country, yet he ruled in a way that met with general approval from most northerners and most Nigerian Muslims as well as most Christians. In 2007, a relatively peaceful election transferred power to Umaru Yar'Adua, making this the first time in Nigerian history that a civilian had followed a civilian in the presidential office. Yar'Adua, who is Muslim, died of natural causes in May 2010 (after a long illness), and his vice president Goodluck Jonathan (who is a Christian) is finishing off his term. The next election will take place in 2011, and Jonathan has announced that he will seek the office. This upsets an informal agreement in Nigeria that the presidency will switch every two terms from Muslim to Christian. Nigeria's electoral history is spotty at best. Most people believe that the elections of 2003 and 2007 were rigged, even though most Nigerians were also satisfied with the results. Should another corrupt election bring a Christian to office out of turn, however, things could fall apart quickly.

The Democratic Republic of Congo

The Democratic Republic of Congo (DRC) has the second largest population in Africa. Approximately 95 percent of the population claims allegiance to some form of Christian faith, making it the most Christian nation on the continent. Half the population is Roman Catholic (29 million members), which places the DRC fifth on the list of largest Catholic countries. The Congolese Catholic Church is also the oldest church in the sub-Saharan region of Africa. Portuguese missionaries arrived in the 1490s, and in the early 1500s Alfonso I, ruler of the Kingdom of the Congo, converted to Christianity. Though the Portuguese slave trade later turned the local people away from Christianity, Catholic Christianity was never totally eliminated from the Congo River basin.

The Congo, which became a royal colony of Belgium in 1885, was considered the personal possession of King Leopold II, who ran the country for the sole purpose of increasing his own wealth. Literally millions of local Africans were worked to death on the colony's rubber plantations. The situation became so appalling that the Belgian government seized control from the king in 1908. In recompense for the abuses of Leopold, the government tried to turn the Congo into a model colony. Forced labor was ended and positive steps were taken to improve the lives of the local people. Catholicism was central to Belgian rule and, based on a concordat signed with the Pope, the state began supporting the missionary and educational efforts of the Catholic Church out of public funds. Other churches were allowed to operate in the region, but they were not similarly supported. For reasons of efficiency in evangelism and effective communication with the government, the various Protestant churches in the Congo began to cooperate with each other as early as the 1920s, setting up a system of "comity" that assigned different geographic regions of the country to different denominations. This system never coalesced into a church union, but it did mean that relatively cordial relations existed among all the groups.

As was the case elsewhere in Africa, local Christians began to express dissatisfaction with foreign control over the churches early in the twentieth century, and a number of African Independent Churches soon sprang up. The most successful of these movements was led by Simon Kimbangu. Kimbangu was a Congolese catechist associated with the British Baptist Missionary Society, and around 1920 he launched his own independent movement of healing and evangelism. Kimbangu's message was not all that different from that of the missionaries – he was strongly opposed to both polygamy and African traditional religion – but he was a charismatic leader who quickly attracted a significant following. He appointed 12 "apostles" to assist him in his work, and within just six months thousands of people had been converted. Worried about his growing influence, the Belgian authorities arrested Kimbangu on a charge of sedition on his 34th birthday (September 12, 1921) and sentenced him to life in prison. He died there in 1951, but his church – the Church of Jesus Christ on Earth by His Special Envoy Simon Kimbangu – survived him. Today the Kimbanguist Church is the largest African Independent Church, claiming 17 million members (with perhaps 9 million members in Congo), and it is a member of the World Council of Churches.

The Congo gained its independence from Belgium in 1960, and the first five years of self-rule were rough. In 1965, a young military officer named Joseph Désiré Mobutu took charge and brought order to the country. That order came with a price, however, in the form of submission to Mobutu as virtual dictator. Mobutu received strong backing from the USA. The Congo is centrally located in the heart of Africa, and America saw it as a strategic place from which to keep an eye on the rest of the continent during the years of the Cold War. This outside support from the United States allowed Mobutu to govern as he pleased, and his personal bank accounts in Switzerland were filled with billions of dollars siphoned from the national treasury.

The domestic policy of Mobutu focused on African authenticity, on making his country as postcolonial as possible. To that end, in 1971 he changed the name of the nation from Congo to Zaire, an African term that means "radiant." Mobutu also sought to remove all traces of colonialism from *Zairewa* Christianity. (*Zairewa* is the possessive form of Zaire.) As part of that project, he decreed that in place of the Christian names they had received at baptism, *Zairewa* Catholics (and all other Christians as well) should adopt new African names. Leading the way, Mobutu changed his own baptismal name from Joseph Désiré to Sese Seko. Those who refused to comply, including priests who continued to baptize babies with Western names, were threatened with fines and imprisonment.

In legislation directed more at Protestants than Catholics, Mobutu declared that only three churches would be allowed to continue to exist in the country: the Roman Catholic Church, the Kimbanguist Church, and the Church of Christ in Zaire – a new denomination that was to be formed by the merger of all other Protestant churches. The new denomination was a loose merger that allowed different Protestant groups to keep most of their own distinctive features – in many ways it was only a slight intensification of the pre-existing comity arrangement – but there was some initial resistance to the idea. Eventually most churches cooperated with the new structure and virtually all the churches also transferred control from the missionaries to local Christian leaders. Catholics, too, were pressured by

Mobutu to make their churches more authentically African. Though many Catholic leaders resented his intrusion at the time, the *Zairewa* Catholic bishops are now quite proud that they were the first to develop a fully indigenous Catholic liturgy in Africa.

Mobutu was forced to resign from office in 1997. He was replaced by Laurent-Désiré Kabila, who almost immediately changed the name of the country back to the Democratic Republic of Congo, or "DRC." Kabila was assassinated in 2001 and was replaced by his son, Joseph Kabila, who remains in office today. Joseph Kabila is a Protestant (Anglican), but he married a Catholic woman named Olive Lembe di Sita in June 2006 with the wedding service being performed by the Catholic archbishop of Kinshasa. Overall, religion does not seem to be a major factor in the way he governs the country. What has been central to his regime has been the attempt to re-establish relative peace in the nation and in central Africa generally after the series of wars that ravaged the eastern part of the Congo and the neighboring states of Uganda and Rwanda during the years 1998 to 2003. Large numbers of refugees were created as a result of these wars, and the challenge of coping with that humanitarian crisis remains a serious concern of both the nation and the Congolese churches today.

Race and Faith in South Africa

South Africa is an exception to many of the generalizations that can be made about the rest of Africa. In most of Africa, colonization involved the imposition of white rule with a minimum of Europeans present to oversee the process. In South Africa, however, colonization meant European settlement, and that settlement began much earlier than the colonization of the rest of the continent. The Dutch arrived in the mid-1600s and set up a colony in the southeastern region of the country near the present-day city of Cape Town. In 1795, the British seized power in Cape Town and the Dutch moved inland. Tensions between the two groups eventually led to the Boer War in the 1890s. The British won the war and established the Union of South Africa in 1910, but the Dutch South Africans (known as "Afrikaners") soon reclaimed functional rule over the country through the ballot box.

The Afrikaners were intent on keeping their own culture "pure" and developed a theory of race relations called "apartheid" to maintain this separateness of peoples, which was based on the writings of the Dutch theologian and politician Abraham Kuyper and appealed to the biblical story of the tower of Babel. Afrikaners argued that God intended the different races to live apart (hence the term "apartheid," meaning aparthood) and that the "superior" races had the responsibility of guardianship (*voogdyskap*), or ruling over others. With those two principles in mind, the Afrikaner Nationalist political party began enacting legislation that mandated racial separation in almost all areas of life – religious, residential, matrimonial, and governmental. They developed a complex racial system that distinguished between whites of European descent, black Africans, "colored" people of mixed-race ancestry, and Indians (a catch-all designation that included most Asians). Whites reserved the best land for themselves and set up separate "homelands" where black Africans were supposed to live. Dependent on the cheap labor of black Africans, white South Africans allowed a variety of slums to grow up around the white cities that dotted the landscape. These slums were later designated "townships," the most famous of which is Soweto, located outside Johannesburg. (Soweto is an abbreviation of "south-west township.")

In the 1960s, about the same time that every other African nation began to push for independence, the black citizens of South Africa began earnest protests against the racist policies of their nation. The African National Congress, the party of Nelson Mandela, was the main political organization fighting to overthrow the apartheid regime in South Africa, and as the resistance became more intense, the government cracked down harder. Many black activists were arrested, some were put to death by the government, and others just disappeared. As the stakes were raised higher and higher, violence also broke out within the black community, as individuals suspected of collaborating with the South African apartheid government were sometimes beaten or killed by those involved in the antiapartheid movement.

While not the main players, the churches were involved in the effort to end apartheid. The Cottesloe Statement, a joint statement issued in 1961 by all the South African churches that were members of the World Council of Churches, condemned both discrimination in the churches (separate denominations for blacks, whites, and coloreds) and the government policy of apartheid in the country as a whole. Later, in 1982, the World Alliance of Reformed Churches, which was led by the black South African theologian Alan Boesak, declared that the theology used to support apartheid was a Christian heresy. Finally, a group of South African Christian leaders published *The Kairos Document* in 1985, which argued that the use of revolutionary violence against unjust governments was sometimes required on Christian grounds. Their logic expanded the classic theory of "just war" to include the concept of just revolution. One of the leading voices behind the document belonged to Frank Chikane, president of the Pentecostal Apostolic Faith Mission.

Beset by internal revolutionaries and scorned by the international community, South Africa finally ended apartheid. In 1990, Nelson Mandela was released from prison and the African National Congress was declared legal. In 1992, the white citizens of South Africa voted officially to end single-race rule. And in 1994, a new multiracial constitution was adopted and Nelson Mandela was installed as president. The long nightmare of apartheid and the war to end apartheid were over. But many scars and sorrows remained, and there was a deep need for reconciliation if the nation was to move ahead constructively. Reconciliation is not, however, the province of government. Governments can deal with matters of justice, but reconciliation is spiritual. Recognizing that reality, President Mandela appointed Archbishop Desmond Tutu of the Anglican Church to lead a Truth and Reconciliation Commission (TRC) to help heal the nation, encourage contrition, and promote forgiveness. Tutu would be the first to say that the work of the TRC was flawed and incomplete, but he would also observe that the task they set for themselves was unprecedented. His watchword was that ultimately there is "no future without forgiveness," and the challenge of the TRC was to provide space where forgiveness could happen. Rarely has despair been more evident in human history than in South Africa during the final years of apartheid. But rarely has any human organization produced more hope than the TRC under the leadership of Desmond Tutu.

Christianity in post-apartheid Africa is booming and, as elsewhere in Africa, the Pentecostal/Charismatic sector is experiencing the fastest growth. This is partly because

Table 9.5   Denominational profile of South African Christian population

Group	Number of adherents	% of Christians in country
AIC*	15,000,000	40
Ref/Presb	5,000,000	13
Pentecostal*	3,500,000	9
Catholic	3,500,000	9
Methodist	3,000,000	8
Anglican	2,000,000	6
Lutheran	1,000,000	3
Other	4,500,000	12
Total	37,500,000	

* There are about 2,000,000 members of the Protestant and Catholic churches that can be considered Charismatic. If those are added to the members of the Pentecostal churches and the AICs, there would be roughly 20,500,000 Pentecostal/Charismatic Christians in South Africa, 55% of the total Christian population.

South Africa has the largest independent church movement on the continent – AICs make up 40 percent of the South African Christian population – but also because transnational Charismatic Christianity is increasingly prominent. Christian television shows produced in the USA and elsewhere along with an increasing number of urban megachurches are preaching a message of divine financial blessing for all who call on God's name and join their organization. But older, more established churches continue to attract millions of followers as well. In South Africa's pluralistic religious marketplace many different kinds of churches are flourishing (see Table 9.5).

Religious Tensions in Ethiopia

Ethiopia is one of only two nations in all of Africa that was never colonized by Europe. One of the main reasons Ethiopia was exempted from colonization was the fact that it was already a Christian nation. Ethiopian Orthodox Christians trace their roots back to the first century when the Bible reports that an Ethiopian court eunuch converted to Christianity, but most historians date the real beginning of Christianity in Ethiopia to the fourth century. Monasticism was introduced to Ethiopia in the sixth century by a group of Orthodox monks from Syria, who are now referred to as the "nine saints."

The Ethiopian Orthodox *Tewahedo* Church (the official name of the Ethiopian Orthodox Church) is the largest Christian subgroup in the country with 35 million members. It is also one of the largest Orthodox Churches in the world. Originally, the ecclesiastical head of the Ethiopian Orthodox Church, who is known as the *abune*, was appointed by the pope of the Coptic Church and quite frequently this person was not an Ethiopian. The highest ranking native Ethiopian official in the Church was the *ichege*. The role of the *ichege* was to be the confessor and advisor of the emperor, to oversee the monasteries, and to serve as interim abune in the event of a vacancy. In 1956, the Ethiopian Orthodox Church declared its full independence from the Coptic Church and began electing its own *abune*. Since then the role of the *ichege* has been eliminated. The current Ethiopian Orthodox Abune Paulos (born 1935) has served as one of the presidents of the World Council of Churches.

Many practices of the Orthodox Ethiopian Church are unique, preserving a number of Jewish elements that other Christian churches have rejected or ignored. For example, Saturday is retained as the Sabbath and is celebrated as a day of fasting each week before worship on Sunday. Ethiopian Orthodox churches are also architecturally modeled after the old Jewish temple in Jerusalem, having a three-part structure with an entrance room for singing and dancing called the *qine mahlet*, an inner room for worship called the *qiddist*, and a small central room called a *meqdes* that only the priests and deacons (and in former times, the king)

Figure 9.8 Carrying the tabot to be rechristened during the festival of Timkat
© PhotoStock-Israel/Alamy

can enter. Inside the *meqdes* is the *tabot* (also called an ark), which is an inscribed stone tablet that represents the tablets of the law that were kept inside the Ark of the Covenant in ancient Israel. If the *tabot* is either desecrated or absent from an Orthodox Church, worship cannot be performed in that building. Once a year, on the festival of Timkat (which celebrates the baptism of Jesus by John the Baptist), the *tabot* is ceremonially removed from the church, carried to a nearby river or stream, and is christened or rebaptized. All the people who are gathered for the ceremony also renew their baptismal vows. (See Figure 9.8.)

Until 1974, Ethiopia was a Christian Kingdom overseen by a Christian emperor. The country's structure was largely feudal, with three-quarters of the population serving functionally as serfs for the wealthy landowners. The last emperor of the country was Haile Selassie, who began his rule in 1930. Haile Selassie was also known as Ras Tafari ("Ras" means "prince" or "ruler" and "Tafari" was his birth name). This honorific title is preserved in the Rastafarian religious movement in Jamaica that believes Haile Selassie was God incarnate. Selassie was deposed in 1974 by Lieutenant Colonel Mengistu Haile Miriam, a Communist with ties to North Korea who undertook a radical reordering of Ethiopian society, including a major land redistribution program. His policies contributed to the famines that devastated Ethiopia in 1984 and 1985, and severe persecution of the churches took place. Mengistu was himself overthrown in 1991, and since that time the nation has been run as a democracy. Since 1999, Ethiopia has had unstable relations with its neighbors Eritrea and Somalia, with active warfare breaking out from time to time.

Even before the end of the Empire in 1974, the Ethiopian government had allowed some non-Orthodox Christians to enter the country and engage in evangelistic activity. The largest non-Orthodox church in the country is the Qale Heywet (Word of Life) Church, originally started by American missionaries (Sudan Interior Mission). The missionaries had to leave the country during World War II, however, and the church became wholly indigenous by the time they returned five years later. This church began as an Evangelical Protestant denomination, but it is now thoroughly Charismatic, and has about five million members. The Mekane

Yesus Church is the third largest church in the country. Started by Pietistic Scandinavian Lutheran Christians, it too has been Pentecostalized. Its membership is approaching four million. In fact, Pentecostal/Charismatic Christianity has become so prominent in Ethiopia – accounting for roughly 15 percent of the population – that the common name for Christians who are neither Orthodox nor Catholic is now "pente," which is shorthand for Pentecostal.

Ethiopia's various religious communities have lived side by side with each other in relative peace for the last several decades. In recent years, however, Muslim–Christian violence has been on the rise. Muslims, who now make up 30 percent of the population, live mainly in the south of the country. This is also where most of Ethiopia's Pentecostal/Charismatic Christians live. Numerous Christian leaders and ordinary church members have been attacked and some churches have been burned. This violence is the result in part of the increasingly radical turn Islam is taking in northeastern Africa generally, but the evangelistic assertiveness of the Pentecostal/Charismatic churches has also contributed to rising tensions. The government has reacted swiftly to quell the violence, replacing some local political leaders who were implicated in the troubles and moving more troops into the area to maintain order, but significant tensions remain.

Like all of Africa, Ethiopia is in a time of transition as a nation, and the Christians of Ethiopia are affected by that transition along with everyone else. Traditional ways of life are strong, and change is not always easy. One indicator of how slowly things can move is that it took until 2007 for the Ethiopian Orthodox Church to religiously approve the use of antiretroviral drugs, in addition to the drinking of holy water, as a remedy for those suffering from HIV/AIDS. But change is coming to Ethiopia nonetheless and, along with people all across the continent, Ethiopian Christians are confronted on a daily basis with the hope and the despair that come with living in an era of transformation.

Notes

1 Mercy Amba Oduyoye, *Daughters of Anowa: African Women and Patriarchy* (Maryknoll, NY: Orbis Books, 1995), p. 9.
2 Vincent J. Donovan, *Christianity Rediscovered* (Maryknoll, NY: Orbis Books, 1978), p. 148.
3 Eliza Griswold, *The Tenth Parallel: Dispatches from the Fault Line Between Christianity and Islam* (New York: Farrar, Straus and Giroux, 2010), pp. 66–73.

Suggestions for Further Reading

Baur, John (1994). *2000 Years of Christianity in Africa.* Nairobi: Pauline Publications Africa.

Bediako, Kwame (2004). *Jesus and the Gospel in Africa: History and Experience.* Maryknoll, NY: Orbis Books.

Eshete, Tibebe (2009). *The Evangelical Movement in Ethiopia: Resistance and Resilience.* Waco, TX: Baylor University Press.

Gifford, Paul (1998). *African Christianity: Its Public Role.* Bloomington: Indiana University Press.

Griswold, Eliza (2010). *The Tenth Parallel: Dispatches from the Fault Line Between Christianity and Islam.* New York: Farrar, Straus and Giroux.

Hastings, Adrian (1989). *African Catholicism: Essays in Discovery.* Philadelphia: Trinity Press International.

Hastings, Adrian (1994). *The Church in Africa, 1450–1950.* Oxford: Oxford University Press.

Isichei, Elizabeth (1995). *A History of Christianity in Africa: From Antiquity to the Present.* Grand Rapids, MI: Eerdmans.

Kalu, Ogbu (2008). *African Pentecostalism: An Introduction.* Oxford: Oxford University Press.

Rittner, Carol, John K. Rioth, and Wendy Whitworth (eds) (2004). *Genocide in Rwanda: Complicity of the Churches?* St Paul, MN: Paragon House.

Sundkler, Bengt and Steed, Christopher (2000). *A History of the Church in Africa.* Cambridge, UK: Cambridge University Press.

Tutu, Desmond (1999). *No Future Without Forgiveness.* New York: Doubleday.

Chapter 10

East Asia

Piety and Politics

Christianity and politics have been linked in East Asia for centuries. The Portuguese arrived with their cannons and crosses at the beginning of the sixteenth century, and the connection between piety and politics was later reinforced by the Western colonization of the region in the nineteenth and early twentieth centuries. Britain, France, Russia, and the United States used negotiation and military force to open the nations of East Asia to both trade and Christianity. Many missionaries who traveled to East Asia during these years were troubled by the unscrupulous practices of European and American colonizers, and some spoke out against abuses. In the end, however, almost all of them cooperated with the colonial powers, reasoning that since the Western "opening" of Asia allowed the gospel to be preached in new lands, it ultimately had to be part of God's grand plan for the world. In light of this history, it is understandable that many East Asians came to view Christianity as a foreign religion, imposed on the region against their will.

East Asia today is clearly postcolonial, and Christianity is becoming ever more at home in the region, but the linkage between faith and politics remains. In Indonesia, for example, citizens are legally required to be members of one of a limited number of approved "world religions." At first, there were only five approved options: Islam, Buddhism, Hinduism, Catholicism, and Protestantism. The list has since been expanded to include, among others, Baha'i, Jehovah's Witnesses, and Confucianism. The Indonesian assumption seems to be that belonging to a world religion makes a person a better citizen in a way that being non-religious or a follower of local religion does not.

Religion and politics have a very different relationship in Vietnam. As a Communist nation, Vietnam is suspicious of religion in general and is especially suspicious of Protestantism because it is often associated with Vietnam's former enemy, the United States. Conversion to Protestantism can result in persecution. The Hmong, a minority ethnic group living in the northern part of the country, have learned this the hard way. In the last two

The World's Christians: Who they are, Where they are, and How they got there, First Edition. Douglas Jacobsen.
© 2011 Douglas Jacobsen. Published 2011 by Blackwell Publishing Ltd.

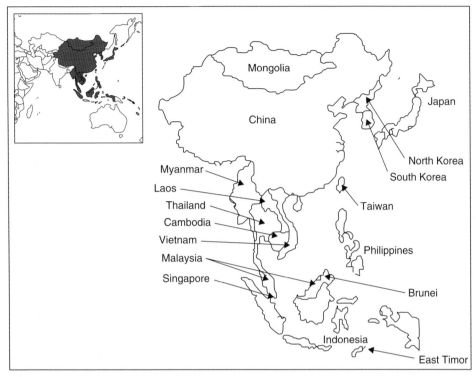

Figure 10.1   Map of East Asia. Map by author. 17 countries: total population 2,100,000,000 (32% of global population); Christian population 205,100,000 (10% of regional population, 10% of global Christian population): Orthodox 100,000, Catholics 100,000,000, Protestants 50,000,000, Pentecostal/Charismatic 55,000,000.

decades, more than half of the Hmong people have converted to Protestant Christianity and the governmental response has been harsh. Hmong Christians have been arrested and beaten, their churches have been destroyed, and Bibles and other religious books have been confiscated. The government rationale for its policy – which is almost the opposite of Indonesia's – is that if the Hmong want to be religious they should follow their own local traditions instead of an imported religion. Becoming nonreligious would also be an allowable choice, but conversion to the "enemy's" Protestant faith is seen as inherently treasonous.

There is no standard East Asian model of how faith and politics should be linked. Sometimes the relationship is straightforward and positive as it is in South Korea, where the last four presidents, starting with Kim Young-sam (elected in 1992), have been Christians. Sometimes the relationship is more tense and oppositional, as is the case in Myanmar where the Karen people, the nation's largest ethnic minority group, have made conversion to Christianity part of their political resistance to the military dictatorship that runs the country. The patterns vary, but politics and religion are intertwined almost everywhere. This does not mean that all of East Asian Christianity is intentionally political. There are many Christians in the region who understand their faith largely in personal terms, focusing on their own salvation and on God's power to heal, to protect them from evil, and to help with family relations. But even for Christians who want to stay out of politics, the political often intrudes. In East Asia, social identity and social relations define the contours of daily existence, and that socially connected character of life makes it hard to disentangle religion from the larger cultural-ethnic-political mix.

The Region in General

East Asia has a long and impressive history, and for centuries was the cultural and economic center of the world. Chinese silk, with its luxurious softness and bold colors, was desired everywhere, and from ancient times through the middle ages, Romans, Persians, and others risked travel on the famous and often dangerous Silk Road to obtain it. Various sea routes were also developed in the eighth century to deliver Chinese goods to Southeast Asia, India, and the Persian Gulf nations. East Asia was not only an exporter of luxury items, it was also the source of many useful technologies. The East invented the stirrup, the wheelbarrow, the crossbow, the magnetic compass, gunpowder, and the moveable type printing press, all long before any of these were known in the West. In the arts, Chinese painting, poetry, and porcelain were without equal in the rest of the world.

During the nineteenth and twentieth centuries the West subjugated most of East Asia, but many historians and economists are predicting that the East will soon rise again to reclaim its historical position as the center of the world. Many who live in East Asia concur, believing that Asia's resurgence is already well underway. Japan has been a leading, though not always a positive, player in this turnaround. Japan was the first East Asian nation to master and then use Western-style modernization for its own purposes, including competition with the West. Part of Japan's competitive plan involved its own program of colonization in East Asia, and to that end Japan annexed Korea in 1910, occupied Manchuria (northeastern China) in 1931, launched a war against China in 1937 to establish Japanese control over the mainland, and subjugated most of Southeast Asia in the late 1930s and early 1940s. The Japanese occupiers could be brutal, and the "Rape of Nanjing," which took place during the Sino-Japanese war of 1937, is remembered as one of the most horrible acts of military violence against civilians in history.

In 1941, the Japanese bombed Pearl Harbor in the Hawaiian Islands, hoping to destroy the United States military presence in the region and guarantee Japan's unchallenged control over East Asia. Japan's motto was "Asia for Asians," which played on rising anti-Western attitudes. By the early 1940s, Japan had driven the European colonial powers out of the Far East, and for a few years Japan ruled a large conquered territory that ranged from Russia in the north to Indonesia in the south. The Japanese Empire was dismantled after World War II, but the dream of freedom from Western colonial control that Japan had spread across the region remained. Thus there was widespread resistance when Western powers attempted to reclaim their old domains after the war. Eventually Indonesia, Malaysia, Burma, the Philippines, Laos, Cambodia, and Vietnam all established themselves as independent self-governing nations, alongside China, Japan, and the Koreas.

The process of independence was complicated by the emergence of the Cold War between the United States and the Soviet Union. The Cold War drew the United States into deeper involvement in East Asia even while the old European colonial powers were withdrawing. The Vietnam War, which lasted from the mid-1960s until 1973, was perceived in the United States as a form of resistance to the worldwide spread of Communism. But within East Asia and in many other parts of the world, this conflict was seen as a last vestige of colonialism, and defeating the United States represented the final step in the process of creating a new postcolonial Asian world.

During the last 30 years, East Asia has experienced significant economic growth and development, led by Japan with the assistance of the so-called "Asian Tigers" of Taiwan, South Korea, Singapore, and Hong Kong, and more recently by China, which has become a huge economic player, not only in Asia but the world. China, the world's most populous nation, is now the globe's second largest producer of goods and services, and is struggling with how best to respond to the growing disparity between the rich and the poor that its economic success has engendered, an ironic development for a state committed to social equality. Not all East Asian countries have experienced similar growth. Economic development in Malaysia, Thailand, and Indonesia has been modest at best, and the economies of Laos, Cambodia, Vietnam, and East Timor are floundering.

The bottom line is that while some people in East Asia are living very comfortably, the vast majority are poor. This disparity is reflected in measures of per capita gross domestic product (GDP) – the value of all the goods and services produced within a nation in a given year divided by the country's population. The 2009 per capita GDP for the world as a whole (as reported by the World Bank) was around $9,000. Japan ($40,000) and South Korea ($18,000) rank well above this global average, but most East Asian countries fall significantly below, including China at $3,800, Indonesia at $2,400, the Philippines at $1,750, and Vietnam at $1,000. (By comparison, the per capita GDP numbers for the United States and the United Kingdom were $46,500 and $35,000 respectively.) What this means is that large numbers of hard-working East Asian families live either in poverty or on the brink of poverty.

East Asia is a complex region with a proud cultural history and a growing economy that is making some individuals incredibly wealthy while large numbers remain impoverished. This is the terrain on which Christianity is making its way in the early twenty-first century as a relatively new Asian religion. In East Asia, Christianity is one among many religions and, while Christianity may be reshaping the mix of Asian faiths, it is itself being influenced by the social dynamics and spiritual traditions that exist in the region.

East Asian Religions

Perhaps the most obvious religious fact about East Asia is that it is home to more than 95 percent of the world's Buddhists. Buddhists account for a majority of the population in Myanmar, Thailand, Laos, Cambodia, Vietnam, and Japan. The actual number of Buddhists in the region is difficult to estimate because Buddhism is not an exclusivist religion. A person can be a little bit Buddhist or very devoutly Buddhist or a hybrid Buddhist, claiming to be Taoist, Shinto, or even Christian while simultaneously identifying as Buddhist. In addition, Buddhist communities generally do not keep membership statistics, so there are no institutional databases to access. By some calculations, as many as half of East Asia's population (one billion people) could be counted as Buddhists, but the most widely accepted estimate is about 350 million.

Buddhism itself is a complex religion containing many different schools of thought. Three of the most important East Asian versions of Buddhism are Theravada, Pure Land, and Zen. Theravada is a conservative form of Buddhism that is monastic in orientation and emphasizes the classic Buddhist goal of the "extinction of the self" (i.e., the dissolution of the ego and the cessation of bodily desires and emotional states that brings about the end of suffering). Theravada Buddhism is dominant in the south coast nations of Thailand, Myanmar, Laos, and Cambodia. Pure Land Buddhism is more popular in China. Rather than seeking the extinction of the self, this school of Buddhism emphasizes the joys of life in heaven – the pure land – which can only be attained through the help of various divine or semidivine intermediaries such as Amitabha, who is the principal buddha of Pure Land Buddhism, or the goddess of mercy Guanyin. In Japan, Zen Buddhism is one of the most popular alternatives. Zen stresses the importance of meditation as the path to enlightenment and rejects the need for assistance from spiritual intermediaries. Zen also minimizes the importance of sacred texts, in contrast to Theravada and Pure Land which greatly value the Buddhist scriptures.

While the significance of Buddhism is enormous, it is actually not the largest religion in East Asia by head count. That designation goes to Chinese traditional religion, which is followed by as many as 400 million people. Chinese traditional religion has never been codified in the same way as Buddhism, Islam, or Christianity. Rather than being tightly defined by doctrine or moral precepts, it is embodied in a loose collection of rituals and practices that serve the spiritual and communal needs of the Chinese people. In its more public expressions, it provides ceremonies for marking the calendar year and celebrating important transitions in the human life cycle. On the individual level, it includes divination (fortune telling), exorcism of demons, and protection from ghosts, as well as the use of traditional medicine and feng-shui (designing and arranging one's living space to maximize the benefit of cosmic forces). The People's Republic of China has tried to suppress traditional religion, calling it superstitious and out of sync with Communism's rational, scientific approach to life, but many follow it anyway. Outside the People's Republic, Chinese traditional religion flourishes in Taiwan and in the many Chinese immigrant communities that exist throughout the nations of Southeast Asia.

Islam is also a significant East Asian religion. Approximately 225 million Muslims live in the region, and Indonesia, with its roughly 180 million Muslim citizens, is the largest Islamic nation in the world. Many Muslims also live in China, Malaysia, Thailand, and the Philippines. East Asian Islam is for the most part comfortable with cultural and religious pluralism. Even in Indonesia, where Muslims form the majority of the population, there has been little pressure to make the nation as a whole officially Islamic, although some provinces within Indonesia (most notably Aceh in the far west) do follow Shari'a law. A few radical Islamic groups can be found in the region, such as Jemaah Islamiya, which advocates the creation of a new Southeast Asian pan-Islamic state, and the separatist movement Abu Sayyaf, which operates mainly on the southern island of Mindanao in the Philippines, but for the most part fundamentalist or jihadist Islam is rare.

Table 10.1 Distribution of three major world religions in East Asia (as % of total country population)

Country	Total population	% Christian	% Muslim	% Buddhist
Brunei	400,000	14	54	1
Cambodia	14,000,000	1	2	86
China	1,315,000,000	5	2	8
East Timor	1,000,000	85	3	0
Indonesia	225,000,000	13	85	1
Japan	127,500,000	2	0	55
Laos	6,000,000	3	0	43
Malaysia	26,000,000	7	48	7
Mongolia	2,750,000	1	5	22
Myanmar	50,000,000	8	2	72
North Korea	22,500,000	2	0	22
Philippines	85,000,000	91	6	0
Singapore	4,500,000	13	18	15
South Korea	48,500,000	28	0	24
Taiwan	23,000,000	6	0	35
Thailand	65,000,000	1	7	86
Vietnam	85,000,000	8	1	50

Other religions in East Asia include Hinduism, with 10 million followers located mainly in Malaysia, Myanmar, and the Indonesian island of Bali; Shamanism, which is the folk religion of Korea; and Shinto, which is a form of religious devotion to the state that is unique to Japan. In addition to these "named" religions, a wide range of local religious practices and traditions also continue to operate in the region, although these are increasingly limited to the highland areas of the smaller islands of Southeast Asia.

What may be the biggest religious story in recent East Asian history, however, is the growth of Christianity. In spite of its inauspicious beginning, coming into East Asia on the coattails of colonialism, Christianity has prospered in its new setting. At present, there are 200 million Christians in East Asia, representing nearly 10 percent of the total regional population. If growth trends continue, it is possible that the number of Christians in the region will surpass the numbers of Muslims within the next two decades. But the issue is not just that East Asia is becoming more Christian, it is also that East Asian Christians are increasingly seeking to make their faith more intentionally Asian.

Asian Culture and Christian Faith

While it is always easy to find exceptions to generalizations, it is still worth noting that an East Asian understanding of religion differs significantly from an American or European understanding. In East Asia, religion is typically viewed as part of culture. Like other dimensions of culture – such as art, literature, folk wisdom, healing practices, and life-cycle rituals – religion is treated as a source of ideas, practices, and attitudes that can be put to use when needed. In this perspective, each individual religion represents a different and distinct clustering of cultural resources, and resources from any of those religious clusters or traditions can be used to meet different religious needs at different points in any person's life, or multiple religious resources can be brought to bear simultaneously when dealing with a specific issue or concern. Thus an individual considering a major life decision might consult a Taoist fortune-teller, offer prayers at a Buddhist shrine, and read the Bible looking for guidance, without sensing any tension or incompatibility among those varied activities.

This is clearly not how most people in the West understand religion. In Europe and in the Americas, religion is usually treated as if it is an either/or proposition. In this framework, a person is supposed to be a member of only one religion at a time. A person can convert from one religion to another but cannot legitimately belong to two religions at the same time. In East Asia, that kind of exclusivity is typically rejected; questions of religious identity are generally more relaxed. Even East Asian Christians – sometimes against the wishes of their Western colleagues and counterparts – are increasingly adopting the attitude that people of different faiths can learn from one another. This does not mean that East Asian Christians mix and match at whim whatever spiritual practices and values they find attractive, but it does mean that dialogue is finding a place alongside dispute in the Christian encounter with East Asian culture and religion. Three dimensions of Asian spirituality are receiving special attention: mindfulness, story, and spirit.

Mindfulness is a central concern of Buddhism and of Asian spirituality in general. Mindfulness means living in the present, being fully aware of one's surroundings and actions. This includes ordinary bodily practices such as breathing mindfully (being aware of the air moving in and out of one's lungs), eating mindfully (chewing one's food unhurriedly), and walking mindfully (placing one foot in front of the other with care and deliberation). But mindfulness is also a matter of attitude, most notably being content with one's life, caring for those in one's immediate vicinity, and undertaking with pleasure the work one has been assigned. The Vietnamese Buddhist teacher Thich Nhat Hanh explains: "If while washing dishes, we think only of the cup of tea that awaits us … we are not alive during the washing of the dishes … [and] if we can't wash the dishes, the chances are we won't be able to drink our tea either. While drinking the cup of tea, we will only be thinking of other things."[1]

This is all very Buddhist, but some Christian leaders like the Vietnamese Cardinal Francis Xavier Nguyen Van Thuan (1928–2002) have also made mindfulness central to Christian spirituality. Nguyen Van Thuan learned the importance of mindfulness while imprisoned by the Communist government of Vietnam for 13 years, from 1975 to 1988. Wanting to do great things for God and struggling to understand how he could possibly serve God or others while in prison, he learned the importance of paying attention to the ordinary dimensions of everyday life. In *The Road of Hope* (2001), which was composed during his incarceration, he explains:

> If you wish to become a saint, do ordinary things well. They may seem insignificant, but pour all your love into them. … You say you are waiting for the "right moment" to do something

truly great. I wonder how many times such occasions will arise in your lifetime. No, take hold of the daily opportunities that arise to perform ordinary work in an extraordinary way.

For Nguyen Van Thuan, performing the many "uneventful, unnoticed, and monotonous" routines of daily life in an extraordinary way was the pathway to mature faith.[2] This is a very different attitude toward life than is typical of Christianity in the busy West, where multitasking and future-planning are a way of life. Nguyen Van Thuan's words are not uniquely Asian – to some degree they also represent the ideals of ancient Western monasticism – but for him and for many other Asian Christians who live uneventful and unnoticed lives of daily drudgery these words of guidance are thoroughly Christian and thoroughly Asian at the same time.

The second dimension, story, provides another point of contact between Christianity and East Asian culture. The Chinese theologian Choan-Seng Song has made this the core of his own reflection on faith. In the West, theology has traditionally been done from the top down. One reads the Bible and studies the Christian tradition in order to apply its principles to life. But Song's story theology begins at the bottom, in the marketplace listening to the stories that people tell about themselves and others. The stories of the marketplace reflect the ambiguities of ordinary life – joy laced with pain, poverty mixed with hope, good and bad blended together. Christianity does not always have answers for these stories, but Song suggests that these stories of life do not necessarily require answers. What emerges from Song's story-laden reflections on faith is not a theology of conclusions, but a vision of a God who walks beside people even when life is unclear, ambiguous, and confused. Once again, this is a thoroughly Christian attitude that is also very Asian. Coming from a Buddhist perspective, Thich Nhat Hanh echoes Song's sentiments almost exactly when he writes: "Some life dilemmas cannot be solved by study or rational thought. We just have to live with them, struggle with them, become one with them. Such dilemmas are not in the realm of the intellect. They come from our feelings and our will, and they penetrate our subconscious and our body, down to the marrow of our bones."[3]

Mindfulness and story together point in the direction of spirit. In the West, Christianity is often presented as a religion of rationality. Doctrine comes first and living comes second. But in East Asia, God is typically experienced first as a source of consolation, comfort, and power and only secondarily (if at all) as the Great Explainer of the world. This experiential faith orientation is rooted in the Asian notion that people need to adjust to reality rather than trying to change reality so it better suits their personal desires. From a contemporary Western perspective this can seem alarmingly passive, but the notion of yielding to the Holy Spirit has been a significant element of Christian spirituality throughout the centuries. It is also a major emphasis within the growing global Pentecostal/Charismatic movement, and that may partly explain why Pentecostal and Charismatic forms of Christianity are growing exponentially in East and South-East Asia.

Politics and Prosperity in the Philippines

The Philippines, with more than 77 million Christians out of a total population of 85 million, is one of only two nations in East Asia where Christians account for a majority of the population. (The only other predominantly Christian nation in East Asia is the tiny country of East Timor, which gained independence from Indonesia in 2002.) Christianity has a long history in the Philippines. The Spanish conquered the islands in the early 1500s and immediately began a program of conversion. By the mid-1700s most of the country had been brought into at least nominal conformity with the Catholic faith.

Catholicism in the Philippines is a cultural faith. While individual devotion is important and personal faith is valued, Christianity is understood to be grounded in the institutional church (the bishops, priests, and religious) and it is a resource for the people as a whole. Roman Catholic Christianity provides the framework for communal life from birth/baptism to maturity/confirmation to marriage to death/last rites. The church encompasses everyone and all of life, but Catholicism is a big tent. The repertoire of faith that Filipinos can draw from includes a wide range of local ideas and behaviors that have been adapted for Christian use, in addition to other formal church liturgies and devotional practices related to Christ, the Virgin Mary, and the saints, that are part of the European Catholic tradition.

The American military took over the Philippines in 1898 during the Spanish–American War, and William Howard Taft (later the 27th President of the United States) was installed as Governor. The United States controlled the islands until 1946 when the Philippines became an independent nation. The predominantly Protestant Americans looked askance at Filipino Catholicism, and Protestant missionaries flooded into the country trying to make converts. Some non-Roman Catholic churches did emerge, including the Philippine Independent Catholic Church (also known as the Aglipayan Church) with five million members, and the Iglesia ni Cristo (founded in 1914 by the prophet Felix Manalo who declared himself God's last messenger on earth) with four million members, but non-Catholic Christians generally had little success in drawing Filipinos away from their Catholic faith. To date, the vast majority of Filipinos – more than 80 percent – remain Catholic.

In addition to holding a prominent place in the culture, the Catholic Church also plays a significant role in politics. This political power of the Church was demonstrated in 1986

Figure 10.2
Archbishop Jaime Cardinal
Sin at a rally in Manila, 2000
© Reuters/Corbis

when Archbishop Jaime Cardinal Sin (1928–2005) encouraged Catholics in Manila and throughout the Philippines to support the People Power protest (known popularly as the EDSA revolution) that ended the corrupt regime of Ferdinand and Imelda Marcos and that installed Corazon Aquino as president. Archbishop Sin intervened in national politics again in 1998 when he issued a catechism about voting premised on the notion that "the Church has the role of critical solidarity with the government in defending the moral order" and, by extension, it also has the right to oppose the government "when moral and Gospel values are at stake."[4] He rejected the notion, advocated by some, that the church should identify one candidate as God's anointed choice, saying instead that God favored charity, justice, honesty, and truth, but most Catholics could read between the lines and discern that the bishop's own preference was for Alfredo Lim, the Mayor of Manila. Lim lost the election to the former movie star Joseph Estrada, but Cardinal Sin later helped orchestrate the removal of Estrada in the second People Power revolution (ESDA II) which took place in 2001.

The Vatican was uneasy with Sin's political involvement, cautioning him several times, but he remained politically active until his death in 2005. After Cardinal Sin's death, Pope Benedict XVI instructed the Philippine bishop's

Figure 10.3   The EDSA I protests, Manila, Philippines, 1986
© Alex Bowie/Getty Images

council to avoid meddling in national politics, and since then the bishops have for the most part acquiesced. Even before the Pope's intervention, it had become evident that the church's political activity had produced only moderate success in achieving its goals. While People Power produced some short-term improvements, things reverted quickly to the status quo after both EDSA revolutions. Corruption continued to be rampant and issues of justice and poverty remained largely unaddressed. Many Filipinos now assume that the Catholic Church has the power to bring down a bad government, but does not necessarily have the capacity to produce genuinely good government. Not surprisingly, many Filipinos have begun to turn elsewhere with their concerns about piety, politics, and poverty, and increasingly, they have sought answers in Charismatic/Pentecostal forms of Christianity.

The most popular religious figure in the Philippines today is a Charismatic Catholic lay preacher named Mariano Z. Velarde, better known as Brother Mike. Brother Mike runs the El Shaddai radio station, and he organizes a wide variety of events in Manila focusing on prayer and healing. His Saturday meetings, held in the grounds of the International Convention Center in the middle of the city, draw 500,000 people or more and the El Shaddai movement has about 10 million followers nationally. Brother Mike has been endorsed by the Catholic hierarchy and a Mass is said at each of his gatherings, but his message is simple, straightforward, and not particularly Catholic: those who bless God through financial gifts given to the El Shaddai ministry will be blessed, and God's blessings are obtained through "positive confession" – that is, by verbally claiming the health and wealth God has promised to everyone.

This kind of preaching has great appeal in the Philippines, where reciprocity is a cultural norm: a person who is given a gift is expected to respond in kind. Brother Mike suggests that giving God a gift in the form of a donation to El Shaddai literally obligates God to bless the giver in return. Such logic is sensible to Filipinos, and it is hugely attractive to the economically disadvantaged people who flock to El Shaddai's meetings and listen to Brother Mike's radio broadcasts. Protestants have their own equivalent to El Shaddai in the Jesus is Lord Fellowship, which claims four million followers. Many critics paint El Shaddai and the Jesus is Lord Fellowship as nothing more than religious scams, bilking the poor, and giving them little or nothing in return. Yet both organizations provide some social services – ranging from schools to low-cost retail stores – and, more importantly, they give their followers a sense of spiritual assurance and personal pride that allows them to live with dignity even in the midst of continuing poverty.

Christian Growth in South Korea

Christianity came relatively late to Korea, but it has blossomed dramatically in the twentieth century and especially in the years following World War II. Catholicism was first introduced in 1784, but persecution prevented the church from establishing solid roots until 1886 when France forced Korea to grant religious freedom to Catholics. The first Protestant missionaries had arrived two years earlier in 1884. Christianity remained a tiny presence in the country until 1907 when the Great Revival occurred and the "Convert a Million Koreans to Christianity" movement ignited a century of phenomenal Protestant church growth. Koreans were attracted to Protestantism in part because of its experiential and emotional dimensions, emphases that were similar to those of traditional Korean shamanism. Protestantism was also bolstered by several Protestants who were prominent leaders of the Korean resistance movement during the Japanese occupation of Korea that began in 1910.

Korea was freed from Japanese occupation by American troops during World War II, but new tensions arose when Communists tried to take over the country. War erupted in June of 1950. When a ceasefire was finally arranged in 1953, the result was a nation divided between North and South, facing each other across a hostile border. Before the war, the majority of Korean Christians had lived in the North. Many of those Christians fled South during the conflict, leaving friends and family behind, and they have been separated ever since. This is a tragedy for the Korean population as a whole, and the Christian community prays constantly for the reunification of the country and its churches. Since the division, Christianity has stagnated under Communist persecution in the North while it has grown dramatically in the South. It is currently estimated that there are more than 13 million Christians in the South and fewer than half a million in the North.

Christians make up about 29 percent of South Korea's population. Protestantism represents the largest bloc of the Christian population and Presbyterianism dominates the South Korean Protestant world. Presbyterianism in South Korea has, however, been beset by tensions and the movement is now divided into more than 80 separate denominations. The Hap Dong Church and the Tong Hap PCK are the largest, claiming two million members each. Korean churches routinely overestimate their numbers, but even if the claimed membership was halved, there would still be more Presbyterians in South Korea than in the United States. Most Korean Presbyterians are evangelical in theological orientation, stressing the need for conversion and affirming the inerrancy of the Bible. And they are politically involved. The current president of South Korea, Lee Myung-Bak, is a Presbyterian and so was former president Kim Young-Sam (1993–98).

The Pentecostal/Charismatic movement is also quite large and growing and is represented most visibly by the Yoido Full Gospel Church led by the Reverend David Yonggi Cho. Located in downtown Seoul, this church (which has several campuses in the city, but considers itself an extended congregation rather than a denomination) claims more than half a million members. Routinely describing itself as the largest church in the world, the Yoido Church has become a model for megachurches globally. Being Pentecostal, the leadership of the Yoido Church gives the Holy Spirit credit for its phenomenal growth, but organizational finesse has played a huge role: the Yoido Church is a well-oiled, carefully run machine. Worship is timed to the minute and services last precisely one hour, which is necessary since there are seven services each Sunday and thousands of worshippers need to be moved in and out of the main building during the 30-minute break between those worship services (see Plate 15).

The key factor in Yoido's growth has been the cell group. Cell groups are small gatherings of five to fifteen people who meet regularly in their homes between weekly worship services for the purposes of prayer, mutual support, and evangelism. The goal is both fellowship and growth. People are attracted to the Yoido Church not so much because of the massive worship services, but because of the appeal of small group membership. In a modern impersonal city like Seoul, cell groups provide a human point of contact and a sense of community. As soon as a cell group reaches 15–20 members, it divides in two and the process starts over again. The cell group concept was invented at the Yoido Church, but it is now a staple of church growth worldwide, adopted by Anglican, Methodist, Presbyterian, Baptist, and other churches as well as by many Pentecostal groups.

The growth of both Protestantism and the Pentecostal/Charismatic movement has been tremendous during the last half century, but growth seems to be leveling off in both camps. Perhaps these forms of Christianity have simply reached their saturation point. But Protestantism, in particular, may also be hurting itself. In the past, Protestantism had a strong reputation for both morality and care for the common good, but a number of recent scandals have marred that image. These include the misuse of power by President Kim Young Sam's son and also the collapse of a downtown department store that caused the death of more than 500 people after the Presbyterian owner had been warned about the building's structural problems. There have also been several incidents where Protestants have desecrated Buddhist or other public religious sites, raising questions about Protestant civility in a religiously pluralistic society.

The most significant growth in South Korean Christianity is now taking place within the Catholic domain, and the public reputation of Catholicism is also on the rise. Catholics currently account for about 10 percent of the Korean population, but the numbers are changing. The reasons for this new growth spurt are not entirely clear, but one element may be that Catholics generally express more respect for traditional Korean ways of life, including Buddhism, than other Christians. Catholics have also become more visible politically. Two recent presidents, Kim Dae-Jung (1998–2003) and Roh Moo-Hyun (2003–08), were Catholic and both were known for their support of human rights and democracy.

Indonesia's Religious Variety and Violence

Indonesia claimed independence from Dutch rule in the late 1940s. After more than a decade of political instability, President Sukarno assumed power in 1960 and immediately began trying to unify the country under his command. He dissolved the nation's political parties and set up a National Front that was designed to foster consensus within the nation as a whole. To aid in that task, Sukarno developed a philosophy called "*Pancasila*," meaning "five pillars." The five affirmations of *Pancasila* are belief in one God, the dignity of all people, the unity of Indonesia, democracy guided by wisdom, and social justice as a governing principle for the nation. Sukarno was attempting to develop a public philosophy for Indonesia that could be affirmed by the country's Muslim majority but that would also be acceptable to the nation's many minority groups, including its Christians.

In 1967, Sukarno was overthrown by a military revolt and General Suharto assumed the presidency. Suharto affirmed Sukarno's philosophy of *Pancasila*, but he was also intent on exercising greater control over the population as a whole. Part of that control included the suppression of Indonesia's many local, animistic religions, and all Indonesians were required to become members of one of five "monotheistic" world religions: Islam, Buddhism, Hinduism, Catholicism, or Protestantism. (Indonesian Buddhists and Hindus are technically supposed to affirm monotheism as a tenet of their faith, though neither Buddhism nor Hinduism traditionally teaches belief in one supreme God.) At present, Islam is by far the largest Indonesian religion, accounting for 85 percent of the population; Protestantism is second with 10 percent of the population; and Catholicism is third with 3 percent. The Buddhist and Hindu communities each claim only about 1 percent of the population.

More than 800 different ethnic communities can be identified within the Indonesian population, and these groups have responded differently to Christianity. The largest ethnic community is the Javanese, and Christianity has made some inroads with this group: approximately 11 percent are Christian. The next largest ethnic groups are the Sundanese and the Madurese, with virtually no Christian presence. Chinese immigrants constitute the fourth largest ethnic group, and almost half of the members of this group are now Christian. With regard to the rest of Indonesia's smaller ethnic communities, the picture is similarly mixed. Islam claims a supermajority (two-thirds or more of the membership) in 350 (60 percent) of these groups, while Christianity claims a supermajority in about 250 (40 percent). This does not mean that Christians make up 40 percent of the Indonesian ethnic minority population, however, because most of the Christianized groups are small in size whereas most Muslim groups tend to be larger. Regionally, Christianity has a stronger presence in the eastern half of the country and is less well represented in the west (see Figure 10.4).

In recent years, Indonesia has experienced a significant amount of interethnic and interreligious violence, most of it involving conflict between Muslims and Christians. Violence has been especially prevalent in those parts of the country where ethnic groups that are predominantly Christian live side by side with those that are predominantly Muslim. In Central Sulawesi and the Maluku islands, for example, thousands of people have been killed and hundreds of villages have been destroyed during the last two decades as a result of Muslim–Christian violence. But tensions have also erupted in the western regions of the

Plate 1   Matthew the Poor/Yūsuf Iskandar

Plate 2   Coptic Pope Shenouda III
© KHALED EL-FIQI/epa/Corbis

Plate 3 Ancient Armenian church near Lake Van, Turkey

© Dennis Cox/Alamy

Plate 4 Aerial view of St Sava Serbian Orthodox Church (Belgrade, Serbia)

Vlado Marinkovic; www.pbase.com/vmarinkovic/favourites

Plate 5   Hill of Crosses, Siauliai, Lithuania
http://en.wikipedia.org/wiki/File:Hill-of-crosses-siauliai.jpg. Photo by Mannobult, licensed under Creative Commons

Plate 6   The Queen of Heaven, the Black Madonna of Czestochowa
Jasna Gora Monastery, Czestochowa, Poland/The Bridgeman Art Library

Plate 7   Christ the Savior Church, Moscow, destroyed in 1931
Wikipedia

Plate 8 Christ the Savior Church, Moscow, rebuilt in 2000

© Galina Barskaya/Fotolia.com

Plate 9 Orthodox Cathedral of the Ascension, Almaty, Kazakhstan
© Wiskerke/Alamy

Plate 10 Cathedral of the Epiphany (CSI), Dornakal, India

© Revd Dr Paul M Collins; http://inculturation.chi.ac.uk

Plate 11 Young Muslim demonstrators shout slogans as they march in central Paris during a protest against the new law banning religious symbols in French state schools, February 14, 2004

© Charles Platiau/Reuters/Corbis

Plate 12 Pope Benedict XVI (R) meets France's President Nicolas Sarkozy at the Vatican, December 20, 2007

© Reuters/Corbis

Plate 13 Victims of the Rwandan genocide lying outside a Catholic Church
© Baci/Corbis

Plate 14 Members of the Cherubim and Seraphim Church (AIC), West Africa
Eternal Sacred Order of the Cherubim and Seraphim on Victoria Island, Lagos, Nigeria. Photograph by Eliot Elisofon, 1959.
EEPA EECL 4903. Eliot Elisofon Photographic Archives. National Museum of African Art, Smithsonian Institution

Plate 15 Yoido Full Gospel Church, Seoul, Korea, July 27, 2008
© Pascal Deloche/Godong/Corbis

Plate 16   Zhongguancun Christian Church, Haidian District, Beijing (TSPM/CCC)
© Jason C.Y. Kwong

Plate 17   Golden Lamp Church, Linfen, Shanxi province, China; now closed by the authorities
© Andy Wong/AP/Press Association Images

Plate 18 Our Lady of Guadalupe
Topfoto/The Granger Collection

Plate 19 Universal Church of the Kingdom of God, Brazil
© David Ivanowski

Plate 20   "This Home is Catholic" (*Este Hogar es Catolico*) door sign
© Chacpol

Plate 21 Rick Warren's Saddleback Church, Lake Forest, May 20, 2008
© Ann Johansson/Corbis

Plate 22 Martin Luther King, Jr. preaching at Mason Temple, Memphis, Tennessee
© Richard L. Copley/AFSCME

Plate 23 Paul Gauguin: *Two Tahitian Women*, 1899 (oil on canvas) (*Les seins aux fleurs rouges*)
© akg-images/Erich Lessing

Plate 24   Paul Gauguin: *Haere Pape*, 1892 (oil on canvas)
© The Barnes Foundation, Merion, Pennsylvania/The Bridgeman Art Library

Plate 25 Detail of a painting of Tiwi art on display at the beautifully preserved Catholic church in Nguiu, Bathurst Islands, Tiwi Group, Northern Territory, Australia

Carole-Anne Fooks/Australian Image Originals/www.livingtravel.com.au

Plate 26 Icon of Symeon the Stylite

© Topfoto/Ullstein Bild

Plate 27   Ancient cross marking the purported burial site of St Thomas in Mylapore (near Chennai), India
Photograph reproduced courtesy of Bernardo Michael

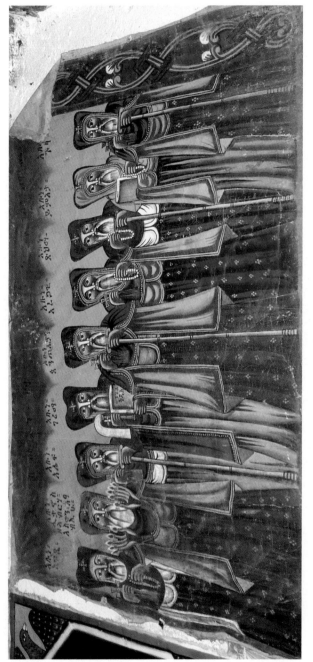

Plate 28 Icon of the "Nine Saints" painted on a church wall in Ethiopia
© Ondřej Žváček, http://commons.wikimedia.org/wiki/File:Nine_Saints.jpg

Plate 29 Icon of the Triumph of Orthodoxy, Cretan School (16th century)
Benaki Museum, Athens, Greece/Gift of Helen Stathatos/The Bridgeman Art Library

Plate 30 Icon depicting Saints Cyril and Methodius, Varna
© José F. Poblete/CORBIS

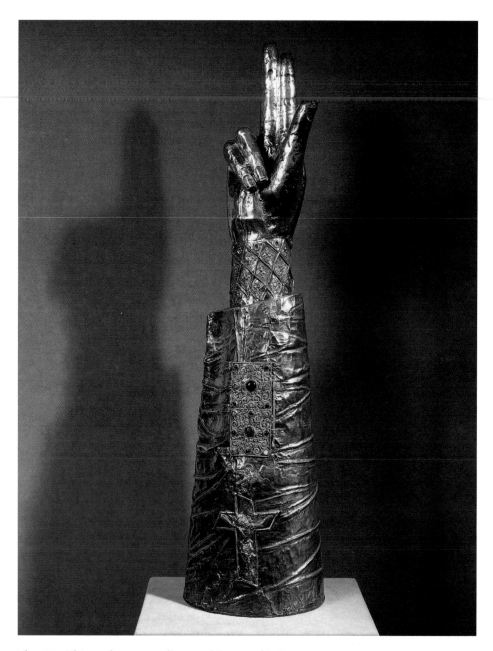

Plate 31 Thirteenth-century reliquary of the arm of St George
Gianni Dagli Orti/The Art Archive/Alamy

Plate 32 Andrei Rublev icon of John the Baptist
© The Art Gallery Collection/Alamy

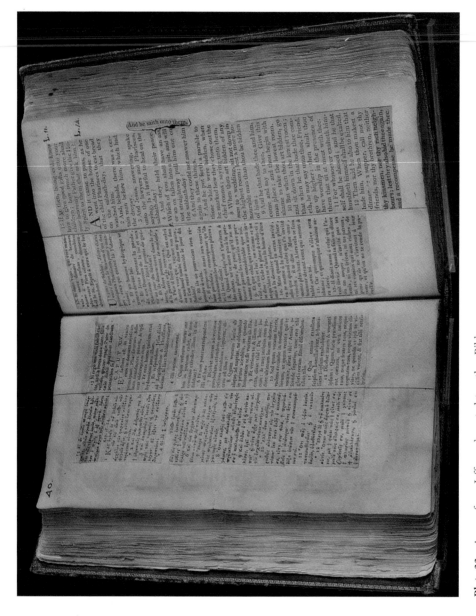

Plate 33 A page from Jefferson's pasted-together Bible

By kind permission of the Division of Political History, National Museum of American History, Smithsonian Institution

Plate 34 Baroque church, Steingaden, Germany
© Bildarchiv Monheim GmbH/Alamy

JEAN,

Roy de Congo,

à la tête de ses armées et le premier fait Chrétiens.

Tiré de l'Histoire des Voyages.

Paris chez Duflos rue St Victor.

A. P. D. R.

Plate 35 The Christian King Nzinga Nkuwu (João I) of Congo (copper engraving by Pierre Duflos, 1780)

The Stapleton Collection/The Bridgeman Art Library

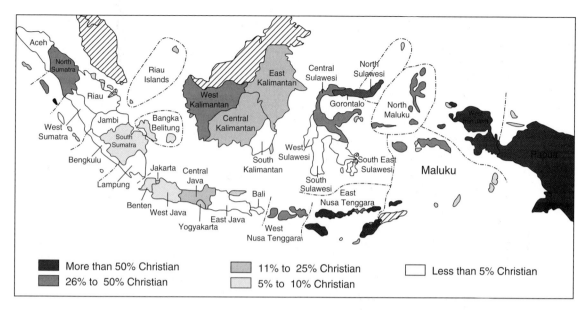

Figure 10.4   Map of Indonesia showing distribution of Christians (% of total population in region). Map by author.

country where Islam is especially strong. In Bandung state, a group called the Anti-Apostasy Movement of the Indonesian Ulema Congregation Forum monitors Christian activities and often tries to squash them.

Because the majority of those killed have been Christians – some put the estimate as high as 90 percent – charges of overt religious persecution have been made. This perspective certainly rings true in those regions like Sulawesi where radical Islamic groups like Laskar Jihad have been active and some local political leaders are clearly biased against Christians. But it is important to point out that Christians are not always innocent victims; in some instances they have instigated the violence. It is also necessary to remember that religion is only one factor contributing to these clashes. Long-standing ethnic tensions have also played a role and social and economic developments have often exacerbated the situation.

Christianity has a long history in Indonesia, and it is the majority faith in three of the country's provincial jurisdictions. In terms of sheer numbers, there are three times as many Christians in Indonesia as there are in the Netherlands (Indonesia's former colonial ruler), and there are probably 10 or 20 times as many Christians in church on Sunday. Denominationally, most of Indonesia's 29 million Christians fall into four main categories: Catholic, Reformed, Lutheran, and Pentecostal/Charismatic. Catholicism, which was first introduced to Indonesia by the Portuguese in the early 1500s, currently claims seven million members. Reformed Protestantism, brought to the islands by the Dutch in the 1600s, is close behind with six and a half million. Indonesia's Lutherans, who trace their roots to the

Figure 10.5   Reformed church (next to mosque) in Malang, East Java, Indonesia
© Dario De Santis

work of pietistic German missionaries who came to the region in the late nineteenth century, number five million. Finally, Pentecostal/Charismatic Christianity, a twentieth century latecomer which is largely indigenous in origin and leadership, has grown spectacularly during the last half century and now claims about 10 million adherents.

All four of these groups have been challenged by the recent upsurge in interreligious violence and they are trying to develop new programs that will encourage peaceable relations and mutual good will rather than continued conflict. Even the Pentecostal/Charismatic churches that have traditionally shied away from anything political have become involved in this endeavor: the Bethel Church of Indonesia, for example, has recently added a focus on "blessing the city" (being good citizens) to its older emphases on healing and spiritual empowerment. None of these churches – least of all the Pentecostals – sees politics as its first calling, but they have all come to see community involvement as necessary.

The Complexities of Christianity in China

China is not only the largest nation in East Asia, it is the largest nation in the world, and it is a place where Christianity has a long and complicated history. First introduced to China in the seventh century by a Persian monk named Alopen, Christianity was banned from the

Empire in 845. Four hundred years later, Franciscan monks reintroduced Christianity to China, but they too were soon banned. Around 1600, the Jesuits made a third attempt, and they were moderately successful, but their mission also fell on hard times. The Christianity that exists in China today – with the exception of a few small Catholic communities left from the Jesuit years – is the product of a fourth initiative, involving both Catholics and Protestants, that began in the early nineteenth century in tandem with the West's colonization of the region. But Christianity in China is also increasingly a home-grown affair, being defined and structured along thoroughly Chinese lines and often having a distinctly Pentecostal/Charismatic flavor.

As a nation, modern China was created in 1912 when the Ming Empire came to an end and the Chinese Republic was born. Sun Yat-sen had led the way toward democracy, but the older and more well-established General Yuan Shikai became the first official President. When Yuan died suddenly in 1916, the country fell into chaos. In the next decades, the two strongest leaders who emerged were Chiang Kai-shek, head of the Nationalist Party, and Mao Zedung, chairman of the Communist Party. In the years following World War II, civil war erupted between these two parties. Beaten in the north by the Communists, Chiang withdrew to the south and was eventually pushed entirely off the mainland to Taiwan where he set up his own alternative Nationalist Chinese government. On the mainland, however, the Communists were triumphant, and a new People's Republic of China (PRC) was inaugurated under Mao's rule in 1949. The PRC continues to see Taiwan as a part of China and is committed to reuniting the island with the rest of the country.

Long before the creation of the PRC, the rulers of China had determined that religion is something that needs to be kept under strict control. Religion can wreak havoc on a society, and it has frequently done so in China. In the two hundred years between 1700 and 1900, for example, there were five major religiously inspired uprisings in China. Three of these were led by Muslims, one was led by a Buddhist secret society (the White Lotus), and the most catastrophic of all, the Taiping Rebellion, which resulted in an estimated 25 million deaths, was led by an indigenous Chinese Christian leader (Hong Xiuquan). Add in the Opium Wars of the mid-1800s and the so-called Boxer Rebellion (1899–1901), both of which had religious dimensions, and it seems obvious that religion has the power to disturb the social peace.

Given China's long-standing efforts to control religion, no one expected the PRC to give religion a free hand. The only question was how harsh the control would be. Mao Zedung and the other leaders of the new PRC were Communists. They believed that religion was the product of irrational fears and economic oppression and that it would simply wither away as soon as the socialist ideal became reality. Wanting to make sure religious opposition would not hinder the creation of the new socialist China, the government required all religious groups to pledge their patriotic support for the PRC's socialist goals and to declare themselves to be fully independent of foreign control.

Catholic and Protestant reactions to the new requirements differed greatly. For Catholics, the reaction was basically negative. At the time of the founding of the People's Republic, there were approximately three million Catholic Christians in China. For Roman Catholics, independence from "foreign control" was impossible, since allegiance to the Pope – a foreign leader – was both a core teaching of faith and a deeply ingrained religious practice.

In addition to Catholicism's theological commitment to papal authority, the Vatican also encouraged Catholics to resist the new socialist policies of the republic. Bishops were given instructions to avoid cooperation with the new government whenever possible and to actively oppose Communist directives whenever they appeared to conflict with Christian faith and morals. While the Chinese Catholic leadership occasionally expressed support for certain particular patriotic causes, including speaking out against the military intervention of the United States in the Korean War during the early 1950s, the Catholic Church generally stood aloof from the Communist state, exhibiting independence, mixed sometimes with active resistance, that eventually led to the arrest and detention of many Catholic bishops and priests.

The Protestant community was initially much smaller than the Catholic population, with only about a million members, and its response was more mixed. The issue of independence from foreign control was not itself a significant concern for most Protestants. Long before the government of China began to advocate a "three self" ideal of churchly independence – self-governing, self-supporting, and self-propagating – most Chinese Protestant leaders had already embraced those values. In fact, some Protestants saw the new government regulations as giving them the opportunity finally to attain complete freedom from missionary oversight. The Protestant response to the demand of support for the socialist cause was, however, more varied. Some Protestants, like the YMCA (Young Men's Christian Association) leader Wu Yaozung (Y. T. Wu), were pleased to cooperate because they believed the new Communist government represented an important positive step toward the realization of the kingdom of God on earth. Others, such as Ni Tuosheng (Watchman Nee), a businessman who was also the founder of the Little Flock local church movement, rejected the new patriotic requirement because he was ideologically opposed to both Communist atheism and socialist economics. Still others, like the well-known Protestant dissident Wang Mingdao, refused to comply because they had spiritual reservations about mixing faith with politics in any form and because they believed that fellowship with "false" Christians (those outside their own organization) would threaten their own salvation.

At first the government of the PRC was content to merely poke and prod the Protestant and Catholic Churches toward compliance, but eventually the state adopted a more forceful stance. In 1955 it launched the Protestant Three-Self Patriotic Movement and two years later the government created the Chinese Catholic Patriotic Association (1957). While the stated goal of these two organizations was purely administrative – merely to "coordinate" church activity with government policy – they soon took on the role of being the state-approved governing bodies for the Protestant and Catholic Churches themselves, with the government ordering all Christians to join the appropriate association. Some Christians complied, many did not, and tensions between the joiners and the resisters was often intense.

Joiners, both Protestant and Catholic, were convinced that cooperation with the People's Republic was unavoidable and necessary if Christianity was going to survive in the new regime. Some even believed that God was at work in the new government, citing social improvements like the eradication of opium abuse as evidence of the government's good faith and intentions. But many Catholic and Protestant leaders remained unconvinced, refusing to cooperate with the new patriotic associations and denouncing those who did.

In response, the government initiated a major persecution of all unco-operative Christians. The result was a deep and painful split between the Chinese patriotic Christians and the dissident or underground Christians in both the Catholic and non-Catholic Christian communities.

Dissident Protestants and dissident Catholics were subject to the same kind of repression, but the Protestant churches were generally able to adapt more easily. When a Protestant leader was arrested or imprisoned, another member of that group could easily step forward to assume leadership. Catholics did not have the same flexibility, especially at the level of bishop. The Pope was supposed to appoint bishops, but China had prevented communication with the Pope. Finally, under significant pressure from the government, the Catholic Patriotic Association began consecrating new bishops without papal approval. Pope Pius XII responded by threatening to excommunicate those involved in making such appointments, but the process moved ahead anyway. Had the pontiff followed through with his threat of excommunication, the new bishops would have been declared formally schismatic and no longer part of the global Catholic Church. But the Vatican decided on a more politically shrewd response. The pope declared the newly installed bishops "valid, but illicit," and the ambiguity of that wording was meant to send a very explicitly mixed message. On the one hand, faithful Chinese Catholics could be assured that the sacraments being administered by the new bishops would be considered genuine and efficacious by the Church as a whole. On the other hand, Rome made it clear that the new Chinese method for selecting bishops was thoroughly unacceptable.

In the year 1966, however, that kind of nuance lost all significance as the Cultural Revolution sprang into existence, defining all of reality in terms of stark good and bad. Launched by Mao Zedung to consolidate his power within the Party and to further his vision of the Communist cause, the Cultural Revolution sought to cleanse China of the "four olds" that were holding back progress: old customs, old culture, old habits, and old ideas. Religion was "old" on all four counts and it had to be destroyed. To that end, thousands of members of a youth militia called the Red Guard were given free rein to arrest, mock, torture, and abuse anyone or anything that smelled of the past. Religious leaders were especially singled out for "re-education," and virtually all of the nation's churches, mosques, temples, and monasteries were either closed or totally destroyed. Christianity was crushed and the patriotic Protestant and Catholic associations were shut down. But while Christians suffered, they did not suffer alone. Members of other religious groups, ordinary citizens, and even some Communist Party members received equally horrendous treatment at the hands of the Red Guards.

The goal of the Cultural Revolution had been to destroy religion, but ironically that is not what happened. Rather than eliminating Christianity, the arrest and detention of the clergy forced Christian laypeople to take responsibility for their own religious lives in new ways. Thus lay Catholics continued to meet on their own to worship God as best they could without the aid of priests. Grandmothers, who often acted as midwives, baptized Catholic infants to keep the intergenerational chains of faith intact, and Chinese Catholics developed a new appreciation of their identity as a people of God and not just as members of the church. In the Protestant world a similar development took place. Given the need for secrecy, Protestants met quietly in homes to avoid detection, but with time many of these small churches became too large to avoid detection, so they divided. The result was a burgeoning of new house churches and of new networks connecting them to each other. With time, some of these networks became quite large. For example, the Yin Shang network of house churches, founded during this time, now claims five million members. The required secrecy also reshaped the character of many Protestant churches, making them more suspicious of outsiders and pushing them increasingly toward a Pentecostal/Charismatic style of faith because they felt they had no option other than to rely on the Holy Spirit in a time of terrible trial when all human hope seemed lost.

Starting in the mid-1970s, Deng Xiaoping and a circle of other pragmatically minded Communist leaders slowly began to steer the People's Republic in a new direction, away from the extremes of the Cultural Revolution and back toward normality. They wrote a new constitution, adopted a positive attitude toward economic modernization, and rethought the country's policies related to religion. The result has been an incredible transformation. While China remains committed to socialism, socialism is now defined more flexibly. The Chinese government can still be an authoritarian state – as demonstrated by the violent suppression of prodemocracy protests in Tiananmen Square in 1989, the repression of the Falun Gong movement in 1999, and the recent crackdowns in Tibet and Urumqi – but there is no question that China has become a much more open society.

Adjusting to this new reality has been difficult for the churches because the ground rules are not entirely clear. The new government policy guarantees religious freedom for Chinese citizens, but it also reserves the right of the state to control religion when necessary. It declares that religions that undermine the socialist cause or that promote "abnormal" beliefs and practices will not be tolerated, creating ambiguity since interpretations of what is normal or what is seen as undermining socialism can vary greatly from locale to locale. In some regions of China, religion is booming; in others, it is facing significant government opposition.

Overall, however, the trend is clearly toward greater freedom, and Christianity in China is growing by leaps and bounds because of that. The precise number of Christians in China today is hard to estimate. The government usually says there are only about 20 million Christians in the country, but some observers say there may be 150 million or more. A reasonable estimate seems to be around 65 million: 12 million Catholics, maybe 15 million traditional Protestants, and somewhere between 35 and 40 million Pentecostal/Charismatic believers, numbers that reflect tremendous growth on the part of Catholics and non-Catholics alike.

There are various social explanations for this growth, most of them associated with China's policy of rapid modernization. Massive projects like the Yangtze River Dam displaced millions, and advances in agriculture changed the economic landscape. Rural-to-urban migration has become very common, and it is projected that in the decade 2010 to 2020 as many as 200 million additional agriculture workers will migrate to China's ever-growing cities. University education is booming, and young adults in particular are searching for meaning. For them, the future seems both exhilaratingly open, but also frighteningly unknown. In this changing environment, Christianity offers both a sense of belonging (because the church can become a new community for those who feel "lost" socially or geographically) and a moral point of reference in a world where so many other behavioral guidelines have been swept away.

Figure 10.6 Christians attend Sunday service at Shouwang Church in Beijing's Haidian district, October 3, 2010. Shouwang is a "house church," not officially sanctioned by the government
© Petar Kujundzic/Reuters

The growth of Protestantism and Pentecostal/Charismatic Christianity has also been aided by the movement's entrepreneurial character. In the same way that small businesses have mushroomed everywhere in China, Protestant and Pentecostal/Charismatic churches have grown because anyone with energy and vision can start a new congregation. By way of contrast, the Chinese Catholic Church is both much more hierarchical in structure and much more traditional in attitude. A majority of Catholics in China still live in villages (many of them located in Hebei Province southwest of Beijing) that are populated almost entirely by Catholics. It is common in China to think of Catholicism as an ethnic faith because it is so closely tied to Catholic family lineage and to Catholic village culture. Protestantism and Pentecostal/Charismatic Christianity are, by contrast, more individualistic, so they are more easily maintained when a person moves from village to town to city.

Non-Catholic Christianity in contemporary China continues to be divided between the Three-Self Patriotic Movement and the related China Christian Council (TSPM/CCC), which represent the old "above ground" church, and the unregistered "underground" house churches. That kind of language is, however, becoming increasingly anachronistic. Rather than being clumped into just two categories, Chinese churches now fall along a spectrum of options ranging from the government-registered TSPM/CCC churches (see Plate 16) through a variety of open, but unregistered churches (some of which are very large) in many of China's rapidly growing cities (see Plate 17) to traditional "underground" churches, which are found mostly in the more rural areas of the country (see Figure 10.6).

All of these non-Catholic churches share much in common theologically. They express high regard for the Bible, emphasize personal faith and practice, and generally affirm the historical teachings of Christianity as expressed in documents such as the Apostles' Creed and the Nicene Creed, but all three kinds of churches are also dealing with tensions created by the rapid growth of Pentecostal/Charismatic forms of Christianity. The leadership of the TSPM/CCC is most concerned, expressing criticism about Pentecostal/Charismatic emphasis on the supernatural and the more subjective dimensions of faith. Given the huge role that superstition and supernaturalism have played in historical Chinese folk religion – facets of traditional Chinese culture that Chinese Communists still see as irrational and dangerous – most TSPM/CCC leaders want Christianity to position itself as a rational and scientific faith rather than as a spirit-filled movement.

Churches not associated with the TSPM/CCC have generally moved in the opposite direction. Rather than resisting Pentecostal/Charismatic developments, they have embraced them, even though the transition has not always been easy. Most of these churches believe in the miraculous power of the Holy Spirit and in God's ability to heal the sick. However, there are different opinions regarding some manifestations of the Holy Spirit, especially speaking in tongues. In 1998, four of the largest Chinese house church networks (including the Fangcheng network which claims 10 million members) drafted a conciliatory statement of faith intended to prevent fractures within the movement along Charismatic versus non-Charismatic lines. On the critical issue of speaking in tongues, this statement took a carefully worded middle position that neither forbade the practice nor encouraged it.

The TSPM/CCC churches and the unregistered churches also tend to have different views regarding the social implications of the gospel. The TSPM/CCC churches are likely to stress the social side of Christianity – its implications for life in this world. Bishop K. H. Ting, the leading theological spokesperson for the TSPM/CCC, who taught for years at Nanjing Seminary, says bluntly: "Christ is not so small as to concern himself only with religious or spiritual or ecclesiastical things."[5] In his view, Christ is leading everyone in the whole world, Christians and non-Christians alike, toward peace, justice, and harmony, and the job of Christians is to cooperate with that process wherever it leads, including the political arena. In contrast, most unregistered churches consider evangelism and personal salvation to be the primary focus of Christianity. They excel at person-to-person evangelism, primarily at the local level but "foreign missions" are also underway, most visibly in the "Back to Jerusalem" movement which has the goal of evangelizing all of the nations between China and the Middle East. The unregistered churches remain cautious about direct participation in government-run initiatives, but some of them now stress the need to be "good neighbors" to all the people around them and are developing programs that they hope will both address the needs of society and honor Christ by improving the public image of the church.

In contemporary China, Catholicism exists in a world not connected at all with other forms of Christianity. In fact, most Chinese consider Catholicism to be a separate and distinct religion that is not connected to non-Catholic Christianity at all. Theologically, there is and always has been only one Catholic Church in China, and this is true despite the visible split that exists between the open and approved patriotic Catholic Church and the unregistered and illegal underground Catholic community. Since the 1980s, however, the gap between these two expressions of the Catholic tradition in China has been narrowing. Slowly, and often painfully, the "underground" church is being reabsorbed into the governmentally recognized Catholic Church in China.

A tale of two bishops illustrates both the joy and sorrow of this process. In 1955, Bishop Gong Pinmei of Shanghai was arrested along with Aloysius Jin Luxian, rector of the

Catholic seminary in Shanghai. They were among thousands of Catholics imprisoned by the government. Some of the detainees were tortured, some died in prison, and Gong and Jin each spent decades in jail. Jin was the first of the two to be released. When he was allowed to return to Shanghai in 1982, he was stunned by what he saw. Catholic Masses were crowded and parishioners were hungry for spiritual guidance. Despite his years in prison, Jin decided to set aside his bitterness and join in the work. He accepted the post of Bishop of Shanghai and immediately began working for further improvements. Largely as a result of his efforts, the patriotic Catholic Church was allowed in 1989 to reintroduce prayers for the Pope into the Mass. Under Bishop Jin's leadership the church in China was also allowed, for the first time, to create its own Catholic Bishops Council that was free from government control. Jin remains cautious, and he explicitly rejected an invitation to assume the top leadership position within the Catholic Patriotic Association, but he appears convinced that cooperation is the best way forward for both the church and the state.

Bishop Gong (known as Cardinal Kung in the West) was released from prison in 1985 – three years after Jin – and he spent his first year out of jail in Shanghai with Bishop Jin. Jin assumed that he and Gong were friends, but in 1987 Gong moved to the United States (for health reasons) and he immediately became an outspoken critic of both the Chinese government and the patriotic Catholic Church. In particular, he condemned Jin by name as a traitor to the Catholic faith. Gong kept up his denunciations of Jin and the patriotic Catholic Church until his death in 2000 and, since then, the Cardinal Kung Foundation has carried on his work, roundly criticizing any form of Catholic co-operation with the government and documenting the continuing persecution of underground Catholic bishops and priests.

The tide of history seems, however, to be on the side of Bishop Jin. More and more, the bishops within the patriotic church are asking the Vatican to regularize their appointments. This often happens in secret and is not announced even after the fact, but it is now estimated that 80 percent of the bishops in the public Catholic Church in China have received the Pope's approval. This has dramatically diminished the spiritual differences between the state-approved and underground churches, and in many locations that distinction itself is becoming a relic of the past. In fact, in some dioceses, the bishops from the patriotic and the underground wings of the local Catholic Church live together amicably in the same rectory, jointly offering the Eucharist at Mass. Today the public Catholic churches in China are generally full, and most laypeople enthusiastically support their priests and bishops, whom they see as being simultaneously patriotic and loyal to the pope.

To be sure, there are still some places where the divide between the public church and the Catholic underground is deep and bitter, and in some places local government officials continue to repress the underground church. Past abuses can be hard to forget, and sometimes there is intense animosity between those who suffered and those who did not. In full awareness of these realities, Pope Benedict XVI made reconciliation the core message of the pastoral letter he addressed to the Catholic community in China in May 2007. Acknowledging that the journey to full fellowship within the Chinese Catholic Church will take years to accomplish, the Pope called on Chinese Catholics to commit themselves to the cause of unity both for the sake of the faith and for the sake of their nation. The Pope also acknowledged that careful bargaining with the state would need to be part of the process of completing the normalization of the Catholic Church in the PRC, since technically the church is still prohibited from acknowledging the full authority of the pope.

Events of the last half century have made it clear that politics is unavoidable for the churches in China. Once the government makes religion its business, religious leaders have no option but to take politics seriously. Mixing faith and politics in the contemporary world is not easy, but many Christians in East Asia consider it to be part of their calling. They would say that if Christianity is to play a constructive role in the region, it needs to be integrated into the full fabric of life, and politics is part of that fabric. Christians in East Asia are aware that religion can create tension when it is injected into the political process and it can sometimes even produce violence, but their hope is that Christianity can also enhance the common good and "bless the nations" where Christians live.

Notes

1 Jennifer Schwamm Willis (ed.), *A Lifetime of Peace: Essential Writings by and about Thich Nhat Hanh* (New York: Marlowe and Company, 2003), pp. 70–1.
2 Francis Xavier Nguyen Vam Thuan, *The Road of Hope: A Gospel from Prison* (Boston: Pauline Books and Media, 2001), pp. 8, 186–7.
3 *A Lifetime of Peace*, p. 7.

4 Jaime Cardinal Sin, "On Christian Participation in Elections of May 11, 1998," http://geociti.es/CapitolHill/Senate/3455/elect1.html (accessed November 11, 2010).
5 K. H. Ting, *God is Love* (Colorado Springs: Cook Communications, 2004), p. 111.

Suggestions for Further Reading

Aragon, Lorraine V. (2000). *Fields of the Lord: Animism, Christian Minorities, and State Development in Indonesia*. Honolulu: University of Hawai'i Press.

Buswell, Robert E. Jr. and Timothy S. Lee (eds) (2006). *Christianity in Korea*. Honolulu: University of Hawai'i Press.

Charbonnier, Jean-Pierre (2007). *Christians in China, A.D. 600 to 2000*. San Francisco: Ignatius Press.

Evers, V. (2005). *The Churches in Asia*. Delhi: ISPCK.

Fox, Thomas C. (2002). *Pentecost in Asia: A New Way of Being Church*. Maryknoll, NY: Orbis Books.

Friend, Theodore (ed.) (2006). *Religion and Religiosity in the Philippines and Indonesia: Essays on State, Security, and Public Creeds*. Washington, DC: Southeast Asia Study Program.

Griswold, Eliza (2010). *The Tenth Parallel: Dispatches from the Faulty Line Between Christianity and Islam*. New York: Farrar, Straus and Giroux.

Kindopp, Jason and Carol Lee Hamrin (eds) (2004). *God and Caesar in China: Policy Implications of Church–State Tensions*. Washington, DC: Brookings Institution.

Lee, Timothy S. (2010) *Born Again: Evangelicalism in Korea*. Honolulu: University of Hawai'i Press.

Madsen, Richard (1998). *China's Catholics: Tragedy and Hope in an Emerging Civil Society*. Berkeley: University of California Press.

Phan, Peter (ed.) (2011). *Christianities in Asia*. Oxford: Wiley-Blackwell.

Ting, K. H. (2004). *God is Love*. Colorado Springs: Cook Communications.

Wesley, Luke (2004). *The Church in China: Persecuted, Pentecostal, and Powerful*. Baguio, Philippines: AJPS Books.

Whyte, Bob (1988). *Unfinished Encounter: China and Christianity*. Harrisburg, PA: Moorehouse Publishing.

Wiegle, Katherine L. (2005). *Investing in Miracles: El Shaddai and the Transformation of Popular Catholicism in the Philippines*. Honolulu: University of Hawai'i Press.

Xi, Lian (2010). *Redeemed by Fire: The Rise of Popular Christianity in Modern China*. New Haven, CT: Yale University Press.

Yang, Huilin and Daniel H. N. Yeung (eds) (2006). *Sino-Christian Studies in China*. Newcastle, UK: Cambridge Scholars Press.

Chapter 11

Latin America
After Monopoly

More than half a billion Christians live in Latin America – 24 percent of the total world Christian population and 40 percent of the world's Catholics – making this region the most Christian place on earth. For the last hundred years, Latin American Christianity has been growing exponentially, and most of that growth has been biological. There are now eight times more people in Latin America than there were in 1900, and accordingly there are almost eight times the number of Christians. While the expansion of Christianity in Africa and Asia has been fueled to a significant degree by people converting from non-Christian religions to Christianity, the growth of Christianity in Latin America has been almost entirely due to the region's high birth rate.

A hundred years ago, the Roman Catholic Church was so dominant in the region that it was effectively a religious monopoly. Only 1.5 percent of the population belonged to non-Catholic Christian churches. (In 1900, all of these non-Catholic Christians – who were called *evangélicos* in Spanish and Portuguese – were Protestants. Today the term *evangélico* is applied indiscriminately both to Protestants and to Pentecostal/Charismatic Christians.) The remaining 5 percent of the population was either nonreligious or affiliated with some non-Christian religious group.

But these numbers tell only part of the story. The whole culture of Latin America was historically Catholic down to its smallest details. The yearly calendar was built around Catholic holy days. Catholic rituals marked rites of passage (birth, adulthood, marriage, and death). People saw the world through Catholic eyes and they experienced the world through Catholic categories of emotion. Non-Catholics were in some sense nonpersons. In many countries, for example, Protestant marriages were not legally recognized, and sometimes Protestant couples were prosecuted for sex crimes because they were "living in sin." After the early 1800s, Catholicism was no longer the officially established religion in most countries – there was some kind of legal separation of church and state in most Latin

The World's Christians: Who they are, Where they are, and How they got there, First Edition. Douglas Jacobsen.
© 2011 Douglas Jacobsen. Published 2011 by Blackwell Publishing Ltd.

Figure 11.1   Map of Latin America (smaller Caribbean nations are not shown – see Figure 11.6 on p. 221). Map by author. Total population 560,000,000 (9% of global population); Christian population 507,000,000 (91% of regional population, 24% of global Christian population): Orthodox 500,000, Catholics 395,000,000,* Protestants 11,500,000, Pentecostal/Charismatic 100,000,000.*
* The estimated 100,000,000 members of the Catholic Charismatic Renewal are evenly split between these two categories.

American nations by the mid-nineteenth century – but even without political support, and sometimes despite serious opposition by anticlerical (antichurch) governments, the Catholic Church still functioned like a regional religious monopoly until the middle of the twentieth century.

Then things began to change. Increasingly choice became part of the Latin American religious experience, and today even in Catholic strongholds like Colombia, Mexico, and Ecuador the religious landscape is becoming diverse. Catholicism is still the majority religion almost everywhere, but Catholics no longer control the whole religious market. The most important driving force behind this change has been the phenomenal growth of the Pentecostal/Charismatic movement in the last three or four decades. At present, roughly 30 percent of the region's population is Pentecostal/Charismatic, with Charismatic Catholics outnumbering non-Catholic *evangélico* Pentecostal/Charismatic Christians by more than two to one. Figure 11.2 illustrates the size of the shift that has occurred in the religious make-up of the Latin American population and visually displays the loss of Catholicism's former monopoly status.

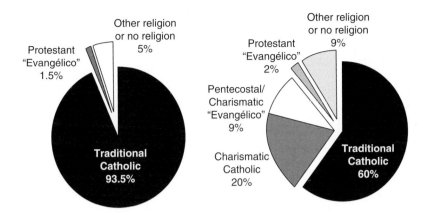

Figure 11.2   The religious profile of Latin America in 1900 (left) and 2005 (right)

Learning to Choose

In Latin America today, religious identity is no longer indelibly assigned at birth. Individuals have to decide for themselves how they will identify themselves and with whom they will religiously affiliate. The idea of making "a personal decision for Christ" has been part of the normal pathway to membership in some *evangélico* churches for decades, but the need to make a conscious decision about religion is now increasingly becoming part of the Catholic experience as well. The rise of religious choice means that people born into Catholic families now have to consciously decide if they want to stay Catholic and, if so, they have to decide what kind of Catholic they will be.

The Vatican is very aware of how much Latin America has changed. In fact, when the late Pope John Paul II issued his call for a "new evangelism" within the Catholic world, he had Latin America largely in mind. This new evangelism focuses on conversion understood in a Catholic sense as the lifelong process of turning away from sin and toward Christ, rather than on conversion understood in a Protestant or Pentecostal/Charismatic sense as an event. In the past, it was assumed that the Catholic orientation of the culture (the Catholic calendar, Catholic-informed public laws, and the peer pressure of being part of a national Catholic community) would, working together with the normal religious activities of the Catholic Church, be sufficient to encourage lives of conversion. But in many Latin American countries that old Catholic social infrastructure has fallen apart, and alternative religious options – including a "no religion" option – have become increasingly available. Being Latin American and being Catholic are no longer one and the same. Particularly worrisome to many Catholic leaders is that the growth of religious diversity can be self-perpetuating: as non-Catholic numbers grow, it becomes more socially acceptable to choose to be non-Catholic.

Acknowledging this new context of faith, the Catholic Church has begun to compete for members in additional ways, involving both offensive and defensive strategies. Offensively, and acting out of the assumption that people who feel warmly toward the Catholic faith will not go looking somewhere else for spiritual nurture, the Catholic Church has given much more attention to programs that emphasize the emotional and experiential dimensions of faith. The most successful of these initiatives by far is the Catholic Charismatic Renewal that now involves millions of Latin American Catholics. Defensively, Catholics in the region have employed a variety of means to hamper the growth of non-Catholic religion, including lobbying for legislation to restrict the activities of religious sects, developing programs to help Catholics resist being proselytized, and sometimes intimidating non-Catholics into silence through threats and occasional violence.

But despite this Catholic resistance, other forms of faith – and especially Pentecostal/ Charismatic Christianity – are growing. One of the main reasons this is happening is that there is a severe shortage of Catholic clergy in the region. The current ratio of parishioners to priests in Latin America is roughly 12,000 to one. That makes it impossible for any Catholic priest to address all the religious needs that exist within his parish. Some Latin American Catholics rarely see a priest, much less talk with one. When people are looking for spiritual guidance it is therefore not surprising that they sometimes turn to the Protestant or Pentecostal/Charismatic churches for assistance.

The growth of the Pentecostal/Charismatic movement, in particular, also seems related to urbanization – the stunning rise of megacities all across Latin America. São Paulo, Mexico City, Bogotá, Caracas, Rio de Janeiro, and Buenos Aires are now among the world's largest cities, and they are all encircled by slums, places of seemingly endless squalor and ceaseless violence where new residents often settle after arriving from the countryside. To date, the Catholic Church has been only marginally successful in providing social and religious support to the urban poor, while some of the Pentecostal/Charismatic churches have been remarkably successful in these settings. Rather than building churches "for the poor," Pentecostal/Charismatic Christians have been building churches "of the poor," led by those who once were or still are poor themselves, and that has made a huge difference.

The Pentecostal/Charismatic movement has been spectacularly successful in Latin America, but growth has not been uniform. The number of people who fit into the four categories of traditional Catholicism, Charismatic Catholicism, *evangélico* Protestantism, and *evangélico* Pentecostal/Charismatic Christianity varies dramatically from country to country. The religious profiles of the 10 largest countries of Latin America, which together account for 87 percent of the population in the region as a whole, illustrate this variety (see Table 11.1). As is clear from this table, Brazil, Chile, and Guatemala clearly reflect the new demographics of religion in the area, while Mexico, Ecuador, and Peru still look very much like the "old" Latin America that is slowly dissolving away throughout most of the continent.

Twenty years ago, many scholars were predicting that the result of this process of transition would be a newly *evangélico* Latin America. Protestant-style religiosity seemed ready to overwhelm the continent. But that has not taken place, and expectations have changed. In Guatemala, for example, *evangélico* growth (Protestant and Pentecostal/Charismatic Christians combined) has stalled in the last 10 to 15 years, and some scholars now speculate that non-Catholic forms of Christianity may have reached their saturation point in Guatemalan society. The same pattern is beginning to emerge elsewhere. It now looks as though Catholicism will remain the dominant faith in most places, but it will have nothing like the monopoly status it once enjoyed, which means that the Catholicism that remains will not be old-style Latin American Catholicism, but something quite new and different.

Table 11.1   Christian profiles of the 10 largest nations of Latin America (estimated size of traditional and charismatic populations within the Catholic Church and the *evangélico* churches

Country	Population	% Christian	% Traditional Catholic	% Charismatic Catholic	% Protestant Evangélico	% Pentecostal/ Charismatic Evangélico
Brazil	186,500,000	90	45	30	3	12
Mexico	107,000,000	94	79	9	4	2
Colombia	45,500,000	96	65	25	1	5
Argentina	39,000,000	91	78	12	2	8
Peru	28,000,000	90	75	7	2	6
Venezuela	26,500,000	95	78	12	1	4
Chile	16,500,000	85	55	15	3	12
Ecuador	13,500,000	97	83	8	1	5
Guatemala	13,000,000	82	27	27	3	25
Cuba	11,250,000	47	39	3	1	4
Total	486,750,000	91	62	19	2	8

The Complex History of Church and State

The Roman Catholic Church had a monopoly on religious power in Latin America from the 1500s to the mid-twentieth century, but that does not mean that relations between the Catholic Church and the political rulers of Latin America were always cordial. In fact, the history of church–state relations in Latin America is complex, convoluted, and full of conflict.

During the early days of Spanish and Portuguese colonization, church and state were basically inseparable. The pope had delegated control of the church in the newly discovered Americas to the political rulers of Spain and Portugal – a power that was called *patronato* in Spanish and *padroado* in Portuguese. In effect, the church was a wholly state-controlled organization. No consultation with the pope was necessary even in the appointment of bishops. Why would the pope agree to such an arrangement? His hope seems to have been that it would encourage the Spanish and Portuguese monarchs to govern their newly conquered lands in accordance with Catholic truth and values. The pope also adopted this stance because he had no other realistic options. There was no other way to oversee and govern the Catholic Church in the New World.

Though they were Christians, the monarchs of Spain and Portugal did not always make faith a priority. Often the most important concern seemed to be extracting as much wealth as possible from Latin America in the shortest amount of time. To that end, the native people were put to work in the gold and silver mines of the continent, and later African slaves – more than 10 million between the years 1650 and 1860 – were brought to the region to do this work. A handful of church leaders spoke out in opposition to the mistreatment of indigenous and African people – most notably Bartolomé de Las Casas, whose *History of the Destruction of the Indians* (1552) chronicled the oppression of native people – and some action was taken to curb the worst abuses, but many church officials either remained silent or actively supported the exploitation.

When Latin America achieved independence from European rule in the early decades of the nineteenth century little changed. The leaders of the Latin American independence movements were by and large wealthy local landowners (called *caudillos*) who had little interest in altering any of the underlying social and economic structures of the region. The *caudillos* had a division of opinion, however, with regard to the church. Some of them were secularists who espoused anticlerical views and resented the privileges and influence of the church. For them, the acceptable alternatives were either to assume total control over the church (claim the powers of *patronato* as their own) or to severely limit the church's influence. Other more conservative political leaders in the newly independent nations of Latin America were much more loyal to the church. Rather than seeking to limit its power, these conservatives welcomed the benefits that a strong church could confer: an obedient citizenry, religious support for their policies, and salvation in the world to come. Throughout the nineteenth and twentieth centuries these two views clashed repeatedly, resulting in dramatic and sometimes violent swings of public policy from prochurch to antichurch and then back again. The focus of the church during this time was often on its own self-preservation and on the consolidation of power during times of friendly government rule.

In the early years of the twentieth century, the Catholic Church in Europe began rethinking issues of church and state and adopting new views about workers' rights, justice, and critical political engagement. Many of these new views slowly drifted over to Latin America and began to affect developments in the region in positive ways. The movement called Catholic Action – a kind of moderate Catholic social gospel – was especially prominent during the years 1905 to 1940. But then in the 1960s the political map was redrawn once again as military dictatorships took control of many Latin American nations. Most of these military leaders were intent on keeping the poor in their place and on supporting policies that benefitted the wealthy. These military dictatorships arose during the iciest years of the Cold War, and the Marxist revolt in Cuba that took place in 1959 allowed many of these Latin American dictators to defend their actions as part of the worldwide fight against Communism. But the violence used by these governments against so-called "leftists" was often extreme. Thousands of ordinary citizens were arrested and many were tortured and killed, including priests and religious workers.

In some Latin American nations, the Catholic Church gave its blessing to these military governments and their fight against Communism. This was, for example, the case in Argentina where the church was largely complicit with the government in fighting a "dirty war" against social justice advocates, Communist revolutionaries, and anyone else who accidentally got in the way. Elsewhere, in Chile for example, the church was much more proactive and courageous in taking a public stand against violence and repression. One of the most outspoken leaders of this resistance movement was Oscar Romero, the Archbishop of El Salvador from 1977 to 1980, who finally "commanded" the Catholic members of the military to stop killing people. In response, Romero himself was assassinated just a few days later. Eventually, the Catholic Church as a whole concluded the situation was getting out of control, and it began to take a more consistent stand against oppression and for justice.

Latin American Catholicism's new emphasis on justice was to some degree an outcome of the Second Vatican Council (1962–65) which promoted the notion that matters of justice and human rights were deeply connected with Christian faith. Following Vatican II, the Council of Latin American Bishops (also known as CELAM for its Spanish name, the *Consejo Episcopal Latinoamericano*) met in the Colombian city of Medellin in 1968 to discuss how to apply the teachings of Vatican II to Latin America. CELAM reached the conclusion that the church had to display a "preferential option for the poor" in matters of public policy. Rather than seeing itself as a partner of the wealthy and those in power, the church redefined its role as that of advocate for the poor. On that basis, the church reconceptualized its public responsibilities, focusing on alleviating pain whenever possible, working for justice where injustice was the norm, and helping to educate the poor so they could better defend their own rights as human beings.

For many, what had previously been questionable – social protest like that of Bartolomé de Las Casas – now became the Catholic ideal. When it was articulated formally, this new stance became known as liberation theology, a new kind of Catholic religious reflection developed by people like Gustavo Gutiérrez in Peru and the Boff brothers (Leonardo and Clodovis) in Brazil. Liberation theology argued that justice was an essential element of truth, saying that for too long "truth" had been defined in abstract ways that had nothing to do with how people actually lived. "Truth" had been twisted to support injustice rather than justice, misleading people into believing that God wanted the rich to be rich and the poor to be poor and that pain and suffering were "gifts" that helped people become more spiritual. To counterbalance that kind of wealth-justifying theology, liberationists said that the first responsibility of any genuinely Christian theologian was to join in the people's struggle for justice. Informed and shaped by their participation in that struggle, theologians would then be equipped to reflect properly on how God, sin, salvation, and the saints were related to life in the real world where oppression and suffering were so pervasive. Some critics argued that liberation theology made theology entirely political and not spiritual at all. But liberationists replied that the whole prior history of the church in Latin America was dripping with political support for the wealthy. Liberation theology was accordingly not a politicization of theology, but a redirection of an already political Christianity toward the needs of the poor.

During the late 1980s and 1990s, many of Latin America's military dictatorships came to an end, and most governments in the region became much more democratic. As that shift occurred, the highest leadership within the church came to view the liberationist and progressive elements within Latin American Catholicism as less necessary than before or even as problematic. Pope John Paul II gave his support to this shift in attitudes, condemning several prominent liberation theologians whom he thought needed to be reined in and appointing a new flock of conservative bishops whom he hoped would push the liberationist message to the margins of church life. Today, the moral-political energy of the Catholic Church in Latin America is much more likely to be directed against issues like abortion and gay rights than against economic inequality and political oppression. Still, the influence of liberation theology remains, visible in the nearly universal belief within contemporary Latin American Catholicism that working for the good of society requires that special attention be given to the needs of the poor. That would not have been the case in the mid-twentieth century.

Popular Catholicism: The Importance of Mary

The full story of Catholicism in Latin America involves much more than politics, and much more than the institutional church. There is also a "popular" strand of Catholicism in the region – often called "the people's church" – that sometimes seems to runs on an almost separate track from the formal routines and teachings of the Roman Catholic Church. This popular version of Catholicism developed early in the colonial period as the indigenous and *mestizo* (mixed race) people of the region tried to translate European Catholicism into ideas and practices that made sense within the categories of the indigenous cultures.

Saints play a major role in Latin American Catholicism, and no saint is more popular than Mary, the Virgin Mother of Jesus. More than any other place on earth, Latin America is the land of the Virgin, and this is the case for one simple reason: Mary revealed the mercy of God to the people of Latin America in a way that the official church leadership could not. The God of the institutional Catholic Church was inextricably blended together with God as represented by the conquistadors – a frightening and powerful deity who came to America to overthrow the local gods and goddesses and to rule in their place. By contrast, Mary came on God's behalf to help and to serve. She came to Latin America to pick up the pieces after the conquest, embracing the indigenous people as they were – poor and humble and broken – and affirming their human worth. The God of the conquistadors and colonial rulers might have elicited respect and obedience, but the God of Mary was (and is) loved. Official Catholic theology says that these two Gods are one and the same, but the heart of Latin American Catholicism belongs to the God of Mary.

Stories about Mary are everywhere in Latin America and almost every country has its own Marian patroness or protector. The most famous Mary of the region is the Virgin of Guadalupe, who has many titles, including the "Patroness of Latin America," the "celestial missionary of the New World," and the "Mother of the Americas." As traditionally told, the Virgin of Guadalupe first appeared to Cuauhtlatoatzin, a Mexican indigenous Christian whose baptismal name was Juan Diego, in the year 1531. The appearance of the Virgin was remarkable because of her physical attributes: she looked like an indigenous Mexican, dark-skinned and dressed in the local garb, rather than a European Madonna. It was also remarkable because of what Mary said: she told Cuauhtlatoatzin that she came as a merciful mother who wanted to give her love, compassion, help, and protection to all the inhabitants of the land. With that single message, Mary changed Catholicism from being an outsider's religion into a religion that was embraced by the indigenous people as their own. After the encounter, Juan Diego discovered that the image of Mary he had seen had been miraculously imprinted on his *tilma* (see Plate 18), a roughly woven cloak or shawl worn exclusively by peasants. That garment now hangs on display in the Basilica of Our Lady of Guadalupe in Mexico City where 15 million people come to see it every year.

Similar stories can be told of many other apparitions of Mary – or sometimes miraculous appearances of carved statues or paintings of Mary that took place throughout the colonial period (from the 1500s to the 1820s) – and it was almost always people of humble origins who received the visitation. In Brazil in 1717, three local fisherman hauled a black statue of the Virgin Mary, 30 inches (76 cm) tall, out of the Paraiba River near São Paulo. No one knew how it got there. The three men had fished all day and caught nothing, but after deciding to continue fishing "with faith in the *Virgin Aparecida*" (the Virgin "who appeared"), they caught a net full of fish. The statue was kept in one of the men's homes for several years until a small chapel was built for it in 1743. In 1930, Pope Pius XII named her the patroness of Brazil. Today the Virgin of Aparecida is housed in a spectacular basilica in São Paulo (the second largest Catholic church in the world, which holds 45,000 people) where it is venerated each year by more than seven million visitors.

In Costa Rica, the Virgin made her first appearance in 1635 when the Feast of Holy Angels was being celebrated in the city of Cartago. Indians and *mestizos* were banned from Cartago, and it is symbolic that Mary appeared outside the city and that she was found by a poor *mestizo* woman named Juana Pereira. Her formal name is Our Lady of the Angels, but locally the Mary of Costa Rica is known as "*La Negrita*," the "little black one." *La Negrita* is a small statue, about three inches (7.6 cm) tall, that Juana found perched on a rock by the side of the footpath leading to Cartago. She took the statue home with her, but it kept disappearing only to reappear on the rock where it was originally found. Eventually it became clear that Mary wanted a shrine built at the site where Indians and *mestizos* could come and be comforted by the Virgin. She now resides in a beautiful basilica in Cartago and each year on August 2 (her feast day) more than a third of the population of Costa Rica – a million and a half people – come to Cartago to honor her presence among them.

Similar stories could be told about many other Marys of Latin America – Our Lady of Luján in Argentina, Our Lady of Copacabana in Bolivia, Our Lady of Charity of El Cobre in Cuba, Our Lady of Quinche in Ecuador, Our Lady of Mercy in Peru, Our Lady of Cormoto in Venezuela. Their stories underscore the dignity of the poor and lowly, and many of the stories also borrow significantly from the religious ideas and practices of the past. The site where the Virgin of Guadalupe first appeared to Juan Diego, for example, was a hill on which the local goddess Tonantzín was formerly worshiped, and many scholars have suggested that veneration of the Virgin of Guadalupe was originally a way for native people to continue to worship Tonantzín in a manner that was acceptable to the new Catholic rulers of the land. That interpretation may have some merit, but it misses the most important point. The appearances of Mary provided Latin America with a way to make Catholicism its own, a way to fashion Catholicism into a distinctly Latin American form of Christian faith. With eyes on Mary, the focus of Catholicism turned away from politics and wealth toward the inner spiritual longings of the human heart. This process began among the indigenous and *mestizo* populations, but it soon spread to the whole population because the needs that Mary met were needs that everyone felt to some degree.

Non-Catholic Christianity

While Catholicism has always been the majority expression of Christianity in Latin America, Protestant Christianity is not an exotic import that has just arrived in the region. Protestants have been present in Latin America in small numbers for centuries, and their numbers jumped significantly during the nineteenth century when some of the more liberal-leaning governments of Latin America encouraged Protestant immigration in hopes of lessening

Catholicism's influence in society. Most of these early Protestant immigrants belonged to communities that were simultaneously ethnic and religious, such as Italian Waldensians, German Lutherans, and Russian Mennonites, and for the most part they resettled as groups and largely kept to themselves, avoiding both political engagement and evangelism. In the late nineteenth and early twentieth centuries, a new wave of more missionary-minded Protestants began to arrive, mostly from the United States. They often managed to recreate some local version of their "home" denomination (Baptist, Episcopal, Methodist, Presbyterian, Disciples of Christ, etc.) in the region, but most of these transplanted Protestant churches failed to put down deep roots and they attracted only a modest following. By the mid-twentieth century, all of them together accounted for only about 2 percent of the population.

In contrast to these traditional Protestant churches, the Pentecostal/Charismatic movement has had much greater success in Latin America, and much of the success of the movement has been due to the fact that it is largely a home-grown faith, rather than an exotic import. Many Latin American Pentecostal churches originated in the region. The Pentecostal movement in Chile, for example, was established in 1909 by Willis C. Hoover (a leader in the Chilean Methodist Church) when he shared his own Pentecostal experience of baptism in the Spirit and speaking in tongues first with his congregation and then with the denomination as a whole. In 1912, Romanita Carbajal de Valensuela launched the Pentecostal movement in Mexico when she started the Apostolic Church of Faith in Jesus Christ, a "oneness" or "Jesus only" Pentecostal church, which rejects the doctrine of the Trinity as traditionally understood and emphasizes the need for baptism by immersion and speaking in tongues as part of the process of salvation. Other new Pentecostal churches were founded during the early twentieth century in Argentina, Brazil, Colombia, Guatemala, Peru, Nicaragua, the Caribbean and elsewhere. Much of the success of these churches is due to the fact that, even if they were sometimes originally started by non-Latin American missionaries, local people often rose quickly through the ranks to attain positions of leadership. For the most part, these Pentecostal churches were much more strapped for funds than the older historic Protestant churches and they had fewer educational resources, but by 1960 there were as many Pentecostal Christians in Latin America as there were traditional Protestants.

Since 1960, the Pentecostal/Charismatic movement has exploded throughout the region, producing a wide variety of new Pentecostal and neo-Charismatic denominations. The spiritual excitement associated with these new churches is reflected to some degree in their names: God Is Love, Waves of Love and Peace, Vision of the Future, Word of God, Prince of Peace, and Universal Church of the Kingdom of God (see Plate 19). Many of these denominations champion the "prosperity gospel," promising financial blessings for those who put their trust and their meager resources into the work of the church. But what may set them apart even more is their willingness to go where the people are, into the slums of the cities, becoming part of the neighborhoods, being available when and where they are needed, praying with and for gang members, drug addicts, struggling single parents, and anyone else who needs their help.

Even though the Pentecostal/Charismatic movement first took off among the poor, however, its membership is no longer confined to that social class. People from all sectors and walks of life have become involved as the movement has grown. Today, 9 percent of the Latin American population is involved in the *evangélico* (as opposed to Catholic) Pentecostal/Charismatic movement. Meanwhile the Protestant movement in Latin America remains comparatively small, still accounting for only about 2 percent of the overall population.

The Catholic Charismatic Renewal

The Catholic Charismatic Renewal began in North America in 1967, but it was quickly exported to Catholics around the world, arriving in Latin America in the early 1970s. During the early years, the movement was sometimes called Catholic Pentecostalism because many Catholics who became involved in the movement had been in contact with non-Catholic Pentecostal Christians and their religious experiences paralleled those of Pentecostals: baptism in the Spirit, speaking in tongues, healing, and other spiritual gifts. By the late 1970s, however, the Catholic wing of the movement had established its own separate identity as the Catholic Charismatic Renewal, and contacts with *evangélico* Pentecostal/Charismatic Christians began to decline.

Two of the most prominent early promoters of the Renewal in the region were Francis McNutt, a Dominican priest, and Edward Dougherty, a Jesuit priest, both from the United States. As spiritual entrepreneurs and masterful salesmen, McNutt and Dougherty raised up a wave of local leaders who began helping them spread the message around the continent. In the earliest years, the movement operated outside the formal structures of the church and under the radar of many bishops, but within a few years the Renewal caught the eye of the church hierarchy and many bishops came out in support of the movement. Bishop Diego Jaramillo of Colombia was one of the first to do so. Sensing the Renewal's potential to help the Catholic cause in Latin America, Jaramillo described the movement as "one of the most serious pastoral efforts of the church to attract the multitudes to the faith and conversion through the action of the Holy Spirit."[1] Some bishops, however, were more cautious or even openly critical of the movement. One concern was that, rather than shoring up the borders of Catholicism, the Renewal might actually become a stepping stone for people to move away from traditional Catholicism. Other bishops, especially those in Brazil, feared the movement was an attempt by conservative Catholics to derail the efforts of liberation.

With mixed support, the Catholic Renewal grew relatively slowly in the 1970s, and by the end of that decade the total number involved in the movement was still well under 1 percent of the total Catholic population. But then two things happened. First, many more bishops became convinced that the Renewal had the potential to be a positive force within the Catholic Church. It seemed not to be a stepping stone to Protestantism, but rather a powerful means of retaining the Catholic faithful. Second, the leaders of the Renewal themselves adopted a bolder strategy for getting the message out. They went public, holding mass rallies and healing services in soccer stadiums and large auditoriums, and they later launched radio and television programs to spread the word. Simultaneously, they encouraged members of the Renewal to go door to door, sharing their spiritual experience with others – something Catholics had never done before. Finally bishops, priests, and Catholic lay leaders began organizing Charismatic prayer groups in dioceses and parishes all across the region.

As a result of all these activities, there are now tens of millions of Catholics involved in the movement – more than 20 percent of all the Catholics in the region. As is true of almost every other dimension of religion in Latin America, the effect has been regionally uneven. In some countries (in Brazil, Colombia, and Guatemala, for example), 35 percent or more of the Catholic population is or has been involved in the Renewal movement. Elsewhere (in places like Paraguay, Costa Rica, and Peru) the numbers are much smaller. It is difficult to measure the size of the Renewal with precision because membership lists are not kept and because people sometimes move in and then out of the movement. But directly through active participation and indirectly through families, friends, and neighbors, the impact of the Renewal on Latin American Catholicism has been enormous. It has reinvigorated the spiritual lives of millions of people and has deepened their commitment to the Catholic Church. This is especially true for women, who make up two-thirds of the movement. It may also have saved the Catholic Church in Latin America from being overwhelmed by the "invasion" of the *evangélico* Pentecostal/Charismatic "sects" – the derogatory term used by some Catholic leaders to warn Catholics away from any fraternizing with non-Catholic Christians.

Charismatic Competition in Brazil

Today there are more Catholics in Brazil than in any other country in the world. Brazil has been a solidly Catholic nation for centuries. Begun as a Portuguese (rather than Spanish) colony, Brazil moved relatively smoothly from colonial status into independence during the early 1800s under the governorship of the royal regent Pedro I, the son of the Portuguese King João VI. Because the transition went so smoothly, Brazil was largely spared from the antichurch sentiments that were part of many independence movements in Spanish Latin America. Under Brazil's first constitution (instituted in 1824), Catholicism was named the official religion of the nation. Legal separation of church and state took place in 1891, but the Catholic Church continued to enjoy a privileged position in society. In 1934, the constitution was rewritten to give Catholicism back some of the benefits lost in 1891, including a substantial government subsidy to fund Catholic schools and charitable organizations.

Confident in its Catholic identity, Brazil was relatively tolerant of Protestants, who had been present in the region since the colonial period, and that tolerance was facilitated by the fact that non-Catholic Christianity was never a threat. As late as 1950, Protestants made up only 2 or 3 percent of the total population. The Brazilian government and the Catholic Church were less accommodating of the Afro-Brazilian religions of Condomblé and Umbanda – hybrid religions developed by African slaves and their descendants that mixed African spirituality with elements of Christianity and Latin American indigenous religion. Those religions were illegal up until the 1950s and could be practiced only in secret. In the mid-twentieth century Brazil looked like a traditional Catholic country that was destined to remain so for years to come.

But that is not what happened. Rather than being a bastion of loyal, but somewhat stodgy, traditional Catholicism, Brazil has become a hotbed of religious fervor and change. Some of that change looks bad for the Catholic Church. *Evangélico* Pentecostal/Charismatic churches have mushroomed, Afro-Brazilian religions have been legalized and are now visible everywhere, and the Catholic population has declined. But a broader spiritual leavening of society has also been taking place and that leavening has helped the Catholic Church as much as any other religious group in the country. More people seem to be more interested in religion, whatever the religion is. This change is palpable within the Catholic Church where only about a quarter of the membership was religiously active half a century ago and today almost half the Catholics in the country attend church regularly.

One reason for the overall increase in religiosity is that religious leaders have developed better ways of "marketing" their faith. During the 1960s, 1970s, and 1980s, progressive Catholics took the lead, founding base communities – small groups engaged in Bible study and social analysis – in Catholic parishes all across the country. The goal was to energize Catholicism at the grassroots, among the poor who had formerly been involved only tangentially in the life of the Church – and the means of doing this was a new emphasis on social justice. The base community movement was quite successful, especially between the years 1965 and 1985 when the military ruled the country, but there was a kind of built-in limitation to the numbers of people who could be attracted that way. The motivation for involvement was rooted in a sense of spiritual duty mixed with hope for personal growth and self-improvement, but involvement in a base community was often time-consuming (involving many meetings and many other hours spent trying to improve the local community) and doing good out of a sense of duty does not appeal to everyone.

What proved to be more appealing was the spiritual power, health, acceptance, and simple fun that a new generation of Pentecostal/Charismatic churches began offering urban Brazilians in the late 1970s and early 1980s. One researcher explains:

> People live monotonous lives in their neighborhoods, where there is nothing to do on Sundays; the neighborhood is ugly and has no services, no movie theater, no soccer field. In those places, the only way to have an enjoyable experience is to go to the Pentecostal church, where you are going to have an impressive aesthetic experience, with music and dance, because they are not just looking for the truth but may only want to spend a pleasant moment, meet or make friends, feel part of a community.[2]

When the new national Constitution went into effect in 1988 – a Constitution that for the first time established full religious freedom in Brazil, creating a truly unfettered marketplace of religion – the Pentecostal/Charismatic churches were ready to compete and their numbers skyrocketed. The ranks of Pentecostal/Charismatic Christians, which had increased from 2 percent of the population in 1950 to 6 percent in 1980, rose to about 10 percent by 2000. By that time there were five Pentecostal/Charismatic denominations in Brazil that had more than a million members each, including Assemblies of God, with eight million members, followed in order of size by the Universal Church of the Kingdom of God, the Christian Congregation of Brazil, the God Is Love Church, and Brazil for Christ.

Of all these churches, the organization that has attracted the most attention is the Universal Church of the Kingdom of God (*Ingeja Universaldo Reino de Deus*), which is often identified simply as the IURD. Founded by Edir Macedo, a former state lottery official, in Rio de Janeiro in 1977, the IURD understood from the beginning that it needed to actively advertise if its message was going to reach the masses, so IURD started its own television station, more than 60 radio stations, a newspaper, and a book publishing company. It sometimes uses controversial methods to gain attention. In one particularly infamous incident that took place in 1995, one of the senior pastors of the church kicked and slapped a ceramic replica of the Virgin of Aparecida on national TV to demonstrate that this "horrible disgraceful doll" had no power and deserved no respect. However, the main message of the church is positive: that God wants to bless his faithful followers with health and prosperity as well as with future salvation. This is a message that has appealed to many Brazilians.

Primarily a church of the urban poor, the IURD has taken a strong stand against the Afro-Brazilian religions, offering services of exorcism for those who have previously been involved in what the church sees as the demonic practices of Condomblé and Umbanda. More recently, the IURD has also been competing with the Catholic Church for middle-class members, especially women, running a series of television ads in 2008 supporting the use of birth control (which the Catholic Church strongly opposes) and launching a television Christian soap opera called "Storm of Love." Since most Catholic churches are open 24 hours a day, potential Catholic converts assume that churches should be open all the time – so the church buildings of the IURD are open 24 hours a day too. More recently, the IURD has also become involved in politics, partly to protect its rights and partly to influence the direction of society. Currently, about 40 members of the church have been elected to the Brazilian Congress (about 7 percent of the total), and they represent political parties with views that range across the political spectrum from left to right.

Pentecostal/Charismatic growth caused the Catholic Church in Brazil to radically reconsider its own strategies for maintaining members and encouraging them to be more active. They pinned many of their hopes on the Catholic Charismatic Renewal, and in the person of Padre Marcelo Rossi they found someone who could compete with *evangélico* churches like the IURD. A 6 foot 4 inch (193 cm) former aerobics teacher who was ordained as a priest in 1994, Rossi says explicitly that "it was Bishop Edir Macedo [of the IURD] who woke us up"[3] to the need for Catholics to pitch their message to the Brazilian people in a way never done before: outside the church in the public square. Rossi's own medium for doing this is music, performed in large concert venues and sold on CDs (approaching 20 million in sales). But he is also a parish priest who says Mass daily in a refurbished factory in downtown São Paulo that draws 30,000 people daily. (There are plans underway to build a new 65,000-seat church in the same neighborhood.) In addition to being a priest and musical performer, Rossi is a talented preacher who can explain Catholic theology in ways that help ordinary people to see how faith is connected with their lives.

The Catholic Church is expanding its services and outreach in other ways as well. There are now two Catholic television networks in Brazil – Rede Brasil Cristão (the Christian Brazil Network) and Redevida (the Life Network) – both of which carry predominantly Charismatic programs. The church has expanded its specialized ministries, including exorcism and divine healing, to compete with *evangélico* churches like the IURD. Healing and exorcism are both part of the long history of Catholicism, so these are not new additions to the tradition, but they are being emphasized and performed in newly visible ways. Like the *evangélico* Pentecostal/Charismatic movement in Brazil, the Catholic Renewal is a grassroots movement. In Catholic churches all across the country, small groups of spirit-filled believers gather weekly for times of prayer and mutual encouragement.

After three decades of postmonopoly competition, there is considerable debate about Brazil's religious future. Some observers believe the Pentecostal/Charismatic churches will continue to grow at a rapid rate and might even become the majority religion by the year 2050. Others predict religious stability, citing

Figure 11.3   Padre Marcelo Rossi participates in an outdoor mass, November 2, 2000, in São Paulo, Brazil
© Mauricio Lima/AFP/Getty Images

smaller rates of decline in Catholic Church membership and slower rates of growth in the Pentecostal/Charismatic movement. Obviously, the future cannot be predicted today any better than it could have been predicted in the mid-twentieth century. What is clear, however, is that Brazil is a bellwether for the region as a whole, and its future will have enormous consequences for the rest of the region.

Holding the Line in Mexico

Mexico, which has the second largest population of Catholics in the world, is almost 90 percent Catholic and, despite years of antagonism between church and state, Catholicism continues to have enormous influence in society. Non-Catholic Christians currently account for only about 6 percent of the population – much lower than the number in Brazil – but that represents a significant gain from the beginning of the twentieth century when they represented less than 0.5 percent of the Mexican people. Many of Mexico's non-Catholic churches are aggressively evangelistic, but even so the movement is growing only slowly and few expect its numbers to rise dramatically in the near future.

One of the reasons the Catholic Church is doing so well today is because it learned long ago how to fight for its rights and influence. The history of church–state relations in Mexico is contentious and bloody. The leaders of the Mexican War of Independence (1810–21) were political "liberals" who believed the state should be run on secular principles and that the influence of the church should be restricted to purely spiritual concerns. In the 1820s and early 1830s, these liberals tried and failed to limit the church's role in society. But in the 1850s a new liberal leader, Benito Juárez, came to power and he was much more successful in stripping the church of its privileges and property. The church fought back hard, first by excommunicating people who bought confiscated church lands and withholding the sacraments from those who supported Juárez's anticlerical policies, and later with organized violence in the form of the War of Reform (1858–61).

Figure 11.4　Catholic fighters of the Cristero Rebellion (1926–29)

During the presidency of Díaz Porfirio (1864–1911), the Catholic Church and government settled into an uneasy but workable truce, until the Mexican Revolution (1910–17) upset that balance and brought a stridently secular and antichurch government back into office. The new Constitution, written in 1917, established religious freedom as the law of the land, banned religion from the public schools, seized all religiously owned buildings and land, and forbade clergy from holding office and from criticizing the state. The Catholic reaction, once again, was war. The Cristero Rebellion (1926–29) included, on the Catholic side, the planned assassinations of secular teachers and, on the government side, the promise to murder one priest for every teacher killed. Many priests and bishops went underground, and the Catholic Church essentially stopped functioning. As many as 90,000 people were killed. After the war ended, the church was severely repressed. By the mid-1930s only about 350 priests were left in the country, and laypeople had to take upon themselves the responsibility of keeping the Catholic faith alive. In the 1940s, a series of informal but relatively permanent arrangements allowed the church to begin to function once again, but it was not until 1992 that Mexico finally adopted a new legal code that formally acknowledged the existence of the Catholic Church.

This history underscores the tenacity of popular support for the Catholic Church in the face of governmental opposition, and it also goes a long way toward explaining how the Catholic Church is still able to maintain its dominance in the country. Catholicism in Mexico is strong because it has learned how to engender loyalty in its bishops, priests, religious brothers and sisters, and lay members without any assistance from the state. And that skill has helped the Catholic Church resist the *evangélico* "invasion" that has taken place in the last half century. Beginning in the mid-twentieth century, one of the ways this was done was by persuading Catholics to put signs on their doors saying: "This home is Catholic. We do not accept Protestant propaganda" (see Plate 20). And for the most part, *evangélico* growth was kept to a minimum – at least until the 1970s.

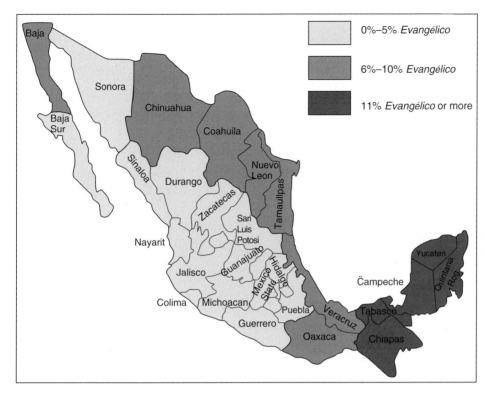

Figure 11.5 *Evangélico* (non-Catholic) Christianity in Mexico. Map by author.

In 1970, non-Catholics still represented only 2 percent of the Mexican population, while 93 percent remained solidly Catholic, but since then the *evangélico* population has been slowly growing – up to 5 percent by the year 2000. The success of non-Catholic churches in Mexico has been geographically uneven (see Figure 11.5). *Evangélico* Christianity has made its deepest inroads in the Mexican southeast, where the Indian population has responded favorably. It has also enjoyed modest success in the north along the border with the United States and on the east coast. Central Mexico and the west coast remain almost totally Catholic.

Two characteristics of the Mexican *evangélico* population make it stand out as distinctive. First, only 20 percent of *evangélicos* in Mexico are Pentecostal or Charismatic compared with 75 percent for Latin America as a whole. Second, Mexico has an unusually high concentration of newer, more doctrinally creative non-Catholic churches than anywhere else in Latin America (see Table 11.2). In particular, Jehovah's Witnesses, Seventh Day Adventists, and Mormons are well represented as is *La Luz del Mundo*, an indigenous church started by Samuel Joaquin Flores in the early twentieth century that rejects the divinity of Christ. While the Catholic leadership of Mexico is opposed to all forms of non-Catholic Christianity, it finds these four groups especially troublesome because of their strong emphasis on door-to-door evangelism.

As in Brazil, one strategy the Mexican Catholic Church has adopted to combat *evangélico* Christianity is support of the Catholic Charismatic Renewal. But the Renewal movement in

Table 11.2   The 10 largest non-Catholic churches in Mexico

Church name	Founded	Current membership (estimated)
Jehovah's Witnesses	1923	1,500,000
National Presbyterian Church	1872	1,500,000
Seventh Day Adventist Church	1893	750,000
Union of Independent Evangelical Churches	1923	750,000
Church of Jesus Christ of Latter Day Saints (Mormon)	1879	750,000
Assemblies of God	1915	600,000
Light of the World (*La Luz del Mundo*)	1940	500,000
Methodist Church of Mexico	1873	350,000
Apostolic Church of Faith in Jesus Christ	1914	200,000
Church of God in the Republic of Mexico	1920	200,000

Mexico is much smaller than it is in Brazil, and it has never received the complete support of all the Catholic bishops. The main line of defense thus remains the strengthening of anti-*evangélico* resolve within the Catholic community itself. This strategy has been effective to date partly because Catholicism and national identity are still quite strongly connected in Mexico; being non-Catholic is still, for many Mexicans, tantamount to not really being Mexican at all. But attitudes are changing and it is uncertain how much longer this hold-the-line attitude will be effective.

But competition with non-Catholic Christians is not the Catholic Church's only problem nor is it the church's greatest current challenge. Perhaps the most significant issue facing the Mexican Catholic Church today – at least in the eyes of the bishops – is how to be a public force for morality in Mexican society. The Constitution forbids the involvement of the church in political affairs, but the church feels an increasing responsibility to shape public policy, especially on issues of sexual ethics, and it is getting both direct and indirect encouragement from the Vatican to do so. Abortion is one of these issues that the church is trying to address. Abortion has been illegal in Mexico for decades, but recently there has been increasing pressure to liberalize those laws. Mexico City's decision in 2007 to relax its laws regarding abortion was seen by many Catholic leaders as the potential beginning of a national trend, and they decided to organize in opposition. Rather than addressing the issue on a national level, however – a strategy that would likely have been seen as "political" and thus illegal – the church adopted a much lower-profile local response. And it proved quite effective. In the years 2008 and 2009, more than a third of the Mexican states passed legislation that further restricted the availability of abortion and increased the penalties associated with it.

The church has to be careful, however, not to overstep its bounds, and not just because of legal limits on its activity. Opinion polls show that while Mexicans respect the Catholic Church and its moral teachings, they do not necessarily want the church telling them what to do politically. Mexican Catholics seem to be sending a message to the church that they will listen to its "opinions" – teachings that the Catholic leadership considers morally

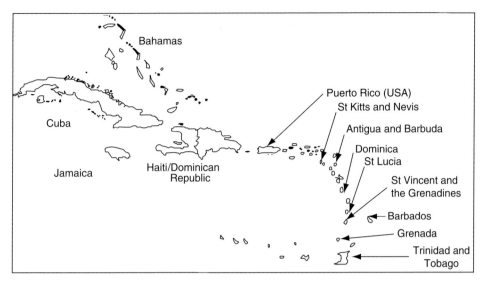

Figure 11.6 The island nations of the Caribbean. Map by author.

binding rules and not opinions at all – but that they will decide for themselves how they will behave as Catholics in public life. What this underscores is that even in a country as solidly Catholic as Mexico, the church does not have the monolithic influence on the moral and spiritual life of the people that it once had.

The Caribbean Difference

The Caribbean is very different geographically, culturally, and religiously than the rest of Latin America. Geographically the Caribbean is a territory of many separate island nations and territories (see Figure 11.6), and island nations often develop their own peculiar personalities. In the Caribbean this natural tendency was heightened by a complex colonial history. Spain originally controlled the whole region, but as early as the 1600s, other European nations moved in to establish their own presence in the area. While their interests were primarily mercantile, these new colonial powers, especially Britain and the Netherlands, introduced Protestantism to the region as well. The islands were also home to millions of African slaves – more than a third of the 12 million slaves brought to the New World ended up in the Caribbean – and after the end of slavery the British also brought thousands of indentured servants to the islands from India and China. The Asian Indian community, in particular, also grew during the early years of the twentieth century as a result of voluntary immigration.

The legacy of this complex history is evident both in the mixed ethnic composition of the islands and in the diverse religious profile of the region (see Table 11.3). As is true in the rest of Latin America, Catholics account for a majority of the Caribbean population (56 percent), but non-Catholic Christianity accounts for a larger proportion of the population here (17 percent) than anywhere else. The Caribbean is also the only subregion of Latin America in which

Table 11.3   Religious profiles of five largest independent Caribbean nations

Country	Population	% Catholic	% Protestant	% Pentecostal/ Charismatic	% Hindu	% Muslim
Cuba	11,250,000	42	1	4	–	–
Dominican Republic	9,000,000	80	4	11	–	–
Haiti	8,500,000	70	5	15	–	–
Jamaica	2,700,000	5	30	30	–	–
Trinidad & Tobago	1,300,000	25	20	10	25	5

Protestant and Pentecostal/Charismatic Christians combined constitute a majority of the population in some countries. These include Antigua and Barbuda (80 percent), the Bahamas (76 percent), Barbados (90 percent), Jamaica (55 percent), St Kitts and Nevis (84 percent), and St Vincent and the Grenadines (81 percent). Taking a different perspective, Christianity is also weaker here than anywhere else in Latin America with Christians accounting for only 73 percent of the overall Caribbean population. About half of the non-Christian population of the islands is nonreligious, with the great majority of these people living in Cuba. The other half of the non-Christian population is composed of members of various non-Christian religions, with places like Trinidad and Tobago, Suriname, and Guyana standing out as distinctive because of their significant Hindu and Muslim populations. (While Suriname and Guyana are geographically located on the South African mainland and not in the Caribbean, they are usually culturally considered part of the Caribbean.)

What is also pervasive, but much harder to measure, is the variety of Afro-Caribbean religions that flourish in the region, such as Santería in Cuba, Vodou in Haiti, Zion Revival in Jamaica, and Spiritual Baptists in St Vincent and the Grenadines. These religions were originally developed during the colonial era by African slaves, who took the ideas and practices of West African religion and mixed them with bits and pieces of Christianity to produce spiritual movements that helped them survive the harshness of slavery. They are still very much alive today; people commonly say, for example, that Haiti is 70 percent Catholic, but 100 percent Vodou. While Vodou has incorporated a number of Christian elements into its rituals and understanding of the world, Vodou and Christianity still remain very different religions at their cores, and this is true of most other Afro-Caribbean religions as well. This does not mean that they are necessarily incompatible. Christianity is a religion of salvation, focusing on the ultimate destiny of one's soul. By contrast, Vodou is a religion of the here and now, a religion that provides its devotees with assistance for dealing with pain and suffering in the present. It is not unreasonable, therefore, for Haitians to be Catholic with regard to their future salvation and Vodou when dealing with the trials of ordinary life that abound in Haiti.

Cuba stands out as the only nation in the Caribbean – and the only nation in all of the Americas – that has been under long-term Communist rule. When Fidel Castro and the

Communist Party took control of the island in 1959, most Cubans were more than pleased to be rid of the nation's former dictatorial ruler, Fulgencio Batista. In fact, most Catholic and Protestant churches held services of thanksgiving to God for the success of the revolution. But in light of the Cold War and given the churches' great fear of Communist atheism, that spirit of thanksgiving did not last long. Many missionary-led churches pulled foreign personnel off the island during the early years of Castro's rule. This is a shame because there is some evidence that Castro might have been willing to negotiate a strategic alliance with the churches had they adopted a socialist perspective on public life, but most of the churches were committed to the right of private property and were unwilling to move in his direction.

During the 1960s, 1970s, and 1980s, the churches of Cuba slowly lost members as the influence of Communism in Cuban life increased, but since the end of the Cold War in 1990, the churches have begun to revive. This revival has been aided by the fact that the prohibition that excluded religious believers from membership in the Communist Party was discarded in 1991 and that the state redefined itself as "lay" (nonreligious) in contrast to being atheistic (antireligious) in 1992. One of the most important signals of Cuba's new openness to religion was the nation's hosting of a visit by Pope John Paul II in 1998. The trip took years to negotiate, and the Catholic Church hoped the visit would change the way Christians were treated in Cuba. It seems that those hopes are being fulfilled. While visiting Cuba, John Paul II blessed the first stone of what he hoped would be a new seminary for training Cuban priests. In November 2010, that seminary – the first major Catholic structure built in the country in the last 50 years – opened its doors, with President Raul Castro (Fidel Castro's brother) participating in the ceremony. It does seem as if a new day may be dawning.

Finally, one other "nation" of the Caribbean requires attention here, even though it is technically part of the United States and not an independent country at all. That nation is Puerto Rico, one of the 14 territories that the United States owns and governs around the world. Some residents of Puerto Rico consider their nation to be an "occupied" territory and would like independence, but the majority of the people seem content, at least for the time being, with the country's territorial status. Religiously, Puerto Rico is significantly more Christian than the Caribbean as a whole. In fact, it is one of the most Christian nations on earth, with 97 percent of its people calling themselves Christians of one kind or another. About 60 percent of the island is traditionally Catholic, and the remaining Christian population is roughly evenly divided among Charismatic Catholics, Protestants, and non-Catholic Pentecostal/Charismatic Christians.

The brief descriptions provided in this chapter only begin to scratch the surface of the Christian and religious diversity that exists in Latin America today. Religious dynamics in Guatemala, Argentina, or Bolivia, for example, would be quite different from those in either Mexico or Brazil. The significance of non-Christian religion is also increasing throughout the region, including both the renewal of indigenous religions and the importation of other religions from around the globe. What that means is that the already complex religious profile of Latin America is becoming more complex every day. Any notion of religious monopoly is clearly a thing of the past. Like much of the rest of the world, Latin America is now a place where people have to decide whether to be religious or not and, if so, what religion they will be.

Notes

1 Quoted in R. Andrew Chesnut, *Competitive Spirits: Latin America's New Religious Economy* (Oxford: Oxford University Press, 2003), p. 72.

2 Quoted in Raúl Zibechi, "How Brazil Benefits from Being World's Most Pentecostal Country" (October 15, 2008) at http://www.brazzil.com/articles/197-october-2008/10120-how-brazil-benefits-from-being-worlds-most-pentecostal-country.html (accessed October 21, 2009).

3 Quoted in Chesnut, *Competitive Spirits,* p. 81.

Suggestions for Further Reading

Boff, Leonardo and Clodovis Boff (1987). *Introducing Liberation Theology.* Maryknoll, NY: Orbis.

Burdick, John (1993). *Looking for God in Brazil: The Progressive Catholic Church in Urban Brazil's Religious Arena.* Berkeley: University of California Press.

Camp, Roderic Ai (1997). *Crossing Swords: Politics and Religion in Mexico.* Oxford: Oxford University Press.

Chesnut, R. Andrew (2003). *Competitive Spirits: Latin America's New Religious Economy.* Oxford: Oxford University Press.

Freston, Paul (ed.) (2008). *Evangelical Christianity and Democracy in Latin America.* Oxford: Oxford University Press.

Gill, Anthony (1998). *Render Unto Caesar: The Catholic Church and the State in Latin America.* Chicago: University of Chicago Press.

González, Ondina E. and Justo L. González (2008). *Christianity in Latin America: A History.* Cambridge, UK: Cambridge University Press.

Martin, David (1990). *Tongues of Fire: The Explosion of Protestantism in Latin America.* Oxford: Blackwell.

Penyak, Lee M. and Walter J. Petry (eds) (2009). *Religion and Society in Latin America: Interpretive Essays from Conquest to Present.* Maryknoll, NY: Orbis.

Sigmund, Paul E. (ed.) (1999). *Religious Freedom and Evangelization in Latin America: The Challenge of Religious Pluralism.* Maryknoll, NY: Orbis.

Steigenga, Timothy J. and Edward L. Cleary (eds) (2007). *Conversion of a Continent: Contemporary Religious Change in Latin America.* New Brunswick, NJ: Rutgers University Press.

Chapter 12

North America

Faith in a Free Market

Christianity in North America has been more restless than in most other parts of the world. From the very beginning of the North American "experiment" (as the European colonial ventures were sometimes called), Christians in this part of the world have been intent on developing new and better ways of being Christian. This is partly because North America is a land of immigrants where people from many different Christian churches and from many different world religions have settled side by side, with no single group having the power to make everyone else conform to their vision of reality. That diversity led naturally to the religious competition that is so much of American religious life today. But the dynamism of faith in North America has also been deeply affected by the notion of voluntarism. To have faith or not is seen as a choice – it is a personal matter of the will – and that too has helped foster a market mentality with regard to religion in this region of the world.

If all of this sounds decidedly Protestant, that is because it is. More than anywhere else, North America is Protestant turf. Roughly half of the local population is Protestant and all of those Protestants taken together account for almost a third of all the Protestants in the world. In the recent past, Protestantism was even more dominant. In 1970, the region's population was 65 percent Protestant and in 1900 it was more than 80 percent Protestant. As a result, North American culture as a whole bears a Protestant stamp. This is so much the case that even Catholics – with the exception of the French Catholic population in Canada – behave in an almost Protestant fashion in comparison to Catholics in the rest of the world. North American Catholics think on their own and they sometimes question Vatican decisions. This independence of thought has occasionally been a source of frustration for the Catholic leadership in Rome. In fact, "Americanism" was condemned as a heresy by the pope in the late 1800s, but the Vatican has also at times praised American Catholicism for its postethnic character and its ideological flexibility.

The World's Christians: Who they are, Where they are, and How they got there, First Edition. Douglas Jacobsen.
© 2011 Douglas Jacobsen. Published 2011 by Blackwell Publishing Ltd.

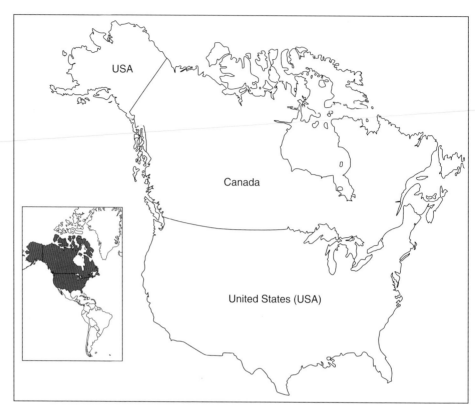

Figure 12.1   Map of North America. Map by author.
Total population 340,000,000 (5% of global population); Christian population 260,000,000 (76% of regional population, 13% of global Christian population): Orthodox 3,000,000, Catholics 85,000,000, Protestants 132,000,000 (includes LDS Church), Pentecostal/Charismatic 40,000,000.

The competitive Protestant ethos of Christianity in North America has given rise to a unique form of church organization called denominationalism, an idea that now is so common around the globe that it seems almost natural, but it is not. For most of Christian history, the majority of Christians lived in locations where there was only one kind of Christian church (Catholic or Orthodox or Lutheran, etc.). That one local church was seen as being the true church of Jesus Christ on earth and all other churches were seen as deficient or heretical. But in North America, Christians have come to assume that Christianity can take a variety of different forms, each of which embodies its own particular interpretation of Christianity, but none of which is automatically considered heretical. These churches are "denominated," that is, they are specifically named varieties of the same basic religion. Rather than being seen as heretics or enemies, other kinds of Christians are viewed simultaneously as brothers and sisters in faith and as friendly religious rivals. This cheery denominational understanding of Christian diversity originated in North America, but in the last century it has become the style of faith almost everywhere, a sign of how pervasive the influential North American Christianity has become within the global matrix of Christianity.

Until the mid-twentieth century, most North American denominations tended to operate like national franchises, meaning that all the congregations of a given denomination shared certain family resemblances wherever they were located. One could assume, for example, that a Methodist church would differ from a Presbyterian church in relatively predictable ways, whether they were located in the east or the west or the north or the south of the nation. In recent decades, however, denominational identities have become much blurrier and less distinct, and denominational loyalties have declined. Today it is the character of the local congregation that matters to most North Americans, and denominational affiliation is clearly secondary. Many local congregations are now denominationally unaffiliated and many other congregations that maintain ties with a denomination downplay those connections, identifying themselves with only a location (like the Church of Smithville or Johnstown) or a generic adjective (like Church of the Good Shepherd or Redeemer Church) and not with the name of the denomination itself. In addition, many contemporary North American Christians see themselves as freelance believers who feel no need to attach themselves to any congregation or denomination. They practice their religion entirely on their own.

While these trends can be observed to some degree everywhere in North America, it is important to remember that this region is made up of only two countries – the United States and Canada – and these two nations are in some ways very different from each other. Because attention to the United States tends to overwhelm attention given to Canada, this chapter begins with a discussion of Christianity in Canada before shifting its focus to the United States.

Christianity in Canada

The history of Christianity in Canada serves as a reminder that the religious history of North America could have taken a very different road. Rather than being settled by Protestants, Canada was colonized by French Catholics who had every intention of making Canada as Catholic as Latin America. But in 1763, the British took control and Protestantism began to flourish, and by the late 1800s nearly 60 percent of the population was Protestant. Since then, Protestant numbers have declined while Catholicism has held steady at about 40 percent of the population. Protestant losses were especially pronounced in the last half of the twentieth century, and Protestants now make up only about 30 percent of the Canadian population.

From the time the British took control, Canada has been a composite country containing two separate and distinct "nations": one French and Catholic, the other British and Protestant. Sometimes called the "two solitudes," Catholic and Protestant Canada can still be located geographically today, with most of the Catholic population being found in Quebec and most of the Protestant population in Newfoundland and the west. The presence of many "First Nations" people (Native Americans) adds another layer of complexity to Canadian society and religion.

Always religiously and ethnically diverse, Canada has generally been at ease adding other people and faiths to its population, allowing new immigrants to keep their ethnic and religious

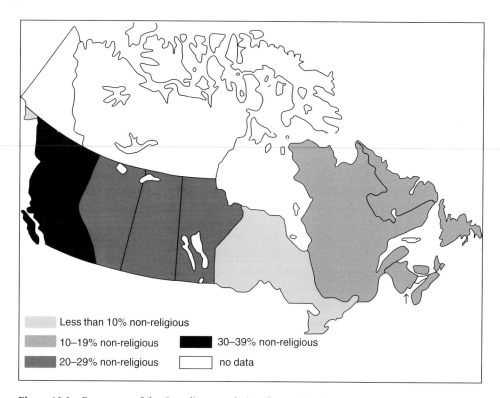

Figure 12.2   Percentage of the Canadian population (by province) reporting no religious affiliation. Map by author.

identities largely intact. Canada has never tried to blend everyone together into one great "melting pot" of culture, the approach perceived as the ideal in the United States. Because of this, Canada has found it relatively unproblematic to move in recent years from seeing itself as a Christian nation to seeing itself as a post-Christian, religiously pluralistic society, while many people in the United States remain firmly committed to keeping the United States "Christian." A corollary of this development is that many Canadians are suspicious of religious groups that they see as being overly aggressive in seeking converts. As one Canadian religious researcher explains: "We [Canadians] don't look favourably on groups that want to 'convert' other people to their way of thinking, particularly vulnerable people such as children, immigrants, and the elderly ... The pluralist ideal seems to translate into Canadian groups not so much competing for truth as coexisting to service the needs of their affiliates."[1]

Easygoing they may be, but many Canadians, especially the nation's church leaders, are worried about the state of religion in the country, and especially by the fact that more and more people seem to be dropping out of organized religion. While most Canadians continue to identify themselves as Christians, church membership and attendance have declined significantly in the last half century. In 1960, 99 percent of Canadians said that they were members of some church or religious community, and today that number is 83 percent. In 1960, 67 percent of Canadians attended religious services on a weekly basis, but fewer than

20 percent do so now. Self-conscious secularity is also on the rise. In 1960, it was rare for a Canadian to admit to being nonreligious. Today, more than 20 percent of the population claims that label. In general, the people in Eastern Canada remain more committed to their churches than those in the west, but church membership and attendance have declined everywhere (see Figure 12.2).[2]

The status of religion in Canada may not, however, be as dire as the raw numbers seem to imply. Even with relatively low public participation in religious activities, most Canadians continue to think of themselves as religious people. More than half say that God is "very important" in their lives, and another 30 percent indicate that God is at least "moderately important." Almost two-thirds say that religion gives them comfort and strength, and more than half report that they pray, meditate, read sacred texts, or engage in some kind of worship every month. What has changed is that much of this activity now takes place in private rather than in a church context. Canadians are holding onto the aspects of Christianity that attract them, then weaving them together with other ideas and practices to create their own individual tapestries of faith. Sometimes they describe themselves as being "spiritual, but not religious" – a label that seems to apply to a sizeable portion of the population. More than 20 percent of Canadian adults say they engage in private religious practices on a regular basis even though they rarely or never participate in public church worship.[3]

About 40 percent of Canadians have changed their religious affiliation at least once in their lives, usually as a result of a personal search for alternatives rather than in response to some newly advertised packaging of religion. No one knows whether this self-driven style of Canadian spirituality can sustain itself in the future. Some scholars predict that Canada will follow the same trajectory as Western Europe and become increasingly secular in the years ahead. Others are urging the churches to meet nonattending members where they already are, revamping themselves in order to connect more effectively with contemporary spiritual needs. If that happens, Christianity in Canada may well begin to look more like Christianity in the United States, not Europe.

Christianity in the United States

More Christians live in the United States than in any other country in the world – about 235 million – and American society as a whole is one of the most religiously active in the world. More than 90 percent of Americans believe in God and, according to the World Values Survey, 84 percent of them pray or meditate on a regular basis, 72 percent say God is "very important" in their lives, and 36 percent say they attend religious worship services once a week or more. The last figure may be slightly overstated – people tend to inflate their church attendance record – but still at least a quarter of the United States population is in church every Sunday.

People who study religion often ask themselves why religion remains such a vital and vibrant part of American life while it has stagnated or declined in most of Europe, and the answer that is often given is "competition." It is the massive and diverse infrastructure of Christianity in America, with each denomination or religious organization trying to develop new religious "products" that fit the needs and desires of its religious "customers," that

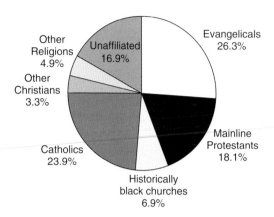

Figure 12.3   Religion in the USA using "American" categories of description

Source: Numbers come from the *U.S. Religious Landscape Survey—Religious Affiliation: Diverse and Dynamic* (Washington, DC: The Pew Forum on Religion and Public Life, 2008), available at http://religions.pewforum.org/pdf/report-religious-landscape-study-full.pdf.

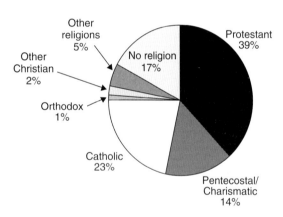

Figure 12.4   Religion in the USA using four world Christian traditions as categories of description

drives the engine of religious life in America. In Europe the options are relatively limited, and if people cannot find a religious option they like they just drop out. But the United States offers its residents literally thousands of Christian alternatives to choose from and almost everyone can find some kind of religion they like. That is what keeps people involved and that is what keeps them active.

Because the American religious landscape is so complex, scholars have developed a variety of different classification systems to map the terrain. The most commonly used map of American religion – the one most frequently referenced in news articles and sociological surveys – identifies five major clusters of Christians: mainline Protestants, Evangelicals, historically black churches, Catholics, and a final catch-all group called simply "other Christians." (See Figure 12.3.)

This American map of Christianity differs from the four-tradition model of Christianity used throughout this book, and the differences are instructive. It is noteworthy, for example, that Pentecostal/Charismatic Christianity does not appear on the American map as a separate category, that Orthodox Christianity is subsumed under the category of "other Christians," and that Protestantism is divided into three separate groups (mainline, Evangelical, and black church). The American map also indicates that the United States is still a predominantly Protestant nation, with just over 51 percent of the population falling into that category. But if the four-tradition model were used instead, many Evangelical Protestants would be reclassified as Pentecostal/Charismatic Christians and the overall number of Protestants in America would drop to just under 40 percent (see Figure 12.4) – a finding that would be unsettling to many American Protestants who still think of the United States as "their" land. Labeling religion is always fraught with difficulties, and in the United States this is especially the case. This chapter will accordingly use both sets of labels – the American map and the four-tradition model – to explain the state of Christianity in the region today.

As is the case in Canada, religiosity is distributed unevenly across the geography of the nation, and like Canada the West Coast of the country is considerably less religious than the East. But the real story is where religion is hottest, and that is in the South. Nine states – Alabama, Arkansas, Georgia, Louisiana, Mississippi, North Carolina, South Carolina, Tennessee, and Texas – stand out as significantly more religiously active than the rest of the country, with the sole exception of Utah where the Mormon population is also highly active.

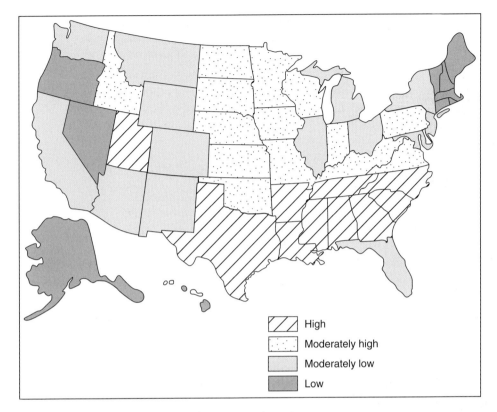

Figure 12.5   Church attendance rates by state. Map by author.

(See Figure 12.5 which uses church attendance rates to map levels of religiosity by state.) These states in the South constitute the traditional "Bible belt" of America, which also extends northward in slightly less intense form to include most of the Midwest.

Protestantism in the United States: Mainline and Evangelical

Discussions about Protestantism in the United States often hinge on differentiating between mainline Protestants and Evangelicals. These two large groups are often treated as if they are functional opposites, with members of the mainline churches being defined as "liberals" or "progressives," while Evangelicals are assumed to be "conservative" or even "fundamentalist" in orientation. But that bipolar depiction of mainline versus Evangelical differences does not accurately reflect what is going on. In reality, mainline Protestantism and Evangelicalism represent two very different ways of clumping groups of American Protestants together. Mainline Protestantism is defined institutionally and refers to a small group of historical Protestant denominations: the United Methodist Church, the Evangelical Lutheran Church in America (ELCA), the Presbyterian Church USA, the Episcopal Church, the American Baptist Church, the United Church of Christ, the Disciples of Christ, and the

Table 12.1   The mainline Protestant denominations in the USA

Denomination	Current membership
United Methodist Church	8,000,000
Evangelical Lutheran Church in America	4,800,000
Presbyterian Church USA	3,000,000
Episcopal Church	2,200,000
American Baptist Church	1,300,000
United Church of Christ	1,200,000
Disciples of Christ	700,000
Reformed Church in America	275,000

Reformed Church in America (see Table 12.1). By contrast, Evangelicalism is defined attitudinally as a loosely organized movement of individuals, churches, denominations, and parachurch organizations that share a handful of common experiences and convictions, including being "born again" and believing that the Bible is the literal Word of God.

Mainline Protestantism and Evangelicalism have very different histories. The mainline denominations arrived in North America early, often as the first churches in the towns founded by European settlers. Consequently, mainline Protestantism remains stronger along the east coast, where older cities and villages often have mainline Protestant churches in the center of downtown near the courthouse or town hall. Both the locations and the impressive sizes of these mainline church buildings illustrate why these churches are called mainline. These were the churches of the town leaders, the respectable people, the main players in society. Their faith was interwoven with the social fabric of the whole community so that being a member of a mainline congregation said not only that you were a Christian, but also that you were a responsible, respected member of the local community.

The Evangelical movement has a very different origin, with roots going back to the "Great Awakening" that took place between the years 1730 and 1755 when itinerant ministers traveled from town to town, preaching to crowds, often in the open air and frequently on days other than Sunday. They would jump on a hay wagon or would mount the courthouse steps and hold forth on the evils of sin and the need for spiritual "new birth." Some of the preachers of the era were stunning orators. It was said, for example, that George Whitefield (1714–70) could bring a crowd to tears merely by pronouncing the world "Mesopotamia." But it was not just their oratory that set these Evangelical preachers apart; it was also the message itself – a message that had nothing to do with respectability and social standing, but instead was all about individual salvation and the need for conversion.

Before the Great Awakening, most Protestants in the British colonies that would later become the United States – that is, most mainline Protestants – had assumed that salvation was a process. That process began when an infant was baptized and then progressed slowly through years of Christian instruction and worship. But the revivalists of the Great Awakening believed that God could work much faster. Salvation could be attained in an instant through the experience of conversion, a moment that was often deeply emotional.

Overcome by guilt and fearful of being sent to hell for their sins, people confessed their faults and found forgiveness through God's grace. For them, the gospel was the "good news" (or the "evangel," from which the word evangelical is derived), and they were convinced that others needed to hear that message too. Today, Evangelicals are found everywhere in the United States, but they are concentrated in the so-called "Bible belt" of the South and Midwest.

There are some broad theological differences between Evangelicals and mainline Protestants, but comparison is difficult because Evangelicals are largely defined by what they believe in common while mainline Protestants, who are bound together institutionally rather then ideologically, are much more varied in their beliefs. As a group, Evangelicals tend to be religiously self-confident, bold in their assurance that they have answers for the religious questions of humankind. Typically, American Evangelicals affirm four core beliefs: (1) that Christ's death and resurrection are the only source of salvation, (2) that the Bible is the inerrant Word of God, (3) that everyone must have a personal conversion experience, and (4) that Christians have a duty to evangelize (to try to convert) others. Undoubtedly the best known American Evangelical is Billy Graham (born 1918), who for decades preached the evangelical Christian message to large gatherings (called "crusades") in crowded sports stadiums and other large venues all around the world. Graham's sermons were always peppered with his famous phrase, "the Bible says."

The typical mainline Protestant would be more hesitant than the typical Evangelical to claim to have answers for other people's spiritual questions. Faith is viewed as a journey that can take different forms during different stages of life, and the journey can be marked by doubt as well as by confidence. Mainline Protestants often describe God as a God of grace, rather than vengeance. It is assumed that people other than Christians will undoubtedly show up in heaven, so evangelism and conversion have become less crucial. Most mainline Protestants consider the Bible to contain the Word of God, but they also believe it is an ancient document that needs to be carefully interpreted, and not all of it still applies to life today. Some portions of the Bible seem to have no connection with contemporary culture and many mainline Protestants are comfortable just ignoring them. What mainline Protestants generally want their churches to be today are places of welcome where everyone feels included and affirmed, not places where people are told they are going to hell. They see the real core of Christian living not in doctrinal precision or spiritual fervor, but in living the "Golden Rule," following Jesus's commandment to love others in the same way that we love ourselves.

For whatever reason – scholars disagree about the causes – mainline Protestantism in the United States has declined precipitously in membership over the last 40 years. Mainline churches have lost more than 25 percent of their membership since 1970, and when adjusted for population growth, their membership is down almost 50 percent. Mainline Protestantism has also lost much of its former power and influence. Until the middle of the twentieth century, when mainline Protestant leaders spoke – individuals like the theologian Reinhold Niebuhr or the New York City preacher Harry Emerson Fosdick – almost everyone in the nation listened, or at least the "important" people listened. That is no longer the case, and some commentators now refer to mainline Protestantism as the "oldline" or the "sideline." Regardless of their losses, the mainline Protestant churches retain a sense of responsibility for speaking to, and speaking for, the center of American faith and life, a center that is becoming more diverse every day. In that context, they see their task as helping members remain grounded in their own traditions while building bridges of understanding and co-operation with other Christians and with people of other faiths or of no faith at all. For millions of Americans, that is the only kind of Christianity that makes sense in the contemporary world.

The recent history of Evangelicalism is very different from that of mainline Protestantism, because their pattern has been one of growth rather than decline. In 1970, Evangelicals comprised perhaps 15 percent of the United States population (about 30 million people). Today, as much as 25 to 30 percent of the population (up to 90 million people) says it is Evangelical, and Evangelicals have become a huge force in both American politics and American business, spawning a wide variety of evangelically oriented books, movies, music, and almost any other commodity one could want. In the world of religious competition that is America, Evangelicals have clearly outperformed their mainline Protestant neighbors.

The competitive advantage that Evangelicals enjoy seems to be at least partially a result of their ability to mix certitude in matters of doctrine with flexibility in church programming. The last 40 years have been a time of tremendous transition in the United States, and the consistency of the Evangelical theological message has been reassuring for many people, a point of stability in a changing world. Simultaneously, Evangelical churches – many of them with minimal or nonexistent denominational ties – have developed a broad range of innovative programs to attract new members. The nondenominational Evangelical megachurches that can now be found in almost every large American town have been especially adept at this task. Many of these churches conduct intensive surveys of the local community to assess needs, and then design church programs in response, a process very similar to the kind of market research a for-profit company would typically undertake before launching a new product. Megachurch pastors such as Rick Warren of Saddleback Church in southern California (see Plate 21) see no problem with this. They would not deny that research and planning are involved, but they would say this is perfectly fine because the goal is spiritual: to religiously serve people where they are.

Serving people where they are does not, however, mean Evangelical pastors are content to let them stay there. Warren in particular has proved himself to be a master at moving people from where they are to where he believes they really ought to be. His book *The Purpose Driven Life: What on Earth Am I Here For?* has sold more than 40 million copies, and the main point of the book is that life is not about satisfying one's own needs. The opening lines of the book read: "It's not about you. The purpose of your life is far greater than your personal fulfillment, your peace of mind, or even your happiness."[4] According to Warren, the real purpose of life is to know God and to serve others, and Saddleback Church oversees more than 200 programs designed to help members do just that through worship, counseling, Bible study, local and global outreach, support for those in need, and small groups meeting in homes. Many other Evangelical churches engage in similar activities on a smaller scale: developing creative new programs that meet the needs of their members and also provide members with opportunities to use their gifts to help others. Though many Evangelical churches champion "traditional family values" – one man and one woman faithfully married to each other and raising their kids together – they often have more programs to support single parents and divorced men and women than can be found at most mainline churches.

During the last several decades, the differences between Evangelicalism and mainline Protestantism have become seemingly more oppositional, partly because they overlap with political differences and American political differences have become so much more contentious during this time. Evangelicals generally tend toward the conservative politics of the Religious Right and the Republican Party, while the leadership of the mainline churches (though not always the people in the pews) tends to support a variety of more progressive policy options usually associated with the Democratic Party. This division is by no means absolute. Millions of Evangelicals are Democrats and many mainline Christians are Republicans, but as groups the political profiles of Evangelicals and mainline Protestants do diverge significantly.

But while there are many differences between these two groups, the similarities between Evangelicals and mainline Protestants have also been increasing in recent years. There is, for example, a new sense of energy and excitement within many mainline churches about spirituality and spiritual growth. Mainline congregations now sponsor small group meetings for Bible study and encourage parishioners to explore the spiritual disciplines of prayer, service, fasting, and meditation. Some mainline churches have adopted contemporary styles of worship and offer healing ministries to their members. These are activities that formerly would have been seen as prototypically Evangelical. A similar move toward the middle is evident in Evangelicalism, where some churches are now experimenting with a variety of more typically mainline elements of worship like lighting candles, reciting creeds, offering formal rather than extemporaneous prayers, and wearing liturgical robes. Some Evangelicals are also engaging in conversations about social justice, the environment, and interreligious dialogue that are more characteristic of the mainline. Many of the old markers of difference between Evangelicals and the mainline are still in place, but others are clearly in transition and may well disappear in the coming years.

The Fuzziness of Pentecostal/Charismatic Identity in America

The modern Pentecostal movement has deep roots in the United States. The Azusa Street Revival that took place in Los Angeles in 1906, led by William J. Seymour, played a critical role in developing a movement mentality among the many different people who were beginning to champion this new Spirit-centered vision of Christianity. Many of the oldest and best known classical Pentecostal denominations in the world began in America in the early decades of the twentieth century. Roughly 5 percent of the United States population belongs to a classical Pentecostal church. The four largest of the classical Pentecostal denominations are the Church of God in Christ (COGIC) with about five and a half million members, the Assemblies of God (AG) with almost three million, the Pentecostal Assemblies of the World (PAW) with about one and a half million, and the Church of God (Cleveland, Tennessee) with about 750,000.

In the 1960s and 1970s the United States also played a central role in creating the Charismatic movement that has since spread the Pentecostal message of spirit-filled

Christianity to Catholic and Protestant churches around the world. One recent survey suggests that 30 percent or more of all the Catholic and Protestant Christians in the United States can be described as functionally Pentecostal/Charismatic.[5] Though that may be an overestimate, there is no doubt that Pentecostal/Charismatic numbers are huge. Nonetheless, the visibility of Pentecostal/Charismatic Christianity is generally less than one might expect, and this is due at least in part to the fact that many Pentecostal/Charismatic Christians in the United States don't know what to call themselves.

This problem began in the 1980s when two very public scandals erupted in the Pentecostal/Charismatic movement and tarnished the name. First, Jim Bakker of the Praise the Lord (PTL) television network admitted to having a sexual affair and was later convicted of accounting fraud (partly to conceal hush money paid to his mistress), and then Jimmy Swaggart, another well-known Pentecostal television preacher, confessed to having sex with prostitutes. To dissociate themselves from these scandals, many Pentecostal/Charismatic Christians began calling themselves Evangelicals, a switch in terminology that was made easier by the fact that services of worship in the Pentecostal/Charismatic and Evangelical churches had already become quite similar. Speaking in tongues and prophecy were receiving less emphasis in many Pentecostal/Charismatic churches, while Evangelical churches were adding Charismatic elements like contemporary Christian music and prayers for healing to their services of worship. During these years, a number of neo-Charismatic churches were also launched that intentionally blurred the line between Evangelical and Pentecostal/Charismatic varieties of faith, with Calvary Chapel, a church in California founded by Chuck Smith in 1965, leading the way. By the late 1980s Calvary Chapel had grown into a fellowship of several hundred congregations.

Today, no one is quite sure how to identify, label, or count Pentecostal/Charismatic Christians in the United States or whether it is even helpful to try to distinguish them from other Spirit-aware, Evangelical-style Christians. Perhaps as many as half the Evangelicals in the country could be described as Charismatic to some degree, but no one has a strong desire to draw that line. Pentecostal/Charismatic Christians like blending in, and non-Charismatic Evangelicals like the fact that including Pentecostal/Charismatic Christians boosts the overall Evangelical numbers and makes the movement as a whole look larger and more important. The situation is so murky that J. Lee Grady, editor of the Charismatic Christian magazine *Charisma*, declared in mid-2009 that the label "Charismatic" was simply dead. Grady was not saying that the Holy Spirit had stopped doing miracles, but rather that the old label had stopped being helpful, and "it really doesn't matter what we label the next movement."[6]

Despite this ambiguity of labeling and terminology, the Pentecostal/Charismatic movement in the United States does seem to be doing quite well. Somewhere between 35 and 40 million people are likely involved. This number includes the 15 million members of the classical Pentecostal denominations, an additional five million Catholic Charismatics, five million or more people who are members of the various neo-Charismatic and Spirit-filled non-denominational churches that have been founded in the last three or four decades, and somewhere in excess of 10 million additional Christian believers who talk and behave like Pentecostal/Charismatic Christians but who choose to identify themselves simply as Evangelical Christians with no adjective to indicate their Pentecostal/Charismatic orientation.

Table 12.2 Historically black churches with more than one million members

Denomination	Year founded	Current membership
Church of God in Christ	1907	5,500,000
National Baptist Convention, USA	1880	5,000,000
National Baptist Convention of America	1915	3,500,000
African Methodist Episcopal Church	1816	2,500,000
National Missionary Baptist Convention of America	1988	2,500,000
Progressive National Baptist Convention	1961	2,500,000
Pentecostal Assemblies of the World	1906	1,500,000
African Methodist Episcopal Zion Church	1821	1,500,000

The Historically Black Protestant Churches

During the colonial period, white Christians in America were deeply divided over the issue of whether black slaves should be baptized or instructed in Christian faith. Despite that white Christian ambivalence, a black church soon emerged. At first it existed as an "invisible institution" within the slave population, meeting secretly at night to avoid detection, but in the early 1800s a number of predominantly African-American denominations were formed within the free black population. The oldest of these denominations is the African Methodist Episcopal (AME) Church, founded by Richard Allen in Philadelphia in 1816. Today, however, only about 12 percent of African American Protestants are Methodists. The largest single black denomination is the Church of God in Christ, a Pentecostal denomination with more than five million members, but more than 60 percent of African American Christians are Baptists of one kind or another (see Table 12.2).

Doctrinal disputes have frequently been the cause for establishing new Protestant denominations, but that has rarely been the case in the historically black churches in the United States. Even today most black Methodists affirm the same doctrines as white Methodists, and most black Baptists believe the same kinds of things that white Baptists believe. Rather than theological differences, it was ethical concerns that drove the creation of the black church. In the nineteenth and early twentieth centuries, most white Protestants in America thought race was a topic that fell outside the realm of ethics. Whites commonly believed that God had simply created the races unequal, and their unequal treatment in society reflected the created order. Even many white abolitionists who believed slavery was a sin still held this view of race. But most African Americans believed that God created everyone to be equal and that racial prejudice was a sin. Because of their commitment to equality, black Christians felt compelled to create their own new churches where everyone would be welcomed equally regardless of race. These new racially inclusive churches became predominantly black churches because most white Christians refused to join them.

The Civil Rights Movement of the 1960s expressed this inclusivity of spirit. Led by people like Martin Luther King, Jr. and Fannie Lou Hamer, and by organizations like the

Figure 12.6   Bishop T. D. Jakes of the Potter's House Church
© Barry Brecheisen/ WireImage/Getty Images

Southern Christian Leadership Conference, the Civil Rights movement combined the words of the Bible and the words of the United States Constitution to demand freedom and equality for all people. The goal of the movement was modest – racial integration and the willingness to live and work together as equals – but the cost was high, with hundreds of black Christians (along with some white supporters) being jailed and beaten, and some killed, for protesting the legal but immoral relegation of black people to second-class citizenship. The Civil Rights movement was undergirded by Christian principles from start to finish. Almost all of the leaders were members of the Protestant clergy, and songs rooted in the Christian tradition helped sustain supporters through the worst periods of persecution. Most of King's speeches were, in fact, sermons, and his last oratory ("I Have Seen the Promised Land") was delivered from the pulpit of Mason Temple, the headquarters of the Church of God in Christ in Memphis, Tennessee, on the night before his assassination (see Plate 22).

Since the end of the Civil Rights era, the intellectual leaders of the movement – black theologians and "womanist" theologians (black Christian feminists) – have become somewhat more radical, while the pastors and institutional leaders of the denominations have remained relatively conservative in their views. That gap in attitudes and expectations has sometimes caused tensions, but the threats that African Americans (especially those living in the nation's cities) have faced together – ranging from crack cocaine to crime to crumbling schools systems – have helped keep the black church together. Compelled to respond to these challenges, the historically black churches have developed new programs designed to keep their children safe in the cities, to care for aging seniors, to reintegrate people who have served prison terms back into the community, and to help single mothers feed their families. Because of this work, the urban black church remains a respected institution within the African American community, though its resources have often been stretched very thin.

In recent years an alternative wing of the black church has also emerged that focuses more intentionally on the new black middle class and the religious hopes and fears that characterize the spirituality of this relatively affluent sector of the African American community. One of the most visible examples of this new kind of church is The Potter's House in Dallas, Texas. Founded and led by the flamboyant Rev. Thomas Dexter Jakes (born 1957), The Potter's House is a megachurch with a membership that exceeds 30,000. Jakes (see Figure 12.6) is both a spiritual leader and a religious entrepreneur, and his message is a mix of old-time Pentecostal religion (he was raised in the Oneness or "Jesus Only" Pentecostal tradition that rejects the traditional formulation of the Christian trinity), the prosperity gospel, advice about gender roles and family relations, and instruction about the attitudes and habits of life needed for success in life and in business. He is the author of more than 25 bestselling books and has produced two feature-length movies. Critics say that Jakes has turned Christianity into little more than a religious commodity and that he does not sufficiently acknowledge the historical and social factors that continue to hamper African Americans in the United States today. But others see Jakes and The Potter's House as the model for what a successful, mainstreamed black church can and should be.

Catholicism in Transition

When the United States declared its independence in 1776 less than 1 percent of the population was Catholic, but by the middle of the nineteenth century the Roman Catholic Church was the largest single Christian entity in the nation. Catholic growth was fueled by waves of immigration. The Irish were the first to arrive in large numbers, and they were followed by Germans, Poles, and Italians. The sheer numbers of new parishioners overwhelmed the institutional resources of the church, and, especially during the early years of the nineteenth century, laypeople often took the lead in establishing new parishes and finding priests to serve them. This was a very American way to proceed, but it was not particularly Catholic. As the growth of the church hierarchy slowly caught up with the growth of the Catholic population as a whole, newly appointed bishops took control of the church back from the laity.

Up until the middle of the twentieth century, Catholicism existed largely as a separate subculture within the American social order. This was partly a matter of ethnicity. For many Catholic immigrants the church served as a kind of halfway house that preserved the cultural ways of the old world and eased the transition to life in America. But even after the influence of ethnicity waned, the Catholic Church continued to function as a kind of separate world that existed apart from mainstream America. This was largely a result of Catholic choice, a reasonable reaction to the anti-Catholic prejudices of the majority Protestant population. Catholics organized their own "parochial" school system to educate their children, they created a separate hospital system to care for their sick, and they developed their own philanthropic and social clubs like the Knights of Columbus where they could relax in their free time. The continuation of their religious segregation was also guaranteed by the fact that the Catholic Church deemed attendance at the religious services of any other group, including Protestant churches, to be a serious sin. At the intimate levels of family, friendship, and faith, Catholics remained in their own separate world long after they began to blend more readily into public American life at work, in government, and in the military.

By the 1950s, Catholic separation from larger public life in America was coming to an end and a major transformation was beginning. Protestant Americans finally began accepting Catholics as their Christian equals and many Catholic communities, in response, began to downplay some of their more distinctively Catholic (or distinctively ethnic) ways of life. In 1960, a major milestone in American history was reached with the election of John F. Kennedy as the first Catholic President of the United States. Then the post-World War II baby boom generation (a population cohort more prone than most to criticize its parents than previous generations were) pushed the transformational process further along by openly questioning the folkways and even some of the doctrinal beliefs of the Catholic past. Finally, the *aggiornamento* (bringing up to date) of the Second Vatican Council spurred change and development in Catholicism around the world, including the United States. Today Catholics are part of the mainstream of American religious life, even though their regional distribution across the nation is somewhat uneven, with many more Catholics living in the Northeast and the Southwest than in the so-called Deep South (see Figure 12.7).

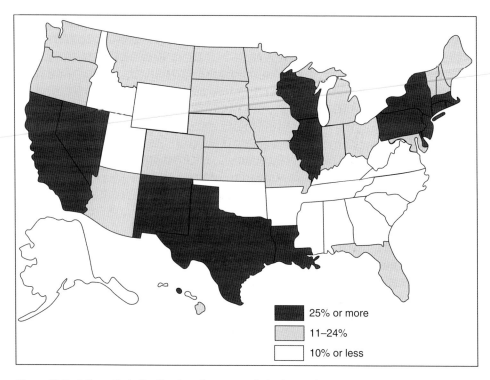

Figure 12.7   Where Catholics live (% of state population). Map by author.

Being mainstream has not, however, necessarily guaranteed religious success. In fact, many commentators describe the recent history of American Catholicism in negative terms, rather than positive. The data is incontestable. Weekly attendance at Mass has dropped dramatically, the percentage of Catholic children currently enrolled in Catholic schools is less than half of what it was in the 1960s, and the numbers of priests and religious brothers and sisters are significantly lower than they were in the mid-twentieth century even though the Catholic population has almost doubled since then. Catholics are also defecting from the faith in record numbers: only two-thirds of those born into Catholic homes remain Catholics as adults. In fact, if all those Americans who are "formerly Catholic" were to be gathered into their own denomination, it would be the second largest denomination in the country, smaller than the Catholic Church itself but larger than the Southern Baptist Church (which has 16 million members).

The 75 million Americans who remain members of the Catholic Church can be divided into three groups: about a third are highly engaged, another third are loosely connected (showing up at Christmas and Easter and at family events like baptisms), and a final third are essentially nonpracticing, having little if any interaction with the church after baptism. Catholics are not only distancing themselves from the church in terms of attendance, they are also moving away from the church intellectually. Many American Catholics are particularly disenchanted with the teachings of the church as they apply to sexuality and human reproduction. Surveys show that about 90 percent of sexually active American Catholic women use birth control, about 65 percent of American Catholics believe that sex between consenting unmarried adults is not immoral, and about 40 percent of Catholics are prochoice on the issue of abortion, in spite of the fact that birth control, premarital sex, and abortion are all thoroughly and unambiguously condemned by the Catholic Church. The Catholic pedophile crisis that erupted into public view in 2002 – a crisis that centered not only on the abuse of young boys and girls by Catholic priests, but also on the church's slowness to respond – drove a further wedge between Catholic laypeople and the church hierarchy and has cost the church dearly in terms of both moral standing and money (almost a billion dollars has now been paid out to victims).

But despite these challenges and troubles, not everything is going downhill in American Catholicism, and there are some positive countertrends. Perhaps the most significant is the new religious activism of the Catholic laity. As the numbers of priests, brothers, and sisters have declined, Catholic laypeople all across the nation have stepped into leadership roles. The office of deacon is a case in point. By the mid-twentieth century, the office of "permanent deacon" (different from the office of "transitional deacon," which is a step on the way to priestly ordination) had become largely extinct within the Catholic Church. But starting around 1970 the office was revived, and now there are more than 13,000 permanent deacons (all of them men) in the American Catholic Church. Others (including many women) are becoming lay ecclesial ministers, a new office established on the basis of a passage in the most recent edition of the *Catholic Catechism* that stipulates that "the laity can also feel called, or in fact be called, to cooperate with their pastors in the service of the ecclesial community, for the sake of its growth and life." The office of lay ecclesial minister is defined differently from parish to parish, with titles like director of religious education, youth minister, liturgical director, or pastoral coordinator. At present, there are roughly 40,000 lay ecclesiastical ministers in the American Catholic Church, almost the same as the number of priests.

The new sense of spiritual energy among the laity is found not only among conservative loyalists in the church, but also among some Catholics who are rather cynical about the church as an institution. For example, Kerry Kennedy, the niece of US President John F. Kennedy and a well-known human rights activist, has recently written:

> I've come to realize that Catholicism is far more important than the pope and the bishops, our statues and icons, the confessional, the rosary beads, the smell of wax candles and incense, and our fabulous pageantry. Rather, Catholicism, in the end, is about creating a society based on a shared vision of God as exemplified by Christ, his commitment to justice and peace, and, most of all, his love. … When I become incensed by the latest outrageous pronouncement of a wayward bishop, I try to remember that perhaps at this moment in history the Holy Spirit is sending lay Catholics an empowering message that we can no longer be passive in our faith and blindly follow the hierarchy; instead, we must take personal responsibility to act on the word of Christ despite the impediments placed in our path.[7]

All of this positive energy within the American Catholic Church makes it awkward to describe American Catholicism as in a state of decline, but it is also not quite accurate to say that the church is flourishing when there is such widespread disagreement among American Catholics about the current status of the church and its future direction. Some Catholics, like Kerry Kennedy, hope for a relatively radical restructuring of the church, perhaps even including the eventual ordination of women. But many others, including most of the church hierarchy, would bemoan Kennedy's attitude as part of the problem. For them, Kennedy's criticism of the church is an expression of the "culture of dissent" that is slowly destroying the church from within. They would call Kennedy a "cafeteria Catholic" – a person who thinks she can pick and choose what appeals to her from the wide variety of Catholic offerings and can ignore the rest. By contrast, these more conservative Catholic leaders would define "real" Catholics as people who seek to obey everything the church teaches, not just the items they happen to agree with.

The other great unknown in American Catholicism is how it will be shaped in coming years by the growing numbers of Hispanics in the nation. At present, fully one third of the American Catholic population is Hispanic, and it is predicted that a majority of Catholics in the United States will be Hispanic by 2050. The Catholic Church in America has already become fully multicultural. In Los Angeles, for example, Mass is said in more than three dozen languages every Sunday. Because of that diversity the Catholic leadership is already more international in its orientation than the population of the United States as a whole. The growing Hispanic membership of the Church may strengthen that internationalist perspective, but it might also recenter attention away from the larger world, placing greater emphasis on domestic American problems and concerns.

Orthodoxy in the United States

Orthodoxy has been present in North America since the late 1700s when an Alaskan mission was established by its near neighbor Russia. Russian Orthodoxy is still quite visible in Alaska today. The number of Orthodox Christians in the United States grew in the late 1800s as Orthodox Christians from Eastern Europe began to enter the country in significant number. The majority of the earliest immigrants were Greek, followed later by Orthodox believers from Serbia, Romania, Russia, the Ukraine, the Middle East, and elsewhere. Today there are about two million Orthodox Christians in the United States, divided among more than 30 different Orthodox "jurisdictions" found across the nation. The largest is the Orthodox Church in America (OCA), which has more than a million members. This church has roots in the Russian Orthodox mission in Alaska and became autocephalous in 1970, making it the only Orthodox church in the United States with that status.

For the last half century the greatest challenge facing Orthodoxy in the United States has been its own inner diversity. According to Orthodox canon law, there should be only one Orthodox church in each nation, and most certainly there should be only one bishop in any given city or town. Yet because of the immigration patterns in the United States, different jurisdictions sometimes exist within a few blocks of one another, with each representing a different ethnic group trying to preserve its own distinctive Orthodox traditions. But despite some fears that merger would result in loss of ethnic identities, a movement toward Orthodox unity is slowly gaining momentum.

This process of emerging unification is represented most visibly in the Standing Conference of Orthodox Bishops in America (SCOBA), founded in 1960, which is an association of nine groups representing more than 80 percent of the Orthodox Christians in the country. But the organization that has been pursuing the unity of the Orthodoxy most aggressively in recent years is the Orthodox Christian Laity (OCL). Founded in 1987 by a group of Greek Orthodox Christians from Chicago, its membership has since expanded considerably. In 2000, the OCL released a document titled "An Orthodox Christian Church in the United States: Unified and Self-Governed" that asks the Ecumenical Patriarch of Constantinople to call for the creation of a new unified autocephalous Orthodox Church in the United States (combining all the various Orthodox churches, including the OCA) with the process of unification to be overseen by SCOBA. The sentiments of the document have been widely affirmed by Orthodox groups in the United States, but less enthusiasm is being expressed from Orthodox leaders outside the United States who worry that unification of Orthodoxy in America will cause American members to feel less attached to their ethnic mother churches overseas.

But unified or not, Orthodoxy in the United States is slowly becoming ethnically "American" rather than Greek or Russian or Romanian. Orthodox churches are being established with congregants from a wide variety of ethnic backgrounds and far away from urban immigrant neighborhoods. One driving force behind this development is the growing number of people who convert to Orthodoxy from non-Orthodox backgrounds. Many of these converts have come to Orthodoxy from Evangelical Protestantism. Because these new members were trained as evangelicals to be bold in their personal expressions of faith, they sometimes carry this attitude into their new-found Orthodox faith. One such convert, the popular Christian writer Frederica Mathewes-Green, says bluntly: "When I became Orthodox I didn't become Russian, Finnish, or Serbian. I'm here for the faith, not the pierogis; I don't know how to do Greek dancing or paint Ukrainian eggs." Describing her conversion, Mathewes-Green adds: "Orthodoxy initially struck me as strange and off-putting: beautiful but rigorous, and focused much more on God than on me. Western Christianity of many stripes has tended in recent decades to become somewhat soft and emotional – in a sense, consumer-focused. Orthodoxy has missed that bandwagon and still stubbornly addresses its energy toward worshipping God."[8]

Ironically, Orthodoxy in America has become religiously competitive by deciding not to be competitive. For many individuals, and for many Evangelicals in particular, it is precisely the God-centered, human-comfort-denying aspects of Orthodoxy that are most appealing. Amid the welter of nicely packaged and ready-to-buy versions of Christianity that are available in the United States, Orthodoxy somehow seems to stand out as more authentic, a way to "go organic" spiritually by adopting a purer form of faith that is less adulterated with the consumer contaminants of other American churches.

The Church of Jesus Christ of Latter Day Saints

In addition to being a place where all four of the world's major Christian traditions have flourished, the United States has also been an incubator of several entirely new Christian churches constructed from scratch within the American context. The largest and most influential of these groups is the Church of Jesus Christ of Latter Day Saints (LDS), founded by Joseph Smith, Jr., in the early 1800s. The LDS Church currently has 13 million members worldwide,

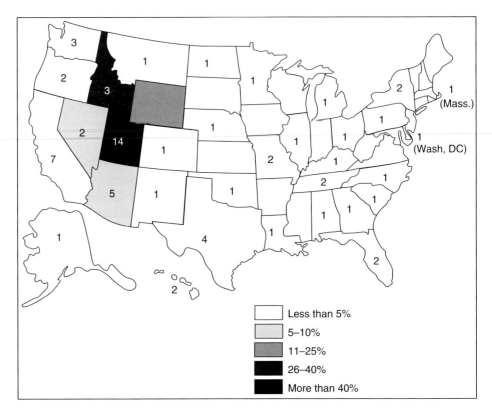

Figure 12.8   Where Mormons live (% of state population). Map by author.
Note: Numbers indicate how many temples have been built in each state; no number means none exists.

including almost six million members in the United States. Commonly known as Mormons, the LDS is the fourth largest denomination in the nation, exceeded in membership only by Catholics, Southern Baptists, and United Methodists. The LDS Church is headquartered in Salt Lake City in the state of Utah, the home state for a majority of their American members. But Mormon congregations (called "wards") and temples (buildings used for special ceremonies, but not weekly worship) are found throughout the country (see Figure 12.8).

There are no clergy in the LDS Church. Leadership positions in a ward are assigned on a rotating basis, and local leaders serve as volunteers without pay. But the church overall is characterized by a strong sense of authority. The LDS Church is led by a president who functions as a "prophet, seer, and revelator" for the Mormon community as a whole. The president is assisted by two counselors, and these three people together are known collectively as the "First Presidency." A group of 12 apostles, called the Quorum of Twelve, helps in oversight of the church. The LDS Church is unique in its emphasis on the notion of priesthood for all male church members. Mormon boys can be ordained into the Aaronic priesthood at age 12 and the Melchizedek priesthood at age 18. Women cannot be ordained to the priesthood, but Mormons believe in "continuing revelation" and assume that God can still communicate new information about proper Christian practice and belief to the church's leadership. In 1978, the First Presidency announced that they had received a new revelation allowing "all worthy male members of the Church [to be] ordained to the priesthood without regard for race or color,"[9] overturning an earlier ban on priesthood for men of African descent.

Mormons hold a variety of doctrines that set them apart from most other Christians. They believe, for example, that Jesus visited North America after his death and resurrection and that the record of his visit is described in the *Book of Mormon*. The LDS Church considers as scripture not only the Bible, but also three additional books: the *Book of Mormon*, *The Doctrine and Covenants of the Church of Jesus Christ of Latter Day Saints*, and *The Pearl of Great Price*. Mormons also believe that marriage is eternal and that marriages and baptisms can be undertaken on behalf of people who are dead. The Mormon understanding of God's character is particularly controversial: the church teaches that God has a physical body and is married. Mormons also believe that almost everyone will go to heaven, but that there are three levels of heaven (telestial, terrestrial, and celestial) and only faithful Mormons will be allowed into the highest and holiest (the celestial).

In actuality, individual Mormons hold many different views about all of these theological matters, and there is much less dogmatism about belief in the Mormon church than most outsiders would suspect, but there is no disputing the fact that taken as a whole LDS teachings vary significantly from the teachings of most other Christian churches. This is so much the case that many other Christians have questioned whether Mormons should really be called Christians at all. This is an attitude that deeply offends members of the LDS Church. In their eyes, the Mormon Church is the most truly Christian church on earth. They believe that the Christian movement as a whole fell into apostasy very early in its history and that true Christianity then ceased to exist until it was restored in the nineteenth century by the revelations given to Joseph Smith and by the restoration of the ancient biblical priesthood.

But while Mormon beliefs may be considered unusual or even heretical by some American Christians, their way of life is often considered to be exemplary. Members of the LDS Church are known for their strong family values, their self-discipline and hard work, and their honesty. Mormons are viewed by many people – and not just their fellow church members – as ideal Americans. In fact, most LDS men were Boy Scouts in their youth, members of one of the most "all American" organizations in the country. Mormon wards do not have church youth groups like most other American denominations. Instead, they sponsor special Mormon-only Boy Scout troops as their main youth activity. Mormon young people also attend "seminary" during their high school years, daily hour-long training sessions held before the start of the school day. Perhaps the best known activity of the church is the two-year missionary program, undertaken by about 30 percent of Mormon men and about 15 percent of Mormon women, which places Mormon young people in locations around the world where they go in pairs from door to door sharing the Mormon gospel.

The Mormon church is creative and idealistic in seeking converts, but to some degree that is true of most churches in North America. Churches in this region of the world have no other option than to constantly seek new members or die. To that end the churches of North America are continually assessing themselves, trying to remain relevant and attractive to members and new converts alike. The fact that some groups, like the Orthodox, are able to attract and keep members by refusing to change their ways of life are the exceptions that prove the rule: their steadfastness can be attractive in a world where every other option is in a state of perpetual change.

In recent years, the religious profile of North America has become increasingly complex as new immigrants from Asia, Africa, and Latin America have imported their traditions of faith into the region. Many of these immigrants are not Christians, and the widening range of religious pluralism can be a challenge for some Christians who have never before had neighbors who were practicing Buddhists, Muslims, or Hindus. However, many of these new immigrants are Christians, and their growing presence in the United States is also having an impact on the churches. As Korean Presbyterians, members of African Independent Churches, Latin American Catholics, and many other kinds of Christians make their way to North America they are adding ever more richness to a free market of religion that is already overflowing with alternatives.

Notes

1 Reginald W. Bibby, *Restless Gods: The Renaissance of Religion in Canada* (Toronto: Stoddart, 2002), p. 65.

2 Colin Lindsay, "Canadians Attend Weekly Religious Services Less than 20 Years Ago," *The General Social Survey: Matter of Fact, no. 3:* (Statistics Canada, June 2008), pp. 1–3.

3 Warren Clark and Grant Schellenberg, "Who's Religious?" *Canadian Social Trends* (Summer 2006), pp. 2–8.

4 Rick Warren, *The Purpose Driven Life: What on Earth Am I Here For?* (Grand Rapids, MI: Zondervan, 2002), p. 17.

5 *Spirit and Power: A 10-Country Survey of Pentecostals* (Washington, DC: The Pew Forum on Religion and Public Life, 2006), p. 91.

6 J. Lee Grady, "The Charismatic Movement: Dead or Alive?" *Charisma* (June 30, 2009), online at http://www.charismamag.com/index.php/fire-in-my-bones/22455-the-charismatic-movement-dead-or-alive(accessed October 4, 2009).

7 Kerry Kennedy, *Being Catholic Now: Prominent Americans Talk About Change in the Church and the Quest for Meaning* (New York: Three Rivers, 2008), pp. xxxii–xxxiii.

8 Frederica Mathewes-Green, *At the Corner of East and Now: A Modern Life in Ancient Christian Orthodoxy* (New York: Putnam, 1999), pp. 10, 11.

9 *The Doctrine and Covenants of the Church of Jesus Christ of Latter Day Saints* (Salt Lake City, Church of Jesus Christ of Latter Day Saints, n.d.), p. 294.

Suggestions for Further Reading

Badillo, David A. (2006). *Latinos and the New Immigrant Church*. Baltimore, MD: The Johns Hopkins University Press.

Bass, Diana Butler (2006). *Christianity for the Rest of Us: How the Neighborhood Church is Transforming the Faith*. San Francisco: HarperSanFrancisco.

Bibby, Reginald W. (2002). *Restless Gods: The Renaissance of Religion in Canada*. Toronto: Stoddart.

Bramadat, Paul and David Seljak (eds) (2008). *Christianity and Ethnicity in Canada*. Toronto: University of Toronto Press.

Carroll, Bret E. (2000). *The Routledge Historical Atlas of Religion in America*. London: Routledge.

Dolan, Jay P. (2002). *In Search of an American Catholicism: A History of Religion and Culture in Tension*. Oxford: Oxford University Press.

Eck, Diana L. (2001). *A New Religious America: How a "Christian Country" Has Become the World's Most Religiously Diverse Nation*. San Francisco: HarperSanFrancisco.

Finke, Roger and Rodney Stark (2005). *The Churching of America, 1776–2005: Winners and Losers in Our Religious Economy*. New Brunswick, NJ: Rutgers University Press.

Froehle, Bryan T. and Mary L. Gautier (2000). *Catholicism USA: A Portrait of the Catholic Church in the United States*. Maryknoll, NY: Orbis.

Noll, Mark A. (2001). *American Evangelical Christianity: An Introduction*. Oxford: Blackwell.

Ostling, Richard N. and Joan K. Ostling (2007). *Mormon America: The Power and the Promise*. New York: HarperOne.

Pinn, Anthony B. (2002). *The Black Church in the Post-Civil Rights Era*. Maryknoll, NY: Orbis.

Putnam, Robert D. and David E. Campbell (2010). *American Grace: How Religion Divides and Unites Us*. New York: Simon and Schuster.

Synan, Vinson (2001). *The Century of the Holy Spirit: 100 Years of Pentecostal and Charismatic Renewal, 1901–2001*. Nashville, TN: Thomas Nelson.

Wuthnow, Robert (2009). *Boundless Faith: The Global Outreach of American Churches*. Berkeley: University of California Press.

Chapter 13

Oceania

Experiments in Identity

Christianity was introduced to Oceania – Australia and the island societies of the Pacific – more recently than it was to any other region of the world, and it was also introduced more successfully here than almost anywhere else. Although Christianity was brought to Oceania only a little more than two centuries ago, it has now been adopted by 70 percent of the population. Functionally, there are two very different cultures of Christianity within the region. In most of the island nations, where European settlement has been minimal, Christians are in the majority and Christianity is a significant social and political force. Fully 90 percent of the indigenous population of the Pacific is Christian. In Australia and New Zealand, however, where the descendants of European (mostly British and Irish) settlers comprise the majority of the population, Christianity is so much on the decline that some Christians think of themselves as members of an endangered species of faith. It is the growing absence of Christianity within this European settler population that brings the overall Christian percentage of the region down to 70 percent.

In most of the island nations and territories of Oceania, old religious traditions have been rejected and the vast majority of people now identify thoroughly with Christianity, so much so that to be an indigenous Pacific islander is almost synonymous with being Christian. The contrast between the "heathen" past and the Christian present can at first appear totally discontinuous, but closer inspection often reveals that many of the themes and orientations of traditional religion have been braided into the Christian identity of the present. Sometimes a quiet nostalgia for what has been lost can be sensed beneath the public and usually very Christian rhetoric of the people. While Christianity is incontestably the dominant religion of the region, Oceania's adoption of Christianity is still an experiment that is not quite finished. Though conversion to Christianity has

The World's Christians: Who they are, Where they are, and How they got there, First Edition. Douglas Jacobsen.
© 2011 Douglas Jacobsen. Published 2011 by Blackwell Publishing Ltd.

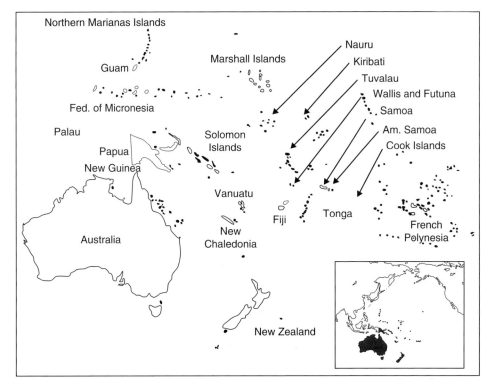

Figure 13.1   Map of Oceania. Map by author.
Total population 34,000,000 (1% of global population); Christian population 24,000,000 (71% of regional population, 1% of global Christian population): Orthodox 700,000, Catholics 9,200,000, Protestants 10,300,000, Pentecostal/Charismatic 3,800,000.

been genuine and runs deep, Pacific Christianity is still in the process of development and maturation.

A very different kind of religious experimentation is taking place in Australia and New Zealand, which both seem to be laboratories for jettisoning a dominant religion without adopting a new one. In the Anglo-Pacific world of Australia and New Zealand, Christians now account for only about 60 percent of the overall population, down from close to 90 percent at the end of World War II. Church attendance is also relatively low with only about 15 percent of the population showing up weekly. The number of people reporting "no belief" on census forms has also skyrocketed. In Australia one out of every five people now claims to be nonreligious, and in New Zealand two out of every five people respond that way. But here, too, surface appearances may be misleading. Some scholars suggest that rather than being steadfastly secular, Australians and New Zealanders simply wear their faith in a more relaxed fashion than people in other parts of the world. Whether in Australia, New Zealand, or the island nations of the Pacific, religious identity is a work in progress throughout Oceania.

Oceania and the West

Oceania is a huge area, consisting of more than 20 million square miles of sea and land (twice the size of Europe), but as a global region it is often overlooked. There are many more references in the news to the Pacific Rim (the nations that surround the Pacific) than there are to the Pacific itself. In fact, Oceania is often treated as if it is simply empty space. This is where outside nations test their missiles because they assume no one will be hurt regardless of where they land. But Oceania is not empty. It is home for 34 million people, and the region has been inhabited for tens of thousands of years. Though that number of people may seem small in comparison to the world as a whole, making up less than 1 percent of the world's population, Oceania is home to about one-fifth of all the world's languages and about one-quarter of its different religions.

The cultural richness of the region is in many ways a function of its geography. Each island – and there are thousands of them – is its own little world, and the people on each of those different islands developed their own unique ways of understanding themselves and their place in the universe. And even on the bigger islands, the indigenous people were often isolated from each other by the ruggedness of the land. On the island of New Guinea, for example, there are more than 800 different clans and tribes, each with its own distinctive language and way of life. A similar situation existed in Australia, where the many different Aboriginal people of the continent were separated by the sheer size of the country and by the arid, essentially uninhabitable, character of most of the land.

The global isolation of the south Pacific came to an end in the 1770s, when the English sailor Captain James Cook "discovered" and then mapped the territory during three separate voyages through the region. The European settlement of Australia began almost immediately, with the British Crown Colony of New South Wales initiated in 1788. A host of other settlers, explorers, missionaries, and merchants followed in the nineteenth century. Stories from the early years of interaction between the West and the Pacific included some terrifying accounts of cannibalism and human sacrifice, but the more popular picture that emerged in the West was of a peaceful and tranquil Oceania that resembled the Garden of Eden. The French painter Paul Gauguin (1848–1903) helped create this image via his simple but strikingly beautiful paintings of life in French Polynesia (Plates 23 and 24), and in the early twentieth century the anthropologist Margaret Mead (1901–78) reinforced that paradisiacal vision of life on the islands in her book, *Coming of Age in Samoa* (1928), which described Samoa as a place where life was easy, sex was unencumbered by guilt, and the neuroses of the West were unknown.

Based on this positive but mythical portrait of the region, many anthropologists and other scholars criticized the modernization and Christianization of Oceania as immoral – as the willful destruction of the fragile and beautiful cultures of the Pacific that had taken thousands of years to evolve. But the people of Oceania themselves generally adopted a rather different perspective. For them, many of the material, cultural, and religious goods of the West (ranging from iron axe heads to Christianity) seemed superior to anything they previously possessed, and they felt no reason to reject them simply for the sake of preserving their old ways of life. For some, the desire for Western material goods in particular – items like radios, cookware, and "exotic" foods such as canned peaches that sometimes during World War II seemed to appear literally out of nowhere in parachute drops of supplies – became a major driving force in life, even to the point of evolving into religion-like movements (called "cargo cults") that focused on the hope that new shipments of foreign goods would soon appear in abundance. The John Frum movement in Vanuatu that began shortly after the end of World War II, for example, was based on the hope that an American soldier would soon return to the island, bringing prosperity to everyone who followed him. While many of these movements dissolved quite quickly, 5 percent of the Vanuatuan population (about 10,000 people out of Vanuatu's total population of 215,000) still believe that the mythical John Frum is coming, and they celebrate his hoped-for appearance every February 15.

But while many Pacific people welcomed interaction with the West, it was not without cost. Almost as soon as the lands of the Pacific were "discovered," Europeans began to colonize and control the region. In Australia and New Zealand, colonization took the form of immigrant settlement, with whites taking the best lands for themselves and relegating the indigenous people (Aborigines and Torres Strait Islanders in Australia and Māoris in New Zealand) to less desirable locations. This state of affairs continues to be the norm in Australia, but the Māoris in New Zealand have been able to reclaim some lands based on stipulations in the Treaty of Waitangi that they signed with the British crown in 1840.

Political independence arrived late in the region. At the end of World War II, none of today's Pacific island nations was independent. Today there are 12 independent small island nations in the region (in addition to Australia and New Zealand), but an almost equal number of island territories are still controlled by foreign powers, including Guam, the Northern Mariana Islands, and American Samoa, which are territories of the United States, and New Caledonia, Wallis and Futuna, and French Polynesia, which are governed by France.

Christianity and the Indigenous People of the Pacific

The earliest efforts to Christianize the Pacific began in the seventeenth century when Jesuit missionaries from the Philippines fanned out across the Pacific region, but these early missionary ventures produced little lasting change. The more significant effort to evangelize the region began in the nineteenth century, with Protestants taking the lead and with Catholics following quickly in their wake. By the early twentieth century, most indigenous residents of the region had been exposed to Christianity in one form or another, and many had converted. Missionaries played an important role in this process, but local Pacific evangelists and catechists did the lion's share of the work.

Looking back on the pre-Christian era, it is common for people in the region to describe the past as a period of religious darkness in contrast to the light of Christianity in which they now live. In Australia, for example, some Aboriginal Christians refer to the past as "Devil time" – a time when "the Devil tempted people to live wrong: living wild, naked, swearing, fighting, dancing corroborees [ritual ceremonies], practicing polygyny and child marriage, murdering each other, crying over dead bodies, and continually reincarnating themselves."[1] By contrast, they call the present "God time," a time of salvation and advance.

In New Guinea people similarly speak of the present as "God's time," saying "now is now, and before is before," and there is no desire to turn the clock back.[2] Almost everywhere in Oceania the Christian present is described as far superior to the pre-Christian past.

Catholics and Protestants, however, tend to describe the relative merits and demerits of the past in slightly different ways. The Catholics of Oceania are usually more positive about the past, characterizing the older religious ways of the Pacific as inadequate and incomplete, but not as completely mistaken. They argue that the old ways of life contained some elements of goodness and truth, but those elements pointed toward and found fulfillment in the fuller revelation from God they discovered in the Catholic tradition. Most Protestants, by contrast, posit a sharper difference between the pagan past and the Christian present. The old ways are described as totally mistaken, and rejecting them is a prerequisite for accepting the new message of Jesus. Stated in this way, the Protestant position sounds strict and unbending, but Protestant practice is often more nuanced. Many Protestants distinguish between beliefs and practices that are cultural and those that are religious. The old religious ways have to be discarded, but beliefs and practices that are deemed purely cultural can be retained and can sometimes even be positively incorporated into Christian faith. A well-known example of such cultural incorporation is described in the book *Peace Child* (1975), written by a Canadian Protestant missionary in New Guinea. He used the cultural practice of making peace between warring tribes through the gift of a child from one tribe to another – a "peace child" – as a metaphor for explaining Christ's role as the Son of God who was given to humanity to establish peace between God and humankind.[3]

Aware of the break between the deficient ways of the past and the Christian present, many Pacific island Christians are convinced that another rupture in time is imminent. That new rupture will signal the beginning of the "end times," an era culminating in Christ's return to earth and the end of human history. Many believe that a figure known as the antichrist will appear during these years. He will set up a worldwide government and will require his followers to be marked with "the triple six" (666). Those who resist him in the name of Jesus will be killed, but eventually Christ will intervene, defeat the antichrist, and take all faithful Christians home to heaven. Some believe that the end times have already begun, so Christ might return at any moment. Many local Christians believed, for example, that the Gulf War of 1990 (the first invasion of Iraq by the United States military) was evidence that the end times were already under way. Because only those who are living pure and holy lives at the moment Christ returns to earth will be rescued out of the world by Jesus, this belief puts enormous pressure on Christians to constantly "watch their walk" so they will be ready to meet Christ when he comes. This apocalyptic understanding of the future can be found among Christians in many other parts of the world, but in Oceania it is an especially common perspective, evident within the Catholic Church as well as within the Protestant and Pentecostal/Charismatic communities.

In Oceania, the adoption of Christianity has typically been a communal process, not an individual experience, and the conversion of a community often took place in two steps. In the first step, the practices of Christianity were appropriated as a second set of rules alongside traditional ways of life so they could be tested to see if and how well they worked. Could Christianity protect people from the curses of the dead? Could Christianity ensure a good harvest? Did Christianity make life better in any tangible way? Often the younger people of the community undertook this testing with the tacit approval of the elders, and the chiefs or "big men" of the community sat back to observe what happened. In New Guinea, one local believer describes this experience as being "split down the middle, our old customs are still all there, and the custom of the whites have arrived ... We have not yet ceased the old customs, they are all still there, and we mix them up ... and make something of them."[4] An Aboriginal spokesperson from Australia said similarly in the late 1950s, we "believe in both ways – our own and the Christian. ... We believe in the old Law and we want to keep it; and we believe in the Bible too. So we have selected the good laws from both and put them together."[5]

After Christianity had proven itself in practice, the process moved into a second or deeper stage of conversion, defined by the decision to embrace Christianity as the core identity of the community. This was typically perceived as a fairly dramatic break with the past, as a point of no return with regard to the religious and cultural development of the group. But even in this second stage of conversion, the ways of the past were not always obliterated. Traces or remnants were sometimes allowed to remain so they could be possibly be retrieved in extreme situations. After one New Guinea village became decisively Christian, for example, the sacred bones of minor ancestors were dumped in the latrine, but the bones of more powerful ancestors were transferred from the centrally located ritual house to a remote cave in the forest, just in case they might be needed someday.

Identity in Oceania involves a holistic understanding of the world that combines religion with a strongly developed sense of place (including the residents of that place) and a strong loyalty to the local community (which is frequently defined politically). These three elements of life – religion, place/people, and community/politics – constantly interact, and conflicts can emerge, but ideally all three will operate in harmony with each other. Because this is the case, most societies in Oceania tend toward local uniformity. In terms of religion, this means that conversion is never merely personal. It involves the entirety of the people, it involves a new understanding of the land, and it involves politics. Usually this also means that most villages and neighborhoods – or an entire nation, if it is small – will be dominated by one particular Christian denomination.

Christianity in Non-Australian Oceania: An Overview

The complicated geography of Oceania can be considerably simplified if the area is conceptualized in terms of three large cultural subregions: Melanesia, Micronesia, and Polynesia (Figure 13.2).

Melanesia, which means "black islands," accounts for roughly 60 percent of the non-Australian population of the Pacific. The islands of this subregion are generally larger than the islands of Polynesia or Micronesia, allowing more than one people group or culture to exist side by side. Because of this, Melanesian societies are often more complex than those found in the rest of the Pacific. Religiously, the population of Melanesia is 48 percent Protestant, 29 percent Catholic, and 13 percent Pentecostal/Charismatic. Each of the island nations of Melanesia has its own unique denominational configuration based on its missionary past, and in most cases one denomination dominates each country or territory

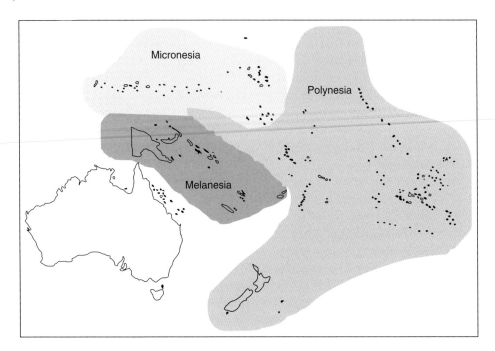

Figure 13.2　Map of Melanesia, Micronesia, and Polynesia. Map by author.

(see Table 13.1). Thus, the Anglican Church of Melanesia accounts for three-quarters of all the Protestants in the Solomon Islands. In Fiji, almost all the Protestants are Methodists, and in Vanuatu most people are Presbyterians. This same pattern also applies to Papua New Guinea despite having a population of almost six million people. More than half the Protestants of Papua New Guinea are associated with the United Church (a merger of the Methodists and Presbyterians) and another 30 percent are Lutheran. New Caledonia, which is a French territory, is the only place in Melanesia where the Christian population is predominantly Catholic.

Micronesia, which means "small islands," has the smallest population of the three subregions, with only 5 percent of the total Pacific island population. Squeezed between the Pacific and Southeast Asia, Micronesia is defined by its unique mix of Pacific and Asian cultures. Micronesia also has a longer colonial history than the rest of Oceania. Originally subjugated by Spain in the seventeenth century, the islands were sold to Germany in the late nineteenth century. Most of Micronesia was then incorporated into the growing Japanese Empire during the years leading up to World War II, and after the war it became a trust territory of the United Nations. The various nations of the region began to claim independence in the late 1960s, but Guam and the Northern Mariana Islands remain possessions of the United States. Religiously, Micronesia is distinguished by its predominantly Catholic identity (see Table 13.2). Sixty percent of the Micronesian population is Catholic, 22 percent Protestant, and 12 percent Pentecostal/Charismatic. In both Guam and the Northern Marianas Islands, eight out of ten people identify themselves as members of the

Table 13.1 Religious profile of Melanesia

Country/territory	Population	% Catholic	% Protestant	Main Denomination	% Pentecostal/Charismatic
Fiji	850,000	10	30	Methodist	15
Papua New Guinea	5,750,000	33	50	United Church	12
Solomon Islands	525,000	15	65	Anglican	15
Vanuatu	215,000	15	63	Presbyterian	15
New Caledonia	240,000	55	20	Catholic	5
Total	7,580,000	29	48		13

Table 13.2 Religious profile of Micronesia

Country/territory	Population	% Catholic	% Protestant	% Pentecostal/Charismatic
Kiribati	105,000	55	30	10
Marshall Islands	65,000	10	45	40
Fed. of Micronesia	110,000	55	30	8
Nauru	12,000	30	37	8
Palau	20,000	45	45	5
Guam (USA)	170,000	80	10	6
N. Mariana Islands (USA)	80,000	80	2	8
Total	562,000	60	22	12

Catholic Church. The one significant exception to this Catholic dominance in the region is found in the Marshall Islands, the only place where Protestant missionaries arrived ahead of the Catholics. Only 10 percent of the population of the Marshall Islands is Catholic and the rest are divided fairly evenly between Protestantism, represented primarily by the Congregational Church, and the Pentecostal/Charismatic movement, represented primarily by the Assemblies of God.

Polynesia means "many islands," and Polynesia (with the exception of New Zealand) is indeed a region of many small islands stretched out over thousands of miles of ocean. Because the Polynesians were a seafaring people, however, they were able to maintain a common metaculture that united the islands despite the vast distances separating them. New Zealand (known as Aotearoa in the local Māori language) is by far the largest Polynesian nation and also among the last to be settled. The Māoris arrived about 800 years ago; white, European settlement began in the early 1800s. The islands of Hawai'i represent the northern border of the region (though they are not included here because they are part of the United States). Taken as a whole, the current population of Polynesia is 35 percent Protestant, 15 percent Catholic, and 10 percent Pentecostal/Charismatic (see Table 13.3). But those numbers hide a major discrepancy between the religious profile of New Zealand and the rest of the islands of Polynesia: only 56 percent of the population of New Zealand is Christian compared to 92 percent for the rest of Polynesia.

Table 13.3   Religious profile of Polynesia

Country/Territory	Population	% Catholic	% Protestant	Main Denomination	% Pentecostal/ Charismatic	% LDS
New Zealand	4,100,000	12	33	Anglican	10	1
Samoa	180,000	18	40	Congregational	12	25
Tonga	110,000	15	36	Free Wesleyan	10	32
Tuvalu	10,000	1	84	Congregational	5	–
American Samoa (USA)	70,000	18	38	Congregational	14	25
Cook Islands (NZ)	20,000	20	60	Congregational	10	5
French Polynesia (Fr.)	260,000	38	35	Congregational	10	5
Wallis and Futuna (Fr.)	15,000	96	1	Catholic	1	–
Total	4,765,000	14	34	–	10	3
Total (without NZ)	665,000	27	38		11	16

In contrast to Melanesia, where each island nation or territory has its own distinct and different denominational identity, the islands of Polynesia are remarkably similar in their religious profiles. Everywhere, except in French Polynesia, Protestants form the largest Christian bloc, and almost everywhere in Polynesia the Protestants are Congregationalists, tracing their roots to the London Missionary Society (LMS) that began work in the region in Tahiti in 1797. The only exceptions to Congregationalism's dominance are found in Tonga, where most Protestants are Methodists, and in New Zealand, where most are Anglican. Catholics usually form the next largest group on each of the islands with 15 to 20 percent of the population, and Pentecostals – almost all of them members of the Assemblies of God – account for about 10 percent of each island's residents. What makes Polynesia's religious profile truly unique, however, is the significant presence of the Church of Jesus Christ of Latter Day Saints (LDS). Members of the LDS account for 16 percent of the total island population (apart from New Zealand), and they represent 25 percent or more of the population in Samoa, Tonga, and American Samoa. The LDS Church has three temples in the region, in addition to many local congregations (called "wards"), and it has built a university in Hawai'i to serve the educational needs of its Polynesian members.

New Zealand is a very different place from the rest of Polynesia, distinguished both by its geographic size (representing 97 percent of all the land in Polynesia) and its population, which is six times larger than all the other islands combined. At present, the population of New Zealand is predominantly of European origin (about 80 percent). Fifteen percent of the population is Polynesian (10 percent Māori and 5 percent other Polynesian people). Christianity first came to New Zealand/Aotearoa in 1814, when the Reverend Samuel Marsden preached a Christmas Day sermon to a gathered crowd of Māori at the Bay of Islands in northeast New Zealand. Marsden left soon after his sermon, but before the next Anglican missionary made his appearance in 1823 a substantial number of Māoris had already become Christians through the efforts of local converts. By 1840, the year the

Māori signed the Treaty of Waitangi with the British crown that gave Britain governmental control of the region, half the Māori population had converted. The treaty guaranteed that Māoris would have continued use of the land, but as more and more Europeans arrived, the outnumbered Māori people were slowly pushed out of the way. Most European settlers were Christians – a mix of Anglicans, Presbyterians, and Methodists – and many were devout. Soon, 90 percent of the New Zealand population was Christian, a proportion that remained constant through World War II.

Figure 13.3   T. W. Ratana
Courtesy of Uri Whakatupuranga Ratana Archives

Today, only 55 percent of New Zealanders call themselves Christian. The drop in Christian numbers began during the last decades of the twentieth century, and that trend has continued in the early years of the twenty-first century. Based on the number of people who call themselves explicitly "not religious" (40 percent), New Zealand now ranks as one of the most secular nations on earth, in the same category as Sweden and France. But when New Zealanders are asked how important God is in their lives, 23 percent of New Zealanders say "very important" compared to only 7 percent in Sweden and 11 percent in France.[6] The decline of Christianity in New Zealand has been mostly a Protestant phenomenon. Catholics have generally held steady, and their church attendance rates remain relatively high. The Māori population is also more religious than the general population, with roughly 70 percent calling themselves Christian.

The six largest churches in New Zealand are the Anglican Church (accounting for 15 percent of the New Zealand population), the Catholic Church (12 percent), the Presbyterian Church (10 percent), the Methodist Church (2.5 percent), the Church of Jesus Christ of Latter Day Saints (1.5 percent), and the Ratana Church (1 percent). The Ratana church is a predominantly Māori organization begun in the year 1925 by an Anglican layman named Tahupotiki Wiremu Ratana (1873–1939; see Figure 13.3). The special revelations he received from the Holy Spirit (*Wairua Tabu*) prompted a revival within the Māori Anglican world, focusing on the gift of healing and on spiritual visions. While the Ratana Church remains relatively small in size (about 50,000 members), it has been historically influential in defending Māori rights, and it continues to serve as an important symbol of Maori identity today. Despite significant losses in membership, the Anglican Church remains the largest of New Zealand's denominations, and in recent years it has put significant effort into becoming a truly multiracial, multiethnic church for all the people of New Zealand. It now routinely describes itself not simply as Anglican, but as a church of "three streams": the Māori, the Pakeha (European), and the Pasefika (Polynesian).

Religion, Eethnicity, and Politics in Fiji

Of all the nations in the Pacific, Fiji is the most troubled politically, and those troubles are linked to Christianity and its role in society. In Fiji, as elsewhere in the Pacific, it is assumed that religion (*lotu*), place/people (*vanua*), and community/government (*matanitu*) should exist in harmony with each other. But that is not currently the case, and there are significant differences about how to proceed. Most of the indigenous Fijians – more than 90 percent of whom are Christian, of which two-thirds are Methodists – think the answer is clear: they represent the *vanua*, their form of Christianity should be the *lotu* for everyone, and the *matanitu* should support the practices of their form of Christianity while serving the needs of the indigenous people (not the immigrant population) of the islands.

However, indigenous Fijians now account for only slightly more than half the population of Fiji. About 40 percent of the population is Indo-Fijian, descendents of Indian "coolies" (cheap laborers) brought to the islands between the years 1880 and 1915 to work on the sugar plantations owned by the British colonial elites who ran the country. Most of these Indo-Fijians are either Hindu (75 percent) or Muslim (15 percent). Only 6 percent are Christian. Many indigenous Fijians think of their Indian neighbors as interlopers who don't really belong on their land; they are not part of the *vanua*. As one Christian chief put it: "This is not their country … They still speak Hindi. They still eat curry. They are not Christians."[7] Land is an issue in Fiji as it is everywhere in the Pacific, and in Fiji most of the land – more than 90 percent – has been designated for indigenous ownership only. This means that most Indo-Fijians can only rent or lease the land on which they live and they have to find employment in businesses like shop-keeping, tourism, and driving taxis which are not dependent on owning land.

This combination of cultural prejudice and legal bias is a recipe for trouble, and tensions between the indigenous Fijian population and the Indo-Fijian population have been evident in the politics of the island for years. Fiji gained independence from Great Britain in 1970, and the transition went fairly smoothly until 1987 when a pro-Indo-Fijian government was elected to office. Indigenous Fijians were shocked and responded with a set of back-to-back coups that kicked out the new government, re-established indigenous Fijian rule over the nation, and rewrote the constitution to guarantee permanent indigenous Fijian control of the island. Under pressure from the international community, that new constitution was revised in 1997 and many of the most blatantly anti-Indian elements were deleted. Those changes empowered the Indo-Fijian Labour Party and after a long campaign they won the next election. Once again indigenous Fijians were outraged. They staged yet another coup, toppling the government in 2000, and finally managed to legally put the indigenous Fijian United Party into power in 2001. In 2006 there was one more coup, but this time both the cause and the outcome were different. The leader of the coup was the military commander Frank Bainimarama, who is an indigenous Fijian, but his stated goal was to create a new postethnic, postindigenous, pluralist government that would treat everyone fairly and equally.

In the midst of all these changes of government, the Methodist Church has consistently supported indigenous Fijian privilege over the political rights of Indo-Fijians. The proindigenous Fijian coups of 1987 and 2000 were praised by church leaders as good and necessary, while Bainimarama's 2006 coup has been criticized as evil and illegal. Methodists, in cooperation with a coalition of other conservative Protestant and Pentecostal/Charismatic Christians, have called for an end to Bainimarama's military government and for new elections. They have also continued to support the notion that Fiji should be governed by indigenous Fijians for indigenous Fijians and that the whole nation should be Christian. Their ideal is to see Fiji become "God's Treasured Possession"[8] – a place where everyone loves Jesus and God's law is obeyed. For that to happen, of course, the Indo-Fijian population would have to be either converted or eliminated from the island. Sometimes the Methodist Church seems uncertain which of these two options is preferable. They have engaged in various attempts to convert Indo-Fijians, but violence has also sometimes been part of the mix. In one particularly troubling incident in 1998, members of a Methodist Youth Fellowship burned down four Hindu temples in the city of Lautoko after spending the previous eight hours in prayer at their church. When arrested, they defended their actions by saying the Bible demanded that "the idols must be destroyed."[9]

Figure 13.4   Frank Bainimarama (leader of 2006 coup)
© Torsten Blackwood/AFP/Getty Images

The Bainimarama government has placed a number of restrictions on the Methodist Church, including banning the church's annual meeting (which culminates in a popular church choir competition) because it has tended in the past to take on overtones of being an antigovernment rally. Bainimarama says the Methodist Church long ago ceased to be a true church and instead has become little more than an ethnically based, religious political party. Leaders of the Catholic Church in Fiji (which has about 85,000 members) generally share Bainimarama's opinion, and they have embraced his agenda as being in line with the demands of Christian justice, even though they condemned the military coup by which he came to power. But many people, both in Fiji and around the world, are beginning to lose hope in Bainimarama's vision of Fijian justice. Despite numerous calls for new elections, the military remains firmly in charge, and its control is getting tighter and more restrictive with time. In light of that fact, world opinion is slowly shifting toward the Methodists. Even the World Council of Churches, which is usually very sensitive regarding questions of justice and human rights, has begun to speak up on behalf of the Fijian Methodist Church, criticizing the Bainimarama government for its undemocratic practices.

No one is sure what will happen next. Ethnic, religious, and governmental tensions will likely continue to simmer in Fiji for years to come, and perhaps this is a vision into the future of the Pacific islands as a group. Most of these nations are becoming more pluralistic every day, and how the Christians of the area respond to that growing social complexity will determine whether the future is peaceful or troubled. It is unlikely that any other country will implode in the way that Fiji has – the demographic mix on Fiji is unique – but tensions between a solidly Christian notion of national identity and a more pluralistic notion of political life may well emerge in other Pacific nations in the coming decades.

Christianity and the Relaxed Spirituality of Australia

Compared to the other nations of the region, Australia is the looming giant of the Pacific. Covering more than seven and a half million square kilometers and home to 21 million people, it represents more than 90 percent of both the land and the population of Oceania.

Perhaps because of its size, Australia is a confident place, and Australians are known world-wide for their friendly and laid-back approach to life. They bring that same relaxed attitude to religion. For most Australians, religion is not something to worry or fuss about. In fact, most Australians generally try to avoid the topic in conversation, and if they are required to say something it often comes out as inarticulate, mumbling about "the man upstairs" or a reference to some cosmic spirit of the universe that exists who-knows-where. But despite this seeming lack of interest in religion, Australians are not typically antireligious. Only one out of every ten Australians is a self-described atheist, and the rest embrace some kind of spirituality or belief in God; almost two-thirds call themselves Christian. What Australians clearly do not like, however, is pushy faith – aggressive religion that tries to force itself on others, telling people what they have to believe and what they should and should not do. There is a name for that kind of religion in Australia. It is called "wowserism." And no one, not even the most serious and dedicated religious believer, wants to be a wowser.

The root of Australia's relaxed or indifferent attitude toward religion, and its opposition to wowserism, goes back to the beginning of the colony in 1788. Australia was a British penal colony, a place to send criminals where they could redeem themselves though hard work. Most of the prisoners sent to Australia were not overly religious, but Britain was a Christian nation and wanted to make sure its Australian convicts had the religious resources they needed to improve their lives, so a series of chaplains were sent to help them mend their ways. Australia was obviously not a choice ministerial appointment, and many of the individuals who took the position were driven to do so by their own personal religious fervor. These were true believers who wanted to change the colonists into devout and loyal Christians like themselves. In a word, they were wowsers, and the convicts in Australia typically had scant interest in their stuffy, middle class, rules-abiding religion. It is thus not surprising that when the Reverend James Denny visited the colony in 1824, he found it to be "the most godless place under heaven."[10]

But Australia quickly developed beyond its unsavory beginnings, and the steadily increasing European settler population became more Christian as the years went along. Besides the original colony of New South Wales, new settlements were begun in Victoria, Tasmania, South Australia, Queensland, Western Australia, and the Northern Territory. These various separate colonies were federated into the independent Commonwealth of Australia in 1901.

In that same year, the national census found that 96 percent of the Australian population was Christian: 40 percent were Anglican, 22 percent Catholic, and 34 percent were members of other churches. Those figures held roughly even until 1950, and then they began to decline. In 1975, only eight out of every ten Australians were still calling themselves Christians, and the relative size of the churches had shifted so that there was a relatively even distribution of Anglicans, Catholics, and "other Christians" in the nation. By the year 2000, the number of Australians calling themselves Christian had dropped to 69 percent, and the relative size of the churches had shifted once again, with the Catholic Church taking the lead (27 percent of the population) followed by the Anglicans and "other Christians" at 21 percent each. Today, only 60 percent of the population is Christian: 24 percent Catholic, 14 percent Anglican, 11 percent other Protestant, 8 percent Pentecostal/Charismatic, and 3 percent Orthodox (see Figure 13.5).

Anglicanism in Australia

When British settlement began, the Church of England (Anglicanism) functioned as the established church of Australia, but it was never formally declared the state church. When the Constitution of the Commonwealth was drafted in the late 1890s, religious freedom was written into the document. The Anglican Church remained the single largest church in the nation, but by the early twentieth century the influence of the church was noticeably diminishing. In 1907, a survey conducted in the city of Brisbane found that only 15,000 of the city's 130,000 self-proclaimed Anglicans (less than 12 percent) were showing up for worship each week. Brisbane is known for its liberal tendencies, so this figure is not necessarily reflective of national trends – in conservative Sydney, the numbers would have been much higher – but it foreshadowed what was to happen in the rest of Australian Anglicanism. In the 1950s, about 30 percent of all Anglicans attended church weekly; by 1970, only one out of every four Anglicans was in church on Sunday morning; today, only 5 percent of the Anglican population attends worship regularly. Factoring in the declining size of the Anglican Church as a whole, the number of Anglicans attending worship on any given Sunday in contemporary Australia is equivalent to only one-fifteenth of the number attending in 1950.

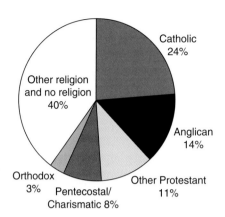

Figure 13.5   The religious profile of Australia

Today the Anglican Church accounts for about 14 percent of the Australian population, and fewer than half of children raised as Anglicans continue to identify with that church as adults. Those who remain are often described as falling into two groups: progressives and evangelicals. The progressive wing tends to support the ordination of women and, more recently, the ordination of gays and lesbians. The evangelical wing of the church, which is centered in Sydney, takes a more conservative tack. Anglican evangelicals from Australia participated in a boycott of the 2008 Lambeth Conference (the 10-yearly meeting of the world Anglican Communion) that was orchestrated by the conservative Anglican churches of Africa, and they have become involved in conservative politics at home – partly through an organization called the "Festival of Light" (organized in 1973), which changed its name to "Family Voice Australia" in July 2008. That kind of political activism is, however, unlikely to attract many ordinary Australians back to the church. It smacks of wowserism and, even apart from that, roughly three-quarters of the population think that religion and politics should have nothing to do with each other.

Catholicism in Australia

Catholics arrived in Australia aboard the first ship of convicts in 1788. Almost all of them were Irish, and religion was part of their non-British identity. They had no priest to serve them until a fellow convict, a priest named James Dixon, began to circulate among them, celebrating Mass, in 1803. Dixon's meandering was put to an end in 1804 after the Castle Hill Rebellion, in which Catholics played a major role, and Australian Catholics were once again priestless. In 1820, a new priest arrived, and there has been continuity in Catholic leadership since that time. As the colony matured, the education of children became a pressing social concern, and a separate Catholic parochial school system was set up in the 1860s, staffed mainly by the Sisters of St Joseph. The Catholic Church currently operates 1,300 primary schools in Australia, along with more than 400 secondary schools and two universities. This educational system has been a huge factor in maintaining and reinforcing the identity of the Catholic community, and a majority (64 percent) of Australians who are raised as Catholics remain Catholic as adults.

Catholic identity has also been strengthened in the decades following World War II by an influx of more than a million new Catholics from Italy, Germany, Croatia, Hungary, and elsewhere in Europe. Religion plays a huge role in these immigrant communities, and that energy has bubbled over into the Catholic Church as a whole. The result is a successful and flourishing church, where almost half the membership attends Mass weekly. Today Catholics account for 40 percent of all the Christians in the country, and they are among the most religiously active of all Australians. In October 2010, Australian Catholics also got a huge boost from the Vatican when it named Mary MacKillop the first Australian-born Catholic saint. MacKillop, the cofounder of the Sisters of St Joseph, is widely respected by Australian Catholics and non-Catholics alike.

Orthodoxy in Australia

There are presently about 600,000 Orthodox Christians (Chalcedonian and Miaphysite combined) living in Australia, which accounts for about 3 percent of the Australian population and almost all of the Orthodox Christians in the Pacific. The Greek community is the largest, with more than 100 parishes, the Serbian Orthodox Church has almost 50 parishes, and the Coptic Orthodox Church has 20. Other Orthodox communions represented in Australia include the Antiochene, Armenian, Belarusian, Macedonian, Malanka Syrian, Romanian, Russian, and Syrian. Most Orthodox Christians are relatively recent immigrants, arriving after 1950, and the churches of these communities serve as centers of cultural identity as well as places of worship. Partly because of that the Orthodox community has the highest retention rate of any religious group in Australia, nearly 80 percent.

Regionally, Orthodoxy is strongest in New South Wales and Victoria, but the Orthodox populations of Queensland and South Australia are on the rise. At present most priests and bishops still come from Europe and the Mediterranean, but some Orthodox communities (most notably the Greek and Coptic) have begun building schools and monasteries that will allow Australian Orthodoxy to produce its own leadership pool. It is possible that the many different Orthodox Christians of Australia will eventually create a single Australian Orthodox Church, but for now most Orthodox Christians in Australia are quite content in their different and diverse ethnic communities.

Pentecostal/Charismatic Christianity in Australia

It is difficult to determine the size of the Pentecostal/Charismatic community in Australia. Estimates vary from as low as 1 percent of the population to almost 20 percent; a figure around 8 percent seems reasonable. There has been some kind of Pentecostal/Charismatic

Figure 13.6 Entrance to Saint Shenouda Coptic monastery (New South Wales, Australia). Photo by author.

presence in Australia since the late 1800s. In fact, Australian Congregational minister John Alexander Dowie, who moved to the United States in 1888, is partly responsible for forming the Pentecostal/Charismatic movement in early twentieth-century America. Over the years a number of prominent American Pentecostal/Charismatic preachers have returned the favor and visited Australia, including the flamboyant Aimee Semple McPherson. More recently, David Yonggi Cho, pastor of the Yoido Full Gospel Church in Seoul, Korea, has tried to influence Pentecostal/Charismatic developments in the country. Despite such efforts, Australians have generally not embraced Pentecostal/Charismatic Christianity with the same enthusiasm that is evident in Africa and Latin America. The intense and exuberant spirituality of the movement contrasts with the much more modest and relaxed spirituality that prevails in Australia as a whole. Several Pentecostal/Charismatic megachurches have, however, made some inroads, especially in South Australia and New South Wales.

The best known of these new megachurches is the Hillsong Church located in Baulkham Hills, a northwest suburb of Sydney. Hillsong, which is associated with the Australian Christian Churches (formerly the Assemblies of God in Australia), was founded by the husband and wife team of Brian and Bobbie Houston (see Figure 13.7) in 1983. It currently has 15 extension campuses in the greater Sydney area and another in Brisbane, and it has established a variety of international congregations in cities as far away as London, Kiev, Cape Town, Stockholm, and Paris. The main church seats 3,500 and is filled to capacity for multiple services every week. The yearly Hillsong Conference attracts about 30,000 people from all around the world, and Hillsong Television is broadcast in more than 150 countries. The heart of the Hillsong phenomenon is its music, with millions of albums sold globally. Hillsong provides a hip, fun, and entertaining alternative to the blander diet of worship served up at most traditional Christian churches in Australia, but it is difficult

(a)

(b)

Figure 13.7a   Hillsong Church, Australia
Courtesy of the Hillsong Church, Australia

Figure 13.7b   Pastor Bobbie Houston
from Hillsong Church, Australia
Courtesy of the Hillsong Church, Australia

to reproduce outside an urban setting. Nonetheless, there is little doubt that Hillsong and other large Pentecostal/Charismatic churches like Paradise Church in Adelaide (also associated with the Australian Christian Churches denomination) are resculpting the shape of Christianity in Australia.

Australian Aboriginal Christianity

The history of Christianity's interaction with the Australian Aboriginal population is complex and in many ways contradictory. Christianity was, on the one hand, used as an ideological weapon against the Aboriginal people, justifying the British takeover of their land and relegating them to almost subhuman status. On the other hand, Christian missionaries were often the most outspoken defenders of the Aboriginal people and their ways of life. Still, even well-intentioned missionaries were often thoroughly paternalistic, treating the Aborigines as if they were incapable of making their own assessments of the Christian gospel and its application to their lives and culture. Christianity was "white law" that remained a largely foreign import to Aboriginal society.

A key turning point came when Aboriginal Christians themselves created the Aboriginal Evangelical Fellowship in 1971. Since that time, several indigenous revivals have taken place and currently 70 percent of the Aboriginal population is Christian (Aborigines account for about 2 percent of the total Australian population). Many Aboriginal Christians in Australia today, probably a majority, are Pentecostal/Charismatic in orientation, and they are developing their own indigenous Christian beliefs, rituals, material culture, and art (see Plate 25). They have also begun to hold Christian corroborees, ritual gatherings where the events of "Dream Time" (the sacred world) are theatrically performed, and they are developing a new theology of the land that focuses on respect for "Mother Earth." Some white Christian leaders express concern that Aboriginal Christianity is not "orthodox" – not sufficiently attuned to the traditional theological ideas of Western Christianity – and they describe it as a syncretistic mix of Christianity and Aboriginal religion. But from the perspective of most Aboriginal Christians, these new versions of Christianity are allowing them to feel authentically Aboriginal and Christian for the first time.

Australia, along with the rest of Oceania, is a place of new and shifting identities. It has been the home for the Aboriginal people for millennia, but the encounter with the West that has taken place during the last two centuries has reshuffled the cultural resources of the area, requiring everyone to rethink their national, communal, and even personal identities. So far, this process has been generally favorable to Christianity, which is now the dominant religion of the Pacific. However, the examples of Australia and New Zealand illustrate that the fortunes of any religion, including Christianity, can change quite quickly. The dynamics of globalism have changed and continue to change the ground rules of cultural and religious identity everywhere, and those dynamics are especially dramatic and visible in Oceania.

Notes

1 Quoted in Heather McDonald, *Blood, Bones, and Spirit: Aboriginal Christianity in an East Kimberley Town* (Melbourne: Melbourne University Press, 2001), pp. 76–7.

2 Joel Robbins, *Becoming Sinners: Christianity and Moral Torment in a Papua New Guinea Society* (Berkeley: University of California Press, 2004), p. 164.

3 See Don Richardson, *Peace Child* (Seattle: YWAM Publishing, 2007).

4 Quoted in Holger Jebens, *Pathways to Heaven: Contesting Mainline and Fundamentalist Christianity in Papua New Guinea* (Oxford: Berghahn Books, 2005), p. 109.

5 Quoted in Tony Swain and Garry Trompf, *The Religions of Oceania* (New York: Routledge, 1995), p. 91.

6 Statistics come from the World Values Survey, online at www.worldvaluessurvey.org/ (accessed September 16, 2009).

7 Quoted in Matt Tomlinson, *In God's Image: The Metaculture of Fijian Christianity* (Berkeley: University of California Press, 2009), p. 164.

8 Quoted in Lynda Newland, "Religion and Politics: The Christian Churches and the 2006 Coup in Fiji" in Jon Fraenkel, Stewart Firth, and Brij V. Lal (eds), *The 2006 Military Takeover in Fiji* (Canberra: ANU E Press, 2009), pp. 187–208. Available online at http://epress.anu.edu.au/coup_coup/pdf/whole_book.pdf (accessed November 17, 2010).

9 Quoted in Matt Tomlinson, *In God's Image*, p. 168.

10 Quoted in Tom Frame, *Losing My Religion: Unbelief in Australia* (Sydney: University of New South Wales Press, 2009), p. 43.

Suggestions for Further Reading

Bouma, Gary (2006). *Australian Soul: Religion and Spirituality in the Twenty-First Century.* Cambridge, UK: Cambridge University Press.

Breward, Ian (2001). *A History of the Churches in Australasia.* Oxford: Oxford University Press.

Frame, Tom (2009). *Losing My Religion: Unbelief in Australia.* Sydney: University of New South Wales Press.

Jebens, Holger (2005). *Pathways to Heaven: Contesting Mainline and Fundamentalist Christianity in Papua New Guinea.* New York: Berghahn Books.

McDonald, Heather (2001). *Blood, Bones, and Spirit: Aboriginal Christianity in an East Kimberley Town.* Melbourne: Melbourne University Press.

Piggin, Stuart (1996). *Evangelical Christianity in Australia: Spirit, Word, and World.* Oxford: Oxford University Press.

Robbins, Joel (2004). *Becoming Sinners: Christianity and Moral Torment in a Papua New Guinea Society*. Berkeley: University of California Press.

Swain, Tony and Gary Trompf (1995). *The Religions of Oceania*. London: Routledge.

Tacey, David (2000). *Re-Enchantment: The New Australian Spirituality*. Sydney: HarperCollins.

Thompson, Roger C. (1994). *Religion in Australia: A History*. Oxford: Oxford University Press.

Tomlinson, Matt (2009). *In God's Image: The Metaculture of Fijian Christianity*. Berkeley: University of California Press.

Part III   How They Got There

Introduction

Christianity is a historical religion, focusing on real events that happened in real time, and it is a communal religion that involves relationships between flesh and blood human beings. Ideas about God and doctrine – the stuff of theology – have played a significant role in the history of the Christian movement, but ideas are best understood in their social contexts. The following chapters combine these two dimensions of Christianity, or as they are called here "convictions" (beliefs and practices) and "encounters" (social history), in a narrative of growth and change that begins in the hinterlands of first century Palestine and ends with Christianity's global presence in the world today. The story of Christianity moves forward in fits and starts and sometimes takes off in new directions that would have been impossible to predict in advance, but this is how Christianity became the global religion it is today.

The stories and developments included in the following four chapters illustrate the Christian movement as a whole in all its persistent diversity rather than dwelling on one particular region or time period. Countless important and interesting facts about the movement have been left out because of space limitations. Roughly equal space is given to the first and second millennia of Christian history, and the chapters try to give the Christian East and the Christian West, and in more recent centuries the Christian South, equal consideration in the telling of the story.

The title of Part III is "How they got there," and the word "there" refers both to geography and theology (i.e., to the variety of the Christian traditions and subtraditions as they exist today). The following chapters explain how and why the geographic territory of Christianity has expanded and contracted during the last 2,000 years and describes the different Christian movements, traditions, communities, and formally organized churches that have emerged, grown, changed, and sometimes shrunk or collapsed along the way.

Each of the following four chapters is organized in the same way. After a brief introduction to the time period as a whole, the first half of each chapter focuses on the core convictions

The World's Christians: Who they are, Where they are, and How they got there, First Edition. Douglas Jacobsen.
© 2011 Douglas Jacobsen. Published 2011 by Blackwell Publishing Ltd.

of the Christian communities that flourished during that era, sketching what could be called the internal history of the movement. This part of each chapter explains how Christians got "there" in terms of theological understanding and church practices. The second half of each chapter then discusses how these Christian communities changed and developed, based on their encounters with other cultural, political, and religious realities. This part of the story could be called the external history of Christianity, and it has much more to do with how Christianity got "there" in terms of geography. These two dimensions, the internal and the external, have always been closely related in Christian history, but they are separated here for the sake of clarity.

The chapters themselves are self-explanatory and need no further introduction here, except for a word about the sometimes confusing problem of vocabulary when dealing with the Christian churches of the East. Because the Christian East has been relatively under-studied and because it has also been generally neglected in most older histories of Christianity, there is no commonly agreed upon set of labels for describing the three main Christian traditions of the East. This book will use the terms (1) Orthodox, (2) Miaphysite, and (3) Church of the East.

Orthodox in this sense refers to the Orthodox churches that affirm the Chalcedonian Creed written in the year 451. Most of the Orthodox Christians in the world today are Orthodox in this sense of the term. The *Miaphysite* churches (Coptic Orthodox, Syrian Orthodox, Ethiopian Orthodox, and Armenian Apostolic) also consider themselves "Orthodox" (as their names imply) and they are sometimes referred to collectively as the "Oriental Orthodox Churches," but these churches have historically rejected the Chalcedonian Creed and they represent a different tradition of "Orthodox" Christian faith and life. To avoid confusion they will be called simply Miaphysite. Most Miaphysite Christians today live in the Middle East and North Africa. The third eastern tradition is the *Church of the East*. This church, which many people call the Nestorian Church even though members of the Church of the East do not like that label, was centered in the Persian Empire (modern day Iran and Iraq). It was once a huge movement, but is very small today. It is important to remember that the "Church of the East" (upper-case singular "Church") is a specific ecclesiastical organization and should not be confused with the "churches of the East" (lower-case plural "churches") that refer to all three of these Eastern Christian traditions.

Chapter 14

The Ancient Tradition

Beginnings to 500

During the first five hundred years of its existence, the small religious movement begun by Jesus developed a broad following that by the year 500 included 45 to 50 million members (15 percent of the world's total population) spread out across a huge region of the world extending from Spain in the west to India in the east and from Ireland in the north to Ethiopia in the south. From the very beginning, leaders of the movement expressed a wide variety of opinions about God, Jesus, humankind, and the world in general, variety that only increased as the Christian movement encountered new cultures. But another process was also underway: the slow coalescence of a theological center. By the middle of the third century, a general consensus was in place, the nub of which eventually developed into what can be called "the Ancient Tradition" of the Christian religion. This Ancient Tradition did not define every Christian doctrine and practice, but instead provided something like a north star for Christians scattered all across what is now the Middle East, northern Africa, and southern Europe – a handful of common convictions that helped guide these Christians generally in the same direction despite all the local diversity that existed within the movement.

Knowledge of what took place during the first five centuries of the Christian movement is geographically uneven because the sources of that history (such as written documents, historic buildings, and art) have been preserved better in some regions than in others. This unevenness of information has deeply colored the traditional telling of the story. In particular, the narrative of Christianity within the Roman Empire, where relatively high quality records do exist, has tended to overshadow all others. While there is no doubt that developments within the Roman Empire were tremendously important for Christianity's growth and expansion as a world religion, the full story must include what took place outside of Rome as well.

The World's Christians: Who they are, Where they are, and How they got there, First Edition. Douglas Jacobsen.
© 2011 Douglas Jacobsen. Published 2011 by Blackwell Publishing Ltd.

Viewed through a Roman lens, the history of Christianity is one of expanding influence and power within the world, and the theme of that story is the political victory of Christianity over the old gods of the pagan Roman Empire. But Christians living in Persia and further east had a very different story, and even within the Roman Empire this unidirectional story of Christian triumph became hard to maintain when, in the early fifth century, the western provinces of the Empire were invaded by various "barbarian" tribes that threatened both the Roman and Christian identity of the region. Viewed from a global perspective, the history of Christianity is not a story of simple unidirectional development, but is instead a much more interesting story of how a new religion took root in many different places in many different ways. By the year 500, Christianity had become the most successful and most multicultural religious movement the world had ever seen. Well before the dawn of the modern global age, Christianity had become the first great "world religion."

Convictions

Christianity did not spring into existence with its core convictions already neatly defined. It began instead as a somewhat rag-tag affair; the early followers of Jesus were not even sure what to call themselves. At first, they described themselves somewhat vaguely as "followers of the way." Only later did other people – people outside the movement – recognize its distinctiveness and begin to call them "Christians," meaning followers of Christ. But even after Christianity had a name, many questions of identity remained. Was Christianity a new kind of Judaism or was it something else? Was Christianity supposed to organize itself as a movement designed to last for centuries or was the end of the world so close that such effort made no sense? And what exactly was the Christian message? Obviously Jesus had preached "good news," but who was this Jesus? How were his followers to explain him, what he had done, and why was his message so important?

It took the Christian movement roughly two centuries of exploration and experimentation to sort out these questions and come to some general agreement. By the year 250, a middle ground was emerging, a rough consensus of opinion. Once again, the issue of naming arose. What should this new Christian majority be called? The most common appellation was "the Church," though some called it "the Great Church" to distinguish it from the variety of smaller Christian alternatives that continued to exist outside of this great church. Others preferred the word "catholic," meaning broad-minded in spirit and universal in scope, and still others favored the term "orthodox," meaning of a right or proper opinion. For simplicity's sakes, this majority or mainstream perspective within the Christian movement will be called here simply the "Ancient Tradition."

The Ancient Tradition was a big tent. It allowed for considerable variety in Christian practice and ideas, and it was multicultural in membership, incorporating three major language groups (Greek, Latin, and Syriac) and numerous smaller ones (e.g., Armenian, Georgian, Gothic). The tradition itself was defined by a handful of convictions that transcended all these differences. When the Ancient Tradition first coalesced, it took the form of a broad but informal consensus that was affirmed by a loose network of impor-tant urban Christian leaders, bishops of the major cities in the ancient world. Starting

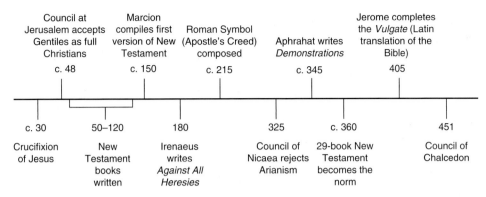

Figure 14.1 Timeline for the Ancient Tradition

around 300, the Ancient Tradition developed into a much more formal sense of identity, reflected in the agreement that was reached about the contents of the New Testament and articulated in a number of significant Christian creeds (short summaries of Christian faith and practice).

The Ancient Tradition never included all of the Christians in the world. A variety of smaller Christian traditions continued to flourish outside the movement. These alternative groups differed from the Ancient Tradition, but they were not necessarily "less" Christian. In fact, some commentators have suggested that at least some of these nonmainstream versions of Christianity may have had more in common with the original message of Jesus than the version provided by the Ancient Tradition itself, especially regarding spiritual freedom and respect for women. Nonetheless, it is clear that the Ancient Tradition included the great majority of Christians who were living during this period and that it exercised far greater influence on subsequent Christian history than any of the other smaller Christian groups that existed during this era.

The first two centuries: a time of exploration

After Jesus's death, his closest followers were at first disoriented. They had come to believe that he was the prophesied Messiah of Judaism and, despite Jesus's own reluctance to become a political leader, they seem to have hoped that somehow Jesus himself would fully usher in the kingdom of God about which he spoke so frequently. But then he was killed, and all seemed lost. It was not until they became convinced of his resurrection and were "filled with the Holy Spirit" on the day of Pentecost that the disciples regained their equilibrium and began the work of organizing the Christian community and sharing the good news of Jesus with others.

Originally, the Jesus movement was entirely Jewish, but the message that Jesus preached was expansive, and soon a number of Gentiles (non-Jews) were attracted to the movement. A man called Paul, who was himself Jewish, soon became the leader of a subgroup within the Jesus movement who felt that Gentiles should be admitted into the Christian community on an equal footing with Jews. Paul was an unusual follower of Jesus. He had never met

Jesus and he had originally viewed the Jesus movement as a heresy within Judaism. But then, while traveling to Damascus with the goal of stifling the small Christian community that had emerged there, he was knocked to the ground by a powerful vision of Jesus that convinced him to abandon his anti-Christian crusade and become an evangelist for Christianity instead. Paul would subsequently become one of the greatest Christian missionaries of all time, preaching the gospel and starting churches in cities across Asia Minor (now Turkey) and Greece. Many of the letters he wrote to the churches he founded were preserved and are now included in the New Testament.

Paul's vision of an expansive and culturally embracing Christianity conflicted with the opinion of many core leaders of the movement in Jerusalem. Headed by James and Peter, who had both known Jesus while he was alive, the Christians of Jerusalem believed that becoming a Christian also necessarily entailed becoming a Jew, which meant following Jewish law, including circumcision for men. Paul reported in his letters that he boldly confronted these leaders at a special council in Jerusalem (held around the year 48), and with the help of Peter ultimately convinced most of them to accept Gentiles into the movement as equals. The only condition was that these new Gentile converts needed to show some degree of respect for their Jewish fellow-believers by avoiding truly offensive behavior such as eating food containing blood, food sacrificed to idols, or animals that had been strangled. And they were also to avoid all forms of sexual immorality. As for Jewish Christians, the assumption seems to have been that they would continue to follow Jewish rules and ritual practices. With this agreement in hand, the early Christian movement was suddenly bicultural, clearing the first hurdle on the way to becoming a truly multicultural global religion.

Early Christianity was an urban movement, and it typically attracted more adherents from the lower levels of society than from the higher. Urban life in the ancient world was challenging for everyone, but especially for the poor, who were often new arrivals in town and lacked any social support system. Average life expectancy was around 25 years, and women were typically married by the age of 14. In this context, the local Christian church could serve as a kind of family where the young and the old, men and women, and the rich and the poor cared for each other. The early Christian churches were communities of refuge for people in need of assistance within the rough and tumble of the world's ancient urban centers. This was perhaps especially so for the women who then (as now) formed the majority of the movement's membership. Women carrying the burdens of life (bearing and caring for children, preparing food, tending the sick) found in Christianity a religious movement that both valued those tasks and assisted them in carrying them out. The early Christians not only believed in the reality of divine healing, they also cared for the infirm and offered assistance to both their own members and others during times of famine or plague.

But while Christians seemed able to work together when the issues had to do with basic human needs, they could be considerably more contentious when it came to other matters. Leadership was one point of disagreement. Even during Jesus's lifetime, tensions had arisen among his followers over who should have more power and authority within the movement. After Christ's death, the main dispute centered on whether the church should be overseen by what might be called "settled leadership" – a formally selected president or bishop who served as the institutional leader of a local congregation – or by "charismatic" leaders who were either self-appointed or chosen by informal acclamation on the basis of the power of the Spirit they possessed. This latter group included spirit-inspired prophets, gifted teachers, martyrs (people who were persecuted because of their Christianity, but remained faithful), and, slightly later, an assortment of hermits and ascetics who distinguished themselves from ordinary Christians by the rigors (some would say the excesses) of their spiritual self-discipline.

Leadership conflicts were intense and ongoing. Ignatius, bishop of the church in Antioch in the early second century, asserted bluntly that anything done without his approval or oversight was wrong simply because it was done without him. In the mid-second century, a new movement led by Monatus and two female collaborators named Priscilla and Maximilla championed the cause of spirit-filled prophets who, in essence, served as mediums speaking the word of God directly to the community of believers. Clement and Origen, successive directors of a Christian school in Alexandria, Egypt – probably the first formally organized school in the history of the movement – favored, not surprisingly, a more intellectual model of leadership. They suggested that it was the more educated who should guide the less educated toward Christian maturity. The writings of the New Testament leave room for all of these different kinds of leadership, but eventually the mainstream Christian movement opted for an institutional structure that gave power to the settled leadership of the bishops. This decision essentially shut women out of positions of authority since the office of bishop, unlike that of prophet or teacher, had come to be reserved only for men. Partly because of this, some women were attracted to nonmainstream versions of Christianity (especially Gnostic) in which women had more opportunities to lead.

Early Christians also clashed over Jewish–Gentile relations. While Paul had opened space for a Gentile form of Christianity to exist – one not bound by Jewish laws and religious regulation – Jewish Christianity did not cease and some Jewish-Christian leaders continued to insist that only those who were circumcised could be considered fully Christian. At the other extreme, Marcion of Sinope (a city located on the southeast coast of the Black Sea) argued that Christianity and Judaism were two totally separate and distinct religions. Marcion believed that the physical world that had been created by the Jewish God Yahweh was evil and that Jesus had come to reveal a totally different God and to rescue people out of the pain of physical existence. Marcion's version of Christianity included strict moral guidelines and a variety of practices like vegetarianism that were designed to wean people from their attachments to the present world.

Another area of dispute in the early church was discipline. What was the proper response to individuals who committed obviously immoral acts (sins) after they had been baptized as Christians and become members of the movement? It was widely assumed that the waters of baptism washed away the guilt of earlier sins, but was there any remedy for sins committed after baptism? Some said that Christians who relapsed into sin were lost forever. A more lenient approach appeared in an early Christian book called *The Shepherd* (or *The Shepherd of Hermas*) that said that Christians could be allowed just one opportunity for repentance and forgiveness after baptism. Over time, various forms of penance were designed to help restore wayward members to fellowship even after repeated episodes of sin. Church discipline has remained a contentious topic throughout the centuries, and debates about appropriate rigor or moderation continue today.

Finally, there were many disputes in the early Christian movement about ideas. Disagreements about how best to describe the person of Jesus – whether as an angel, a prophet, a phantom appearance of God on earth, or somehow God in genuine human form – produced considerable heat and friction. Arguments about the work of Christ – how Jesus's life, death, and resurrection healed the human condition and made reconciliation with God possible – were also intense. These disputes about the person and work of Jesus in turn gave rise to a host of related questions: did God create this world, or is this world a kind of prison from which Christ releases people? What precisely is the human defect that Christ came to correct or heal? Are souls created at birth or are they pre-existent, merely entering a human body at birth? How is the universe constructed, and what invisible spiritual beings oversee its workings? Do human beings have free will? What kinds of experiences are characteristic of a genuine encounter with God, and which are not? What role should reason and logic play in religious faith, if any at all?

A broad range of answers were offered to these questions, and many options were explored. Gnostic Christians were especially active in proposing new ideas, so much so that they are sometimes called the first Christian theologians. Gnosticism was a kind of New Age movement within early Christianity that was spiritual in tone, intellectual in content, and esoteric in orientation. Gnostic Christians used the categories of Greek philosophy and metaphysics to explore what they saw as the deeper meanings that were hidden inside the basic Christian message. Gnostic ideas were creative and often insightful, but they were often so abstract and intellectual in nature that they were difficult to connect to the practical concerns of ordinary Christians caught up in the hustle and bustle of daily life. Some of the more extreme Gnostic ideas – including the suggestion that Jesus had not really died on the cross – troubled other Christians, and this eventually produced a significant anti-Gnostic movement within the early Christian movement. The consensus that finally emerged in the form of the Ancient Tradition favored a more practical and concrete form of Christianity, even though it was sometimes enriched by Gnostic insights.

Two men in particular helped to crystallize the Christian mindset that would come to dominate the movement. One of them was Irenaeus (his birth date is unknown, but he died in 202), who was the Bishop of Lugdunum (Lyon) in what is now southern France, and his main role was negative or exclusionary. His two most famous books are entitled *Against All Heresies* and the *Refutation and Overthrow of Knowledge Falsely So Called*. As these titles imply, his goal was to define the boundaries of the movement as clearly as possible, and eliminating some of the movement's fuzziness likely helped it to endure. Cyprian (208–58), the bishop of Carthage who lived a generation after Irenaeus, shared many of his predecessor's concerns, but Cyprian's focus was on institutional structure much more than theology. Cyprian said that being a Christian meant being part of the Christian community, asserting that "One cannot have God as Father who does not have the church as mother." Since the church had such an important role, it was crucial to determine which Christian group or groups represented the one true church. Cyprian's proposal, following a suggestion made earlier by Irenaeus, was that the true Christian community was defined by a lineage of leadership that could be traced back through history to the apostles that Jesus had appointed to be in charge of the church and ultimately to Jesus himself. This idea of the historical continuity of Christian leadership, which eventually was given the name "apostolic succession," is still an important element in many Christian traditions (especially the Catholic, Orthodox, and Anglican).

Creating the Christian Bible

The creation of the Christian Bible also helped to consolidate the Ancient Tradition and it confirmed Christianity's character as a religion of the book. This cannot be said of all religions; most religions are grounded in oral tradition rather than in written scriptures. But as the child of Judaism – another book-centered religion – Christianity was largely destined to become a scriptural faith itself. The Greek term *biblios* (from which the word "Bible" is derived) simply means "book," and that is fitting since the object called a book is largely a Christian invention. Most writing of the time was done on scrolls – long pieces of paper that were rolled up for storage – but Christians found scrolls unwieldy. They wanted a format that would make it easy to find specific passages of scripture more quickly, and books – writing inscribed on separate leaves of paper that are bound together at the spine – were the answer. So Christians wrote books, not scrolls, and the Bible soon became "the Book" for the movement as a whole.

The Christian Bible consists of two parts: the Jewish (or Hebrew) Scriptures, which Christians call the Old Testament, and the New Testament, which focuses on Jesus and the earliest years of the Christian movement. Christians did not choose the contents of the Old Testament, but simply accepted what Judaism had already decided should be there. Defining the content of the New Testament was more challenging. The movement was awash in books, because early Christians were prolific writers who understood the power of the pen. Many of these books were about Jesus, and some included wonderful, but clearly fictional, stories about Jesus's youth: making clay sparrows come alive and fly away, lengthening a board his father had cut too short, raising a playmate from the dead. Other writers recounted the mighty actions of the apostles, with Peter, Thomas, John, and Paul getting the most attention. Some were didactic, giving instructions about what to believe or how to act. Some discussed the metaphysical intricacies of the universe, describing worlds within worlds and the complicated orders of angels who oversaw them. Some composed Christian poetry, others wrote prose. Some focused on the apocalyptic end of the world, while others penned treatises designed to help the movement organize itself for the long haul.

At first, no one felt any urgency about collecting the writings of the movement into one book. The assumption of many early Christians was that the end of history was at hand, so there was no need to plan for the future. But as time moved along and the world did not come to an end, the notion of putting together a Christian companion to the Hebrew Bible grew in appeal. This slowly emerging conclusion was given a huge boost when the anti-Jewish Christian thinker Marcion co-opted the process by cobbling together his own version of what the Christian book should look like. But when other Christians looked at Marcion's Bible, many were disturbed. He had bound together the four Gospels (those by Matthew, Mark, Luke, and John) and the writings of Paul along with the Acts of the Apostles, but he had edited these works to remove any positive references to Jews or Judaism. In response to Marcion's new biblical text, supporters of the emerging Ancient Tradition felt compelled to develop their own alternative collection of Christian writings to replace Marcion's compilation.

Although there was some debate about which documents should and should not be included in the New Testament, the actual process was not particularly difficult. From the beginning, some books were deemed to be so special – most notably the four Gospels of Matthew, Mark, Luke, and John and various collections of the letters of Paul – that they were treated as "sacred" from the very beginning. Other writings, while they were considered interesting and even inspiring, were never taken seriously as candidates for inclusion in the Christian scriptures. Books like the *Infancy Gospel of Thomas* (which tells the story of the clay sparrows) or the *Acts of Thecla* (a female companion of Paul) belong in this class. Finally, there was a short list of texts, including the book of Revelation, the "pastoral epistles" (1 and 2 Timothy and Titus), the *Letter of Barnabas*, the *Didache*, the first *Letter of Clement*, and *The Shepherd*, about which opinion was divided.

Various lists of the books in the New Testament, most of them quite similar, circulated throughout the Christian movement during the second, third, and early fourth centuries, but by the mid-300s that list was becoming finalized around the 27 that now form the standard "canon" of the New Testament. In the West, this new 27-book list became normative in 405 when Jerome's (c.340–420) Vulgate, a Latin translation of the Hebrew and Greek original manuscripts of the Bible, was completed. The Greek-speaking wing of the Ancient Church accepted the new canon at roughly the same time, although they placed the book of Revelation in a slightly different category than was the case in the West. The book of Revelation was included in the Greek text of the Bible, but it was not read during public worship because its wild symbolism was so prone to fanatical misinterpretation. The third (and smallest) language group within the Ancient Tradition, the Syriac-speaking Christians of the East, moved in a slightly different direction. Their translation of the New Testament, called the *Peshitta*, contained only 22 books, leaving out the short letters of 2 Peter, 2 and 3 John, and Jude, because their authorship was unclear, and the book of Revelation because of its controversial content. Modern versions of the *Peshitta*, however, often add these five books back into the canon so that the Syriac text now aligns with the rest of the Christian world.

The Standard 27-book Canon of the New Testament

The Four Gospels: Matthew, Mark, Luke, John

The Acts of the Apostles

Letters attributed to the Apostle Paul: Romans, 1 and 2 Corinthians, Galatians, Ephesians, Philippians, Colossians, 1 and 2 Thessalonians, 1 and 2 Timothy, Titus, Philemon

Other Letters: Hebrews, James, 1 and 2 Peter, 1, 2, and 3 John, Jude

The Book of Revelation

Since the fourth century, the New Testament (in its Latin, Greek, or Syriac form) has been accepted by virtually every Christian community in the world as the foundational text of the Christian religion. Christians have frequently argued with each other about very basic issues, but the New Testament itself has been exempt from serious debate. The interpretation of the New Testament has produced controversy upon controversy, but the text itself has not been contested. The creation of the New Testament is undoubtedly one of the greatest accomplishments of the Ancient Tradition.

Codifying core Christian beliefs

The other great accomplishment of the Ancient Tradition was the composition of a series of different creeds: brief summaries of core Christian beliefs that were intended to serve as shorthand guides for Christian belief and for the proper interpretation of the Bible. Creeds were also helpful for instructing converts prior to baptism, for corporately affirming the faith during worship, and for identifying heresy (ideas and ideals deemed to be improper or mistaken). The goal of almost all these creeds was to express the core convictions of the Christian faith in clear and unambiguous terms that avoided the idiosyncrasies of any particular time and place. But no written document can ever fully transcend the limitations of its own particular context and the language in which it is written, and because of that each of the ancient creeds has its own distinct emphases, even though there is considerable overlap in what all of them say.

One of the oldest Christian creeds, known as the Roman Symbol or the Interrogatory Creed of Hippolytus, dating from about the year 215, was written in Latin and comes from the church at Rome. It was composed in an interrogatory style and was likely used as a question–answer prelude to the ritual act of baptism for new members. As was typical of Latin culture and Latin-speaking Christianity, this statement is short and straightforward. Its reference to Pontius Pilate, the Roman official who ordered the execution of Jesus, also situates the Christian faith in "real time" as opposed to mythic history.

> Do you believe in God the Father All Governing? Do you believe in Christ Jesus, the Son of God, Who was begotten by the Holy Spirit from the Virgin Mary, Who was crucified under Pontius Pilate, and died and was buried and rose the third day living from the dead, and ascended into the heavens, and sat down on the right hand of the Father, and will come to judge the living and the dead? Do you believe in the Holy Spirit, in the holy Church, and in the resurrection of the body?[1]

This creed was later enlarged and slightly modified around the year 700 to become the "Apostles' Creed" – a creed that is still recited in many churches today.

The Creed of Nicaea, written about a hundred years later in 325, was composed in Greek, a language and culture generally considered to be more philosophical in orientation than Latin. This creed was also written in response to a very specific theological question. Arius, a deacon from the church in Alexandria (in Egypt), was promoting the idea that, rather than being fully divine, Jesus was almost God, but not quite. Arius said that Christ, the Son of God who was incarnate in Jesus, was less divine than God the Father because the Son had been begotten in time, while the Father was timeless and eternal. Most of the bishops gathered at Nicaea were opposed to this Arian proposal and wanted to condemn his views as strongly as possible. Seeking both to philosophically clarify Christian teaching and to explicitly condemn Arius, the 325 version of the Nicene Creed reads:

We believe in one God, the Father All Governing, creator of all things visible and invisible; And in one Lord Jesus Christ, the Son of God, begotten of the Father as only begotten, that is, from the essence of the Father, God from God, Light from Light, true God from True God, begotten not created, of the same essence as the Father, through whom all things came into being, both in heaven and in earth; Who for us men and for our salvation came down and was incarnate, becoming human. He suffered and the third day he rose, and ascended into the heavens. And he will come again to judge both the living and the dead. And we believe in the Holy Spirit. But, to those who say, "once he was not" or "he was not before his generation," or "he came to be out of nothing," or who assert that he is a creature, or changeable, or mutable, the Catholic and Apostolic Church anathematizes [condemns] them.[2]

Syriac-speaking Christians tended to favor a more literary and poetic style of expression, and they typically linked doctrine (ideas) with ethics (behavior) in their understanding of faith. There is no document in the Syriac subtradition that precisely parallels the formality of either the Roman Symbol or the Nicene Creed, but an excerpt from the book *Demonstrations* by Aphrahat the "Persian Sage" (270–345) provides a rough equivalent. The distinctive spirit of Syriac Christianity is clearly visible in this passage:

Now this is faith:
When a man believes in God the Lord of all,
Who made the heavens and the earth and the seas and all that is in them;
And made Adam in His image;
And He gave the Law to Moses;
Who sent of His Spirit in the prophets;
Who sent His Messiah into the world.
And that a man should believe in the resurrection of the dead;
And in the sacrament of baptism.
This is the faith of the Church of God.
And that a man should separate himself from observing hours and Sabbaths and moons and seasons,
And divinations and sorceries and astrology and magic,
From fornication and reveling and vain doctrines which are instruments of the Evil One,
From the blandishment of honeyed words, from blasphemy and from adultery.
These are the works of the faith which is based on the true Rock which is Christ,
On Whom the whole building is raised.[3]

The creedal highpoint of the Ancient Tradition, which was also the beginning of its end, came with the writing of the Chalcedonian Creed in the year 451. The Council of Chalcedon was called to settle once and for all the vexing question of how the human and the divine were related in Jesus. While the Council of Nicaea had attempted to settle the matter, differences of opinion had continued and arguments had rambled on. In compromise language that attempted to satisfy all the contending parties, the Chalcedonian Creed declared that Christ was "perfect both in his deity and also in humanness" and that these two "natures" (the human and the divine) were united in one "person." The creed further stated that because the human and the divine were united in Christ from the moment of conception, the proper title for his mother Mary was *Theotokos*, meaning "the one who bears God" or, translated more freely, the "Mother of God."

Those present at the council hoped this formulation of Christology would be the last word on the topic, but that was not to be the case. Conflicts continued, and the theological camaraderie that had kept the Ancient Tradition together for more than two centuries began to unravel. By the middle of the sixth century, the consensus of the Ancient Tradition had dissolved and three new Christian subtraditions had arisen to take its place (a story told in the following chapter). Although the Creed of Chalcedon failed to stem that division, its longer legacy has been more successful. Today almost all the world's Christians affirm the Chalcedonian Creed as the proper starting point for reflection on the person and work of Christ.

Encounters

At the same time as the Christian movement was consolidating its core convictions in the form of the Ancient Tradition, it was simultaneously encountering a variety of new political, cultural, and religious realities as it spread out from its original base in Palestine. While the Ancient Tradition acted as a centering force within the movement as a whole, these new encounters nudged the growing Christian movement in a number of different, sometimes contradictory, directions. Thus even though many of the core convictions of Christians living in the Persian Empire were nearly identical to those of Christians living in the Roman Empire, the histories of the two groups slowly diverged as they grappled with different local conditions. In the Roman Empire, Christianity became the imperial faith of the land, intimately wedded to the state; in Persia and in India, Christianity became a persistent minority religion; and in a variety of other settings, Christianity became the ethnic faith of different local people groups.

Christianity in the Roman Empire: from persecuted minority to imperial church

The ancient Roman Empire was one of the best organized civilizations the world has ever seen. Founded in 27 BCE, the Roman Empire was the continuation, with a new political leadership structure, of the Roman Republic, which had been founded around 500 BCE. Roman territory had expanded slowly from the regions immediately surrounding the city of Rome to include a huge area surrounding the Mediterranean Sea and then stretching north all the way to Great Britain (see Figure 14.2). As the Empire grew it absorbed the cultures and values of many of the people it conquered, making Roman culture richly diverse. At the same time, however, Rome was thoroughly unified: one emperor oversaw the policies of the state and one law was enforced throughout the entire domain.

The history of the Christian movement in the Roman Empire is, like the Empire itself, rich and complex, but the underlying plot is simple: Christianity began as a small, persecuted religious sect and eventually became the government-backed religion of the realm. This is obviously a story of success, but it is also the story of a movement's altered self-understanding.

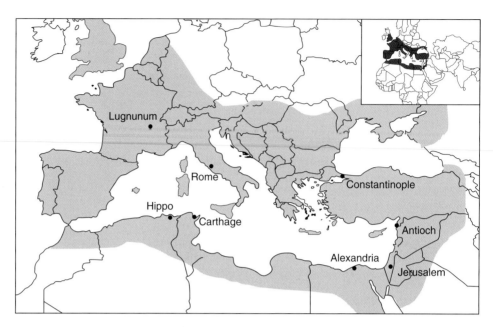

Figure 14.2   Roman Empire at peak size (showing major cities and modern national boundaries). Map by author.

The original Christian message had a political component to the extent that Jesus's frequent references to the "kingdom of God" called into question the absoluteness of the Roman state, although early Christians themselves were virtually never involved in the actual political intrigues of the Empire. Yet Christianity had become the favored faith of the realm by the early 300s, and it became the official religion of the state before the year 400. After that, the church was deeply and inevitably linked to the political activities of the Empire, and the new imperial church came to think of itself as duty-bound to dictate the religious and moral norms of society.

In the first century, of course, that turn of events was literally unimaginable. Christianity began as a tiny speck of religious activity, barely on the radar of the Roman world. For the most part Christianity grew largely out of sight, taking root among the poor and powerless. It spread first to the cities because those were the easiest places to reach. The missionary travels of the apostle Paul illustrate that the growth of Christianity followed the many ship routes that criss-crossed the Mediterranean Sea. By the middle of the second century there was hardly a Roman seaport or major urban center where Christianity had not been planted. While Christianity remained very small in terms of overall numbers, geographically it was becoming at home throughout the Empire.

As urban religious minorities, Christians were easy scapegoats in times of social unrest, and their talk of eating the body and blood of Jesus (i.e., the Eucharist) did little to assuage the fears and suspicions of their Roman neighbors. So when Rome went up in flames in the year 64 and people began to accuse the Emperor Nero of starting the conflagration, he lost no time in blaming the catastrophe on the Christians. And the charge stuck because many thought that Christians just might be strange enough to have done

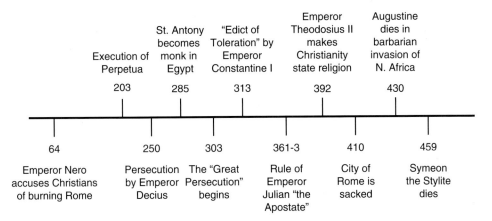

Figure 14.3 Timeline of Christianity and the Roman Empire

it. Nero arrested a number of Christians, tortured some to obtain false confessions, and coated others with pitch and set them on fire to serve as lanterns for parties at the imperial residence.

As gruesome as this episode was, it would be a mistake to see this kind of intentional, state-sanctioned persecution as the normal experience of Christians in the early centuries of the movement. Generally, Christians lived at peace with their neighbors, and persecution was relatively rare. When violence occasionally erupted, it was usually the unplanned by-product of some local social or political upheaval. In such times, Christians were occasionally lynched by neighborhood mobs or were snatched up by the regional authorities to serve as victims for the "games" held in the many circuses and coliseums that dotted the Roman world. One of the most famous martyrdoms of the time – the execution of the young mother Vibia Perpetua in 203 – is set in this context. The tale is heart-wrenching. Her father pleaded with her to compromise just a bit and save her life for the sake of her baby son, but Perpetua never wavered. The wild animals were set loose on her, and she was gored by a wild bull. Finding herself still alive, she quickly rose to her feet and fixed her disheveled hair in order to die with dignity. At the end, she helped the frightened young gladiator finish the job by guiding his sword to her own neck.

Perpetua's story was an encouragement to the Christian community, but her experience was, in general, rare before the year 250. After that date, however, the persecution of Christians became much more systematic and intense. The Roman Empire as a whole was beginning to feel the first tremors of its ultimate demise. The economy was becoming shaky, newly aggressive foreign populations were rattling their swords along the northern border of the Empire, and citizens in general were feeling edgy. As one means of dealing with the deteriorating situation, the Empire was divided into two large administrative subunits (Eastern and Western regions largely following the Latin–Greek language divide that existed within the Empire) in an attempt to make governance easier. But tensions and troubles continued and it did not take long for the imperial soothsayers to propose a reason: the gods of Rome were angry because they were being neglected. The Emperor Decius (249–51) responded by ordering everyone to reaffirm their religious devotion to the gods in a series of public ceremonies scheduled throughout the Empire.

For Christians this was a problem. While loyalty to the state was permitted, engaging in the public worship of the pagan gods of Rome was not. Some Christians acquiesced, either doing what was required or bribing an official to say they had. But other Christians resisted the order, and the Emperor felt compelled to act. The persecution of Christians became an imperial policy enforced on an empire-wide basis, and the goal was not merely the persecution of individuals but the eradication of Christianity. Many Christians were arrested and some were put to death; Christian buildings were destroyed, Christian scriptures were confiscated and burned, and Christian leaders were pressured to recant their faith in public, hoping their failure would undermine the morale of the Christian community as a whole. This state-sanctioned persecution continued on and off for more than 50 years, with the most intense violence taking place during the Great Persecution that was initiated by Emperor Diocletian (284–305) in the year 303.

But after 10 years of suffering, at the seeming height of the persecution, a stunning development took place. A new Emperor came to power, and not only did he stop the persecution, he became a Christian himself. His name was Constantine, and he was the son of Constantius, the "caesar" or assistant emperor of the Western administrative region of the Roman Empire. When his father died, Constantine's troops proclaimed him emperor-to-be, and after a series of battles with other contenders, Constantine eventually secured the throne. It is said that on the eve of one of those battles for his throne, Constantine had a dream that led him to mark the shields of his soldiers with the letters *chi* and *rho*. He later discovered that this was a Christian symbol – *chi* and *rho* are the first two Greek letters in the word "Christ." Convinced that the God of the Christians had helped him win the imperial office, he showed his gratitude by almost immediately, in cooperation with the Eastern Emperor Licinius, issuing an Edict of Toleration in the year 313 that stopped the persecution. When Licinius later reneged on that agreement, Constantine went to war against him, and eventually established himself as the sole ruler of the Empire. He would serve in that position until 337.

The depth of Constantine's "conversion" has been debated. Perhaps it was just pragmatic. The Roman Empire was a multiethnic, multicultural state that had long relied on the pagan faith of Rome as a social glue to hold itself together. That glue seemed to be losing its holding power, and perhaps Constantine thought Christianity was the best alternative available. The growth of Christianity between the years 250 and the end of the persecution in 313 makes this a plausible interpretation. In 250, Christians accounted for roughly 2 percent of the imperial population. By 313, they probably made up 15 percent of the population. Constantine may have reasoned that a religion that could grow so dramatically under such adverse conditions was clearly the wave of the future. Still, Constantine's conversion could also have been genuinely religious, and, regardless of how it began, Constantine seems to have become a convinced Christian by the end of his life.

Whatever the motivation behind it, Constantine's conversion thoroughly changed the context of Roman Christianity. The state that had formerly persecuted the church now became its greatest patron. Old church buildings were restored and new churches were constructed. Bishops were welcomed in the royal court and living martyrs (i.e., Christians who had been severely persecuted, but who survived) were treated like heroes. In order to help the Christian community better organize itself and codify its beliefs, Constantine himself convened the Council of Nicaea, inviting bishops from all across the land to attend at his expense. On the more explicitly political side of things, Constantine modified a number of Roman laws to make them more compatible with Christian values (typically making the law more forgiving and less harsh) and he undertook the construction of a new capital for the Empire at Constantinople (modern day Istanbul). Sometimes called "the New Rome," Constantinople was essentially built from scratch so that, unlike the original Rome, it would be unpolluted by any prior worship of the pagan gods.

Christians who lived through this transition saw it as miraculous. Constantine was perceived as almost the equal of Christ. He was the instrument of God's rule on earth, the earthly king of God's kingdom come to earth. But Constantine's successors were less supportive of the Ancient Tradition than Constantine himself, and for some time the ultimate outcome was unclear. Constantine's son, the Emperor Constantius (337–61), was a supporter of Arius, while the Emperor Julian (361–63), who was known as "Julian the Apostate," favored the restoration of Roman paganism. Subsequent rulers tended to be more supportive of the Ancient Tradition, but not always consistently so.

Figure 14.4   Head of the giant statue of the Emperor Constantine in the courtyard of the Palazzo dei Conservatori, Rome, Italy
© Michael Juno/Alamy

It was only when Theodosius came to the throne in 378 that the Ancient Tradition once again took center stage. In 392, Theodosius made Christianity the official religion of the state, condemning all expressions of Christian faith and banning all public pagan ceremonies. The once-persecuted church now became the imperial church of the realm, the favored and protected religion of the state, and in an unsettling turn of events it became the persecutor of other religions it deemed offensive. Christianity was not, however, merely the religion of the state – it had also become the religion of the Roman majority. By the middle of the fourth century more than half the Roman population had converted, and by the year 400 close to 80 percent of the population was at least nominally Christian. Any tension between being Roman and being Christian evaporated, and Christianity became the new civil religion that kept the mighty Roman Empire intact.

Most Christians welcomed the imperialization of Christianity, but it posed new challenges for their religious lives. Persevering in the face of martyrdom had previously been the mark of the faithful. How were Christians to express their faithfulness when the era of martyrdom had ended? In a word, the answer was monasticism.

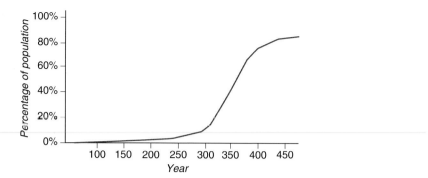

Figure 14.5   Estimated growth of Christianity as a percentage of the Roman population

Some Christians in Syria and Egypt had long engaged in various practices of asceticism (the denial of physical pleasures and the intentional abuse of the body) as a way to discipline their thoughts and emotions and to become completely focused on God. Asceticism was a kind of self-martyrdom that proved one's spiritual mettle. As it became increasingly easy to be a Christian in the newly Christian Roman Empire, more and more people felt a need to adopt this stricter style of Christian life. Many of the most serious Christian ascetics began to move to the desert where they could pursue their spiritual practices alone, just as Christ had spent time in the desert alone with God. Anthony the Great (251–356) was one of the first Roman citizens to follow this path, leaving civilization in the year 285, even before the Empire became Christian, to live alone in the wastelands of the Nitrian Desert of northern Egypt. Individuals like Anthony would later be called "monks," a word derived from the Greek word *monos*, which means "alone." But the Christian monks of the desert soon found that solitude was hard to maintain. As stories of the lives and power of the desert fathers and mothers drifted back into mainstream society, thousands of people flocked to the desert seeking guidance and blessing from these living saints.

The most famous monk of the era was Symeon, who lived in Syria and died in the year 459. During his lifetime Symeon was known as "the great wonder of the world," and Christians came from as far away as Spain and Britain to request healing, prayer, and instruction. The crush of the crowds became so great that Symeon eventually built a tower that enabled him to see and hear everyone better. In bits and stages, Symeon increased the height of this tower until it reached almost 50 feet (15.24 m), and for 37 years he lived on the tiny three foot (nearly 1m) square platform at the top. He prayed all night, ministered to the needs of the people all day, and rarely slept or ate. His ascetic regime was so strict that some wondered if he truly was a human being, and occasionally some doubters would climb up the tower to investigate – usually being converted on the spot. Atop his tower, it was almost as if Symeon was already in heaven, serving as humanity's personal mediator with God (see Plate 26). In an age when the imperial church was taking hold and when God was beginning to seem more distant than in the past, the wonder-working monks of the desert provided the Christian community with an alternative, more personal means of connecting with God.

The rise of this new class of holy men and women ultimately reconfigured the church, changing it into a two-tiered hierarchy. Monastic, ascetic Christians occupied the top spiritual tier, while ordinary Christians living in the world occupied the bottom tier. The unintended message for the masses was that most people were simply incapable of living truly serious Christian lives, since total dedication to God required living like the monks and nuns of the desert. The Christian movement struggled with the implications of this two-tiered hierarchy of spirituality for centuries to come.

By the year 400, many Roman Christians felt as if they were living at the culmination of history. They thought the millennium itself – the thousand-year period of peace and prosperity that is foretold in the Christian Scripture – had arrived. The fact that those outside the Roman Empire did not share their experience or their perspective seemed inconsequential. In fact, most Roman Christians felt little or no compulsion to evangelize the rest of the world; they were not even sure that people in the rest of the world were fully human. Then the unthinkable happened: a group of non-Roman barbarians who had embraced the heretical Christianity of Arius sacked the city of Rome in the year 410. Later a host of other barbarian groups overran most of the western half of the Empire. How could this happen? How could the kingdom of God on earth be attacked? How could the Christian Empire fail?

Two answers were given. In the West, where the barbarian incursions had taken place, it was Augustine of Hippo (354–430), a bishop in what is now northeastern Algeria, who formulated the best response. Augustine argued in *The City of God* that the Roman Empire was not, in fact, the promised millennium and that Christians might well have to live through times of trial and suffering. The present age was a time of testing, a time when the "city of God" (defined by the love of God and others) and the "city of man" (defined by the love of self) existed in tension. In such an age, the proper Christian stance was to remain faithful and patient in the midst of suffering and to long for the day in heaven when God would end all sorrow. Christians living in the eastern half of the Empire had a much more militant and this-worldly response. In their view, the sacking of Rome and the barbarian incursions were merely temporary setbacks. They saw no reason to rethink their imperial faith, and remained hopeful that the Christian Empire would soon reconquer the West and restore the full glory of God's visible kingdom on earth. These two different responses to the barbarian invasion presaged the slow divide within the Roman imperial church that eventually produced the separate Western Catholic and Eastern Orthodox Christian traditions.

Christians in India and Persia: persistent religious minorities

The history of Christianity outside Rome followed a very different path than it did within the Roman Empire, and nowhere is this more obvious than in India and Persia. In these lands, Christianity never was in contention for becoming the state religion, and Christians never accounted for more than a modest percentage of the population. The Roman story of moving from persecution to power makes no sense here. Instead, the main narrative is one of persistence and survival.

India

The story of Christianity in India stretches back to the first century. Christians in India say that Thomas, one of the original 12 disciples of Jesus, was the first person to bring the gospel to their land. According to their account, Thomas came to the southwest coast of India (to what is now the state of Kerala) and established a number of Christian communities there before moving on to the southeast region of India (Tamil Nadu) where he died. There are Christians in India today who claim to trace their roots to the apostle Thomas, and they maintain his burial place at Mylapore, near the modern city of Chennai (see Plate 27). For years, historians dismissed this account as fabrication, but recent documentation of the early trade routes that crossed the Arabian Sea from Egypt to the west coast of India makes the story plausible. Regardless of the precise details, it is clear that Christianity arrived in India at a very early date.

Christianity soon developed its own local style of faith in its new Indian setting. The eventual outcome was that Christians in India became entrenched minorities within the local social order, in essence becoming a new caste within the social hierarchy of southern India. Given the lack of written records, the historical process that led to this state of affairs can only be surmised. After an initial burst of growth, the Thomas Christian community appears to have reached an apex at perhaps 20 percent of the local population. As conversions slowed and then finally ceased, the group reoriented itself toward the consolidation of its own community and peaceable coexistence with the surrounding majority non-Christian (Hindu) population.

The concept of caste – a socially defined hierarchy of status – provided a means of making this transition. Caste was often defined in part by religion, and religion became the main factor in the emerging Thomas Christian caste. Eventually the Thomas Christians achieved a relatively high caste identity, and they have survived as a minority community within the general population of India for almost two thousand years. There is a tendency for minority cultures to merge into the majority culture over time, and the fact that Indian Christians have been able to persist for centuries while maintaining cordial relations with their non-Christian neighbors is a tribute both to their tenacity and to the historical hospitality of Indian culture as a whole. (Today, one-third of the population of Kerala is Christian, but only a small portion of that number can trace their roots to the original Thomas community of Christians.)

Persia

A similar but more complicated and much more painful history of Christianity as a minority religion took place in Persia. Christianity was introduced to Persia in the early second century by way of the desert trade routes that connected the Mediterranean world with Central Asia. The cities strung along this route were complex settlements where members of different religions and cultures mixed, and the Christianity that took root in these cities reflected that diversity. Gnostic-style speculation about Christian beliefs, which was often vehemently condemned within the Roman Christian world, tended to receive a cautious welcome in the region because it provided a way of explaining Christianity to a world in which ideas were more fluid than they were in Rome.

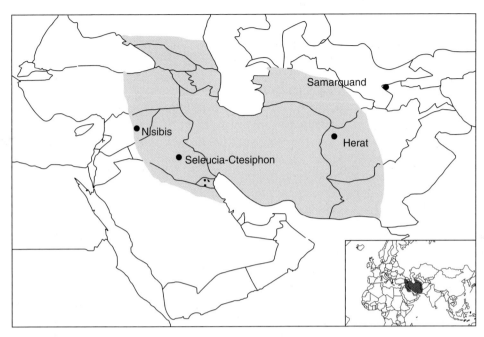

Figure 14.6   Sasanian Empire, c. 250 size (showing major cities and modern national boundaries). Map by author.

Another distinctive element in Persian Christianity was introduced by the merchant missionaries who brought Christianity to the region: the use of Syriac, a form of Aramaic that was very similar to the language spoken by Jesus and by many other Palestinian Jews. The continuing use of Syriac as the language of Christianity guaranteed that Persian Christians would maintain a lively (though often contentious) relationship with Judaism.

Finally, the Christians of Persia had a distinctly more ascetic understanding of Christian life than was common in the Roman Empire. Celibacy was honored, perhaps because it distinguished Christians from the mainstream Zoroastrian population that placed great value on having large families. The importance of celibacy is explained in the *Acts of Thomas*, a Christian book that was very popular in Persia. In that story, the apostle Thomas interrupts a young couple on their wedding night and convinces them to refrain from what he calls "filthy intercourse." He tells them that celibacy will free them from all the afflictions and troubles of child-rearing, and they will be able then to devote themselves entirely to God.

During the first two centuries of Christian history, Persia was ruled by the Parthians, a seminomadic people whose Persian "empire" was essentially a coalition of many small regional principalities. That looseness of control, which allowed for considerable freedom at the local level, was a boon for early Christians who generally deemed Persia to be a safer place to live than Rome. In the 220s, however, the Parthians were overthrown by the Sasanians who were more intent on imposing a centrally controlled uniformity on the Persian Empire, and that uniformity included a newly aggressive form of Zoroastrianism. During the Parthian era, Zoroastrianism existed as a relatively tolerant Persian folk religion. Under the Sasanians, Zoroastrianism became the official state religion and, even though people were not required to convert, everyone was required to show public respect for Zoroastrian values and moral practices. This change put Christians at risk.

Zoroastrians see the world as a spiritual battlefield where the forces of good and the powers of evil continually clash. In this warfare, the behavior of humans is a key factor in how that conflict will culminate, and everyone in Persia was expected to support the side of goodness against evil and death. Viewed from this perspective, a number of Christian practices were deeply offensive because they seemed to aid the powers of evil rather than good. One such behavior was burying the dead, a practice that was very important to Christians because it was modeled on the burial of Christ. In contrast, Zoroastrians believed that corpses were permeated with evil and that burial defiled the goodness of the earth. Rather than burying their dead, Zoroastrians placed them on raised platforms or towers where their bodies could be eaten by vultures and would never touch the ground. Zoroastrians also differed from Christians regarding sexuality and procreation. Having children – producing new human life – was seen as a way of combating the forces of death and evil, so couples were expected to have as many children as possible. Given that profamily stance, the Christian community's emphasis on celibacy seemed like a pact with the devil, an intentional effort to undercut all that was good about life.

Tensions between the Christians and the Zoroastrians were rising throughout the third century, but the Persian Christian community was generally exempt from overt persecution until the fourth century. Then the ascension of Constantine to the Roman imperial throne changed the equation. With Constantine's conversion to Christianity, Christians in Persia suddenly came to be seen as not only anti-Zoroastrian but as potentially in league with Persia's greatest enemy. Things were made worse when Constantine wrote to the Sasanian ruler Shapur II in 315 instructing him, in somewhat paternalistic language, to make sure the Christians of his realm were treated fairly. Viewing Constantine's words as a veiled threat, Shapur decided it was best to simply rid Persia of its subversive Christian population. The "Great Persecution" of Christians began in earnest around 340 and lasted until 401. It was both brutal and systematic. Nearly 200,000 Christians were put to death before the end of the century, often in gruesome and sadistic ways like throwing people into pits of rats to be eaten alive, and orchestrating mass crucifixions. There was a short suspension of the violence in the early 400s, but a Second Persecution began in the early 440s and lasted until around 460 with perhaps another 200,000 Christians killed before the attacks finally subsided. Eventually, the Sasanian government concluded that persecution was ineffective. Despite more than a century of oppression, the Christian community had not disappeared but had amazingly held relatively steady in numbers. Also, the Christian movement made some adjustments to Persian culture, most notably in the area of family and children, including a recommendation that priests marry. The government accordingly adopted a new policy of grudging tolerance with regard to the Christian movement.

With the cessation of persecution, Christians in Persia finally had the opportunity to put their own house in order. The situation had become complex, since two different Christian populations lived side by side. One consisted of native Persian people who had converted to Christianity; the other consisted of Roman Christian citizens who had been captured and deported to various regions of Persia during the many Roman–Persian wars of the era. These two communities of Christians spoke different languages and had separate hierarchies of

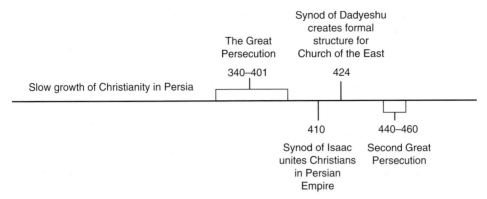

Figure 14.7   Timeline of Christianity in Persia

bishops and priests. In the year 410, the Synod of Isaac began the work of reconciling these two communities and of setting up a single nationwide church organization. The Synod of Dadyeshu, which took place in 424, ratified the creation of this newly unified "Church of the East" and formally declared independence from the Imperial Church of the Roman Empire. This declaration of independence was in many ways a political necessity. It was a way of saying that Persian Christians were loyal citizens and not political subversives who secretly favored Roman Christians over their Persian Zoroastrian neighbors. At the same time, the creation of a distinctly separate Church of the East was also a declaration of spiritual independence, a pronouncement that the Roman model was not the only way to be Christian. But still, Christians in Persia continued to see themselves as part of the unified Ancient Tradition of Christianity, even though they expressed that faith in their own distinctively Persian way.

With persecution ended, the Church of the East truly flourished for the first time. During the last half of the fifth century, they remained a religious minority in Persia proper (comprising perhaps 30 percent of the total Persian population), but they had a thriving missionary outreach to the rest of the world. Just as Christianity had been introduced to Persia by merchants and missionaries from the West, Persian Christians spread their message eastwards by the same means. Within a few decades, the Church of the East established Christian communities in almost all of the major cities along the famous Silk Road that connected Persia with the Far East. By the year 500, the 40 or so bishops who led the Church of the East were overseeing a vast transnational domain that included all of Central Asia from Baghdad to the oasis city of Turpan (sometimes spelled "Turfan") in what is now western China.

Within this territory, Christians associated with the Church of the East were a small minority, and they held virtually no political power. Perhaps they hoped for something more. Perhaps they hoped that the rulers where they lived would convert to Christianity like Constantine and begin to favor Christianity over the other religions of the area. But if that was the case, there is no evidence to support it. The more likely case is that their own experiences of severe persecution led them to be wary of close church–state alliances. Although they were clearly missionary-minded, they were content to follow their own rules and ways of life without oppression and had no desire to politically impose their faith on others.

Other Christianities

Alongside the imperial Christianity of Rome and the minority Christianity of India and Persia, a variety of other embodiments of Christianity also flourished during this time – versions of Christianity that were often very closely connected with one particular nation or people.

The two oldest Christian churches of this kind can be found in Armenia and Georgia, two neighboring nations in the Caucasus (the land between the Black Sea and the Caspian Sea). Christianity became the national religion of Armenia in the early 300s after King Tiridates III was healed by the prayers of Gregory (later known as "the Illuminator") who was both a Christian and the son of the king's chief rival. Tiridates' conversion was undoubtedly elicited by gratitude for his divine healing, but it was also a means of unifying the kingdom since it arrived via the family of his main political enemy. Christianity might have become simply the state religion of the land – a kind of mini-imperial Christianity – but history intervened. In 387, Armenia lost its independence and was partitioned by Persia and Rome, making the nation and the state two very different things. Fractured by their enemies, the Armenian people turned to Christianity to bind them together. As a people, they all read one Armenian translation of the Bible and belonged to the one Armenian Church that was overseen by a church officer called a *catholicos*. Perhaps fittingly for this kind of ethnically identified church, the position of Armenian catholicos was hereditary, vested in the family of Gregory the Illuminator until the thirteenth century. A similar story can be told about the neighboring nation of Georgia that embraced Christianity around the year 340. For Georgians, too, Christianity became the core of their corporate identity, helping them to maintain a powerful sense of religious nationalism even while their historic homeland was divided, redivided, and ruled by many different overlords over the course of the complex history of the Caucuses.

In Ireland a very different kind of Christianity took form. Christianity was planted in Ireland in the early 400s by Palladius, a missionary from Gaul (France) who worked mainly in the south, and by Patrick, a Briton who worked mainly in the north. Palladius and Patrick intended to introduce a kind of standard-brand Roman Christianity to the island, but a much more particular brand actually took root in the region. Irish ethnicity and ways of life reshaped Irish Christianity into a new form of faith that was organized along the lines of social clans, monasticism, and open air preaching, and that merged the earthiness of Irish culture into the often other-worldly faith of Rome. Even today Celtic Christianity maintains its own distinctive sense of spirituality, a tribute to Ireland's unique blend of ethnicity and faith.

Yet a third distinct style of ethnic Christianity developed nearly half a world away in the Kingdom of Axum (now Ethiopia) in northern Africa. A shipwreck deposited a well-educated Christian named Frumentius on the Axumite coast in the mid-300s. He was taken to the royal court where he rose to high office and gradually introduced Christianity to the leaders of the country. His foundational efforts were built upon by the "nine saints" who arrived in Axum from Syria in the late fifth century (see Plate 28). The miraculous deeds of these nine monks convinced the population as a whole to join the movement. Details are lost in history, but it is clear that the Christianity of Axum quickly developed its own unique style and practices, including Saturday worship. Christianity and Axumite culture eventually merged completely, and despite pressure from Islam the ethnic Christianity of Ethiopia remained the dominant religion of the region until well into the twentieth century.

There are many other examples of local-based, ethnic-centered forms of Christianity that can be identified during these years. For example, the Donatist Church in North Africa that was almost entirely Berber in ethnic composition; several Bedouin subgroups living in the Arabian peninsula became Christian *en masse*; and various "barbarian" nations living along the northern border of the Roman Empire (e.g., Goths and Vandals) adopted Arian Christianity as their national faith in the mid-fourth century as a result of the efforts of the Roman missionary Ulfilas (310–83). All of these groups deserve a place in the global history of the Christian movement.

At the end of its first five centuries of existence, Christianity had made an impressive start for a new religion. It had not only survived, but had consolidated its core convictions in the creation of the Christian Bible and in the articulated creeds of the movement. And it had become a world religion in the then known world, with followers spread all across the Afro-Eurasian land mass. Yet not all the signs were positive. The Roman Empire, the home of most of the world's Christians, seemed on the brink of dissolution. Christians in Persia had survived a period of horrible persecution and had emerged surprisingly strong, but no one knew if the persecution was truly at an end. And the variety of smaller Christian churches or movements that had emerged remained just that, small and fragile experiments in Christian faith. Despite its very strong start, Christianity's future remained uncertain in the year 500.

Notes

1 John H. Leith (ed.), *Creeds of the Churches: A Reader in Christian Doctrine from the Bible to the Present* (Richmond, VA: John Knox Press, 1973), p. 23.

2 Ibid., pp. 30–1.

3 Quoted in Samuel Hugh Moffett, *A History of Christianity in Asia* (New York: HarperCollins, 1992), p. 130.

Suggestions for Further Reading

Baumer, Christoph (2006). *The Church of the East: An Illustrated History of Assyrian Christianity*. London: I. B. Taurus.

Casiday, Augustine and Frederick W. Norris (eds) (2007). *Cambridge History of Christianity: Volume 2, Constantine to c.600*. Cambridge, UK: Cambridge University Press.

Erhman, Bart D. (2003). *Lost Scriptures: Books That Did Not Make It Into the New Testament*. New York: Oxford University Press.

Esler, Philip F. (ed.) (2000). *The Early Christian World* (2 vols). New York: Routledge.

Freeman, Charles (2009). *A New History of Early Christianity*. New Haven, CT: Yale University Press.

Frend, W. H. C. (1984). *The Rise of Christianity*. Philadelphia: Fortress Press.

Grillmeier, Aloys (1975). *Christ in Christian Tradition: From the Apostolic Age to Chalcedon (451)*, 2nd edn, trans. John Bowden. Atlanta, GA: John Knox.

Harmless, William (2004). *Desert Christians: An Introduction to the Literature of Early Monasticism*. Oxford: Oxford University Press.

Johnson, Luke Timothy (2009). *Among the Gentiles: Greco-Roman Religion and Christianity*. New Haven, CT: Yale University Press.

McDonald, Lee Martin and James A. Sanders (eds) (2002). *The Canon Debate*. Peabody, MA: Hendrickson.

Mitchell, Margaret M. and Francis M. Young (eds) (2006). *The Cambridge History of Christianity, Volume 1: Origins to Constantine*. Cambridge, UK: Cambridge University Press.

Moffett, Samuel Hugh (1992). *A History of Christianity in Asia: Beginnings to 1500*. New York: HarperCollins.

Rubenstein, Richard E. (1999). *When Jesus Became God: The Struggle to Define Christianity During the Last Days of Rome*. New York: Harcourt.

Stark, Rodney (2006). *Cities of God: The Real Story of How Christianity Became an Urban Movement and Conquered Rome*. New York: HarperOne.

Wilken, Robert Louis (2003). *The Spirit of Early Christian Thought: Seeking the Face of God*. New Haven, CT: Yale University Press.

Chapter 15

The Great Division and the Age of the East

500 to 1000

As the fifth century came to a close, the historic consensus of the Christian movement, as embodied in the Ancient Tradition, was under severe strain. The Christian Roman Empire had been functioning as the Ancient Tradition's great defender, but that supportive role was becoming increasingly difficult to maintain since the Empire itself was beginning to crumble. The West – meaning the Latin-speaking western half of the old Roman Empire – had already been lost to invading barbarian tribes, and the eastern half of the Empire was already far along the path toward becoming the smaller and entirely Greek-speaking Byzantine Empire. In the mid-seventh century, the size of the Byzantine Empire would shrink even further in response to Islamic growth and expansion.

Well before Islam came on the scene, however, the early Christian movement had lost much of the connectedness it had enjoyed in the fourth and fifth centuries. In fact, the sixth century became one of the most important watersheds in Christian history as the Ancient Tradition of the early centuries underwent a "Great Division," producing four new and distinct Christian subtraditions: Orthodox, Miaphysite, Church of the East, and Catholic. Two of these groups – the Catholic and the Orthodox – are still quite prominent today; the other two are largely unknown because they were devastated in the fourteenth century and have never recovered. During the years under examination here (500–1000), however, these two traditions – the Miaphysite and the Church of the East – were major players in the unfolding history of Christianity.

The Great Division took place in two stages (see Figure 15.1). The first stage occurred during the sixth century, and it was relatively dramatic. During this first phase, the Church of the East, which was centered in Persia, and the newly formed Miaphysite tradition, located mainly in Syria and Egypt (see Figure 15.2), established their complete independence both from each other and from the Imperial Church of the Roman Empire. The cause of this division was largely theological: the Imperial Church continued to defend the creed

The World's Christians: Who they are, Where they are, and How they got there, First Edition. Douglas Jacobsen.
© 2011 Douglas Jacobsen. Published 2011 by Blackwell Publishing Ltd.

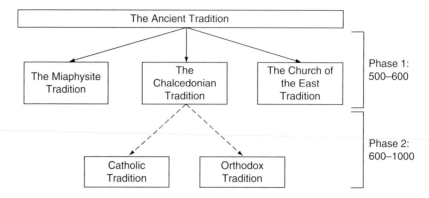

Figure 15.1   The Great Division

that had been issued by the Council of Chalcedon – a creed that was supposed to make the Ancient Tradition permanent – while the Church of the East and the Miaphysite tradition rejected that creed, each for different reasons. Thus three new traditions were in place by the close of this first stage of the Great Division: the Miaphysite, the Church of the East, and the Chalcedonian tradition.

The second stage of the Great Division was a much slower process with very little of the obvious contentiousness that had defined the first. It took place entirely within the movement's Chalcedonian wing and was characterized by the slow drifting apart of the eastern (Latin-speaking) and western (Greek-speaking) halves of the old Roman Imperial Church. The majority of Christians in both of these regions continued to affirm the theological conclusions pronounced at the Council of Chalcedon, but over time that shared affirmation lost the power to hold the two wings of the old Imperial Church together. The causes of this drift were as much sociological as they were theological. The historical experiences of these two regions were very different from each other – social chaos in the West and imperial continuity in the East – and they produced different spiritual needs. There was no single watershed event to signal a final break between them, but well before the year 1000 the "Catholic" tradition of the West and the "Orthodox" tradition of the Byzantine Empire had gone their separate ways.

In addition to the Great Division, the other major development that took place during this era was the rise of Islam. The impact of Islam on the history of Christianity has been immense. Islam began in the early 600s when the Prophet Muhammad began receiving revelations from Allah – revelations that would later be recorded in the *Quran* – and it soon became the fastest growing religious movement the world had ever seen. By the early 700s, the followers of Islam had conquered all of North Africa, all of the Middle East (including Persia), and almost all of the Iberian Peninsula. Within these conquered territories, many of which had formerly been part of the Christian Roman Empire, the status of Christianity changed suddenly from being the favored religion to being merely a tolerated religion.

Many Christians found it difficult to adjust to the new landscape, especially Christians associated with the Imperial Church of the Byzantine (Eastern Roman) Empire. They were used to being in charge and were unsettled by their loss of power. But some Christian

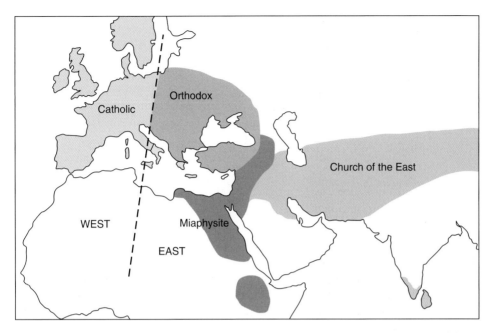

Figure 15.2   Christian "East" and "West" and the general geographic locations of the four major traditions, 500–1000. Map by author.

communities welcomed the arrival of Muslim rule. This was the case, for example, in many parts of Syria and Egypt where Miaphysite Christians had been bitterly persecuted by the Byzantine state. Members of the Church of the East, located mostly in religiously Zoroastrian Persia, also welcomed Muslim rule. In Persia, Christianity had never been more than a tolerated religion, and Christians found Muslim rule generally less oppressive than Zoroastrian rule. The regional expansion of Islam had one other benefit for Christians: by conquering large regions of formerly Christian territory and separating the competing Christian factions that had emerged during the first stage of the Great Division, Islam likely reduced the amount of Christian versus Christian violence that otherwise might have taken place.

Because so much of the action that took place during this period occurred in the East, it seems only reasonable to call these years collectively the "Age of the East." The "East" in the history of Christianity refers to all the lands east of a line roughly extending from Finland in the north to the "heel" of Italy in the south (see Figure 15.2). The "West" was a considerably smaller area, confined to what is now known as Western Europe. Between the years 500 and 1000, the West was experiencing a period of significant social and political disorder, so much so that this period of Western history is sometimes called the "Dark Ages." The West also lagged behind the East in terms of religious developments, since the Catholic tradition was only slowly coming to see itself as an independent Christian tradition during the period.

Convictions

The Council of Chalcedon (451) was supposed to have consolidated the Ancient Tradition for all time, yet less than a century later the theological common ground of the ancient church had crumbled and been replaced with a new divided terrain. The flashpoint for division was exactly what Chalcedon had tried to resolve: the relationship between the human and the divine in the person of Christ. Each of the four new traditions – Church of the East, Miaphysite, Orthodox, and Catholic – held its own distinctive and slightly different understanding of Christology, but these sometimes seemingly minor differences of theology often pointed toward much deeper divisions among the groups that existed on the level of Christian practice and spirituality.

The Church of the East, which is sometimes called the "Nestorian Church," took many of its main theological cues from Nestorius (386–451), who served as Patriarch of Constantinople for three years from 428 to 431 before being removed from office for his Christological views. He tended to emphasize the human side of Christ more than the divine, and the Church of the East followed suit. The Miaphysite tradition adopted the opposite approach, stressing the divinity of Christ much more than his humanity. The emerging Orthodox and Roman Catholic traditions were both originally defined by their loyalty to the doctrinal formula of the Council of Chalcedon, but each of these traditions also added its own new emphases. In the Orthodox East, the leaders of the Orthodox tradition were seeking to expand the thin consensus of Chalcedon into a much larger theological worldview than the original framers of the document had imagined; and in the Catholic West, the Chalcedonian formulation was amended by adding a short new clause to the Creed redefining the relationship between Christ and the Holy Spirit. Given the divisions that existed among these groups, the core convictions of each have to be explained separately.

The Church of the East

The Church of the East had become quasi-independent well before the year 500, partly because it spoke its own language (Syriac) and was immersed in its own culture (Persian). But the Christians of Persia had also become uneasy with certain emphases within the Ancient Tradition. For example, when the leaders of the Ancient Tradition condemned the views of Nestorius at the Council of Ephesus in 431 – views that were generally held in favor by Persian Christians – the Church of the East took offense. Despite that, the Church of the East tried to maintain some sense of theological fellowship with the Orthodox Church of Byzantium, even going so far as to change some of its own religious phraseology at a council held in 544 to bring it generally more in line with the wording of the Council of Chalcedon. But when the Second Council of Constantinople, held in 553, condemned another theological hero of the Church of the East, Theodore of Mopsuestia, cooperation ended. After that, there was no turning back, and the Church of the East went its own independent way.

Theologically, the Church of the East stressed the humanity of Jesus both as necessary for the salvation of humankind and as a model for how Christians themselves were supposed to live. The divinity of Christ was never forgotten, but the distinctive emphasis of this tradition was on the human side. Giwargis (George) I, the Catholicos (ecclesiastical head) of the Church of the East from 661 to 680, explained that it was Christ the human who demonstrated to other humans that they too could someday overcome sin and death and could rise to life eternal with God, saying:

> If Christ had not been truly human and accepted death in his humanity for our sake – being innocent of sin – and had not God who is in him raised him up, it would not have been possible for us sinners, condemned to death, to acquire hope of resurrection from the dead; for if it had been God who died and rose – in accordance with the wicked utterance of the blasphemers – then it would only be God, and those who are innocent, like him, who would be held worthy of the resurrection.[1]

Some other Church of the East leaders were even more creative in their explanations of the life and work of Jesus. Catholicos Timothy I (in office 780–823), for example, argued that Christ "paid to God the debt of all the creatures"[2] before he was baptized by John the Baptist, and then the rest of his life – the three years recorded in the Gospels including the crucifixion – were devoted strictly to showing his disciples how they as human beings should live and worship God.

The humanity of Christ also provided a model of how the presence of God – the filling of the Holy Spirit – could be experienced by Christian believers. In the same way that Jesus became Christ (the anointed one) through a special anointing by God, individual Christians could enjoy a similar, though not quite identical, anointing or filling of the Holy Spirit in their own lives. John of Dalyatha (c. 690–780), one of the most famous monks in the Church of the East tradition, described this anointing of God's Spirit in almost Pentecostal terms, saying it was like fire, love, and intoxication all mixed together: "Love bursts forth within the heart, and the heart becomes hot, so that it kindles and burns the whole body with the force of [God's] love. … I have frequently heard … the brethren crying out when … in the intoxication of Christ's love."[3]

This vision of divine love prompted the Church of the East to became one of the most missionary-minded churches in Christian history. Evangelism by the Church of the East was distinguished by its genuine sense of concern for others. No one expressed this attitude more eloquently than the monk Isaac of Nineveh (also known as Isaac the Syrian) who died around the year 700. For Isaac, the goal of the Christian life was to obtain a merciful heart, the same merciful heart that Jesus possessed, full of love for

> all of creation, for men, for birds, for animals, and even for demons. At the remembrance and at the sight of them, the merciful man's eyes fill with tears which arise from the great compassion that urges his heart. It grows tender and cannot endure hearing or seeing any injury or slight sorrow to anything in creation. Because of this, such a man continually offers tearful prayer even for irrational animals and for the enemies of truth and for all who harm it, that they may be guarded and forgiven.[4]

In addition to emphasizing love and mercy, the Church of the East also developed a style of theology that allowed them to engage others with an openness that was unusual for the time. Following the insights of Theodore of Mopsuestia (350–428), the Church of the East asserted that all human beings possess a significant capacity to do good, even though they are fallen and prone to sin. This attitude allowed them to be less judgmental of others than many Christian groups. The Church of the East also developed its own distinctive method of biblical interpretation, reading the Bible as a historical document describing a series of very particular events through which God was revealing moral and spiritual truth to human-kind. Rather than picturing the Christian tradition as possessing all truth for all time, the Church of the East saw itself as being the caretaker of a set of historically revealed ideas about God and the world that, while true, were not necessarily complete. This open-ended understanding of the relationship between truth and the Christian message had a dramatic impact on how the Church of the East related to members of non-Christian religions.

The Miaphysite tradition

The Miaphysite tradition, like the Church of the East, had roots that predated the Council of Chalcedon, going back to Cyril of Alexandria (378–444), one of the great champions of the full divinity of Christ in the years leading up to Chalcedon. The main Christological emphasis of the Miaphysite tradition was that Christ was God. Miaphysite Christians believed that Christ had a human body and even a human mind and soul, but in some sense that was beside the point. It was Christ's divinity that mattered. The term *miaphysite* means "one nature," and Miaphysites affirmed that the human and the divine had merged together in Christ into one nature – a combined human–divine essence in which the glory of divin-ity thoroughly outshone the comparatively miniscule light of Christ's humanity. Miaphysite Christians were convinced that the Chalcedonian Creed had erred in its (to their way of thinking) overemphasis on the duality of Christ's human and divine characteristics. For Miaphysites, it was God who walked the earth in Christ, not just a man. It was God who suffered on the cross. And somehow God had even experienced death as part of the process of saving humankind.

Saying that God had suffered or that God had died was shocking to many Christians. Severus of Antioch (465–518), the most articulate theologian of the early Miaphysite move-ment, tried to explain the Miaphysite position by saying that God's experience of pain and death was a free decision and not a necessity. He said that, in Christ, God was:

> united to a body with a rational and intelligent soul, but he permitted it to suffer naturally from the blows of pain … on the cross, when he might have deadened these also as God, but he was not desirous of this, for it was not for himself, but for our race, that he was purchasing the suc-cesses of victory. Therefore he permitted his body to suffer, while even he himself also was not alien from suffering, for he was united to a suffering body … He is said also to have tasted death for us … for he went down into Sheol with his soul.[5]

According to this Miaphysite view of salvation, humankind could not be freed from the grip of death unless God somehow experienced the pain of death and then destroyed death from the inside out through his own divine resurrection. No mere mortal could overcome death in that way; only God could, and God did that in Christ.

Most Christians who identified themselves with the Miaphysite tradition lived within the boundaries of the Byzantine state, and their views about God's suffering sounded like heresy to most leaders of the Byzantine Imperial Church. In the mid-sixth century, the pro-Chalcedonian Byzantine Emperor Justinian (527–65) launched a massive campaign designed to either convert Miaphysites back to Orthodoxy or drive them out of the empire. The persecution was severe, including the execution of some Miaphysite leaders, but rather than undercutting Miaphysite resolve, the violence made them more determined. In Egypt, the Patriarch Theodosius I left the Orthodox Church in the year 536 to become the first pope of the Miaphysite Coptic Church. The division became more widespread under the leadership of Jacob Baradeus, the Metropolitan of the Church at Edessa (near the Persian border). Over the course of three decades traveling secretly around the Byzantine Empire to avoid arrest – and with more than a little help from the Empress Theodora, who opposed her husband Justinian's anti-Miaphysite policies – Jacob managed to ordain thousands of new Miaphysite priests and deacons, more than two dozen bishops, and two patriarchs. By the time of his death in the year 578, a whole new Miaphysite church hierarchy had been established, and the split with Chalcedonian Christianity had become final.

Miaphysitism was especially strong in Egypt, perhaps because it rebutted the antidivine views of Arius that had been popular in Egypt in earlier years. But the Miaphysite movement also gained a significant following in Ethiopia (through the influence of Egypt), in Syria, and later in Armenia where the Armenian Church formally adopted a Miaphysite understanding of Christ at the Second Council of Dvin in the year 554. Given the geographic expansiveness of the movement, its largely underground character, and its no-compromise, protest-oriented mentality, the Miaphysite tradition had a hard time remaining institutionally united. Miaphysite leaders often criticized each other for differing on various fine points of doctrine or for being insufficiently dogmatic in their opposition to Chalcedonian Orthodoxy. By the end of the sixth century as many as 20 incompatible Miaphysite subgroups had emerged. But after this initially fractious period, the movement entered an era of consolidation. In the end, four churches emerged as the main carriers of the Miaphysite tradition: the Coptic Orthodox Church of Egypt, the Ethiopian Orthodox Church, the Syrian Orthodox Church (which is sometimes also called the Jacobite or West Syriac Church), and the Armenian Apostolic Church. All of these churches remain in existence today.

The Orthodox tradition

The Christians who ultimately aligned themselves with the emerging Orthodox tradition saw themselves as simply carrying forward the Ancient Tradition of the Chalcedonian Creed. But no tradition is written in stone – cultures change even when change comes slowly – and in the early seventh century these Orthodox Christians were slowly awakening to the fact that their own convictions had begun to develop beyond (but not in opposition to) the formulas of Chalcedon. A key event in this coming to consciousness was a dispute with the Byzantine Emperor Heraclius, who ruled from 610 to 641. Byzantium was at war with Persia, and Heraclius decided to try to broker a compromise agreement between the Chalcedonian and Miaphysite Christians of his realm in order to strengthen the unity of the empire for battle. His new proposal was called "monothelitism" (meaning "one will"), and the hope was that it would transcend and heal the Chalcedonian–Miaphysite divide. Monothelitism affirmed the two natures of Christ (human and divine), but then argued that these two natures were expressed through a single shared will, so functionally Christ's natures were merged even though technically they remained separate. Heraclius thought this was a brilliant compromise, but, as is often the case with compromises that are dictated from the top down, the new formula satisfied no one. Heraclius finally had to resort to force in an attempt to get everyone to agree, but the use of violence just hardened the resistance of both Chalcedonians and Miaphysites.

The most eloquent antimonothelite spokesperson for the Chalcedonian (Orthodox) faction was Maximus (580–662), who is also known as "Maximus the Confessor." Maximus received this title because he continued to confess the convictions of his faith, rejecting Heraclius's new "heresy," even after he was arrested and tortured by having his right hand severed and his tongue cut out. Maximus was firm in his conviction that the doctrine of one will was a denial of the full humanity of Christ and was therefore inconsistent with the standard of Christology set forth in the Chalcedonian Creed. For Maximus, the "hypostatic union" of the human and the divine in Christ – which involved union without merger or "confusion" – was the key not only for understanding the person of Jesus, but also for understanding the fundamental structure of reality.

Maximus believed that somehow the whole created order – everyone and everything in the universe – was potentially, and in many ways was already, hypostatically united with God in a manner that paralleled the divine–human union that existed in Christ. For Maximus, God was present everywhere, human life existed within a divine plan that included the whole universe, and the limited (creation) and the limitless (the Creator) were mysteriously bound together.

In this union, the created world remained the created world and God remained God, but somehow the two came together in a way that made possible not just the redemption of humankind, but the redemption of the whole universe. At present, that mystery was visible only in the life of Christ, but someday the full "mystery of Christ" would be plainly revealed for all to see. Maximus explained:

> Because of Christ – or rather, the whole mystery of Christ – all the ages of time and the beings within those ages have received their beginning and end in Christ. For union between a limit of the ages and limitlessness, between measure and immeasurability, between finitude and infinity, between Creator and creation, between rest and motion, was conceived before the ages. … For truly he who is the Creator of the essence of created beings by nature had also to become the very Author of the deification of creatures by grace … and in the future he will by grace confer on those created beings the knowledge of what they themselves and other beings are in essence.[6]

For Maximus, the salvation effected by Christ – the action that reconciled God and human-kind – was found in the Incarnation itself, the union of the human and divine that was embodied in Jesus of Nazareth. A century later, this same theme re-emerged in slightly different form during another conflict between the Orthodox tradition and the Byzantine state, which is known as the Iconoclastic Controversy. Icons are religious paintings of Christ,

Mary (*Theotokos*), figures from the Bible, and saints from various ages, and they had become popular objects of veneration within the Chalcedonian Byzantine Church. In 730, however, the Emperor Leo III banned the veneration of these images. The Empire had lost considerable territory to the armies of Islam, and Leo decided that God was punishing the empire for the sin of idolatry and was perhaps favoring the Muslim army because Islam banned the use of human images in art. Leo hoped that God would grant him victory in battle if he destroyed all the idolatrous icons in his realm.

Those who, with Leo, opposed the veneration of icons were called iconoclasts (icon destroyers) while supporters were known as iconophiles (icon lovers). The most outspoken iconophile was Manṣūr ibn Sarjūn (676–749) – known in the West as John of Damascus – who lived outside the Byzantine Empire in Muslim-held territory where he could publish his views without fear of arrest. Manṣūr's defense of the icons was based on the mystery of the Incarnation as articulated by Maximus, but it was expressed in much simpler form. He wrote:

> In former times God, who is without form or body, could never be depicted. But now when God is seen in the flesh conversing with men, I make an image of the God whom I see. I do not worship matter; I worship the Creator of matter who became matter for my sake, who willed to take His abode in matter; who worked out my salvation through matter.[7]

The veneration of icons was valid because God's union with humankind in Christ had sanctified not merely Christ's body, but all matter – everything from flesh and blood to the paint used for the icons. Even if the masses of Orthodox believers did not fully understand the complicated theology behind this, the practice of venerating icons gave them a lived sense of participating in the mystery of salvation as both Maximus and Manṣūr described it.

Theologically, the Iconoclastic Controversy came to an end at the Second Council of Nicaea (787) when the Orthodox Church affirmed the veneration of icons. The political conclusion of the episode had to wait another half century, until 843, when the Empress Theodora finally placed the full power of the state behind the declaration of the council. This conclusion of the Iconoclastic Controversy became known as the "Triumph of Orthodoxy" (see Plate 29). This affirmation of the iconophile position can also be seen as the coming of age of the Orthodox tradition as a whole, and Orthodox churches around the world celebrate that fact every year when they commemorate the Triumph of Orthodoxy on the first Sunday of Great Lent (six weeks before Easter or "Pascha" as it is called in the Orthodox tradition). The theology of Orthodoxy that was developed between the years 600 and 850 continues to define the attitudes and spirituality of Orthodox Christianity around the world today.

The slowly emerging Catholic tradition

While the three Eastern traditions were busy declaring their independence from each other and defining their differences, Christians in the western half of the old Roman Empire were trying simply to keep their faith alive. The West had been overrun by non-Roman armies in the fifth century and, despite a very serious effort by the Emperor Justinian to retake the region in the mid-sixth century, Roman rule was never restored. As the macrostructures of society collapsed, localism became the norm. A variety of petty monarchs, many of them simply local warlords, marked off pockets of territory under their control. In this unsettled era, Christians in the West had little time or opportunity for conscious tradition building. Still, some of the developments that took place during these five hundred years paved the way for the subsequent full coalescence of the Catholic tradition in the eleventh, twelfth, and thirteenth centuries.

One of the most important developments during this time was the increasingly centralized leadership of the Western, Latin-speaking church in the office of the Bishop of Rome, who is also known as the Pope. The old Roman Imperial Church had been overseen by a Pentarchy of Patriarchs, the bishops of the five most important Christian cities in the Empire (Rome, Alexandria, Antioch, Jerusalem, and Constantinople). Almost from the beginning, the Bishop of Rome had played a special role within the Christian movement. Rome was the capital of the Empire and, therefore, the most important Roman city. Furthermore, the Bishop of Rome was considered to be the successor of Peter, the head of the 12 disciples who had worked alongside Jesus. As long as the Roman Empire included both the East and West, the role of the Pope as the "vicar of Peter" was held in check by the prestige and power of the bishops of the other major Roman cities in the Pentarchy. When communication between East and West decreased, however, the leadership claims of the bishops of Rome escalated, becoming more strident and less collegial because there really was no one with whom he could or had to consult. The claim that the Pope is the rightful head of the entire world Christian movement would later became a core belief within the Roman Catholic tradition, even though the Orthodox Church and many other Christians have never accepted that claim.

The emerging Catholic identity of the Western church is also evident in the addition of the word *filioque* to the Nicene Creed as it was typically recited in the liturgy of the Eucharist. The Latin word *filioque* means "and the Son." The original wording of the Creed said that the Holy Spirit (the third member of the Christian Trinity) proceeded from the Father. The addition of *filioque* changed the Creed to say that the Spirit proceeded from the Father *and the Son*. This change was first made in Spain in the year 589, when the Visigothic Kingdom was in the midst of converting from Arian Christianity to Catholic Christianity, and it may have been added as a way of underscoring the full divinity of Christ (a belief that was denied by Arian Christians). Whatever the possible theological reasons for the change, what was more significant in historical perspective was the fact that the change was made without any consultation with the Orthodox churches in the East. Prior to this time, any change in the wording of a major creed would have been seen as requiring universal (both Eastern and Western) Christian agreement. Failure to consult before making this change was an affront to the Orthodox Christians of the East, which formally condemned the addition at the Fourth Council of Chalcedon held in 879–80, but it was simultaneously a sign that the Western church was coming to see itself as religiously independent from the East.

The spiritual orientations of the East and West were also diverging during these years with regard to their conceptions of human nature and salvation. In particular, the West was adopting a much more pessimistic view of human nature than was common in the East.

Perhaps it was the social unsettledness of the region that gave rise to this way of thinking, but the writings of Augustine of Hippo, the fifth-century North African bishop, also played a major role. Augustine had lived through the first "barbarian" invasion of the West, and he had become convinced that every human being is born corrupted by "original sin" and totally estranged from God. Eastern Christianity had a relatively more positive evaluation of human nature and humanity's relationship with God, and it was this gut-level difference of spirituality, as much as any formal institutional or theological differences, that slowly drove the East and the West apart.

Encounters

The world changed significantly during the years 500 to 1000, and Christianity changed with it. One of the most disruptive and creative developments of the period was the rise of Islam. Islam redrew the map of the world. Within a century and a half of the death of Muhammad, Islamic armies had subjugated all of Persia and most of Central Asia, decimated the Byzantine Middle East, conquered North Africa and Spain, and almost overrun France on the way to creating the largest empire the world had ever seen (see Figure 15.3). As millions of Christians were engulfed by this new Islamic Empire, they struggled to develop new ways of practicing their faith in a thoroughly altered social environment.

At roughly the same time, the great *Völkerwanderung* – the "wandering of people" – was taking place in Europe. The Goths arrived in the 400s, and a host of other Slavic and Germanic groups – Alans, Angles, Bulgars, Franks, Frisians, Huns, Khazars, Russians, Sabirs, Saxons, Suevi, and others – followed in their wake, cramming into the region like commuters into a subway car, jostling each other for space to breathe. The main influx was over by about 800, but then the Vikings of Norway began to ransack the coastal settlements of Europe and (in the tenth century) the Magyars of Hungary began the plundering by horseback of the inland towns of the continent. The resulting map of Europe was highly fragmented – little kingdoms and principalities were created everywhere – but Western Europe was becoming simpler with regard to religion. While almost none of these European newcomers had been Christians when they arrived, almost all of them had become Christians by the year 1000, with the Vikings and the Magyars being among the last to convert.

Meanwhile, the Church of the East was expanding its sphere of influence toward Asia and interacting with the religions of the Far East. That contact contributed to a flourishing of Persian Christian literature and to an extension of Christian missionary activity all the way to China. Taken together, the rise of Islam, the wandering people in Europe, and the opening of communication between Europe and Asia led to a massive shift in the global balance of power, altering the experiences and identities of people all over the world. The impact on Christianity varied according to locale. In some places conditions for Christians improved; in other places, life became considerably more difficult. Sometimes encountering new religious, political, and cultural realities prompted change within the Christian movement, and sometimes the encountering of difference hardened existing Christian identities.

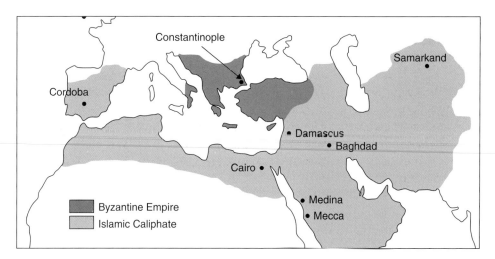

Figure 15.3   Byzantine and Arab Empires, c. 800. Map by author.

Encountering Islam

Muhammad, the founder of Islam, was born around 570 and died in the year 632. When he was 40 years old, he began receiving the revelations from Allah that would later be collected in the *Quran*. Taking a stand for strict monotheism, in opposition to the historical polytheism of the Arab Bedouin tribes, Muhammad preached a message that combined religious piety and social policy in a seamless approach to life that centered on submission to the will of God. After initially meeting resistance, he was eventually successful in uniting the warring tribes of Arabia into a disciplined and committed Muslim *ummah* (community). Agreeing to refrain from warfare among themselves, the Muslim tribes of Arabia began raiding the neighboring nations – standard international relations for the times – and suddenly they found themselves conquering huge tracts of land from the Byzantine and Persian Empires that were exhausted from years of battling each other. Much of that land was filled with Christians.

At first, the lives of Christians in the new Islamic Empire changed relatively little, with the exception of a list of rules designed to minimize the public visibility of the church. For example, Christians were forbidden from displaying the cross in public, and they were told to keep their church bells silent. From time to time, a church building might also be seized and turned into a mosque for Muslim prayers, but generally Christians themselves were not abused. According to the *Quran*, Christians (along with Jews) were *Ahl al-Kitāb* ("people of the book"), and as such they were free to practice their own religion. Because they were non-Muslims, they were required to pay an extra tax (*jizya*) to the new Islamic state – a financial burden that even in the earliest days of Muslim rule encouraged some Christians to convert to Islam – but during the early years of Islamic Empire the leadership generally discouraged conversion. This was especially the case during the largely Arab-run Umayyad Caliphate (661–750).

That policy changed to some degree under the Abbasid Caliphate (750–1258), which was multinational in character, rather than being simply Arab, and was deeply concerned about how to maintain a sense of cohesion within its large and diverse empire. The policy of the Abbasids was to unite the Caliphate on a foundation of shared faith rather than Arab culture, and obviously Islam was that faith. What this meant for Christians was that the pressure to convert suddenly intensified, and bowing to that pressure many Christians did in fact become Muslim. (Obviously some Christians converted for purely religious reasons, finding Islam a superior religion, but social pressure was always part of the mix.) While local patterns of Christian decline varied, the total Christian population in the conquered territories soon dropped significantly. By year 1000, Christians probably made up only about half of the population in the Muslim territories that had formerly been under Christian rule.

In these Muslim-ruled lands, Christians (who were classified as *dhimmis*) generally lived in self-contained communities called *millets*. The legal classification of *dhimmi* protected the religious and cultural rights of Christians – they could practice their faith in their *millet* – but it also limited their participation in society as a whole. Christians from different subtraditions were usually organized into separate *millets*, and each *millet* was expected to act like a minigovernment within the state, policing its own population, providing its own education, and being communally responsible for the taxes assigned. The *dhimmi* structure fused religious identity with ethnic or subgroup identity and in doing so it transformed the leadership of the *millet* from a purely religious office into a role that combined faith and politics – and that changed the character of the people who sought the office, for it now appealed to those who sought power and wealth as well as those who felt religiously called to leadership. While the structures of the *dhimmi* system were basically the same everywhere, the three Christian traditions of the East reacted to the experience of Muslim rule quite differently.

The Orthodox experience

The Orthodox tradition tended to view Islam in the same way that it viewed every other alternative religious movement: it was heresy. This position was articulated by Manṣūr ibn Sarjūn (John of Damascus) in his book the *Fount of Knowledge* where he identifies "the superstition of the Ishmaelites" as just one of 103 different heresies that Christians had to guard themselves against. In his brief description of Islam, Manṣūr was curt and rude. He called Muhammad a false prophet and lambasted the *Quran* as full of strange and ridiculous claims.

It is somewhat surprising that Manṣūr was so negative in his assessment of Islam given his own personal history. He had been raised in Damascus, the capital of the Umayyad Caliphate, and his father, who was also a Christian, had been the caliph's chief financial advisor. Manṣūr later inherited that position and served the caliph for a number of years before retiring to become a monk. He knew the Umayyad court well, and he had been treated with respect. Manṣūr also knew that had he been a resident of the Byzantine Empire, his life would likely have been more difficult than it was under Muslim rule. He lived during the most contentious years of the Iconoclastic Controversy, and Manṣūr's pro-icon writings would have been banned in Byzantium. Manṣūr could express his views freely only because the Umayyad Caliphate protected him from arrest by the Byzantine state. But as an Orthodox Christian Manṣūr had deeply internalized the need to resist any and all deviations from the Orthodox way, regardless of whether the fight was against the enemies of the icons or

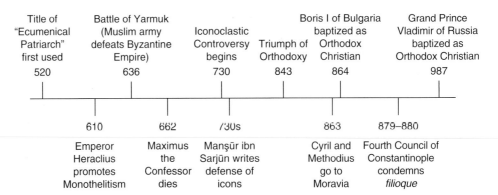

Figure 15.4   Timeline of Orthodox Church in the Byzantine Empire, 500–1000

against his friends and protectors in the Umayyad court. For Manṣūr, truth was truth, and the kindness of heretics did nothing to lessen the error of their ways.

Within the Muslim world, Orthodox Christians were known as Melkite or Rum Christians. Melkite means "of the king" and Rum means "Rome." Both labels were meant to indicate that this particular kind of Christianity was connected with the Byzantine (Roman) Empire and its emperor or king. But despite the fact that Orthodox Christians were verbally associated with an enemy state, Orthodox Christians seemed to have fared no worse under Muslim rule than Miaphysite Christians or members of the Church of the East. While Byzantine Orthodox Christians saw themselves as locked in battle with the new Islamic Empire that had swallowed up much of their former land, the Caliphate apparently viewed the Christians of the Byzantine Empire as only a modest threat.

The growth of Islam led to one very significant institutional development within the Orthodox world itself: the Patriarch of Constantinople gained new status. The Patriarch of Constantinople had already begun calling himself the Ecumenical Patriarch – the Patriarch of the "whole world" – in the late sixth century before the rise of the Islamic Empire. But the Islamic capture of the cities of Alexandria, Antioch, and Jerusalem (the other three eastern patriarchates) meant that Constantinople was the one patriarchate still supported by a Christian Empire. Using that status to his advantage, the Ecumenical Patriarch expanded the definition of his role. The claims of the Ecumenical Patriarch never came close to matching the claims being made by the papacy, but the Ecumenical Patriarchate did become more assertive in its relations to the rest of the Orthodox world, and that was not always appreciated.

The Miaphysite experience

The rule of Islam was generally welcomed by Miaphysite Christians, at least at first, since the Caliphate was less oppressive than the Byzantine Empire, which had been persecuting them for decades. This does not mean that the Miaphysite Christians of Egypt, Syria, and Palestine thought well of their new Islamic overlords. Miasphysites were countercultural Christians, religious resistance fighters seeking to preserve the purity of their own very specific Christian faith in a world where they thought truth and righteousness were always under attack. Islam was clearly part of that attack, so it was viewed negatively even if Islamic rule was better than Byzantine rule.

Miaphysite sectarianism was especially strong in Egypt, where it was wedded to Coptic ethnic identity. The Copts were native Egyptians, the ancient people of the land as opposed to new Greek-speaking or Arabic-speaking immigrants. While some Coptic Christians held positions of prominence, especially in the fields of medicine and finance, the Miaphysite majority was located mainly in the countryside, and this rural character of the movement made it harder for the Muslim leadership to control the community than if it had been concentrated in the cities. Within this rural Christian world, monasticism provided the structure that held the Miaphysite movement together. Rural monasteries often functioned as local banks and grain storage facilities as well as being places of spiritual retreat, and as "full service" organizations they quite naturally became the new centers around which an alternative, resistant-to-conversion Coptic culture developed.

Secure in this separate world, Coptic Christians could be feisty defenders of their own rights. This is reflected in the fact that between the years 725 and 773 there were six Coptic uprisings in Egypt designed not so much to overthrow Muslim rule as to keep that rule within tolerable limits. In the ninth and tenth centuries, the Coptic Christians of Egypt also received aid from their Nubian (Christian) Miaphysite neighbors to the south, especially from Georgios I (King of Nubia 860–920) who is said to have placed the Coptic community under his personal protection. The countercultural attitude of the Coptic church, combined with support from Nubia, helped this particular Miaphysite community resist the pressures of Islam more successfully than most other churches in the region. Although membership eventually declined and the Coptic language fell into disuse (except for liturgical purposes) around the year 1000, the Coptic community remained adamant in defending its faith and civil rights, an attitude that still endures in Coptic Orthodoxy today.

The Church of the East experience
The Church of the East had become used to being a *dhimmi* community long before the Arab conquest of Persia that took place in the mid-seventh century, having existed for centuries as a minority religious body in a Zoroastrian state. The transition to Muslim rule was hardly noticeable except that the conditions of life improved slightly. The Sasanian Empire had barely tolerated Christianity, but the new Muslim leadership viewed Christianity as a kindred faith. The Church of the East may also have been treated with greater respect than other Christians because most Muslims believed the Church of the East's understanding of Christ had some resemblance to their own. Muslims venerate Jesus as a prophet, but not as God incarnate, and the Church of the East's emphasis on Christ's humanity was more palatable to most Muslims than other Christian positions that more strongly emphasized Christ's divinity.

In light of its new and somewhat improved quality of life under Islamic rule, the Church of the East actually blossomed. During the initial years of Muslim governance, its membership grew (primarily as a result of converts from Zoroastrianism, a religion that was viewed in a highly unfavorable light by the new Muslim rulers. New monasteries and churches had to be built to keep up with the growth. The social dynamic changed when the Abbasids came to power. Under increasing pressure to submit to Islam, the Christian population within the Persian heartland began to decline, even though the Church of the East as

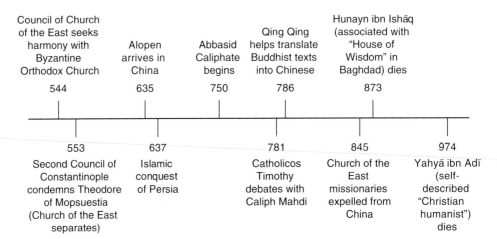

Figure 15.5   Timeline for Church of the East, 500–1000

a whole continued to expand in non-Muslim territory further East. The Christian communities of India and Sri Lanka formally joined the Church of the East network during these years as did new Christian communities as far away as China, Tibet, and the Uighur Khaganate. By the year 1000, the international organization of the Church of the East included more than 70 bishoprics (up from about 45 in the year 500) that were organized into 15 provinces scattered throughout the vastness of Central Asia.

The original language of the Church of the East was Syriac, but in the eighth century – about the same time that the Abbasid Caliphate came into existence and moved the capital of the Muslim world from Damascus to Baghdad – the Christians of Persia began the switch to Arabic. Fluency in Arabic opened a whole new realm of possibilities for relationships between Christians and Muslims. Members of the Church of the East had always been skilled at living side by side with people of other faiths, so negotiating difference was an old habit, but the Abbasid Caliphate's public philosophy of unity added a new urgency to the task. Dialogue with Muslim leaders became a necessary part of trying to keep the practice of "co-living" alive in the region.

Dialogue with the Caliphate could be dangerous. When Christians engaged in conversation with the Abbasid court or the Caliph himself it was like a mouse dancing with a cat, and the Christian mouse knew that the Muslim cat could pounce any time it wanted. Timothy I, who served as Catholicos of the Church of the East from 780 to 823, was given the opportunity to dialogue with the Abbasid Caliph Muhammad ibn Mansur al-Mahdi, who ruled from 775 to 785. Early in his reign, Al-Mahdi had instigated a short but severe persecution of the Church of the East, but he later mellowed and became more accommodating. In general, Al-Mahdi seems to have thought Christianity was both illogical and unnecessarily complicated. He asked Timothy repeatedly why Christians described God as a Trinity instead of simply as one. He asked how Christ could be both human and divine, when it is impossible to be two things at once. He asked why there were four Gospels: could no one get the story straight? And he asked what Christians thought of the Prophet Muhammad.

The last question was obviously the most dangerous for Timothy, but his carefully crafted answer reveals a very different understanding of Islam than was expressed, for example, by Manṣūr ibn Sarjūn who had flippantly denounced Islam as mere heresy. Timothy respectfully said:

> Muhammad is worthy of all praise by all reasonable people, O my Sovereign. He walked in the path of the prophets and trod in the track of the lovers of God. … He turned his face from idols and their worshippers, whether those idols were those of his own kinsmen or strangers, and he honored and worshipped only one God. Because of this God has honored him exceedingly and brought low before his feet two powerful kingdoms [the Roman and Persian Empires] … He further extended the power of his authority through the Commander of the Faithful and his children from east to west and from north to south. Who will not praise, O our victorious King, the one whom God has praised, and will not weave a crown of glory and majesty to the one whom God has glorified and exalted? These and similar things I and all God-lovers utter about Muhammad.[8]

Christians associated with the Church of the East tradition tended to see partial truth in many places and they tried to honor truth wherever it was found. In keeping with that attitude, Timothy gave Muhammad credit for all the good he had done and for the many successes he had achieved. As a Christian, Timothy continued to assert that ultimately Christ's message surpassed the revelation of Muhammad, but he felt no need to diminish the accomplishments of Muhammad.

A similar attitude of respect is present in the writings of other Church of the East Christian scholars who were associated with the House of Wisdom (*Bayt al-Hikma*), a library and translation facility established in Baghdad in the early 800s by the Abassid Calpih al-Ma'mun (813–33). Hunayn ibn Ishīq (808–73) and Yahyā ibn Adī (893–974) are especially noteworthy. These Christian academicians were attracted to the works of Aristotle (which they translated) because they found his concrete, scientific style of philosophy to be more compatible with Church of the East theology than the philosophy of other Greek thinkers like Plato who were more poetic and abstract in their thinking. Aristotle's logic also provided Church of the East Christians with a religiously neutral philosophical platform for talking with Muslim scholars about God and the world – and talk they did. In particular, the open-minded and open-hearted Yahyī ibn Adī, who described himself as a Christian humanist, welcomed fellowship with all other genuine humanists from whatever traditions they might come. His embracing vision of Christian faith and philosophy served the Church of the East well as it sought to defend itself and maintain its standing within Persian society during the later years of Abassid rule.

Encountering Chinese culture and religion

Church of the East Christians had been living in what is now part of far western China (the cities of Kashgar and Turpan) since before 500, but the first planned evangelistic endeavor took place in 635 when a monk named Alopen (likely a Chinese transliteration of "Abraham") arrived in the capital of the Tang Empire, Chang'an (modern Xi'an). The Tang Dynasty ruled China from 618 to 907, and it was huge both in numbers, with a population approaching 80 million, and in territory, including almost all of present-day China. China was the trade capital of the world, and emissaries from other nations were constantly coming to Chang'an seeking to establish amicable relations with the Empire. Alopen likely traveled to China as a member of that kind of trade delegation from Persia, but his personal goals were religious.

Alopen was apparently well received by the Chinese government, and within just a few years of arriving he had received approval to construct Christian monasteries throughout the whole of China. No one knows how many monasteries were actually built, but the locations of at least 11 are known. These monasteries were not necessarily large enterprises – some undoubtedly consisted of nothing more than a series of shallow caves dug into the face of a cliff like those found all along the Silk Road – but, however small these monastic communities may have been, they served as seedbeds for further Christian growth. Alopen quickly began the work of translating the Christian message into Chinese. Taking many of his cues from Buddhism, which had arrived in China several centuries before Christianity and had been relatively successful as a missionary religion, Alopen composed a number of Christian *sutras* (short doctrinal treatises written in a literary style borrowed from Buddhism) that were designed to explain the Christian gospel using cultural categories that were familiar to the Chinese people.

In describing the annunciation and birth of Christ, Alopen explained:

> God caused the Cool Breeze to come upon a chosen young woman called Mo Yan, who had no husband, and she became pregnant. The whole world saw this, and understood what God had wrought. … Mo Yan gave birth to a boy and called him Ye Su, who is the Messiah and whose father is the Cool Breeze. … When Ye Su was born, the whole world saw a bright mystery in the Heavens. Everyone saw from their homes a star as big as a wagon wheel.

Alopen not only retold the story of Jesus in a Chinese idiom, he took pains to underscore the universal character of the Christian message. Thus he asserted that God "is in everything and everywhere. Humanity lives only because it is filled with God's life-giving breath. … The sacred spirit of God works in everybody, bringing all to fullness."[9]

Later, Church of the East monks became even more adept in Chinese translation and more engaged in dialogue with other religions, especially Buddhism. In fact, it appears that in the late 700s the Christian monk Qing Qing helped the Buddhist missionary Prajna translate a number of Buddhist texts from Sanskrit into Chinese. Eventually Christianity became known as the "religion of light" or the "luminous religion" and it gained stature as a venerable and respected faith. The liturgical sutra "In Praise of the Three Sacred Powers," which dates from the late eighth century (perhaps written by Qing Qing himself), reflects this increasing sense of Christian at-homeness in Chinese society and its use of the word "Allaha" for God reflects the Church of the East's own encounter with Islam:

> The highest skies are in love with You.
> The great Earth opens its palms in peace.
> Our truest being is anchored in Your Purity.
> You are Allaha: Compassionate Father of the Three.

Everything praises you, sounding its true note.
All the Enlightened chant praises –
Every being takes its refuge in You
And the light of Your Holy Compassion frees us all. …

You live perpetually in light,
the light which enters every sphere.
Yet you have never been seen.
No eye can see Your Form
or Your Unclouded Nature. …

Great Teacher, I stand in awe of the Father.
Great Teacher, I am awed by the Holy Lord.
Great Teacher, I am speechless before the King of the Dharma.
Great Teacher, I am dazzled by the Enlightened Mind –
Great Teacher, you do everything to save us.

Everything looks to You, without thinking.
Shower us with Your Healing Rain!
Help us to overcome, give life to what has withered,
And water the roots of kindness in us.[10]

Even though Christianity seems to have been favorably received by the Chinese, its existence
in the region was relatively short-lived. In the 840s, the Tang Dynasty took an inward turn,
becoming suspicious of everything non-Chinese, and especially of non-Chinese religion.
The Manichaeans were the first to be affected, with the Emperor Wuzong banning them
from China in the year 843. Two years later, the Buddhist, Zoroastrian, and Christian communities were expelled as well. Within a matter of decades, few if any Christians were left in
China. A common explanation for Christianity's rapid demise is that, no matter how positively the Church of the East may have been regarded, it remained a largely foreign faith
practiced mostly by foreign monks and merchants living on Chinese soil. It did not have
deep roots. In reality, however, we know very little about this ancient period of Chinese
Christianity. It is clear that the Church of the East did not establish a permanent presence
in China, but it may be inappropriate to view this effort as a failure. An alternative interpretation would be to understand this engagement as a first experiment in Christian–Chinese
relations, one that revealed a potentially deep compatibility even though it came to a
politically dictated abrupt end in the mid-ninth century.

Encountering the new peoples of Europe

The encounter of Christianity with the new peoples that were streaming into Europe produced two very different stories in the regions that we now call Western and Eastern Europe.
In Western Europe, the process was generally incremental, with small kingdom after small
kingdom slowly turning away from paganism and embracing Catholic Christianity.
Sometimes the mechanism of Christianization was the conversion of the ruler; sometimes
it was the result of the miracle-working feats of wandering monks and missionaries. In
some cases, the Pope was involved in the process; at other times, he was not. Generalizations

are difficult to make. In what is now Eastern Europe, the process of conversion to Christianity was much more political. To become a Christian nation in Eastern Europe almost always entailed entering into some kind of political alliance with the Byzantine Empire. As a result, it was sometimes hard to see the difference between evangelism and diplomacy. In the end, however, the results were largely the same. Almost all of Europe, both East and West, had become Christian by the year 1000.

Western Europe

Christians living in Western Europe before the beginning of the Germanic "invasion" of the region had rarely tried to convert the "uncivilized" people who resided outside the borders of the Empire. Many Roman citizens thought these "barbarians" might, in fact, not be fully human. They were unsure if the gospel really applied to them. There were a few exceptions to this view of things. Ulfilas had evangelized the Goths in the mid-300s and Patrick and Palladius had taken it upon themselves to convert the wild people of Ireland in the 400s, but that was not the norm. After 500, however, more and more Roman Christian citizens found themselves living side by side with "barbarian" people, and those barbarians turned out not to be quite so barbaric after all. As the myth of difference slowly evaporated, the newly arrived and still arriving Germanic people who were flooding into the region became apt candidates for conversion.

A key turning point occurred around the year 600 when Pope Gregory I (590–604) is said to have come across a group of young Angli (Anglo-Saxons from England) who were being sold in the slave market at Rome. In a famous play on words he proclaimed that someone needed to preach the gospel to these "angelic" people of the north. Later, the Pope himself arranged to send a formal mission to King Ethelbert of Kent, located in southeastern England. The papal delegation was led by a monk named Augustine (not Augustine of Hippo, but a friend of Gregory from his prepapal years), and it included more than 40 church dignitaries all decked out in their finest ecclesiastical garb. The King was not entirely ignorant of Christianity because his wife, Bertha, was a Frankish Christian. Soon after meeting with Augustine, Ethelbert formally converted to Christianity and most of his Kentish people followed his example. Augustine subsequently became the first Archbishop of Canterbury – the most important Christian office in the region – and within a century most of England's other small Anglo-Saxon kingdoms had become Christian as well.

Not every nation was converted by pomp and ceremony, however. Some embraced the Christian faith because of the sanctity and wonder-working power of the various holy men and women (mostly monks and nuns) who meandered their way across the continent seeking converts and founding new monasteries. Individuals like Columbanus (540–16), Willibrord (658–739), Boniface (672–754), and Leoba (700–79) amazed ordinary people with their magical powers. Leoba, for example, was revered as a woman who could control violent storms, and Boniface was known for his courage in confronting local gods. Clearly having such people as friends was an advantage for any rulers. And conversion brought other resources too: communities of monks or nuns who could provide spiritual advice, prayers for the prosperity of the region, intellectual power in the form of literary skill, and engineering skills including the ability to clear forests and drain swamps to create new farmland. By the close of the period in the year 1000, virtually all of Western Europe had become at least nominally Christian, with Scandinavians being the last to let go of their ancient pagan traditions.

Whatever the particular pathway to conversion, the process almost always included some accommodation to local religious ideas, practices, and piety. Most varieties of pre-Christian European paganism emphasized the spiritual significance of certain sacred hills or groves of trees. These sacred sites were often selected as locations for the building of new churches, and wood from the trees of the sacred grove was sometimes used to construct the edifice, maintaining the material continuity of the place while simultaneously demonstrating the superior power of the Christian God. Numerous pagan symbols and ideas were incorporated into European Christianity as a way of building bridges of understanding between the old beliefs of a people and their new-found Christian faith. Most missionaries hoped that some day these accommodations could be purged from the churches, but they considered them to be necessary in the short run. As Pope Gregory himself said: "There is no doubt that it is impossible to efface everything at once from their obdurate minds; because he who endeavors to ascend to the highest place, rises by degrees or steps, and not by leaps."[11]

A Christian poem called the "Dream of the Rood," composed around the year 750 by a writer named Caedmon, illustrates the way that pagan sensibilities were used to Christian effect. Listeners who were familiar with the pagan practice of venerating sacred trees would have resonated with the cross – the "tree" or the "rood" on which Christ died – who does the speaking.

> I could have felled, but I stood fast.
> The young hero stripped himself – he, God Almighty –
> strong and stout-minded. He mounted high gallows,
> bold before many, when he would loose mankind.
> I shook when that Man clasped me. I dared, still, not bow to earth,
> fall to earth's fields, but had to stand fast.
> Rood was I reared. I lifted a mighty King,
> Lord of the heavens, dared not to bend.
> With dark nails they drove me through: on me those sores are seen,
> open malice-wounds. I dared not scathe anyone.
> They mocked us both, we two together. All wet with blood I was,
> poured out from that Man's side, after ghost he gave up …
> Now has the time come
> when they will honor me far and wide,
> men over earth, and all this great creation,
> will pray for themselves to this beacon. On me God's son
> suffered awhile. Therefore I, glorious now,
> rise under heaven, and I may heal
> any of those who will reverence me.[12]

By the year 800, the process of conversion was well on its way to completion and the time had come for someone to try to consolidate the Catholic Christians of Western Europe into one common society. All of these Christians already belonged to one church – the Catholic Church, headed by the Pope in Rome – so it seemed sensible to try to unite them within one empire as well. Charlemagne, in cooperation with Pope Leo III (795–816), decided to make the attempt. Born in 742 into the royal Carolingian house, Charlemagne assumed the title

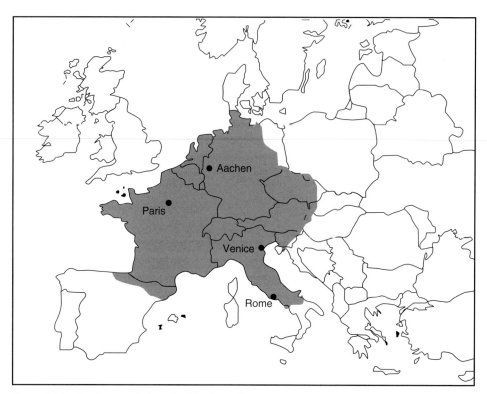

Figure 15.6   Charlemagne's domain. Map by author.

King of the Franks in 768. The Frankish Kingdom was already the largest political entity in Europe, and Charlemagne enlarged it further so that his rule eventually included almost three-quarters of the continental landmass of Western Europe, with his capital in Aachen (see Figure 15.6).

But being a mere king, even of a very large kingdom, was not what Charlemagne wanted. He wanted to revive the Christian Empire in the West and he wanted to rule that domain. That dream took a huge step forward when on Christmas day in 800 Charlemagne, while attending Mass at St Peter's Church in Rome, was crowned "Emperor of the Romans" by Pope Leo III. Charlemagne tried to rule as a good Christian emperor. He reformed the church within his realm, eliminating abuses, creating an efficiently run system of oversight, and improving the education of the clergy. He also entered into negotiation with the Byzantine Empire, hoping to re-establish the old East–West framework of the ancient Roman Empire, though he never did get the full recognition he desired. And he sought to be a good supporter of the papacy.

In the end, however, his empire largely died with him. After his death, the lands Charlemagne ruled were divided among his sons, and the "Holy Roman Empire" became an ever-changing kaleidoscope of glued-together kingdoms and principalities in the general region of what is now Germany, Switzerland, and parts of Italy and France. The Holy Roman Empire continued to be a significant political force in European history, lasting in some form until 1806, but it never became the grand Christian imperial reality Charlemagne had hoped it would become. And yet the dream remained, and the goal of creating a new Christian empire changed the dynamics of church and state relations in Western Europe forever, setting the stage for the ongoing clash of popes and political rulers for centuries to come.

As a Christian emperor, Charlemagne had come to see himself as necessarily exercising authority over both the state and the church in a manner similar to the way Byzantine emperors governed both church and state in the East. The popes, however, believed that God had given them authority over both the church and the state and therefore political power was theirs to dispense as Christ's vicar on earth. From the papal perspective, the proper role of the emperor was to be subservient to the spiritual authority of the pope and to make sure that other rulers followed suit. Tensions between these two views of the Christian state flared up time and time again in the two centuries after Charlemagne's death. Those tensions would not be resolved until the eleventh or twelfth centuries, and even then the solution would only be temporary.

While these political issues are hugely important, the real heart of the Christian movement in Western Europe during the years 500 to 1000 was not found in politics, but in the monasteries. Western monasticism traces its roots to Benedict of Nursia (480–547), who took the relatively extreme views of monasticism as they existed in the East and refitted them for the very different context of the West. In the East – in Egypt and Syria – monasticism had largely been about fleeing the world in order to prove one's spiritual mettle in the wilderness in combat with the devil. The working assumption was that the Christian Empire was a safe place for ordinary Christians, but God's athletes needed something more. In the West, however, that model did not make sense. Society was falling apart, and rather than being schools for spiritual athleticism, monasteries were becoming some of the only islands of order, tranquility, and learning left in the region. When Benedict wrote his monastic "Rule" – a set of guidelines for how local monasteries were to be organized – he had this new situation in mind. Rather than encouraging spiritual extremism, he encouraged moderation, and rather than making everything a matter of pure spirituality, he said monastic life should be defined by its alternating rhythm of work, prayer, rest, and study. During the five hundred years being examined here, it was this practice of moderate monasticism that, more than anything else, allowed Christianity to survive the disruptions of the era. And later, after 1000, it was the Benedictine monastic movement that supplied the energy and ideals that were needed for Catholic Christianity to truly blossom in the high medieval period that followed.

Eastern Europe

The task of evangelizing new immigrants and establishing a Christian political order in the East was very different from that of the West. Christianization in the East was almost always associated with politics, in this case meaning some kind of political alliance with the Byzantine Empire. Sometimes the possibility of an alliance with Byzantium was a positive factor in the process, at other times it was not. The Christian histories of Bulgaria (located just north of Greece), Moravia (located in what is now the Czech Republic), and Russia give a sense of how this Byzantine dynamic could play itself out differently in alternative contexts.

For the Bulgarian Khan (King) Boris I (852–89), the power of the Byzantine Empire was a problem. Boris had decided to convert to Christianity, but he was worried that, given the geographic closeness of his country to Byzantium, conversion to Orthodox Christianity would almost automatically make the Bulgarian people subservient to the Byzantine Empire. Hoping to preserve Bulgarian independence, Boris tried to strike a deal with Rome rather than with Constantinople, so he (and his people) would become Catholic rather than Orthodox. When the Byzantine Emperor Michael III learned of this plan, he quickly amassed an army on the Bulgarian border and blocked the mouth of the Danube with his ships. Cowed by the display of military power, Boris had a change of heart and was baptized into the Byzantine Orthodox Church, with the Emperor Michael III serving as his baptismal godfather.

Baptized or not, Boris still did not like playing second fiddle to the Byzantine Empire, and he hoped that raising the status of the archbishop of Bulgaria to the level of patriarch might help establish Bulgaria's religious and political independence. Soon Boris was again in correspondence with Rome, hoping to persuade the pope to accommodate his plans, and once again the Byzantine emperor managed to disrupt those negotiations. In the end, Bulgaria agreed to banish Catholic clergy from its territory in exchange for having its Orthodox church declared formally "autonomous" from Constantinople – just a notch below the full independence Boris had wanted. This seems to have been a satisfactory compromise, and thereafter Boris welcomed Byzantine missionaries into his lands to help complete the Christianization of his people. Relations between Byzantium and the Bulgarian state remained contentious for centuries, however, and concerns of religious independence were often part of the mix.

A rather different situation existed in the Kingdom of Moravia, located in Central Europe. The threat to Moravian independence did not come from the Byzantine state, but from the aggressive religiopolitical aspirations of Moravia's Frankish Catholic neighbors. The Moravian King Ratislav wrote to Constantinople in the mid-800s asking for spiritual and political assistance. The response – which was undoubtedly less than he hoped for, since Ratislav wanted political as well as religious assistance – was the sending of two Orthodox missionaries, Cyril and Methodius, to translate the Bible into the Slavic language and to help Ratislav's people learn the basic doctrines of Christian faith (see Plate 30). These two missionaries were a gifted pair – they were brothers who had served as diplomats and teachers before becoming monks – but they were unable to assist Ratislav in his attempt to maintain the political and spiritual independence of his realm. The position of the Moravian kingdom continued to weaken in relation to France, and soon the two Orthodox missionaries were forced out of the region by the Frankish clergy. In 864, the Frankish King Louis the German finally invaded the region and subjugated the Moravian people. Ratislav himself was arrested, blinded, and thrown in jail, where he died.

A more successful negotiation, with a far more pleasant ending, took place between Kievan Russia and Byzantium in the late 900s. The Russian people (the Rus) had their origins in Scandinavia, but after settling down among the Slavic tribes along the Dnieper they lost their native language and became part of the Slavic cultural world. Lured by trade with the Byzantine Empire, the Rus slowly migrated south to the region of Kiev, which was located along one of the main trade routes heading out of Constantinople, and by the mid-900s some Russian leaders had been attracted to Christianity as well. One of the most prominent was Olga, the mother of the reigning monarch Svyatoslav and grandmother of

Vladimir, who eventually succeeded to the throne. But while Olga was a Christian, her son and grandson remained solidly pagan. Aware that many of Russia's main trading partners in Scandinavia and Eastern Europe were becoming Christian, the Russian leadership began to wonder if it would be to their advantage to follow suit.

When Vladimir became Grand Prince of the Rus in 977, he was still considering his options. As the story is told, he sent out envoys to examine four possibilities: Western Catholic Christianity, Eastern Orthodox Christianity, Judaism, and Islam. Judaism would require circumcision and Islam would require giving up alcohol, so Vladimir cut his options to either Catholic or Orthodox Christianity. Unimpressed with Catholic worship and overwhelmed by the beauty of Orthodox worship, Vladimir decided to become Orthodox. His conversion seems to have been genuinely religious, but it was also highly political – he was, after all, a grand prince. As part of the price for his conversion, Vladimir negotiated his own marriage to Anna, the sister of the Byzantine Emperor Basil II, and in exchange for her hand he gave back to Basil the Black Sea port city of Cherson, which he had been holding hostage until the marriage was complete. Following his baptism in 987, Vladimir then helped Basil put down an attempted military coup within the Byzantine Empire. He also became an energetic promoter of Christianity in Russia, sometimes to the point of ruthlessness in his fight against paganism. Perhaps not surprisingly his campaign was only modestly successful: only about a dozen Christian churches existed in Russia at the time of his death. Vladimir's son, Jaroslav the Wise (1015–54), was much more successful in establishing Orthodoxy in Russia by persuasion rather than coercion, and he made it the dominant faith of the people.

As the year 1000 approached, Christians around the world, and especially within the Byzantine Empire, must have felt confident that the Christian movement as a whole was in good shape. While the Byzantine emperors still viewed Islam as a threat and still considered the loss of large sections of formerly Christian territory in the Middle East and North Africa a terrible tragedy, Orthodox gains in the north had largely made up for losses in the south. Christians living in Islamic territory were also relatively upbeat. For the Church of the East, Muslim rule was better than Zoroastrian, and for the Miaphysites, life under Islam was generally no worse than Byzantine persecution. Things were not perfect – living under Muslim rule could be a burden – but it was bearable. In the West, it also looked as if the social disruptions of the previous five centuries were coming to an end, and the future looked relatively bright. As the next five centuries unfolded (1000–1500), the hopes of the West would be met and far exceeded, while the experiences of Christians in the East would be much worse than anyone could possibly have imagined.

Notes

1   Quoted in Sebastian Brock, *Fire from Heaven: Studies in Syriac Theology and Liturgy* (Burlington, VT: Ashgate, 2006), p. 175.

2   "Dialogue of Patriarch Timothy I and the Caliph Mahdi," in N. A. Newman (ed.), *The Early Christian-Muslim Dialogue: A Collection of Documents from the First Three Islamic Centuries* (Hatfield, PA: Interdisciplinary Biblical Research Institute, 1993), p. 187.

3   *The Wisdom of the Pearlers: An Anthology of Syriac Christian Mysticism*, trans. with an introduction by Brian E. Colless (Kalamazoo, MI: Cistercian Publications, 2008), pp. 158–9.

4   Isaac of Nineveh, *On the Ascetical Life*, trans. Mary Hansbury (Crestwood, NY: St Vladimir's Seminary Press, 1989), p. 12.

5   Severus of Antioch, "LXV. From the Letter of the Same Holy Severus to Eupraxius the Chamberlain, and about the Questions Which He Addressed to Him," in E. W. Brooks (ed. and trans.), *A Collection of Letters of Severus of Antioch from Numerous Syriac Manuscripts*. Online at http://www.ccel.org/p/pearse/morefathers/severus_coll_3_letters.htm (accessed February 24, 2009).

6   Maximus the Confessor, *On the Cosmic Mystery of Jesus Christ: Selected Writings from St Maximus the Confessor*, trans. Paul M. Blowers and Robert Louis Wilken (Crestwood, NY: St Vladimir's Seminary Press, 2003), pp. 123, 125, 128.

7   John of Damascus, *On the Divine Images: Three Apologies Against Those Who Attack the Divine Images*, trans. David Anderson (Crestwood, NY: St Vladimir's Seminary Press, 1980), p. 23.

8   "Dialogue of Patriarch Timothy I and the Caliph Mahdi" in N. A. Newman (ed.), *The Early Christian-Muslim Dialogue: A Collection of Documents from the First Three Islamic Centuries* (Hatfield, PA: Interdisciplinary Biblical Research Institute, 1993), pp. 218–19.

9   Martin Palmer, *The Jesus Sutras: Rediscovering the Lost Scrolls of Taoist Christianity* (New York: Ballantine, 2001), pp. 159–60, 166.

10 Ibid., pp. 202–4.

11 Bede, *Historia Ecclesiastica* 1.30. Online at http://www.fordham.edu/halsall/basis/bede-book1.html (accessed March 9, 2009).

12 "The Dream of the Rood." Online at http://faculty.uca.edu/jona/texts/rood.htm (accessed March 12, 2009).

Suggestions for Further Reading

Baumer, Christoph (2006). *The Church of the East: An Illustrated History of Assyrian Christianity*. London: I. B. Taurus.

Brock, Sebastian P. (2005). *Spirituality in the Syriac Tradition*. Kerala: St Ephrem Ecumenical Research Institute.

Brown, Peter (2003). *The Rise of Western Christendom: Triumph and Diversity, AD200 – 1000*. Oxford: Blackwell.

Fletcher, Richard (1997). *The Barbarian Conversion: From Paganism to Christianity*. Berkeley: University of California Press.

Fletcher, Richard (2003). *The Cross and the Crescent: Christianity from Muhammad to the Reformation*. New York: Viking.

Griffith, Sidney H. (2008). *The Church in the Shadow of the Mosque: Christians and Muslims in the World of Islam*. Princeton, NJ: Princeton University Press.

Hamilton, Bernard (2003). *The Christian World of the Middle Ages*. Stroud, UK: Sutton Publishing.

Herrin, Judith (2007). *Byzantium: The Surprising Life of a Medieval Empire*. Princeton, NJ: Princeton University Press.

Jenkins, Philip (2008). *The Lost History of Christianity: The Thousand-Year Golden Age of the Church in the Middle East, Africa, and Asia – and How It Died*. New York: HarperOne.

Louth, Andrew (2007). *Greek East and Latin West: The Church AD 681–1071*. Crestwood, NY: St Vladimir's Seminary Press.

Meyendorff, John (1989). *Imperial Unity and Christian Divisions*. Crestwood, NY: St Vladimir's Seminary Press.

Moffett, Samuel Hugh (1992). *A History of Christianity in Asia: Beginnings to 1500*. New York: HarperCollins.

Noble, Thomas F. X. and Julia M. H. Smith (eds) (2008). *The Cambridge History of Christianity: Early Medieval Christianities, c.600–c.1000*. Cambridge, UK: Cambridge University Press.

Palmer, Martin (2001). *The Jesus Sutras: Rediscovering the Lost Scrolls of Taoist Christianity*. New York: Ballantine.

Chapter 16

The Rise of the West and Decline of the East

1000 to 1500

The global center of Christianity shifted dramatically away from the East and toward the West between the years 1000 and 1500. The transformation resulted both from the unprecedented rise of the Christian West and from the equally stunning decline of Christianity in the East. In the West, ideas and attitudes that had been incubating for decades blossomed into a new vision of the Catholic Church as the champion and defender of Christianity and of Catholicism as the organizing principle of European society. Meanwhile, in much of the East, Christianity was pushed to the brink of oblivion. The Church of the East declined precipitously, and the Miaphysite churches also suffered terrible losses. The Orthodox Church declined, too, when the Byzantine Empire was defeated by the Islamic Ottoman Empire, but its losses were less than those of the other Eastern churches.

At the beginning of this period, it would have been impossible to predict how powerful and how aggressive Western Christianity would become in the next five hundred years. As the first millennium drew to a close, there was meager evidence of Catholicism's future strength. Though nearly all the rulers of Western Europe were Christian, few of them were models of Christian virtue, and the Catholic Church itself was not in the best of shape. There were a few bright spots, like the newly established Benedictine Abbey in Cluny, France, but the overall picture did not inspire much hope. The tremendous flourishing of Western Christianity that took place during this period was a surprise for everyone.

It would have been equally difficult to predict the decline of the East. In the year 1000, it still looked as if the East would remain a significant center of Christianity. In Byzantium, the boundaries of the realm had expanded under the rule of Basil II (976–1025) to their largest scope since the mid-600s. The Miaphysite churches and the Church of the East also seemed relatively healthy. The rate of membership decline in these churches seemed to be slowing as the year 1000 approached, and it looked as if Christian adherents might be stabilizing at around 30 to 40 percent of the regional population. The nearly total collapse of

The World's Christians: Who they are, Where they are, and How they got there, First Edition. Douglas Jacobsen.
© 2011 Douglas Jacobsen. Published 2011 by Blackwell Publishing Ltd.

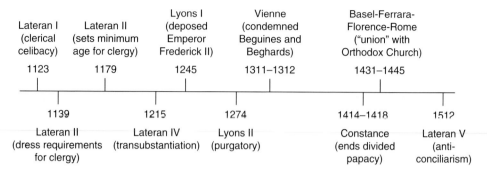

Figure 16.1   Ten General Councils of the Catholic Church, 1123–1512

Christianity in the East that took place during the following centuries was as unexpected as the rise of the Catholic West.

Taken as a whole, the years from 1000 to 1500 represent a major watershed in the development of global Christianity. Before the year 1000, Christianity was centered in the East, and it was embodied in four strong but independent traditions. Five hundred years later, the global center of Christianity had shifted from Asia to Europe, and the Western Catholic tradition, which had previously been the weakest of the four, had become the dominant carrier of the Christian religion. The Christian East has never recovered from the devastation of these years, and the ascendancy of the West has continued. Today, fully half the world's Christians are Catholic and a majority of the rest of the world's Christian population also traces its roots to the Western tradition. By contrast, less than 15 percent of Christians in the world today are members of any of the three historical traditions of the East.

Convictions

The five centuries from 1000 to 1500 were a time of almost frenzied institutional activity for the Catholic tradition. According to the reckoning of the Catholic Church, there have been 21 general councils in the two thousand-year history of Christianity; nine of these general councils were held between the years 1000 and 1500, and a tenth was held just after the end of the period in 1517 and belongs to the same sequence. Thus half of all the recognized general councils of the Catholic Church took place during this segment of time (see Figure 16.1). This activity was all part of a single extended process of development that resulted in the maturation and codification of Catholicism as a Christian tradition that was fully separate and distinct from Eastern Orthodoxy. Many of the key religious convictions that still define Catholicism today were first articulated during this period, including priestly celibacy, belief in Purgatory, praying the rosary, and the seven sacraments. This period also produced a major enlargement in the power and authority of the popes, a much clearer theological explanation of salvation, and the beginning of the Catholic university system. For Catholicism, this was a time of unprecedented growth and consolidation.

Developments within the Eastern traditions were less dramatic, but still significant. In the Orthodox Church of the Byzantine Empire, the role of experience in the Christian life was seriously rethought. Also during this time, the Russian Orthodox Church began to translate the sometimes esoteric theology of Greek-speaking Orthodoxy into its own simpler and more narrative style of faith. Focused on mere survival, the Miaphysite churches and the Church of the East had less time and energy for reflection on religious identity or theology. An important exception occurred in the twelfth and thirteenth centuries when the Ethiopian Orthodox Church, which was Miaphysite in orientation, but remained independent of Muslim rule, developed a creative new interpretation of its history and identity that emphasized Christianity's continuity with, rather than difference from, Judaism.

The Catholic tradition

Because the Catholic tradition is "catholic," which means all-encompassing, broad generalizations about the tradition can be misleading. Catholicism embraces paradox. It can be highly rational and decidedly mystical at the same time. It can be overwhelmingly institutional and thoroughly spiritual simultaneously. It contains contradictory impulses that can push it toward service and compassion in one moment and toward power and control in the next. Many of these paradoxes were built into the Catholic tradition during the years examined in this chapter.

At the core of this newly self-confident and independent Catholic identity was the idea of the church as the institutional carrier of salvation. This was an old idea, dating back to people like the third-century Bishop Cyprian of Carthage (see Chapter 14) who said that the church was the necessary spiritual mother of everyone who was a Christian. But in this later period, Cyprian's metaphorical description of the church's role in salvation was updated and systematically institutionalized. This process obviously affected the church as an institution as well, making it more distinct from society as a whole and more hierarchical in its organizational structure. As the church was restructured and the process of salvation was more concretely codified, salvation seemed more assured, but perhaps it also came to seem more routine.

The Catholic Church of the year 1000 had been designated to be the carrier of salvation, but at times it did not look particularly holy; it did not look like the highway to heaven it was supposed to be. The church was headed by bishops and largely administered by local priests, but many bishops were lacking in piety and many priests were not well trained. Most bishops were wealthy. They held church property in their own names, and they had many of the same responsibilities and duties as any other wealthy landowner, including community governance and defense. Because of that, local rulers usually wanted to have a say in who was picked as bishop, and they generally wanted bishops to be worldly wise, knowing how to handle life in the here and now. As for priests, many lived just like everyone else – they were local peasants with a religious calling. Some were devout and a few were moderately well trained, but many were not. They were typically given a bit of farmland for their sustenance or a very small stipend, and they had to make ends meet as best they could. Since there were not yet any formal rules about priests being celibate, many of them were married or lived with a concubine (someone who was functionally a wife, but whom they could not marry for some legal or social reason). There was nothing particularly immoral about this, but priests with wives and children often had a family stake in how local conflicts were resolved, so it was hard for priests to serve as neutral pastors or confessors for everyone in the community.

In the eleventh century, the church decided to reform this state of affairs at both the priestly and episcopal levels, and the main force behind that reform was Pope Gregory VII who occupied the papal throne from 1073 to 1085. Before he was pope, he had been a monk named Hildebrand, and he was deeply influenced by a relatively new form of monastic piety associated with the monastery of Cluny in southern France (founded in 910). Most Catholic monasteries operated as local organizations unconnected with any monastic order, but Cluny had created a large network of monasteries in France, northern Spain, and northern Italy that were all committed to the same rigorous interpretation of Benedict's Rule. Gregory liked both the strictness of Cluny and its hierarchical organization, and those ideals became the core of his plan for reforming the church.

Gregory had a high view of his own office. In his encyclical *Dictatus Papae* (c.1075) he said among others things that the papacy had "never erred; nor will it err to all eternity." As the protector and defender of truth and as the apostolic successor to Peter the apostle, the pope's job was to govern the church with a firm hand and to guide it in the right direction. Gregory wanted to eliminate ethical abuses among the clergy, so for the first time it was stipulated that all priests, not just bishops, were to live celibate lives. But some abuses were part of the church structure itself. These included simony (the selling of clerical offices to the highest bidder), nepotism (favoring one's own relatives in appointments to clerical office), and lay investiture (which gave local rulers, who were laypeople, the right to appoint individuals to the office of bishop). These abuses were more difficult to address because powerful people had a stake in keeping things the way they were.

Gregory's most persistent opponent was the Holy Roman Emperor Henry IV, who shared his predecessor Charlemagne's opinion that emperors ought to be able to control the church in their own realm, and he very much wanted to retain the right to select bishops in his own territories. He detested the views of Pope Gregory VII and refused to follow them, which led to a showdown, called the "investiture controversy." The Pope excommunicated the Emperor and deposed him from office. When his political power base began to crumble, Henry decided his only option was to accept the Pope's new rules, and he traveled to the Pope's castle at Canossa in northern Italy in January, 1077 to beg for forgiveness. Gregory kept him waiting at the gate for three days in the snow, but finally relented. Henry was forgiven, reconciled with the Pope, and his rule was restored. But he never forgot the embarrassment he had suffered at Gregory's hand. In 1085, Emperor Henry invaded Italy and literally chased Gregory out of the papal office. Attempts to reform the system of lay investiture continued for decades, until 1122 when Pope Calixtus II and the Holy Roman Emperor Henry V signed a formal agreement at the Concordat of Worms defining the relationship between church and state. Tensions between popes and political rulers lingered on even after that, however, and they still sometimes bubble up today.

Overall, the investiture controversy had the general effect of strengthening papal power, and the popes who governed the church in ensuing decades often made bold claims about the scope of their power. For example, Pope Innocent III (1198–1216) used the analogy of the sun and the moon to compare the church and state, saying that while the state ruled over people's bodies, the church ruled over their souls. He thus reasoned that in the same way that "the moon derives its light from the sun ... so too the royal power derives the splendor of its dignity from the pontifical authority." But the boldest statement of all came from Pope Boniface VIII (1294–1303) who declared bluntly in his papal bull *Unam Sanctam* that "it is absolutely necessary for salvation that every human creature be subject to the Roman Pontiff." The church, he said, had absolute power, including the power of dispensing or withholding salvation itself.

During this period of Catholic history, salvation was construed as a kind of legal transaction between individuals and God, and the church was essentially the brokering house for God's grace on earth. The theological framework for this new vision of salvation was developed by Anselm of Canterbury (1033–1109), who in his book *Cur Deus Homo* (usually translated *Why God Became Man*) used the analogy of offended honor to explain humanity's predicament with God and the nature of salvation. Anselm defines sin as an offense against God's honor. Offending the honor of another human being can be rectified by making appropriate recompense – admitting one's error, asking forgiveness, and offering some appropriate gift to make things right. But offending God creates a problem because God is infinite; thus sin's offense against God's honor is also infinite and no finite human being can ever make right an infinite wrong. Happily, Anselm says, the God-Man Jesus, who was himself both human and divine, took on himself the work of reconciling God and humankind, paying the infinite penalty of humanity's offense through his death on the cross.

According to the Catholic theology developed in this medieval period, the grace or merits of Christ's infinite sacrifice had been deposited in the spiritual treasury of the church, and they were available to individual sinners through the clergy and the sacraments they administered to the faithful. Earlier in Catholic history the notion of "sacrament" was somewhat fluid, but in the twelfth century the term was restricted to seven very specific ritual actions: baptism, the Eucharist, confirmation, penance (including the confession of sin, sorrow for sin, various "acts of penance," and absolution by a priest), extreme unction ("anointing of the sick"), marriage, and holy orders (ordination to the clergy). Understood as component parts of one overall system, the seven sacraments provided a comprehensive cradle-to-grave method for obtaining salvation – the only route to salvation that was guaranteed. In 1439, this list was made part of official Catholic teaching at the Council of Florence.

During the medieval centuries, fear was a primary motivator of religious faith and practice, and the greatest fear was to die with a serious sin unconfessed – a state of being that would send one directly to hell forever. But increasingly, Western Europeans also began to worry about what happened to people who died in a state of partial sinfulness, having confessed and been forgiven of all their major sins, but having not yet been fully cleansed from all their minor sins and sinful impulses. This was the state in which most people died. Obviously they would need to be perfected before entering heaven – only the truly pure and holy could stand without fear in God's presence – but it was unclear how this would happen. The Second Council of Lyon (1274) answered that question by proclaiming the doctrine of purgatory, which was understood at the time as a place one was sent after death to be painfully punished until the last drop of sin and sinfulness had been driven out of one's heart. These punishments of purgatory were deemed to be as terrible as the pains of hell itself except for the fact that they were temporary. (Most Catholics today have a much more

Figure 16.2   Fourteenth-century Italian Renaissance poet Dante Alighieri holding his book *Divine Comedy* against a backdrop of Hell, Purgatory, and Paradise in a 1465 painting by Domenico Michelino (Purgatory is the "seven-storey mountain" in the background)
© David Lees/Time Life Pictures/Getty Images

nuanced view of what is involved in the experience of purgatory.)

Fear of hell drove people to the sacraments, but fear of purgatory drove them to seek out other sources of grace or perform various works of righteousness that they hoped would shorten their time in purgatory. These remedies included prayer, fasting, and giving alms to the poor. Taking special vows of religious obligation were thought to help as well – either lifelong vows as monks or nuns or short-term vows related to some specific time period (such as Lent) or act (such as pilgrimage). Saints, the great Christians of the past, were petitioned for aid, and it was generally assumed that such requests had a better chance of being answered if spoken in close proximity to a relic of that saint – a preserved piece of the saint's body or some object, such as clothing, that was intimately associated with the saint (see Plate 31). Each saint and each relic had its own unique power, and churches that possessed extensive relic collections often became important destinations for pilgrimage. Beginning in this era, the church also occasionally offered people special dispensations of grace called indulgences, legal documents issued by the church releasing individuals from some or all of the punishments they deserved in purgatory. The first widespread use of indulgences took place during the Crusades, when soldiers were sometimes promised plenary indulgences (granting full release from the punishments of purgatory and immediate entrance into heaven) if they were killed in action while fighting to regain the Holy Land. Later, the church began to sell indulgences (partial or plenary) as a fund-raising practice to help support the administrative offices of the Vatican and to construct large-scale buildings such as St Peter's Basilica in Rome.

Fear was not, of course, the only religious emotion of the time. Some believers, then as now, were motivated almost purely by the love of God and others. No one exemplified this more fully than Francis of Assisi (1182–1226), perhaps the most beloved figure in all of Catholic history. Francis was the son of a wealthy cloth merchant in the town of Assisi, located in central Italy about 80 miles north of Rome. After living a carefree life as a youth, his life was turned upside down by God in his early twenties. Leaving the good life behind, he began attending to the needs of the local leper colony and begging door to door for his own food. Increasingly he spoke of his attraction to "Lady Poverty," and he sought to become a troubadour for God – a joyful follower of Jesus who tried to live in the same simple way as Christ himself. His positive faith was contagious, and others began to join his cause.

Contemporaries like Peter Waldo, who was a generation older than Francis, attracted followers to a similar what-would-Jesus-do style of Christian living, and a movement of

Catholic women called "beguines" (located mainly in what is now Belgium and the Netherlands) also embodied this new style of piety. What set all of these "apostolic life" movements apart from the Catholic mainstream was their positive view of God, focusing on love rather than vengeance. The individual histories of these movements differ considerably. The Waldensian movement, founded by Peter Waldo, was ultimately condemned by the church because neither Peter nor his followers would submit their spiritual opinions to the judgment of the church. The beguines were condemned on similar grounds. But Francis vowed his obedience to the church, and his movement became a new kind of monastic organization, a "mendicant" (wandering, rather than cloistered) order of monks called Franciscans.

The eleventh, twelfth, and thirteenth centuries were times of relative wealth in Western Europe. That wealth produced the leisure needed for study, and soon universities were being created all over Europe. The University of Bologna is often credited with being the first, but the University of Paris soon took center stage, and it was an Italian theology professor at the University of Paris who set the standard for Catholic intellectual life. His name was Thomas Aquinas (1225–74), and he is still the most revered "doctor of the Church" (authoritative teacher) in all of Catholic history.

Aquinas's style of teaching and writing is known as scholasticism, and its aim is to take belief and turn it into genuine knowledge. The method for doing this is reason: the careful, systematic weighing of alternative arguments about the world, seeking to discover the logic that already exists in the world as God has designed it. Aquinas was not a scientist in the sense of starting with the simple observation of things and trying to explain how it all made sense in a purely reasonable or natural fashion. He was a theologian who began with the assumption that what the Bible said and what the church taught was true. But given those parameters, he then examined every expressed opinion on the basis of reason, trying to see what made sense, what seemed logical and illogical, and what had to be assumed in order for all the teachings of the church to fit together in a single all-encompassing understanding of reality. His greatest work was entitled the *Summa Theologica*, his attempt to sum up all that could humanly be known on the basis of scripture, church teaching, reason, and the observation of the world. It was, and is, an amazing accomplishment, and it expresses the deep conviction that lay at the heart of the Catholic intellectual tradition as it was emerging in the thirteenth century when Aquinas wrote, that God is rational, that the world is orderly, that the teachings of the church are true, and that everything works together exactly as God planned it. This view of the world is one in which people do not have to live in fear, but can confidently place their trust in the reasonable and predictable ways of God, and in the church as God's representative body on earth.

But almost as soon as this rational Christian view of the world had been articulated, it was called into question by two catastrophes that shook Europe's Catholic faith to its roots. The first was a natural disaster: the Black Death – a deadly epidemic of bubonic plague that swept through Europe in the years 1347 to 1350 (see Figure 16.3). A third of the population died, and in some regions the mortality rate was well over 50 percent. People did not know why God was punishing them, which was the only way they could interpret the event, and their cries to God yielded no help. It was all irrational – pure pain, pure emotion.

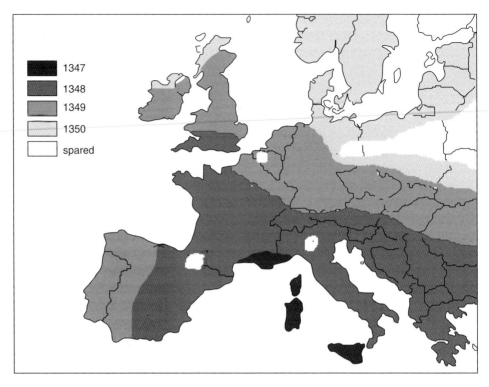

Figure 16.3   The path of the Black Death. Map by author.

The second disaster was spiritual in character, taking the form of a divided papacy that lasted for almost 40 years from 1378 to 1417. During this era, two competing lines of popes existed alongside each other, one in Rome and the other in Avignon in southern France, and no one was sure which of these popes represented the one true church of Christ on earth. If, as Pope Boniface had said around the year 1300, "it is absolutely necessary for salvation that every human creature be subject to the Roman Pontiff," this posed a very real and genuine spiritual problem. Which pope was the right one? To which should one submit? In response to this unprecedented situation, some Catholic theologians began to suggest that councils, not popes, should ultimately define what the church is and what it stands for. For more than a century after the resolution of the problem, popes repeatedly had to defend themselves and their authority against this "conciliar" understanding of power and authority within the church.

By the mid-fifteenth century, life in Western Europe had bounced back from the Black Death and the divided papacy, and the Catholic Church had returned to normal – almost, but not quite. A new layer of mystery had been added to the medieval view of God and a new mystical strand of Catholic piety had risen to prominence. No one expressed this attitude more eloquently than the woman known as Julian of Norwich (1342–c.1416), who was an English anchoress (a woman who was not a nun but lived a solitary religious life). She had lived through the disasters of the plague and the divided papacy, and she developed a new, more delicate and fragile vision of reality than had been typical in Catholicism before. In her visions, Julian describes the world as God revealed it to her:

[God] showed me something small, no bigger than a hazelnut, lying in the palm of my hand. … I looked at it with the eyes of my understanding and thought: What can this be? I was amazed that it could last, for I thought that because of its littleness it would suddenly have fallen into nothing. And I was answered in my understanding: It lasts and always will, because God loves it; and thus everything has being through the love of God.[1]

In Julian's perspective, the question was not why bad things sometimes happen, but how anything as small and fragile as the world could even exist, and her answer was that it exists simply because God loves it. Julian's vision of life and faith represented a dramatic shift away from the fear-centered spirituality of the high medieval period and toward a spirituality of trust and love. In fact, rather than picturing God as a ruler or judge, Julian sometimes described Christ as a loving mother: "The mother can give her child to suck of her milk, but our precious Mother Jesus can feed us with himself, and does, most courteously and most tenderly, with the blessed sacrament, which is the precious food of true life."[2] Julian was not critical of the institutional church, and she believed the sacraments were necessary for salvation, but at the same time the core of her spirituality lay elsewhere, in mystical experience and the love of God.

As the era came to an end, the Catholic tradition was becoming ever more internally rich and diverse. The core planks of Catholic belief and practice had been firmly established in the eleventh through the thirteenth centuries, and a wealth of other forms of piety and devotion were springing up around that core. But new problems were appearing on the horizon. The various nations of Europe were becoming increasingly independent and were beginning to question how much authority the pope should have within their domains. The old clerical abuses of simony and nepotism had crept back into the church, the business of indulgences was getting out of hand, and the printing press was allowing alternative "heretical" Christian views to be disseminated across the continent with greater ease than ever before. All of these concerns, both positive and the negative, would crash together dramatically in the sixteenth century.

Developments in the Orthodox tradition

The main contours of Orthodox tradition had been established in the eighth and ninth centuries, so developments from 1000 to 1500 can be seen as a fine tuning rather than as a major readjustment, but significant changes did take place. Perhaps the key theological issue of the period was whether Christians could still hope to experience the presence of God in their lives in the same dramatic ways that had been possible during the first few centuries of the Christian movement. Increasingly, Orthodox Christians were coming to assume that such experiences should not be expected in the present. This response reflected how routine Orthodox life in the Byzantine Empire had become. The old dream that the Byzantine Christian Empire was the beginning of Christ's reign on earth and would eventually include the whole world had faded into the background and spiritual expectations had shrunk as the Empire had slowly adjusted to its losses to Islam and its smaller size. The Byzantine court was still grand, perhaps grander than ever, but hopes and expectations had been tempered.

The spiritual apathy associated with these developments was condemned by Symeon (942–1022), who was known as the "New Theologian" (Symeon is the third Orthodox saint to be given the title "theologian," the other two are John the Apostle and the fourth-century Gregory of Nazianzus). Symeon preached that the passionate experience of God was still possible and that the wondrous experiences of the early church fathers and mothers could be reproduced in the present day. Symeon knew this was possible because he claimed to have experienced it himself.

Symeon's opponents accused him not only of spiritual pride but also of lying, yet he held his ground:

> The men … whom I call heretics are those who say that there is no one in our time and in our midst who is able to keep the Gospel commandments and become like the holy Fathers … [and experience] the illumination and reception of the Holy Ghost … Those who make these claims shut up the heaven that Christ opened for us, and cut off the way that he inaugurated for us.

Symeon believed it was not only possible but necessary for Christian believers to experience the life-changing presence of God in their lives. He implored others to:

> come, learn that it is not merely in the future, but even now that the unutterable treasure … lies open … I entreat you all … to endeavor to become partakers of such a life. It is the light of God, the Holy Ghost himself, who sanctifies those who partake of Him and who makes them gods by adoption. … just as friend speaks to friend face to face, so He who by nature is God speaks to those who by grace He has begotten as gods.[3]

While Symeon's claims seemed outrageous to some of his contemporaries, the Orthodox tradition as a whole slowly came to agree with him and to see Symeon as being in agreement with views that had been around since the time of Maximus the Confessor. The reasoning was that if salvation involved a process of actual deification, surely that process must have an experiential component. Could someone become deified and feel nothing?

The limits of religious experience were, however, placed under scrutiny yet again three hundred years later when the Hesychast movement began to advocate a new kind of spirituality focusing on the repetition of the "Jesus Prayer." In its longest form the Jesus Prayer consists of only 12 words, "Lord Jesus Christ, Son of God, have mercy on me, a sinner," and sometimes it is abbreviated even further, with the shortest form being simply "Jesus." The slow repetition of this prayer, accompanied by various body positions and breathing techniques, was suppose to promote the stillness of soul (hesychasm means "silence" or "stillness") that its practitioners believed was necessary in order to experience the face-to-face vision of God described by Symeon. While the physical techniques used by the Hesychasts raised questions for some, it was their claim that they could "see" God that produced the strongest opposition. Critics said that the Bible clearly stated that no one can see God and live, and they accused the Hesychasts of being heretics.

Gregory Palamas (1296–1359), a monk from Mount Athos (the most famous Orthodox monastery in the world, located in what is now northern Greece) and later Archbishop of Thessalonica (also in northern Greece), came to the Hesychasts' defense. Gregory said that the vision of God experienced by Hesychasts was the same as the vision of Christ experienced by the four disciples who accompanied Jesus to Mount Tabor and saw him "transfigured before them" when "his face shone like the sun and his clothes became dazzling white" (Matthew 17:1–2). Gregory argued that the light that shone from Jesus's face was not the light of the *essence* of God, which he agreed no one could see and remain alive, but it was instead a manifestation of the *energies* of God. He explained that the relationship between the essence and energies of God is like that between the sun and its rays. They are not identical, but they are indivisible; the sun cannot be the sun without shining, and the rays of sunshine obviously cannot exist without the sun. The energies of God are not God in God's essence, but they are truly divine nonetheless.

The distinction provided by Gregory is important to the Orthodox tradition not only because it defended Hesychasm, but also because it provided new language for explaining how human beings could be deified by their participation in the mystery of Christ and yet not become identical to Christ himself. The deification of humankind involved being immersed in and filled by the energies of God; Christ, by contrast, possessed the pure essence of God. Christians throughout the Eastern world had struggled to understand how humanity could know God at all when God was so totally transcendent and beyond all human comprehension. Gregory's distinction between the energies and essence of God provided an answer.

While the Byzantine Empire and the Patriarchate of Constantinople was the center of Orthodox faith during the early part of these centuries, Russian Orthodoxy was slowly coming into its own and by the late fifteenth century would challenge Constantinople for leadership of the Orthodox movement as a whole. Theologically, Russian Orthodoxy remained dependent on the Byzantine Church, but Russian Christians were generally more interested in life than theology. Given the orientation, the experientialism of the Hesychast movement was deeply appealing to many Russians, and many other models of holy living were also attractive, including "holy fools" – people who purposely flouted the rules of society to make a spiritual point. Perhaps the most famous fool for Christ during these years was Basil of Moscow (1468–1552), a figure similar to Robin Hood, who shoplifted goods and gave them to the poor. *Startsy*, elders or holy men who served as spiritual advisors for both monks and laypeople, were also venerated. Sergius of Radonezh (1314–92) was the most prominent, and he and his followers are credited with founding more than 400 new monasteries that served as centers of spiritual counsel for Orthodox Christians from all walks of life. This was also the golden age of Russian icon painting, and iconographers like Andrei Rublev (c.1370–c.1430) developed a distinctly Russian style of iconography that was more personal and intimate in character than the much stiffer imperial style that predominated in the Byzantine Empire (see Plate 32).

Ethiopian Christianity and other smaller Christian movements

Only a handful of historical documents related to the history of Ethiopian Orthodox Christianity survive, but that evidence indicates that the Christianity of this region changed significantly during the years from 1000 to 1500, emerging with the inauguration of the new Zagwe ruling dynasty in the mid-1100s. The Christian movement had originally been

Figure 16.4   St George's Carved Stone Church
(Lalibela, Ethiopia)
© Gavin Hellier/Superstock

located in the northern part of the country, but the spread of Islam all down the east coast of Africa had forced the Christian community to move inland to the highlands north of Addis Ababa. The Ethiopian church remained linked with the Coptic church in Egypt, and the *abuna,* the chief religious officer of the Ethiopian church, was appointed by the Coptic pope. During the Zagwe Dynasty, the kings of Ethiopia also took a variety of religious roles upon themselves, especially King Lalibela, who reigned from 1190 to 1225. Lalibela's greatest accomplishment was the building of a new religious center for the nation, which he called the New Jerusalem, near the city of Roha (which is now known as Lalibela). The river that runs through this territory was renamed the Jordan, and a series of new churches were built by carving them down into the earth out of solid rock (see Figure 16.4). It seems obvious that the place was meant to be a pilgrimage site, but little if anything is known about its specific function within the Orthodox church of the time.

The Zagwe Dynasty was overthrown in 1270 by a new "Solomonic" dynasty that claimed to represent the ancient traditions of the nation. The Solomonids claimed a lineage that went back two thousand years to the Israelite King Solomon and his Ethiopian Queen Sheba and, in keeping with that historical narrative, they accentuated the Jewish character of Ethiopian society and religion, exemplified in such practices as male circumcision. *Kibre Negest*, a book written during this time to bolster the claims of the new Solomonic dynasty, provided a chronicle of Ethiopia's mixed Jewish–Christian heritage, ending with the promise that God would continue to reward the Solomonic kings of Ethiopia for their moral and religious leadership, granting them "more glory, and grace, and majesty than for all the other kings of the earth."[4]

While the *Kibre Negest* implied that the kings of Ethiopia were the religious leaders of the land, spiritual authority was actually concentrated in the monastic communities of the region. Because of this, a theological fracture that emerged in the early 1400s between the monasteries in the north and the monasteries in the south caused significant alarm. The main dispute concerned the appropriate day on which to celebrate weekly Christian worship – either on Saturday (the Jewish Sabbath) or on Sunday (which was the common Christian practice elsewhere). A compromise was reached around the year 1450 that allowed worship on both days. At about the same time, the Ethiopian church began the practice of having a *tabot* (or ark) in every church building. The *tabot*, made from flat pieces of inscribed stone or wood that are usually about 6 inches (15.24 cm) square, symbolizes the tablets of the law that were kept in the "ark of the covenant" in ancient Israel. Both the church's "double Sabbath" and its congregational *tabots* are indicators of the Judaic character that Ethiopian Christianity was assuming.

In many ways, Ethiopian Orthodoxy lies outside of either Eastern or Western Christianity. It is simply different, and as such it is representative of several other varieties of Christianity that existed around the world in these centuries that were also simply "other." Each was its own experiment with being Christian. The Christianity of India, for example, maintained itself for long periods of time without any priests and developed its own lay-centered faith. The Christianity of China was a very different kind of experiment, one that was more open to cooperation with other religions, with one leader of the Chinese Christian church serving for a while as the government overseer of the Manichaean religious community as well as the Christian. The mobile Christianity of Central Asia, where some churches had no fixed places of worship but instead met in tents and migrated with the people, represents a third alternative. The stories of these small and scattered Christian groups, like the story of Ethiopian Christianity, are known only in snippets, but they serve as concrete reminders that global experimentation with Christianity has been taking place for centuries.

Encounters

During the period from 1000 to 1500 Christian encounters with others became significantly more confrontational. In the West, Christianity adopted a strikingly aggressive and often violent posture toward Islam, toward pagan religions (both at home in Europe and later abroad), and toward heretics of all kinds. The West was also assertive in its relations with the Christian churches of the East. Partly in reaction to the new aggressiveness of western Christianity, Islam also became much more confrontational during these years, especially in its attitude toward the Christians of the East. By the early fourteenth century, that confrontational stance had become positively brutal, and the final result was the effective elimination of Christianity from vast regions of the East where it had previously had significant representation.

Catholicism's confrontations with otherness

As Catholicism became stronger and better organized in the West, its main means of relating to the non-Catholic world became increasingly hostile. Led by popes who viewed themselves as the vicars of Christ on earth, Catholic Christians came to believe their church had never erred and that their God-given role on earth was to impose their own perfected version of Christian faith on everyone else. Anyone who held religious views different from the Catholic consensus was treated as an enemy who needed to be confronted and then either converted or defeated. There were no other options.

This can appear to be an incredibly arrogant stance, but Catholics of the time considered it to be merciful since they believed that the Catholic Church provided the only means through which salvation and eternal life in heaven could be obtained. Persuasion was always the preferred means for recruiting new Catholic believers, and several new monastic preaching orders were created to help with that goal. These included the Franciscans and the Dominicans; members of both groups were known as "friars." But in instances when persuasion failed, or when a particular group was obviously opposed to the Christian gospel, many Catholics assumed that force was a valid alternative – and, over time, it became easier to turn to violence more quickly. Eventually crusading (doing battle for Christ) became a way of life, and it was taken up by monks and laypeople alike. The famous monk and preacher Bernard of Clairvaux (1109–53) even went so far as to invent a new word for the killing of heretics and evildoers: *malecide*. While homicide continued to be seen as a sin, *malecide* was considered a righteous act of faith.

There were a few exceptions to this pervasive sense of agreement that violence was justified if it advanced the Christian cause, and perhaps the most outspoken critic of this view was the Majorcan writer Raymond Lull (1223–1315). Part linguist, part scientist, and thoroughly brilliant, Lull spoke a variety of languages and he was convinced that Christian truth could make its case based on reason and persuasion alone. He visited North Africa several times, and eventually decided that it might be possible to unify the three great monotheistic traditions of the world – Christianity, Judaism, and Islam – rather than viewing them as necessary competitors in a global race for converts. But his views would still be considered radical by many people today, and they were clearly not appreciated in his own time. Much the same can be said for Francis of Assisi, who during the Fifth Crusade (1213–21) took it upon himself to wander across the battle lines to talk with the Sultan Malik al-Kamil. He hoped both to convert the sultan and to make peace, and most of his contemporaries thought he was crazy for having tried.

Catholicism's newly confrontational attitude toward the rest of the world was first developed in Spain, or Al-Andalus as it was known to Muslims. In the early 700s, the Iberian peninsula had been conquered by the Umayyad Caliphate, leaving only a thin strip of land in the far north under Christian control. Almost immediately the Christians in the region began to fight back, slowly regaining control of the peninsula. The *reconquista,* as it came to be called, was not an organized "crusade," but was instead a piecemeal affair with different Christian kingdoms slowly extending their borders further and further south. By 1100, roughly half the region was back in Christian hands. By 1250, the only remaining Muslim territory was the Kingdom of Granada in the far south (see Figure 16.5). The *reconquista* demonstrated that force could be effective in the defense of faith, and it also reinforced the idea that any given society could tolerate only one religion.

During the *reconquista* there was always a sizeable borderland that separated Christian Spain from Muslim-dominated Al-Andalus. Religious life in this borderland was often complex, since local compromises had to be worked out among Christians, Muslims, and Jews who were living alongside each other. But in regions that were solidly controlled by either Muslims or Christians there was generally much less room for flexibility or religious compromise. In Christian-controlled lands, in particular, diversity was rarely tolerated, and Muslims and Jews were often forced to convert. These converts were called New Christians or *conversos.* Some of these *conversos* continued to practice their old religions in private, but if they were discovered, they were severely punished. Once the whole peninsula was in Christian hands, pressure to convert became even more intense. In the year 1492, the same year that Granada (the last Muslim kingdom) was finally captured, Jews were given the choice of either becoming Christians or leaving the country. Ten years later, Muslims were given the same ultimatum. By that time few, if any, Christians in the West believed that a religiously diverse society was possible. Religious uniformity was considered the only guarantee of social stability.

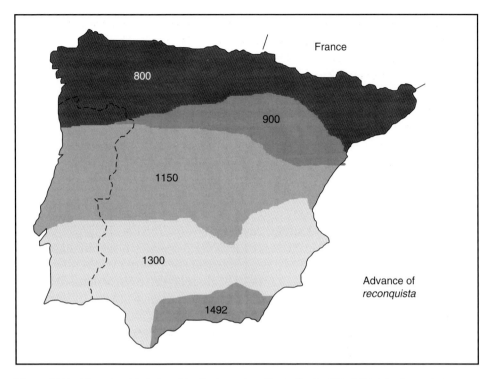

Figure 16.5   Changing Christian–Muslim boundary line in Spain, 800–1492. Map by author.

A similar reconquest took place in Sicily, contributing to Catholicism's growing reliance on the use of force to make the world Christian. Up until the mid-900s, Sicily had been part of the Byzantine Empire, but in the late 900s the island was conquered by a Muslim army based in North Africa. A hundred years later, the Normans, who had taken up residence in southern Italy, began a counterattack. By 1100, the island was back in Christian hands, and Islam was driven back to Africa. Two things distinguished the Sicilian experience from that of Spain. First, the Sicilian initiative had the explicit blessing of the pope, the first time such a thing had happened. Second, many of the residents of the conquered territory were Orthodox Christians, which complicated the re-Christianization process. Could newly Catholic Sicily countenance the presence of Orthodox Christians? The basic answer was "no." Over the course of the twelfth century, the Orthodox Christians of the island were slowly, but forcibly, Latinized (made subservient to the pope and Catholic doctrine), even though they were allowed to continue worshiping in the Byzantine style. These Christians are called Italo-Catholics, and about 50,000 can still be found in the region today.

But the reconquests of Spain and Sicily were only a warm-up for the main event, the Catholic Crusades that took place in the Middle East during the twelfth and thirteenth centuries. The first Crusade was instigated by Pope Urban II (1088–99) in the year 1095 after he received a request for military aid from the Byzantine Empire. Instead of merely assisting Byzantium, Urban called upon the Catholic people of the West to rescue Jerusalem from the "filthy grip" of the Muslims who controlled it. To make the endeavor more

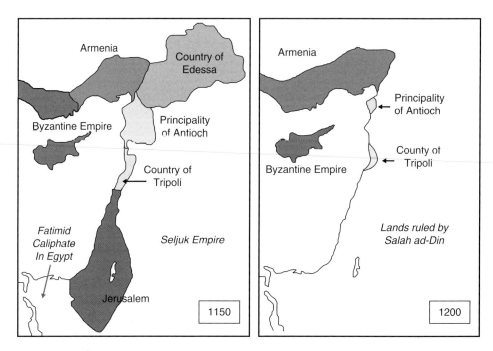

Figure 16.6   Map of the Crusader states, c. 1150 (left) and c. 1200 (right). Maps by author.

attractive, he promised that those who took up the sword against Islam would be greatly rewarded by God for their efforts, hinting that perhaps all their sins would be forgiven. Later popes made the connection between crusading for Christ and the forgiveness of sins much more explicit. Around 100,000 people responded to Pope Urban's call and started on their way across Europe toward the Middle East. Very few of these people were trained soldiers, and they left a path of sorrow and destruction in their wake as they plundered towns for supplies, commandeered crops from local farmers, and often killed any Jews unlucky enough to wander into their path.

By the time it arrived in the Middle East, the Crusader army numbered only 15,000, but those who were left were all relatively well-trained soldiers. Working together, they were remarkably successful in capturing the coastline and in establishing a string of Crusader kingdoms in the region (see Figure 16.6). Their success was due in part to the relative disarray that existed within the Muslim world at that time, but that situation soon changed. Under the leadership of Nur ad-Din (1156–74), the new regional ruler of the Seljuk Turks, Muslims began to fight back, and under his successor, Salah ad-Din Yusuf ibn Ayyub (1174–93) – known as Saladin in the West – the Muslim counterattack became an irresistible force. By the end of the 1200s the Crusader enterprise had collapsed, and the Middle East was again under Muslim rule (see Figure 16.6). Faced with defeat, Catholic Christians in the West latched on to rumors about a large Christian kingdom somewhere east of the Muslim-controlled territory of the Middle East. Their plan was to find that kingdom and then create an anti-Muslim alliance that could attack the Muslim world from two directions. The kingdom was never found, but European Christians spent several centuries looking for it.

Meanwhile, European Catholics were fighting other religious battles closer to home. Paganism still persisted in the Baltic region (present-day Estonia, Latvia, and Lithuania), and the Teutonic Knights and the Sword Brethren (or Livonian Knights) were sent to remedy that situation. These were military monastic orders. Members took monastic vows, but their monastic service took the form of warring in the name of Christ. The Northern Crusade, as it was called, lasted from about 1200 to 1400, and when it was over, Europe's last bastion of paganism was no more. Over the course of the Crusade, however, the conversion of pagans ceased to be the only objective. Orthodox Christians were also sometimes targeted for conversion as the Latin West extended its reach into Eastern Orthodox territory.

At about the same time, a different kind of religious warfare was taking place in southern France, where the enemies of God were not pagans but heretics. In this case, the heretics were Albigensians (also known as Cathars), Christians who championed a Gnostic-like faith that stressed asceticism and secret wisdom. Members of the movement were mercilessly hunted down during the Albigensian Crusade that was undertaken by the French government with the blessing of the pope. The crusade began in 1209 and was largely over by 1229, but a small remnant of Cathars escaped to a fortress hideaway called Monségur in the Pyrenean mountains between France and Spain. That fortress was finally captured in 1244, and on the same day, 220 Albigensians were burned alive by the victorious Catholic forces as a warning to anyone else who might be attracted to Cathari ideas.

In the mid-1400s, this same crusading spirit was being exported overseas. The Portuguese and Spanish played leading roles in this endeavor since they were the first Europeans to "discover" the rest of the world. Providing guidance for the work, Pope Nicholas V (1447–55) published the papal bull *Romanus Pontifex* (1445) that gave Christian explorers the right to seize the lands of Muslims, pagans, and infidels, and to enslave the people of any regions if doing so would assist in their conversion. *Romanus Pontifex* reformulated the old crusader ideal for new international settings, and the results were disastrous for the people who were encountered, especially in what would later become Latin America.

Starting in 1513, for example, Spanish conquistadors were required to read a statement (in Spanish), called a *Requerimiento*, to any new people they encountered in the Americas, informing them of their need to submit to the Catholic Church and to the monarchs of Spain. If they submitted, they were promised "many privileges and exemptions." If they refused or seemed to refuse, which must have been the case often since the indigenous people of the region could not speak Spanish, the *Requerimiento* said:

> With the help of God, we shall powerfully enter into your country, and shall make war against you in all ways and manners that we can, and shall subject you to the yoke and obedience of the Church and of their Highnesses; we shall take you and your wives and your children, and shall make slaves of them, and as such shall sell and dispose of them as their Highnesses may command; and we shall take away your goods, and shall do all the mischief and damage that we can … [and] the deaths and losses which shall accrue from this are your fault, and not that of their Highnesses, or ours.[5]

Most modern readers will find this statement shocking, but it would not have shocked most Catholic Christians of the period because violence had come to define the standard relationship between Catholicism and and all varieties of otherness that were not Catholic.

The Catholic West and the Orthodox East

The only place where some ambiguity existed in this us-versus-them Catholic view of the world was in the church's relationship with the different Christian communities of the East. This was especially the case with the Orthodox Church, which, at the beginning of this period, many Catholics still considered a kind of sibling church, part of the same family of faith. Both churches – the Catholic and the Orthodox – were rooted in the Imperial church of the old Roman Empire, yet they were far from identical. The two churches had never spoken the same language (the West spoke Latin and the East spoke Greek), and their historical experiences had been pushing them in different directions for centuries. The end result of these divergent developments was schism – a formal split between the two churches – and the date of that schism is traditionally given as 1054.

As with many other events of this period, however, the actual facts about what took place in the supposed schism of 1054 are unclear. Acting on the instructions of Pope Leo IX (1049–54), the papal legate who was visiting Constantinople excommunicated Michael Cerularius, the Patriarch of Constantinople. Within two weeks, Patriarch Michael excommunicated the Pope in return. The Patriarch didn't know it, but Pope Leo had died before the excommunication was even issued. What did these actions mean? No one was quite sure. Neither church had formally declared the other church heretical, so excommunication applied only to the individuals involved (one of whom was dead) and not to the churches as a whole, but a new bitterness entered the relationship. In fact, one of the reasons Pope Urban II responded so quickly upon receiving a request for military assistance from the Byzantine Emperor was that he hoped a crusade might help the Catholic and Orthodox Churches heal the division that had taken place. When the armies of the West arrived in the East, however, they found that face-to-face relations with the Orthodox population often led to worse relations, not better, and many church leaders in the West soon became convinced that the Orthodox Church was in need of serious religious correction.

The Fourth Crusade provided an opportunity to act on that newly developed attitude. Instead of proceeding to the Holy Land, the Fourth Crusade was diverted to Constantinople. The reasons for the diversion are complicated, including both financial considerations and a desire for retribution for an attack on Catholic traders and merchants living in Constantinople that had taken place in 1182. More important than why the attack took place, however, is what happened. After a 10-month siege, the Western armies breached the walls in April of 1204 and captured the city. In the chaos that followed, churches were looted, Orthodox Christian women were raped, and the Crusaders and their financial supporters hauled off as much booty as they could carry. Pope Innocent appears to have been genuinely shocked by the event, and he denounced the violence. But when the Latin army decided to stay put and to set up a new Latin Kingdom in the heart of the old Byzantine Empire, the Pope could not resist the temptation to cooperate. Soon the Catholic Church was working hand in hand with the rulers of the new Latin Empire to either restructure the Orthodox Church along Roman lines or, when necessary, to replace it with a new Latin Catholic hierarchy (the same thing that had been done earlier with Italo-Catholics in Sicily). Latin rule lasted until 1261, and for that whole time the Orthodox Christians of the East felt violated by the Catholic Christians who were governing the region (see Figure 16.7).

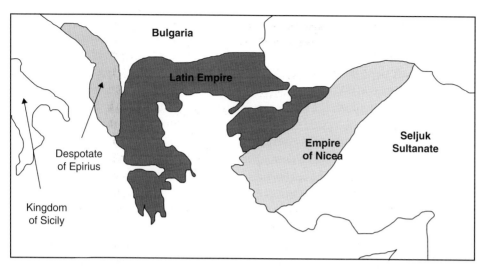

Figure 16.7   Latin Empire in former Byzantine territory, 1204–61. Map by author.

When Emperor Michael Palaeologus recaptured Constantinople in 1261 and re-established the Byzantine Empire, the first reaction of the West was to call for another crusade to retake the region. That outcome was prevented only by Michael's own willingness to submit to Rome and become a Catholic himself, at least in name, as a way of buying time for the Empire and the Orthodox Church to recover. But Rome was never satisfied with the mere compliance of the Emperor; it wanted complete "reunion," meaning the total submission of the Orthodox Church to the control of Rome. Thus when the Byzantine Empire found itself once again under threat of a Muslim attack in the late 1400s and asked once again for help, the stated price for help from the West was the prior submission of the Orthodox Church to the pope. That submission was made at the Council of Florence in 1439, but the declaration of union between the Catholic and Orthodox Churches was denounced within the Orthodox world before the ink was dry on the page – and no help for the beleaguered Byzantine Empire was ever forthcoming from the West. The only really lasting effect of this attempted "union" was the further weakening and division of the Orthodox Church itself.

The Catholic Church followed the same basic pattern in its relationships with the other churches of the East: occasionally extending minimal help, frequently engaging in conflict, and always attempting to subsume the non-Catholic Churches of the East into the overarching structure of the Catholic Church under the leadership of the pope. It should come as no surprise that some members of the various Eastern churches were attracted to the possibility of union with Rome. This was, in part, a pragmatic consideration – the Catholic Church had resources the East did not and perhaps union with Rome would aid in the Eastern Christian struggle for survival – but it was also, in part, the expression of a genuine concern for Christian unity. Driven by these mixed motives, representatives from many of these churches, including the Armenian Orthodox, Syrian Orthodox, Church of the East, and Coptic Orthodox, attended the Council of Florence (the full name of this meeting was the Council of Basel-Ferrara-Florence-Rome, since it moved from city to city, meeting intermittently from 1431 to 1445) where they negotiated different degrees of fellowship or union with the Catholic Church.

For the most part, these negotiations resulted in the division of the various Eastern churches rather than in the merger of any single church in its entirety into the Catholic fold, and the long-term result was the emergence of parallel Catholic and non-Catholic organizations within the different churches of the region. For example, while the Syrian Orthodox Church (Miaphysite) continued to exist, a new Syrian Catholic Church was organized alongside it, composed of former Syrian Orthodox individuals and congregations that embraced union with Rome. Similar Catholic churches were formed by dissident members leaving the Coptic Orthodox Church, the Armenian Church, the Church of the East, and every other Christian community in the East. These Eastern Catholic Churches are called by a variety of terms: Greek Catholics, Oriental Catholics, Catholics of the Eastern Rite, or "uniate" (a term that is considered derogatory). What makes these churches distinctive is that while they have all submitted to the authority of the pope and accepted the dictates of Catholic theology, they continue to follow their own historically Eastern ways of worshiping. The process of creating these churches began at the Council of Florence, and was formalized later.

The one unique church in this regard is the Maronite Church. The Maronite movement emerged as a small but separate church in the Lebanon Mountains in the seventh century, and their commitment to monothelitism (see Chapter 15) kept them separate from all the other churches in the region. The Maronites were fighters who wanted to be free of Muslim control and they warmly embraced the French Catholic Crusaders when they arrived in the Middle East, entering quickly into full communion with the Catholic Church. This is the only church in the East that became entirely merged into the Catholic tradition. The Catholic identity of the Maronite Church remains strong today, as does its special relationship with France.

The collapse of Christianity in the East

Many factors, both positive and negative, contributed to the decline of Christianity in the East that occurred between 1000 and 1500. In part, the decline was prompted by new developments within Islam itself, especially the rise of the Sufi movement which introduced a new and more personal dimension to the Muslim experience. Sufi Islam was positively appealing to many Christians. But numerous other Christians gave up their faith largely to avoid ever-increasing persecution, which increased markedly after 1300. Finally, a third factor in the growth of Islam and collapse of Christianity was the fact that Islam could be practiced almost anywhere, and Christianity could not. For Islam, any piece of ground could be designated a mosque; a building was not necessary. By contrast, Eastern Christianity was dependent on a material culture that included church buildings, monasteries, icons, plates and cups to celebrate the Eucharist, and graveyards in which to be buried. As Christian resources declined, that material culture became more and more difficult to sustain.

The histories of the different Christian peoples of the East are linked to the histories of the various Muslim empires that rose and fell during these years. The most important of these empires are listed in Table 16.1 along with the general attitude toward Christianity that

Table 16.1   Major Muslim empires, indicating general attitude toward Christianity

Empire	Dates	Location	Attitude toward Christianity
Fatimid Caliphate	909–1171	North Africa, Egypt, Palestine	Mostly tolerant
Seljuk Empire	1037–1194	Central Asia, Middle East, Turkey	Moderate to harsh
Mongol Empire(s)	1206–1368	China, Central Asia, Persia, Russia, Turkey	First supportive, then very harsh
Mamluk Sultanate	1250–1517	Egypt, Middle East	Moderate to harsh
Ottoman Empire	1299–1923	Turkey, Balkans, Middle East, Egypt, North Africa, Persia	Moderate
Timurid Empire	1370–1526	Persia, Caucuses, and Central Asia	Very harsh

characterized each of these regimes. While the overall pattern for Christianity was one of decline, each Christian community experienced that decline in its own way. The histories of three different regions – Egypt, Persia/Central Asia, and the Byzantine Empire – provide some sense of how diverse those experiences could be.

Egypt

The Fatimid Caliphate, which began in 909, took control of Egypt in 969. For the most part the Fatimids, who were followers of Shi'a Islam, were well disposed to the Copts and their Christian faith. The Coptic Pope Abraham (976–79) had a close relationship with the Fatimid Caliph al-Mu'izz li Din Allah (932–75), and their personal ties helped establish good relations between Muslims and Christians during the early years of the new caliphate. That peace was disturbed during the first decade of the eleventh century by Caliph al-Hakim Bi-Amr Allah, who began a harsh and unexpected persecution of Christians in the year 1004. Church buildings and monasteries were destroyed, the celebration of church festivals was prohibited, and Christians were forced to wear distinctive clothing. Many Copts thought this was the beginning of the end, a final massive push to eliminate Christianity from the Egyptian landscape. But after 10 years, the persecution ceased as quickly as it had started, and al-Hakim ordered the return of church property, the rebuilding of destroyed church buildings, and the lifting of social restrictions. Christians who had converted to Islam under threat of violence were offered the option of reconversion to Christianity, an act that was unprecedented in the history of Muslim–Christian relations.

During the rest of the eleventh century and much of the twelfth, Fatimid Egypt experienced something of a golden age when scholarship flourished and life was generally good, and this was true for Christians and Jews as well as for Muslims. But the Western Crusades ended this period of calm. The Crusades prompted intense anti-Christian feeling throughout the Middle East, and local Christian populations were often the main objects for that animosity, even though many of them were deeply opposed to the Crusader's war effort.

In general, the Coptic Christians of Egypt were less affected by the Crusades than many other Christians in the East. Christianity had always held some leadership positions in the government, and this continued during the Crusades. Most Christians also voiced their strong support for the anti-Crusader cause. This was especially true during the reign of

Salah ad-Din (1174–93), and Salah ad-Din, in return, showed public respect for the Coptic church. Starting in the mid-twelfth century, however, governmental oppression of Christians began to increase. Christians were required, once again, to wear distinctive clothing, they were taxed excessively to help pay for the war, they were banned from various public posts, and they were increasingly the target of local mob violence. The Coptic population was still large and strong enough to absorb it all, but life was not easy. In part because they were under threat, Coptic Christians felt a need to reaffirm their faith, and a tremendous amount of Christian literature was produced during the early thirteenth century. In particular, three brothers of the Ibn al-'Assal family (Al-Safi, Abu al-Farag, and Abu Ishaq) produced literally hundreds of works dealing with church law, systematic theology, religious psychology, and the philosophical defense of Christian beliefs.

The Mamluk Empire assumed control of Egypt in 1250. Even though they were at war with the Christian Crusaders of the West, the Mamluk leadership, in keeping with the historical teachings of Islam, initially treated the Coptic Christian population with relative tolerance. But a new breed of local anti-Christian Muslim preachers was trying to turn Egyptian popular opinion in the opposite direction. Based on the fact that some Christians continued to hold relatively high office in the government, these radical preachers accused the government of allowing Coptic Christians to dominate the country. While that charge was patently false, the Mamluk government felt compelled to initiate a variety of new restrictions on Christians. This did not assuage the anger of the masses, however, and Muslim mobs, often with the aid of sympathetic local government officials, sometimes violently took matters into their own hands.

The attacks on Christians were especially harsh during the years 1301, 1321, and 1354, and the accumulating impact of these violent episodes was devastating. By 1400, much of the material infrastructure of the Coptic church had been destroyed and the Coptic community had been relegated to the margins of society. Many Christians converted to Islam during these years, sometimes because it was the only way to stay alive. Some of these conversions were merely public displays, and many *musalima* (Coptic Christians who converted to Islam) continued to practice Christianity in private. But Coptic Orthodoxy is a tradition that stresses communal faith and public worship, so private Christianity is hard to sustain. By 1500, after two centuries of persecution, the Christian percentage of the total Egyptian population had been roughly cut in half, dropping from approximately 30 percent to perhaps 15 percent – a mere remnant of the ancient Coptic church of the past.

Persia and Central Asia

The history of Christianity in Persia and Central Asia mimics the history of Christianity in Egypt, except that the high points of the story are higher and the low points are significantly lower. The eleventh and twelfth centuries were largely inconsequential in terms of either losses or gains for Christians in the region. At the start of the period, Abbasid rule was slowly crumbling while the power of the Seljuk Turks was increasing, but the Seljuks themselves were in some sense only passing through the territory on the way from their original homeland in Central Asia to Turkey, where they eventually settled down. The big change for Christians in Persia and Central Asia came in the 1200s when the Mongol Empire extended its rule into the region.

The Mongol Empire was founded by Temujin (known in the West as Genghis Khan), who created a new alliance of nomadic Mongolian tribes in 1206. By the time of his death in 1227, his empire extended from the Pacific Ocean to the Caspian Sea, and by 1275 the Mongol Empire (divided into a number of separate jurisdictions or khanates) ruled all of China, Tibet, Russia, and Persia. The religion of the Mongols was shamanism – a nature-centered form of religion that emphasizes communication with the spirits – and their public policy supported religious freedom. Christianity, in particular, was highly respected by the Mongols for a variety of reasons: some of the tribes that made up Temujin's original coalition were predominantly Christian in religious orientation, many Christian holy men and women had visionary

Figure 16.8   The Mongol Emperor Hulegu with his Christian wife, Sorkaktani-beki
Courtesy of Sotheby's

powers that the Mongols respected, and a number of Mongol khans had Christian wives or mothers. The most prominent of these women was Sorkaktani-beki, a member of the Church of the East, who was the wife of Temujin's son, Tolui, and the mother of three Mongol Emperors: Kublai (who began the Yuan Dynasty in China), Mongke (who ruled the Golden Horde in Central Asia), and Hulegu (who was married to a Christian and ruled over the Il-khan Empire in Persia – see Figure 16.8). Because of this Christian connection, many members of the Church of the East began to hope that one of the Mongol rulers might convert to Christianity himself.

This hope was part of the Christian mentality at the time that Hulegu drove the Seljuk Turks out of Persia in the late 1250s, and it sparked a response that would later come back to haunt the Christians of the region. During the initial Mongol attack, Christians were often spared from violence while Muslim citizens were killed in droves. This disparity of treatment had various causes, but one was that some of the invading Mongol generals were Christians themselves, and they went out of their way to protect their Christian coreligionists. In Baghdad, Mosul, and Damascus, three of the most important cities in the region, new policies of religious freedom were announced almost as soon as these cities were captured. Local Christians were overjoyed and, in retrospect, they were overexuberant. They marched in the streets carrying the cross. They rang their church bells. They drank wine in public. And they mocked the powerlessness of their Muslim neighbors to do anything about it. They were certain the era of Islamic rule was permanently over. But it was not. In Damascus, the Mongol troops withdrew after only six months, and once back in power the Muslim majority attacked the Christians of the city with terrible vengeance, paying them back many times over for the arrogance they had displayed when Hulegu's army was in charge.

In the rest of Central Asia, Christians enjoyed a longer period of freedom, but it too came to an end when a new Mongol ruler, named Ghazan, came to the throne. Ghazan, who ruled from 1295 to 1304, had converted to Islam from Buddhism as part of his pathway to the throne. As if to prove the sincerity of his conversion, one of Ghazan's first acts in office was to mandate the destruction of all Christian churches, Jewish synagogues, and Buddhist temples in his realm. The announcement of this policy also opened the door for Muslim citizens to take their own more personal revenge on non-Muslim neighbors. The situation quickly became unruly, and finally Ghazan himself intervened and restored a modicum of order. But intermittent violence continued through the remaining years of his reign, and conditions for Christians deteriorated even more under his successor, Oljeitu (1304–16). Within 20 harsh years, the church hierarchy had been crushed and most Church of the East buildings had been reduced to rubble. The last known general gathering of Church of the East leaders in the Ilkhanate of Persia occurred during a synod held in 1318. After that, it was simply too dangerous to meet.

But worse was yet to come. In 1370, a new Muslim leader appeared on the scene, Timur Leng (founder of the Timurid Empire, known as Tamburlaine in the West), whose goal was to become a great Muslim caliph and cleanse the land of all non-Muslims. Timur Leng was merciless, often overseeing the execution of Christians and other infidels in person. In fact, he was so ruthless that some Muslim contemporaries questioned whether anyone who committed such evil acts could be a Muslim at all. By the time of his death in 1405, there was little Christianity left to salvage anywhere in Central Asia, and Christianity had been decimated in Persia as well. The magnitude of the decline is illustrated by the shrinking list of cities in the region with resident Church of the East bishops. In the year 1000, 68 cities were on that list. By 1238, there were 24, and, after Timur Leng, there were only 7, and all of them were struggling to survive. Sometime near the end of the fifteenth century, the Church of the East decided to make the office of church patriarch hereditary, since they thought it would likely be impossible in the future to gather enough bishops together to select a successor by convocation. By the year 1500, only the tiniest remnant of Christians remained in Persia and Central Asia, and that remains the case today.

The Byzantine Empire

In the year 1000, the Byzantine Empire seemed to be on an upswing. The Emperor Basil II, ruler from 976 to 1025, extended the Byzantine territories to their largest reach since the rise of Islam. But in 1071, the mighty Byzantine army was defeated by the Seljuk Turks, a new upstart power in the region, at the Battle of Manzikert. This defeat did not result in the immediate fall of the Byzantine Empire, but most of Asia Minor (Turkey) was lost by the end of the eleventh century. The Orthodox populations within the conquered territories were treated reasonably well, but the Muslim victory at Manzikert initiated a slow process of conversion that resulted in the eventual diminution of Christianity in the region.

As the Turkish armies advanced, the Byzantine Emperor wrote to Pope Urban II asking for the West to provide military assistance. The Crusader army did respond, and the establishment of several Crusader states in the Middle East distracted the attention of the Muslim powers in the region away from the Byzantine Empire long enough to allow the empire time to recover some of its lost territory. The Crusader armies also helped the Armenian community, which had immigrated from the Caucuses (between the Black Sea and the Caspian Sea) into what is now south-central Turkey, to set up their own new Christian kingdom that lasted from roughly the late eleventh century until the early thirteenth.

This generally positive relationship between the Byzantine Empire and the Western Crusaders ended in 1204 when the Fourth Crusade conquered Constantinople. Crusader

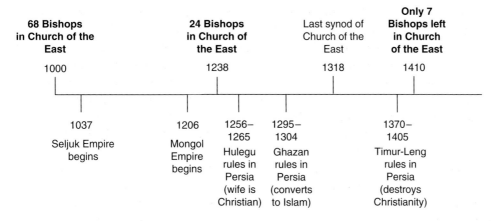

Figure 16.9   Timeline of Christian decline in Persia

rule continued for another half century, and by the time Byzantine autonomy was restored in 1261 both the status and the power of the empire had been permanently damaged. During the thirteenth century the Byzantine Empire slowly crumbled into near oblivion as the Christian kingdoms of Bulgaria and Serbia nibbled away at its western border while the Ottoman Turks (who replaced the Seljuks) advanced in the east. After the rapidly growing Ottoman Empire defeated the Serbs and Bulgarians in the late 1300s, Constantinople was surrounded by Muslim enemies. In 1453, Constantinople itself was captured, and Byzantium – the last remnant of the once mighty Roman Empire – finally came to an end. By the mid-1500s, the Ottoman Empire had further extended its realm to include what is now Romania, Hungary, Moldova, and the Ukraine, in addition to ruling the Middle East, the Caucuses, and most of North Africa. Catholic Christians in Western Europe began to fear that they too might fall prey to the Ottoman advance and come under Muslim rule themselves.

Christians in these newly conquered Ottoman territories rarely suffered the kind of persecution that was common in Egypt and Persia. The Ottoman Empire needed the Christians of the region to help them keep the state running, so they took pains not to ostracize them. There was, however, one glaring exception to this overall pattern of relatively benign rule: the Janissary system. The Janissary was an elite division of the Ottoman army that had special duties, including the protection of the Sultan. Janissaries were slaves of a sort, who were forcibly taken from their families at a young age and raised to be soldiers. They were castrated and were expected to remain celibate for life. After 1400, most of the "recruits" for the Janissary system came from Christian families in the Ottoman-occupied territories. It was almost like a living tax – a certain percentage of Christian boys were collected every year, converted to Islam, and turned into Muslim soldiers. This was surely a source of great sorrow for thousands of Christian families in the region.

For the Orthodox world as a whole, the loss of Constantinople and the end of the Byzantine Empire had a disorienting effect. Constantinople was the center of the Orthodox Christian world. It was a holy city, under the direct protection of *Theotokos* (Mary, the Mother of God), and it was the place from which God's rule was supposed to slowly emanate to all the rest of the world. Christians wondered how it could possibly have fallen into the hands of infidels. Some Orthodox Christians suggested that the loss of Constantinople signaled the end of the world, while others thought it was a punishment of the Patriarchate for having agreed to union with Rome at the Council of Florence. Whatever the response, the fall of Constantinople required a rethinking of identity for Orthodoxy as a whole.

For more than a thousand years, the Orthodox assumption had been that Christianity and the empire were two sides of the same reality – two different expressions of the reign of God on earth. But even before the fall of Constantinople, Orthodox Christians in some places like Serbia and Bulgaria – places that had reason to resent the sometimes oppressive control of the Byzantine Empire and the Patriarch of Constantinople – had begun to develop an alternative national sense of religious identity. Eventually the nationalist model of Orthodoxy would become the new norm. In Russia, however, Orthodox religious nationalism would soon morph into a new vision of empire, with the Patriarch of Moscow claiming that his city was the "third Rome" and that he should accordingly be recognized as the new international head of the Orthodox world. The reasoning was simple and historical. The Christian movement had originally been centered in Rome, but because that city was polluted by centuries of pagan sacrifice, Constantine decided to build a "new Rome" that was entirely free from pagan influence at Constantinople. Now that this "second Rome" had also become corrupt and had fallen into heresy through its union with Catholicism, God was raising up a third Rome in the new Russian Empire that he hoped would endure until the end of time. This vision of Moscow as the third Rome remains powerful in Russian Orthodoxy even today.

The years 1000 to 1500 were a time of massive change in the global profile of Christianity. When the era began, the center of the Christian world was still located in the East; by the time it ended, the influence of the East had declined dramatically and, despite Russia's new aspirations, the Catholic Church of the West had indisputably become the major carrier of the Christian tradition. Along with that geographic shift, there had also been a change in attitude. The Christian traditions of the East had generally championed an expansive vision of salvation (deification) and had been modest in their attempts (or simply unable) to impose their Christian ideas and values on others. But as the East declined, those views became less influential and the West's more narrowly defined view of salvation and its more aggressive stance toward others became the Christian norm.

Notes

1   Julian of Norwich, *Showings*, trans. Edmund Colledge and James Walsh (Mahwah, NJ: Paulist Press, 1978), p. 183.

2   Ibid., p. 298.

3   Symeon the New Theologian, *The Discourses*, trans. C. J. deCatanzaro (Mahwah, NJ: Paulist Press, 1980), pp. 312, 355, 357, 365.

4   *Kebra Nagast*, trans. E. A. Wallis Budge (London: Oxford University Press, 1932), available online at http://www.sacred-texts.com/chr/kn/ (accessed June 19, 2009).

5   Lee M. Penyak and Walter J. Petry (eds), *Religion in Latin America: A Documentary History* (Maryknoll, NY: Orbis, 2006), pp. 26–7.

Suggestions for Further Reading

Angold, Michael (ed.) (2006). *Eastern Christianity: The Cambridge History of Christianity, Vol. 5.* Cambridge, UK: Cambridge University Press.

Armour, Rollin, Sr. (2002). *Islam, Christianity, and the West: A Troubled History.* Maryknoll, NY: Orbis.

Bornstein, Daniel Ethan and Denis R. Janz (eds) (2007). *Medieval Christianity: A People's History of Christianity.* Minneapolis: Fortress Press.

Duffy, Eamon (2006). *Saints and Sinners: A History of the Popes*, 3rd edn. New Haven, CT: Yale University Press.

Lowney, Chris (2005). *A Vanished World: Muslims, Christians, and Jews in Medieval Spain.* Oxford: Oxford University Press.

Moffett, Samuel Hugh (1992). *A History of Christianity in Asia: Beginnings to 1500.* New York: HarperCollins.

Moses, Paul (2009). *The Saint and the Sultan: The Crusades, Islam, and Francis of Assisi's Mission of Peace.* New York: Doubleday.

Papadakis, Aristides and John Meyendorf (1994). *The Christian East and the Rise of the Papacy: The Church AD 1071–1453.* Crestwood, NY: St Vladimir's Seminary Press.

Rubin, Miri and Walter Simons (eds) (2009). *Christianity in Western Europe c. 1100 – c. 1500: The Cambridge History of Christianity, Vol. 4.* Cambridge, UK: Cambridge University Press.

Volz, Carl A. (1997). *The Medieval Church.* Nashville, TN: Abingdon Press.

Walsh, Michael (2003). *Warriors of the Lord: The Military Orders of Christendom.* Grand Rapids, MI: Eerdmans.

Chapter 17

Christianity in a Global Era

1500 to the Present

The world has changed more in the last five hundred years than in all of previous human history, with change following change so quickly that sometimes people haven't had the time to adjust to one new reality before another comes along and reconfigures the world in yet a different way. The term "future shock" has been used to describe this modern experience of life – wave after wave of the future crashing onto the shore of the present so quickly that people floundering in the surf have no time to stop and catch their breath. The pace and scope of change in the modern world – for historians, this means everything after the year 1500 – has affected everyone and everything. Christianity is no exception, and the Christianity that exists around the globe today is stunningly different from Christianity as it existed at the close of the fifteenth century.

In the year 1500, no one really knew what it meant to live on a globe. The Chinese may have sailed around the world as early as 1421, but they then returned home and destroyed all their great seafaring ships, so their accomplishment made no difference to the way people viewed the world. By the mid-fifteenth century, a few European mariners were becoming convinced that the world was round, but no one experienced that as a fact until a handful of sailors, traveling with Ferdinand Magellan, circumnavigated the world in the years between 1519 and 1521. Magellan himself died en route. The discovery that the earth was a globe – a small planet suspended in space rotating around the sun – was at first so shocking that many people, including most Christians, refused to believe it. The Italian scientist Galileo Galilei was condemned by the Catholic Church as a heretic in 1632 for publishing his heliocentric (sun-centered rather than earth-centered) views about the universe. Only in the last few centuries have humans had the capacity to picture their world as an interconnected "global" community.

The World's Christians: Who they are, Where they are, and How they got there, First Edition. Douglas Jacobsen.
© 2011 Douglas Jacobsen. Published 2011 by Blackwell Publishing Ltd.

An equally shocking discovery was that human cultures around the globe have developed in very different ways, and the new cultural exchanges that took place during this era persistently hammered that reality home. For Christians, this growing awareness of human diversity raised the question of salvation in a new way: how exactly did the Christian gospel apply to all these very different kinds of people around the world, some of whom seemed to have no awareness of their own need for salvation? It also forced Christians to rethink what was central and indispensable to their own practice of Christianity, what was flexible and able to be reshaped to better fit local customs and ways of thinking and what was not.

The pace of change in ordinary, everyday experience has become extraordinary. In 1455, the use of a new movable type printing press allowed the Gutenberg Bible to be distributed throughout Europe at an unheard-of speed. But the capacity for mass communication has been revolutionized even more by the inventions of the telegraph, radio, telephone, television, and now computers and the internet. The discovery of bacteria and viruses, and of drugs to combat disease, altered the way people thought about health, sickness, and dying, and the electric light bulb made it possible for people to work all day and all night. New pesticides, herbicides, and fertilizers allowed farmers to grow crops in sizes and proportions unlike anything seen before. Bicycles, trains, automobiles, and planes made it possible to travel near and far with relative ease. And for the first time in history, new weapons have made it possible for humanity to bring about its own cataclysmic extinction.

Christians, like everyone else, have had to adapt to this newly globalized world, and that already complicated task was made even more complex by the creation of two new Christian traditions: Protestantism and the Pentecostal/Charismatic movement. The processes of globalization have helped to introduce Christianity to more regions of the world than ever before, but it has also created a dazzling panorama of difference within the Christian tradition itself that makes the diversity of the past look pale by comparison. This chapter describes how all of this happened, bringing the long story of Christianity up to the present.

Convictions

In 1500, there were basically two ways to be Christian: one could be either Catholic or Orthodox. The two formerly great traditions of the Miaphysite movement and the Church of the East continued to exist, but they had become small, largely hereditary communities struggling simply to survive. Of the two viable options, Catholicism was clearly the stronger of the two, and it looked as if it was poised to dominate the Christian world. But then suddenly a new movement emerged out of Catholicism that was committed to rearranging and redefining many of the core convictions of the Catholic tradition. That movement became known as Protestantism, and it quickly established itself as a major religious player in the European context and later on the global stage. Then, around the year 1900, when Protestantism was at the peak of its power in Western culture, another tradition, the Pentecostal/Charismatic movement, emerged out of Protestantism and began to develop its own new and powerful vision of Christian faith and life.

The history and varieties of Protestantism

The Protestant tradition began in the early sixteenth century, and it soon came to see itself, and to be seen by others, as a radical alternative to Catholicism. That difference – Protestantism versus Catholicism – produced significant spiritual and political tension in Europe, resulting in years of religious warfare as Protestants and Catholics squared off against each other in battle. Yet Protestantism first emerged as a movement of reform within the Catholic Church itself, and some Protestants (mostly Anglicans and Lutherans) continue to see themselves not as opponents of Catholic Christianity, but as reformers who seek to renew and improve all that is best in what they would call the catholic (with a lower-case "c") tradition.

In 1500, the Catholic Church was already in the midst of a slow process of transition. The goal of overseeing a united Christian Europe with the pope as the supreme spiritual leader and political kingmaker was no longer a viable option. Rising national pride and monarchical self-confidence had undermined the pope's political strength and religious authority. Rulers all across Europe were making special arrangements with Rome that gave the kings and queens of Europe more power in their domains. The monarchs of Spain and Portugal had even cajoled Rome into giving them total control over the Catholic Church in the new lands they were colonizing in the Americas – the power of *patronato* in Spanish or *padroado* in Portuguese. Apart from these political developments, the papacy was also in a state of relative spiritual decline. Luxury had become the norm in Rome. Popes lived very well – they saw themselves as religious royalty – and their pampered lifestyles were hard to reconcile with the asceticism that had been such a large part of Christian spirituality in the past. Many Catholic leaders were calling for some kind of reform.

Another issue confronting Catholicism was the emergence of significantly different religious emphases in the various regions of Europe. In Italy, for example, Christian spirituality, at least among the wealthy, had become merged with the life-affirming and optimistic worldview of the Renaissance. God was not seen as fearsome, but as playful – as a creator who wanted people to be creative and to enjoy the beauty and wonder of the natural world and human culture. Less affluent Catholics in Italy were also interested in the good life, but they typically expressed their more modest aspirations by bargaining with God, Mary, or a local saint, promising to perform certain acts of devotion in exchange for some requested blessing. In Spain, a quite different kind of Catholicism prevailed, one that was strict, disciplined, militant, and intent on subjecting the whole world to Christ. In northern Europe (in what is now Germany and the Low Countries), yet another form of Catholic piety held sway, focusing mainly on personal matters of salvation and religious duties. Northern Europeans wanted to know how to avoid hell and shorten their time in purgatory, and they rejected the optimism of upper-class Italian Catholicism, the religious bargaining of lower-class Italians, and the self-confident militarism of Spain. Northern Europeans were looking for something else, and that search ultimately led to the Protestant Reformation.

Taken together, the new nationalism, the desire for church leaders to lead more modest lives, and regional differences of spirituality created a volatile mix that exploded in the Protestant movement. Martin Luther (1483–1546) lit the match that started the Protestant fire, but at least at first he was a reluctant radical. He was a professor, doing his scholarly work of carefully examining Catholic teaching and religious practice, and he was also a local Catholic priest, trying his best to protect and nurture the spirituality of the people in his parish. He was vexed by the increasingly glib way that indulgences – church-issued documents that guaranteed various kinds of relief from punishment in purgatory – were being sold in his diocese. In the year 1517, he issued a formal, academic invitation, written in Latin, for Catholic scholars to debate the theology and practice of selling indulgences. He nailed that invitation to the door of the church in Wittenburg, Germany, which served as a kind of bulletin board for the University of Wittenburg where Luther taught, and he waited for a response. That invitation to debate became known as the *95 Theses*, and the response was greater than anything Luther expected. Almost immediately, the *95 Theses* were translated into German, reprinted, and distributed all over northern Europe, sparking the religious firestorm that turned into the Protestant movement.

Luther was surprised by that result, but not necessarily disappointed. In many ways, the practice of selling indulgences was just the tip of an iceberg. The deeper problem, according to Luther, was how the Catholicism of his day encouraged the kind of fear that drove people to buy indulgences. Like most other German Catholics, Luther had grown up fearing God because God seemed so intent on sending people to hell as a consequence of every unconfessed sin. Luther had responded to his own fear by becoming a monk and trying to live a perfect life, but he was driven to the point of despair when he realized perfection was impossible. With the help of his monastic supervisor, Johann von Staupitz (1460–1524), and as a result of his own careful rereading of the Bible, Luther came to a new understanding of God – a vision that accentuated God's love for humankind, rather than God's role as vengeful judge. That new view of God changed everything and became the key tenet of the Protestant movement. Luther continued to believe that the church and the sacraments were important aids for faith, but ultimately the church, the sacraments, the saints, and every other form of religious mediation between God and the individual were secondary. In the eyes of the Catholic Church, this was obvious heresy. On June 15, 1520, Pope Leo X issued the papal bull *Exsurge Domine* condemning Luther's views and ordering him to recant. When Luther received the document, he and his students burned it in a bonfire; he was officially excommunicated the following January.

Had Luther lived earlier, he would likely have been burned as a heretic. This had been the fate of previous reformers like John Wycliffe (1328–84) and Jan Hus (1369–1415), both of whom held views similar to Luther's. But Luther lived in the sixteenth century, not the fourteenth or fifteenth, and local rulers were now more willing and able to defy the church. Luther's local ruler was Duke Frederick "the Wise" of Saxony – one of the most important political leaders within the Holy Roman Empire – and he had no intention of letting the church or the empire crush his favorite professor. Frederick's protection allowed Luther and the infant Protestant movement to survive. Luther's success in challenging the Catholic monopoly soon prompted similar movements all over Europe, and the Protestant Reformation – the term "Protestant" was first used in 1529 – was the result. The newly available printing press was a key factor in the rapid dispersal of Protestant ideas. Luther was a brilliant writer of tracts (short booklets strongly expressing one particular point of view), and his tracts circulated throughout Europe by the thousands. His ideas about grace, faith, and God, along with his diatribes against indulgences, were especially welcomed in urban centers and among the new, literate middle class. Soon Protestantism had spread to Switzerland, the Netherlands, Scandinavia, Britain, France, Poland, and Hungary.

The history of Protestantism is convoluted and complex and it is not possible here to provide any full account of the many different varieties of Protestantism that have emerged over the centuries (see Chapter 3 for a brief outline of these developments). What can be said is that lacking any central governing authority, Protestantism spawned thousands of separate denominations and schools of thought. The resulting Protestant landscape is incredibly complex, but that complexity can be simplified to some degree by identifying three large-scale patterns that have emerged. Since Protestantism as a whole centers on the Bible, these three forms or styles of Protestantism can be viewed as alternative modes of biblical interpretation. The first group sees its main task as systematically explaining the core message of the Bible. The second group focuses on reading the Bible through the lens of religious experience. The third group views the Bible largely as a moral guidebook for Christian living.

Protestants in the Reformed tradition – that is, people who follow the model of Protestantism developed initially by the French/Swiss theologian John Calvin (1509–64) – emphasize the first approach, the systematic theological explication of the biblical message. In the seventeenth and eighteenth centuries, this variety of Protestantism produced a wealth of important theological writings that translated the narrative language and symbolism of the Bible into the much less ambiguous language of philosophy. At first, this made Christianity appear truer, more rational, and empirically grounded and not just a matter of belief. But changes in philosophy and science in the nineteenth and twentieth centuries have forced Protestants in the Reformed tradition to reassess their theology. In particular, modern science questioned the Genesis account of creation and advances in biblical scholarship raised questions about whether the Gospels were historically accurate. Some Protestants embraced these new views of science and biblical scholarship and began to reformulate their understanding of the Bible in the light of those findings – a task which has proven to be never-ending because science and biblical scholarship are themselves always changing. Others decided to reaffirm the ideas of older Reformed theology in largely unchanged form, and they developed a new theory to defend their views focusing on the inerrancy of the Bible in all matters of faith and fact, including science. Today, people aligned with the first group are often called liberal or progressive Protestants, while those in the second group are called conservatives or fundamentalists.

But not all Protestants emphasized theology. Some placed greater emphasis on feelings or experience. The Pietist movement, which began in Germany around the year 1600, was characterized by the belief that the key marker of faith was the experience of conversion – the moment when a person suddenly feels forgiven by God. After an individual experiences the love of God through conversion, then it is possible for that person to trust God about the rest of life. In the eighteenth century, a variety of Pietistic Protestant preachers (especially in the English-speaking world) developed a range of revivalistic techniques designed to elicit conversions. Their sermons were fiery, their audiences were large, conversions were public, and – as in other modern mass gatherings of people like football games and rock concerts – emotions ran high. In the eighteenth century, revival meetings led by George Whitefield (1714–70) helped to spark a Great Awakening among American and English Protestants; in the nineteenth century, revivalism was further developed by people like Dwight L. Moody (1837–99); and in the twentieth century, Billy Graham (born 1918) exported a modified version of Protestant revivalism around the world. Graham's particular kind of revivalism mixed Pietistic-style faith with a moderate form of Protestant fundamentalism to create the modern Evangelical movement, a version of Christianity that since the 1960s has become enormously popular not only in North America but also in Africa and Asia.

There were, however, nonrevivalistic ways of linking experience with Protestant faith, and the views of the German theologian Friedrich Schleiermacher (1768–1834) deserve special attention because of their wide-ranging influence. Schleiermacher, who was raised in a Pietist family, argued that underneath the changeable superficial emotions of life, all people know deep down that they are not the source of their own existence. Life is a gift, and humans have an "absolute dependence" on something or someone else who is the Giver of that gift. For Schleiermacher that Giver was properly called God, and he thought it was simply reasonable – an acknowledgment of reality – to place faith or trust in God experienced in that way. Schleiermacher believed that every human experienced this feeling of absolute dependence to some degree. For him, Christianity was the highest expression of this universal experience, but other religions and even secular culture and science contained glimmers of it. Schleiermacher's perspective laid the groundwork for the kind of positive Christian dialogue with other religions and with the arts and sciences that is so prevalent in progressive Protestant churches today.

A third subgroup of Protestants sought to base their faith in ethics or morality, rather than in either theology or spiritual feelings. For this group, faith means trying to live in the same way that Jesus himself lived. The earliest Protestants to take this approach were the Anabaptists. For them, faith was not so much a matter of belief or feeling as it was a way of life. Citing Jesus's commandment to "turn the other cheek" when attacked, Anabaptists concluded that loving one's enemies meant a commitment to pacifism. Contemporary Anabaptists still revere Dirk Willems, a sixteenth-century Dutch Mennonite who gave up his life for this vision of the gospel. Willems had been arrested for his faith and was facing execution. He managed to escape from jail, but when the pursuing jailer fell through the ice, Willems returned to rescue him. As a result, Willems was recaptured and summarily executed, paying a steep price for his neighbor-loving, nonviolent understanding of faith (Figure 17.1).

Other Protestants besides the Anabaptists linked faith and morality in different ways. In the eighteenth century, for example, Thomas Jefferson (the third President of the United States and principal author of the Declaration of Independence) espoused a morally centered Protestantism as the core of Christianity. Jefferson was a rationalist who was disconcerted by the many miracle stories in the Bible, but he loved the moral teachings of Jesus. In fact, he tried to "improve" the Bible so that it would be easier to discern those core teachings of Jesus. With scissors in hand, he read through the Bible and clipped out all the good parts – the passages that he thought represented the moral gold of the text – leaving behind all the doctrinal and supernatural dross. He then pasted those clippings together to create his own new and improved morality-centered New Testament (Plate 33).

The twentieth century sparked a host of morality-centered Protestant movements, including the Christian labor union movement in Europe and the Social Gospel, women's

Figure 17.1   Dirk Willems rescuing his pursuer. Etching by Jan Luyken
The Martyrs Mirror, 1685 edition. Etchings by Jan Luyken. Courtesy of the Mennonite Library & Archives, Bethel College, North Newton, Kansas

rights, temperance, and Civil Rights movements in the United States. In South Africa, morality-centered Christianity expressed in the *ubuntu* theology of the Anglican Archbishop Desmond Tutu was influential in ending the rule of apartheid. In recent years, it has been the dominant form of "above ground" Protestantism in China, exemplified in the work and writings of Bishop K. H. Ting. The causes championed by morality-centered Protestants have not always been compatible, but they have all been motivated by the same basic impulse.

The Pentecostal/Charismatic movement

Because of its young age, the Pentecostal/Charismatic movement is still somewhat pliable and its boundaries are still relatively fluid. It is also far less institutionalized than Catholicism, Orthodoxy, or even Protestantism, and it has produced far fewer printed documents. These characteristics make it difficult to count the movement's membership with precision and to construct an orderly organizational flowchart that describes how the community operates. But the core convictions of the movement are clear nonetheless. For Pentecostal/Charismatic Christians, it is the direct experience of God and the supernatural work of the Holy Spirit in the world that matter. Members of this tradition expect to see miracles virtually every day, and they expect to feel God with their bodies, rejecting the notion that "head knowledge" of God is sufficient to change anyone.

The Pentecostal/Charismatic tradition arose in slightly different forms in different nations around the world at roughly the same time in the early twentieth century, but the

Figure 17.2   William J. Seymour with other leaders of the Azusa Street revival (Seymour is second from right in front row)
Photograph courtesy of the Flower Pentecostal Heritage Center, Missouri

worldwide epicenter of the movement was a revival that took place in Los Angeles, California, during the years 1906 to 1908 at a run-down church on Azusa Street. William Seymour (1870–1922), the child of former slaves, was the leader in charge, and the Azusa Street Revival, as it came to be called, was the Grand Central Station of the newly emerging movement. People from all over the world made their way to Los Angeles to get "baptized in the Spirit" and then returned home empowered by the Spirit and ready to spread the word. From the very beginning, the Pentecostal/Charismatic tradition was transnational in both scope and character. It was also multiracial in composition and economically centered among the poor – characteristics that still define the movement today.

The theology and spiritual roots of the Pentecostal/Charismatic tradition are more complex than it might at first appear, incorporating elements from Protestantism, Orthodoxy, and Catholicism in a distinctive blend of practices and beliefs. Historically, the Pentecostal/Charismatic tradition emerged out of Protestant Pietism, and especially out of the "Holiness" wing of the Pietistic movement. The Holiness movement proposed the possibility of a "second work of grace" (also called "sanctification") that provides the believer with full freedom from sin, a new spirit of godliness, and the ability to proclaim the gospel with power. This language has similarities with the way salvation is described in the Orthodox tradition (as deification), and that similarity is not coincidental. John Wesley, the founder of Methodism and the theological hero of the Holiness movement, was deeply influenced by his reading of Eastern Christian theology, and he intentionally incorporated some Orthodox emphases into his theology. The Holiness theology of conversion followed by sanctification moved the Orthodox aspects of Wesleyanism to center stage. Then the Pentecostal/Charismatic movement went one step further, adding "baptism in the Spirit" to their theology and arriving at the "full gospel" message of Pentecostal/Charismatic faith.

Although the Pentecostal/Charismatic tradition has its roots in the Holiness movement and borrows some of its ideas indirectly from Orthodoxy, it also resonates with some of the key convictions of Catholic Christianity, most notably its sacramentalism – the belief that ritual actions and material objects can become vehicles of God's grace. Pentecostal/Charismatic Christians lay hands on people when they pray for them; they anoint people with oil; they pray over small scraps of cloth and send them to people who are sick so they will be healed; they clap, dance, shout, and sing, and they raise their hands in praise of God, using their whole bodies as well as their minds in worship. The particular actions or objects may be distinctively Pentecostal/Charismatic, but the general principle is consonant with Catholic sacramentalism.

Non-Pentecostal/Charismatic Christians, especially those from the West, tend to assume that the passages in the Bible that speak of angels and demons are meant to be interpreted metaphorically. In contrast, most Pentecostal/Charismatic Christians believe that the world is full of invisible spirit beings like angels and demons that actively interact with living human beings. This view is, in fact, held by the majority of the world's six billion people, who not only believe that the earth is full of angels and demons and other spiritual forces, but claim to have had first-hand experience of them. Pentecostal/Charismatic Christians consider spiritual beings to be significant players in daily life, and they promise that people who turn their lives over to Jesus and seek the filling of the Holy Spirit will be freed from demonic oppression and will be helped by angels.

The Pentecostal/Charismatic movement is grounded in a robust mix of Christian convictions that includes the West's long-standing emphasis on forgiveness of sins, Protestantism's focus on the Bible as the Word of God, Orthodoxy's understanding of deification (or being filled with the Spirit of God), Catholicism's sacramental imagination and practice, and humanity's almost ubiquitous belief in the power of invisible spiritual beings that serve the purposes of either goodness or evil. It is a hybrid Christian movement with powerful appeal. In just over a century, the Pentecostal/Charismatic movement has grown to include more than a sixth of all the world's Christians, making it the fastest growing religious movement in human history.

Catholicism

Catholicism has changed significantly during the last five centuries. Many of those changes would have taken place with or without the rise of Protestantism or the Pentecostal/Charismatic movement, but there is no question that the two new traditions had an impact. The Catholic Church responded to Protestantism by correcting obvious abuses and simultaneously rearticulating Catholicism's well-established core convictions. This was done principally at the Council of Trent (1545 to 1563), which also rebuffed Protestant criticism that said Catholics had to "earn" their salvation while Protestants trusted in God's grace. The bishops who gathered at Trent affirmed that they believed in grace as much as any

Protestant, but they also believed in human responsibility. Moral effort was the way that Christians cooperated with and showed their gratitude to God for the free gift of saving grace. Convinced that Catholic theology was already correct and complete, the Catholic bishops perceived that their main challenge was educational, nurturing proper belief and practice within the Catholic community. To that end, the newly formed Society of Jesus (the Jesuits) spent the next century founding hundreds of seminaries and colleges across Europe and around the world to educate Catholics about what they ought to believe.

Another response to Protestantism was that the church began a worldwide building campaign. It was apparent that Catholics needed to *feel* more Catholic, so ornate new Baroque style churches were designed and constructed with the hope of overwhelming worshipers with their heavenly beauty (see Plate 34). These churches were full of paintings, sculptures, stained glass windows, and statues of saints that communicated a sense of what heaven was supposed to be like and that were also intended to serve as reminders that the Catholic Church alone provided the only sure means of getting to heaven. Part of this strategy was to make Protestant churches and Protestant faith in general seem, in comparison, not only theologically mistaken but also simply lacking in sacredness. This strategy was relatively effective, and even today many Catholics find Protestant churches to be sterile meeting places and not "real" churches, not sacred buildings at all.

The Baroque era lasted about two centuries, from roughly 1600 to 1800. It helped restore and buttress Catholicism, but it eventually became less appealing and less convincing. Across Europe, people shifted their attention away from the heavenly future and toward the earthly present. Catholics – even devout, practicing Catholics who attended Mass regularly – began to wonder how Catholic faith was connected to life in the present world. The Catholic leadership generally ignored them, until a tipping point was reached with the French Revolution of the late 1700s. As the leaders of the French Revolution became ever more radical and anti-Catholic, the church became ever more reactionary and antidemocratic. When the Revolution finally failed, the church took the lead in trying to restore Europe to its old hierarchical and monarchical ways. The Catholic motto was "throne and altar," and the church was soon opposing anything that seemed even remotely modern. Newspapers were bad, and so were labor unions. Public education was bad, and so was government record keeping related to births, deaths, and marriages. Science was bad, and so was biblical scholarship and archeology. The most important pope during these years was Pius IX (Pio Nono in Italian), the longest ruling pontiff in history (1846–78), who was jokingly referred to as "Pope No-No" because of his condemnation of all modern developments. It was as if the Catholic Church had decided that the world should simply never change, and the church's self-assigned role was to be an anchor, trying to drag the world to a full stop.

But, of course, change kept coming, and slowly the Catholic Church realized that adjustments were required if it was to remain relevant and meaningful to the people it served. One powerful symbol of change occurred in the year 1929 when the church finally gave up its campaign to regain the Papal States, a territory in central Italy that the papacy had ruled as a separate nation since the eighth century. Italian nationalists had taken control of the region in 1870 and had subsequently integrated the Papal States into the newly unified Italy state. (The Catholic Church still owns a small piece of land in Italy called Vatican City, but the Vatican's 109 acres is miniscule compared to the roughly 16,000 square miles that made up the old Papal States.) The popes hoped that giving up their territorial claim would strengthen their standing as spokesmen for justice and moral purity in human society. Faced with the relentless and seemingly irreversible growth of democracy, the popes recognized that they would have to rely on the laity if Catholic values were to be preserved in the world. During the first half of the twentieth century, "Catholic Action" programs encouraged laypeople to do just that: use their influence to help maintain the Catholicity of the nations within which they lived. Lay activism has become an increasingly significant part of Catholic spirituality ever since, represented in groups and movements as divergent as Opus Dei, liberation theology, and the Catholic Charismatic Renewal.

The church also very cautiously began to give Catholic intellectuals space to reflect on how the Catholic faith might maintain its viability in the modern world. The papal encyclical *Humani Generis*, issued by Pope Pius XII in 1950, was a milestone in this regard. The bulk of the document warns against scholarly work that seeks too blatantly to overthrow the historical teachings of the church, but then acknowledges that "whatever new truth the sincere human mind is able to find, certainly cannot be opposed to truth already acquired, since God, the highest Truth, has created and guides the human intellect." As long as Catholic scholars were willing to weigh their findings "with painstaking care and a balanced judgment," they could proceed. And proceed they did, with intellectuals like Marie-Dominique Chenu, Yves Congar, Henri de Lubac, Jacques Maritain, Karl Rahner, and Edward Schillebeeckx leading the way. Some of these theologians were silenced by the church for a portion of their careers, but Catholic scholars are now active and energetic participants in public discourse throughout the world.

Catholic engagement with the modern global world culminated in the Second Vatican Council, held in four sessions between the years 1962 and 1965. The spirit of the meeting as a whole is captured in the words of the pastoral constitution *Gaudium et Spes*, issued by Pope Paul VI at the close of the Council: "The joys and the hopes, the griefs and the anxieties of the men of this age, especially those who are poor or in any way afflicted, these are the joys and hopes, the griefs and anxieties of the followers of Christ. Indeed, nothing genuinely human fails to raise an echo in their hearts." But as open-hearted and forward looking as the council was, the years since have not been easy. Some Catholics were disturbed by the jettisoning of old rituals and ways of life, while others thought the council did not go far enough in reformulating Catholicism for the modern age. Everyone would agree, however, that the council helped to foster a deeper and broader sense of Catholicism's global reach, a fact underscored by Pope John Paul II's (1978–2005) 104 international trips, visiting Catholics in every corner of the globe. Even though Catholic laypeople and leaders from around the world sometimes find the arcane ways of the Vatican frustrating to deal with, no other Christian body has done more to foster theological unity and cultural pluralism at the same time.

Eastern Orthodoxy

Few changes or additions have been made to the core doctrines of the Orthodox churches since 1500. Perseverance, and not innovation or development, has generally been seen as the more important task, especially for Orthodox Christians who have been living in predominantly Muslim nations or, during the twentieth century, under Communist dictatorships. But perseverance or self-protection has also been part of Orthodoxy's ongoing efforts to ward off what many Orthodox Christians see as the pernicious influence of the West.

During the last five hundred years, Catholic and Protestant Christians have repeatedly tried to woo Orthodox Christians away from their own tradition so they could remake them into good Western-style believers. And sometimes they have succeeded. Cyril Lucaris, the contested Patriarch of Constantinople (1620–38), for example, was convinced of the truth of Calvinist doctrine, and German Pietists made significant inroads into Russian Orthodoxy during the eighteenth century. An even more substantial challenge over the last three centuries has been the Catholic Church policy of trying to create new "Eastern rite" or "uniate" Catholic churches from breakaway subunits of the various Orthodox churches. The papal encyclical *Allatae Sunt* (1755) laid out the blueprint for this activity, and there are now about 20 different "Eastern Rite" Catholic churches scattered across the Middle East and Eastern Europe. In response to all these pressures, many Orthodox leaders have favored a "repeating theology"[1] – repeating the historical convictions of the past as a way of protecting Orthodoxy from any inappropriate innovations that might spring from non-Orthodox influences.

One particularly significant example of Orthodoxy's resistance to change took place in seventeenth-century Russia when Nikon was selected to be the new Patriarch of Moscow in 1652. He had not sought the post, but once in office he took his role seriously. Since Moscow was now the "Third Rome" – the successor of Constantinople and functional center of the Orthodox world – the Patriarch of Moscow saw himself as necessarily needing to become more global and less idiosyncratically Russian in his religious perspective, and he thought the Russian church as a whole needed to move in that direction, too. In particular, Nikon wanted to bring Russian practice into closer alignment with the Byzantine traditions of the Greek-speaking Orthodox world. Many Russians refused to go along with Nikon's suggestions, however, and when the Patriarch tried to force his views on the church, a massive schism resulted with an Old Believers (or Old Ritualists) movement breaking away from the mainstream Russian Orthodox Church. This schism has never healed, and today there are still about 2,500,000 Old Believers in Russia and the Russian diaspora.

During the last five or six decades, the Orthodox tradition as a whole has become considerably more open to fellowship and conversation with other Christian traditions. This is evident in the fact that 15 autocephalous Orthodox churches are today members of the World Council of Churches (WCC), a predominantly Protestant body founded in 1948. The Orthodox have had a significant influence within the WCC, often serving as a counterbalance to the more progressive Protestant views of some member churches. That role has sometimes been frustrating. In the 1990s, the Orthodox churches came close to resigning from the WCC en masse as a protest against what they saw as an overemphasis on matters of political liberation, gender orientation, and women's equality, but the WCC backed off from some of its more controversial positions and the Orthodox churches continued as members. The Orthodox churches have also in recent years reached out to the historical Miaphysite churches (which the Orthodox often call "Oriental Orthodox churches"), seeking to broker a possible reunion between the two traditions. A joint statement issued in 1990 concluded that, despite the bitter theological disputes of the past, the Christological statements of the two traditions were not in conflict and the mutual condemnations of the two traditions were rescinded. While full unity has not yet been achieved, there is now more cooperation between these two traditions than ever before.

Encounters

The last five centuries have been a time of overwhelming change in human history, and the single best word for describing those changes is globalization. Globalization is a complicated, and often contentious, process. By itself, the term globalization refers simply to the increasingly interconnected character of the world in which we live, but it can be helpful to distinguish between two very different processes and outcomes of globalization which have been termed *grobalization* and *glocalization*.[2] Grobalization takes place when powerful global actors export or impose their ways of doing things on others. This is sometimes also called the McDonaldization of the world. The ultimate end of grobalization taken to its logical conclusion would be worldwide homogeneity, with everyone listening to the same songs, wearing the same styles of clothing, and eating the same prepackaged food. Glocalization is almost the opposite. In glocalization, local entrepreneurs – and these include social and cultural entrepreneurs as well as business entrepreneurs – creatively mix together bits and pieces from different cultures of the world to create new hybrid realities. Fusion restaurants that bring together different styles of ethnic cuisine to create new and interesting dishes illustrate this kind of glocalization, as does blended music that mixes sounds from different styles or cultures. With regard to religion, grobalization implies the spread of one, largely unchanged, variety of faith around the world. By contrast, glocalization implies indigenization, enculturation, and local adaptation.

During the last five centuries, the main grobal actors on the world stage have been a series of European empires that have been intent on reproducing their own cultures in different regions of the world (see Table 17.1). Christianity has not always been a main focus of these empires, but both Catholicism and Protestantism have been part of their grobal influence. In the second half of the twentieth century, grobalism took on a new dynamic with the rise of the Cold War: the attempted ideological division of the world into two competing camps, one committed to the exportation of democratic capitalism mixed with Christian or "Judeo-Christian" values and the other committed to the exportation of Communism mixed with atheism. In the last few decades, and especially since the fall of Communism in the USSR, pure capitalism as embodied in various large international corporations has driven most grobal developments worldwide.

In contrast to these highly visible sources of grobalism, most glocal developments – whether economic, cultural, or religious – have taken place beneath the radar of publically "newsworthy" visibility. This is certainly true in the history of Christianity where the names of many of the most important glocalizers of the past have been lost to history. But that is the nature of glocalism – it is a local-global phenomenon with the accent on the local use or adaptation of global resources or ideas. Glocalism is not necessarily institutionalized or permanent. Instead it is often in flux, reacting to, shifting with, and creatively negotiating

Table 17.1 Modern European empires

Empire	Beginning date	Effective ending date	Main regional focus	Main religious orientation
Portuguese	late 1400s	decline in 1700s/ ends mid-1900s	Brazil, Africa, and the East Indies	Catholic
Spanish	late 1400s	decline in 1700s/ ends c.1900	Latin America and the Philippines	Catholic
Dutch	late 1500s	ends mid-1900s	The East Indies	Protestant
British	early 1600s	ends mid-1900s	North America, Africa, India	Protestant
French	early 1600s	ends mid-1900s	Africa and Southeast Asia	Catholic

space between the grobal products being foisted upon the world and the values, ways of life, and material products of local cultures.

The rest of this chapter sketches out some of the most significant developments in recent Christian history on this background grid of grobalization and glocalization. The goal of this very brief overview is to provide an impressionistic image of how the global Christian community has changed and developed over time. For clarity's sake, each of the last five centuries is discussed separately and in relatively equal space. The trajectory of the narrative as a whole is one in which the historical "center" of Christianity in Europe and North America has slowly dissipated so that the world's Christians are scattered all around the globe with no place or region able to be identified as the single center of the movement.

Sixteenth century: Catholic globalization

The sixteenth century was the age of the European Reformation, one of the most significant turning points in Christian history. This is when Lutheranism, Anglicanism, the Anabaptist movement, and Reformed Protestantism all got their start. But just as significantly, and maybe more so, this was a century of global Catholic expansion.

During these years, the Catholic nations of Spain and Portugal began the most impressive project of Christian globalization the world had ever seen. Portugal took the lead, spreading its influence south along the west coast of Africa, then north along the east coast, and finally on to India and Southeast Asia (present-day Indonesia). Spain set out in the opposite direction, crossing the Atlantic and exploring the Americas. Hoping to prevent conflicts between these two powerful Catholic nations, Pope Alexander VI issued the bull *Inter Caetera* in the year 1493, which established a dividing line, with lands to the west granted to Spain and to the east to Portugal (Figure 17.3).

Spain had a clear goal in its American venture: to produce wealth and to grobally replicate Spanish Catholic society in the New World. To that end, cities were built, churches were constructed, monasteries were founded, and universities were established. When they encountered indigenous people (*indígenas*), the Spanish pattern was generally to conquer

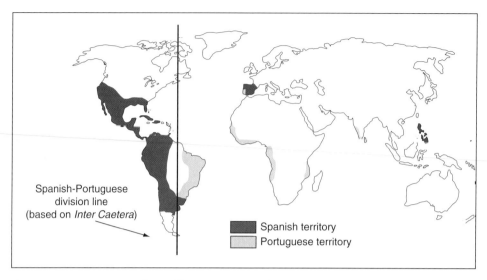

Figure 17.3   Portuguese and Spanish empires, sixteenth century. Map by author.

them, dismantle their political structures, put them to work on large plantations (*encomiendas*), and then convert them. This last task was assigned to hundreds of missionary monks, mostly Franciscans and Dominicans, who were "assisted" by the Spanish military presence in the region. The assumption, in keeping with the crusader logic of the medieval period, was that both force and persuasion were necessary. The Spanish Catholic theologian Juan Ginés de Sepúlveda (1489–1573) explained that "useful terror" could be very effective in helping "the light of truth scatter the darkness of error … [and] break bad habits."[3]

The treatment of the indigenous people of the Americas was often brutal, and the Dominican priest Bartolomé de las Casas protested that abuse as early as 1516. Las Casas had originally come to the region as an *encomiendera* – an owner of an *encomienda* – but he was revolted by the treatment of *indígenas* and turned to religion to salve his conscience. His complaints seem to have secured some immediate improvements in the local situation, but they were insufficient to end the general mistreatment that continued throughout the sixteenth century.

Despite the abuses, many *indígenas* seem genuinely to have embraced Christianity as their own preferred religion, but the Catholicism of the indigenous population was never an exact reproduction of European Catholicism. It mixed together European faith with local customs and understandings of reality to create new glocal versions of Catholicism that better served the needs and aspirations of local people. The Virgin Mary plays a large role in many of these localized forms of indigenous Catholicism in Latin America and that pattern started in 1531 when the Virgin Mary is said to have appeared to Cuauhtlatoatzin (Juan Diego) in what is now Mexico. Mary told Cuauhtlatoatzin that she loved the native inhabitants of the land and approved of their faith, and the Virgin of Guadalupe, as she is now known, has been a symbol of glocal faith ever since.

In the other half of the sixteenth-century Catholic world, the Portuguese adopted a different strategy. In their colonial ventures, the Portuguese embraced glocalization in Africa but were boldly grobal in India. The Portuguese encounter with Africa began in the late fifteenth century, and its stimulus was trade, mostly slave trade. The Portuguese traders preferred dealing with Christian partners in Africa rather than pagan ones, so evangelism became part of their business strategy. In the Congo, King Nzinga Nkuwu became a Christian in the year 1491 and, after his baptism, assumed the name João I (Plate 35). When João died in 1509, he was succeeded by another Christian, Afonso I (1509–43), and then a long line of Christian kings of the Congo continued to rule into the 1700s. Congolese Christianity mixed a range of thoroughly African ideas about the spirit world with doctrines taught by the Portuguese missionaries. The saints of Portuguese Catholicism were sometimes reconceived as African ancestors, and Catholic mysticism sometimes looked like spirit possession. Whatever its particulars, Congolese Christianity was clearly glocal in character and the Portuguese seemed unperturbed by that fact.

The Portuguese took a very different approach in India. The first Portuguese encounter with India took place in 1498 when Vasco da Gama arrived on the west coast of India, near present-day Calicut (or Kozhikode), seeking, as he said, "Christians and spices." The Portuguese hope was to break the Muslim monopoly over the Asian spice trade and simultaneously to find Christians who could become their allies in the fight to free the Holy Land from Muslim domination. The Portuguese did find Christians in India, but not the kind they were looking for. The Christians of India's west coast were associated with the Church of the East, and their beliefs and behaviors were quickly deemed heretical and in need of serious correction. The Portuguese began that task almost immediately, formally establishing an Office of Inquisition in 1560 to root out and put on trial any Indian Christian professing heretical (i.e., non-Catholic) beliefs. More than 16,000 Indians were arrested and around a hundred were sentenced to death. The culmination of this process came in 1599, when the Portuguese summoned all local Christians to the specially convened Synod of Diamper where they demanded full submission to Catholic Christianity and to the pope as its head. They then burned all the ancient writings of the Indian Christian community that they had collected so there could be no going back to the old, mistaken ways of the past. It would be hard to find a more explicit case of Christian grobalization.

Seventeenth century: learning tolerance

In Europe, the seventeenth century was the time when Protestantism finally became a fixture on the continent and when Protestants (of various kinds) and Catholics realized they needed to learn how to live peaceably alongside each other. For more than a century, the Catholic kings and queens of Europe had been trying to crush the movement, and they had been successful in rolling it back in several regions where Protestants had originally made serious inroads, including Poland, Belgium, France, Austria, and Bohemia (the present-day Czech Republic). A variety of means had been employed, including military intervention, with the Thirty Years War (1618–48) being the last chapter in that sorry history of interreligious violence. The Peace of Westphalia that ended the Thirty Years War proposed a checkerboard solution to the problem of religious difference. Henceforth each local European state or territory would determine its own religious identity based on the religious preference of its ruler. The assumption, however, was that one and only one religion would be allowed in each location. There were some exceptions to this rule, but very few. Most Europeans could not imagine that a religiously pluralistic state could survive.

A slightly different dynamic prevailed in Great Britain where the battle in the English Civil War (1642–51) was not between Catholics and Protestants, but between two different forms of Protestantism: the Royalists were almost all Anglicans, while the Parliamentarians, who opposed the absolute power of the king, were mainly Puritans or Presbyterians. While the Parliamentarians won the Civil War, they ultimately lost the support of the English people, and the Anglican tradition emerged victorious when the monarchy was restored in 1660. But it was a chastened Church of England that returned to power and in 1689 Parliament passed an Act of Toleration that allowed Dissenters (Protestants who were not members of the Church of England) a limited set of religious rights.

Neither the Peace of Westphalia nor the English Act of Toleration resulted in full religious freedom. What emerged instead was a form of rough toleration, with Catholics and different kinds of Protestants sequestered into separate national or regional enclaves and still viewing each other as enemies – and sometimes violence continued to flare up at the boundary lines where different religions touched, as was the case in Northern Ireland until very recently.

The first extension of Protestantism beyond the shores of Europe took place within this context of religious warfare followed by limited religious toleration and local religious homogeneity, and the primary place where this extension took place was North America. The Protestant (mostly British) colonization of North America generally followed a pattern that can be called "displacement settlement" with British immigrants displacing American Indians from their lands so they could then settle on those lands themselves – a policy later continued by the United States government as the boundary of the nation was pushed ever further westward under the banner of "Manifest Destiny" during the nineteenth century. This was a very different style of colonization than had prevailed in Latin America. Puritans and other British settlers did not enslave the Indian population, nor did they try very hard to convert them. Overall, there was little mixing of the two cultures (European and Native American). As a result, the colonization of North America produced a very different form of Christian globalization: British America was a simple extension – a transplanting – of European Protestantism to the other side of the Atlantic Ocean.

While some of the English citizens who came to North America were motivated by economics, many were in search of religious freedom. The most articulate of these Protestants were the Puritans who settled in the region of the United States now known as New England. The Puritans who moved to the New World were not missionaries. They were religious refugees who wanted to create their own settlements where they could practice their own religion as they pleased, and they hoped that everyone who disagreed with them would stay away. The Puritan vision was utopian, expressed eloquently by John Winthrop in a 1630 speech to the people on board the ship *Arbella* before they disembarked to found the city of Boston. His theme was love, and he challenged the new colonists to make New England an exemplary Christian "city set upon a hill," a culture and way of life that would be a model for the rest of the world to follow. The idea was essentially to start over from scratch, using the Bible as their guide, to build a new and perfect Christian society, one that might become the first ray of the dawning millennium of God's reign on earth.

But the Puritan dream did not last. Scores of non-Puritan settlers entered the region, and despite the best efforts of the Puritan government to keep the place pure – including hanging the Quaker preacher Mary Dyer on Boston Common in June 1660 – the Puritan monopoly came to an end. Puritan devotion also waned with time. The sons and daughters of the settlers could not keep up the red-hot fervor of the founders. As a result, a new kind of Christian society slowly emerged in New England and in the rest of British America. This new society was religiously pluralistic – narrowly so, consisting mainly of various kinds of Protestants – but still, because there was no one central government to make one form of Protestantism normative, people had to begin to learn how to live with each other as neighbors despite their religious disagreements.

A very different encounter was taking place in the Catholic world at the same time, one involving the recently formed Society of Jesus, the Jesuits. The Jesuit order was created in the mid-sixteenth century to "enter upon hospital and missionary work … [and] go without question wherever the pope might direct." The Jesuits were directed to Asia and to China in particular. When Matteo Ricci (1552–1610) first arrived in China, he spent his time learning the Chinese language and studying Chinese culture in conversation with the scholars of the imperial court. Once he had established his scholarly credentials, Ricci and his Jesuit colleagues began the task of explaining Christianity to these intellectuals in ways they could understand and would hopefully find appealing, a task that continued throughout the seventeenth century. The Jesuits' ultimate goal was to help Chinese Christians create an authentic new Chinese understanding of Catholic faith and life – a task that required considerable reflection on what was and was not appropriate. The Jesuits were convinced glocalists; they believed that Christian faith had to be adapted to different cultures.

A defining issue was whether Chinese Christians should take part in the seasonal rites of traditional Chinese religion and the veneration of ancestors. The Jesuit response was "yes," but others disagreed. For most Catholics living in the seventeenth century, the spiritual flexibility of the Jesuits was inconceivable. When Christians in Europe could only just tolerate each other, the Jesuits' open embrace of Chinese culture was problematic. Members of other Catholic orders that were working in China, especially the Franciscans and Dominicans, concluded that the Jesuit policy sanctioned idolatry. They complained loudly to Rome, creating what is known as the Chinese Rites Controversy. Eventually, Pope Clement XI condemned the Jesuit position. That condemnation stood until the mid-twentieth century when the Catholic Church finally reversed its decision and allowed Catholics in China once again to take part in public Confucian ceremonies and to pay honor to their ancestors. In 1958, Pope John XXIII went even further, referring to Ricci as the "the model of missionaries" in his encyclical *Princeps Pastorum*.

Eighteenth century: church, state, and slavery

When the eighteenth century began, Christianity and the state had been glued together for more than 1,300 years. By the time the century ended, separation of church and state was well on the way to becoming the new norm. In the Roman Empire, Theodosius I had merged the two in the year 392; in Armenia and Georgia, Christianity and ethnic nationhood had been joined at least as long; and in the Muslim world, Christians had been organized into *millets* – effectively little religioethnic ministates – since the seventh century. Christians had all but forgotten that the movement began as a nonstate organization, a person-to-person association of believers in Jesus. In the eighteenth century that vision was recovered, but the transition was not easy.

In Europe, the separation of church and state was fueled largely by the ideas of the Enlightenment – a century-long period, running from the late 1600s to the end of the 1700s, when a number of leading intellectuals began to champion the role of reason (as opposed to passion or religious belief) in scholarly inquiry and in social life. In England, Enlightenment thinkers were often devout Christians, including John Tillotson (1630–94), who was the Archbishop of Canterbury and thus the head of the Church of England. But in France, the Enlightenment typically had an antireligious or anti-Catholic edge to it, partly because the Catholic Church had so much more power in France than the Church of England had in Great Britain. The best estimate is that in the eighteenth century the Catholic Church owned about a third of all the land in France. Enlightened French thinkers were anxious to break what they saw as the church's stranglehold on society, and the French Revolution (1789–99) gave them that opportunity.

The motto of the French Revolution was *liberté, égalité, fraternité* (liberty, equality, solidarity). At first, the goal was to make both the church and the state subservient to those ideals, but as the Revolution progressed it became more radical, eventually leading to the execution of King Louis XVI and the decision to completely destroy the Catholic Church with the intention of remaking France into a thoroughly postreligious society. In one of many horrific episodes, 16 Carmelite nuns who were discovered by the Committee of Surveillance while they were hiding in Compiègne (a city located about 50 miles north of Paris) were brought to the capital and executed by guillotine on July 17, 1794. A Catholic counterrevolt had begun in the area of the Vendeé the year before, and it too was bloodily suppressed with perhaps a quarter of the 800,000 residents slaughtered in the process. Eventually the Revolution exhausted itself, Napoleon Bonaparte assumed power in France, and the special status of the Catholic Church in French society was partially restored. But the ideal of democracy had become wedded in France to an antireligious understanding of church–state separation. For many in the Catholic Church, this meant that democracy was seen as evil by definition; for the proponents of democracy, it meant that democracy almost necessarily had to be anticlerical. Both attitudes were soon exported throughout the Catholic world, shaping developments in Latin America as much as in Europe.

In North America, church–state separation followed a different route. Once again a revolution was involved, but the American Revolution was not at all antireligious. In fact, many of the leading American revolutionaries were Christians who championed the cause of church–state separation as the best thing that could happen to religion. Several factors help explain the difference from France. First, North America was a land of many churches rather than one established state church, so there was no monolithic religious institution against which to revolt. Second, the churches had little, if any, real power over the governments of the colonies. Third, the Great Awakening, a revival that swept across the British North American colonies in the 1730s and 1740s, had convinced many Christians that state support was unnecessary for the flourishing of Christian faith. The leaders of the Great Awakening – who often preached in the open air and drew crowds that numbered in the thousands – had changed the religious terrain of North America through persuasion alone,

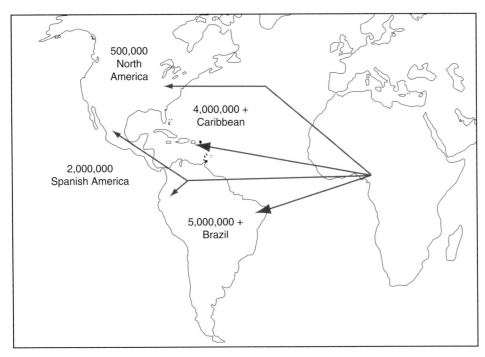

500,000
North
America

4,000,000 +
Caribbean

2,000,000
Spanish America

5,000,000 +
Brazil

Figure 17.4   African slaves brought to the Americas, 1650–1860. Map by author.

and many American Protestants had become convinced that true religion could never be advanced by violence or force. They therefore stoutly opposed the creation of any religious establishment (official state church) in the new United States. What they wanted, instead, was religious and political freedom so that true faith could flourish. Separation of church and state was perceived as an aid to true religion, not a hindrance.

The separation of church and state and the concomitant rise of religious freedom signaled a massive change in the way Christians viewed the world, and today most Christians assume that support of religious freedom is a Christian virtue and that the separation of church and state is the way things are supposed to be. But this is a very recent experiment – it is only two hundred years old – and it may not be permanent. Some countries in Western Europe still have formal state churches and many of the Orthodox churches and the political rulers in predominantly Orthodox lands have never fully embraced the notion of church–state separation. A number of Christian leaders in Africa and some theocratic Protestant and Catholic thinkers in the West also seem willing to reconsider the notion that church and state should be kept apart. Nonetheless, the idea of church–state separation and the religious freedom it implies has had an enormous influence on global Christianity, reinforcing and validating glocal developments around the world.

The Christian story of the eighteenth century is not, however, only about freedom. It is also about slavery. About 12 million Africans were brought to the Americas and sold as slaves during the four centuries of the Atlantic slave trade, the late 1400s to 1866 (see Figure 17.4). The peak of this trade took place in the eighteenth century when 4,000,000 Africans were shipped to the Caribbean, more than 2,000,000 to Brazil, and about 200,000 to British colonies in North America. Virtually all of this immoral traffic in human lives was overseen by the Christian nations of Europe. Religion was not the driving force behind the slave trade – money was – but the churches cooperated with the slave "industry," sometimes even baptizing victims before they were shipped overseas, branding them with a cross to indicate that they were Christians.

How could Christians, especially Christians who were beginning to champion religious freedom and democracy, also support the slave trade? For many Christians, the answer was biblical: a straightforward reading of the New Testament seemed to say that slavery was part of normal human society. Masters were supposed to act kindly toward their slaves, but the institution itself was not condemned. As for African slavery in particular, the story of the cursing of the descendants of Ham, the son of Noah, found in the ninth chapter of Genesis, was used to justify the enterprise. In that passage, Noah curses Ham's son Canaan, saying his descendants were damned to be "the lowest of slaves" forever (Genesis 9:25). But it was not only Christians who supported and were complicit in the slave trade. Europeans as a whole supported it, including many post-Christian Enlightenment thinkers who thought that freedom applied only to rational human beings. Viewed in this light, Africans and other "savages" who were deemed not rational did not need to be free, nor did women, who were similarly seen to be less than fully rational.

Ironically, the slave trade itself promoted the glocal development of Christianity in the Americas. A significant number of slaves brought to the Americas were Christians from the kingdom of the Congo. These individuals had been raised as Christians from birth and they brought their faith with them to the Americas where they helped create a separate black Christianity that differed significantly from the Christianity of the masters who enslaved them. In North Carolina, for example – where Congolese slaves were more common than anywhere else in North America – Christian slaves from the Congo helped articulate the linkage between salvation and freedom that is still so central to the Black Church in the United States today. The words for salvation (*kanga*) and freedom (*lukangu*) in the Kongo language are etymologically related,[4] and for Congolese Christian slaves in North America the meanings of these two words converged even more strongly than they ever had in Africa. Salvation was freedom and freedom was salvation, and the two were inseparable. The other region of the Americas where Congolese slaves were especially prominent was Brazil, and the various forms of Afro-Brazilian religion that developed in the *quilombos* (settlements of runaway slaves in the backlands of Brazil) often included elements of Congolese Christianity. This development presaged the great variety of Christian-influenced Afro-Brazilian and Afro-Caribbean glocalized religions that still flourish in Latin America today.

Nineteenth century: Christian growth and Protestant globalization

The main Christian story of the nineteenth century was growth, and especially Protestant growth. During this period, the Christian population of the world shot dramatically upward from 22 percent of the global population to 34 percent (see Table 17.2 for Christian population growth by continent). That kind of dramatic growth demands explanation. As it turns out, roughly three-quarters of this gain was the result of natural population growth,

Table 17.2   Distribution of Christian population by continent, 1800 and 1900

Continent	Christians 1800 (in millions)	% of all Christians	Christians 1900 (in millions)	% of all Christians	Relative gain/loss
Europe	180	83	380	68	−15%
Latin America	21	10	62	11	+1%
North America	7	3	78	14	+11%
Africa	3	1	9	2	+1%
Asia/Pacific	6	3	26	5	+2%
Total	217		555		

especially in the regions of the world that were already predominantly Christian: Europe, North America, and Latin America. Europeans and Americans together accounted for 25 percent of the global population in 1800, but by 1900 they comprised 34 percent. The remaining 3 percent gain in the growth of Christianity worldwide can be explained largely as the result of the Protestant missionary movement which made significant advances in Africa and Asia during this time.

Despite Protestantism's growth, Catholicism remained the world's largest Christian tradition, accounting for just over half the world's Christians in 1800 and also in 1900. This is somewhat surprising given that there was a lull in Catholic missionary activity for much of this century. In fact, the year 1800 marks the low ebb in Catholic missions with only about 200 missionaries worldwide. Later in the century, the Catholic missionary spirit revived and a host of new missionary orders were formed. Where the big shift came globally was in the relative sizes of Orthodoxy and Protestantism. In 1800, Orthodoxy represented 27 percent of all the Christians in the world, while Protestantism accounted for only 22 percent. By 1900, those numbers were reversed, with Protestants now claiming 27 percent of all the world's Christians and Orthodoxy falling to 22 percent.

Prior to the nineteenth century, Protestants generally had been content to keep to themselves and stay at home in Europe and in the mostly Protestant British colonies of North America. But in the nineteenth century Protestant missions became "big business." European state churches and American denominations organized major missionary ventures, and many others were supported by new, free-standing missionary organizations like the British and Foreign Bible Society (formed in 1804), the American Board of Commissioners for Foreign Missions (1810), and the China Inland Mission (1865). Thousands of Protestant missionaries were sent around the world, making their way to the smallest islands in the Pacific and to the most remote regions of Africa. The only place they did not go in significant numbers was Latin America.

Protestant missionary activity, not surprisingly, tended to follow the boundary lines of the new Protestant empires – especially the British Empire – that dominated the world during these years. Missionaries were rarely paid servants of any state, but missionary activity frequently piggy-backed on Europe's imperial network because that network provided both personal protection and ease of access to the nations the missionaries wanted to evangelize.

China is a case in point. Protestant missionaries benefitted enormously from the outcome of the so-called "Opium Wars," the first of which was fought from 1839 to 1842 and the second from 1856 to 1860. These wars were fought by Great Britain for the purpose of "opening" China to Western trade, and especially to the sale of opium, which the British traders were pushing on the Chinese people. The treaties that ended these wars included not just new freedom for traders and drug dealers, but also freedom for missionaries who were now guaranteed access to the inland areas of China that had formerly been off limits. Many missionaries felt that the association with opium was unfortunate, but their theology assured them that God had opened the doors of China in response to their prayers, and the means by which God had chosen to do that was not their concern.

Most Protestant missionary initiatives concentrated on individual conversion, but they also stressed the Bible and education. The logic was straightforward. In order to be a good Protestant one had to be able to read the Bible, so people had to be taught to read and the Bible had to be translated into the local language. The schools organized by the Protestant missionaries taught much more than just reading and the Bible, however. In essence they became outposts of Western civilization, inculcating in students a Western sense of time, individualism, social hierarchy, self-discipline, and dress. And that was fine with most missionaries, who were sure that their culture, as well as their faith, was far superior to the cultures of the people they were trying to "save." There is no question that most Protestant missionaries were grobalists.

But Protestant schooling – and the Protestant ethos in general – was also an incubator of glocal creativity. New Christians were told to read the Bible for themselves. They were told to interpret the Bible, applying it to their own lives and the culture in which they lived. And they did just that, with the resultant indigenization of faith looking nothing like anything the world had seen before. In Africa, Independent or African-Initiated Churches (AICs) began to emerge all across the continent. In 1872 the Kiyoka (Burning) movement erupted in Angola and, in 1888, the Native Baptist Church was formed in Nigeria. Thousands of other African-grown churches soon followed. Similar developments took place in Asia and around the world. Perhaps the largest of these movements, and certainly the most politically volatile, was the *Taiping Tianguo* (the Heavenly Kingdom of Great Peace) that arose in China and was led by Hong Xiuquan.

Hong had become a Christian by reading a small volume of nine tracts composed by Afa Liang, a Chinese Christian who served as the translator for a Scottish Presbyterian minister. The tracts illuminated the meaning of a visionary dream Hong had experienced several years earlier, that told Hong he was Jesus's younger brother, the second son of God, who had been sent to earth to inaugurate the promised kingdom of God that would bring heavenly peace to the world. Convinced that he had a special role to play in the Christianization of China, Hong gathered a significant following over the next several years, eventually organized into what was essentially a new Christian state within the Chinese state. When Hong and his followers began to move north toward Beijing in the early 1850s, the Chinese government felt compelled to act and tried to crush the movement. But it was not easy. Hong himself died in 1864, but his followers fought on until 1871.

Figure 17.5   Hong Xiuquan, leader of the *Taiping Tianguo*
© akg-images

When it was all over, as many as 25 million people had died as a result of the conflict, making the *Taiping Tianguo*, the Taiping Rebellion, the bloodiest revolt in Chinese history.

The creativity unleashed by Protestantism was not, however, limited only to the "mission field." Protestants in Europe and America were also experimenting with radically new ways of understanding the Christian message. One of the most enduring of the new American approaches was initiated by Joseph Smith while he was living in rural New York State. He told his followers that the angel Moroni had shown him a new set of scriptures in addition to the Bible – the *Book of Mormon*, the *Pearl of Great Price*, and the *Doctrine and Covenants* – that taught that God the Creator had once been human and had slowly attained divinity. They too, if they were faithful, could follow that path and someday become gods themselves. It was all very different from traditional Christianity; in fact, Smith believed that all the rest of Christian history was in error and that his own new church represented the "Restoration" of true Christian faith. Today, the Church of Jesus Christ of Latter Day Saints, also known as the Mormon church, has six million followers in the United States and roughly the same number scattered across the rest of the world.

In Europe, the creativity of Protestantism produced a rush of philosophical and theological inventiveness. The German philosopher G. F. W. Hegel (1770–1831) had originally studied to become a Lutheran minister, and he wondered why both philosophy and religion talked so much about absolute and changeless truth, when the world itself was in the process of constant change. In response to that quandary, Hegel developed an influential new philosophy that envisioned God or Spirit or the "Absolute" as an ever-unfolding reality that was always in the process of change. Hegel's reconceptualization of God and the universe became the foundation for a host of other developments in nineteenth- and twentieth-century European thought, including both Marxism and eventually process theology.

This same Protestant creativity can also be observed within changing attitudes toward slavery in British and American Protestantism. For centuries, Christians had lived comfortably with slavery, but suddenly opinion began to turn against the practice. In England it was the evangelical leader William Wilberforce (1759–1833) who became the champion of the antislavery cause. In the United States, Frederick Douglass (1818–95) was perhaps the most outspoken, making a sharp distinction between what he called "the Christianity of Christ" and "the corrupt, slaveholding, women-whipping, cradle-plundering, partial and hypocritical Christianity of this land."[5] What was at stake here was not just the new Abolitionist ethic that Douglass, Wilberforce, and others articulated, but more importantly a new way of reading the Bible that made this Abolitionist interpretation of Christianity possible. To arrive at this conclusion one had to read the Bible against the grain of its surface meaning, which seemed to accept slavery as a fact of everyday life. What Abolitionists argued, however, was that, beneath the surface meaning of the text, the deeper message of the Bible was one of equality and liberty for all. This new way of reading the Bible paved the path for progressive Christians later to make the same kinds of arguments for the equality and human rights of all people, including women and GLBT individuals, in both church and society.

The story of Protestant globalization and the creative energy it set loose in the world is very obviously not the whole of the nineteenth-century history of Christianity any more than Catholic globalization was the whole of the sixteenth-century history. However, it was those Protestant developments, more than anything else, that set the stage for the theological and practical transformations that have convulsed Christian history in the twentieth and twenty-first centuries.

Twentieth century: the redistribution of faith

For the Christian world the twentieth century was a time of great change. It began hopefully, with progress in the air. In 1901 the American Protestant missionary activist John R. Mott (1865–1955) pronounced that it was reasonable to expect "the evangelization of the world in this generation." Christians in Europe and the United States – both Catholics and Protestants – anticipated that the social and economic order, not just individuals, might soon be redeemed and made whole. The unspoken assumption was that modern Euro-American Christian civilization was nearing its own Christian perfection. Advance was inevitable, and soon the world in its entirety would embrace the Christian message and way of life.

Then things began to fall apart. World War I – "the Great War," as it was called – shattered the illusion of progress when the soil of Europe soaked up the blood of supposedly civilized Christians barbarously killing each other for a cause no one could adequately explain. As the war began to wind down, the influenza pandemic of 1918 and 1919 spiraled up, killing perhaps 40 million people worldwide. Then the Great Depression hit, driving the world economy into the ground, and World War II followed soon after, with the horror of the Holocaust and the terror of nuclear weapons. The peace that finally ensued was hardly a peace at all, as the world settled into a massive Cold War that pitted the United States and its capitalist allies against the Soviet Union and its Communist alliance (see Figure 17.6).

Christian hope and idealism took a beating during these decades, and a more realistic Christian view of the world emerged in both the United States and Europe. In Europe, Christian realism quickly turned into simple secularism, and the state took over more and more of the old functions of religion – defining morality, caring for the sick and needy, and providing a sense of meaning and purpose without any reference to God. The Lutheran minister and theologian Dietrich Bonhoeffer had seen this coming. During World War II, Bonhoeffer was part of the Confessing Church movement – a movement within German Protestantism that rejected Nazi demands that the church's understanding of Christianity be made to conform with their ideology of the *Volk* (the Aryan nation) and the state. Arrested for his part in a failed conspiracy to assassinate the German leader Adolf Hitler and writing from prison, Bonhoeffer reflected on Christianity and society. He said that the myth of Christian civilization was dead. Instead, the world had entered a "religionless time," and Bonhoeffer warned that the followers of Jesus needed to thoroughly rethink how they were called to live and who God was. The old ways and the old ideals no longer worked. Bonhoeffer was pessimistic about the ability of the Christian movement – at least in Europe – to change, and he feared it might just die. Some still think that Christianity in Europe is on the way to extinction.

Christian realism in the United States followed a different path. Rather than declining, Christianity flourished in the years after the war as soldiers returned home and started their lives over, bent on living "normal" lives with their families in the new neat and clean suburbs

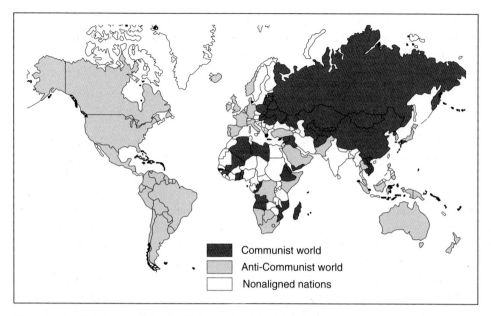

Figure 17.6   Global map of the Cold War, c. 1980. Map by author.

that were being built around the edges of the nation's cities. More than ever, Christianity and the "American way of life" seemed to coalesce as the United States defined itself as a God-fearing nation with responsibility for defending the world from the militant, grobal atheism of the Soviet Union. Some dissident movements questioned some parts of this American vision of righteousness – the Civil Rights Movement and the antiwar movement directed against United States involvement in Vietnam – but many of these dissident movements also appealed to Christian values (like love and peace) and to American values (like freedom and self-determination) to make their case. If Christian realism seemed to veer toward secularism in Europe, it veered toward American exceptionalism in the United States – the belief that the American way of life was the best and most Christian model of society on earth.

Much of the rest of the world saw things differently. The first decades of the century had been years of ever-growing domination by Europeans. In Africa, the European race to establish colonies on the continent, called the "Scramble for Africa," was reaching its peak. By 1915, every African nation, with the exceptions of Ethiopia and Liberia, was under European rule. In the Middle East, France and Great Britain divided the territories of the old Ottoman Empire between themselves after the defeat of the Ottomans in World War I. Meanwhile, the British Raj (Rule) still governed India; the French were expanding their Indochinese Empire from Vietnam into Cambodia, Thailand, and Laos; and the Dutch were still in charge of the Southeast Asian islands that would eventually become Indonesia. In all these lands, Christian missionaries were hard at work, trying to convert "the natives."

But resistance was growing. As early as 1900, the members of the Righteous Harmony Society (the so-called "Boxers") had tried to drive all Westerners and Christians out of

China in a bloody uprising known as the Boxer Rebellion (1900–01). It was not successful, but it presaged what was to take place all around the world in the two decades following World War II. During those years, the worldwide network of European colonies collapsed as local leaders pushed for self-government and as the European powers decided the fight to keep control of their former colonial holdings was neither feasible nor affordable.

In the many new postcolonial nations that were emerging around the world, there was a strong sense of the need for independence not only from political control, but also from Euro-American culture. This was reflected within Christianity in the form of a call for a moratorium on all Western missionary activity. Christians around the world said it was time for the "older churches" of Europe and North America to give the "younger churches" of Africa and Asia – a category that included both locally initiated "independent" African and Asian churches as well as many former "missionary churches" that were trying to break free of Western control – a chance to grow and mature in their own ways and on their own terms.

While a full moratorium was never enacted, many Western Christian churches did scale back their missionary efforts to some degree and all of them tried to become much more respectful of the local cultures in the regions where they were still active. During this time the idea of "inculturation" became the new watchword in mission – an understanding of cross-cultural Christian cooperation that viewed mission as a two-way street of mutual enrichment rather than as a one-way delivery system bringing Western Christian truth to the rest of the world. As Pope John Paul II explained in his encyclical *Slavorum Apostoli* (1985), inculturation involved both "the incarnation of the Gospel in native cultures and the introduction of these cultures into the life of the Church."[6]

It was in these years after the European colonial era came to an end – after the middle of the twentieth century – that Christianity became a truly global movement in a new way. The measure was no longer the mere presence of Christianity in all the various countries of the world; it was the increasingly even dispersal of the Christian population worldwide. Thus while 68 percent of the world's Christians still lived in Europe in 1900, only 27 percent of the world's Christian population is located there now. The rest live in Latin America (24 percent), Africa (20 percent), Asia and the Pacific (16 percent), and North America (13 percent) – and the evenness of that distribution is flattening out more every day (see Table 17.3).

As with the growth of Christianity in the nineteenth century, it is worth asking what factors have driven this twentieth-century shift in global Christian demographics. Once again, differential birth rates have played a major role, accounting for about one third of the change. During the twentieth century, the European percentage of the world's population fell from 24 to 12 percent, while the African percentage jumped from 8 to 13 percent, Latin America rose from 5 to 9 percent, and Asia moved from 57 to 60 percent. Secularization in Europe also had an impact, explaining another third of the shift. In 1900 roughly 95 percent of the population of Europe was Christian, but by 2000 that had number fallen to 78 percent.

The rest of the change, however, was more positively religious in character: it came from conversion and it was located primarily in Africa and Asia. Population growth was also a major factor in these areas, but the impact of conversions was enormous. To illustrate, the population of Africa is currently six times larger than it was in 1900, but the Christian population is 46 times bigger. In Asia and the Pacific, the population is currently four times what it was in 1900, but the Christian population is 12 times greater than it was a hundred years ago.

Table 17.3 Distribution of global Christian population by continent, 1900 and 2000

Continent	Christians 1900 (in millions)	% of all Christians	Christians 2000 (in millions)	% of all Christians	Relative gain/loss
Europe	380	68	565	27	−41%
Latin America	62	11	505	24	+13%
North America	78	14	260	13	−1%
Africa	9	2	415	20	+18%
Asia/Pacific	26	5	310	16	+11%
Total	555		2055		

A majority of this new growth has taken place within the Pentecostal/Charismatic movement. Today fewer than 5 percent of the Christians in Europe are Pentecostal/Charismatic, but more than 25 percent of all the Christians in Africa are Pentecostal/Charismatic and that number rises to more than 30 percent in Asia. The reason for this attraction to Pentecostal/Charismatic Christianity is multifaceted, but the fact that Pentecostal/Charismatic Christianity comes with no colonial baggage – it has never been associated with any political empire – is significant. In a sense, Pentecostal/Charismatic Christianity is postcolonial by nature. It encourages local Christian autonomy and cultural adaptation (glocalism) wherever it goes, and that has made it an especially attractive form of faith in the global south.

Christians today are more evenly distributed around the world than they have been at any other time in the past. Arriving at this state of relative parity has required a huge transfer of Christian numbers away from the "North" (Europe) and toward the "South" (Africa, Asia, and Latin America). This is so much the case that some scholars now predict that the future of Christianity lies in the global south. That may become true in the future, but it is not an accurate description of the present. Right now the Christian world is better described either as "flat" or multicentered. Europe and North America continue to be Christian powerhouses in terms of missions, money, and education. Their leadership status within the global Christian community is no longer unchallenged, but it has not been entirely obliterated either. Brazil, South Korea, and Nigeria now exist as alternative centers of global Christianity, and numerous other nations are poised to join that circle of leading Christian nations, but these countries are taking their places alongside Europe and North America, they are not replacing them – at least, not yet.

The last five hundred years of Christian history have been an almost unbelievably complex time of growth, expansion, reconsideration of core convictions, and theological creativity. As a result, Christianity in every region of the globe has become more self-aware, more articulate, and in many ways more particular. Yet at the same time, the Christian world, along with the world as a whole, has become smaller and more interconnected, which means there are currently more conversations going on among the world's many different kinds of Christians than ever before. Predictions about what might result from this new mix of diversity and dialogue differ wildly. Some hope that a new sense of Christian unity will ultimately evolve; others believe that Christianity will soon shatter into a host of different separate and distinct Christianities – different and distinct religions, albeit all centered on the person of Jesus. Given the quirkiness of the past, most historians would refrain from choosing either side in that debate, but one thing is clear: the next few decades will be a time of continuing change and transformation within the Christian world, making our own age one of the most significant periods in the history and development of the Christian religion.

Notes

1   George A. Maloney, *A History of Orthodox Theology since 1453* (Belmont, MA: Nordland, 1976), p. 318.

2   The terms come from George Ritzer, *The Globalization of Nothing 2* (Thousand Oaks, CA: Pine Forge Press, 2007).

3   Quoted in Luis N. Rivera, *A Violent Evangelism: The Political and Religious Conquest of the Americas* (Louisville, KY: Westminster/John Knox, 1992), p. 220.

4   John K. Thornton, *The Kongolese Saint Anthony: Dona Beatriz Kimpa Vita and the Antonian Movement,* 1684–1706 (Cambridge, UK: Cambridge University Press, 1998), pp. 212–13.

5   Frederick Douglass, *The Narrative of the Life of Frederick Douglass, An American Slave* (New York: Signet, 1968), p. 120.

6   *Slavorum Apostoli,* online at http://www.vatican.va/holy_father/john_paul_ii/encyclicals/documents/hf_jp-ii_enc_19850602_slavorum-apostoli_en.html (accessed August 5, 2009).

Suggestions for Further Reading

Davies, Noel and Martin Conway (2008). *World Christianity in the 20th Century*. London: SCM.

Gilley, Sheridan and Brian Stanley (eds) (2006). *The Cambridge History of Christianity: World Christianities c.1815–c.1914*. Cambridge, UK: Cambridge University Press.

Hsia, R. Po-Chia (2005). *The World of Catholic Renewal 1540–1770*, 2nd edn. Cambridge, UK: Cambridge University Press.

Jenkins, Philip (2007). *The Next Christendom: The Coming of Global Christianity*, revised edn. New York: Oxford University Press.

Jenkins, Philip (2008). *The New Faces of Christianity: Believing the Bible in the Global South*. New York: Oxford University Press.

Kim, Sebastian and Kirsteen Kim (2008). *Christianity as a World Religion*. London: Continuum.

Linden, Ian (2009). *Global Catholicism: Diversity and Change Since Vatican II*. New York: Columbia University Press.

MacCulloch, Diarmaid (2005). *The Reformation*. New York: Penguin.

McLeod, Hugh (ed.) (2006). *The Cambridge History of Christianity: World Christianities c.1914–c.2000*. Cambridge, UK: Cambridge University Press.

Miller, Glenn T. (1997). *The Modern Church: From the Dawn of the Reformation to the Eve of the Third Millennium*. Nashville, TN: Abingdon.

Neill, Stephen (1986). *A History of Christian Missions*, 2nd edn. London: Penguin.

Robert, Dana L. (2009). *Christian Mission: How Christianity Became a World Religion*. Oxford: Wiley-Blackwell.

Sanneh, Lamin (2008). *Disciples of All Nations: Pillars of World Christianity*. Oxford: Oxford University Press.

Ward, W. R. (1995). *Christianity Under the Ancien Régime 1648–1789*. Cambridge, UK: Cambridge University Press.

Index

Aachen 314
Abbasid Caliphate 304–5, 307,
    308–9, 340
Abolitionists 369
Aboriginal Evangelical
    Fellowship 264
Aboriginals 250, 251, 253, 264–5
abortion
    laws on 142, 220
    pro-choice Catholics on 241
Abraham (Prophet) 68
Abraham, Coptic Pope 339
Abu Sayyaf (separatist
    movement) 184
Aceh 184
Act of Toleration (England 1689) 362
Acts of the Apostles 275
Acts of Thecla 276
Acts of Thomas 287
Adelaide 264
Adelaja, Sunday 107, 108
affirmative action (for Dalits) 127
Afghanistan 110, 113, 114–15, 116
Africa
    Anglicanism 150, 151, 165, 169,
        170, 174, 175, 352

Catholic populations 27, 33
    European race to establish
        colonies 371
    Evangelical movement enormously
        popular in 351
    life expectancy in 160
    Methodism 165
    Orthodox population 13
    Pentecostal/Charismatic
        Christians 51, 56, 60
    Portuguese glocalization in 361
    Protestantism 39
    spread of Islam down east
        coast 330
    see also East Africa; North Africa;
        South Africa; Sub-Saharan Africa
African-Americans 8
    Baptist 237
    independent holiness 60
    Methodist 237
    threats faced together 238
African National Congress 175
Afrikaner Nationalist party 174
Afro-Brazilian religions 214, 215, 216,
    222, 366
Afro-Caribbean religions 222, 366

Aglipayan Church 188
Ahl al-Kitāb 68, 304
AICs (African Independent/
    Initiated Churches) 58, 162, 167,
    246, 368
    largest 173, 176
Akinola, Peter, Anglican Bishop 171
Alabama 230
Al-Andalus 332
Alaska 242
Albania 13, 25, 91, 93
    declared fully atheistic 92
    independence (early 1900s) 95
al-Bashir, Omar Hasan Ahmad 160
Albigensian Crusade (1209–29) 335
Aleksy II, Patriarch of Moscow 105
Alexander VI, Pope 359
Alexandria 273, 277, 302
    Islamic capture of 306
    Patriarchs of 22–3
    see also Clement of Alexandria;
        Cyril of Alexandria; Origen of
        Alexandria
Alfonso I, Christian King of the
    Congo 172, 361
Algeria 72, 285

The World's Christians: Who they are, Where they are, and How they got there, First Edition. Douglas Jacobsen.
© 2011 Douglas Jacobsen. Published 2011 by Blackwell Publishing Ltd.

Al-Hakim bi Amr Allah, Fatimid
    Caliph 339
Allen, Richard 237
al-Mahdi, Muhammad ibn Mansur,
    Abbasid Caliph 308–9
al-Ma'mun, Abbasid Caliph 309
al-Mu'izz li Din Allah, Fatimid
    Caliph 339
Alopen 194, 309–10
Alpha Course 134, 135–6
al-Qaeda 114
Amalapuram 125
amaNazaretha church 60
Amazing Grace (Newton) 41
AME (African Methodist Episcopal)
    Church 237
American Baptist Church 231
American Board of Commissioners
    for Foreign Missions 367
American Revolution (1776) 45, 364
American Samoa 251, 256
Americanization 14
Amitabha 184
Anabaptists 46, 107, 351, 359
Ancient Tradition 269–92
    Great Division 293–318
Andhra Pradesh 125
Anglican Church of Melanesia 254
Anglicanism 10, 39, 41, 44, 86, 110,
    257, 275, 348
    African 165, 169, 170, 174, 175, 352
    cell group concept adopted by 191
    churches that self-consciously
        identify with 150
    CSI and 124
    de facto state church in southern
        American colonies 45
    devout 257
    English Royalists (17th-c.) 362
    Evangelical 151, 261
    high-church 74
    moderate 46, 152
    Progressive 151, 152, 261
    start of 359
    see also Anglo-Catholics; Church of
        England; Evangelicalism;
        GAFCON

Anglo-Catholics 8, 151, 152
Anglo-Saxons 312
Angola 368
animistic religions 192
Anna, Byzantine princess 317
Annan, Kofi 155
anointing 28, 297, 323, 354
Anselm of Canterbury 29, 136, 323
Anthony (Egyptian monk) 68, 77, 284
Anti-Apostasy Movement of the
    Indonesian Ulema Congregation
    Forum 193
anticlericalism 140–1, 204, 208, 217, 364
Antigua and Barbuda 222
Antioch
    bishops of 273, 302
    Islamic capture of 306
    Orthodox Church of 19
    Patriarchs of 22–3
    see also Ignatius of Antioch; Severus
        of Antioch
anti-Semitism 86, 105
    Polish national extremists 100
apartheid 174, 175, 352
Aphrahat (the Persian Sage) 278
Apostles 3, 14, 59, 274
    see also John; Paul; Peter; Thomas
Apostles' Creed 199, 277
Apostolic Church of Faith in Jesus
    Christ 212
Aquinas, Thomas 29, 325
Aquino, Corazon 188
Arabia/Arabs 3, 291, 304
Arabic language 70, 307, 308
Aramaic 287
Archbishops of Canterbury 152, 165
    see also Augustine; Tillotson;
        Williams
Argentina 223
    church complicit with government
        in "dirty war" 208
    Orthodox presence 13
    Our Lady of Luján 211
    Pentecostal churches 212
Aristotle 309
Arius/Arian Christianity 277, 283,
    285, 291, 299, 302

Ark of the Covenant 177, 330
Arkansas 230
Armenia 69, 290
    Christianity and ethnic
        nationhood 363
    massacre of Christians in
        Turkey 76, 80, 81, 82
    see also Republic of Armenia
Armenian Apostolic Church 299
Armenian language 270
Armenian Orthodox and Apostolic
    Church 20, 72, 73, 74–5, 80, 83,
    112, 268, 290, 299
    dissident members leaving 338
    semiautonomous jurisdictions 82
Arminianism 43
arrests 2, 82, 92, 93, 147, 173, 175,
    181, 196, 200–1, 208, 259, 281,
    282, 300, 316, 351, 361, 370
    free rein to 197
Aryan nation 370
Ashafa, Muhammad Nurayn 171–2
Ashimolowo, Matthew 153
Asia 368
    Catholic populations 27, 33
    Evangelical movement enormously
        popular in 351
    Jesuits directed to 363
    Orthodox presence 13
    Pentecostal/Charismatic
        community 51, 56, 60
    Protestantism 39, 74
    spice trade 361
    see also Central Asia; East Asia;
        South Asia; Southeast Asia
Asia Minor 2, 67, 272, 342
Asian Indian community 221
Asian Tigers 183
assassinations 174, 208, 238
    failed 147, 370
    secular teachers 218
    Theo van Gogh 144
    targeted 140–1
Assemblies of God 59, 215, 235, 255,
    256, 263
    see also Australian Christian
        Churches

Ateek, Naim 86
atheism 260, 371
   Communist 25, 36, 92, 93, 100,
     196, 223, 358
   militant, grobal 371
Athenagoras I, Orthodox Patriarch 98
Augustine, Archbishop of
   Canterbury 312
Augustine of Hippo, St 28, 35, 67,
   285, 303
Auschwitz-Birkenau 100
Australia 4, 259–65
   Anglicanism 260, 261
   Catholicism 260, 261–2
   Christianity on the decline 248
   immigrant settlement 251
   Orthodoxy 13, 260, 262
   Pentecostal/Charismatic
     Christianity 260, 262–4
   religious experimentation 249
   see also Aboriginals; New South
     Wales; Northern Territory;
     Queensland; South Australia;
     Tasmania; Victoria; Western
     Australia
Australian Christian Churches
   263, 264
Austria 137, 138–9, 361
Austrian Empire 99
Austro-Hungarian Empire 106
authoritarianism 198
autocephalous churches 19–20, 24,
   88–90, 106, 242, 243, 357
autochthonous churches 58
Avignon 326
Axum 290–1
Azariah, V. S., Anglican Bishop of
   Dornakal 110, 130
Azerbaijan 80, 112, 113
Azusa Street Revival (LA 1906–08) 8,
   51, 60, 235, 353

baby boom generation 239
"Back to Jerusalem" movement 200
Baghdad 74, 289, 308, 341
   Christian sites targeted by Islamic
     extremists 76

House of Wisdom 309
Baha'i faith 180
Bahamas 222
Bahrain 72
Bainimarama, Frank 259
Bakker, Jim 170, 236
Bakker, Tammy 170
Bali 185
Balkans 97–8
   see also Albania; Bosnia; Bulgaria;
     Croatia; Greece; Macedonia;
     Moldova; Montenegro; Romania;
     Serbia
Baltic region 98
   paganism persistent in 335
   see also Estonia; Latvia; Lithuania
Bandung 193
Bangladesh 115–16
baptism 14, 18, 28, 31, 52, 53, 57,
   60, 188, 197, 213, 278, 317, 323,
   354, 361
   ceremony to renew vows 177
   children slowly own 19
   church attendance for 133,
     149, 240
   creeds helpful for instructing
     converts prior to 277
   desire for 32
   mass 79
   need emphasized by
     immersion 212
   new African names adopted at 173
   question–answer prelude to 277
   sins washed away by 3–4, 273
   undertaken on behalf of dead
     people 245
Baptists 10, 39, 44, 60, 74
   African-American Christians who
     are 237
   black 237
   cell group concept adopted by 191
   Charismatic Christian 57
   immigrants in Latin America 212
   Naga Christian 118
   number of adherents 124,
     142, 240
   rules and dogma 107

   see also American Baptist Church;
     Anabaptists; Carey; Graham;
     Kimbangu; Obasanjo; Southern
     Baptist Church; Spiritual Baptists
Baradeus, Jacob, Metropolitan of
   Edessa 299
Barbados 222
barbarians 291, 293, 303, 312
Barbuda 222
Baroque style churches 355
Barth, Karl 147, 148
Basil II, Byzantine Emperor 23, 317,
   319, 342
Basil of Caesarea 68
Basil of Moscow 329
Batista, Fulgencio 223
Bayt al-Hikma 309
Bedouins 291, 304
beguines 325
Beijing 368
Belarus 88, 91, 94, 101, 102–3
Belgium 137, 139, 158, 161,
   325, 361
   Congo, colony and independence
     172, 173
Belgrade 96
Belzec 100
Benedict XVI, Pope 10, 123, 151,
   188–9, 201
Benedict of Nursia 315
Benedictines 29, 315, 319, 322
Bengali language 123
Berbers 3, 291
Berlin 158
Bernard of Clairvaux 332
Bertha (wife of King Ethelbert) 312
Bhutan 115, 116
Bible 32, 51, 129, 134, 161, 168, 176,
   259, 325, 328, 362
   affirming the inerrancy of 191,
     233, 350
   belief in 2, 55, 232, 253
   churches that express high regard
     for 199
   confiscated 181
   core message of 350
   creation of 275–7, 291

Bible (*cont'd*)
  icons and figures from 300–1
  Orthodoxy and Catholicism share
    the same 35
  power as a physical object 128
  Protestant commitment to 10, 38,
    40–1, 42, 46, 47, 52, 233, 350, 354
  translations of 68, 123, 162, 290,
    316, 350, 368
  words of US Constitution
    combined with words of 238
  see also British and Foreign Bible
    Society; Gutenberg Bible; New
    Testament; Old Testament; *also*
    under following Bible *headings*
Bible belts
  Norway 149
  US South and Midwest 231, 233
Bible reading 3, 186, 187, 349,
  351, 369
  devotional 149
  historical document 298
  literal 162
  New Christians and 368
  new way of 369
  teaching 123, 367–8
  through the lens of religious
    experience 350
Bible schools 59
Bible stories
  familiarity with 132
  icons depicting 14
  miracle 351
Bible study 7, 26, 41, 125, 187, 234
  careful 46
  Evangelical 49
  mainline congregations
    sponsor 235
  progressive Catholics and 215
birth control 216, 241
BJP (Bharatiya Janata Party) 120, 121
black churches 230, 237–8, 366
Black Death (1347–50) 325
Black Madonna icon (Poland) 99
Black Sea 273, 290, 317, 342
Boer War (1890s) 174
Boesak, Alan 175

Boff brothers (Clodovis and
  Leonardo) 209
Bogotá 206
Bohemia 361
Bolivia 223
  Our Lady of Copacabana 211
Bolshevik Revolution (1917) 92, 102
Bonhoeffer, Dietrich 147, 370
Boniface 312
Boniface VIII, Pope 326, 323
Book of Mormon 245, 369
Boris I, Bulgarian Khan 316
Bosnia-Herzegovina 91, 93, 95
Boston 362–3
Botswana 160
Boutros-Ghālī, Boutros 79
Boxer Rebellion (China 1899–1901)
  195, 372
Brahmans 127
Brazil 206, 209, 214–17, 223, 373
  African slaves shipped to 366
  black statue of Virgin hauled out
    of river 210–11
  Catholic Renewal
    movement 213–14, 219–20
  Constitutions (1824/1988)
    214, 215
  Independent Spirit-filled
    churches 58
  number of Catholics 10
  Orthodox presence 13
  Pentecostal/Charismatic movement
    212, 215–17
  Protestants in the population 214
  slaves 366
  see also Afro-Brazilian religions
Brazil for Christ Church 215
Brazilian Congress 216
Brest-Litovsk Union (1595) 106
Brethren 74, 142
Brisbane 261, 263
Britain *see* United Kingdom
British Africa 161
British and Foreign Bible Society 367
British Baptist Missionary
  Society 173
British Crown 250, 251, 257

British Empire 367
British Mandate 71, 84
British Raj 115, 371
Broad Church Anglican
  moderates 152
Brother Mike (Mariano Z.
  Velarde) 189–90
bubonic plague 325
Buddhism 111, 115, 180, 191, 192,
  195, 246, 311
  destruction of temples 341–2
  mindfulness in 186, 187
  numbers 183–4
  predominant 116
  ruler who converted to Islam
    from 341
  texts translated from Sanskrit into
    Chinese 310
  see also Pure Land; Theravada;
    White Lotus; Zen
Buenos Aires 206
Bulgaria 13, 24, 25, 80, 88, 91, 93,
  315–16, 343, 344
  independence (early 1900s) 95
Bultmann, Rudolph 148
Burma 182
  see also Myanmar
Burundi 160
Byzantine Empire 21, 22–4,
  139, 293, 294, 304, 305,
  314, 339, 342–4
  attempted military coup
    within 317
  defeated by Ottoman Empire 319
  Miaphysite Christians persecuted
    by 306
  near oblivion 343
  Orthodox Church of 296, 316,
    320–1, 327, 329
  papal request for military aid
    from 333, 336
  political alliance with 312, 315
  re-established (1261) 337
  trade with 316
  see also Basil II; Heraclius; Justinian;
    Michael III; Michael VIII;
    Theodora

Caedmon 313

Calcutta *see* Kolkata; Teresa of
    Calcutta

Calicut (Kozhikode) 361

California 8, 51, 60, 234, 236

Calixtus II, Pope 322

Calvary Chapel 236

Calvin, John 46, 350

Calvinist tradition 43, 357

Cambodia 182, 183, 371
    Theravada Buddhism dominant
        in 184

Canada 227–9, 230
    French Catholic population 225

Canossa 322

Cape Town 174, 263

Cappadocia 68

Caracas 206

Carbajal de Valensuela,
    Romanita 212

Cardinal Kung Foundation 201

Carey, William 123

Caribbean 153, 212, 221–3
    Africans shipped to 365–6
    slaves 366
    see also Cuba; Haiti; Puerto Rico

Carmelite nuns 364

Cartago 211

Caspian Sea 290, 341, 342

caste system 112, 116, 121, 127,
    128, 130
    denounced by Protestant
        Christians 123

Castle Hill Rebellion (1804) 261

Castro, Fidel 222–3

Castro, Raul 223

Catechism of the Catholic Church 28,
    32, 33, 241

catechists 161–2, 173, 188, 251

Cathars 335

Catherine of Sienna 28–9

Catholic Action 208

Catholic Bishops Council
    (China) 201

Catholic Church in Fiji 259

Catholic identity 106
    decisive 9

encouraging a more proactive sense
    of 37
national identity and 98, 99,
    100, 220
predominant 254

Catholic Patriotic Association
    (China) 196, 197, 201

Catholic Pentecostalism 213

Catholic schools 214, 239, 240, 262

Catholicism 7, 8–9, 21, 26–37, 116,
    137, 195–6, 198, 225, 253, 257,
    261–2, 321–7, 354
    abuse of young boys and girls by
        priests 241
    allowed to continue to exist 173
    Anglican priests and bishops
        welcomed into 151
    anti-Protestant 218
    assassinations of secular
        teachers 218
    attempt to break political power
        of 141
    attitudes and actions protested 39
    Baroque era helped restore and
        buttress 355
    bonds between Polish culture
        and 100
    Central European 93, 94, 98–101
    champion and defender of
        Christianity 319
    change and development in 239
    change that looks bad for 215
    church and state issues 208
    church attendance 240, 257
    confession of sins 43
    consideration of Protestant
        tradition 10
    declaration of union between
        Orthodox Churches and 337
    decline in Church membership 217
    disenchantment with teachings
        of 240
    dissident 197
    Eastern rite 72, 89, 357
    engagement with Orthodoxy 98
    frontal attack on the Church 143
    full submission to 361

general councils of the Church 320
goal to energize at grassroots 215
healing and exorcism 217
home of some of the most famous
    saints 140
hostile means of relating to
    non-Catholic world 331
Hutu killing of Tutsis aided by 157
imposed by force 98
Indian 122–3, 129–30
indigenous 360
IURD competing for middle-class
    members 216
Latin-based Christianity 90
Maronite Church and 73, 338
membership of church (England &
    Wales/Ireland/Scotland) 152
militant 348
modern democracy 140
need to submit to monarchs of
    Spain and 335
new movement emerged out
    of 347
nominal conformity with 188
North American 225
notion of vocation or serving
    God 41
official religion 214
old social infrastructure fallen
    apart 205
persecution of Church
    members 152
policy that ended special status
    of 144
popular 143, 210–11
positive about the past 252
predominant 93, 146
prevalence in Spain 140
Protestant challenges to 46
Protestant salvation shares much
    with 42
public reputation of 191
rearticulating well-established core
    convictions 354
reliance on use of force 333
religious freedom 140, 190
religious monopoly 203, 207

Catholicism (*cont'd*)
  role of laypeople 134
  "second Rome" corrupt and into
    heresy through union with 344
  special privileges 142
  strongholds of 204
  supernatural spiritual power a
    special challenge for 167
  supremacy of Pope and
    doctrine 106
  upper-class 348
  vision as organizing principle of
    European society 319
  way paved for full coalescence
    of 302
  Western Europe and faith
    inseparably linked 139
  see also Anglo-Catholics; Catholic
    Patriotic Association; CCC; CCR;
    Chinese Catholic Church;
    Eastern Catholic Churches;
    liturgy; Opus Dei; Popes; Syrian
    Catholic Church; theology;
    Vatican
Caucasus 342, 343
caudillos 208
CCC (China Christian Council) 199,
  200
CCR (Catholic Charismatic
  Renewal) 57–8, 206, 213–14,
  216, 219–20, 236, 356
CELAM (*Consejo Episcopal
  Latinoamericano*) 33, 209
celibacy 287, 288
  Janissary 343
  priestly 320, 321, 322
Central America 4
  see also Costa Rica; El Salvador;
    Guatemala; Nicaragua
Central Asia 4, 65, 66, 110–15, 289,
  339, 340–2
  Christianity obliterated in most of 74
  Church of the East spread
    throughout 73, 308
  desert trade routes that connected
    the Mediterranean world
    with 286

Islamic armies subjugated most
  of 303
little Christianity left to salvage
  anywhere in 342
mobile Christianity 331
Central Europe 93, 94, 98–101, 316
Chaghatai 112
Chakkarai, V. 121
Chalcedonian Creed *see* Council
  of Chalcedon
Chalcedonian Orthodoxy 72, 262,
  300, 301
  opposition to 299
Chang'an 74, 309–10
Charisma (magazine) 236
Charismatic Christianity 57–8, 189
  preachers/leaders 169, 170,
    173, 263
  transnational 176
  see also CCR; Pentecostal/
    Charismatic movement
Charlemagne, King of the Franks
  and Holy Roman Emperor
  139, 313–15, 322
Chelmo 100
Chenchiah, P. 129
Chennai 121, 125, 286
Chenu, Marie-Dominique 356
Cherson 317
Chiang Kai-shek 195
Chicago 243
Chikane, Frank 175
Chile 206, 208
  Pentecostal movement 60, 212
Chilean Methodist Church 212
China 5, 289, 308
  Buddhism 184, 310
  Christianity 194–202, 303,
    310–11, 331
  Church of the East planted in 73
  economic growth and
    development 183
  GDP 183
  indentured servants from 221
  involvement in Africa 160
  Jesuits directed to 363
  Mongol rule of 341

Muslims in 184
Pentecostal/Charismatic
  movement 60
Protestantism 38, 39, 367–8
suppression of traditional
  religion 184
see also Boxer Rebellion; CCC;
  Chang'an; Cultural Revolution;
  Opium Wars; Qing; Silk Road;
  Taiping Rebellion; Tang Dynasty;
  Wuzong; Yuan Dynasty
China Inland Mission 367
Chinese Catholic Church 199,
  200, 201
Chinese Empire 112
Chinese language 363
Chinese Rites Controversy 363
Christ of India parades 130
Christian III, King of Denmark 148
Christian Congregation
  of Brazil 215
Christian labor union movement 351
Christianization
  China 368
  Eastern Europe 315, 316
  India 123
  Indonesia 192
  Oceania/Pacific 250, 251
  Roman Empire 102
  Western Europe 311
church and state 95, 105, 289,
  315, 322–3
  antagonism between 217
  complex history of 207–9
  separation of 45, 46, 97, 142, 144,
    203, 214, 364, 365
  wedded together in
    Christendom 139, 140
Church of Christ in Zaire 173
Church of Denmark 148, 149
Church of England 8, 47, 261
  Catholicism (16th-c.) and 46
  decimated 153
  Evangelicals within 151
  number of active members falling
    dramatically 150
  religious head of 152, 165, 364

religious rights for Protestants not members of 362

women priests 151

Church of God 235

Church of God Mission 170

Church of Jesus Christ of Latter Day Saints *see* Mormons

Church of North India 124

Church of the East 8, 75, 112, 268, 306, 321, 337, 341, 347

buildings reduced to rubble 342

Christians of India's west coast associated with 361

decline of 319

dissident members leaving 338

founding of 121

independence from Imperial Church of Roman Empire 289, 293–4

Islam and 295, 307–9, 310–11, 317

language and culture 296

missionaries 74, 289, 297

sphere of influence 303

spread of 73

theological hero condemned 296

theology 297–8

thousands of churches in far-reaching zone 4–5

see also Giwargis I; Nestorian Church; Timothy I

churchless Christianity 126

Circle of Concerned African Women Theologians 168

circumcision 116, 272, 273, 317, 330

Civil Rights movement (US) 49, 237–8, 352, 371

class membership 112

Classical Pentecostalism 57, 235, 236

Clement XI, Pope 363

Clement of Alexandria 273

Cleveland 235

Cluny monastery 319, 322

COGIC (Church of God in Christ) 235, 237, 238

Cold War 159, 160, 173, 182–3, 223, 370

military dictatorships during iciest years of 208

Colombia 204, 212, 213, 214

see also Bogotá; Medellin

Columbanus, St 312

Committee of Surveillance 364

Committee of Union and Progress *see* Young Turks

Commonwealth of Australia 260, 261

communal consciousness 28–9

Communion *see* Eucharist

Communism 24–5, 100, 114, 118, 177, 184, 190, 223, 358

biased against religion 88

Catholics encouraged to oppose directives 196

collapse of 82, 91–2, 96, 97, 102, 103, 106, 107, 112, 113

crucible of 92–3

dictatorships 357

facets of traditional culture seen as irrational and dangerous 200

imprisonment by government 186

long-term rule 222–3

resistance to worldwide spread of 183

threat of 36

worldwide fight against 208

Communist Party

China 195, 197

Cuba 223

Compiègne 364

Concordat of Worms (1122) 322

concubines 321

Condomblé 214, 216

Confessing Church movement 370

confessionalism 46

confirmation 28, 188, 323

Confucianism 180, 363

Congar, Yves 356

Congo 161, 172, 361, 366

see also DRC; Zaire

Congolese Catholic Church 172

Congregation for the Doctrine of the Faith 123

Congregationalists 45, 124, 255, 256, 263

Congress Party (India) 120

conquistadors 210, 335

Constantine, Roman Emperor 282–3, 288

Constantinople 283, 302, 316

conquered 342, 343

Crusader ransacking of 23

recaptured (1261) 337

Second Council (553) 296

see also Istanbul; Patriarchs of Constantinople

Constantius I, Roman Emperor 282

Constantius II, Roman Emperor 283

contemplative theology 17

conversion 74, 99, 123–4, 140, 151, 172, 243, 288, 312–13, 335

centrality of 124

conquest and 188

debated 282

dramatic 41

encouraging 119, 128

forced 106, 114

illegal 68

potential 216

resulting in persecution 180–1

salvation attained in an instant through 232

self-conscious 46

stressing the need for 190–1

style of Protestantism that focuses on 149

conversion to Islam 165, 341, 343

encouraged 304

merely public displays 340

under threat of violence 339

Cook, Capt. James 250

Coptic culture 3

Coptic language 307

Coptic Nationalism 20, 79–80

Coptic Orthodox Church 20, 72, 77–80, 83, 268, 299, 307, 337, 339–40

dissident members leaving 338

Ethiopian Orthodox declares full independence from 176–7

faith and ethnicity 75

official head of 77, 79

parishes in Australia 262

Costa Rica 211, 214
Cottesloe Statement (1961) 175
Council of Basel-Ferrara-Florence-
    Rome (1431–45)
Council of Chalcedon (451) 20, 22,
    268, 278–9, 294, 296, 298,
    299–300
    Fourth (879–80) 302
Council of Ephesus (431) 296
Council of Florence (1439) 23, 337,
    338, 343
Council of Florence-Ferrara
    (1438–39) 102
Council of Latin American Bishops
    see CELAM
Council of Nicaea (325) 22, 199,
    277–8, 283, 302
    Second (787) 22, 301
Council of the Muslim Faith
    (France) 145
Council of Trent (1545–63) 36, 354–5
Counter-Reformation 106
Creed of Nicaea *see* Council
    of Nicaea
Cristero Rebellion (1926–29) 218
Croatia 91, 94, 95, 97, 98, 262
crucifixion and resurrection 2, 3–4,
    31, 55, 83, 274, 277, 297, 298
Crusades 23, 26, 35, 68, 69, 73, 89, 98,
    233, 332–40, 342–3
    first widespread use of
        indulgences 324
    see also reconquista
CSI (Church of South India) 124, 125
    Cathedral of the Epiphany 130
Cuauhtlatoatzin 210, 360
Cuba 208, 222–3
    Our Lady of Charity of
        El Cobre 211
Cultural Revolution (China 1966)
    197, 198
Cursillo de Cristiandad
    movement 140
Cyprian, Bishop of Carthage 67,
    274, 321
Cyril (Orthodox missionary) 316
Cyril of Alexandria 298

Cyril Lucaris, Patriarch of
    Constantinople 357
Czech Republic 91, 137, 138–9,
    315, 361
Czechoslovakia (former) 91
Czestochowa 99

Dalits 123, 127–8
Dallas 238
Damascus 272, 308, 341
    see also John of Damascus
Danube, River 91, 316
Dark Ages 295
Darwinian evolution 47
Decius, Roman Emperor 281–2
Declaration of the Rights of Man and
    of the Citizen (France 1789) 144
Deep South 239
deification 17–18, 55, 300, 328, 329,
    344, 353, 354
Democratic Party (US) 235
Denmark 146, 148, 149
De Nobili, Roberto 123
denominationalism 45, 57, 226
dharma 119, 311
dhimmis 71, 305, 307
Dhinakaran, D. G. S. 125–6
Díaz, Porfirio 218
Diego, Juan *see* Cuauhtlatoatzin
Diocletian, Roman Emperor 282
disciples 2, 4, 49, 129, 271, 297,
    302, 329
    see also Apostles
Disciples of Christ (Protestant
    denomination) 212, 231
Dissenters 362
Dixon, James 261
Dnieper, River 316
*Doctrine and Covenants of the Church
    of Jesus Christ of Latter Day
    Saints* 245
Dominicans 213, 331, 360, 363
Donatist Church 291
door-to-door evangelism 219
Dornakal 130
Dougherty, Edward 213
Douglass, Frederick 369

Dowie, John Alexander 263
DRC (Democratic Republic of
    Congo) 172–4
Duma (Russia) 104
Durham, William 51, 52
Dutch South Africans 174
Dyer, Mary 363

Early Byzantine Era (500–1000) 21,
    22–3
East Africa 162
East Asia 4–5, 180–202
    Catholicism introduced to 36
East Pakistan *see* Bangladesh
East Timor 183, 187–8
Eastern Catholic Churches 338
Eastern Europe 4, 13, 88–109,
    242, 317
    conversion to Christianity 312
    Eastern Rite Catholic churches 357
Eastern Orthodoxy *see* Orthodoxy
Eastern Roman Empire 22, 90, 294
Ecuador 204, 206
    Our Lady of Quinche 211
ecumenical councils 22
Ecumenical Patriarch *see* Patriarchs
    of Constantinople
Ecumenical Protestantism 48–9
Edessa 299
Edict of Toleration (313) 282
EDSA revolutions (Philippines
    1986/2001) 188, 189
Educación para la Ciudadanía 142–3
education 36, 74, 104, 119, 127, 140,
    160, 166, 170, 172, 262, 305, 355,
    367–8, 373
    cheap 161
    church control of 99
    clergy 314
    innovative programs 107
    mutual recognition of degrees 59
    obtaining a minimal level of 56
    poor children living in urban
        slums 135
    religious 25, 105, 142–3, 149, 241
    shahs of Iran encouraging 113
    university 198, 256

Edwards, Jonathan 42
Egypt 67–8, 77–80, 286
   Christians 72, 78–9, 284,
      293, 294–5, 299, 306–7, 330,
      339–40, 343
   fundamentalist Islam 80
   Mamluk Empire assume control
      (1250) 340
   Miaphysitism especially strong
      in 299
   monasticism 315
   Muslim rule welcomed 295
   Orthodox population 13, 72, 77
   spirituality and survival 77–80
   see also Alexandria; Coptic
      Orthodox Church
El Salvador 208
El Shaddai movement 189–90
ELCA (Evangelical Lutheran Church
   in America) 231
Elizabeth I, Queen of England 46
Embassy of God Church 107–8
encomiendera 360
England 312, 369
   Enlightenment thinkers 364
   see also Church of England
England and Wales
   Church membership 152
   public faith of 46
English Civil War (1642–51) 362
Enlightenment (European) 36, 47,
   364, 366
Episcopal Church 212, 231
   see also AME
Equatorial Guinea 160
Eritrea 177
Estonia 91, 94, 101, 102–3
Estrada, Joseph 188
Ethelbert, King of Kent 312
Ethiopia 158, 161, 269, 290, 291
   Jewish character of society and
      religion 330
   monasticism introduced to 176
   religious tensions 176–8
Ethiopian Orthodox Tewahedo
   Church 13, 20, 83, 164, 268, 299,
   321, 329–31

antiretroviral drugs approved
   by 178
Church full independence from
   Coptic Church 176–7
ethnic cleansing 76, 81, 88, 96
ethnicity 116, 239
   bonds of 112
   faith and 74–6, 81–2, 94, 95–8, 118,
      257–9, 290
   nationality and 88
   new nations defined by 92
Eucharist 4, 19, 28, 31–2, 35, 134, 201,
   280, 302, 323, 338
Europe *see* Central Europe; Eastern
   Europe; Northern Europe;
   Southern Europe; Western
   Europe; *also under individual*
   country names
Eusebius of Caesarea 2
Evangelicalism 39, 48, 177,
   190–1, 369
   American 49, 230–6, 243
   Anglican 151, 261
   growing tensions 152
   roots of the movement 49
   see also Aboriginal Evangelical
      Fellowship; Graham
evangelicos 39, 203, 204, 205, 206, 213,
   214, 215, 216, 217, 218
   growing 219
excommunication 167, 217, 322,
   336, 349
   threat of 197
exorcism 167, 217
extremism 100, 315
   Islamic 76, 145
   see also fundamentalism

FABC (Federation of Asian Bishops'
   Conferences) 33
Falun Gong 198
Family Voice Australia 261
Fangcheng (house church
   network) 200
Far East 182
Farraj, Ya'quob 74
Farsi 112

Fatah 86
Fatimid Caliphate 339
Felicitas 67
feminists 60, 134
   black Christian 238
Ferdinand and Isabella, King and
   Queen of Spain 140
Festival of Light organization 261
Fifth Crusade (1213–21) 332
Fiji 254
   religion, ethnicity and
      politics 257–9
Fijian Methodist Church 259
Finland 146, 148, 295
First Crusade (1088–99) 333–4
First Vatican Council (1870) 33
Flores, Samuel Joaquin 219
Florida 118
Focolare movement 135
folk religion 185, 186, 200, 287
Fosdick, Harry Emerson 233
Fourth Crusade (1204) 23,
   336, 342
France 73, 137, 138–9, 143–5, 158,
   190, 257, 274, 316, 326, 361
   almost overrun by Islamic
      armies 303
   belief in God 133
   Catholic missionaries in Africa 161
   Enlightenment 364
   Islam 143, 144–5
   Ottoman lands divided among
      Britain and 71, 371
   Pacific territories governed by 251
   Protestantism spread to 45–6, 350
   trade and Christianity in East
      Asia 180
   see also Cluny; French Revolution
Francis of Assisi 135, 324–5, 332
Franciscans 195, 325, 331, 360, 363
Franco, Gen. Francisco 141, 142
Franks 73, 312, 316
   see also Charlemagne; Louis the
      German
fraud 108, 119, 236
Frederick the Wise, Duke of
   Saxony 349

Freedom of Conscience Act (Russia 1990) 104
French Polynesia 250, 251
French Revolution (1789) 36, 140, 144, 355, 364
Freudianism 47
Frumentius 290
fundamentalism 48, 118, 136, 231, 350, 351
  Islamic 74, 76, 80, 114, 184

Gabon 160
Gabriel, Sahar 77
GAFCON (Global Anglican Future Conference) 151
Galilee 1
Galileo Galilei 29, 346
Gandhi, Mohandas (Mahatma) 115, 120, 121, 128
Gauguin, Paul 250
Gaul 290
gays and lesbians 29, 142, 151, 261
GDP (gross domestic product) 101, 160, 183
Genesis 350, 366
Geneva 148
Genghis Khan 341
genocide 80–2, 84, 88
  worst in modern history 157
George I *see* Giwargis I
Georgia (Caucasus) 91, 94, 101, 102–3, 290
  Christianity and ethnic nationhood 363
  language 270
Georgia (US) 230
Georgios I, King of Nubia 307
German Empire 99
German Lutherans 114, 212
  see also Bonhoeffer
German Pietism 46–7, 350
  missionaries 194
  significant inroads into Russian Orthodoxy 357
German Protestantism 39, 45–6, 370
  state churches 44
Germanic groups 303, 312

Germany 8, 108, 138, 139, 143, 158, 314
  Catholic influx into Australia from 262
  Micronesian islands sold to 254
  Muslims 143
  Nazi regime welcomed and supported by Christians 147
  numbers of Catholics and Protestants roughly even 146
  officially-sanctioned religion in parts of 46
  religious nationalism harnessed for use in war against 92
  see also Luther; Lutheranism
Ghana 153, 157, 159
Ghazan, Mongol ruler 341–2
Ginés de Sepúlveda, Juan 360
Giwargis I, Catholicos of Church of the East 297
GLBT individuals 369
glocalization 358–9
Gnosticism 273, 274, 335
Goa 122–3
God Is Love Church 212, 215
Golden Horde 90–1, 341
Golden Rule 1, 159, 233
Golwalkar, Madhavrao Sadashivrao 120
Gong Pinmei, Bishop of Shanghai 200–1
Gospels 2, 56, 96, 125, 188, 275–6, 297, 308, 328
  small group study of 135
  whether historically accurate 350
Gothic language 270
Goths 3, 291, 302, 303
  evangelized 312
Grady, J. Lee 236
Graham, Billy 40, 118, 233, 351
Granada 332
Great Awakening (1730–55) 232, 350, 364–5
Great Depression (1930s) 370
Great Persecution (303) 282, 288
Great Schism (1054) 22, 98, 336

Greco-Turkish War (1922) 82
Greece 13, 89, 91, 93, 272, 328
  political and religious independence (1832–33) 95
  tension with Catholic Christianity 97
Greek Catholic Church 97
  Ukrainian 106–7
Greek language 3, 21, 22, 90, 95, 336
Greek Orthodox Church 9, 73, 82, 83, 88, 90, 97, 243
  declaration of autonomy (1833) 24
Gregory I, Pope 312, 313
Gregory VII, Pope 322
Gregory of Nazianzus 328
Gregory of Nyssa 18, 68
Gregory the Illuminator 290
grobalization 358, 359, 361, 368
Grundtvig, N. S. F. 149
Guadalupe Virgin 210, 211, 360
Guam 251, 254
Guanyin 184
Guatemala 206, 212, 214, 223
Gulf War (1990) 252
Gutenberg Bible 347
Gutiérrez, Gustavo 209
Guyana 222

Haile Selassie, Emperor of Ethiopia 177
Haiti 222
Hamas 86
Hamer, Fannie Lou 237
Hanafi tradition 113–14
Hap Dong Church 190
Hausa 171
Hawai'i 182, 255, 256
healing ministry 167, 217
Hebei Province 199
Hebrew culture 3
Hegel, G. W. F. 369
Henry IV, Holy Roman Emperor 322
Henry V, Holy Roman Emperor 322
Henry VIII, King of England 46
Heraclius, Byzantine Emperor 299–300

heresy 20, 98, 102, 122, 175, 226, 245, 277, 285, 299, 300, 306, 327, 328, 331, 336, 344, 349, 361
  Albigensian 335
  Americanism condemned as 225
  Communism as 92
  Galileo condemned by Catholic Church 346
  Islam denounced/viewed as 22, 305, 309
  Jesus movement viewed as 272
  killing of heretics 332
Hesychast movement 328–9
hijab 144–5
Hildebrand *see* Gregory VII
Hillsong Church 263–4
Himalayan nations *see* Bhutan; Nepal
Hindi languages 258
  and subdialects 112
Hindu Right 120
Hindu Sangh Parivar movement 127–8
Hinduism 111, 115, 119, 120, 129, 180, 183–4, 192, 246, 258, 259, 286
  Brahmin 123
  discrimination banned within 127
  high-caste 121, 127, 128
  internationally known feminist who became Christian 60
  low-caste 116, 127, 128, 130
  number of followers 185
  significant populations 222
  social philosophy of 127
Hinn, Benny 125
Hispanics 242
Hitler, Adolf 84, 147, 370
HIV/AIDS 155, 160, 178
Hlond, August, Polish Archbishop 100
Hmong people 180–1
Holocaust 84, 86, 370
holy orders 28, 323
Hong Kong 183
Hong Xiuquan 195, 368
Hoover, Willis C. 60, 212
Hopkins, Gerard Manley 27
house churches 197–8, 199, 200

Houston, Brian and Bobbie 263
Hulegu, Mongol Emperor 341
human reproduction 240
Hunayn ibn Ishīq 309
Hungary 91, 94, 98, 262, 303, 343
  constitution guarantees religious freedom 99
  Protestantism 46, 350
Hus, Jan 349
Hutus 157
Hyderabad 117, 125

Iberian Peninsula 294
  conquered by Umayyad Caliphate 332
  see also Portugal; Spain
Iceland 146, 148
  Kvennakirrkjan 134, 135–6
Ichege, office of 176–7
Iconoclastic Controversy 300, 301, 305
icons 9, 14–15, 22, 50, 99, 241, 338
  famous 86
  golden age of Russian painting 329
  veneration of 26, 301
Idahosa, Benson 170
identity 102, 108, 270
  blurring of 8
  cultural 70, 116–17, 265
  distinctive 22, 94, 95
  ethnic 14, 70, 95, 307
  important symbol of 257
  linguistic 70
  multilayered sense of 112
  reconstructing 89
  regional 70, 138
  religious 14, 24, 49, 57, 79, 81, 265
  shared 70
  social 127, 182
  struggle to reclaim 92
  see also Catholic identity; Jewish identity; national identity
Igbo (Ibo) 171
Iglesia ni Cristo 188
Ignatius Loyola 140
Ignatius of Antioch, Bishop 273
immigration 221

Baptist 212
Catholic 262
Catholic growth fueled by waves of 239
ethnic and religious identities intact 228
Protestant 211–12
Imperial Church of the Roman Empire 289, 293–4, 336
  churches rooted in 335
  overseen by Pentarchy of Patriarchs 302
incense 9, 129, 241
indentured servants from 221
Independent churches 57, 58, 72, 89, 163, 168
  see also AICs
India 2, 3, 108, 110, 115, 269
  Catholicism 36, 122–3
  Christianity 111, 116–30, 285, 286, 290, 331
  indentured servants from 221
  language groups 112
  sea routes developed to deliver Chinese goods to 182
  see also Andhra Pradesh; Bengali; Buddhism; Calicut; CSI; Dalits; Hinduism; Hyderabad; Kashmir; Kerala; Malabar; Meghalaya; Mizoram; Nagaland; Pune; Punjabi groups; Tamil Nadu
Indian Constitution 127
Indians (Latin American) 211, 219
indígenas 360
Indochinese Empire 371
Indo-Fijians 258, 259
Indonesia 181, 182, 183, 185, 371
  approved world religions 180
  religious variety and violence 192–4
  Shari'a law in far west 184
  see also Aceh; Bali; Bandung; East Timor; Suharto; Sukarno; Sulawesi
Infancy Gospel of Thomas 276
infidels 335, 344
  execution of 342

Innocent III, Pope 322–3, 336
Inquisition 26, 123, 361
intellectualism 136
Interrogatory Creed of Hippolytus *see*
    Roman Symbol
Iran 74, 110
    declared an Islamic Republic 113
    official language 112
    shahs encouraging Western-style
        education 113
Iraq 5, 71, 72, 142
    Christians leaving in droves 77
    first invasion by United States 252
    see also Baghdad; Mosul
Ireland 137, 269, 312
    belief in God 133
    Catholic Church membership 152
    ethnicity and faith 290
    highest church attendance in the
        world 133
    religiosity 138
    see also Northern Ireland
Irenaeus, Bishop of Lugdunum
    (Lyon) 274
Iron Curtain 91
Isaac of Nineveh (the Syrian) 297
Iskandar, Yūsuf *see* Matthew
    the Poor
Islam 90, 97, 104, 139, 180,
    192–3, 327
    aggressive and violent posture
        toward 331
    Arabic language and 70
    armies of 68, 301, 303
    Christian conversion made
        illegal 68
    Church of the East and 295, 307–9,
        310–11, 317
    denounced as heresy 309
    driven back to Africa 333
    expansion/growth of 293, 295,
        306, 338
    fundamentalist 74, 80, 114, 184
    heartland of 69
    historic teachings of 340
    holy war against 98
    jihadist 184

no easy differentiation between
    religion and state 75
    pressure from 13, 291, 307–8
    radical 114, 144, 178,
        184, 193
    rise of 22, 294, 303, 342
    shared allegiance to 74
    Shari'a law 143, 171, 184
    spiritual tradition within 114
    spread down east coast of
        Africa 330
    suppressed 114
    taking up the sword against
        333–4
    territory lost to 23
    treatment of women in 144
    viewed as a threat 317
    visibility in Western Europe 143,
        144
    see also conversion to Islam;
        Muhammad; Ottoman Empire;
        Quran; Shi'ite Muslims; Sufism;
        Sunni Muslims
Islamic Empire 112, 303, 304, 306
Islamic law 81, 113–14, 114–15
Islamic Republic of Pakistan 118
Islamic State of Iraq (extremist
    group) 76
Israel 67, 69, 70, 83–6, 177, 330
    creation as Jewish homeland
        (1947) 72
    shared opposition to policies of
        government 83
    see also Zionism
Istanbul 70, 283
    anti-Greek riots (1955) 82
Italian Waldensians 212
Italo-Catholics 333, 336
Italy 137, 138–9, 295, 314, 333
    belief in God 133–4
    Catholic immigrants in
        Australia 262
    Christian spirituality among the
        wealthy 348
    influence in Ethiopia 158
    monasteries 322
    number of Catholics 10

religiosity 138
    see also Focolare; Sicily; Vatican
IURD *(Ingeja Universaldo Reino de*
    Deus) 216, 217

Jacobite Church 299
Jakes, Thomas Dexter 238
Jamaica 177, 222
James, St 272
Janissary system 343
Japan
    economic growth and
        development 183
    occupation of Korea (1910) 190
    Shinto 185
    Western-style modernization 182
    Zen Buddhism 184
Japanese Empire 182, 254
Jaramillo, Bishop Diego 213
Jaroslav the Wise 217
Jasna Gora monastery 99
Jefferson, Thomas 47, 351
Jehovah's Witnesses 39, 180, 219
Jemaah Islamiya 184
Jerome 68, 276
Jerusalem 1, 50, 67, 177, 272, 302
    Catholic people called upon to
        rescue 333–4
    Church of the Holy Sepulcher 83
    Global Anglican Future
        Conference 151
    Islamic capture of 306
    Patriarchs of 22–3
    St George's Cathedral 86
Jesuits 36, 123, 195, 213
    founder of 140
    missionaries from Philippines 251
    seminaries and colleges across
        Europe 355
Jesus of Nazareth 67, 168
    broad following 269
    crucifixion and resurrection 2, 3–4,
        31, 55, 83, 274, 277, 297, 298
    in India 111
    language spoken by 287
    Messiah belief 271
    moral teachings of 351

number of followers 69
teachings of 1–2, 47
union of human and divine
    embodied in 300
    see also Golden Rule
Jesus Calls (ministry) 125, 126
Jesus Prayer (Orthodox) 17, 23, 328
Jewish Christians 272
"Jewish Fascism" 105
Jewish identity 84
"Jewish problem" 86
Jews 2, 111, 168, 177, 271–2, 304, 330,
    334, 339
    considered to be cousins in faith
        with Christians 68
    demand that all should convert to
        Catholic Christianity 140
    destruction of synagogues 341
    dislike for 100
    executed in Nazi death camps 100
    feast of Pentecost 50
    local compromises among
        Christians, Muslims and 332
    moral teaching which encourages
        respect for Christians and 114
    scriptures 1, 275
    second-class citizens 144
    see also anti-Semitism; Israel;
        Judaism; Palestine
Jin Luxian, Aloysius 200–1
John, St (Apostle) 275, 328
John XXIII, Pope 36, 363
John the Baptist 177, 297
John of Dalyatha 297
John of Damascus *see* Mansur ibn
    Sarjun
John Paul II, Pope 10, 97, 100–1, 135,
    143, 205, 209, 223, 356
    election (1978) 142
    Fides et ratio (1998) 136
    Slavorum Apostoli (1985) 372
Jonathan, Goodluck 172
Jordan 70, 71–2
Jordan, River 330
joy 54
Jão I (Nzinga Nkuwu), Christian King
    of the Congo 361

Jão VI, King of Portugal 214
Juárez, Benito 217
Judaism 97, 144, 270, 273, 317, 321
    affirmed by Jesus 1
    Islam as successor of 22
    Jesus movement viewed as heresy
        within 272
    Persian Christians' relationship
        with 287
    prophesied Messiah of 271
Julian, Roman Emperor 283
Julian of Norwich 326–7
just war 175
Justinian, Byzantine Emperor 299,
    301–2

Kabila, Joseph 174
Kabila, Laurent-Désiré 174
Kaduna 170, 171
Kairos Document (1985) 175
Karen people 181
Karunya University 125
Kashgar 309
Kashmir 117
Kazakhstan 74, 112, 113
    Christian population 114
Kazimierz, Jan, Polish King 99
Kennedy, John F. 239, 241
Kennedy, Kerry 241, 242
Kentish people 312
Kenya 163
    African Creed developed by
        Masai 168
Kerala 122, 123, 286
Khtai 112
Khurusan 112
Khwarrazmshahs 112
Kibre Negest 330
Kiev 106, 107, 263, 316
Kim Dae-Jung 191
Kim Young-sam 181, 191
Kimbangu, Simon 173
Kimbanguist Church 173
King, Martin Luther 237
King's Capital 108
Kingsway International Christian
    Center 153

Kinshasa 174
Kirill I, Patriarch of Moscow 105
Kiyoka (Burning) movement 368
Kolkata 123
Komanapalli, Ernest and Rachael 125
Kongo language 366
Korea 182
    folk religion 185
    see also North Korea; South Korea
Korean War (early 1950s) 196
Kosovo 91
Kublai Khan 341
Kung, Cardinal *see* Gong Pinmei
Küng, Hans 148
Kurdistan 77
Kuwait 71, 72
Kuyper, Abraham 148, 174
Kyrgyzstan 74, 112, 113
    Christian population 114

La Negrita 211
laïcité 144–5
Lalibela, King of Ethiopia 330
Lambeth Conference (2008) 151, 261
Laos 182, 183, 371
    Theravada Buddhism dominant
        in 184
Laplace, Pierre-Simon 136–7
Las Casas, Bartolomé de 207–8, 209,
    360
Laskar Jihad 193
Late Byzantine Era (1000–1500)
    21, 23
Latin (language) 21, 23, 90, 277, 336,
    349
Latin America 34, 203–24, 335, 364
    Catholic conquest of 36
    Catholic Easter-time festivals 129–30
    demographic center of Catholic
        world 27
    liberation theology 126, 209
    Orthodox presence 13
    Pentecostal/Charismatic
        community 51, 56, 60
    Protestantism 38, 39, 203
    see also CELAM; Central America;
        FABC

Latvia 91, 94, 101, 102–3
Lautoko 259
LDS *see* Mormons
Lebanon 69–70, 71
    Maronite militias 76
    see also Maronite Church
Lee Myung-Bak 191
leftists 208
Legio Maria movement 163
Lembe di Sita, Olive 174
Lenshina, Alice 168
Leo III, Pope 138, 313, 314
Leo III, Byzantine Emperor 301
Leo IX, Pope 336
Leo X, Pope 349
Leoba, St 312
Leopold II, King of Belgium 172
Le Pen, Jean-Marie 144
Liang, Afa 368
liberation theology 33, 126,
    209, 356
    Dalit version of 128
Liberia 158
Libya 72
Licinius, Eastern Emperor 282
Lim, Alfredo 188
linguistic division/diversity 90,
    112, 281
literacy 160
Lithuania 91, 94, 98
    Catholicism intertwined with
        identity 98
Little Flock 196
liturgy 8, 9, 14, 54, 72
    Catholic 174, 188, 241, 302
    Church of the East 310
    Coptic 307
    Evangelical 235
    Lutheran 134
    Orthodox 8, 9, 14, 72, 95, 102, 106
Livonian Brothers of the Sword/
    Knights 98, 335
Locke, John 47
London 153, 263
    Holy Trinity Church, Brompton
        134
London Missionary Society 256

Los Angeles 242
    see also Azusa Street Revival
Louis XVI, King of France 364
Louis the German, Frankish King 316
Louisiana 230
Low Countries 46
    see also Belgium; Luxembourg;
        Netherlands
Lubac, Henri de 356
Lubich, Chiara 135
Luke (Gospel) 125
Lukijan, Pantelić, Bishop of Buda 96
Lull, Raymond 332
Luther, Martin 8, 40, 43, 44, 46, 149,
    348–50
Lutheran World Federation 59
Lutheranism 10, 39, 44, 57, 74, 99,
    165, 193–4, 226, 254, 348, 369
    majority population 146
    Pietistic Scandinavian 178
    principle of public service 149
    start of 359
    state church/official religion 46,
        148–9
    see also ELCA; German Lutherans;
        United Evangelical Lutheran
        Church
Luxembourg 137, 138–9
Luz del Mundo, La 219
Lviv 107

Macedo, Bishop Edir 216
Macedonia 13, 80, 91, 93, 95, 262
MacKillop, Mary 262
Macrina 68
Madras *see* Chennai
Madrid 143
Magellan, Ferdinand 346
Magyars 303
mahdi figure 113
Majdanek 100
Malabar 122
malaria 155
Malawi 160
Malaysia 182, 183, 184, 185
malecide 332
Mamluk Empire 340

Manalo, Felix 188
Manchuria 182
Mandela, Nelson 175
Manichaeans 311, 331
Manila 188, 189
Manna International 125, 126
Mansur ibn Sarjun (John of
    Damascus) 18, 301, 305
Manzikert, Battle of (1071) 23, 342
Mao Zedung 195, 197
Māoris 251, 255, 256–7
    important symbol of identity 257
Mar Thoma Syrian Church 122
Marcion of Sinope 273, 275–6
Marcos, Ferdinand and Imelda 188
Maritain, Jacques 356
Maron, John 72
Maronite Church 70, 72–3, 75,
    76, 338
marriage 28, 53, 54, 71, 188, 317,
    323, 355
    affirmed 26
    child 123, 251
    Christian-Muslim 68
    dead people 245
    gay 142, 143
    not legally recognized 203
    polygamous 162, 167
    priestly 167
Marsden, Samuel 256
Marshall Islands 255
martyrdom 80, 281, 283–4
    tradition that emphasizes
        possibility of 113
    training toward 78
Marx, Karl 93
Marxism 47, 208, 369
mass crucifixions 288
Mathewes-Green, Frederica 243
Matthew the Poor 77–8, 79, 80
Maximus the Confessor 18,
    300–1, 328
McNutt, Francis 213
McPherson, Aimee Semple 54, 263
Mead, Margaret 250
Medellin 209
meditation 184

Mediterranean 68, 69, 139, 155, 262, 279, 280
  desert trade routes that connected Central Asia with 286
  holy war against Islam in 98
  Roman 90
Medvedev, Dmitry A. 105
megachurches 38, 234, 238, 263
megacities 206
Meghalaya 118
Melanesia 253, 256
Melkite Christians 306
Memphis 238
mendicants 325
Mengistu, Lt.-Col. Haile Miriam 177
Mennonites 46, 107, 212, 351
Messiah 1, 271, 278, 310
  see also mahdi
mestizo people 210, 211
Methodism 10, 44, 47, 57, 60, 74, 124, 212, 227, 258
  African 165
  African-American 237
  cell group concept adopted by 191
  devout 257
  founder of 353
  merger of Presbyterians and 254
  support for indigenous privilege over political rights 258–9
  see also AME; United Methodists; World Methodist Council
Methodist Youth Fellowship 259
Methodius 316
Mexican Revolution (1910–17) 218
Mexican War of Independence (1810–21) 217
Mexico 4, 204, 217–21, 223, 360
  number of Catholics 10
  Pentecostal movement launched in 212
Mexico City 206, 220
  Basilica of Our Lady of Guadalupe 210
Miaphysite tradition 8, 72, 262, 293, 294, 296, 298–9, 300, 321, 338
  decline in 319
  Islam and 306–7, 317

Orthodox churches seeking reunion with 20, 357–8
  persecution by Byzantine state 295
  struggle to survive 347
Michael III, Byzantine Emperor 316
Michael VIII Palaeologus, Byzantine Emperor 337
Michael Cerularius, Patriarch of Constantinople 336
Micronesia 253
  unique mix of Pacific and Asian cultures 254
Middle East 4, 63, 65, 66, 67–87, 269, 334
  active sea route connecting India with 121
  African interaction with 155
  anti-Christian feeling throughout 339
  Eastern Rite Catholic churches 357
  French Catholic Crusaders warmly embraced 338
  goal of evangelizing all nations between China and 200
  loss of large sections of formerly Christian territory 317
  Muslim conquest of 22–3, 294, 303
  original heartland of Orthodoxy 13
  potential ally in the East against Muslims of 122
  weariness of Christians in 130
  see also Silk Road
Miesko I, Polish King 99
Milingo, Emmanuel, Archbishop of Lusaka 167
military dictatorships 181, 208, 209, 223
millets 71, 75, 95, 305, 363
Mindanao 184
Mindszenty, Jozsef, Cardinal 98
minority groups 71, 74, 81, 106–7
  ethnic 116, 157, 180–1, 192, 212
  religious 285, 286
miracles 10, 58, 59, 236, 311, 351, 352
  belief in 26, 53, 56, 167
  downplayed 162
  healing 162
  power to work 50

  working 162
missionaries 127, 180, 223, 290, 313
  accused of misrepresenting gospel 162
  American 177, 212
  Anglican 256
  Apostle Paul as 272
  Baptist 173
  Buddhist 310
  Catholic 73, 161, 367
  Church of the East 74, 289, 297
  in China 303
  German Pietistic 194
  Jesuit 251, 363
  miracles and 162, 311
  Orthodox 316
  Pentecostal/Charismatic 108
  Portuguese 172
  Protestant 123, 188, 190, 212, 252, 255, 367, 368
  well-intentioned 264
Missionaries of Charity 123
Mississippi 230
Mizoram 118
Mobutu, Joseph Désiré (Sese Seko) 173, 174
Moghals 112
Moldova 91, 94, 101, 102–3, 343
Moltman, Jürgen 148
monasticism/monasteries 17, 31, 72, 78, 135, 176, 184, 187, 262, 283–4, 285, 290, 312, 338, 349, 359
  approval to construct 310
  destroyed 197, 339
  fortified 99
  mendicant 325
  Middle Eastern Syro-Egyptian ideal 68
  military orders 335
  moderate 315
  most famous in the world 328
  Nestorian 73–4
  new preaching orders 331
  relatively extreme views of 315
  reopened 103, 106
  ruined 110
  rural 307

monasticism/monasteries (*cont'd*)
  small 21
  theological fracture between 330
  see also Benedictines; Cluny;
    Dominicans; Franciscans; Jasna
    Gora; Mount Athos; St Macarios
Mongke, Mongol Emperor 341
Mongol Empire 90, 340–1
Mongolia 74
Mongols 112
monotheism 68, 192, 304, 332
monothelitism 299–300, 338
Monségur 335
Montenegro 91, 93, 95
Moody, Dwight L. 351
morality 147
Moravia 315, 316
Mormons 8, 39, 219, 230, 243–5, 257
  number of followers 369
  significant presence in
    Polynesia 256
Moroni (angel) 369
Moscow 24, 102, 114
  Christ the Savior Church 103
  Patriarchate of 104, 106, 344; *see
    also* Aleksy II; Basil of Moscow;
    Kirill I; Nikon; Tikhon
Mosul 341
Mother Teresa *see* Teresa of Calcutta
Mott, John R. 370
Mount Athos (Orthodox
  monastery) 328
Mugabe, Robert 160
Muhammad (Prophet) 113, 294, 304,
  305, 308–9
  number of followers 69
Mukarrasin 77–8
Mukti Mission 60, 124, 125
multiculturalism 112, 242
Mumbai 124
Muslim militias 171
Mutara IV, Rwandan King 157
Myanmar 181, 183, 184, 185
Myland, David Wesley 52

Nagaland 118
Namibia 159

Nanjing Seminary 200
Napoleon Bonaparte 144, 364
National Catholicism 141
National Front
  France 144
  Indonesia 192
national identity 24, 79, 86, 95, 96, 97,
  105, 116–17, 120
  Catholicism and 98, 99, 100, 220
  independent nations trying to
    formulate 113
  spiritual carrier of 103
nationalism 24, 25, 77, 84, 348, 355
  aggressive 105
  ethnic 80, 98
  religious 20, 92, 95, 97, 98, 290, 344
  strong sense of 99
  see also Coptic Nationalism
Nationalist Party (China) 195
nationality
  ethnicity and 88
  faith/religion and 74–5, 95, 100
Native Americans 227
  little mixing of Europeans and 362
Native Baptist Church (Nigeria) 368
Natrun valley 77
Nazi Germany 147, 370
  death camps 100
Nebi Uri 86
négritude 159
Nehru, Jawaharlal 111, 117, 120, 121
neo-Charismatic churches 57, 58,
  212, 236
Nepal 115, 116
nepotism 327
Nero, Roman Emperor 280–1
Nestorian Church 8, 73–4, 75, 112,
  268, 296
Nestorius, Patriarch of
  Constantinople 296
Netherlands 137, 138, 158, 221, 325
  numbers of Catholics and
    Protestants roughly even 146
  Oecumenische Vrouwensynoden
    gatherings 134
  Protestant state churches 44
  Protestantism spread to 350

tensions between Muslims and
  non-Muslims 143–4
three times as many Christians in
  Indonesia as in 193
New Caledonia 251, 254
New England 362–3
  Puritan Congregational Church 45
New Guinea 250, 252, 253
New South Wales 250, 260, 262, 263
New Testament 3, 50, 162, 271, 272,
  273, 366
  defining the content of 275
  interpretation of 276–7
  morality-centered 351
New York City 233
New York State 369
New Zealand 4
  Anglicanism 256, 257
  Christianity on the decline 248
  immigrant settlement 251
  religious experimentation 249
  religious profile 256
  see also Māoris
Newfoundland 227
Newton, John 41
Nguyen Van Thuan, Francis Xavier,
  Cardinal 186–7
Ni Tuosheng (Watchman Nee) 196
Nicaragua 212
Nicene Creed *see* Council of Nicaea
Nicholas V, Pope 335
Niebuhr, Reinhold 233
Nigeria 153
  Christianity and Islam 169–72
  Native Baptist Church 368
Nigerian Anglican Church 169
Nikon, Patriarch of Moscow 102
Nitrian Desert 284
Nkrumah, Kwame 159
nondenominationalists 74
Normans 333
North Africa 28, 65, 66, 67–87, 139,
  155, 269, 332
  Donatist Church 291
  Islam conquers 294, 303
  loss of large sections of formerly
    Christian territory 317

Sicily conquered by Muslim army
  based in 333
  weariness of Christians in 130
North America 4, 225–47, 362
  Catholic Charismatic Renewal 213
  Catholic population 27, 33, 34
  Evangelical movement enormously
    popular in 351
  immoral freedom and godless
    materialism 105
  Orthodox population 13
  Protestantism 39
  slaves to British colonies in 366
  see also Canada; United States
North Carolina 230, 366
North Korea 177, 190
Northern Crusade (*c.*1200–1400) 335
Northern Europe 349
  Catholic piety 348
  Protestantism 39, 45, 46
Northern Ireland 152, 362
Northern Mariana Islands 251, 254
Northern Territory (Australia) 260
Norway 146, 148, 149, 303
  first children born to single
    mothers 147
Nowa Huta Lord's Ark Church 100
Nur ad-Din, regional ruler of Seljuk
  Turks 334
Nyerere, Julius 159

Obasanjo, Gen. Olusegun 172
Oberprokuror 102
OCA (Orthodox Church in
  America) 242, 243
Oceania 248–66
  see also Australia; New Zealand;
    Pacific islands
OCL (Orthodox Christian Laity) 243
Oduyoye, Mercy Amba 168
Old Testament 96, 275
Olga of Kiev 316–17
Oljeitu, Mongol ruler 342
Ondetto, Blasio Simeo Malkio 168
OPEC (Organization of Petroleum-
  Exporting Countries) 72
Opium Wars (mid-1800s) 195, 368

Opus Dei 140, 356
ordination 20, 28, 34, 41, 49, 124, 163,
  216, 241, 245, 299, 323
  boys 244
  gays and lesbians 151, 261
  married men as bishops 167
  women 79, 149, 151, 152, 242, 261
Oriental Orthodoxy *see* Miaphysite
  tradition
Origen of Alexandria 67–8, 273
original sin 31, 303
Orthodoxy 8–9, 13–25, 230, 242–3,
  245–6, 317, 333, 357–8
  antagonism between Roman
    Catholic Churches and 89
  consideration of Protestant
    tradition 10
  conversion to 316
  crusade against 98
  declaration of union between
    Catholics and 337
  decline of 319
  developments in the tradition
    327–9
  Eastern Europe the center of 88
  establishing by persuasion 317
  Islam viewed as heresy 305
  predominant 106–7, 365
  role of experience in the Christian
    life 320–1
  Russia as defender of 101, 102
  see also Armenian Orthodox;
    Coptic Orthodox; Ethiopian
    Orthodox; Greek Orthodox;
    Iconoclastic Controversy; OCA;
    OCL; Romanian Orthodox;
    Russian Orthodox; SCOBA;
    Serbian Orthodox; Syrian
    Orthodox; Triumph of
    Orthodoxy; Ukrainian Orthodox
orthopathy 5
Osama bin Laden 114
Ottoman Empire 23, 24, 70–2, 80–1,
  91, 94, 95, 102
  Byzantine Empire defeated by 319
  Serbs and Bulgarians defeated
    by 343

World War I defeat of 371
  see also Sinan Pasha
Our Lady of Cormoto
  (Venezuela) 211
Our Lady of the Angels *see La Negrita*

Pacific islands 4, 248, 249, 259
  Christianity and indigenous
    people 251–3
  see also Melanesia; Micronesia;
    Polynesia
Pacific Rim 250
pacifism 46, 107, 351
Padre Pio 135
paganism 252, 270, 282, 283, 311,
  313, 344, 361
  aggressive and violent posture
    toward 331
  crusade against 98
  Europe's last bastion of 312, 335
  fight against 317
  Orthodoxy presented as
    improvement on and correction
    of 22
Pakistan 115
  Christians in 116
  Kashmir claimed by India
    and 117
  partition (1972) 116
  see also Bangladesh; Islamic
    Republic of Pakistan
Palamas, Gregory, Archbishop of
  Thessalonica 17, 23, 328–9
Palestine/Palestinian territories 1, 67,
  70, 71, 74, 83, 84–6, 267, 279, 306
Palladius 290, 312
pan-Arabism 70, 74
pan-Islamism 184
  rising tide of 74
Pancasila philosophy
  (Indonesia) 192
Panikkar, Raimundo 123
papal bulls
  Exsurge Domine (1520) 349
  Inter Caetera (1493) 359, 360
  Romanus Pontifex (1445) 335
  Unam Sanctam (1302) 323

papal encyclicals
  Allatae Sunt (1755) 357
  Dictatus Papae (*c.*1075) 322
  Fides et ratio (1998) 136
  Humani Generis (1950) 356
  Princeps Pastorum (1958)
  Slavorum Apostoli (1985) 372
papal infallibility 33
Papal States 35, 36, 356
  campaign to regain 355
Papua New Guinea 254
parables 3
Paradise Church 264
Paraguay 214
Paraiba River 210
Paris 263
Parliamentarians (English Civil
    War) 362
Parthia 2, 287
paternalism 124, 264, 288
Patriarchs of Constantinople 9, 22–3,
    95, 101–2, 243, 306, 344
  see also Cyril Lucaris; Michael
    Cerularius; Nestorius
Patrick (Ireland) 290, 312
patriotism 82, 88, 100, 106,
    195, 200
  see also Catholic Patriotic
    Association; CCC; TSPM
Paul the Apostle 3, 67, 271, 272, 273,
    275, 276
  missionary travels of 280
Paul VI, Pope 356
Paulos, Ethiopian Orthodox
    Abune 177
Pavle, Serbian Orthodox Patriarch 96
PAW (Pentecostal Assemblies of the
    World) 235
Peace of Westphalia (1648) 46, 361,
    362
Pearl Harbor (1941) 182
Pearl of Great Price, The 245
pedophile crisis 241
Pedro I (Brazil) 214
penance 28, 323, 273, 323
  and reconciliation 31
Pentarchy 302

Pentecostal Apostolic Faith
    Mission 175
Pentecostal/Charismatic movement 5,
    7, 8, 50–61, 194, 212, 216, 252,
    253, 256, 347
  cell group concept adopted by 191
  claims about size worldwide 11
  Eastern European 89
  entrepreneurial 57
  evangélico 203, 206, 213, 214,
    215, 217
  faith defined by emphasis 10
  growth of 191, 199, 200
  Indian 124–6
  largest church in Europe 108
  speaking in tongues 26, 52, 57,
    58, 59, 60, 125, 134, 200, 212,
    213, 236
  see also CCR; Classical
    Pentecostalism; Independent
    churches; neo-Charismatic
    churches; PWF; Spirit-filled
    Christianity
People Power protests (Philippines)
  see EDSA
People's Party (Spain) 142
Pereira, Juana 211
Perpetua *see* Vibia Perpetua
persecution 20, 46, 78, 80, 82, 93, 100,
    102, 126, 152, 190, 273, 279, 283,
    306, 317, 343
  bitter 295
  Communist 190
  conversion can result in 180–1
  developing a history that
    emphasized 96
  documenting 201
  ever-increasing 338
  exemption from 288
  harsh 110, 339
  horrible 291
  ineffective 288
  intermittent 84
  major 197
  moving to power from 285
  not uncommon 116
  outright 68

overt 193, 288
  rough 98
  severe 106, 177, 289, 299, 308
  state-sanctioned 281, 282
  structure of life that would
    minimize risk of 74
  systematic and intense 281
  two centuries of 340
  unexpected 339
  worst periods of 238
Persia 310
  Arab conquest of 307
  Byzantium at war with 299
  Christianity 77, 285–7, 288–91,
    296, 303, 308, 340, 342
  culture 3, 296
  Il-khanate 341, 342
  Islam conquers/subjugates 294,
    303
  Mongol rule of 341
  Muslim rule welcomed 295
Persian Empire 73, 112, 287,
    304, 309
  core convictions of Christians 279
Persian Gulf nations 182
Peru 206, 209, 214
  Our Lady of Mercy 211
  Pentecostal churches 212
Peshitta 276
Peter the Apostle 32, 272, 275, 302,
    322
Peter I (the Great), Tsar of Russia 102
Philadelphia 237
Philippines 182, 183, 251
  Muslims in 184
  number of Catholics 10
  politics and prosperity 187–90
  see also Aquino; Manila; Marcos;
    Mindanao; Sin (Cardinal)
phyletism 20, 95
Pietism 149, 178
  see also German Pietism
Pius IX, Pope 36, 355
Pius XII, Pope 98, 197, 211, 356
Plato 309
PLO (Palestinian Liberation
    Organization) 86

Poland 94, 98, 99–101
    Protestantism spread to 45–6,
        350, 361
polygamy 162, 167, 173
Polynesia 253, 255–6, 257
    see also French Polynesia
polytheism 304
Pontius Pilate 277
Popes
    Coptic: *see* Abraham; Shenouda III;
        Theodosius I
    Roman Catholic: *see* Alexander VI;
        Benedict XVI; Boniface VIII;
        Calixtus II; Clement XI;
        Gregory I; Gregory VII; Innocent
        III; John XXIII; John Paul II;
        Leo III; Leo IX; Leo X; Nicholas
        V; Paul VI; Pius IX; Pius XII;
        Urban II
Portugal 137, 158, 180, 193, 207, 214,
        335, 348
    belief there was a Christian
        monarch in the East 122
    Catholic conquest of Latin
        America 36
    Christian globalization 359
    colonial Africa 161
    glocalization in Africa 361
    missionaries in Africa 172
    religiosity 138
Potter's House, The 238
Prajna 310
prayer 7, 77, 93, 134, 186, 284, 290,
        312, 315
    Catholic 28, 31, 135, 138, 189, 201,
        217, 324
    Christian and Muslim neighbors
        come together in 86
    Church of the East 297
    Coptic 79
    dedication in 46
    Evangelical 235, 236
    Methodist 259
    Muslim 304
    Orthodox 9, 17, 19, 23
    Pentecostal/Charismatic 53, 57,
        191, 214, 236

Protestant 41, 46, 49, 125, 147,
        149, 235
    see also Jesus Prayer
predestination 43
premarital sex 241
Presbyterian Church USA 231
Presbyterianism 44, 74, 124, 142, 212,
        227, 257
    cell group concept adopted by 191
    devout 257
    English Parliamentarians
        (17th-c.) 362
    Korean 190–1, 246
    merger of Methodism and 254
    Scottish 46, 368
Prince of Peace Church 212
procreation 288
Protestantism 7, 38–49, 74, 82, 116,
        137, 146–9, 195, 198, 253, 347,
        348–52, 361
    anti-Catholic prejudices 239
    changing attitudes toward
        slavery 369
    church–state 148
    conversion can result in
        persecution 180–1
    cordial relations between Catholics
        and 99
    country suspicious of 180
    creativity unleashed 369
    dissident 197
    Eastern European 89
    Ecumenical 48–9
    Evangelical 48–9, 230–5
    evangélico 203, 206
    flourishing 227
    grassroots vitality 134
    growth of 191, 199, 366, 367
    historically black churches 237–8
    history and varieties of 348–52
    house churches 197–8, 199, 200
    immigrants in Latin
        America 211–12
    Indian 122, 123–4, 130
    introduced to the Caribbean 221
    Koreans attracted to 190
    legislation directed at 173

Mainline 230–5
    missionary-minded 212
    modified revivalism 351
    morality-centered 352
    North American 225, 226
    numbers declined 227
    old ways described as totally
        mistaken 252
    Pentecostal/Charismatic movement
        a new kind of 52
    predominant 188, 230,
        255, 357
    second-class citizens 144
    social activism 123, 124
    spread of 45–6, 350, 361
    Western European 146–52
    see also Anglicanism; Baptists;
        Calvinist tradition;
        Congregationalists; Ecumenical
        Protestantism; German
        Protestantism; Lutheranism;
        Methodism; Presbyterianism;
        Reformed Protestantism; state
        churches; theology; TSPM
PSOE (Spanish Socialist Workers
        Party) 142–3
PTL (Praise the Lord) television
        show 170, 236
Puerto Rico 223
Pune 60, 124
Punjabi groups 116, 118
Pure Land Buddhism 184
purgatory 32, 35, 320, 323–4,
        348, 349
Puritans 42, 45, 46, 362–3
Putin, Vladimir V. 105
PWF (Pentecostal World
        Fellowship) 59
Pyrenean mountains 335

Qale Heywet Church 177
Qatar 72
Qing Qing 310
Quakers 363
Quebec 227
Queensland 260, 262
Quran 70, 294, 304, 305

Rahner, Karl 147, 148, 356
Ramabai, Pandita 60
Rape of Nanjing (1937) 182
Rastafarians 177
Ratana, Tahupotiki Wiremu 257
Ratana Church 257
Ratislav, Moravian King 316
Ratzinger, Joseph, Cardinal 123
    see also Benedict XVI
reconciliation 17, 53, 175, 201, 274
    penance and 31
reconquista 332
Red Guards 197
red-letter Christians 2
Rede Brasil Cristão (Catholic
    television network) 216
Redevida (Catholic television
    network) 216
Reformation 36, 348, 349, 359
Reformed Church in America 232
Reformed Protestantism 10, 43, 44,
    46, 99, 124, 165, 193, 350
    start of 359
    see also World Alliance of Reformed
    Churches
religiosity, measures of 138–9, 143
    distributed unevenly 230
    overall increase in 215
    Protestant-style 206
religious freedom 59, 82, 121, 145,
    190, 366
    constitutions and 99, 118, 148, 215,
    218, 261
    embraced 106, 140
    end of Communist rule 107
    established as law of the land 218
    established on condition 144
    genuine 97, 119
    government policy guarantees 198
    modern conceptions as basic
    human right 40
    promised 142
    settlers in search of 362
    shift toward more 93
    support of 341, 365
    tolerance of another faith not the
    same as 68

religious nationalism 92, 95, 290, 344
Religious Right (US) 120, 235
religious sects 206
Renaissance 348
repression 197, 198, 201, 208, 218
Republic of Armenia 80, 82
Republican Party (US) 235
Requerimiento 335
resurrection *see* crucifixion and
    resurrection
Revelation (book) 276
revivalism 42, 49, 125, 162, 232, 257
    modified 351
    see also Azusa Street Revival; Great
    Awakening; Great Revival; Zion
    Revival
Riccardi, Andrea 135
Ricci, Matteo 363
Righteous Harmony Society *see* Boxer
    Rebellion
Rio de Janeiro 206, 216
ritual immolation 123
Rodriguez Zapatero, José Luis 142, 143
Roh Moo-Hyun 191
Roha (Lalibela) 330
Roman Catholic Church *see*
    Catholicism
Roman Empire 68, 102, 112, 138–9,
    269–70, 279–85, 287, 302,
    306, 309
    barbarian nations along the
    northern border 291
    bilingualism 21, 90
    breadbasket of 67
    last remnant of 343
    one of the most important political
    leaders within 349
    significant political force in
    European history 314–15
    see also Charlemagne; Eastern
    Roman Empire; Frederick the
    Wise; Henry IV; Henry V;
    Imperial Church; Theodosius I;
    Western Roman Empire
Roman Symbol 277, 278
Romania 91, 93, 242
    independence (late 1800s) 24, 95

Romanian Orthodox Church 9, 13,
    24, 88, 243, 343
    strained relationship between
    Greek Catholic Church and 97
Rome 37, 302, 316, 326
    Sant'Egidio Community 135
    slave market 312
    St Peter's 314, 324
Romero, Oscar, Archbishop of El
    Salvador 208
Rossi, Padre Marcelo 216
Roy, Ram Mohan 129
Royalists (English Civil War) 362
RSS (Rashtriya Swayamsevak
    Sangh) 120
Rublev, Andrei 329
Rum Christians 306
rural-to-urban migration 198
Rus (Russian people) 316
Russia 182, 315
    Communist period (1917–91) 91,
    92–3, 102, 103, 114
    establishing Orthodoxy by
    persuasion 317
    geographic center of Orthodoxy 13
    Mongol rule of 341
    Orthodoxy's resistance to
    change 357
    religious nationalism 344
    subjugated by Islamic Mongol
    Empire 90
    trade and Christianity in East
    Asia 180
    see also Soviet Union; *also under
    following* Russian *headings*
Russian Empire 24, 92, 99, 114, 344
    God raising up a third Rome
    in 344
    transition to Communist-run
    USSR 113
Russian Federation 94, 101, 103,
    104, 105
Russian Orthodox Church 9, 19, 24,
    88, 94–5, 101–6, 108, 113, 114, 243
    challenge for leadership of
    Orthodox movement 329
    efforts to squash 92

narrative style of faith 321
number of members 13
schism 357
sphere of influence 93
visible in Alaska 242
vision of Moscow as third
Rome 344
Rwanda 157, 174

Sabbath 177, 330
sacraments 27–8, 45, 354
withholding 217
see also anointing; baptism;
confirmation; Eucharist; holy
orders; marriage; penance
Saddam Hussein 77
Saddleback Church 234
Saladin (Salah ad-Din Yusuf ibn
Ayyub) 334, 339–40
Salt Lake City 244
salvation 3, 200, 208, 209, 222, 251,
278, 347
American Evangelical 233
Black Church in US 366
Catholic 30–2, 123, 320, 321, 323,
326, 327, 331, 348, 354
Church of the East 296, 344
East Asian 181–2
Miaphysite 298
Orthodox 17–19, 75, 300, 301, 302,
328, 353
Pentecostal/Charismatic 55–6, 125,
153, 212, 216
Protestant 41, 42–4, 124, 196,
232, 354
Samanids 112
Samoa 250–1, 256
Samuel, Vinay 124
San Giovanni Rotondo 135
sanctification 353
Sangh Parivar 120–1
Santería 222
São Paulo 206, 210, 216
Sarkozy, Nicolas 145
Sasanian Empire 112, 287–8, 307
Saudi Arabia 72
involvement in Africa 160

Sava (Serbian saint) 96
Sawaswati, Pandita Ramabai 124–5
Scandinavia 316, 317
paganism 312
Pietistic Christians 149
Protestantism 44, 45–6, 350
state churches 148–9
see also Denmark; Finland; Norway;
Sweden
Scheduled Castes 127, 128
Schillebeeckx, Edward 148, 356
schism 163, 197
Modernist-Fundamentalist in
Protestant 47–8
Russian Orthodox 102, 357
see also Great Schism
Schleiermacher, Friedrich 351
scholasticism 325
SCOBA (Standing Conference of
Orthodox Bishops in
America) 242–3
Scotland
Catholic Church membership 152
Presbyterianism 46, 368
Scythia 2
Second Council of Dvin (554) 299
Second Council of Lyon (1274) 323
Second Vatican Council (1962–65)
36–7, 134, 135, 140, 141–2, 209
change and development in
Catholicism around the
world 239, 356
secularism 120, 145, 153, 370, 371
anticlerical views 208
churches that have tended to
internalize 147
philosophy of regional unity that
rejects 74
rise of 136
self-conscious 229
shallow 100
state should be run on principles
of 217
symbol of radical Islam staunchly
opposed to 144
Seidnaya Orthodox Christian
Convent 86

Seljuk Turks 23, 334, 340, 341, 343
Byzantine army defeated by
(1071) 342
Senegal 159
Senghor, Léopold 159
Seoul *see* Yoido
Serbia 25, 80, 91, 93, 242, 343, 344
ethnic cleansing/fighting
(1990s) 96–7
independence (late 1800s) 95
see also Belgrade
Serbian Orthodox Church 88, 96–7,
262
Sergius of Radonezh 329
Sevan, Lake 80
Seventh Day Adventists 219
Severus of Antioch 298
sexual ethics 151, 152
sexuality 142, 240–1
unencumbered by guilt 250
Zoroastrians and 288
Seymour, William J. 8, 60, 235, 353
shamanism 111, 185, 341
Shanghai 201
Shapur II, Sasanian ruler 288
Shari'a law 143, 171, 184
Sheba, Ethiopian Queen 330
Shembe, Isaiah 60
Shenouda III, Coptic Orthodox
Pope 77, 78–80
Shepherd, The 273, 276
Shi'ite Muslims 110, 113, 339
Shinto 183, 185
Siauliai 98
Siberia 82
Sicily 333, 336
Sierra Leone 160
Sigismund III Vasa, Polish King 106
Sikhs 118
Silk Road 110, 111, 182, 310
Simons, Menno 46
simony 322, 327
Sin, Archbishop Jaime, Cardinal 188
Sinan Pasha, Ottoman Emperor 96
Singapore 183
Sinhalese people 116
Sino-Japanese war (1937–45) 182

sins 42, 95, 163, 273
    Christians who relapsed into 273
    confession of 43
    fear of being sent to hell for 233
    forgiveness of 2, 55, 169, 323, 334,
        354
    mortal 31
    pleasures to be avoided 56
    serious 100
    turning away from 205
    venial 31
Sisters of St Joseph 262
slave trade 155, 207, 214, 221, 222,
        312, 365–6
    changing attitudes toward 369
Slavic groups 303, 316
Slavic language 316
Slovak Republic 91, 94, 98
Slovenia 94, 98
slums 206
Smith, Chuck 236
Smith, Joseph 243, 369
sniffers (in Legio Maria Church) 163
Sobibor 100
Social Gospel 351
social norms 142
socialism 118, 141, 195–6, 223
    God-free 100
    natural 159
    religions that undermine not
        tolerated 198
Society of Jesus *see* Jesuits
Sofia-mássor liturgy 134
Solidarity Movement (Poland) 100
Solomon, Israelite King 330
Solomon Islands 254
Solomonic dynasty 330
Somalia 177
Song Choan-Seng 187
Sorkaktani-beki 341
South Africa 60, 160
    antiapartheid movement
        49, 175
    morality-centered Christianity 352
    race and faith 174–6
South America 4, 164
    see also Latin America

South Asia 4, 110–31
    ethnic and cultural groups and
        subgroups 112
South Australia 260, 262, 263
South Carolina 230
South Korea 181, 183, 190–1, 373
    Catholicism first introduced
        (1784) 190
    Presbyterianism 190–1, 246
    see also Kim Dae-Jung; Kim
        Young-sam; Lee Myung-Bak;
        Roh Moo-Hyun; Yoido
Southeast Asia 185, 254, 359, 371
    Chinese traditional religion 184
    Church of the East planted in 73
    subjugated (1930s and 1940s) 182
Southern Baptist Church 240, 244
Southern Christian Leadership
    Conference 238
Southern Europe 269
Soviet Union 72, 98, 159, 371
    antireligious rhetoric 92
    Cold War between US and 182–3,
        370
    dissolution/collapse (1991) 82,
        91–2, 102, 103, 106, 112, 113
    militant, grobal atheism 371
Soweto 175
Spain 2, 137, 158, 207, 269, 335
    belief in God 133–4
    Catholic conquest of Latin
        America 36
    Catholicism's newly confrontational
        attitude first developed in 332
    Christian globalization 359
    Christian monarch in the East
        belief 122
    church and politics 140–3
    control of Caribbean 221
    Islamic armies conquer 303
    militant Catholicism 348
    monasteries 322
    Philippines conquered by 188
    religiosity 138–9, 143
    see also Al-Andalus; Inquisition
Spanish-American War (1898) 188
Spanish Civil War (1936–39) 140–1

Spanish Constitution (1978) 142
speaking in tongues 26, 52, 57, 58, 59,
        60, 125, 134, 200, 212, 213, 236
Spener, Philip Jakob 46
Spirit-filled Christianity 50, 54, 58, 60
Spirit-inspired prophets 162
Spiritual Baptists 222
spirituality 69, 77, 80, 108, 123, 135,
        136, 187, 285, 296, 315
    African 166, 214
    African-American 238
    Asian 186
    Australian 259–65
    Canadian 229
    Catholic 27–30, 327, 348, 349, 356
    Celtic Christian 290
    Dalit 128
    Eastern Christianity 303
    Evangelical 235
    Hesychast 328
    Indian/Hindu 123, 129
    Orthodox 14–17, 301
    Pentecostal/Charismatic 51–4, 58,
        263
    Protestant 38, 40–1, 235, 348
Sri Lanka 115, 116, 308
St Kitts & Nevis 222
St Macarios monastery 77
St Vincent & Grenadines 222
Stalin, Joseph 82, 92, 106
state churches 44–5, 148–9
Staupitz, Johann von 349
stigmata 135
Stockholm 263
Sub-Saharan Africa 4, 155–79
Sudan 160
Sudan Interior Mission 177
Sufism 86, 114, 171, 338
Suharto, Gen. Raden 192
Sukarno, Achmed 192
Sulawesi 193
Sun Yat-sen 195
Sunni Muslims 110, 113
    fundamentalist 114
supernaturalism 54, 134, 162, 167,
        200, 351, 352
superstition 26, 184, 200, 305

Suriname 222
sutras 310
Svyatoslav I of Kiev 317
Swaggart, Jimmy 236
Sweden 99, 146, 257
   church attendance 133
Swedish Lutheran Church 134, 148
Switzerland 137, 138, 146, 314
   bank accounts siphoned 173
   Protestant 44, 46, 147, 350
   see also Calvin; Geneva
Sword Brethren *see* Livonian Brothers
   of the Sword
Sydney 261
   Baulkham Hills 263
Syllabus of Errors (1864) 36
Symeon the New Theologian 23,
   284, 328
symphonia 20, 95, 105
Synod of Dadyeshu (424) 289
Synod of Diamper (1599) 361
Synod of Isaac (410) 289
Synod structure 102
Syria 68, 70, 71, 81, 86, 176, 290,
   293, 299
   Christians 284
   monasticism 315
   Muslim rule welcomed 295
   see also Damascus
Syriac language 270, 276, 278, 287,
   296, 308
Syrian Catholic Church 338
Syrian Orthodox Church 20, 72, 73,
   83, 112, 121, 268, 299, 337, 338
Syro-Malabar Catholic Church 122

Tabor, Mount 329
Taft, William Howard 188
Tahiti 256
Taiping Rebellion (1851–64) 195,
   368–9
Taiwan 183, 195
   Chinese traditional religion 184
Tajikistan 74, 110, 112, 113
Taliban 114–15
Tamburlaine *see* Timur Leng
Tamil Nadu 123, 126, 129, 286

Tamils 116
Tandon, Purushottamdas 119
Tang Dynasty 309–10, 311
Tanzania 159
Taoists 183, 186
Tasmania 260
television 216
temple prostitution 123
Temujin (Genghis Khan) 341
Tennessee 230, 235, 238
Teoctist, Orthodox Patriarch 97
Teresa of Avila, St 140
Teresa of Calcutta, Mother 32, 123
Tertullian 67
Teutonic knights 98, 335
Texas 230, 238
Thailand 183, 184, 371
Theodora, Byzantine Empress 22,
   299, 301
Theodore of Mopsuestia 296, 298
Theodosius I, Holy Roman
   Emperor 283, 363
Theodosius I, Patriarch and
   Miaphysite Coptic Pope 299
theology 4, 63, 67, 126, 137, 175, 187,
   267, 277, 293–4
   Aboriginal 264
   Catholic 16, 18, 22, 29, 30, 32, 33,
      36, 98, 123, 148, 149, 196, 200,
      210, 216, 323, 338, 349, 355
   Church of the East 296, 297–8, 309
   Dalit 128
   Evangelical 233, 234
   Gnostic Christian 274
   Korean Presbyterian 190–1
   Methodist 353–4
   Mormon 245
   Orthodox 13–14, 16, 17–18, 20, 21,
      22, 23, 24, 72, 301, 321, 329, 357
   Palestinian Christian 85
   Pentecostal/Charismatic 52, 54, 353
   Protestant 16, 18, 38, 40, 43, 45, 46,
      47, 48, 98, 233, 350, 352, 367, 369
   ubuntu 352
   see also liberation theology
theosis see deification
Theotokos 279, 301, 343

Theravada Buddhism 184
Thich Nhat Hanh 186, 187
Thirty Years War (1618–48) 361
Thomas the Apostle 275, 286, 287
Thomas Christians/Syrian
   churches 121–2, 286
Thomas, M. M. 124
Tiananmen Square protests
   (1989) 198
Tibet 198, 308, 341
Tikhon, Russian Orthodox
   Patriarch 102
Tillich, Paul 148
Tillotson, John, Archbishop of
   Canterbury 364
Timothy I, Catholicos of Church of
   the East 297, 308–9
Timur Leng 74, 342
Timurid Empire 342
Ting, Bishop K. H. 200, 352
Tiridates III, King of Armenia 290
Tito, Josip Broz 95
Tolui Khan 341
Tonantzín 211
Tong Hap PCK 190
Tonga 256
Torres Strait Islanders 251
torture 168, 197, 201, 208, 281, 300
Transylvania 97
TRC (SA Truth and Reconciliation
   Commission) 175
Trdat, Armenian King 74
Treaty of Waitangi (1840) 257
Treblinka 100
Trento 135
tribal associations 112, 127, 171
Trinidad and Tobago 222
Trinity 3, 18, 68, 212
Triumph of Orthodoxy (843) 22, 301
Tsetsis, George 25
TSPM (Three-Self Patriotic Movement,
   China) 196, 197, 199, 200
Tunisia 67
Turkey 69, 71, 74, 80–2, 340
   massacre of Armenian
      Christians 76, 81, 82
   see also Istanbul

Turkmenistan 74, 110, 112, 113

Turks 104

see also Mamluk Empire; Ottoman
Empire; Seljuk Turks; Young
Turks

Turpan 289, 309

Tutsis 157

Tutu, Desmond, Anglican Archbishop
of Cape Town 175, 352

Uganda 174

UGCC (Ukrainian Greek Catholic
Church) 106–7

Uighur Khaganate 308

ujamaa 159

Ukraine 91, 94, 101, 102–3, 105–8,
242, 343

largest church pastored by Nigerian
Pentecostal 169

pluralistic vision of church and
society 103

see also Kiev; Lviv

Ukrainian Orthodox Church 106,
107, 114

Ulfilas (Roman missionary) 291, 312

Umayyad Caliphate 304, 332

Umbanda 214, 216

underground churches *see* house
churches

Uniate churches 72, 106, 357

Union of South Africa 174

United Arab Emirates 72

United Church (PNG) 254

United Church of Christ 40, 231

United Evangelical Lutheran
Church 124

United Kingdom 134, 158, 221

calls to introduce Shari'a law 143

Catholic Church members
subjected to persecution 152

children born out of wedlock 147

colonial policy 161

decline of Christianity 150

GDP 160, 183

Ottoman lands divided among
France and 71, 371

Protestantism 44, 146, 350

rule in India 117

trade and Christianity in East
Asia 180

see also England and Wales;
Scotland; *also under headings
prefixed* "British"

United Methodists 231, 244

United Nations 72, 84–5, 155, 160

Micronesia a trust territory of 254

United States 108, 229–46

aid to Africa 160

Black Church 230, 237–8, 366

Catholicism in transition 239–42

Christian realism 370

Christian television shows 176

Civil Rights movement 49, 237–8,
352, 371

Cold War between Soviet Union
and 182–3, 370

control of Philippines 188

defined as God-fearing 371

Evangelicals 230–6

first invasion of Iraq by 252

GDP 160, 183

influence in Liberia 158

Korean War 196

Mainline Protestants 230–6

military presence 182

Mormons 230, 243–5, 369

number of Catholics 10

one of the most progressive
denominations in 40

Orthodox Christianity 242–3

Pentecostal/Charismatic
movement 235–7

United States Orthodoxy 230, 242–3,
245–6

outspoken critic of Chinese
government and patriotic
Catholic Church 201

Pacific territories/possessions
of 251, 254

Pentecostal/Charismatic
community 51, 230, 235–6

Presbyterians 190

Protestantism 38, 39, 44, 45, 212,
230, 231–5, 237–8

seeking African allies 159

separation of church
and state 365

support for Mobutu in Congo 173

Taliban driven out of power by 115

trade and Christianity in East
Asia 180

Ukrainian Baptist connections
with 107

Vietnam War 183, 371

Universal Church of Christ 7

Universal Church of the Kingdom of
God 212

see also IURD

University of Bologna 325

University of Paris 325

University of Wittenburg 349

unknown languages 50

see also speaking in tongues

unregistered churches 199, 200

untouchables *see* Dalits

UPM (French Union for a Popular
Movement) 145

Urban II, Pope 333, 334, 336, 342

Urmia, Lake 80

Urs von Balthasar, Hans 148

Urumqi 198

use of force 119, 171, 333

USSR *see* Soviet Union

Utah 230, 244

utopia 92–3

Uzbekistan 74, 110, 112, 113

Vajpayee, A. B. 120

Van, Lake 80

Van Gogh, Theo 144

Vandals 291

Vanuatu 254

John Frum movement 251

Vasco da Gama 122, 361

Vatican 32, 35, 137, 167, 196, 197,
201, 205, 220, 262, 324, 355

Concordats with 99, 144

North American Catholics question
decisions 225

Trojan horse serving to Catholicize
all Eastern Europe 107

uneasy with Cardinal's political
involvement 188
see also First Vatican Council;
Second Vatican Council
Velarde, Mariano *see* Brother Mike
Vibia Perpetua 67, 281
Victoria (Australia) 260, 262
Vietnam 180–1, 182, 183, 371
see also Nguyen Van Thuan; Thich
Nhat Hanh
Vikings 303
Virgin Aparecida 211
Virgin Mary 31, 188, 277, 360
importance of 210–11
see also Guadalupe Virgin;
Theotokos
Visigothic Kingdom 302
Vision of the Future Church 212
Vladimir, Grand Prince of the
Rus 317
Vodou 222
Völkerwanderung 303
voogdyskap 174
Vulgate 68, 276

Waldo, Peter 324–5
Wallis and Futuna 251
Wang Mingdao 196
War of Reform (Mexico
1858–61) 217
Warren, Rick 234
Waves of Love and Peace Church 212
wealth accumulation 170
Wesley, John 353–4
West African religion 222
West Indies 7, 222
see also Jamaica
West Syriac Church 299
Western Australia 260
Western Europe 4, 35, 132–54, 295,
303, 312–15, 319, 323, 326
Catholic Christianity and 138–9,
311, 343

division between Eastern and
90, 91
immoral freedom and godless
materialism 105
Protestant-Catholic divide 113
relative wealth 325
state churches 365
Western Roman Empire 35, 90, 301
White Lotus (Buddhist secret
society) 196
Whitefield, George 232, 350
Wilberforce, William 369
Willems, Dirk 351
Williams, Rowan, Archbishop of
Canterbury 152
Willibrord 312
Winthrop, John 362
Wittenburg 8, 349
Wojtyla, Karol, Archbishop of
Krakov 100
see also John Paul II
Word of God Church 212
World Alliance of Reformed
Churches 175
World Bank 183
World Council of Churches 93, 105,
173, 175, 259
concerns that led to creation of 48
headquarters of 148
moderator of the Central
Committee 124
Orthodox influence within 357
presidents of 177
World Methodist Council 59
World Values Survey 229
World War I 71, 370
World War II 82, 84, 177, 251, 257
German Lutherans deported to
Central Asia 114
Korea freed from Japanese
occupation by American
troops 190
Polish anti-Semitism 100

wowserism 260, 261
Wu Yaozung 196
Wuye, James Movel, Pastor 171–2
Wuzong, Chinese Emperor 311
Wycliffe, John 349

Xavier, Francis 123
Xi'an *see* Chang'an

Yahweh 273
Yahyā ibn Adī 309
Yangtze River Dam 198
Yar'Adua, Umaru 172
Yesus Church 178
Yin Shang (network of house
churches) 198
YMCA (Young Men's Christian
Association) 196
Yoido Full Gospel Church 59,
191, 263
Yonggi Cho, Revd David 191, 263
Yoruba 171
Young Turks 71, 80, 81
youth activity 245
Yuan Dynasty 341
Yuan Shikai, Gen. 195
Yugoslavia (former) 91, 94, 95
genocide and ethnic cleansing 88
see also Bosnia-Herzegovina;
Croatia; Macedonia;
Montenegro; Serbia; Slovenia

Zagwe Dynasty 330
Zaire 173
Zairewa Catholics 173–4
Zambia 167
Lumpa Church 168
Zen Buddhism 184
Zimbabwe 159, 160
Zion Revival (Jamaica) 222
Zionism 84, 85
Zoroastrianism 287–8, 289, 295, 307,
311, 317

Executive
Fitness
FOR MEN

Executive Fitness

FOR MEN

Over 50 effective exercises that really do the business!

C R GILLMAN

PIATKUS

To my husband, Nick, and our sons,
Alexander and George.
Also to my godson, Felix, and my
goddaughters, Alice and Eleanor.

First published in paperback in 1997
by Judy Piatkus (Publishers) Ltd
5 Windmill Street, London W1P 1HF

**The moral right of the author has been
asserted**

*A catalogue record for this book is available
from the British Library*

ISBN 0 7499 1790 6

Designed by Jerry Goldie
Photographs by Jon Stewart

Data capture and manipulation by
Create Publishing Services, Bath

Printed and bound in Great Britain by
The Bath Press, Bath

Contents

1 Under Starter's Orders 8

2 Take Your Marks 15

3 Get Set, Go
The Executive Fitness
Programme 21

4 Eating Out 98

5 Time to Unwind 112

6 Conclusion 124

Index 126

Acknowledgements

Dare I say that the inspiration for this book was born over an exceedingly boozy supper, at which a dear friend lamented his rapidly fading fitness and crumbling health since he'd become something 'big' in the City. As he dripped tears in his beers, a rather dim light flickered in my numbed brain. Thankfully, I remembered enough of the conversation the next day to quiz him and other friends about why they were unable to get fit via the usual routes. I soon realised that Dave's problem of no spare time and long hours spent sitting at a desk was ubiquitous, and that a book could be of great service to many men in the same position as him. So, thank you to Dave and Britta for that memorable and auspicious dinner party.

My considerable gratitude is due to Lesley Hinchcliffe, without whose expertise this book would not have been possible. A fitness consultant, personal trainer and instructor based in the North-West, she has dedicated her career to promoting and improving the standard of fitness teaching. Her unwavering enthusiasm, cheerfulness and belief in the book made her a delight to work alongside. And a very big thank you also to our respective husbands, who were the poor unfortunate souls regularly put through their paces in order to try out the exercise routines as they were developed.

The Institute of Optimum Nutrition (0181 877 9993), based in Putney, West London, was of great support in the researching of this book. The ION is an independent education trust for the study, research and practice of nutrition. It is non-profit making and the team of doctors, nurses, chemists, environmental health experts, sports scientists, nutritionists and complementary practitioners have helped millions of people by means of their courses, publications, clinics and general enquiry service. Particular thanks go to Lorraine Perretta who gave up her valuable spare time to cast an expert eye over the nutrition chapter of the book.

Thanks also to Steve and Alan for their sterling services as models. They made the exercise shoot great fun despite the hard work. Sorry about the aching muscles lads!

And finally, a big thank you to Rachel Bond at Piatkus who is not only an excellent editor but a delight and a hoot to work with. She manages to combine professionalism with a great sense of humour and aptitude for fun, and this book is all the better for it.

Warning

If you have a medical condition, you should not under any circumstances follow the programme in this book without first consulting your doctor. All guidelines, warnings and precautions should be read carefully. Neither the author nor the publisher can accept any responsibility for injuries or damage arising out of a failure to comply with the same.

The Executive Fitness Programme is designed primarily for men. However, as long as the health questionnaire requirements are satisfied, there is no reason why a woman cannot follow this programme unless she is preganant. If so, she should not attempt it.

1 Under Starter's Orders

Look in the mirror and what do you see? A fairly dapper, well-preserved executive in a crisp suit. Not bad, eh? Now strip down to your briefest briefs and tell me, hand on heart, that you are just as pleased with the image. The effects of a sedentary job combined with the demands of a young family almost certainly means a spreading waistline, and no time to get fit via the normal avenues open to younger men with fewer commitments and more free time to themselves. Hence, the appearance of love handles, the slightly paunchy stomach, a thicker midriff, and a not-so-cute bottom from all that sitting at the desk. You may be able to hold down a pressurised job, but can you hold in your stomach?

It's hardly surprising that executives find themselves in this position, given the hassled and hectic lifestyle they are obliged to lead. I'd wager a dollar to a dime that most of you used to be reasonably active and belonged to a tennis club, or played weekend rugby, or perhaps you fancied yourself as a bit of a runner. It's also a safe bet to hazard the guess that the majority of you lament the passing of this sporting heyday and that it is not lack of willpower that prevents you from being more active but lack of time. Demanding jobs, long hours and domestic commitments sound the death-knell for the fitness days of most of us.

So what is to be done if you are to salvage any remnants of your fast-receding sporting form? It is a fact that health clubs make their profits out of those who stump up the substantial annual fees in a moment of resolute determination to get fit, only to use the facilities exhaustively for three weeks and then never to set a trainer-clad foot in the place again. Not such a surprise really, when you consider it's difficult to fit in time for a game of footie with the kids, let alone a workout at the gym three times a week. No, to get back in shape under these very specific and confining circumstances requires a long-term approach and commitment to health and fitness that, in real terms, is merely a modification to your current lifestyle.

This book is expressly designed to get you toned up and tuned up, so that you will be better equipped to deal with the high demands on your time and the stresses on your body and mind. It is specifically tailored to fit into a lifestyle that involves long hours in the office and travelling, and precious few leisure hours spent catching up with the family. With an investment of relatively little time, a degree of effort and a modicum of self-control, you will look and feel better within weeks. You are not aiming for a perfect six-pack of rippling stomach muscles. Nor are you looking for biceps that can crush walnuts. That physique demands long hours of pushing weights and should only be attempted under expert supervision.

This book is aimed at executives who are rather more rotund than they care for but without being fat (probably); who are beginning to feel the ill-effects of a sedentary lifestyle – fatigue, no energy, constant tiredness, weak muscles – and don't like it very much; who are aware that corporate entertaining, the obligatory boozy leaving parties and unhealthy snacks eaten on the run are taking a toll on their health, and who'd like to reverse this slippery slide towards Wayne and Waynetta-style slobdom before it's too late.

As you progress through these pages, you will come across an exercise programme for time-pressed executives that builds gradually over the weeks at your own pace. If followed in conjunction with healthy eating (see p.98), it will help you to lose weight or tone up with the minimal commitment of only half an hour a day, three times a week. There are also additional exercises to target specific problem areas of the body, and exercises that can be practised in the office, in front of the television, about the home, in a hotel room or while travelling – in fact, just about anywhere.

Although heavy emphasis is placed on a healthy eating regime, I acknowledge that it's not always easy to achieve a balanced diet when you are obliged to attend numerous business lunches, or are at the mercy of catered events and the local pub or greasy-spoon caff at lunchtime. So I've included advice on how to negotiate your way as healthily as possible around restaurant and sandwich bar menus, and noted what snacks to go for when, as you inevitably will, you feel peckish mid-morning or mid-afternoon.

But before you flick to the juicy bits about what you should and shouldn't eat and drink, you must first ask yourself the question: why do I want to get fit?

Benefits

People's motives for getting back in shape vary enormously and are, of course, highly personal. For many, it's because a certain milestone or event is looming – are you approaching the big four-oh? Is it your first time in the fathers' race at the school sports day? Or do you simply feel the time is right to stop the rot? Whatever the reason, the stark facts about the benefits of exercise and fitness should be persuasion enough for us all.

Apart from the obvious physical benefits of a slimmer, firmer, more toned body that is less likely to succumb to illness, there are immeasurable psychological benefits. Exercise is one of the best ways of relieving stress and tension, which can be no bad thing for a front-line executive. It is known to release endorphins (natural chemicals produced in the brain) into the bloodstream. These make us feel happy and relaxed, and far more impervious to pain – a kind of natural 'upper', if you like, the effects of which last long after the exercising has stopped.

Many GPs recognise the connection between being unfit and depression, and in some cases, they have begun to prescribe regular activity to patients rather than dishing out anti-depressant drugs. Moreover, any form of regular exercise, even if brief, will produce the following additional benefits:

- more stamina and muscle strength
- improved flexibility, so less risk of muscle strain or injury
- better, more toned physique
- greater energy
- improved quality of sleep
- stronger bones, so reduced risk of fractures
- improved circulation
- body fat may decrease
- lower blood pressure, if it was high
- weight loss or maintenance at ideal weight
- a more efficient, fitter heart

Despite this overwhelming body of evidence in favour of exercise, the vast majority of the British public remain unconvinced. In fact, The Allied Dunbar National Fitness survey (sponsored by the Sports Council, the Health Education Authority and the Department of Health), carried out in 1990–2, found that 48 per cent of men and 40 per cent of women are overweight even though 80 per cent of those surveyed said they believed in the value of keeping fit. Not enough to do anything about it, though, it seems. This fact is supported by another national survey which found that only a tiny percentage of respondents – 14 per cent of men and 4 per cent of women – took part in regular weekly exercise. According to the Health Survey for England, in 1995, 15 per cent of men and 16.5 per cent of women aged 16-64 were obese, (defined as more than 20 per cent over the acceptable weight for their height). What's even more alarming is that we are rearing a nation of unfit children. The now customary school run in the car has abolished a healthy daily walk, and with the lack of emphasis on sport both at school and at home, our children are missing out on the benefits of regular exercise. This is reflected in the fact that childhood obesity is now more prevalent than at any other time in the history of this country.

Motivation

However much you believe in the merits of exercise, or however badly you want to get fit for whatever reasons, it would be naïve to deny that it's very easy to slip off the path to fitness and back into slothful, sluggish ways. It's hard to raise yourself from the lethargy and permanent fatigue that pervade all we do when our lives are so stressed. Sometimes it feels that the dice are loaded against getting fit when pressures mount at work. In this case, self-motivation is crucial.

You may decide to tell people in the office, family and friends that you are starting a new, fitter approach to life, so that you cannot possibly give up for fear of losing face. Alternatively, starting the programme with a friend or partner can provide morale-boosting support at times of low ebb. And, if you're competitive by nature, you'll also want to achieve better results than your fitness pal, which can spur you on to greater things.

If you are going it alone, a good trick to motivate yourself is to keep a progress diary. Before starting the Executive Fitness Programme, find a safe walking route that's about a mile long (use the mileometer of the car to measure if it's along a road route, or local signs if it's a footpath). Walk or run the route as briskly as you can and then note down the time it took, your pulse rate as soon as you finished (see p.19), and how hard or easy it was to achieve. As the weeks pass and the programme progresses, periodically repeat the route and note down the same details. You will be amazed to see how your performance has improved and this good news will lift your spirits. You can also keep a similar diary for your performance of the Executive Fitness routines, although progress here is more immediately obvious because of the graded nature of the programme.

Another trump card in the motivation deck is to take photographs of yourself at regular intervals throughout the programme. Don't worry, nobody else has to see them unless you don't have a self-timer on your camera. In that case, you'll have to find a loved one or trusted friend to take the photos because, for best effect, you need to wear the bare minimum.

So we can take it as read then that you want to get fit, or you would not be reading this book in the first place. It merely falls to me to give as many helpful tips as possible on the practicalities of achieving your fitness goal, particularly when you are up against the clock. The best way to go about this is to plan your fitness campaign before even you attempt a push-up.

Practicalities and Planning

If you are trying to cram a ten-hour working day (not including commuting) into every twenty-four hours, then you are going to have to slot your exercise times into your schedule if you are ever to succeed. Although the events of your week may change, particularly if you have to travel a great deal as part of your job, once you have got into the habit of exercising for half an hour before breakfast, say, it will become easier for you to schedule it in wherever you may be. Ultimately, exercising will become second nature and you will feel the lack of it if, for some reason, you are forced to miss your regular session. Because of the varying nature of your schedule, first thing in the morning (perhaps setting the alarm half an hour earlier) or last thing at night tend to be the most reliable times for following the routines (certainly these were the favoured hours of my executive 'guinea pigs').

There is no need for special clothing or footwear – anything loose fitting that does not restrict movement will do. Nonetheless, the ritual of putting on the 'right' gear can play a psychological role in building up a routine. In this case, a tracksuit, or T-shirt and shorts, plus training shoes are ideal. Never exercise in normal day shoes.

With the possible travel element of your job in mind, and in recognition of the fact that you will be working out largely at home, this programme has been designed to be performed without special equipment. In this sense, it can be truly performed any time and anywhere – as long as there is enough space for you to lie full length on the floor (not from exertion, I hasten to add!). Nonetheless, in order for you to build up strength and stamina, the programme progresses by increasing the number of repetitions of each exercise and by the addition of hand-held weights (which can be easily improvised). I suggest you use a couple of grocery tins but, if the Executive Fitness Programme is to become part of your way of life, a set of hand weights will be a worthwhile investment.

The same holds true of home exercise equipment. You may well have an exercise bike lying unused from a previous, unsuccessful fitness campaign. In which case, why not get it out, dust it off and use it in conjunction with this programme? As long as exercise equipment is readily available, i.e. not dismantled under the spare bed, and you have the space to use it safely, it can be highly beneficial. You will find some advice on choosing home exercise equipment on p.96.

In fact, whether it is home exercise equipment, using the hotel swimming pool, or taking the children for a walk, it's all grist to the fitness mill and to be encouraged. It's exactly this approach that you should be aiming for – incorporating more activity into your daily life. Obviously, in an ideal world you would be taking part in more sport or fitness activity, but, given the high demands on your time, a game of tennis is probably going to be a pleasant exception rather than the regular rule.

This is why it's sometimes more realistic to examine the immovable events of your daily schedule and assess whether any of them can be made more fitness-friendly. Running or cycling to work can be a nonstarter if you don't have shower facilities in the office, but there's no reason why you cannot get off the bus, train or tube one stop early and briskly walk the remaining distance. Similarly, take the stairs rather than the lift. You can extend this principle into numerous areas of your office and home life, from delivering internal memos by hand instead of using E-mail, to digging out the old push-style lawnmower instead of relying on the effortless petrol-driven version. Use rare free lunchtimes normally spent in the office to go for a brisk walk or even a swim at the nearest pool, or take an exercise class at the local fitness centre. At least you can always shower and brush up afterwards and still be presentable on your return to the office, if a little damp between the toes.

Building activity into your precious leisure hours is also to be applauded, and the family will benefit too. Walks or a weekend swimming party can be fun, yet good for all the family.

How to Use This Book

By now, we are all familiar with the well-documented, basic requirements of a healthy lifestyle – eat a balanced, nutritious diet, don't smoke, don't drink to excess and take regular physical exercise. (Arguably, you could add 'learn to manage stress' to the list but it's hard to quantify since one person's stress is another's pleasure.) Neglect any one element of the 'good health' formula and you will suffer the consequences of the imbalance. At best your enjoyment of life will be curtailed, and at worst your life could be drastically shortened. Putting the emphasis on taking regular exercise and ignoring dietary advice could result in you being fit yet unhealthy.

This book aims to show how all the essential elements of healthy living can be interpreted and assimilated into the stressful, hectic life of a modern-day executive. It is a formula that can carry you healthily into the twenty-first century.

Firstly, you are provided with a tailor-made exercise programme (p.21) that can be easily followed any time, anywhere. This programme can, of course, be supplemented by additional activity, and the overriding principle is to organise yourself into taking a more physical, robust approach to life.

The balanced diet aspect of the equation is addressed in Chapter 4. The advice contained in this chapter will not condemn you to a life of brown lentils and flatulence but rather points you towards ways in which you can get the most nutritious value from your food within the parameters imposed on most executives – that is to say, eating out a great deal. Finally, the Queen song 'Under Pressure' probably sums up how most working parents feel the majority of the time. In Chapter 5 you will find numerous ways in which to unwind, relax and cope with the stress that is so prevalent in society today.

But, before you throw yourself into the action, it's essential to complete the pre-exercise health questionnaire, irrespective of how young or fit you feel. So turn to Chapter 2 for the preliminaries, and then you are under starter's orders.

2 Take Your Marks

Although the brackets of ideal height-to-weight ratios that you see published in slimming books and magazines are quite broad, you yourself will know in your heart of hearts what your optimum weight is and whether or not you are carrying excess pounds. Similarly, you should be aware if you are fit and healthy or otherwise, even though, as we have seen, the statistics imply that the British delude themselves on this issue.

So, rather than rely fully on your own (impartial?) judgement as to your state of health, you should complete the questionnaire on page 16 before attempting any increased physical activity. If you answer Yes to any of the questions, you should consult your GP before embarking on the Executive Fitness exercise routines. If you answer No to all the questions, you have a reasonable assurance of your suitability for a graduated exercise programme.

Irrespective of your answers to the questionnaire, a complete health check from a professional can be a good idea at any time. The first port of call is normally your GP, who is able to look at your general state of health. Not only does the doctor have your medical history on record, but from basic information such as blood pressure and weight he or she will be well equipped to advise you specifically as to the wisdom of adopting a fitness regime or not.

If you are fortunate enough to have private health insurance, you can elect to pay for just about any health test you care to imagine. Some corporate policies offer employees health screening at substantially reduced prices, so it pays to ask at work before forking out. If you are

Pre-Exercise Health Questionnaire

	Yes	No
1. Has your GP ever said you have heart disease, high blood pressure or any other cardiovascular problem?	☐	☐
2. Is there a history of heart disease in your family?	☐	☐
3. Do you ever have pains in your heart and chest, especially when associated with minimal effort?	☐	☐
4. Do you often get headaches, or feel faint or dizzy?	☐	☐
5. Do you suffer from pain or limited movement in any joints, which has been aggravated by exercise or might be made worse with exercise?	☐	☐
6. Are you taking drugs/medication at the moment or recuperating from a recent illness or operation?	☐	☐
7. Are you unaccustomed to exercise and aged over thirty-five?	☐	☐
8. Do you have any other medical condition which you think may affect your ability to participate in exercise?	☐	☐

footing the bill yourself, the big private health companies often run promotional offers in the newspapers, so shop around as prices vary widely. As a generalisation, though, costs for a full health screen start at around £200.

Once you have established that you are healthy enough to proceed with the Executive Fitness Programme, there are a few further items of information to tuck under your belt.

Firstly, you may find if you follow the programme with a friend that you progress at a different pace although, to all intents and purposes, you are putting in the same amount of time and effort. This is due to the fact that we do not all start out equal in the physical fitness stakes. Each individual responds differently to exercise and has a different potential for improvement. There are many factors which affect our optimum fitness levels; some, such as heredity, sex, body type, age and, to some degree, state of health, we cannot alter. Others, such as diet and lifestyle, are areas which we can influence. See Chapter 4 for advice on making dietary changes. We can also take some control over the following aspects of our lifestyle:

Body Types

We are born with a specific body type and although we can control our weight and muscle tone, and in that sense our physique, we cannot alter our general body shape. Endomorphs tend to put on weight more readily than the other two categories but all three can benefit from increased activity, and most people adhering to the general principles of healthy eating and following the Executive Fitness Programme will experience weight loss.

- **ectomorph:** long and lean with narrow shoulders and hips

- **mesomorph:** strong and muscular with broad shoulders and narrow hips

- **endomorph:** short with wide, rounded hips, limbs and face

Smoking

As a smoker you greatly increase your risk of heart disease and lung cancer. Smokers are also at a disadvantage when exercising because they require more oxygen to achieve the same performance as a non-smoker. Smokers may find that in the initial stages, the stamina elements of the routines are somewhat harder than for their non-smoking colleagues.

Alcohol

The health benefits and disadvantages are covered in some detail in Chapter 4 but, in short, alcohol will affect your fitness performance adversely and you should avoid drinking before, during or immediately after exercise.

Under-activity

The medical professions have now categorically made the link between low levels of physical activity and high incidence of coronary heart disease (CHD). It is one of the predetermining factors and, conversely, the risk of CHD is reduced when a person is physically active. Heart disease is the number one killer in Britain: 92,000 men and 78,000 women died from the disease in 1991. One in three British men who die this year will do so as a result of coronary heart disease. Taking a little extra exercise can reduce the chances that you'll be one of them.

Fitness

Once you have got some measure of your health ratings from the questionnaire and health professionals, you can gauge your level of fitness by yourself. As a guideline, the resting pulse rate of an average adult male, awake but at rest, is between 60 and 80 beats per minute (on average, 71 beats per minute). A woman's rate is slightly higher at about 80 beats per minute. As your fitness level increases, these figures will probably drop by anything up to ten beats per minute, giving a resting pulse rate in the 60s during normal activity and a waking pulse rate of about 52 beats per minute.

A waking pulse rate is taken over the duration of a minute immediately you wake in the morning after a full night's sleep. Your pulse rate during a normal morning's activity at work should be about ten beats per minute higher than your waking rate.

Just for interest's sake, as proof of the way that stress affects us physically, take your pulse after a particularly hostile and acrimonious meeting, if proof is needed of how stress affects us physically – it will be conspicuously higher than during normal activity. (See Chapter 5 for further information on combatting stress.)

Main Risk Factors for Coronary Heart Disease

- smoking
- high blood pressure
- physical inactivity
- raised blood cholesterol
- obesity

Warm-up and cool-down

It is a prerequisite of every exercise session that you warm-up before the routine and cool-down afterwards, and its importance cannot be over-stressed. The purpose of a warm-up is:

- to prepare the body for activity (our bodily systems take time to adapt to the increased demands of exercise)
- to maximise performance (there is some evidence to suggest that a suitable warm-up period can lead to improvements of up to 20 per cent in flexibility test ratings)
- to avoid the possibility of suffering muscular soreness and injury.

The warm-up exercises on p.23 will prepare your body for the extra stresses of your exercise routine. All movements should be carried out slowly and smoothly so that the muscles and joints have time to adapt to the new tensions placed upon them. When stretching, do not strain or bounce – approach the point of

How to Monitor Your Pulse

The pulse can be located and measured either at the main artery on the side of the neck, just below the jaw, or on the inside of the wrist in line with the thumb. Simply use the first two fingers of one hand to count the number of beats over a certain period. Obviously a full minute gives the most accurate reading but you can take it over 30 seconds and double it, over 15 seconds and multiply by 4, or over 10 seconds and multiply by 6.

maximum stretch slowly and with control, and return to the start/relaxed position in the same manner.

This warm-up routine has been specifically designed to be completed in a short space of time, in keeping with the theme of this book, yet it comprises all the components of a good warm-up, which are:

- gradually to raise the heart rate and increase the body temperature
- mobilising exercises to take the various joints of the body through their full range of normal movement
- gentle stretching
- to bring your heart rate up to workout level.

If you decide to supplement the exercise routines with some sporting or high energy activities, remember that you must still warm-up and cool-down as for the exercise programme. If it is going to be a particularly demanding activity, extend the period of warm-up by increasing the number of repetitions of each element of the routine. In the same way, if you are exercising in cold conditions or early in the morning more time should be allowed for warm-up.

Just as vital as the warm-up period is a cool-down after the main period of activity is completed. The body's systems pass through a series of adaptations as they return to their normal pre-exercise levels and anything we can do to help this recovery process is useful.

Always keep warm while going through the cool-down process to avoid the risk of injury. Good ways to lower the pulse and cool-down include gentle jogging, skipping and walking, gradually decreasing in intensity, and rhythmic flowing movements. The cool-down routine on p.30 is specifically designed for this programme and easy to remember, because it uses the mobilising elements of the warm-up routine. After an exercise session showers or baths should be warm rather than hot; sauna and steam baths are not advisable.

Discipline Pays Off

Irrespective of your commitments throughout the week, never be tempted to try and cram your minimum requirement of three exercise sessions per week into the weekend or do more than one session per day. It may be hard to force yourself to get up early after a particularly gruelling few days of lengthy meetings but it is a great test of self-discipline and infinitely preferable to overdoing it at the weekend and sustaining an injury.

There are good physiological reasons why the programme is designed as it is. The human body is endlessly adaptable – its capabilities are not fixed. If an exercise programme is well devised and adhered to, only unavoidable illnesses or injuries can prevent your progress towards a fitter and healthier state of being and all its inherent benefits.

Alternative Activities

Your goal is to achieve overall body conditioning. If you are able to supplement the Executive Fitness Programme with some additional sporting activity, you should try to get a balance of the four vital components of a good fitness regime:

- **cardio-respiratory performance** (which improves the efficiency of the heart and lungs, which in turn means a better supply of food and oxygen carried in the blood to the muscles)
- **strength** (which increases the amount of force that a muscle can exert)
- **endurance** (the ability to repeat an action over and over again or sustain muscular contraction)
- **flexibility** (which stretches the muscles).

Obviously there are some sports that are strong in one or other of these three disciplines and there are a few activities which combine all three. Here is a guide to the physiological benefits of different sports:

Aerobic (cardio-respiratory)
Running
Cycling
Swimming
Racket sports: badminton (45 minutes minimum); squash (45 minutes minimum); tennis (one hour minimum)
Ball sports; soccer (60–90 minutes minimum, but five-a-side is even better); rugby (a full game, but seven-a-side is better still); basketball (30 minutes minimum); volleyball (full game); hockey (full game)

Strength/Endurance
Rowing (either on the water or on a machine)
Golf (play 18 holes at a rapid pace and carry your own bag)
Weight training (one hour minimum under supervision)
Horse riding (one hour minimum)
Windsurfing (45 minutes minimum)
Circuit training (45 minutes minimum)

Flexibility
Yoga
Dance
Alexander Technique
Tai chi
Swimming

Combining strength, flexibility and aerobic activity
High/low impact/step aerobics (45-minute workout minimum)
Skiing (full day)
Waterpolo (full game)
Dancing (one hour minimum)

It's impossible to make direct comparisons between the activities since there are so many variables in the standard of skill, the intensity of play, the terrain, etc. However, as a basic rule of thumb, if you exercise hard and get your heart rate up so that you are slightly out of breath, all these activities will have beneficial effects. Swimming is one of the best all-round exercises because not only is it aerobic and works many of the major muscle groups (though you must vary your stroke) but the joints are protected from impact because the water bears the load. You are also exercising against the resistance of the water, so it is more efficient.

3 | Get Set, Go

The Executive Fitness Programme

You are now ready to begin integrating the Executive Fitness Programme into your hectic schedule. To lose weight and to maintain that loss, you must complete at least three 25-minute workouts a week (in combination with eating sensibly). This minimum requirement can, of course, be supplemented with exercise sessions for problem areas (see p.75) or with location workouts (see p.88). Bear in mind that the body needs a chance to rest and exercise sessions should be spread evenly throughout the week wherever possible, so don't try and cram three workouts into one weekend!

Irrespective of how fit you are on starting this regime, the programme is designed progressively and I recommend that you follow it from the starting point, Level One. It is also designed to be flexible enough to fit in with your changing requirements. So, however quickly or slowly you progress, you can hold at any stage of the programme and, as long as you complete three sessions a week, you will maintain your fitness at that level. The programme comprises of four interchangeable routines (A, B, C and D) with three levels of difficulty, Level One being the easiest.

Since this programme is designed to be adapted to your lifestyle, I have purposely omitted the use of any equipment apart from the odd prop such as a chair or desk that could be found in any home, office or hotel room. Once you progress to Levels Two and Three, the difficulty and intensity of the exercise is increased by more repetitions but also by the addition of weight. Initially, start with 1lb hand weights, progressing to 2lbs. If hand-held weights are not available, grocery tins from the kitchen are perfectly adequate. If you are travelling, either shove a couple of tins of beans in your case before you leave home or throw yourself on the mercy of the hotel's kitchen and hope they don't buy catering-size tins.

Chapter 2 explained the importance of a warm-up and cool-down whenever you work out. This set of warm-up and cool-down exercises is specifically designed to warm and stretch out all the major muscles quickly but thoroughly. Once you are familiar with the routine, it should only take you about five minutes at most to complete. It's worth noting that you can also use these stretches at any time to relieve tired or tense muscles, particularly if you've been sitting at a desk or round a board table for too long.

Checklist Reminder

● Don't attempt to start the Executive Fitness Programme without first answering No to all the questions in the Health Questionnaire (see p.16).

● Seek advice about your suitability to undertake an exercise programme from a health professional, e.g. your GP or a private health company, as an optional, additional precaution to the questionnaire.

● Follow the warm-up and cool-down routines at every exercise session. Allow 5 minutes for each.

● Never exercise when under the influence of alcohol or drugs.

● If you are in pain or feel unwell, stop exercising. If the symptoms persist, seek medical advice immediately.

Warm-Up and Stretch-Out

Walk or run upstairs but walk back down. Repeat three times. If you have no access to stairs, march on the spot, lifting your knees up high, until you feel warm (at least three minutes).

Now stretch out your . . . Lower body

1. Stand in a good posture with your feet hip-width apart.

2. Take a large step forward with your right leg and place your weight on the leading leg, bending the knee directly over the ankle and keeping the back leg straight (toes pointing the same way as the leading leg).

3. Press your back heel into the floor, keeping your body upright.

4. Hold for a count of eight.

5. Repeat on the other side.

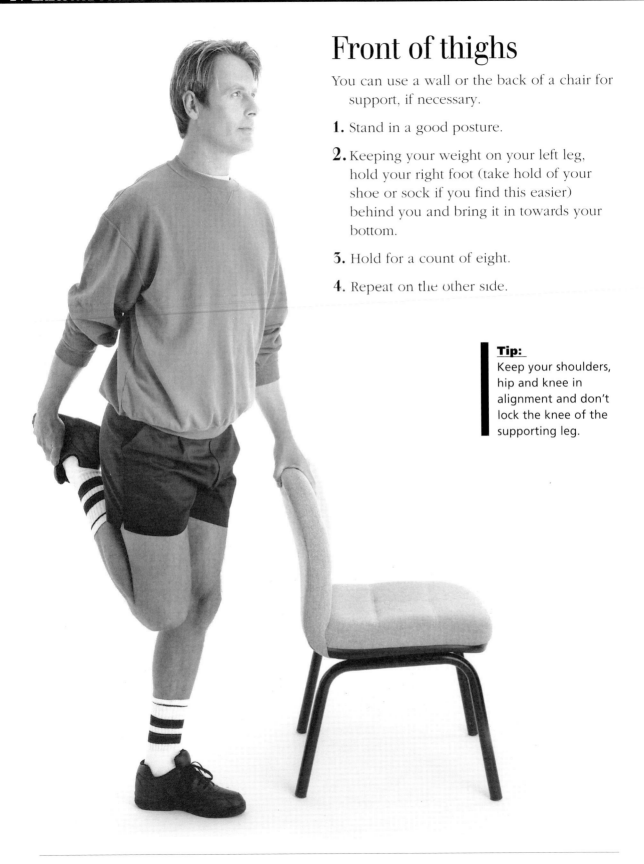

Front of thighs

You can use a wall or the back of a chair for support, if necessary.

1. Stand in a good posture.

2. Keeping your weight on your left leg, hold your right foot (take hold of your shoe or sock if you find this easier) behind you and bring it in towards your bottom.

3. Hold for a count of eight.

4. Repeat on the other side.

Tip:
Keep your shoulders, hip and knee in alignment and don't lock the knee of the supporting leg.

Hamstrings/back of thighs

1. Stand in a good posture.

2. Step forward with your right leg.

3. Transfer the weight back on to your left leg, at the same time bending your left knee and pushing the hips back (as if you were going to sit down).

4. Hold for a count of eight.

5. Repeat on the other side.

Tip:
Place both hands on your left thigh to support your back and let your shoulders fall forward naturally.

Inner thighs

1. Stand with your feet about three feet apart, toes turned out at ten-to-two position.

2. Bend your right knee over the top of your heel and you'll feel the stretch on the inner thigh. If not, try leaning forward very slightly and pushing your hips back.

3. Hold for a count of eight.

4. Repeat on the other side.

Tip:
Keep your weight over the bent knee. Place your hands on your thighs to support your back.

Upper body
Shoulders:

1. Stand in a good posture.

2. Bring your right arm across the front of your chest to point at the side wall. (If support is needed, rest your arm on your left hand.) Keep your arm as straight as possible.

3. Hold for a count of eight.

4. Repeat on the other side.

Tip:
Try to keep your arm raised at shoulder height.

Front of chest/ shoulders

1. Stand in a good posture.

2. Place your hands behind your back and interlock fingers.

3. Try to squeeze the elbows together.

4. Hold for a count of eight.

Shoulders/ upper back

1. Bring your arms in front of you at shoulder height.

2. Interlock your fingers with palms facing in and elbows slightly bent.

3. Drop your chin towards your chest.

4. Now imagine you're separating your shoulder blades by gently rounding your shoulders.

5. Hold for a count of eight.

Arms

1. Stand in a good posture.

2. Take your right arm above your head by the side of your ear.

3. Bend your elbow and drop your arm behind your neck. (If you don't feel the stretch in this position, ease your arm back with your left hand resting behind your elbow).

4. Hold for a count of eight.

5. Repeat on the other side.

Tip:
Try to remain standing tall.

Cool-Down

Just as vital as the warm-up period is the cool-down when you have finished exercising. You may want to throw on an extra layer of clothing, as it is advisable to keep warm while going through the cool-down process to avoid the risk of injury. Gentle jogging, skipping or walking are all acceptable cool-down methods, but a slight adaptation of the warm-up routine is easy to remember and works very well.

Omitting the running up and down stairs stage, repeat the warm-up routine for the upper body and then follow these adaptations for the lower body.

Inner thighs

1. Sit on the floor with the soles of your feet together, and feet pulled in close to the body.

2. Rest your hands on your ankles and lean your body slightly forward from the chest.

3. Hold for a count of eight.

Tip:
If this position is uncomfortable, try putting your hands behind you on the floor for support (as shown) and then lean slightly forward with your chest leading.

Lower legs

1. Sit with your legs out in front, toes pointing towards the ceiling, hands on the floor at the side of your hips or slightly behind you.

2. Sit tall and imagine a string is attached to your toes, pulling them towards your body.

3. Hold for a count of eight.

Upper thighs

1. Lie on your front and rest your head on your left hand.

2. Bend your right leg at the knee and reach round with the right hand to grasp the right foot, shoe or sock and ease it gently towards your bottom.

3. Hold for a count of eight.

4. Repeat on the other side.

Tip:
Press your hips into the mat for greater stretch.

Hamstrings

1. Lie on the floor on your back with your left knee bent.

2. Raise the right leg with the knee slightly bent.

3. Reach behind the leg and hold either above or below the knee, keeping it steady, for a count of eight (or until you feel the stretch). Then ease the leg in a little closer to the body and hold again for a further count of eight or as long as it feels comfortable.

Tip:
Keep your shoulders on the floor and your hips pressed down. Don't let your bottom lift off the ground.

Total body relaxer

(This is a favoured yoga position called The Corpse)

1. Lie down slowly, flat on your back, with your legs together and arms at your sides.

2. Allow the feet to fall gently open, relaxing all the leg and feet muscles.

3. Put your hands palms upwards a few inches away from the body, and let your fingers curl if they want to. Let your arms go limp.

4. Raise your chin and tilt your head back a little. Close your eyes.

5. Let go of all your facial muscles (don't worry if your mouth drops open).

6. Slow down your breathing by inhaling deeply, then exhaling as slowly as you can. Don't breathe again until you have to.

7. Concentrate on your breathing and don't let your mind wander.

8. Stay in this position for as long as you like and then get up slowly.

Executive Fitness Exercise Programme

Instructions

Complete three exercise sessions a week. There are four routines (called A, B, C and D) from which to choose, but if you start with Routine A at the beginning of the week repeat this routine throughout the week (i.e. for your three consecutive sessions) before changing to another routine.

The programme is progressive and allows you to develop at your own pace. Routines A, B, C and D are at the entry standard, Level One. Once you are proficient at each exercise within the routine you can progress to Level Two and eventually Level Three.

You will see that the routines are interchangeable and each will have the desired effect of toning and shaping the body. However, each routine has a slightly different emphasis. Routine A gives general conditioning. Routine B provides a cardio-vascular and interval workout, principally working the heart, lungs and blood supply. Routine C is a top-to-toe programme. And Routine D offers peripheral heart action (PHA) training which means it will get the blood pumping to the extremities of your body. All will help in toning and keeping your body fit, but Routines B and D may be more useful for weight loss whereas Routines A and C provide less rigorous conditioning.

Top Tips

● Having carefully read the exercise instructions, work slowly and in a controlled way (don't rush or jerk) for the best results. Quality is what counts.

● Unless breathing instructions are specifically provided, it's a good tip to exhale with effort and inhale as you relax. Never hold your breath, as this can create undue pressure in the chest and cause a rise in blood pressure.

● Maximum progression: at least three days at each increased set of repeats.

● Don't forget to warm up and cool down every time you exercise.

Routine A
Total Body Conditioning

Wide stance squats

1. Stand with your feet wider than your hips, at the ten-to-two position. Make sure your shoulders are in line, your back is straight and your tummy is tight.

2. Maintaining your upper body position, simply squat and then lift to the starting position without locking your knees. Don't lower and bend knees to less than 90 degrees.

3. Repeat eight times.

Tip:
Don't bend your upper body forward as you lower yourself.

Stride dips

1. From a standing position, stride forward with your left leg, keeping the knee directly over the heel.

2. Raise your trailing right leg on to the toes, with the knee slightly bent.

3. Keep your shoulders directly over the hips (i.e. don't lean forward).

4. Keeping your left (front) knee bent, simply bend both knees and lower the body and then lift up again.

5. Repeat eight times with your left leg leading and then eight times with your right leg leading.

Tip:
Dip only as low as is comfortable and always keep your front knee directly over your ankle, not forward over your toes.

Side bends

1. Stand with your feet wider than your hips and your knees slightly bent. Place the palms of your hands flat against the side of your legs.

2. Slowly bend over to the right, sliding your right hand down towards the knee. Your left hand will automatically slide up towards the hip.

3. Slowly straighten up.

4. Repeat on the other side. Complete a total of 16 repeats.

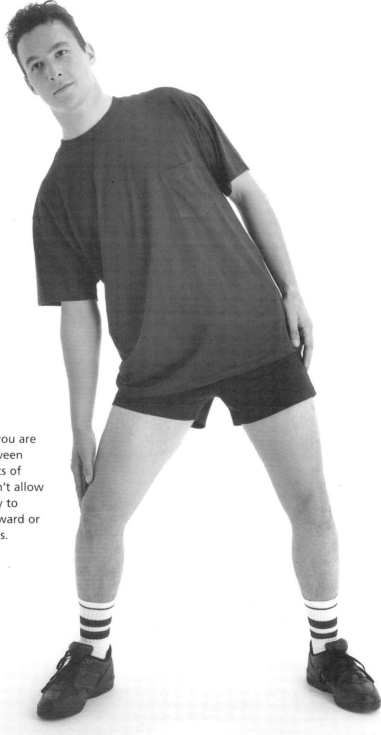

Tip:
Imagine you are held between two sheets of glass. Don't allow your body to move forward or backwards.

Press-ups

If you are unable to perform the full press-up as instructed below, start with the box press-up, then follow with the extended box, until you can complete the full version.

Box press-ups

1. Kneel on all fours with your knees hip-width apart and your hands slightly wider than your shoulders but in line.

2. By bending and straightening your arms (not locking the elbows), rise up and down vertically with your nose touching the ground in the middle of an imaginary line drawn between your hands.

3. Repeat eight times.

Tip:
Always keep your tummy pulled in tight.

Extended box press-ups

1. From the box press-up starting position, walk your hands forward and shift your body weight forward so that your shoulders are still in line with your hands.

2. By bending and straightening the arms (not locking the elbows), rise up and down vertically with your nose touching the ground in the middle of an imaginary line drawn between your hands.

3. Repeat eight times.

Tip:
Always keep your tummy pulled in tight.

Full press-ups

1. From the extended box press-up start position, lift off your knees and take the weight on your toes (feet together).

2. By bending and straightening your arms (not locking the elbows), rise up and down vertically with your nose touching the ground in the middle of an imaginary line drawn between your hands.

3. Repeat eight times.

Tip:
Always keep your tummy pulled in tight.

Abdominals

1. Lie on your back with your knees bent and your feet hip-width apart.

2. To start, raise your head to a position which would enable you to put an imaginary orange under your chin.

3. Place your hands on your upper thighs and, keeping your stomach hollow, slowly slide them up your thigh towards your knees while breathing out.

4. Return to the start position (don't let your head drop back to the floor) and repeat.

5. Repeat eight times.

Tip:
If you find this position difficult, place one hand behind your head for support. Curl up as far as you can and keep your stomach hollowed out. Keep the movements smooth.

Back (erector spinae) strengthener

1. Lying face down with your forehead on the mat, place your hands on the cheeks of your bottom.

2. Very slowly, lift your shoulders and head up, still looking at the floor and keeping your feet firmly on the floor.

3. Lower gently.

4. Repeat four times.

Tip:

This movement should be done very slowly. If you are concerned about your back, use this easier version. Lie with your palms on the floor under your shoulders and elbows tucked in. Just push up gently, keeping your forearms on the floor, until you feel the pull in your lower back. Lower slowly.

Tip:
Extend arm above head
if you find this positon
uncomfortable

Outer thigh (abductors) lift

1. Lie on your side with your head resting on your arm on the floor.

2. Keep your knees bent at a 90 degree angle and lift your upper leg to about 45 degrees.

3. Repeat eight times on each leg.

Outer thigh (abductors) lift

Progression
(Levels 2 and 3):

1. Lie on your side with your legs straight out (don't roll back on to your buttocks), your head resting on one arm on the floor, your other arm in front of your chest for support.

2. Raise the top leg to no more than 45 degrees (about five inches off the floor) and lower.

3. Repeat twelve times with each leg (Level 2), or sixteen times with each leg (Level 3).

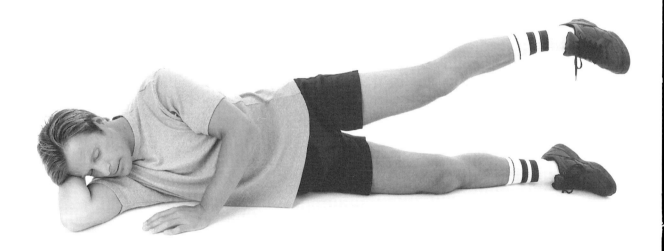

Inner thigh (adductors) lift

1. Lie on your side with your head supported by your arm on the floor.

2. Keeping your lower leg straight, bend your top knee and drop it in front of you, clear of the lower leg.

3. Lift your lower leg, keeping your toe pointing in front of you.

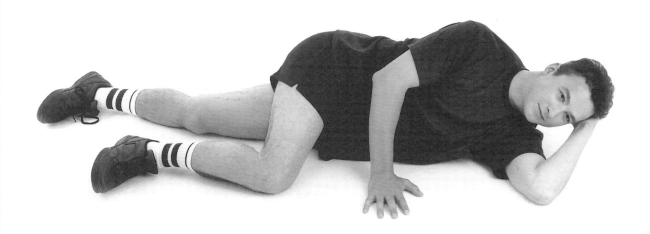

Tip:
Lift your leg only as high as feels comfortable.

Progression Table – Routine A

Exercise	Level One	Level Two	Level Three
Wide stance squats	8 reps	12 reps	12 reps
Stride dips	8 reps R, 8 reps L	12 reps R, 12 reps L	16 reps R, 16 reps L + weights
Side bends	16 reps	24 reps	32 reps + weights
Press-ups	8 reps	12 reps	16 reps
Abdominals	8 reps	16 reps, hands across chest	24 reps, hands lightly held at temples
Back strengthener	4 reps	8 reps	12 reps, hands lightly held at temples
Outer thigh lifts	8 reps R, 8 reps L	12 reps R, 12 reps L, straight leg lifts	16 reps R, 16 reps L, straight leg lifts
Inner thigh lifts	8 reps R, 8 reps L	12 reps R, 12 reps L	16 reps R, 16 reps L

Key: reps = repetitions; R = right side; L = left side.

Routine B

Cardio-vascular to Work the Heart and Lungs. Good for Fat Burning

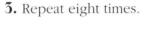

Wide stance squats:

1. Stand with your feet wider than your hips, at the ten-to-two position. Make sure your shoulders are in line, your back is straight and your tummy is tight.

2. Maintaining your upper body position, simply squat and then lift to the starting position, without locking your knees.

3. Repeat eight times.

Stride dips

1. From a standing position, stride forwards with your left leg, keeping your knee directly over your heel.

2. Raise the trailing right leg on to your toes, with your knee slightly bent.

3. Keep your shoulders directly over your hips (i.e. don't lean forward).

4. Keeping your left (front) knee bent, simply bend both knees, lower your body and then lift.

5. Repeat eight times with your left leg leading and then eight times with your right leg leading.

Tips:
Dip only as low as is comfortable and always keep your front knee directly over your ankle, not forward over your toes.

Skipping

With or without a rope, skip on the spot for two minutes or jog round the room, or do some jumping jacks for two minutes. It is important to keep moving.

Bent over row:

1. Kneel on a firm chair with your left leg, and with your left hand supporting your weight on the seat of the chair.

2. Keep your right leg straight and with the foot on the ground wide from the base of the chair.

3. Lean forward with your tummy tight.

4. With your right arm straight, clench your fist and pull it towards your right armpit, elbow pointing towards the ceiling. Keep your arm close to your body and move in a vertical line.

5. Repeat eight times with your right arm, then eight times with your left arm.

Skipping

Again, with or without a rope, skip on the spot for two minutes or jog round the room, or do some jumping jacks for two minutes. Keep moving.

Tricep dips

1. Place a chair against a wall (for safety).

2. With your back to the chair, place both hands on the front edge of the seat, knuckles facing your back (you will be bending down).

3. Bend both knees at right-angles over the top of your heels.

4. Holding your tummy tight, bend your elbows and gently lower your body towards the floor.

5. Breathe out and simultaneously push up as your arms straighten.

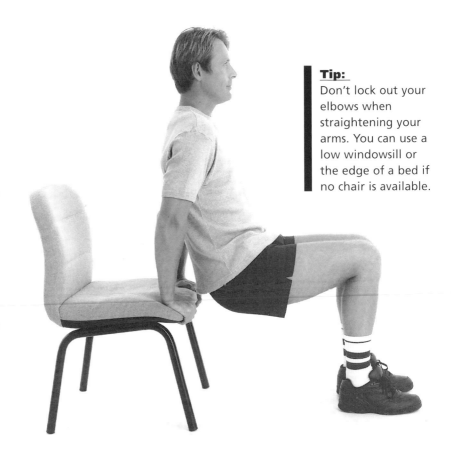

Tip:
Don't lock out your elbows when straightening your arms. You can use a low windowsill or the edge of a bed if no chair is available.

Abdominals

1. Lie on your back with your knees bent and your feet hip-width apart.

2. To start, raise your head to a position in which you could hold an imaginary orange under your chin.

3. Place your hands on your upper thighs and slowly curl up as you reach to tap your hands on the top of your knees, breathing out.

4. Return to the start position (don't let your head drop back to the floor) and repeat.

5. Repeat eight times.

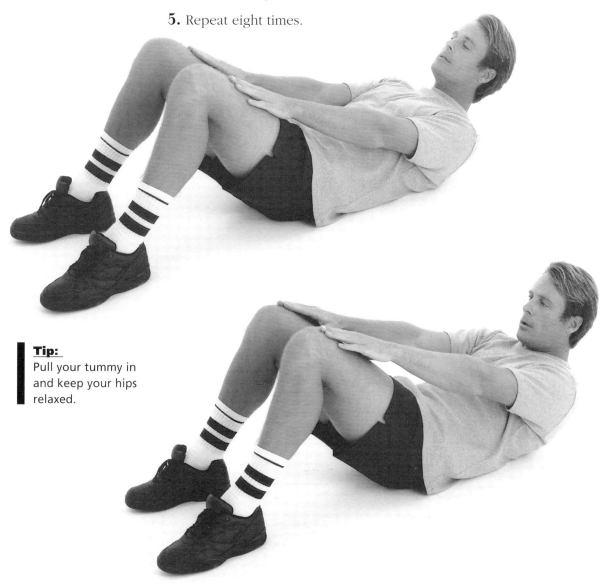

Tip:
Pull your tummy in and keep your hips relaxed.

Back (erector spinae) strengthener

1. Lying face down with your forehead on the floor, place your hands on the cheeks of your bottom.

2. Very slowly, lift your shoulders and head up, still looking down and keeping your feet firmly on the floor.

3. Lower gently.

4. Repeat four times.

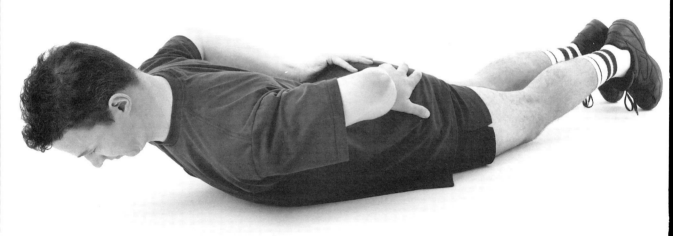

Tip:

If you are concerned about your back, use this easier version. Lie with your palms under your shoulders, elbows tucked in, and just push up gently, keeping your forearms on the floor, until you feel the stretch in your lower back. Lower slowly.

Progression Table – Routine B

Exercise	Level One	Level Two	Level Three
Wide stance squats	8 reps	12 reps	16 reps
Stride dips	8 reps R, 8 reps L	12 reps R, 12 reps L	16 reps R, 16 reps L (weights optional)
Skipping	2 minutes	3 minutes	4 minutes
Bent over row	8 reps R, 8 reps L	12 reps R, 12 reps L + weights	16 reps R, 16 reps L + weights
Skipping	2 minutes	3 minutes	4 minutes
Dips	8 reps	12 reps	16 reps
Abdominals	8 reps	8–12 reps, Hands by ears	8–12 reps, try touching knees with elbows
Back strengthener	4 reps	8 reps	12 reps

Key: reps = repetitions; R = right side; L = left side.

Routine C
Top-to-Toe Programme

Pec-dec (chest)

1. Stand in a good posture, your feet wider than your hips.

2. Bring your arms up at your sides, level with your shoulders, and make right-angles at your elbows, so the lower arm is vertical.

3. Clench your fists.

4. Bring both arms round in front of your face (forearms from wrists to elbows should touch) and back out again.

5. Repeat eight times.

Side bends

1. Stand with your feet wider than your hips and your knees slightly bent. Place the palms of your hands flat against the side of your legs.

2. Slowly bend over to the right, sliding your right hand down towards your knee. Your left hand will automatically slide up towards your hip.

3. Slowly straighten up.

4. Repeat eight times on your right side and then eight times on your left side.

Tip:
Imagine you are held between two sheets of glass and don't let your body move forwards or backwards.

Deltoid raises (shoulders)

1. Stand in a good posture, your feet wider than your hips.

2. Bring your arms to shoulder height in front of you.

3. Fists clenched, knuckles forward, lower your arms slowly and raise them again.

4. Repeat four times.

5. Drop your arms to your sides, knuckles and wrists at the side of your body, then raise your arms to shoulder height and lower again (sideways).

6. Repeat four times.

7. Arms still at your sides, but with your knuckles facing forwards, lift your arms straight back behind you as far as feels comfortable.

8. Repeat four times.

Tip:
Don't swing – the movement should be slow and controlled – don't lock your elbows.

Outer thighs (abductors)

1. Stand with the back of a hard chair to your left side. Hold the chair with your left hand.

2. Put all your weight on your left leg with the knee slightly bent (i.e. not locked).

3. Keep your shoulders in line with your hips, your tummy tight and your back straight.

4. Lift your right leg sideways away from your body to about 45 degrees and lower it back in.

5. Repeat eight times on your right leg and then eight times on your left leg.

Tip:
Keep your upper body straight – don't lean.

Leg raises (inner thigh – adductors)

1. Stand with the back of a hard chair to your left side. Hold the chair with your left hand.

2. Put all your weight on your left leg with your knee slightly bent (i.e. not locked).

3. Keep your shoulders in line with your hips, your tummy tight and your back straight.

4. Bring your right leg across in front of your body towards the chair leg.

5. Repeat eight times on the right leg and eight times on the left leg.

Tip:
Do this exercise slowly. Keep your hips and shoulders square to the front (i.e. don't let your body twist).

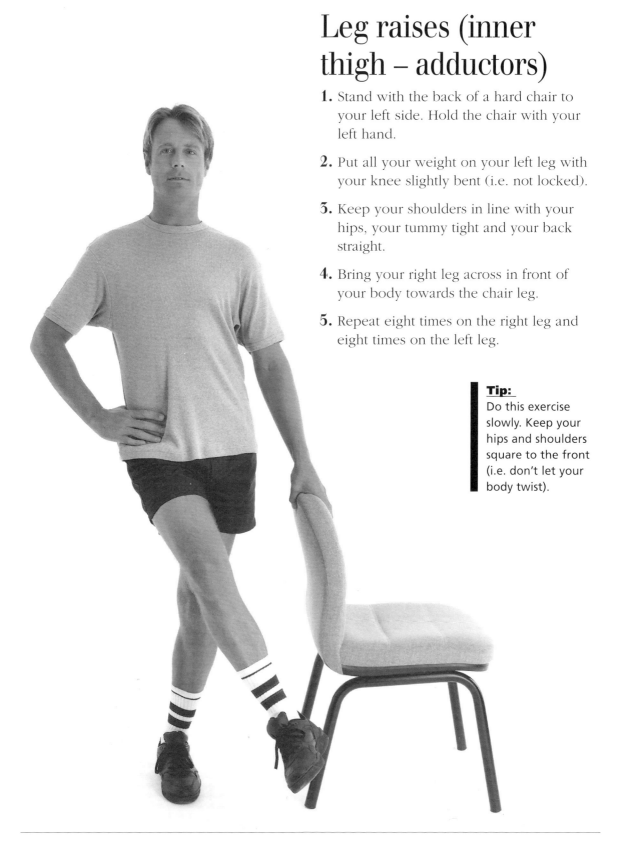

Ski squats

1. Stand in a good posture, feet hip-width apart, directly under your knees and hips.

2. Keeping your tummy tight, push back and down as if you were going to sit down, keeping your heels on the floor and taking your weight on them.

3. Rise to a standing position again without locking your knees.

4. Repeat eight times.

Tip:
Keep your tummy pulled in through-out. If you have difficulty keeping your heels on the floor, stand with your heels raised on a book. Similarly, if you have problems keeping your balance, face the back of a firm chair and hold on with both hands for support.

Abdominals

1. Lie on your back with your knees bent and your feet hip-width apart.

2. Raise your head to a position in which you could hold an imaginary orange under your chin.

3. Place your hands on your upper thighs and slowly curl up as you reach to tap hands on top of your knees, breathing out.

4. Return to the start position (don't let your head drop back to the floor) and repeat.

5. Repeat eight times.

Tip:
Pull your tummy in and keep your hips relaxed. If you find this position difficult, place one hand behind your head for support. Curl up as far as you can and keep your stomach hollowed out. Keep the movements smooth.

Tip:
If you are concerned about your back, use this easier version. Lie with your palms under your shoulders, elbows tucked in and just push up gently, keeping your forearms on the floor, until you feel the pull in your lower back. Lower slowly.

Back (erector spinae) strengthener

1. Lying face down with your forehead on the floor, place your hands on the cheeks of your bottom.

2. Very slowly, lift your shoulders, still looking at the floor keeping your feet firmly on the floor.

3. Lower gently.

4. Repeat four times.

Progression Table – Routine C

Exercise	Level One	Level Two	Level Three
Pec-dec	8 reps	12 reps + weights	16 reps + weights
Side bends	16 reps	24 reps + weights	32 reps +weights
Deltoid raises	4 reps	8 reps + weights	16 reps + weights
Outer thigh lifts	8 reps	16 reps	24 reps
Inner thigh lifts	8 reps	16 reps	24 reps
Ski squats	8 reps	12 reps	16 reps
Abdominals	8 reps	8–12 reps, hands by ears	8–6 reps, elbows to knees
Back strengthener	4 reps	8 reps	12 reps

Key: reps = repetitions; R = right side; L = left side.

Routine D

Peripheral Heart Action

Gets Blood Pumping. Good for Fat Burning

Press-ups

If you are unable to perform the full press-up (see overleaf), start with the box press-up, then go on to the extended box, until you can complete a full press-up.

Box press-up

1. Kneel on all fours with your knees hip-width apart and your hands slightly wider than your shoulders but in line.

2. By bending and straightening your arms (not locking your elbows), rise up and down with your nose touching the ground in the middle of an imaginary line drawn between your hands.

3. Repeat eight times.

Tip:
Always keep your tummy pulled in tight.

Extended box press-up

1. From the box press-up starting position, walk your hands forward and shift your body weight forward so that the shoulders are in line with your hands.

2. By bending and straightening your arms (not locking your elbows), rise up and down with your nose touching the ground in the middle of an imaginary line drawn between the hands.

3. Repeat eight times.

Tip:
Always keep your tummy pulled in tight.

Full Press-up

1. From the extended box press-up start position, lift off your knees and take the weight on your toes (feet together).

2. By bending and straightening your arms (not locking your elbows), rise up and down with your nose touching the ground in the middle of an imaginary line drawn between the hands.

3. Repeat eight times.

Tip:
Always keep your tummy pulled in tight.

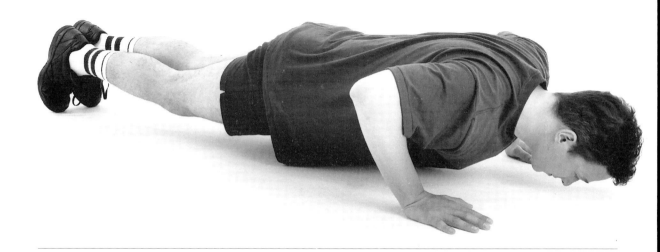

Alternate stride lunges

You may wish to hold a chair at the side for support.

1. Stride forward.

2. Dip your back knee.

3. Step back so that your legs are together.

4. Stride forward again with the other leg leading.

5. Repeat sixteen times in total (i.e. eight lunges with each leg).

Tip:
Don't let the back knee touch the floor. Don't use the momentum of the body to pull you back to an upright position – use the lunges. Don't let your leading knee pass over your toes – keep it over your heel.

Tricep dips

1. Place a chair against a wall (for safety).

2. With your back to the chair, place both hands on the front edge of the seat, knuckles facing your back (you will be bending down).

3. Bend both knees at right-angles over the top of your heels.

4. Holding your tummy tight, bend your elbows and gently lower your body towards the floor.

5. Breathe out and simultaneously push up as your arms straighten.

Tip:
Don't lock out your elbows when straightening your arms. You can use a low windowsill or the edge of a bed if no chair is available.

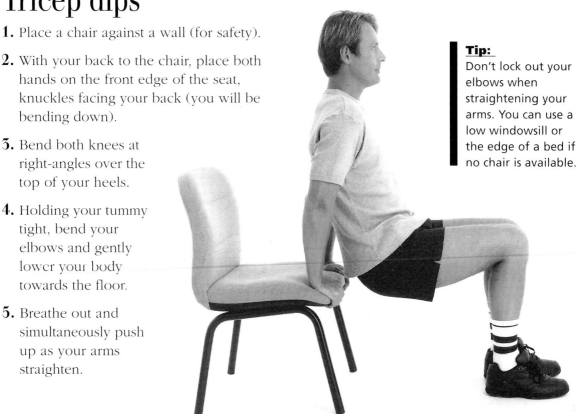

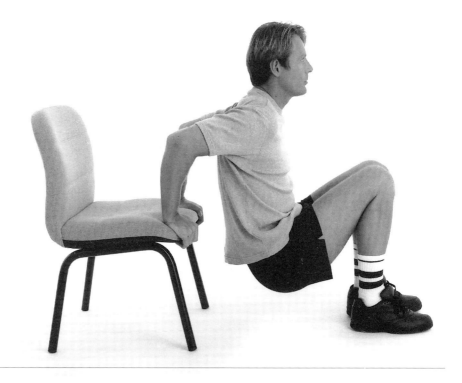

Ski squats

1. Face the back of a hard chair and hold on with both hands, feet hip-width apart, directly under your knees and hips.

2. Keeping your tummy tight, push back and down as if you were going to sit down, keeping your heels on the floor and taking your weight on them.

3. Then rise to a standing position again without locking your knees.

4. Repeat eight times.

Tip:
Keep your tummy pulled in through-out. If you have difficulty keeping your heels on the floor, stand with heels raised on a book.

Abdominals

1. Lie on your back with your knees bent and your feet hip-width apart.

2. To start, raise your head to a position in which you could place an imaginary orange under your chin.

3. Place your hands on your upper thighs and, keeping your stomach hollow, slowly slide them up your thigh towards your knees while breathing out.

4. Return to the start position (don't let your head drop back to the floor) and repeat.

5. Repeat eight times.

Tip:

Tips: Pull your tummy in and keep your hips relaxed. If you find this position difficult, place one hand behind your head for support. Curl up as far as you can and keep your stomach hollowed out. Keep the movements smooth.

Lat pulls

1. Stand in a good posture.

2. Raise your arms above your head, fists clenched, with the inside of your wrist facing forward and hands touching.

3. Pull your arms down and to the side of your body, so that as your hands separate they describe a half circle. End with your elbows in close to your waist and your hands higher than your elbows.

4. Push your arms up again through the same range of movement.

5. Repeat twelve times.

Back (erector spinae) strengthener

1. Lying face down with your forehead on the floor, place your hands on the cheeks of your bottom.

2. Very slowly, lift your shoulders and head up still looking at the floor and, keeping your feet firmly on the floor.

3. Lower gently.

4. Repeat four times.

Tip:
If you are concerned about your back, use this easier version. Lie with your palms under your shoulders, elbows tucked in, and just push up gently, keeping your forearms on the floor, until you feel the pull in your lower back. Lower slowly.

Waist and tummy (abdominals and obliques)

1. Lie on your back with both knees bent and your feet flat on the floor.

2. To start, raise your head to a position in which you could hold an imaginary orange under your chin.

3. Place your right hand behind your head for support.

4. Reach your left hand across to touch your right knee.

5. Return to the start position (don't drop your head to the floor) and repeat on the other side.

6. Repeat eight times on the left and eight times on the right.

Tip:
Squeeze your tummy in and breathe out as you rise.

Progression Table – Routine D

Exercise	Level One	Level Two	Level Three
Press-ups	8 reps	12 reps	16 reps
Alternate stride lunges	16 reps	24 reps	32 reps + weights
Tricep dips	8 reps	12 reps	16 reps
Ski squats	8 reps	12 reps	16 reps
Abdominals	8 reps	16 reps	24 reps
Lat pulls	12 reps	16 reps	24 reps + weights
Back strengthener	4 reps	8 reps	12 reps
Abdominals and obliques	8 reps R, 8 reps L	12 reps R, 12 reps L	24 reps alternate R side-centre-L side

Key: reps = repetitions; R = right side; L = left side.

Problem Areas

Once you start to introduce the Executive Fitness Pogramme into your life on a regular basis, it will not take very long before you start to see results. Within a matter of weeks you will notice a more toned look, and you will feel the beneficial effects even sooner.

Nonetheless, each of us has some part of our body which gives us more cause for concern than the rest. Sadly, there is no such thing as spot reduction from dieting alone. If you work exclusively on a particular area, you can tone the muscle but you will not remove excess fat unless you are cutting down on your food intake and losing weight generally. Regular exercise combined with a healthy eating plan (see p.98) is the only real answer. If you are eating healthily or even sensibly dieting, and following the Executive Fitness Programme, the weight will be starting to drop off by now and there is no harm in targeting specific areas of concern with some supplementary toning.

A steady, slow drop of about 2–3lb a week is the optimum amount to maintain a sustainable loss. Expect to see your greatest loss in the first week, negligible if any loss in the second, and in the third week the drop should level out at a regular amount. Ultimately, whether you decide to diet or to eat sensibly and healthily, it should be combined with regular, low-grade exercise such as the Executive Fitness Programme or brisk walking to lose fat, because at low levels of exercise fat is the main fuel for the muscle. Here are a few additional exercises for sites that commonly prove to be favourite haunts for the demon fat:

To tone up your bottom

Exercise 1

1. Kneel on all-fours but resting on your forearms rather than your hands. Keep your head down.

2. Lift your right knee to a 45 degree angle to the side, then lower it back to the central position without it touching the floor.

3. Repeat sixteen times on each side.

Tip:
Keep your tummy tight throughout and don't let your body swing.

Exercise 2

1. Kneel on all-fours but resting on your forearms rather than your hands. Keep your head down.

2. Lift your right leg behind, with knee bent and foot flexed, until the knee is level with your hips.

3. Bring it down to the start position without the knee touching the floor.

4. Repeat sixteen times on each side.

Tip:
Keep your tummy tight throughout.

To tone up your bottom
Exercise 3

1. Kneel on all-fours but resting on your forearms rather than your hands. Keep your head down.

2. Rest your right knee on your left calf.

3. Lift your right knee behind to hip height and take it back down again to the opposite calf.

4. Repeat twelve times on each side.

Tip:
Keep your tummy
tight throughout.

For a flatter stomach and a trimmer waist

Exercise 1

1. Stand in a good posture, your feet wider than your hips, your knees slightly bent and your tummy tight.

2. Rest your hands on your shoulders with your elbows out to the sides.

3. Keeping your tummy tight and without moving your hips, twist your upper body to the right, then back to centre, and repeat to the left side, all in a continuous, slow and controlled movement.

Tip:
You could use a broom-handle resting behind your shoulders to aid your upper body technique, but don't pull the handle against your neck.

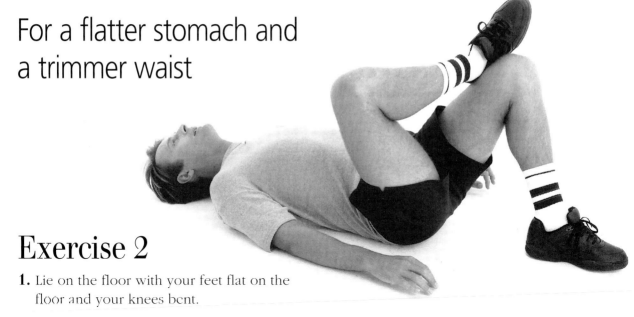

For a flatter stomach and a trimmer waist

Exercise 2

1. Lie on the floor with your feet flat on the floor and your knees bent.

2. Rest your right foot on your left thigh, just below the knee.

3. Place your right arm on the floor beside your body and keep your shoulders flat on the floor.

4. With your left hand behind your head and your elbow out to the side, lift up from the floor, rotating your left shoulder towards your right knee as you rise in a smooth motion.

5. Repeat eight times each side.

Tip:
Keep your elbow out to the side and don't bring it across your face. Breathe out as you come up and keep your tummy pulled in as you do so.

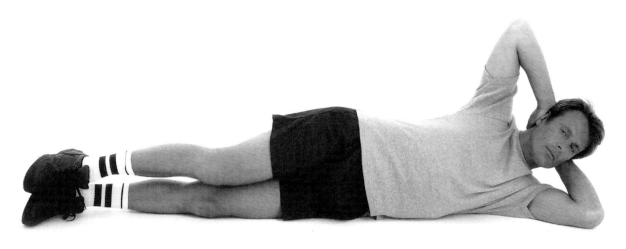

Tip:
Try not to push up with your supporting elbow – use the obliques and abdominal muscles to raise your upper body. This is extremely tough.

Exercise 3

1. Lie on your left side, body straight, making sure you don't roll back on to your buttocks.

2. Place your hands by the side of your head (left hand supporting your head).

3. Lift your upper torso as if you were pulling your right elbow towards your right hip.

4. Repeat eight times each side.

To broaden your shoulders and chest, and strengthen your arms

Exercise 1
(standing dumbbell flye)

1. Standing in a good posture, while holding weights, raise your arms to shoulder level and bend your elbows as if to hug someone.

2. Now bring your forearms together in front of your face, pressing them firmly together, before returning to the starting position.

3. Repeat twelve times.

Tip:
Breathe out as you press your arms together, and breathe in as you return to the start position. If you have access to a bench, this exercise is far more effective when lying flat on the bench and lowering and raising the weights in front of your face.

Exercise 2 (bench press)

1. Lie on your back, knees bent and feet flat on the floor.

2. Holding weights at arm's length above your chest, slowly lower the weights to your chest, making sure your elbows are directly under the weights at all times.

4. As the weights touch your chest, forcefully straighten your arms to press them back to the starting position. Repeat twelve times.

Tip:
Breathe in as you lower, and breathe out as you push upwards. The effect of this exercise can be intensified if done holding a broom-handle, or if you have access to a bar and bench press.

To broaden your shoulders and chest, and strengthen your arms

Exercise 3
(straight arm pull-overs)

1. Lie on your back, knees bent and with both hands clasping a weight held lightly on your sternum (breast bone).

2. Lengthen your arms, but do not lock at the elbows. Lift the weight straight over your head to touch the floor behind your head.

3. Still with arms lengthened, return to the starting position.

4. Repeat twelve times.

Tip:
The action is slow and controlled – don't swing back and forth quickly. Keep your navel pulled into the floor to prevent your back from arching.

Exercise 4 and 5 (press-ups)

The press-up is the best all-round exercise for the upper body, so here are a couple of variations on the standard full press-up:

Inverted press-up

1. Kneel on all-fours with your knees hip-width apart and your hands slightly wider than your shoulders but in line, with your fingers pointing towards each other.

2. Extend your legs and rise on to your toes, keeping your body in a straight line.

3. By bending and straightening your arms (not locking the elbows), rise up and down with your nose touching the ground in between the tips of your fingers.

4. Repeat eight times.

Tip:
Always keep your tummy pulled in tight.

To broaden your shoulders and chest, and strengthen your arms

One-armed Press-up

NB: Only for those who feel fully competent at a full press-up.

1. Kneel on all-fours with your knees hip-width apart and your hands slightly wider than your shoulders but in line.

2. Extend your legs and rise on to your toes, keeping your body in a straight line.

3. Transfer all your body weight on to your right arm and place your left arm behind you to rest on your buttocks.

4. By bending and straightening your right arm (not locking the elbows), rise up and down with your nose touching the ground.

Tip:
Keep your tummy tight throughout to prevent your back from swaying. You may find it easier if you place your feet wider than in a standard full press-up. Remember: this is a very challenging position so start with two reps on each arm and build up to eight very gradually. If it does not feel 'right', please do not attempt it.

Fat busters

Exercising aerobically at a moderate intensity is the best way to burn fat and lose weight. Interval training is a great way to jump-start your cardio-vascular system (heart and lungs) by alternating periods of intense exercise with periods of active rest. It also means you'll be able to slow down and catch your breath before returning to higher-intensity activity.

As your performance improves you can gradually increase the time you spend working out at a greater intensity, but, however long you spend at higher-intensity activity, it should always be balanced by an even longer period of active rest. For example, in a session of twenty to thirty minutes, start with a 1:3 active:rest ratio (e.g. skip for one minute, then walk for four minutes) and repeat four to six times. You can then progress to a 1:2 ratio. Top sportsmen and women train at a ratio of 1:1.

You can, of course, choose your own combination of aerobic activities, but here are a few suggestions to be getting on with.

Outdoors

● Run or skip for two minutes, walk briskly for five minutes.

● Up and down stairs for one minute, walk for two minutes.

● If you are lucky enough to get out for a walk in the country, pick an undulating route and power up the hills, walking regularly in between.

Indoors

● Using the bottom step of the stairs, do two minutes step exercise, alternated with four minutes flat walking.

● In a hotel with a swimming pool, sprint swim for thirty seconds to one minute, alternating with a three-minute freestyle swim.

● If you have any home exercise equipment, increase your level of work (resistance) for two minutes, then lower it for five minutes.

Location Workouts

Incorporating three exercise sessions into your weekly schedule is of paramount importance if you are to get results, and there are numerous opportunities in a busy executive's day when a few moments can be grabbed to practise a little exercise or some relaxation techniques. As we saw in Chapter 1, common sense dictates that if you are trying to stay in shape it's wiser to walk up a flight of stairs than take a lift, to walk the last quarter-mile of your bus or tube journey, to stand and do some buttock clenches when on the phone . . . the list is endless.

However, there may be other scenarios which do not readily spring to mind as the ideal moment for working out but, when needs must, they can present a great opportunity to fit in a little extra toning and shaping.

Workplace workouts

The most important thing to look out for if you are desk-bound is your posture. Office workers have a tendency to bend over their work, rounding their shoulders and with the chest caved in – the classic slouch. Working in this position for long periods causes backache, stiffness and tiredness, not to mention weak back muscles and slack abdominals. At first, correcting your posture will feel most uncomfortable, almost painful, but persevere – not only will you look slimmer with good posture, but you'll be less prone to injuries and back pain.

Once you're consciously making an effort to correct your posture at the desk, you can add to the improvements with a few invaluable exercises which will help to relieve the stresses on your body if you have to remain seated for long periods. None of these is too overt and, if you take a few moments to practise them at intervals throughout the working day, you should reap the benefits of a more relaxed body and a more focused mind.

Six of the best
- Never sit for longer than one hour without moving and stretching.
- Sit over your work. Move your chair nearer your desk so that you don't slouch.
- Sit well back in the chair, keeping your back long and supported, feet flat on the floor about hip-width apart, knees bent at right-angles or slightly above the hips.
- Avoid cupping the phone between your cheek and your shoulder. Switch your phone-holding hand if it's a long conversation.
- Alternate the hand in which you carry your briefcase. Better still, spread the load between two bags so that you are balanced.
- Get out of your chair as often as possible – take phone calls standing up, deliver internal messages and memos in person, do your own photo-copying etc.

To relax the shoulders

1. Sit up straight and in a good posture.

2. Lift both your shoulders up to your ears, breathing in.

3. Squeeze back and pull them back down strongly while breathing out.

4. Repeat three times slowly and three times fast.

To relax the neck

1. Sit up straight and in a good posture.

2. Keeping your shoulders down and level, pull your chin in slightly to keep your neck long.

3. Turn slowly to look over your right shoulder.

4. Return to the centre and lower your head forward until you just feel a gentle stretch in the back of your neck.

5. Return to the centre and repeat on the left side.

To stretch upper and mid-back muscles

1. Sit up straight and in a good posture, with your hands loosely clasped in front of your chest. Pull in your tummy muscles.

2. Turn your palms out and straighten your arms away from you.

3. Return to the starting position.

To stretch the lower back muscles

1. Sit forward in your chair.

2. Bend one leg up and hug your thigh to your chest.

3. Lower the leg to the floor and repeat on the other side.

4. Repeat several times on each side.

To release tension in hands and wrists

1. With your arms down by your sides, make strong fists, then stretch your fingers wide.

2. Repeat as many times as you like.

3. Finish by rotating your hands in perfect circles to both left and right.

4. Finally, lower your arms and shake them out.

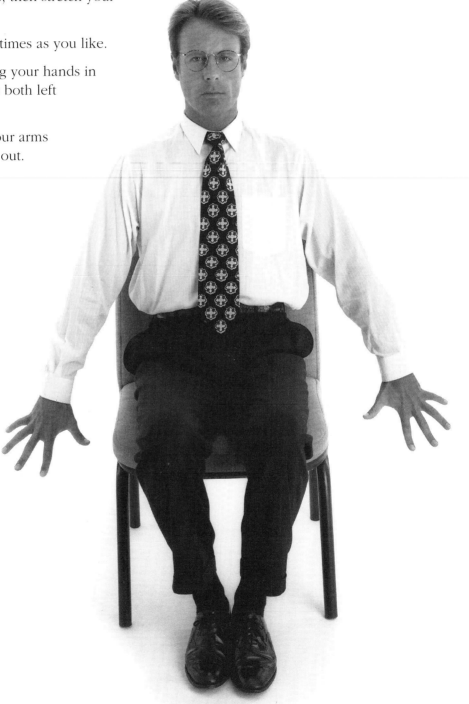

For tired legs, feet and ankles

1. Sit up straight and in a good posture.

2. Keep one foot on the floor and straighten the other out in front of you, placing your hands beside you on the chair for support.

3. In this position, clench and unclench your toes.

4. Now rotate your ankle to form perfect circles to both left and right.

5. Lower your foot to the floor and repeat with the other leg.

Workouts at home

In your own home, the demands of a young family mean that you probably have precious few spare moments to get fit, but at least you're not being observed by strangers as you start contorting yourself while on the telephone.

If you really put your mind to it, there are lots of chances for a quick bit of toning and stretching, and in the most unlikely places. Here are a few ideas to whet your appetite:

While waiting for the kettle to boil

1. Stand with your weight on both feet, but with one leg crossed over the other.

2. Squeeze your buttocks tightly (not the knees).

3. Repeat as often as you like – great for toning the bottom.

When cleaning your teeth

1. Stand in front of the mirror in a good posture, feet wider than your hips, at the ten-to-two position.

2. Keeping your upper body in line, your back straight and your tummy tight, simply squat and then lift to the starting position.

Tip: Don't forget to smile each time you pass the mirror!

Still in the bathroom, try this one to get rid of double chins

1. Let your head go back slightly by lifting your chin.

2. Let your jaw drop open.

3. Make your lower jaw jut right out, then take your bottom teeth right up and over your top teeth and lip.

4. Hold for a count of two, then let your jaw drop open again.

5. Repeat four times, then bring your head erect and, relaxing your face muscles, rest your chin on your chest for a few moments.

If you're chatting in the kitchen

1. Stand about an inch from an empty wall, feet hip-width apart and parallel.

2. Pull in your tummy and, breathing out, slide your back down the wall, keeping your shoulders in contact with the wall and your buttocks tucked under (i.e. taking the strain on your thighs and not on your back). Don't bend your knees more than a 45 degree angle.

3. Maintaining the position, slide up and down the wall several times.

On the phone

1. Hold the handset in one hand and take a telephone directory in the other hand.

2. Hold the book above your head and then lower it behind your head, pointing your elbow towards the ceiling.

3. Repeat several times. This is excellent for strengthening the triceps.

When reading the paper

Instead of sitting in a chair, sit on the floor with your legs apart and place the paper between your legs. If you put your hands on the floor to support yourself you will have a relaxed and easy stretch while you catch up on the world events.

If you like to read in bed

Lie with your head propped on the pillow and pull the soles of your feet together, letting both your knees drop down to wherever is comfortable.

You're not even safe in the bath!

● While the bath is filling, raise one foot on to the side of the bath, bending the supporting leg slightly. With both hands on the thigh of the raised leg, push back with the bottom (a good hamstring stretch).

● To soap a leg, rest your arms on the sides of the bath for support and, pulling in your tummy and without rounding your back, lift one leg at a time, bending the knee (strengthens quadriceps).

Home Exercise Equipment

Exercise bikes, rowing machines, step machines, bouncers etc. will all give good results if used regularly and correctly. However, unless a piece of home fitness equipment is permanently set up and ready for use at best, or at the very least readily available it will not get used. If it's kept under the bed in the spare room, it will almost certainly be doomed to stay there unused until it is finally consigned to the Scout jumble sale. When choosing home equipment, there are several factors to bear in mind before deciding which kind is best for you.

Exercise bikes

Cycling is an aerobic exercise and cycling regularly at low intensity for around thirty minutes is a great way to control and manage your weight. It's a skill that can be easily mastered and is suitable for all levels of fitness and all ages.

An exercise bike should be of reasonably sturdy construction and stability, the resistance, speed and preferably pedal frequency should be clearly displayed, it should be fully adjustable and, of course, comfortable for your size. Don't forget to make sure its dimensions fit its eventual resting place in your home, bearing in mind that you need to allow considerably more space in which to use it than to store it.

Disadvantages: Exercise cycles do not exercise the upper body and take up a lot of room.

Rowing machines

One of the few activities which uses virtually all of the major muscles in the body, rowing is also non-impact, so reducing the risk of injuries. It is aerobic and open to anyone except those with certain back problems and high blood pressure.

Rowing machines fall into two categories, hydraulic and straight-pull machines. The hydraulic variety are much cheaper than the straight pull, which tend to be longer, with electronic feedback and a more realistic rowing motion. Things to look out for in both types of machine are that they are well built and sturdy, have a comfortable seat, swivelling foot plates with straps, full range movement, fully adjustable resistance and workout feedback.

Disadvantages: They are cumbersome, can be noisy, particularly the straight-pull machines, and are not suitable for those suffering from back-ache or high blood pressure. Make sure you can fully extend your legs or you could cause knee injury.

Ski track machines

A natural action which simulates cross-country skiing and uses all the major muscles of the body. They have variable resistance so as to give good progression in an exercise programme and a totally aerobic workout, and are frequently the choice of exercise professionals.

Disadvantages: They take up a lot of room and it can take a couple of weeks to pick up the technique (but persevere - it's well worth it).

Step machines

These machines, simulating the action of climbing stairs, give good aerobic exercise which works the lower body. They offer similar benefits to exercise bikes but tend to take up less space. They are also the quietest piece of home exercise machinery I've come across, which is worth considering if you like to exercise in front of the television.

Disadvantages: They only work the lower body and can put an undue strain on the knees.

Bouncers

Jumping up and down on a mini-trampoline is both aerobic and fun. Bouncing enthusiasts extol the virtues of this simple yet efficient fitness aid. In my experience, when used regularly they can be beneficial, but they take up a

- When lying back in the bath, rest your knees against the bath sides and gently press against them. Hold for several seconds, then relax before trying again. This helps to strengthen and tone the outer thighs and hips.

- Even simply clenching and unclenching your buttocks as you soak will help to produce a firmer posterior.

great deal of room and, unless you have a particularly spacious lounge or spare room, they'll probably only make an appearance on sunny days in the garden.

Disadvantages: *Extremely cumbersome.*

Bull-worker

Rather unfashionable now but, once you've mastered the technique, this hand-held resistance cylinder apparatus can produce good results in terms of muscle definition and muscle building.

Disadvantages: *Purely for strength exercises. There is no cardio-vascular element to the workout, so it should be used in conjunction with flexibility and stretching exercises for full body conditioning.*

Weights

Very useful for resistance work as you advance through the Executive Fitness Programme. Heavy weights should, however, be used only under guidance and not excessively.

Disadvantages: *For strength exercises and should not be used in isolation unless you expressly wish to build muscle.*

In front of the Box

Yet the best time of all for working out is the evening as you chill out in front of the television. Come in, couch potato, your time is up!

- While facing the box, you can easily do all the stretches in the warm-up routine (see p.23) and the office workout, and most of the upper body exercises from the Executive Fitness Programme can be executed while sitting on the edge of an armchair or standing in front of the TV. Of course, the lower limbs take a bit more dedication – watch out for the commercial breaks.

- Finally, get into the habit of getting up to switch channels instead of using the remote controls. You'd be amazed how often you channel-hop.

On the move

You may well find that you spend an inordinate amount of your working life travelling, in cars, taxis, trains or planes. As a passive traveller you have quite a lot of scope for stretching out cramped muscles, and even as a driver you can always grab a few minutes to relieve muscle tension in the inevitable traffic jams.

Make an effort to rotate your wrists and ankles, to shake out your limbs and to stretch your back and shoulders etc. (see Workplace workouts, p.88). If space is too confined to stretch your legs, try to get up and walk about if you're on a train or plane; and, when driving or being driven, stop regularly and get out for a walk about. It's worth adding a few extra minutes to the journey time because you'll feel so much better when you get to your final destination.

4 Eating Out

In health terms, there's little point in toning up your body with the Executive Fitness Programme if you are fuelling yourself with an imbalanced, non-nutritious diet. Exercise must go hand in hand with sensible eating if you are to achieve a healthy body and mind (see also Chapter 5).

Most executives find that the increased demands of work and family mean that you are unable to be as active as you were in younger, more carefree days. It's also a fair bet to suggest that while you may lead a more sedentary life than you would choose, you have probably not cut down on your food intake, and, in many cases increased social and business entertaining probably means that you eat and drink more rather than less. But if you are only a stone to a stone and a half over your optimum weight you can still get away with looking quite presentable in a business suit. And this is where the problem lies. If you don't look sufficiently different to warrant comments from friends and family, nor do you look unsightly for work purposes, there may seem little incentive to put effort into getting back in shape. But, let's face it, you know when you're too fleshy for comfort and you'll also be aware of the ever-increasing side-effects such as lack of energy, constant tiredness, irritability etc.

If you fit into the above category, you will soon find yourself back at your optimum weight by following the Executive Fitness Programme and making sure you eat a healthy diet. What's needed is some common sense in the choices that you make from restaurant menus, sandwich bars and fast food joints; a little self-control (all right, a lot); and some support from your family and friends, in particular from whoever is responsible for shopping and cooking at home, if that's not you.

Once the philosophy of a healthy diet is grasped, it becomes much easier to choose the right options most of the time without becoming a 'calorie bore', and to interpret the tenets of a balanced diet to fit in with your lifestyle.

If you are more than a stone and a half above your 'fighting' weight, you may well decide to restrict your energy intake severely (in other words, to diet) in conjunction with the exercise programme. There is more information on dieting on p.110, but rest assured that you will still see good weight loss results if you merely change your eating habits to a more healthy regime, and the results will almost certainly be more long-lasting than those achieved by stringent dieting.

Healthy Eating

Energy requirements vary from individual to individual and depend on a variety of factors including gender, age, level of physical activity, state of health and metabolic rate. As a rule of thumb, the average man needs 2500 calories (kcals) a day and the average woman 2000, but if you are middle-aged and leading a relatively sedentary lifestyle your daily energy intake should be much lower than that of a young athlete, for example. Nonetheless, irrespective of your individual energy requirements, the proportions of the foods you eat from the main groups (see the table overleaf) should almost always remain the same.

In order to maintain health and to function efficiently, our bodies need fats, carbohydrates, protein, thirteen vitamins and sixteen minerals, and, of course, water is also essential. If we eat a wide range of foods in sensible quantities and proportions, we should be able to obtain optimum levels of every nutrient needed for good health. The British Health Education Authority (HEA) has classified foods into five groups:
- complex carbohydrates
- fruit and vegetables
- milk and dairy products (excluding butter and cream)
- meat, poultry, fish and alternatives, e.g. pulses, eggs, nuts etc. (proteins)
- fatty and sugary foods (simple carbohydrates)

To achieve a balanced diet, the HEA recommends that we include:
- six daily servings of complex carbohydrates
- five servings of fruit or vegetables
- two servings of milk or dairy products
- two servings of protein
- 15–25g (0.5–1oz) of fats and oils

Fat Facts

It only takes an extra 500 calories per day to put on a pound of fat a week in weight.

Food Groups: Making the Switch

Food Group	Choose	Avoid
Carbohydrates	Wholemeal, brown or high-fibre breads, wholegrain breakfast cereals, pasta, rice, potatoes, pulses (beans, lentils, peas)	Sugar-coated cereals, rice breakfast cereals, white bread, biscuits, cakes, pastries
Fruit and vegetables	Fresh, frozen and canned fruit in natural juices, fruit juice and dried fruit, and a wide variety of vegetables	Avoid excessive quantities of fruit at one time, and avoid deep-fried vegetables
Milk and dairy products (excluding butter and cream)	Semi-skimmed or skimmed milk, low-fat yoghurt, low-fat cheeses, reduced-fat versions	Whole milk, full-fat yoghurt, full-fat cheese
Meat, poultry, fish and alternatives (eggs, pulses, nuts)	Lean meat, fish, particularly oily fish (e.g. salmon, mackerel), pulses (e.g. beans, peas, lentils)	Roasted or fried meats and fish
Fatty and sugary foods	Lower-fat and lower-sugar varieties, polyunsaturated spreads (e.g. Flora), skimmed and semi-skimmed milk, grilled, baked, poached, casseroled and steamed foods, bread, fresh, dried and stewed fruit	As milk and dairy products above, plus butter, margarine, cream, chocolate, crisps, biscuits, pastries, cakes, ice cream, sweets, fried and roasted foods, full-fat cheeses (e.g. Cheddar, Stilton), mayonnaise, salad cream, chips, puddings, desserts, ketchups, fizzy drinks

If all that sounds like gobbledygook to you, it is best interpreted as increasing your daily intake of complex carbohydrates such as bread, breakfast cereals, potatoes, rice and pasta, eating more fruit and vegetables, and cutting down on fats, especially saturated fats, and sugar. These simple guidelines will produce a healthy, balanced diet (and its inherent benefits), will result in weight loss if you are over-weight, and, perhaps most importantly, will reduce the risk of heart disease and some diet-related cancers.

Remember that you are not seeking to accomplish the right ratio in every meal or even every day. Aim to balance out your intake in the right proportions from each group over a week or even two weeks, depending on your schedule.

Since these are general guidelines, they should influence the way you think about food in broad terms. However, many executives find themselves with very specific and challenging eating constraints imposed by their work patterns. It's either feast or famine – days of opulent corporate entertaining interspersed with days of travel where you're snacking on the run. With this in mind, I've put together some tips that may be useful for the busy, hungry, corpulent executive.

Help yourself

If you understand or remember nothing else from the HEA recommendations other than to eat more carbohydrates, fruit and vegetables and less fatty and sugary food, you won't go far wrong. But we can take this simplification one step further. If in doubt, target fat and fatty foods to cut out of your diet because, weight for weight, fat has more than twice the calories of starchy, sugary or protein foods.

The other food 'nasty', sugar, can also lurk in unexpected places. It's quite easy to cut out the teaspoon of sugar you add to a cup of tea but did you know that there was at least another teaspoonful hiding in the baked beans on toast you had this lunchtime? Here are some more scary sugar facts:

- an individual bar of plain chocolate contains the equivalent of twelve teaspoons of sugar
- a large slice of fruit cake contains seven teaspoons of sugar
- half a small packet of ginger nuts contains six and a half teaspoons of sugar
- a portion of fruit pie contains four teaspoons of sugar
- two small scoops of non-dairy ice cream contain three teaspoons of sugar
- a large dry vermouth contains one teaspoon of sugar

There is no need to over-react and ruthlessly cut out everything containing fat or sugar. For a start, a no-fat diet can lead to dry, scaly skin and brittle hair, and although refined sugar only gives hollow calories (no nutrients), psychologically a little of what you fancy can occasionally do you good. So, rather than puritanical abstinence or abandoned over-indulgence, I would suggest that the middle ground of sensible moderation is what you should be striving for.

Armed with the above information and official recommendations, it's now up to you to interpret the data and adapt the advice to suit your own lifestyle. For my part, I believe the biggest food dangers for the unaware executive lie between the business hours of eight to six.

Fat Facts

Muscle cannot ever turn into fat.
They are two quite separate tissues.

In the office:

Most vending machines use 'creamers' instead of milk. A creamer is a mixture of vegetable fat and glucose (sugar), which is heavy on calories. If you drink a lot of tea or coffee, you would be better off keeping a tin of powdered skimmed milk or a carton of fresh skimmed milk in the office to add to your tea or coffee – or indeed, drinking it black! Try occasionally to replace a cuppa with a glass of water – you've got to get through those three pints somehow.

If you dash out of the house in the morning after only a slurp of coffee and half a slice of toast you will almost certainly be peckish by mid-morning. A sticky bun or chocolate bar will satisfy the hunger in the short term but you would be far wiser to choose a sandwich or a banana. These alternatives (complex carbohydrates) are far more filling and nutritious than the quick-fix sugary foods (simple carbohydrates), and you are less likely to need something else to eat later in the morning.

If you must snack, look for the savoury varieties but don't be lulled into thinking that if they're not sweet they must be all right. Roasted peanuts and Bombay mix are extremely high in fat and calories. Crisps are marginally better, with the wholewheat variety nosing in front of the others (forget crinkle cut – more surface area means higher fat content). Mini-cheddars are baked and therefore a better option than deep-fried snacks. You may feel virtuous going for the healthy option of peanuts and raisins or yoghurt-coated raisins etc., but these too are high in fat and calories. No, the only snack I can recommend with hand on heart is a bag of Twiglets – they're completely natural and relatively low in fat and calories. In general, if you're peckish between meals it's far wiser to eat a salad roll or chicken sandwich, or some fruit, than to grab a cake, confectionery bar or crisps.

Business lunches

Although you wouldn't be entirely wrong in blaming business lunches for an expanding waistline, they don't have to be the villain of the piece and, with shrewd planning and selection, can even present a few advantages. For instance, it's healthier to eat your main meal earlier in the day rather than late at night and to consume something lighter for supper. (Of course, this assumes that you're not entertaining in the evening as well!) A good restaurant should serve fresh produce freshly cooked rather than the highly processed pre-

Fat Facts

Boys and girls have roughly the same body fat content (16–18 per cent) but after puberty girls tend to gain fat while boys tend to lose it. A slim man has about 12 per cent body fat compared to a slim woman with 23 per cent.

packaged foods we often pick up for lunch at the desk, and the diversity of these dishes can provide all the nutrients needed in a balanced diet. Finally, unless you have the cheek of the devil it's hard to ask for second helpings in a restaurant, so as long as you can perfect tunnel vision where the dessert trolley and cheese board are concerned, it should be difficult to over-eat. (If it's a restaurant that you know piles the plates high, discreetly ask for a smaller portion when ordering.)

Menu selections

Starters

- Choose a wholemeal roll(s) and eat it with just a scrape of butter. Remember the HEA recommends six daily servings of complex carbohydrates, and it's better to take the edge off your hunger with bread than to fill up on higher-energy foods.
- Soup can be an ideal starter, but opt for clear rather than creamy ones.
- Avoid pâtés, which have a high fat content.
- Deep-fried Camembert with a fruit sauce is a definite no-no. In fact, potato skins with sour cream, whitebait or indeed anything deep-fried should be avoided.
- Any fruit or seafood starter is a safe bet but watch out for rich sauces.
- Cured meats and sausages tend to be high in fat and salt.
- Avocados are a mixed blessing – they are a rich source of vitamin E and potassium and have the highest protein content of any fruit. But they also have a very high calorie count, of which up to 80 per cent can be derived from fat. Admittedly, it is monounsaturated fat which is not so damaging but probably best avoided if you're trying to lose weight.
- Artichokes and asparagus are both good choices, but again the sauces, particularly Hollandaise, can blow it, so be restrained.
- Oysters are an excellent choice. In fact, all shellfish are highly nutritious – rich in protein, vitamins and minerals and low in calories. If served with a sauce, look for a tomato-based rather than a cream-based dressing.
- Tomato and mozzarella is a great starter, but go steady on the olive oil dressing (monounsaturated fat).

Main courses

- Shellfish, such as crab or lobster, and fish, particularly oily fish such as salmon, herring or mackerel, are all good choices, preferably grilled or steamed.
- Choose lean meats such as turkey, chicken (without skin), pork

fillet, tenderloin, game and veal, and cut down on red meats.

- Avoid pies, pâtés and sausages.
- Pasta is a good choice but watch out for rich sauces. A tomato-based sauce is usually the best option.
- The method of cooking is often the key to success. Look for dishes that are grilled, steamed, baked or stir-fried and steer clear of the fried and deep-fried options.
- The vegetarian selections on the menu can make a welcome change and, depending on method of cooking, are often a healthy option.
- Opt for jacket (careful with the butter) or boiled potatoes and pass up chips, roasted, mashed and sauté.
- Eat plenty of vegetables or salad with the main course. If your selection is served without veg, get a side order.
- Main-course salads, warm or cold, are a good choice.

Dessert/cheeses

- Fresh fruit or fruit-based desserts (without pastry) are often the best choice.
- Whatever you choose, pass up the cream on top. If you simply must have a topping, choose custard or even low-fat ice cream – better still, plain yoghurt.
- Sorbet is a better choice than most high-fat desserts, although it tends to be high on sugar.
- Don't feel virtuous choosing the cheeseboard instead of a dessert. Full-fat cheeses such as Cheddar and Stilton are very high in fat (up to 35 per cent), so eat them sparingly. Soft cheeses such as Brie and Camembert are only marginally better with, on average, about 26 per cent fat, leaving the low-fat cheeses such as Gouda and Edam as the best options calorie-wise. Nonetheless, cheese provides valuable protein, calcium and vitamin B^{12}, so it has its redeeming features.

Around the world

Eating out can be an important part of our working and social lives and it should be pleasurable for all concerned. After all, it is a sociable way in which to cement relationships and conduct informal business, and you want the atmosphere to be as relaxed as possible. Sad to say for the figure-conscious exec, you will undoubtedly make your lunch companion feel most uncomfortable if you sit fiddling with a small green salad while they wrestle with the chef's special. Fortunately, with a little know-how eating out does not have to mean

Do You Need More Vitamins?
Leading health and nutrition experts agree that there should be no need to take vitamin and mineral supplements if you are eating a balanced diet. However, if you are in any doubt at all about the nutritional value of your diet, a daily multivitamin can do no harm except to your pocket.

pigging out. Here are some pointers to help you find your way around the menus of restaurants whose cooking is based on different gastronomic cultures.

British ✓

Traditional menus tend to be very meat-oriented, so be careful in the cuts you choose. Remember, cut down on red meat and go for more low-fat options such as turkey, chicken (without skin), pork fillet, tenderloin, game and veal. The nursery food staples which have made a popular reappearance in recent years are indulgences that should be enjoyed sparingly, particularly steak and kidney pudding and spotted dick. Suet, after all, is pure fat.

French ✓

With the development of lighter *nouvelle cuisine* dishes back in the eighties, French restaurants became a good option for the careful diner. The main things to watch out for in traditional French cooking are the heavy, creamy sauces such as Mornay, béchamel, Béarnaise and Hollandaise sauces. They are all laden with fat and hence calories. Instead choose a coulis, made of puréed vegetables, or a sauce piquante, with tomatoes, vinegar and shallots. French restaurants offer some cracking and healthy fish dishes (often poached – have you tried quenelles, dumplings made with poached fish and egg whites?), good casseroles and renowned salads. Beware of the cheese trolley: French cheeses tend to be 100 per cent *matière grasse* (very high fat content).

Chinese ✓

Cheap Chinese restaurants and take-aways can use low-quality, fatty meats and rely heavily on flavour enhancers, particularly monosodium glutamate (MSG), which raise blood pressure and the sodium content of food. So always patronise the better-quality restaurants where these practices are not upheld. Healthy options include stir-fry dishes, particularly chicken, vegetable or prawn, steamed fish, and boiled rice or noodles. Beware of spring rolls, wontons (deep-fried dumplings) and fried rice. Lychees are an excellent dessert.

Key

✓ okay

✓✓ pretty good

✓✓✓ excellent

✗ not too bad

✗✗ pretty bad

✗✗✗ definitely a rare treat

Indian ✗

The cooking of the Indian subcontinent relies heavily on frying with ghee (liquid butter) and oil, so be cautious. Tandoori dishes use the traditional cooking method of barbecuing and oven baking with charcoal and are therefore usually a good choice. Doner kebabs which are served in Indian restaurants with nan breads and plain rice are also lower in calories. Dhal (lentils), cucumber or onion raitha (natural yoghurt) and a side salad are a better vegetable side dish choice than some of the oil-laden bhajis. Avoid masala dishes, which are prepared with fresh cream.

Italian ✓✓

Think of Italian food and immediately pasta and pizza spring to mind. The good news is that both do quite well in the nutrition stakes. Pasta uses enriched flours (carbohydrate) made from grain and will keep your hunger satisfied for quite some time. Choose a tomato-based sauce such as marinara (seafood) rather than the cream- butter- or oil-based sauces. Pizzas are also a surprisingly well-balanced meal, with enriched-flour carbohydrates in the dough, vitamins in the tomato sauce and dairy proteins in the cheese, but they are not exactly low in calories. Don't ruin the show by choosing toppings unwisely – avoid salami, pepperoni and many of the meat toppings which are full of salt, fat and calories. Also beat a wide path around breaded and fried meats, and heavy desserts.

Japanese ✓✓✓

In general, Japanese cuisine rates highly on the healthy eating scale. Cooking time is kept to a minimum and fish features prominently, so on the whole Japanese food is low-fat and low-calorie. Best choices include sushi (raw fish), sashimi, sukiyaki, teriyaki, soya beans (tofu and miso), vegetables and rice. The only cautionary note to sound is that too much salty, pickled food is not good for you, and dim sum and tempura are perhaps best avoided.

Mexican ✗✗✗

These dishes are probably best reserved for occasional treats since the calorie count of a Mexican meal is sky-high. The main constituents, corn and beans, are actually very good sources of carbohydrate, but it is the layers of cheese, sour cream and deep-fried accompaniments that cause the damage. Look for rice and beans, flour tortillas such as burritos which are baked, and tacos or tostados. Salsa is fine and guacamole isn't too bad since the fat in the avocado is monounsaturated, but of course it's calorie-heavy. Try to avoid frijoles (refried beans), corn tortillas (fried), and nachos (deep-fried tortilla chips topped with melted cheese and refried beans – about a third of your daily calorie allowance).

Burgers and fast food ✗✗✗

A typical meal in a burger joint or from a fast food take-away is high in saturated fat and low in complex carbohydrates and fibre. So it is very easy to over-eat this type of food and then to feel hungry again soon afterwards. A quarter-pounder with fries and a shake will top the scales at over 1000 calories. Add cheese and it's even higher. A ham-, chicken- or beanburger with a diet soda or fruit juice are your best choices. Good old British fish and chips are no better since they too are drenched in saturated fat. So are the pies, pasties and battered sausages that form the usual alternatives to fish. All these are best left as an enjoyable but occasional treat.

Sandwich shops

In recent years the range of choice on sandwich shop menus has increased hugely and we've come along way from the humble cheese and pickle scenario. Continental breads, exotic fillings and hot as well as cold alternatives all mean that lunch in the office does not have to be a bore. Best of all, sandwich shop proprietors are happy to give you exactly what you want in your sandwich and bill you accordingly, so the health-conscious executive can pander entirely to his or her low-fat, low-sugar, high carbohydrate needs.

- Continental breads such as ciabatta, focaccia (made with olive oil) and pitta are good ways to stock up on carbohydrates.
- Buy rolls rather than sandwiches because they have a better ratio of bread (complex carbohydrate) to filling.
- Ask the sandwich maker to go lightly on the butter/margarine and leave out the mayonnaise (full fat and very high on calories).
- Scotch eggs, sausage rolls, pies and pasties are all extremely calorific and should be avoided.
- A jacket potato with tuna, sweetcorn, baked beans, cottage cheese or low-fat fillings is highly nutritious.
- The can of fizzy drink, chocolate bar and/or bag of crisps you have with your sandwich are full of sugar and fat respectively. You would be better to have another sandwich/roll and accompany it with fruit, and drink water or fruit juice.
- Relishes, sauces, salad cream, mayonnaise and pickles all bump up the calorie and salt content of a sandwich. If you like seasoning stick to pepper, fresh herbs, mustard and vinegar.
- If you must finish your lunch with some-

The Demon Salt

Most people in Britain eat more salt than they need.

Excessive intakes of salt (sodium chloride) are associated with an increased risk of high blood pressure, which can lead to strokes, heart disease and kidney failure. The World Health Organisation recommends a daily intake of 6g (a heaped teaspoon).

thing sweet (our parents have a lot to answer for), and fruit is paling in its appeal next to the cakes, go for scones, custard tarts and rock cakes rather than doughnuts, chocolate cake or fruit cake.

Alcohol

Although heavy drinking at business lunches has declined in popularity, the British consumption of alcohol, and of wine in particular, is rising. It is the alcohol itself in alcoholic drinks that poses the main health hazard, and in broad terms the higher the alcoholic content of a drink (predominantly spirits) the more harm that can be done. Conversely, recent research has shown that drinking in moderation can reduce the risk of heart disease, and in particular around two glasses of red wine a day can lower that risk by between 30–70 per cent, because it is well established that red wine decreases the tendency for blood to clot.

Official advice on alcohol consumption appears to have upped the limits of weekly consumption but offers more leeway for personal interpretation. What the government's 1995 Sensible Drinking Report says is that men who regularly consume 3–4 units of alcohol (see the table over) a day are at low risk, but in the next breath it says that 4 or more units a day is not advised. This is best interpreted as meaning that a man can consume up to 4 units a day (28 units a week) but it is inadvisable on a regular, daily basis. Moreover, the Health Education Authority recommends having at least one or two alcohol-free days a week. This fact, combined with the move towards daily rather than weekly guidelines, is designed to discourage binge-drinking which is the biggest health threat to moderate drinkers. Infrequent 'binge drinking' can, in the worst scenario, cause abnormalities in heart rhythms, leading to alcohol-induced cardiac failure.

Although alcohol is loaded with calories (see table over) that supply almost instant energy to the bloodstream, alcoholic drinks lack most essential nutrients and vitamins. The exceptions are wine and some beers, which contain a few minerals and B vitamins. Despite the well-documented benefits and disadvantages of drinking alcohol, if you are conscious of your energy intake, bear in mind that alcohol is high in calories and they all count towards your daily intake. Beer actually contains fewer calories than wine or spirits, but because it's often consumed in greater quantities, it's the bigger culprit in leading to a drinker's paunch. So choose your bevvy with care. I'm not suggesting you deny yourself wine with your meal, but foregoing a preprandial G&T and a post-dinner port would save you over 200 calories.

How Much Should I Drink?

Nutritionists recommend that we drink at least 3–4 pints of water a day but you can get away with about 2 pints – and that's probably all you have time for. This level of consumption will maintain healthy kidneys and prevent urinary infections. The body needs extra liquids if you have a very high-fibre diet, when your energy expenditure is high, and in hot weather. Alcohol is a diuretic (you produce a greater quantity of urine than the volume of alcohol imbibed), so always drink extra water when drinking alcohol. For more information on alcohol, turn to p.109.

Alcohol Facts

	Equivalent of One Unit	Calories
Spirits	Single pub measure	50 per measure
Port	Single pub measure	75 per measure
Wine	Small glass	85 per glass
Beer, lager or cider:		
Ordinary	half pint or a small can	90 per half pint or small can
Strong	quarter pint or half a small can	350 per pint, 280 per large can, 170 per small can
Low-alcohol	five pints	90 per half pint or small can

How does alcohol affect the body?

Alcohol is absorbed into the body between fifteen and ninety minutes after being consumed. However, it is absorbed more quickly if taken with a fizzy drink such as tonic, soda water, lemonade or fizzy water. The alcohol is broken down by the liver, and it takes approximately one hour to break down each unit of alcohol. Contrary to popular belief, this process cannot be speeded up by exercising or drinking black coffee.

Initially, alcohol can make you feel more relaxed and outgoing. One or two drinks quicken the heart rate but intellectual processes still function normally. Another couple of drinks and your coordination and judgement become impaired; a few more and you're beginning to slur your speech, have a reduced sensitivity to pain and/or are beginning to stagger; any more and you've lost control of voluntary activity, can get blurred vision and are at risk of unconsciousness or coma.

Knowing how many drinks you can have before you reach each level of intoxication depends on your personal tolerance. That is governed by a number of factors including body size, age, sex, amount of body fat, hormone levels, sensitivity to congeners (processing chemicals found in alcoholic drinks), and how regularly you drink. I imagine you will have already established your personal tolerance by bitter experience.

Purely in terms of exercise, alcohol will almost certainly adversely affect your performance. It cannot be used for energy by the exercising muscles as it can only be broken down by the liver. It may make you feel more alert and confident, but even in small amounts it will

● reduce your coordination, reaction time, balance and judgement

- reduce your strength, power, speed and endurance
- make you less able to regulate your body temperature
- reduce blood sugar levels and increase the risk of hypoglycaemia
- increase water excretion and risk of dehydration
- increase your risk of having an accident or injury

The social dangers of drinking and the hazards of drink/driving are well documented, but within the context of this book, the key facts are that drinking more than a couple of units of alcohol will impair your decision-making ability; alcoholic drinks and mixers are high in calories, if you are watching your weight; and you must avoid drinking before, during or immediately after exercise.

Getting the Most From Your Food

Once you've made the effort to eat a balanced, healthy diet, it's a great shame to minimise the effects of your endeavours by making easily rectified mistakes. Here are the facts:

- Smoking gives you a low vitamin C count. So, at the very least, smokers should make sure they get an adequate intake.
- Alcohol has a detrimental effect on nutrients. The purer the alcohol, the worse the damage. Beer is the best option since it is lower in alcohol content and provides B vitamins.
- Don't drink coffee or tea straight after a meal. Caffeine and tannin, which they contain, can impair the absorption of certain vital nutrients and minerals, in particular iron.
- Antibiotics and some prescribed drugs can interfere with the production and use of vitamins and minerals. This is why many GPs recommend a multivitamin supplement after a course of antibiotics.
- Vitamins are lost through cooking and exposure to heat, so raw or lightly steamed vegetables are best.

Weight Loss

The principle of weight loss is an extremely simple equation: energy intake must be less than energy expenditure. So, if you eat less and exercise more, you will lose weight. Put another way, if you are less active than you used to be, it is imperative that you cut your food intake accordingly.

The spanner in the works for the inveterate slimmer is the huge adaptability and survival mechanisms of the human body. Unfortunately for the would-be dieter, a prolonged period of radically reduced energy intake encourages the body to adapt by slowing down the metabolism so that you can function adequately on the new

Hangovers are caused by dehydration (alcohol has a diuretic effect and suppresses the secretion of certain hormones) and the congeners found in alcoholic drinks, and not by the alcohol itself.

reduced level of energy intake. As Jan de Vries points out in his book, *Realistic Weight Control*, people in Third World countries can work well on a diet of one bowl of rice per day because their bodies have become reconciled to it and their metabolisms have slowed accordingly.

Of course, the same principles apply when a very low-calorie diet is followed. In the time it takes for the dieter to reach his or her goal weight, the body has adjusted so that it can function on almost nothing. So, when the dieter decides it is time to start eating sensibly again, the weight lost is quickly regained and proves even harder to shift subsequently, even on a sensible diet. Once the body has learned to function on a daily intake of 400–500 calories, anything in excess, even a modest 1000 calories, will cause a weight gain.

Healthy eating as outlined earlier in this chapter, in conjunction with increased activity or exercise, is the only sure solution to controlled weight loss and, most importantly, weight maintenance. There are those who believe that a fast or several days of stringent dieting is just what is needed psychologically to start a weight-loss programme, but that is where the merits of a crash diet end.

Finally, the way in which weight is lost is also important and the fable of the hare and tortoise can come in handy here. A steady, slow drop of about 2–3lb a week is the optimum amount to maintain a sustainable loss. Expect to see your greatest loss in the first week, negligible if any loss in the second, and in the third week the drop should level out at a regular amount. Ultimately, whether you decide to diet or to eat sensibly and healthily, it should be combined with regular, low-grade exercise such as the Executive Fitness Programme or brisk walking to lose fat, because at low levels of exercise fat is the main fuel for the muscle.

All this is quite a lot of information to take on board, but once you've assimilated it and implemented its principles into your lifestyle it becomes second nature. It's preferable to have the facts so that you can make an informed decision on the degree of change you want to make. And, if you should slip off the road to righteous eating, remember the old adage, 'The battle may be lost, but the war is not over yet.' Simply take a broad brush-stroke approach to eating and drinking rather than panicking and giving up if you have a few days or even a couple of weeks of excess.

Fasting is not recommended but if you decide to start a strict weight-loss regime with one or two days fasting, make sure you drink at least 4 pints of fluid a day, otherwise you will feel dizzy and headachey

5 | Time to Unwind

So much has been written on stress in recent years that you might be forgiven for thinking that we should have it taped by now. Yet still an estimated 75 per cent of all medical complaints are stress-related, and more than 3 million Britons take benzodiazepine drugs (Valium, Librium, Ativan and Mogadon) daily for stress-induced illnesses. Ironically, benzodiazepine addiction is now one of the most common major diseases in the developed world.

Stress: Pros and Cons

Although stress has always been around, it's not hard to see why it is such a scourge of modern society, particularly for executives with young families. There are the obvious pressures of working in a demanding job, the relentless responsibilities of a young family, and the burdens of not enough time in the day. Personal circumstances aside, the pressures of city life itself are stressful – commuting, traffic jams, long queues, noise, light and air pollution, to name but a few. In addition, any changes in our external environment and in our emotional and/or mental state, together with anything that increases the intensity of our lives, whether temporarily or otherwise, is likely to produce stress (see the Stress League Table on p.114)

The effect that such strain has on an individual depends on a number of factors including age, health, previous experience of the stress-inducing factor etc. But the body's response to a stressful situation is the same for us all – namely the 'fight-or-flight' reaction which is a legacy of the survival instincts from our primitive origins. During this involuntary reaction the stress hormone adrenaline is released, causing the heart to pound and your blood pressure to rise. Simultaneously, the blood flow to the digestive system is reduced so that a greater supply can be directed towards the muscles, producing the familiar feelings of butterflies in the stomach. Unfortunately, the rules of acceptable social behaviour mean that there are very few occasions on which the energy from this adrenaline response can be used profitably (unless you make a habit of fisticuffs in the office), and the effects of prolonged stress can become dangerous if the causes are not addressed. When stress is becoming unmanageable, there are certain tell-tale signs to look out for. (See table below)

If these warning signs are consistently ignored, more drastic problems may develop. Adrenaline stimulates the release of fatty acids and glucose into the bloodstream ready to fuel the muscles for 'fight or flight'. When you are under stress for prolonged periods there is a greater risk of strokes and heart disease because of these increased levels of circulating fats and blood cholesterol, and because blood platelets are 'stickier' and so more inclined to form blood clots to block blood vessels.

There are a whole host of remedies for the relief of physical and mental early warning symptoms, but you should be wary of short-term cures. Taking a painkiller to treat a headache or chewing an antacid tablet to cure indigestion will provide momentary relief, but it makes more sense to discover the cause of your stress and address the problems rather than merely treating the symptoms.

Nonetheless, stress is a double-edged sword that should not be

In 1990, 1,672,000 working days were lost through stress or depression, compared with only 542,000 as a result of infection.

The Signs of Stress

Physical early warning signs

- headaches
- indigestion
- persistent diarrhoea
- tiredness
- insomnia
- palpitations
- nervous tics
- teeth grinding
- lower back pain
- chest pain

Mental signs

- feelings of suffocating pressure
- panic attacks
- irritability and short temper, particularly with colleagues and family
- lack of concentration
- poor memory
- intolerance to noise
- uncontrollable emotions
- over-reaction to little things

avoided completely. It is a natural element of all our lives and can be constructive at levels where it improves performance without adverse side-effects. Many of us thrive on the buzz of adrenaline and, when it is for short periods such as to meet a contract deadline, the pressure can be acceptable and even pleasurable. Some people need lots of stress in order to function happily, while others can bear very little; but whatever your individual threshold, stress at your optimum level can amplify your creativity and enjoyment of life.

The danger comes when we deny that we are experiencing stress; if we recognise the fact and deal with it inappropriately, such as by

The Stress League Table

Premier Division

Death of a partner

Divorce or separation

Death of a close relative

Prison sentence

Illness or injury

Getting married

Loss of job

Moving house

First Division

Retirement

Change of job

Money problems

Serious illness in the family

Pregnancy

Sexual problems

New baby

Reconciliation with partner

Death of a close friend

Second Division

A large mortgage

Additional responsibilities at work

Family tensions

Child starting/leaving school

Child leaving home

Office politics

Third Division

Christmas

Holidays

Change in working conditions

Minor traffic offences

Joining/leaving a social group

drinking or smoking heavily to help us through the difficult times; or when there is no release mechanism for the aggressive adrenaline response. Under these circumstances we are setting ourselves up for a fall. After all, it is far better to take preventative measures for dealing with stress than to be forced to change your lifestyle after a heart attack.

Once you have recognised and acknowledged that you are experiencing the adverse effects of stress, it is time to identify the specific causes of your particular unacceptable stress levels. If we accept that the events in the Stress League Table opposite put us under undue pressure, it makes sense, where possible, to avoid more than one of these stress-inducing activities at a time. Try not to move house or start a new job around the time a new baby is due, for example, and generally avoid major changes to the fabric of your life if you are under particular stress from other factors.

What triggers your stress levels is highly personal. You might deal magnificently with pressure at work or personal disasters, but the mere thought of a family Christmas with the in-laws is enough to give you sweaty palms and an overwhelming desire for a stiff drink. In fact Relate, the marriage guidance organisation, report that more people contact them after summer and Christmas holidays than at any other time, so an aversion to 'special' time with relatives is not as unusual as you might think.

Whatever it is that raises your blood pressure, it is imperative that you identify the causes and separate out the constructive and destructive stress-provoking elements in your life. Then, and only then, can you start to take protective or evasive action. Examine how environmental and personal pressures affect your life, and don't limit yourself to workplace stresses alone – you can suffer strain from lack of fulfilment in home and social life just as easily as in career matters. There will be obvious areas where you can eradicate or avoid the causes of stress completely, or reorganise things so that the resultant strain will be manageable. However, we must accept that certain stress-inducing factors are simply unavoidable, and in these cases we must look for a damage limitation exercise.

When you feel yourself getting tensed up, it's essential to set aside a few moments to relax. The fact that you are taking more exercise through the routines of the Executive Fitness Programme and attempting to eat more healthily means that you are already better equipped to deal with stress problems.

Action Plan
Physical Relaxation

Firstly, take control. You will undoubtedly have been exposed to time management experts or managerial and assertiveness training courses throughout your career. Apply these principles of good business management to yourself. After all, you are the one who suffers most from the ill-effects of excess stress. So see things in perspective and control your time and priorities.

Don't allow extra burdens to be imposed on you if you know they will be too much to cope with. Anxiety reduces productivity and increases the likelihood of illness, so you are ultimately doing yourself and your employer a disservice if you take on too much.

Diet

We have seen that both exercise and a balanced diet are essential for good general health, and this is especially important in the Western world where stress reduces our resistance to germs. Exercise promotes concentration and relieves anxiety, while a healthy diet is imperative because the body uses up vital nutrients more quickly when it is under stress. The dietary recommendations of the Health Education Authority will help you withstand the rigours of modern life, but when you find yourself under particular pressure make sure you get plenty of the foods listed below.

Helping yourself to relax when time is in short supply may seem like an indulgence, but it is a good investment in your health and in

	FUNCTION	SOURCES
Complex Carbohydrates	Boost energy	Bread, rice, pulses, oats, pasta, potatoes
Vitamin C	Helps the body fight infection	Fresh fruit, particularly blackcurrants, kiwi and citrus fruits, fruit juice and fresh vegetables
B Vitamins	Maintain a healthy nervous system and release energy	Green vegetables, potatoes, fresh fruit, wholegrain cereals, eggs, dairy products, seafood, lean meat, offal, poultry, pulses, nuts, seeds, dried fruit
Zinc	Helps the body resist infection	Red meat, liver, egg yolks, dairy produce, wholegrain cereals, seafood, particularly shellfish

your relationship with your family and colleagues. Finding ways to unwind physically may not be as difficult as it seems. In the office, practising the exercise routines to relieve tensed muscles (see p.88) will help to dispel mounting physical strain. When you find yourself in a particularly stressful situation which produces 'fight or flight' symptoms, try to find a way to release the energy in some way, even if it's simply running up and down a flight of stairs.

One of the best ways to relax tension in the muscles is to tense and then consciously relax each muscle group. Work systematically through your body from the toes upwards, clenching and unclenching muscles, and finally screw up your face in a tight grimace before letting the muscles relax. It is beneficial if you can sit or even lie with your eyes shut while you go through this procedure. Afterwards simply remain in this relaxed state for a few moments. You'll be amazed how much better you feel – ready to launch yourself into the fray again.

Complementary therapies

Many of the so-called complementary therapies can be hugely beneficial in dealing with stress. The various forms of massage (aromatherapy, shiatsu, marma, tuina, Thai and tangent therapy) can gently relieve the build-up of stress in the muscles, as well as calming the mind. Taking an hour out of your busy schedule for a regular massage is time well spent.

An aromatherapist can tailor the essential oils used in the massage to your specific needs, but cedarwood, petitgrain, Roman chamomile, lavender, sweet marjoram and sandalwood are all soothing oils which may be useful for stress-related problems. As part of a self-care strategy, add literally a few drops of these essential oils to your bath (they are very potent, so don't splash it in like bubble-bath) or they can even be used for inhalation – from your pillow at night or from a handkerchief. Medical herbalists also recommend oats, skullcap and vervain as infusions to be taken throughout the day as a good counter-measure to stress.

In reflexology the feet are massaged to unblock energies throughout the body, to reduce nervous tension and to stimulate the body's own self-healing properties. It's extremely relaxing and can be helpful in identifying the causes of stress in your life. After a course of treatments you will be aware of the points on your feet – or hands – which can be pressed to alleviate individual symptoms by self-massage at home.

Now enjoying a revival after its popularity in Britain in the late seventies, yoga is an Eastern therapy that uses exercise and breathing techniques to calm both the mind and the body. Since it is unlikely that you'll have the time to attend weekly yoga classes, here are a couple of classic yoga relaxation poses to try. And if you find them helpful, there are innumerable yoga books available which can give you further postures for relaxation.

The Corpse or shavasana

(See cool-down exercises, pp.30–33).

1. Lie down slowly, flat on your back, with legs together and at your sides.

2. Allow your feet to fall gently open, relaxing all the leg and feet muscles.

3. Put your hands palms upwards a few inches away from your body, and let your fingers curl if they want to. Let your arms go limp.

4. Raise your chin and tilt your head back a little. Close your eyes.

5. Let go of all your facial muscles (don't worry if your mouth drops open).

6. Slow down your breathing by inhaling deeply, then exhaling as slowly as you can. Don't breathe again until you have to.

7. Concentrate on your breathing and don't let your mind wander.

8. Stay in this position for as long as you like, and then get up slowly.

The Refresher

1. Stand straight, with your legs and feet slightly more than hip-width apart.

2. Allow your body to relax forward, gently letting your head, hands and arms hang forward.

3. Your body will stop in whatever position is comfortable, but will come a little further with practice.

4. Hold the position still for a count of eight.

5. Slowly straighten up, letting your head, hand and arms stay relaxed.

6. Straighten your back, bringing your head up last.

Other ways to de-stress

Getting aggravated appears to me to be all part of the territory when you are a working parent, but you can always try to transfer your nervous energy into physical activity and, preferably, something useful like digging the garden or washing the car. If there is no such outlet or if these feelings persist, then talking about your concerns with people you are close to at work, at home or in the family will help you to deal with the stress, especially the kind that cannot be avoided such as bereavement or divorce. It appears that people who bottle up their problems are more likely to suffer from serious stress-linked illness, including cancer.

And if none of these routes to relaxation appeals, simply doing now and again the things you enjoy, instead of the things you ought to, can relieve feelings of intolerable pressure. Why not listen to some music or read a book instead of doing the monthly accounts? Getting out in the fresh air always pays dividends, and you can kill two birds with one stone if you combine a therapeutic walk in the park with teaching the youngest to ride her bike, for example. Practical or creative hobbies can be immensely rewarding and they provide a rare opportunity for self-expression and great personal satisfaction.

Mental Relaxation

Mental relaxation is just as important as physical repose, if not more so, but sometimes it is harder to achieve. Do you find your mind is racing when you should be catching up on much-needed sleep? Are you still dwelling on problems in the office when you should be concentrating on the plot of Prime Suspect 3?

Breathing

Deep breathing can be a simple key to unlocking mind jams. Taking slow, deep breaths and concentrating on the breathing process calms the mind, helping you to relax, even in the rush hour. To heighten this effect, spiritual teachers recommend imagining the air you inhale is a rich blue colour as you breathe in through your nose for a count of four, holding your breath for a

Don't Fuel Your Stress

● Nicotine, alcohol, caffeine, sugar and non-medical drugs all stimulate the release of noradrenaline (norepi-nephrine), so aggravating stress symptoms.

● Every now and again, replace your normal cuppa with a camomile herbal tea, which is well known for its soothing and calming properties.

● A favourite tonic of the Chinese, ginseng is beneficial in combating many of the symptoms associated with stress. It can be taken in capsule, powder, tea or tonic form, and is available from health stores and Chinese markets.

count of four, and then exhaling through the mouth for a count of four while seeing the air you breathe out as gold. This simple system can be practised anywhere at any time and achieves remarkable results, leaving the mind uplifted and relaxed.

Help from the East

Visualisation and meditation are procedures recommended by all the Eastern philosophies. In its simplest and most common Western form, visualisation can be likened to letting the mind wander or daydreaming. Imagining that you're lying on a tropical beach with Pamela Anderson on the sun lounger next to you is harmless and gives the mind a gentle break.

The Tibetan Buddhists have long used visualisation for healing, and in the West it is used as part of the treatment for cancer. Patients are taught during deep contemplation to make a mental picture of their illness and of the destructive effect their treatment has on it. Following the same principle, visualisation can be used to equally good effect if you practise picturing stress as a burden or weight on your shoulders and then see it lifting clean away. This imagery is, of course, merely my suggestion, and whatever most clearly symbolises your particular stressful situation will produce the best results for you.

Another technique that concentrates on harnessing the power of the mind is autosuggestion. Devised in the late nineteenth century, it emphasises the role of the imagination rather than the will. By using repeated incantations it is possible to clear your mind of all thoughts and worries. The most famous mantra is 'Every day, in every way, I am getting better and better', but you can use any phrase that is pertinent and meaningful to you.

Since the 'fight or flight' reaction is involuntary and often triggered by the unconscious mind, the ability to control your reaction to certain situations is, for most people, extremely difficult to achieve. With this in mind, autogenics was devised to train people how to turn off anxiety and stress reactions and to stimulate the processes of relaxation and rest by 'passive concentration'. There are six basic exercises in body awareness and physical relaxation which, once learnt, can be practised anywhere at any time. It is advisable to take a preliminary course of lessons rather than using 'teach-yourself' tapes, because many people need help to master the concentration techniques.

The simplest form of meditation is quiet contemplation, but in Eastern philosophy it more often involves focusing the mind in order to reach an altered state of consciousness which leads to emotional, spiritual and physical peace and harmony. Transcendental meditation (TM) is a popular technique which produces deep relaxation and benefits to the mind and body. Private and local authority classes are widely available but, with time in short supply, you may have to resort to one of the instructional books although this isn't ideal.

Whatever the method, most people in Britain who turn to meditation are hoping to relieve stress and achieve a state of relaxation. Certainly, as you sit peacefully, you realise that the world is continuing to revolve quite happily without you. Simultaneously your heart rate, breathing rate and metabolism slow down and so the tensions ebb away.

Learn to delegate

The final weapon in the armoury against stress may well go against the grain, but you should enlist some help when you are under pressure. A strong smell of burning martyr wafting from the garage as you try and juggle one hundred and one jobs before setting off on holiday does not make for a jolly atmosphere. Delegate some of the tasks and make it a truly family occasion. Similarly, in the office you will know whether or not you are a good delegator. But rest assured, those who have mastered the art lead less stressful lives than those who have not.

Travel Stress

One of the most stressful aspects of any executive's life can be the amount of travel involved. Not only is it highly time-consuming and fatiguing, but many hours spent on planes and trains and in cars can produce untold physical and mental stress. Long-haul air travel is particularly wearisome because it interferes with the body's circadian rhythms (natural body clock), resulting in what is commonly known as jet-lag.

Jet-lag

The feelings of limbs like lead, heavy eyelids, lack of coordination and concentration, sudden memory loss and mood swings are all symptoms experienced by travellers arriving by plane in a new time zone. You may have adjusted your watch but your internal biological clock has stayed with the timings and routines you left behind you.

In the main, jet-lag is only noticeable when you cross three or more time zones. If you fly in a north–south or south–north direction without any time-zone changes you should not suffer jet-lag, although you will still be exhausted from a long flight. The problems arise with east- and westbound travel, and it can take up to 50 per cent longer to recover from jet-lag after an eastward flight than after a westward flight of the same distance. Flying east (against the sun) reduces the

Feel like a dish rag when you get off a plane? Not only do your clothes feel dishevelled but the stress of flying has increased the production of androgens (male hormones) so increasing sebum production. The result? Greasy Hair!

length of your day, which is much more disruptive to natural cycles than travelling westward (in the same direction as the sun), which extends your day.

Numerous theories and 'cast-iron' recipes for avoiding jet-lag abound – wearing paper bags on your feet is one of the wackiest. In fact, research shows that there is no way of artificially assisting the necessary adjustments to your body rhythms, but undoubtedly there are measures that can be taken to limit its effects.

Preparation

- If you have the choice, try to travel westwards rather than east-wards.
- Ideally, don't pick a flight that forces you to get up too early in the morning, or you will be deprived of sleep before you even start the journey.
- Attempt to schedule in a little R&R on your arrival to help with time adjustments (unlikely, I know).
- Don't be tempted to book the 'red-eye' special that transfers you overnight. Admittedly you can save the cost of an hotel room and reduce the length of time you are away from the office, but arriving between midnight and 6 a.m. in body-clock terms is when you are at your lowest ebb and least well equipped to face arrival procedures and important business meetings.
- Start planning your time-clock change several days before travel-ling. Go to bed an hour or two earlier or later than is customary and adjust mealtimes accordingly too.
- Traffic jams on the way to the airport, delays once you get there and hordes of people milling around the terminal all add to the stress of international travel, but if possible remain calm. After all, it's out of your control, and the extra adrenaline produced under stress only intensifies the problems of time-change travel and its ensuing symp-toms.

On board

- Avoid alcohol, which exacerbates the dehydrating effect of pressurised cabins. Drinking plenty of non-alcoholic fluids can restore the balance. Carbonated or fizzy drinks should be avoided because the bubbles expand in your stomach during the flight, causing heartburn and indigestion.
- Eat light meals that are easy to digest.
- Keep active. Get up and walk about every half hour

Travel or Motion Sickness
The familiar symptoms of nausea and headache are caused by a conflict between what the eye sees and what the inner ear feels. The eyes compensate but the ears do not and so the brain receives conflicting messages. Preventive measures include eating regular snacks rather than full meals, drinking plenty of water or soft drinks and avoiding alcohol. An alternative to the numerous over-the-counter pre-parations for travel sickness is fresh root ginger. Chewed during your journey, it is said to prevent the symptoms of travel sickness.

or so. If space permits, do the exercises recommended for the workplace (see p.88). If not, simply working through the body from the toes up, tensing and releasing muscles to relieve tension and maintain good circulation is helpful.

- Wear loose-fitting, comfortable clothing and kick off your shoes once you are in your seat.
- Remove contact lenses, if you wear them, as the dehydrating cabin atmosphere can irritate your eyes and make lens-wearing uncomfortable.
- Ear-plugs can be your saviour on a long, noisy flight.

On arrival

- If you arrive at night, turn off the lights in your hotel room and rest your eyes, even if you do not sleep. Once day arrives, get out into natural sunlight (assuming there is any) which resets the body's biological clock by stimulating the production of the hormone melatonin. Treatment with melatonin pills is also reported to combat jet-lag.
- Adopt the rhythm of your destination time as soon as possible.

Relaxing en route

Any form of passive travel (air, train, chauffeur) can provide a great opportunity to practise some of the relaxation techniques mentioned earlier in the chapter. Resolutely switch off the mobile phone, put the laptop away and spend a profitable ten minutes recharging your batteries and revitalising your mind and body.

We are always in a hurry to get to our destination, particularly when travelling on business, but if you are driving yourself it is even more important that you set aside a little time for stretching tensed, cramped muscles and relaxing the mind. When driving, posture is just as important as when sitting at the desk in the office. Firstly, make sure your lower back is supported – you can buy special seat implants or lumbar cushions, or a common-or-garden cushion will do. And if you are using a company fleet car, make sure your driving position is adjusted correctly for you. Any driving, but particularly long-distance, high-speed mileage, is very taxing on your concentration. A few moments invested in your physical and mental well-being will make you safer on the road and fresher on arrival.

For further information on any of the complementary therapies mentioned, contact the Institute for Complementary Medecine, PO Box 194, London SE16 1QZ. Telephone: 0171 237 5165.

6 Conclusion

I confess to some difficulty in writing this final chapter because, unlike other books I have written, there is no conclusion to *Executive Fitness for Men*. You don't read the book, complete the programme and there's an end to it. Rather it is an on-going process, something that's assimilated into daily life and which will give long-term benefits for you to enjoy for many years to come.

What I can say is congratulations. If you've been following the routines for some time you should be looking a whole lot better and almost certainly slimmer. And, more importantly, you should be feeling a good deal better, too. I would hope that by now you have more vitality, energy and *joie de vivre*.

Executive Fitness cannot take away the pressures of modern living, nor can it create more free time in a hectic schedule. What it can do is help you cope with those stresses, assist you in accommodating fitness and activity into a busy lifestyle, and encourage you to eat as healthily and nutritiously as possible within the constraints of a 'catered' diet.

The information contained in *Executive Fitness* is merely for your guidance. Once you know the facts, it's up to you to decide when it's prudent to eat sensibly and when it's time to indulge a fancy for something on the 'not recommended' list; whether to exercise or to have a few days off. There's an old saying which seems appropriate here: 'Rules are for the observance of fools and the guidance of others.'

Don't let a desire to lose weight govern your life or a need for a healthy diet ruin the pleasures of eating. Flexibility is the key, and optimum nutrition should be viewed on a broad scale and over a loose timeframe. If you want to go mad and binge on your two-week annual holiday, you can. You simply go back to more sensible eating on your return to home. No guilt, no real damage. That's not to say that you can extend the periods of imprudent eating and no exercise indefinitely, or you'll soon end up back where you started. Just keep a weather eye on things and don't let yourself slip too far.

As you will have seen, healthy eating combined with moderate exercise improves the quality of your life and brings the bonus of weight loss where necessary. If you felt the over-riding need for a stricter diet, I trust you were sensible: starving yourself to lose weight has been shown to be ineffectual. Received wisdom now points the way towards eating to fill yourself up, not to fatten yourself up – more carbohydrates, fruit and vegetables, and less of the fatty and sugary foods. There should no longer be any need for hairshirt tactics to lose weight.

The same holds true for the exercise routines. 'No gain without pain' could not be further from the truth. As you start to enjoy the benefits of a more active way of life, I suspect you will resolve to keep exercise and activity an integral part of your existence. And, again, that is the crucial point. Following the Executive Fitness Programme will definitely make you fitter and will almost certainly help you to lose weight. However, as long as you have accepted and embraced the principles of integrating more activity into your life, it doesn't matter if you cease to follow the programme for a while. Even if you replace the exercise routines with alternative physical activity in your schedule, you can come back to the programme whenever you feel like it, or feel the need for a little extra toning. Admittedly, you'll probably start at a lower level in the routines than the one at which you stopped earlier, but that's part of the beauty and flexibility of the Executive Fitness Programme.

If your aim is to lose weight, you should follow the progressive routines at least until you are at your goal weight. Then keep an open mind. I doubt that you'll want to give up regular exercise once you've reaped its rewards, but it's not a fitness programme that chains you. Regular, moderate activity several times a week is enough to maintain your weight as long as you are eating a reasonably healthy diet.

And there you have it in a polyunsaturated nutshell. All that remains is for me to raise a cheery glass (well, red wine is good for you, after all) and to say *'A votre santé'!*

Index

abdominals 41, 51, 61, 70, 73
  see also stomach
abductors 43, 44, 58
adductors 26, 30, 45, 59
adrenaline 113
aerobic activity 20, 87
alcohol 17, 22, 101, 108-10
  and air travel 122
AAllied Dunbar National Fitness survey
  11
androgens 121
ankles, tired 93
arms 29
  strengthening 82-6
aromatherapy 117
autogenics 120
autosuggestion 120

back (erector spinae)
  strengthening 42, 52, 62, 72
  stretching 91
  upper 28
baths
  after exercise 19
  exercise during 95-7
benefits of exercise 10-11
  four key components 20
bent over row 49
body conditioning, total 35-46
body types 17
bottom toning 76-8, 94
bouncers 96-7
breathing 34, 119-20
Buddhism, Tibetan 120
bull-workers 97
business lunches 102-4

cardio-respiratory performance 20
cardio-vascular programme 47-53
CHD
  see coronary heart disease
chest 28, 54

broadening 82-6
childhood obesity 11
chin, double 94
clothing 12
complementary therapies 117-18, 123
cool-down routine 30-3
  reasons for 19
coronary heart disease 17-18
  and alcohol 108
  and diet 100, 107
  main risk factors 18
  and stress 113

deltoid raises 56-7
depression 10
de Vries, Jan
  Realistic Weight Control 111
diary, progress 11-12
diet 9-10, 75, 98-111, 124-5
  and air travel 122
  alcohol 17, 22, 101, 108-10
  business lunches 102-4
  fast food 107
  food groups 99-100
  international cooking 104-6
  maximising benefits of 110
  in the office 102
  salt 107
  sandwich shops 107-8
  and stress 116-17
  sugar content of foods 101
  supplements 104, 110
  water consumption 108
difficulty, levels of 21
dips
  stride 36, 48
  tricep 50, 68
discipline 19
drinks
  and air travel 122
  coffee and tea 110
  fluid consumption 108, 111

vending machines 102
  see also alcohol
driving 123
drugs 22
  benzodiazepine addiction 112
  prescribed 110

ectomorph 17
endomorph 17
endorphins 10
endurance 20
equipment 13, 21-2, 96-7
exercise bikes 96

fast food 107
fat
  burning 47-53, 64-74, 87
  male and female body content 102
  and muscle 101
  see also diet; weight
feet, tired 93
flexibility 20, 124-5
fluid consumption 111
  water 108

hamstrings 25, 32, 95
hands, tension in 92
health 22
  pre-exercise questionnaire 16
  screening 15-16
Health Survey for England 11
heart
  see cardio-respiratory performance;
  cardio-vascular programme; coronary
  heart disease; peripheral heart action
home
  delegation of chores 121
  exercise equipment 13, 96-7
  relief of stress 119
  workouts 94-7

individual differences 16, 17

Institute for Complementary Medicine 123

jet-lag 121-2, 123

lat pulls 71
leg raises 59
legs 31
    hamstrings 25, 32, 95
    tired 93
lunges, alternate stride 67
lungs
    see cardio-respiratory performance;
    cardio-vascular programme

mantras 120
massage 117
meditation 120-1
melatonin 123
mesomorph 17
minerals 104, 110, 116
motivation 11-12

neck relaxation 90

obesity 11
office see workplace

pec-dec 54
peripheral heart action 64-74
photographs 12
planning 12-13
posture 88, 94
    whilst driving 123
press-ups
    box 38, 64
    extended box 39, 65
    full 40, 66
    inverted 85
    one-armed 86
progression tables
    Routine A 46
    Routine B 53
    Routine C 63
    Routine D 74

pulse rate 18
    how to monitor 19

quadriceps 95

reflexology 117
relaxation
    mental 119-21
    physical 116-19
    total body 33
    whilst travelling 123
rest, active 87
routines, exercise 34
    A 35-46
    B 47-53
    C 54-63
    D 64-74
rowing machines 96

salt 107
sandwiches 107-8
shoes 12
shoulders 27, 28, 56-7
    broadening 82-6
    relaxing 89
showers 19
side bends 37, 55
ski track machines 96
skipping 48, 49, 87
smoking 17, 110
snacks 102, 107-8
sports 20
squats
    ski 60, 69
    wide stance 35, 47
step machines 96
stomach 79-81
    see also abdominals
strength 20
stress 10, 14, 112-15
    league table 114
    mental relaxation 119-21
    physical relaxation 116-19
    and travel 121-3

warning signs 113
swimming 13, 20, 87

telephone exercises 94, 95
thighs 24, 25, 31
    inner (adductors) 26, 30, 45, 59
    outer (abductors) 43, 44, 58
time schedule 8-9, 12, 13, 19, 21
top-to-toe programme 54-63
travel 121-3
    workouts during 97
triceps 50, 68, 95
Twiglets 102

vending machines 102
visualisation 120
vitamins 104, 110, 116

waist 73, 79-81
walking 87
warm-up routine 23-9
    reasons for 18-19
weight
    ideal 15
    mechanics of slimming 110-11
    national statistics 11
    problem areas 75-81
    see also diet; fat
weights 97
    hand 13, 22, 82-4
wine, red 108
workplace
    delegation 121
    and diet 102
    exercises 13, 88-93, 94
    journey to 13, 97
    relief of stress 117
wrists, tension in 92

yoga 20, 117-18
    The Corpse (shavasana) 33, 118
    The Refresher 118

Claire Gillman is a journalist and fitness expert who contributes to many leading magazines and consumer titles. In the past, she has edited *Fitness and Health* magazine and other sporting titles and has been a regular contributor to the *Guardian* newspaper and *Daily Mail* magazine.

Claire has worked extensively with the Parachute Regiment, which was the subject of her first book *PARA: Inside the Parachute Regiment* (Bloomsbury) and led to her second *The Paras Ultimate Fitness* (Hodder & Stoughton). She was the main contributor to *A Guide to Good Health: The Hale Clinic* (Kyle Cathie) and was consultant editor on *Eco Management* (Chancery). She is currently editing a book on esoteric matters entitled *Rainbow Journey* (Hodder). During the course of her writing career, she has appeared on television and given many radio interviews.

She now lives on the edge of the West Pennines with her husband, a former Parachute Regiment Officer, and their two young sons.